The Implications of Knowledge-Based Growth for Micro-Economic Policies

GENERAL EDITOR: PETER HOWITT

The Implications of Knowledge-Based Growth for Micro-Economic Policies

The Industry Canada Research Series

The University of Calgary Press

© Ministry of Supply and Services Canada 1996

ISBN 1-895176-78-6
ISSN 1188-0988   *338.971*

University of Calgary Press   *I34*
2500 University Dr. N.W.
Calgary, Alberta, Canada T2N 1N4

Canadian Cataloguing in Publication Data
    Main entry under title:
    The Implications of Knowledge-Based Growth for Micro-Economic Policies

    (Industry Canada research series, ISSN 1188-0988; VI)
    Issued also in French under title: La croissance fondée sur le savoir et son
    incidence sur les politiques microéconomiques.
    Conference held in Ottawa on March 30-31,1995
        Includes bibliographical references.
        ISBN 1-895176-78-6

    Cat. No. Id53-11/6-1996E

        1. Economic development — Congresses.
        2. Canada — Economic policy — Congresses.
        3. Information technology — Canada — Congresses.
        4. Information theory in economics — Congresses.
        5. Canada — Economic conditions — 1991- — Congresses.
        6. Micro-economics — Congresses.
        I. Howitt, Peter, 1946- .
        II. Canada. Industry Canada.
        III. Series.

HC79.I55I56 1996   338.9'26   C95-980252-5

The University of Calgary Press appreciates the assistance of the Alberta Foundation
for the Arts (a beneficiary of Alberta Lotteries) for its 1996 publishing program.

EDITORIAL & TYPESETTING SERVICES: PMF Editorial Services Inc. and Nicholson
Consultants Inc.
COVER & INTERIOR DESIGN: Brant Cowie/ArtPlus Limited.

Printed and bound in Canada

∞   This book is printed on acid-free paper.

Table of Contents

PART III DINNER SPEECH

PART IV FACILITATING KNOWLEDGE-BASED
GROWTH

PART V CANADA AND THE GLOBAL TELECOMMUNICATIONS REVOLUTION

Preface

DEVELOPING EFFECTIVE POLICIES TO INCREASE JOBS and our standard of living requires the knowledge and understanding of the determinants of economic growth. Although there may be dissension among economists and policy makers on some aspect of the process generating growth, there is a consensus that innovation resulting from the accumulation of knowledge plays a fundamental role. While Canadian industries are currently undergoing significant structural changes to meet new competitive challenges in the global marketplace, ensuring that the new economy is an innovative, knowledge-based one is key to Canada's future success.

The Micro-Economic Policy Analysis Branch of Industry Canada commissioned eleven research papers to broaden and deepen our understanding of key issues relating to the impact of knowledge-based growth on the Canadian economy and the policy implications that arise. The issues examined may be divided into three categories: the sources of knowledge (concepts and measures), designing and assessing innovation policies, and the impact of the global telecommunication revolution on the Canadian economy.

The studies were presented and their findings discussed at the conference "The Micro-Economic Implications of Knowledge-Based Growth" held in Ottawa in March 1995. The papers were subsequently revised in light of comments received from academic, government and business experts who participated in the conference. The final version of these studies and the rapporteur's comments appear in this volume of the Industry Canada Research Series.

The research assembled here will contribute to government policy by bringing us closer to understanding how economic policy can affect the productivity performance and the growth of the Canadian economy. At a more general level, I hope the distribution of pertinent research stimulates policy debate on important micro-economic issues confronting Canada and helps to build a shared vision of economic problems among the wider public.

I would like to take this opportunity to thank all of the authors for their work, particularly Professor Peter Howitt in his capacity both as author and general editor. I know that this volume will be of interest to the policy-making community as well as to everyone interested in economic issues here in Canada and abroad.

JOHN MANLEY
MINISTER OF INDUSTRY

Peter Howitt
Department of Economics
University of Western Ontario
and Canadian Institute for Advanced Research

Introduction

T HE REVIVAL OF GROWTH THEORY led by Romer and Lucas was based initially on very general aggregate models. These models had important macro-economic implications with respect to such issues as the sustainability of growth in the long run and the broad economic determinants of the long-run rate of growth, but they omitted too much detail to be really useful for concrete policy purposes. For example, although the models clearly implied that research and development (R&D) expenditures would be underprovided in the absence of subsidy programs, designing a subsidy program would require facing up to many of the awkward facts not included in the aggregate models such as how to choose the activities that qualify for subsidies, how to structure the subsidies efficiently and whether to target strategic industrial or geographic clusters. None of these questions can be addressed without adding structural content to the original theories.

The revolution in information and communication technologies transforming the global economy is making this gap in endogenous growth theory increasingly serious. Endogenous growth theory is needed to guide the rethinking of many aspects of economic policy called for by this revolution, since it is the only theory we have that focuses on the economy-wide causes and consequences of technological change. However, one quickly runs into the problem that aggregate models are not well suited for dealing with the sorts of structural change we are now experiencing.

This volume deals with this problem by examining some of the detailed structural aspects of the growth process. Together, the papers that follow bring us a little closer to understanding how economic policy might cope with the fundamental technological changes that are continuing to transform the Canadian economy.

SOURCES OF KNOWLEDGE: CONCEPTS AND MEASUREMENT

T HE PAPERS COME IN FOUR GROUPS. The first group deals with a problem of increasing importance and difficulty: economic policy toward technological change and growth must have its impact on the knowledge base of the economy. But most of the economic information available to policy makers, in readily summarized form, is weakest on just this component. We do not have an accurate and detailed portrait of its different parts. While these papers do not resolve the fundamental measurement problems involved, they help to identify important areas for future research, and to give us a clearer picture of certain aspects of the sources of knowledge.

The first paper, by Howitt, deals with problems in constructing and interpreting the national accounts. It identifies several problems in measuring knowledge-based growth using conventional national income accounting procedures and argues that during periods of rapid fundamental technological change, such as we are now experiencing, these problems are likely to result in an underestimate of the growth of output and productivity.

Next, Lee and Has examine data on 55 Canadian industries in an attempt to identify the differences in performance between those that use more or less knowledge. Their paper shows a large degree of heterogeneity within each broad category. It also contains findings that warn against coarse attempts to subsidize high technology at the expense of low-tech industries. Specifically, it finds that although the high-knowledge sector outperforms the medium- and low-knowledge sectors in terms of output and employment, the low-knowledge sector outperforms the high- and medium-knowledge sectors on labour productivity and wage growth.

The paper by Baldwin and Johnson describes some of the interrelationships between different sources of knowledge. In general, one can classify knowledge-creation activities as consisting of either innovation or human capital accumulation. The latter takes place partly in school and partly in the workplace. If policy is to be used to foster one or both of these broad activities, it is important to understand how the activities are interrelated. The paper provides a good example of how survey data can address structural problems like this. It reports a survey of small- and medium-sized growing enterprises, and shows a surprisingly strong positive correlation across these firms between innovation and human capital development. It also finds a lot of heterogeneity across sectors in these activities, thereby giving us more reason to go beyond simple aggregate growth theories that ignore cross-sectoral differences in knowledge creation.

A KNOWLEDGE-BASED APPROACH TO FRAMEWORK POLICY ISSUES

THE SECOND GROUP OF PAPERS attempt to use some of the ideas of endogenous growth theory to examine framework policy issues whose conclusions one might think would be amplified by endogenous growth considerations. That is, parameter changes which would have permanent level effects in the neoclassical growth model tend to induce permanent growth-rate effects in endogenous theory. Thus, policies that would induce a permanent efficiency gain according to the neo-classical model can sometimes induce a permanent increase in the rate of growth. Even without this growth-rate effect, compound interest ensures that the effect on the expected present value of Gross National Product (GNP) is a multiple of a level effect. But with it, this multiplier is likely to be even larger, since one is, in effect, changing the net rate of interest (rate of interest minus growth rate) at which the current level is capitalized. Simple numerical exercises show that this effect can make a huge difference to cost-benefit calculations, even when the change in the growth rate is only a fraction of a percent per year.

Richard Harris opens this set of papers by surveying the rapidly growing literature on the effects of trade liberalization and integration on economic growth. His paper takes a sceptical point of view. While the literature contains interesting analyses, and while Harris argues that a good empirical case can be made that trade liberalization is favourable to economic growth, the evidence is far from conclusive. Part of the problem is that the models coming out of the endogenous growth literature are still too rudimentary, and contain too little detail to isolate and test important channels of transmission. Another reason is that we have little reliable evidence on the relative importance of human capital, investment and domestic R&D on economic growth, and even less information on how these factors interact with international trade flows.

John Whalley surveys the literature on the costs of interprovincial trade barriers. His own previous analysis suggested that these barriers amount to a tempest in a beer mug. That is, the costs are significant in only a few isolated and relatively small industries, the most obvious one being the beer industry. Whalley concludes that considerations of endogenous growth, together with an examination of more recent interprovincial trade data, do little to overturn this conclusion, mainly because the welfare effects running through endogenous technology in a multi-regional world are uncertain not just in magnitude but also in sign. Even more than in the international trade questions examined by Harris, it is hard to identify any specific channel of transmission by which the small static efficiency effects could plausibly be leveraged into something empirically significant.

The final paper in this section is that of Acheson and McFetridge. It re-examines the issue of intellectual property regimes in the light of endogenous growth theory. The paper contains an overview of how intellectual property is protected in Canada and of the various externalities that might be affected by such protection. It argues that endogenous growth theory, as it stands, has too contrived a structure of transaction costs to make intellectual property protection an important aspect of the problem, but that the theory does highlight two important and underexamined aspects of the intellectual property regime: the relationship between current innovators and follow-on innovators, and the relationship between proprietary research and open science. Both relationships are discussed at length in the paper.

FACILITATING KNOWLEDGE-BASED GROWTH

THE THIRD GROUP OF PAPERS deals with policies directed at promoting and facilitating the creation, diffusion and adoption of new technologies. It has been clear from the outset of endogenous growth theory that the increasing returns, externalities and imperfect competition found in the innovation process give a rationale for public intervention. But the developers of the theory have been reluctant to push these policy implications very far, largely because of an awareness that a lot more is involved than is in the models. For example, governments have to choose who gets subsidized, for what activities and according to what arrangements.

Aggregate models in which there is little or no variation along any of these dimensions are not well suited to the question. Nor are models that posit market failure without making reasonable allowance for government failure.

The paper by Lipsey and Carlaw looks at the structural details of various innovation policies in an attempt to determine what distinguishes successful from unsuccessful policies. The authors have assembled files on 30 different cases of innovation policy in Canada and other countries. The paper provides thumbnail sketches of each case and classifies them according to several conventional criteria: successful or unsuccessful, aimed at achieving big leaps in technology or just incremental gains, and attempting to push back the frontiers or just catch up with others. The analysis is organized using the structural view of growth put forth by Lipsey and Bekar who postulate that the effects of technological change depend crucially on the degree to which the change is compatible with the structure of the economy. Their paper also classifies the cases according to the magnitude of the structural change entailed by the attempted innovations. Based on these case studies, the paper suggests that, generally speaking, the chances of a policy succeeding are greater if it aims at incremental changes rather than great leaps; not too much structural change is entailed by the innovations it seeks to promote; and the policy allows flexibility for the private sector to respond to the uncertainties of the innovation process.

This paper breaks new ground in comparative policy studies and is a model of how informed judgment can shed light on a problem that endogenous growth theory raises but has been incapable of resolving.

The other paper in this section, by Acs, de la Mothe and Paquet, looks at the question of whether innovation policy should attempt to be sector-neutral or whether it should be targeted at strategic groups of interlinked industries, regions or firms that generate synergies through technology spillovers and other externalities. The paper argues that Nelson's concept of a national system of innovation should be replaced by a concept based more on the importance of local networks. It discusses the origins of local networks, provides evidence of their growing importance and argues that networks often internalize the externalities of the innovation process. The main policy implications of the analysis are that the "centralized mind set" should be replaced by a bottom-up approach, and that a sub-national infrastructure should be provided to support local interactions. The bottom-up emphasis of this paper echoes the emphasis placed by Lipsey and Carlaw on the need to allow for private sector flexibility in dealing with uncertainty.

CANADA AND THE GLOBAL TELECOMMUNICATIONS REVOLUTION

THE FINAL GROUP OF PAPERS deals with a sector of the Canadian economy that is particularly central to knowledge-based growth – telecommunications. This sector undertakes a sizeable fraction of all R&D spending in the Canadian economy. The resulting innovations affect the efficiency of the entire economy, since communication is vital for linking the whole economy together. Communication networks are, of course, rife with the externalities and spillovers characteristic of the growth process. Moreover, the telecommunications sector is at the heart of the information–communication revolution that underlies so much technological change.

The paper by Röller and Waverman discusses some of the problems involved in measuring the importance of telecommunications infrastructure for the growth process. It points out that there is a positive cross-country correlation between real GDP and the number of telephone main lines. But it also points out that there are causal relationships going in both directions. So one cannot determine, from this correlation alone, which of the following hypotheses has the most truth to it: that telephones facilitate growth, that growth promotes the demand for telephones or that telephone lines are correlated with more fundamental determinants of economic growth. The insights provided by this paper should point toward valuable empirical research.

Bernstein's paper examines the R&D spillovers arising from the telecommunications equipment industry. It estimates the effects on the Canadian manufacturing sector of R&D arising within the sector itself, of R&D done in the United States and of R&D done in the telecommunications equipment sector. The paper finds that the biggest spillover comes from U.S. R&D, but that the spillover from the telecommunications equipment sector is also significant – a 1 percent rise in R&D capital in the telecommunications equipment sector leads to a reduction of 0.011 percent in unit variable costs. The paper also calculates a social rate of return of 55 percent to R&D investment in the telecommunications equipment sector, some three times the private rate of return. Altogether, the paper's findings suggest a strong rationale for government policies to promote R&D in this key sector.

Finally, Globerman's paper examines the economic consequences of the information highway. The paper contains a useful description of what is involved in the information highway, and emphasizes that its economic impact will depend, not on its average productivity, but on its marginal productivity. Globerman takes a sceptical view, arguing that the uses for the information highway that people have imagined so far are already served by existing facilities, almost as well as they would be with a much costlier system. Moreover, it points out grounds for being wary of the externalities argument for government intervention in this area. Of course, the future of technological change is always an uncertain one, and Globerman admits that the visionaries may indeed be right, even though the objective evidence to support their claims appears weak. But his analysis suggests a need for caution before we make huge irreversible infrastructure investments and for a willingness to rely on the same competitive market forces here as in other domains.

CONCLUSION

A S THIS BRIEF INTRODUCTION SUGGESTS, there are few definite conclusions to be drawn from the papers in this volume. Instead, there are some general lessons and a lot of suggestions for future research. It should be remembered that the theory of endogenous growth is still less than a decade old. No one should be surprised that such a comparatively new theory requires further development. Moreover, nothing in this collection of papers suggests that endogenous growth theory provides a misleading approach to the questions involved, just that more structural detail needs to be added. However, with its abundant suggestions as to what details are needed and how they might be provided, this volume is a useful guide for any future work on policy issues related to Canadian economic growth.

Part I   Sources of Knowledge; Concepts and Measurement

Peter Howitt
Department of Economics
University of Western Ontario
and Canadian Institute for Advanced Research

1

On Some Problems in Measuring Knowledge-Based Growth

INTRODUCTION

THE TITLE OF THIS CONFERENCE seems to imply that there is something new about growth being based on knowledge, as does the oft-heard remark that we are now in a knowledge era, in which knowledge is somehow more important than it was in the past. This idea is misleading. It has long been the consensus among economists who have studied the problem that long-term growth is always based on the growth of technical and organizational capabilities. Likewise, every era of rapid sustained growth has been one in which new knowledge transformed peoples' lives. The information revolution we are now living through is dramatically raising the premium on particular kinds of knowledge and skills, while rendering others obsolete. But the same was true of the explosion in technological knowledge in textiles in the late 18th and early 19th centuries, and of technological progress in agriculture in the first half of the 20th century, to pick just two examples.

What is new about knowledge from the economist's point of view is that we are now beginning to incorporate it into our framework of analysis, not as an extraneous outside influence but as one of the main unknowns whose evolution we seek to explain as the outcome of economic forces. Although many of the ideas of endogenous growth theory go back to such writers as Schumpeter, and even as far back as John Rae (1834), and although economic historians and specialists on technology had been analyzing the sources of knowledge and productivity growth for many years before the rise of endogenous growth theory, it was only with the work of Romer (1986), Lucas (1988) and their followers that economists were able to incorporate these ideas into simple dynamic, stochastic, general equilibrium models.

In the simplest aggregate growth models, knowledge is treated much as if it were just another good, capable of being accumulated like capital and aggregated with the same precision (or lack of precision) as capital. Output equals AK, where A measures knowledge and K measures capital, and where there are separate but similar technologies for making A and K grow, each using the existing A and K as an input to the growth process. However, most growth theorists, even within the neoclassical tradition, take seriously the idea that knowledge is not a commodity and cannot be modelled as one. The biggest theoretical accomplishment of endogenous growth theory has been to discover how to modify standard neoclassical general equilibrium models, which were originally designed to deal with the production, exchange and use of commodities, to analyze the production, exchange and use of knowledge, while recognizing some of the essential differences between knowledge and commodities.

Although there has been progress in modelling knowledge at the theoretical level, less progress has been made at the empirical level. If knowledge is indeed different from other goods, then it must be measured differently from other goods, and its relationship to the price system must be different from that of other goods. But, the theoretical foundation on which national income accounting is based is one in which knowledge is fixed and common, where only prices and quantities of commodities need to be measured. Likewise, we have no generally accepted empirical measures of such key theoretical concepts as the stock of technological knowledge, human capital, the resource cost of knowledge acquisition, the rate of innovation or the rate of obsolescence of old knowledge.

To some extent, the situation is one of theory before measurement, to paraphrase one of the apostles of real business cycle theory (Prescott, 1986). But to lay the blame on empirical economists or on data-gathering agencies would be disingenuous. It would be more accurate to say that formal theory is ahead of conceptual clarity. As the Cambridge, United Kingdom side of the Cambridge capital controversy used to insist, the real question is one of meaning, not measurement. Only when theory produces clear conceptual categories will it be possible to measure them accurately.

This paper discusses some of these conceptual issues, suggests ways in which they might be clarified and points out problems they raise for the understanding of technical change and economic growth. It develops the main point that because of our inability to measure properly the inputs and outputs to the creation and use of knowledge, standard measures of Gross National Product (GNP) and productivity give a misleading picture. In particular, our failure to include a separate investment account for knowledge the way we do for physical capital means that much of an economy's annual output is simply missed.

These measurement problems have important implications for measuring growth even in a steady state. But they particularly distort standard measures of growth during a period of transition such as we are going through now when the information revolution has greatly enhanced the opportunities for knowledge creation. In particular, they imply that GNP and productivity may appear to be slowing down when in fact they are surging. The discussion that follows is aimed at clarifying the nature of this measurement problem during such a period of transition as well as during periods of steady-state growth.

Knowledge as a Capital Good?

I DEFINE KNOWLEDGE IN TERMS OF POTENTIALLY OBSERVABLE BEHAVIOUR, as the ability of an individual or group of individuals to undertake, or to instruct or otherwise induce others to undertake, procedures resulting in predictable transformations of material objects.[1] The knowledge can be codified, as when it is transmitted by mathematical theorems or computer programs that can be reproduced through known procedures; or it can be tacit, as when it exists only in the minds of particular individuals or in the established routines of organizations, and is not capable of routine transmission or reproduction.

This definition restricts knowledge to the capabilities of individuals and organizations. It could alternatively be defined as imbedded in goods, as when a computer program is encoded in a file on a diskette. I prefer to think of such a diskette as a unique commodity which can be used in consumption or production, the creation of which required knowledge in the possession of some individual or group of individuals. But there is probably nothing fundamental at stake here. One might just as well think of a properly inscribed diskette in the same terms as a properly indoctrinated graduate student. All that really matters at this stage is to be as clear as possible.

The above definition also rules out knowledge in the abstract. Books, blueprints and computer programs are instruments that different people use to create similar knowledge, not instruments for them merely to use previously existing knowledge. This interpretation alters the usual distinction between the production and diffusion of knowledge, for it implies that the reader creates knowledge much as the writer did. What is different in the two cases is the process by which the knowledge is created, and the degree to which the knowledge being created substitutes for pre-existing knowledge. The writer probably took more time and effort, and the knowledge created during the writing of the book had a greater scarcity value at the time of writing than did the knowledge created by the millionth reader. One reason for defining knowledge this way is that much of what is commonly thought of as costless imitation is, in fact, a costly process that resembles, in many ways, the process of innovation. Any time an individual sets out to learn something, some of it will come from observing what others have done, and some of it will be novel.

A piece of knowledge thus defined is like a capital good. It can be produced, exchanged and used in the production of other goods, or in the production of itself. It can also be stored, although subject to depreciation, as when people forget or let their skills deteriorate, and subject also to obsolescence, as when new knowledge comes along to supersede it. In each case, however, there are important differences between knowledge and capital goods.

Production

THE PRODUCTION OF KNOWLEDGE is, to some extent, a by-product of activities with other purposes, as when people learn from the experience of producing or consuming some good, or when they learn of others' experiences by word of mouth. More generally, it takes place for the same reason as the production of any capital good. Firms spend resources, in the form of research and development (R&D), training, market research, sending people to conferences, etc., with the intended objective of creating knowledge. Households also undergo sacrifices to create knowledge by acquiring an education. Even the activities of learning by doing and learning by using are not as serendipitous as theory often portrays them, as firms can and do go out of their way to experiment, to solicit information from clients and from workers, and to reflect on the lessons of experience.

One big difference between the production of capital goods and the production of knowledge is that the latter typically entails a deeper element of uncertainty. Uncertainty has not yet played a big role in endogenous growth theory, although those working in the evolutionary tradition have rightly focused on it as one of the chief salient characteristics of knowledge. The idea, typical in endogenous growth models, that people have rational expectations about the consequences of innovative activity, is almost a contradiction in terms, since to innovate is to do what no one had thought of before. Of course, when new knowledge consists of the capability of producing new capital goods, then investment in those new capital goods will be subject to the same sort of uncertainty. But to the extent that much physical investment consists of replicating existing capital structures in familiar situations, uncertainty affects it less than it does the creation of new knowledge.

Another difference between the production of capital goods and the production of knowledge is the form of the output. Most types of physical capital take the form of physical implements whose value can be readily appropriated by a single controlling agent, although there are, of course, public capital goods, such as roads and monuments, that entail sizeable transaction costs when appropriated for use. Knowledge, on the other hand, is embodied in people and organizations. In the first case, it takes the form of human capital – a notoriously difficult concept to measure accurately. In the latter case, it takes a form that so far has eluded endogenous growth theory – that of organizational routines.

A digression on organizational routines is in order here, given the difficulty of incorporating them into neoclassical economics. When a large business firm learns to implement new production methods or to reorganize its divisional structure to take better advantage of individual initiative, much of the knowledge is dispersed among the different members of the organization. As in Hayek's (1945) famous vision of the decentralized economy, the organizational routines may allow the knowledge of individual participants to be aggregated efficiently even though no individual has a detailed understanding of the entire operation. In that sense, the organization "possesses" knowledge which may not exist at the individual level. Indeed if, as Hayek can be interpreted as saying, much of the individual knowledge used by the organization is tacit, it may not even be possible for one individual to acquire the knowledge embodied in a large corporation.[2]

Perhaps the most important difference between the production of capital goods and the production of knowledge arises from the fact that many of the methods of producing knowledge use the knowledge of other people or other firms as an input.

That is, one can observe nature or one can observe others, or what others have done. Given the practical difficulty of monitoring what others are observing, this implies a social aspect not necessarily present in other forms of production. This social aspect makes it difficult, and in many cases impossible, to appropriate the full social benefits accruing to the creation of knowledge. Even with patents that fully protect a monopoly of certain types of knowledge that can be codified, there will be a spillover. For example, the ease with which others can reproduce the knowledge I create, once they hear about it, or once they do some reverse engineering, will allow them to generate further knowledge, as one new insight sparks another.

The positive externality from knowledge-generating activities that this implies is a central aspect of almost all endogenous growth theories. It is also present in the production of physical capital (as the original studies of ship and aircraft production indicated) but only to the extent that production of knowledge and capital is a joint activity. It is often just the knowledge emerging from this activity that is hard to appropriate. For instance, an aircraft can be sold, and its benefits appropriated, much as would be the case for any other good, but the producer will not be compensated for all the resulting increases in knowledge of how to improve aircraft production.

The main implication of all these considerations is that most knowledge-creating activities are imperfectly measured. We do have survey-based measures of R&D activities of business firms and government agencies (see Dosi, 1988 for an international comparison of aggregate measures) and, of course, we have measures of input in the educational sector. It is commonly acknowledged, however, that there are lots of informal training, learning, observing, experimenting and other activities taking place within firms and households that go completely unmeasured. More specifically, although wages and other incomes earned by the factors involved may be recorded as part of national income, they are treated as payments for inputs into the creation of goods and services, whereas in truth they are payments for inputs into the creation of knowledge.

EXCHANGE

STRICTLY SPEAKING, THE ABOVE DEFINITION OF KNOWLEDGE implies that it cannot be exchanged between two individuals in the sense usually envisioned by neoclassical price theory. That is, I can share ideas with someone in a conversation or correspondence, and each of us can thereby acquire some of the other's knowledge. One of us might even pay the other for the exchange, as in a consulting relationship. But this "exchange" does not require either of us to give up any of the knowledge being transacted. One way to look at this is to say, as Romer (1990) has emphasized, that knowledge is a "non-rival good," like many public goods, which can be shared by many people without diminishing the amount available to any one of them. But to remain consistent with our definition of knowledge as capability rather than as a disembodied idea, we must instead view any such procedure for "exchanging" information as involving the production of new knowledge. Pure exchange per se is not possible.

While this view of exchange, as necessarily involving an act of creation much like that of the usual notion of production, may strike many economists as odd, it ought to be more common in economics. The standard parable of a pure exchange economy, in which people somehow exchange goods on a large scale without the costly intermediation of business firms that create, operate and maintain markets, and continually strive to improve them, is far removed from anyone's daily life in a modern economy. It is hard to think of any significant transaction activities that people undertake that do not involve establishments that exist mainly to facilitate such transactions – usually business firms but often government or other non-profit agencies. According to the estimates of Wallis and North (1986), the facilitation of transactions absorbs more resources in the U.S. economy than does the pure transformation of inanimate nature. As Clower and Howitt (1995) have argued, the typical act of exchange is one in which two parties – one of which is a specialist business enterprise – lay out resources in order that one of them ends up with money and the other with command over some object or objects. When the object being exchanged is knowledge, the resource cost incurred by the seller need not include a sacrifice of his or her own command over the object.

There is another major difference, however, between the exchange of information and the exchange of capital goods, and that has to do with asymmetric information. A central theme of modern economic theory is that someone wanting to buy something from someone who knows more about it is likely to suffer from problems of moral hazard and adverse selection, and the anticipation of these problems may prevent the transaction from occurring. The problems are unavoidable when knowledge is being traded, in which case, the asymmetry of information that can create market failure is a necessary precondition for there to be a gain from the exchange in the first place. The problems are particularly intractable when tacit knowledge is being sold. Since it cannot be codified, but must instead be taught in a more personal manner, such knowledge is, in the terminology of modern contract theory, non-contractible. Failure of the seller to deliver what was agreed on cannot be remedied easily through the courts – a point which Stigler's (1973) satire on "truth in teaching" illustrates.

Because of these asymmetries of information, together with the difficulty of observing others' use of information, most industrial R&D is done in house (Dosi, 1988) rather than licensed or contracted out. A firm cannot resolve all the agency problems which these asymmetries imply[3] but can presumably internalize them more effectively than can impersonal markets. Although a considerable part of R&D is "sold" to government agencies, private purchases of R&D are relatively scarce.[4] In short, there are few markets in which newly created industrial knowledge is traded, and hence few market prices (as opposed to notoriously unreliable internal transfer prices) to use as a measure of even the private value of R&D. And of course, the problem of appropriability implies that even those prices that do exist do not accurately reflect social values.

USE, DEPRECIATION AND OBSOLESCENCE

KNOWLEDGE CAN BE USED for many of the same general purposes as can commodities. People can use it as a consumption good, as when they read or do research out of pure intellectual curiosity. They can also use it to produce other goods, to create new market opportunities or to generate still more knowledge. Economists have little to say about the purely private activity of consumption that would distinguish knowledge from other commodities. But certain features of knowledge that make its use, as a producer's good, somewhat different from the use of capital goods can be identified.

The first such feature lies at the heart of endogenous growth theory, namely that the use of knowledge necessarily entails increasing returns to scale. As an example, consider a firm attempting to produce a new line of products. If it succeeds, the cost of the R&D which allowed the firm to create the new line will appear as a sunk cost to the firm's subsequent operations. Each time it produces a batch of the new goods, the firm will have to spend more on capital and labour, but it will not have to pay for more knowledge by redoing the R&D.

The problem of increasing returns is that it is incompatible with the standard framework of general equilibrium under perfect competition. Under conditions of competitive equilibrium, firms must be too small to have market power and must earn normal profits. But this would not be an equilibrium situation, if a firm that increased its scale to the point where it had some market power could operate more efficiently and thereby reap supernormal profits. This means that if general equilibrium is modelled in such an economy, there either must be imperfect competition, or the economies of scale must be external to the firms. In the latter case, no individual firm would see itself as being in a position to gain from economies of scale by expanding its operations, since the economies depend on the scale of the entire industry or economy, not of its own operations.

The second feature of knowledge that makes its use in production essentially different from the use of capital goods is that it automatically creates obsolescence of other knowledge, as well as of other capital goods. In the early 19th century, the knowledge of how to build power looms created devastating losses for hand-loom weavers, whose human capital was highly valued. They were quickly rendered obsolete by the new power looms. Knowledge of how to produce and use personal computers and word processors is similarly rendering obsolete typewriters, plants for producing typewriters and the specialized knowledge of how to produce and use typewriters. In short, the creation of new knowledge almost always involves what Schumpeter called creative destruction.

At one level, creative destruction means that the activity of producing knowledge entails negative externalities. As Aghion and Howitt (1992) showed, in the context of a Schumpeterian growth model, there is a rent-seeking aspect to the creation of knowledge which means that, under laissez faire, society may spend more than the optimal amount of resources in the generation of new knowledge. But there is a deeper implication, according to which one of the major uses of knowledge is enabling firms to compete with each other. For, as Schumpeter stressed, the essence of the competitive struggle in a free economy has little to do with whether or not firms take prices as parametric, as in textbook price theory. Instead, it involves the very innovative process that gives rise to creative destruction. The firms that survive this struggle do not respond to adversity by reallocating resources and manipulating prices within known technological parameters. They respond by innovating, by finding previously undiscovered ways to trim costs and open up new markets, and by creating new products that can be sold even in hard times.

The final aspect of knowledge that makes its use different from that of capital is that, to a large extent, it is used not just to produce more goods at a lower cost (as in the case of a pure process innovation) but to produce goods that didn't exist before. Equivalently, knowledge can also be used to raise the quality of previous goods to a level never before experienced. Of course, quality improvements are notoriously hard to measure, and the difficulty of doing so is something that has long plagued the construction of reliable price indexes and measures of real output, at both the aggregate and sectoral levels.

MEASURING OUTPUT, PRODUCTIVITY AND KNOWLEDGE

THE MAIN IMPLICATIONS OF THE ABOVE DISCUSSION for endogenous growth theory can be summarized by saying that the very features which make knowledge distinct from capital goods create four major measurement problems. The first is the "knowledge-input problem." That is, the amount of resources devoted to the creation of knowledge is certainly underestimated by standard measures of R&D activity, by resources used in the educational sector (which exclude a lot of informal activities routinely undertaken by firms and individuals) and by the private cost of education borne by individuals. Many workers, who are counted as engaged in production, management or other non-research activities, spend a considerable amount of their time and energy looking for better ways to produce and sell the output of the enterprise they are employed by and, hence, their compensation should be counted, at least in part, as contributing to the cost of creating knowledge.

The second major measurement problem is the "knowledge-investment problem." That is, the output of knowledge resulting from formal and informal R&D activities is typically not measured at all, because it does not result in an immediate commodity with a market price. From the Haig-Simons point of view, the creation of knowledge ought to be treated like the creation of capital goods since, in either case, there is an expenditure of resources that could alternatively have been used to produce current consumption but which has instead been devoted to the enhancement of future consumption opportunities. Yet the national accounts include no category of final expenditure that would capture a significant amount of the annual increment to society's stock of knowledge the way it captures the annual increment to society's stock of capital – except for the output of the educational sector and for R&D undertaken by or sold to the government sector. None of the new knowledge generated by R&D undertaken by business firms on their own account (which includes most of industrial R&D) results in a direct positive contribution to current

GNP or to the current value added of that sector of the economy, as it would if the resources had instead been devoted to the creation of new capital goods.

To make this point more explicitly, consider the case of a firm that hires additional R&D workers at a cost of $1 million during the current year. The only result of the additional expenditure is a new patent discovered at the very end of the year, which will enable the firm to earn additional profits in future years, with an expected discounted value of $2 million. Since firms are not permitted to capitalize such R&D expenditures, this sequence of events will not result in any increase in current output from that sector as far as the national income accounts are concerned. Likewise, from the income side of the accounts, although there has been an additional $1 million in wages and salaries (assuming that the workers were hired from out of the labour force), there has been an offsetting decrease in profits, since the expenditure by the firm resulted in no increased current revenue. If, instead of the patent, the workers had produced a machine worth $2 million, GNP would have been higher by $2 million.[5]

Of course, to the extent that R&D results in more or better goods being produced, it does eventually affect measured GNP. But new knowledge should also be counted as output when it is created, just as physical investment is counted when it is created even though it eventually has a further effect on GNP by increasing the potential to produce other goods. Furthermore, to the extent that R&D results in better goods, many of its future effects on GNP will not be measured, because of the third major measurement problem, the "quality-improvement problem." As many writers have observed, to the extent that knowledge creation within business firms results in improved goods and services, the practical difficulties of dealing with new goods and quality improvements in constructing price indexes imply that much of the resulting benefit goes unmeasured.

The fourth problem is the "obsolescence problem." If standard measures of GNP ought to include a separate investment account for the production of knowledge then, by the same token, Net National Product (NNP) and national income ought to include a deduction corresponding to the depreciation of the stock of knowledge that takes place as it is superseded, or otherwise reduced in value, by new discoveries and innovations. Furthermore, the creation of new knowledge is also a factor accounting for the depreciation of existing physical capital. Depreciation is a notoriously difficult problem to account for in any case. The timing and extent of replacement investment are endogenous variables that the national income accountant can only capture in rough measure by applying simple mechanical formulas. But the problem becomes even more acute when a wave of innovations accelerates the rate of obsolescence of old knowledge and capital.

In a steady-state economy, the most serious of these measurement problems would be that of quality improvement. Much of the growth of productivity and output, in the long run, is the result of product innovations that generate new and improved goods whose contributions to output are only partially measured. Gordon (1990) for example, has estimated that correcting properly for quality improvements in capital goods alone would at least double the growth rate of aggregate real investment in the United States over the period from 1947 to 1983. Many of the gains from better capital goods are eventually reflected in GNP growth when the improved capital goods boost output in other sectors. But even then, the problem will distort measured productivity growth in different sectors, as when the airline industry is credited with productivity growth that actually occurred in the airframe and engine industries. Furthermore, to the extent that the improved capital goods allow other sectors to create new and improved products, the productivity gains may not even be measured in those sectors, as when more powerful computers allow banks to produce a better quality of service.[6]

By contrast, neither the knowledge-input problem nor the knowledge-investment problem would necessarily create distorted measures of growth in a steady state. Since productivity growth in all sectors would be the same and knowledge inputs would be growing at the same rate as production inputs, the failure to include the knowledge sector when measuring output would not distort growth rates. The effect on the level of output, however, would be potentially quite large. A country that devoted 2.5 percent of its inputs to R&D investment and 20 percent to physical investment would have to add 12.5 percent to the investment component of GNP to correct for this aspect of the knowledge-investment problem, if the two kinds of investment activities yielded the same rate of return. If, as many have argued, R&D investment has a social productivity that is much higher than the social productivity of physical investment, and if the level of knowledge input broadly conceived were much higher than 2.5 percent of total resources, then the unmeasured investment output would be correspondingly higher than 12.5 percent of measured investment.

By the same token, the obsolescence problem by itself would not cause any great distortions in a steady state, where the essential problem for the national income accountant would be to apply the right average rate of depreciation to each class of investment goods. This is, of course, not a trivial problem, but it would exist even in the absence of new knowledge.

During a period of adjustment to a cluster of fundamental innovations, such as we are now experiencing, the combined effect of the four problems probably produces a downward bias in conventional measures of GNP growth and productivity growth. Consider first the quality-improvement problem. Just as it causes part of economic growth to go unmeasured in a steady state, it also causes much of the surge of economic growth resulting from better computers and related goods to go unmeasured. Part of this problem has been dealt with by the adoption, in the United States and Canada, of hedonic measures of quality improvement in the computer industry. But similar measures have not been undertaken in other industries, e.g., the electronic equipment industry that manufactures chips.

Baily and Gordon (1988) have argued that the quality-improvement problem cannot account for much of the slowdown in productivity that took place in the late 1960s and early 1970s, mainly because the failure to measure quality improvements properly has been too steady over time. Moreover, the use of Paasche price indexes in the national income accounts, rather than Divisia indexes, creates a measurement bias in the other direction, especially now that the output of the computer sector has been adjusted to reflect quality improvements more accurately. That is, the output of goods whose quality improvements have been measured will contribute excessively to measured economic growth, since it will be weighted by base period prices that do not reflect the falling real price resulting from technical progress.

Griliches (1994) claims, however, that the fruits of the information revolution have been used disproportionately in sectors where quality improvements are next to impossible to measure. He estimates that over three quarters of the output of the computer industry is used in what he calls the unmeasurable sectors. Furthermore, the information revolution is contributing to an increase in the relative size of the unmeasurable sectors, which Griliches estimates now account for 70 percent of GNP in the United States.

Consider next the knowledge-input problem. When computers first started to change the way work was done throughout the economy, a long period of learning had to take place.[7] At first, people looked for ways in which the new tool could simply replace old ones without a radical change in operating techniques. Although some gains were obtainable in that direction, the added cost of information service departments was often larger than the benefits. Gradually, through a process of trial and error, people are now beginning to exploit the enormous potential of computers, but for many years there were no visible productivity gains associated with the adoption of sophisticated information technologies.

Part of the problem is that the time people spend learning to use computers efficiently, and all the associated costs of training and experimentation, are unmeasured knowledge input. When the opportunities for such knowledge-creating activities are enhanced by the arrival of new fundamental technologies, workers spend less time producing output and more time creating new knowledge. The fact that output does not seem to be rising as fast as before reflects this reduction in real production input. But, since there is no corresponding reduction in measured production input, it appears as if productivity growth has slowed down. Indeed, from a broader perspective, one might see the costly restructuring of firms and the sectoral reallocations involved in learning to exploit fundamental technologies better as an unmeasured knowledge input with similar effects on measured productivity growth.

Next, consider the knowledge-investment problem. Part of the effect of this problem during such a transitional period is the converse of the knowledge-input problem. The learning and restructuring that goes on, as people adjust to a new general-purpose technology, have an unmeasured output, in the form of knowledge accumulation. Even costly mistakes create knowledge of what not to do. If that output were properly measured, it would compensate for the fall in measured output that takes place when firms and workers start devoting more time to learning how to use their new tools.

Even beyond this, however, more workers go into knowledge-creating activities when new opportunities open up because the return to these activities has risen by more than the return to production activities. Thus, it seems likely that the knowledge investment that goes unmeasured is even greater than the fall in output that is measured. So, even if knowledge inputs were measured correctly, the knowledge-investment problem would imply that measured output and productivity growth would fail to reflect what has been, in fact, an increase in overall growth. Neither the inputs nor the outputs of a sector whose productivity and output are growing faster than average would be counted.

Finally, consider the obsolescence problem. To some extent, it moderates the distortions created by the knowledge-investment problem, because the net increase in society's stocks of capital and knowledge resulting from the information revolution would be overstated, if the accelerated obsolescence of pre-existing capital and knowledge were not considered. Thus, if we were to solve the knowledge-investment problem without dealing with the obsolescence problem, we would certainly overstate the gain in NNP and national income taking place during a technological transition, even though measures of GNP and gross productivity would not be affected by the omission.

Aside from this effect, the obsolescence problem generates a separate distortion which reinforces the understatement of productivity gains caused by the other problems during a wave of fundamental innovations. To the extent that unmeasured obsolescence reduces the effective stock of capital, standard measures of total factor productivity (TFP) will overstate the capital services component of inputs to the production process, and will thereby understate the productivity of those inputs.

A FORMAL MODEL

TO MAKE THESE IDEAS MORE CONCRETE, this section presents a simple abstract model to highlight the four measurement problems identified above. The model abstracts from all aspects of human capital, and focuses only on the question of the creation of new knowledge by the business sector. It assumes, for simplicity, that there are only two sectors of the economy: one producing capital goods (sector K) and one producing consumption goods (sector C).

Aggregate output from sector C is governed by the technological relationship:

$$C = Q_c (A_c) F_c (A_c, L_c^p, K) \tag{1}$$

where A_c represents the average stock of knowledge among firms in the C sector; F_c is the measurable number of units of some standardized consumption good being produced; Q_c is the average quality of these goods; L_c^p is the input of production labour in C; and K is the stock of capital. The stock of knowledge embodies both process and product innovations. The former are captured in the F_c function and the latter in the Q_c function.

The flow of aggregate gross output from sector K is governed by the technological relationship:

$$I = Q_k (A_k) F_k (A_k, L_k^p) \tag{2}$$

where the terminology is defined analogously to that of the first equation. For simplicity, and in order to highlight the use of computer capital in other sectors, I suppose that capital is used only in sector C.

The gross flow of new knowledge in the two sectors is governed by the relationships:

$$IA_k = \lambda A_k G_k (L_k^r) \tag{3}$$

$$IA_c = H(A_c, A_k) G_c (L_c^r) \tag{4}$$

where G functions represent the technology of knowledge creation; L^r represents labour input into knowledge creation in the two sectors; and λ is a parameter affecting the productivity of knowledge-creating activities in sector K. A wave of fundamental innovations, such as those involved in the ongoing information revolution, would be represented by an exogenous increase in λ. I suppose that the growth of knowledge in the two sectors is affected not only by current labour inputs but also by the accumulation of past knowledge. Knowledge in sector K is assumed to affect the growth of knowledge in sector C, because more sophisticated capital goods open up opportunities for more sophisticated applications in sector C, as when computers allow banks to invent new kinds of deposits.

The rate of obsolescence of old capital is assumed to be an increasing function of the rate of gross investment (because it takes new investment to render old capital obsolete) and of the rate of creation of new knowledge in sector K. Hence:

$$\dot{K} = \kappa(I, IA_k, K,) \equiv I - \delta(I, IA_k)K \tag{5}$$

where the net-investment function κ is increasing in gross investment I and decreasing in the other two arguments. The depreciation function δ includes the effects of obsolescence as well as physical wear and tear, and is increasing in both arguments.

The rate of obsolescence of old knowledge of either type is also assumed to be an increasing function of the rate of creation of that kind of knowledge. Hence:

$$\dot{A}_i = \alpha_i (IA_i, A_i) \equiv IA_i - \delta_i^a (IA_i)A_i \; ; \; i = c,k \tag{6}$$

21

The final aggregate relationship is the market clearing condition for labour:

$$L_c^p + L_k^p + L_k^r + L_c^r = L \tag{7}$$

where L is the aggregate supply of labour.

To make the measurement problems discussed above operational, I define growth in terms of GNP.[8] Ideally, GNP should include investment in all three categories (physical capital and the two kinds of knowledge):

$$Y \equiv C + \mu I + \mu_c IA_c + \mu_k IA_k \tag{8}$$

where μ refer to shadow prices representing the value to society of incremental units of the respective stocks, in terms of the consumption good. In the standard theory of growth without technological change, there would be just the one μ representing the shadow price of capital, which would be Tobin's q. The rate of growth is therefore:

$$g = (\dot{C}/C)(C/Y) + (\dot{I}/I + \dot{\mu}/\mu)(\mu I/Y) + g_A \tag{9}$$

where g_A represents the direct contribution of growth in investment in knowledge:

$$g_A \equiv \frac{1}{Y}\frac{d}{dt}(\mu_c IA_c + \mu_k IA_k) \tag{10}$$

Total factor productivity growth is g minus the contribution of increased inputs of capital and labour. The latter contributions are measured at market factor prices. The rental price of capital is taken to be the price of capital μ multiplied by the sum $r+\delta$, where r is the long-run average rate of interest and δ the long-run average rate of depreciation of capital:

$$\tau = g - \frac{\mu(r+\delta)\dot{K} + w(\dot{L}_c^p + \dot{L}_k^p)}{Y} \tag{11}$$

TFP growth in producing consumption goods is:

$$\tau_c = \frac{\dot{C}}{C} - \frac{\mu(r+\delta)\dot{K} + w\dot{L}_c^p}{C} \tag{12}$$

The knowledge-input problem can be captured simply by supposing[9] that the measured labour input into production in each sector includes a fraction ϵ_r of workers who are actually engaged in research:

$$Lm_i^p = L_i^p + \epsilon_r L_i^r; \quad i = c,k \quad 0 < \epsilon_q < 1 \tag{13}$$

The quality-improvement problem can be captured by supposing that the measured growth rate of quality improvement for each period in each sector is only the fraction $1 - \epsilon_q$ of the actual growth rate $dln(Q)/dt$. Assume there is some base year in which both actual and measured quality are defined to equal unity. Then measured consumption will differ from real consumption according to:

$$Cm = Q_c (A_c)^{1-\epsilon_q} F_c^p (A_c, L_c^p, K) = Q_c (A_c)^{-\epsilon_q} C \tag{14}$$

Likewise, under the same normalization assumption for the quality of capital goods:

$$Im = Q_k (A_k)^{1-\epsilon_q} F_k^p (A_k, L_c^p) = Q_k (A_k)^{-\epsilon_q} I \tag{15}$$

Because the quality of capital and consumption goods is mismeasured, so are their total quantities and their relative price μ. Assume, however, that the total dollar values of consumption and investment can be measured every year. Then, by dividing these two nominal quantities we get a measure of the relative values of the annual output from the two sectors: $\mu I/C$. The measured relative price will be consistent with this magnitude. Hence:

$$\mu m = \mu (I/Im) / (C/Cm) = (Q_k (A_k)/Qc (A_c))^{\epsilon_q} \mu \tag{16}$$

Equation (16) implies that, as Gordon (1990) has stressed, if quality improvements are larger in capital goods than in consumption goods, then the relative price of capital goods will be overstated.

Under these assumptions, measured output will equal:

$$Ym = Cm + \mu m_0 Im \tag{17}$$

which differs from its real counterpart Y in (8) by:

- not including anything representing current investment in knowledge;

- having measured instead of real consumption and investment; and

- having a fixed, measured relative price of capital instead of the current true relative price.

Note that, aside from the knowledge-investment and the Laspeyres quantity-index problems, the only quality-measurement problem that would distort the measure of GNP is the problem of measuring the quality of consumption goods. Any understatement of physical investment would be offset by an overstatement of the relative price of capital. That is, if the measured base price μm_0 was replaced in (17) by the measured current price μm as defined by (16), measured GNP would equal $Q_c(A_c)^{-\epsilon q}(C+\mu I)$, which differs from Y only by the non-inclusion of knowledge investment and the mismeasurement of the quality of consumption goods.

Corresponding to (17), the measured growth rate of GNP is:

$$gm = (c\frac{\dot{C}m}{Cm} + (1-c)\frac{\dot{I}m}{Im}) = (c\frac{\dot{C}}{C} + (1-c)\frac{\dot{I}}{I}) - \epsilon_q (c\frac{\dot{Q}_c}{Q_c} + (1-c)\frac{\dot{Q}_k}{Q_k}) \tag{18}$$

where c is the measured share of consumption in GNP. The measured rate gm differs from the actual growth rate g defined in (9) in four ways. First, c might not equal the actual share of consumption. Second, gm excludes the g_A term measuring the contribution of knowledge investment. Third, gm makes no allowance for the changing relative price of investment. None of these would matter in a steady state with balanced growth. Fourth, the quality-improvement problem tends to make $gm < g$, since $\epsilon_q > 0$. As discussed above, this last problem would exist even in a steady state with balanced growth.

To discuss the issue of productivity measurement, I first examine the special case in which the economy is in a steady state, where the rate of depreciation δ is constant and known. Then the measured capital stock will be:

$$Km(t) = \int_o^t e^{-\delta(t-\tau)} Im(\tau)d\tau + e^{-\delta t} Km(0) \tag{19}$$

As time passes and the effect of the initial guess $Km(0)$ wears off, the fact that investment is underestimated will imply that the capital stock is also underestimated. Hence, the effects of mismeasurement that tend to underestimate the growth of output will be offset to some extent by underestimation of the growth of capital.

To be more precise, in a steady state with investment growing at the constant proportional rate g, and with the quality of capital goods Q_k growing at the proportional rate ηg $(0<\eta<1)$, the capital stock will be underestimated by proportionately less than investment. That is, in such a steady state:

$$\frac{Km(t)}{K(t)} = \frac{\int_0^\infty e^{-\delta s} I(t-s)Q_k(t-s)^{-\epsilon q}\, ds}{\int_0^\infty e^{-\delta s} I(t-s)\, ds} = \frac{Im(t)}{I(t)} \frac{\int_0^\infty e^{-[\delta+g(1-\eta\epsilon q)]s}\, ds}{\int_0^\infty e^{-(\delta+g)s}\, ds} > \frac{Im(t)}{I(t)} \tag{20}$$

The reason behind this result is that the proportional measurement error in investment grows over time, and the capital stock, which is just a weighted sum of past investments, has a proportional measurement error which is a weighted sum of past proportional measurement errors.

Since the proportional measurement error on depreciation is the same as on the capital stock, it follows that the proportional measurement error on net investment in a steady state will exceed that on gross investment, because depreciation will not be understated by as much as will gross investment:

$$\frac{\dot{K}m(t)}{\dot{K}(t)} < \frac{\dot{I}m(t)}{\dot{I}(t)} \tag{21}$$

Measured TFP growth will be:

$$\tau m = gm - \frac{\mu m(r+\delta)\dot{K}m}{Ym} - \frac{w(1-\epsilon_r)(\dot{L}_c^p + \dot{L}_k^p)}{Ym} \tag{22}$$

In a steady state, the deduction for the growth in capital input in (22) will be understated. According to (16), the proportional measurement error for this deduction would have been the same as for consumption if gross investment had been used but, since net investment is used, the error will be larger than this.

This error in the numerator is offset, however, by the fact that the denominator is also undermeasured. Since the use of a Paasche index does not create any distortion in a steady state with the relative price of capital constant, the analysis following (17) implies that the proportional measurement error of the denominator is also greater than that of consumption. Then in a steady state, where the last term in (22) vanishes, TFP growth will be underestimated by approximately the same amount as GNP growth, and both changes will be attributable to the quality-improvement problem. In transitional periods, however, as mentioned above, all four problems will interact to distort measured TFP growth.

Measured TFP growth in sector C will be:

$$\tau m_c = \frac{\dot{C}m}{Cm} - \frac{\mu m(r+\delta)\dot{K}m}{Cm} - \frac{w(\dot{L}_c^p + \epsilon_r\dot{L}_c^r)}{Cm} \tag{23}$$

A comparison of (12) and (23) shows that, contrary to the case of aggregate TFP growth, the steady-state mismeasurement of TFP growth in sector C is likely to be less than that of GNP growth. For in this case, the underestimate of the numerator in the deduction for growth in capital input is not fully offset by any underestimate in the denominator. That is, according to (16) and (21), the value of net investment will be underestimated relative to consumption.

During transitional periods, the distortion of productivity growth in sector C will be more complicated. In particular, the information revolution is likely at first to create a bigger quality improvement problem for net investment than consumption, thus tending to create an overestimate of TFP growth in the consumption sector. But this will also be offset by the obsolescence problem, which will cause standard accounting procedures to miss the accelerated depreciation of capital. Unmeasured knowledge-input growth in sector C induced by the radical change in capital inputs will also cause TFP growth in sector C to be understated.

Conclusion

IF THE CRITICAL COMPONENT OF THIS PAPER has been larger than the constructive component, this is mainly attributable to the fact that the issue at hand is not likely to be fixed by minor tinkering with national income accounting practices. The underlying problem is that the very conceptual foundations on which national income accounting is based assume away the mainspring of long-term economic growth, by taking knowledge as unchanging and freely available. In such a world, market prices and quantities are all one needs to measure economic activity. In a world where growth is based on the creation, acquisition and use of knowledge, however, we need to look at other magnitudes, and a better conceptual foundation is needed before we know just what magnitudes to look at and how.

The paper suggests some general directions in which to look for better measures. First, to deal with the knowledge-input problem it would be helpful to ask business firms for more detailed information concerning their training, market research, brainstorming, exploration and other activities, both formal and informal. The paper in this volume by Baldwin, Johnson and Pedersen is a good example of what might be learned from asking such questions. At least some attempt could then be made to construct a more comprehensive measure of knowledge input, which could be used to get better measures of productivity in knowledge creation, and could be subtracted from other inputs to get better measures of productivity in narrower production activities. Of course, Canada's experience with the scientific research tax credit scheme in the 1980s shows that there is also a danger of going too far, that it might be possible to construe almost any activity as constituting R&D. But just because a problem is difficult, does not mean that nothing should be done about it.

Better measures of knowledge input would also help in dealing with the knowledge-investment problem. One way of dealing, at least imperfectly, with this issue is to impute, to the resources used in R&D, an investment value equal to the value of the resources used. The characteristic uncertainty and externalities of knowledge investment make this hazardous, since the value of knowledge will have a large random component, and even its expected social value will differ from the expected private value reflected in the value of R&D resources used.

In dealing with the knowledge-investment problem, one can seek better measures of output as well as input. Thus, data on patents and the rate of introduction of new goods,[10] new firms and new jobs all give clues to the extent of knowledge creation. These various quantitative measures have well-known problems,[11] most notably that knowing how many goods, patents, etc., have been created does not indicate what their social or even private value is. But it should be possible to use the sort of hedonic methods to attribute values to these characteristics of new knowledge that have been used since Griliches (1961) to assess the characteristics of new goods in dealing with the quality-adjustment problem. Moreover, a large part of the knowledge-investment problem will be solved if the new satellite accounts being set up by Statistics Canada, as recommended by the 1993 *System of National Accounts*, eventually result in the capitalization of R&D expenditures for national income accounting purposes.

The quality-improvement problem is perhaps the most susceptible to economic analysis, as it has been recognized and dealt with for many years within the economics discipline. What is needed is a more systematic use of hedonic regressions among statistical agencies, as has been done in the case of computers, to deal with quality improvements in other industries. But the use of hedonic measures is itself subject to well-known problems, most notably that measures are crucially dependent on judgments as to how the prices of new goods affect those of old goods in imperfect competition, how the introduction of new goods hastens quality improvements in old goods[12] and, most important in our context, how the sort of deep structural change the world is now undergoing affects the relationships between particular characteristics and social value.[13]

Finally, the obsolescence problem would be mitigated by studies such as Caballero and Jaffe (1993), which has provided at least a preliminary estimate of the rate of obsolescence of patentable ideas. More frequently revised estimates of the rate at which old capital is scrapped would also be helpful, and should be fairly straightforward to obtain. The fact that a large fraction of current investment in recent years has been in new computers, whose rate of obsolescence continues to be much higher than that of the average piece of business equipment, creates an overstatement of net investment that could and should be corrected by surveying business enterprises on the frequency of replacement.

ENDNOTES

1 This definition is broad enough to include knowledge used in service industries, where the material objects can include such items as hair (in the case of haircutting services) or even electrons (in the case of many information services). When all that is received is advice, as in many business service industries, for example, the output of that industry is itself knowledge.

2 Arrow (1994) makes a similar point about Hayek's conception of the use of knowledge.

3 Aghion and Tirole (1994) analyze how these problems might affect the organization of R&D.

4 This is not to deny the existence of joint research ventures and contracted R&D. Rose (1995) presents evidence from a survey of 3566 large R&D-performing firms indicating that 328 of the firms surveyed received funds from another company for conducting research.

5 The working group which produced the international *System of National Accounts* (OECD, Paris, 1993) considered recommending the capitalization of R&D expenditures for just these reasons. In the end, they decided to drop the recommendation, in view of the problems of measuring and evaluating such an intangible investment, although they did recommend the setting up of satellite R&D capital accounts on an experimental basis.

6 This point is made forcefully by Griliches (1994) in a paper summarizing a lifetime of research on the question of measuring the productivity gains from R&D and attributing them to the right sector.

7 David (1991) presents a provocative discussion of this problem.

8 See Usher (1980) for a comprehensive treatment of alternative measures of economic growth, including a discussion of the implications of different measures for the knowledge-investment problem.

9 Of course, statistical agencies cannot make any such supposition. They do the best they can, which we suppose, for simplicity, leaves a constant fraction of research workers misrepresented as being engaged in production.

10 See Klenow (1994), for example.

11 See Griliches (1979), for example.

12 This is the famous "sailing-ship" phenomenon that many economic historians have commented on.

13 See Jorgensen and Landau (1989) and Gordon (1990) for recent discussions of these problems.

ACKNOWLEDGEMENTS

USEFUL COMMENTS AND SUGGESTIONS were gratefully received from John Baldwin, Mike Denny, Fred Gault, Kishori Lal, Antoine Rose, David Rose, T.K. Rymes and Michael Wolfson, none of whom should necessarily be interpreted as agreeing with the contents of the paper.

BIBLIOGRAPHY

Aghion, Philippe and Peter Howitt. "A Model of Growth through Creative Destruction." *Econometrica.* 60, (March 1992): 323-351.

Aghion, Philippe and Jean Tirole. "On the Management of Innovation." *Quarterly Journal of Economics.* 109, (November 1994): 1185-1209.

Arrow, Kenneth J. "Methodological Individualism and Social Knowledge." *American Economic Review.* 84, (May 1994): 1-9.

Baily, Martin Neil and Robert J. Gordon. "The Productivity Slowdown, Measurement Issues, and the Explosion of Computer Power." *Brooking Papers on Economic Activity.* 2, (1988): 347-420.

Caballero, Ricardo J. and Adam B. Jaffe. "How High are the Giants' Shoulders: An Empirical Assessment of Knowledge Spillovers and Creative Destruction in a Model of Economic Growth." In *NBER Macroeconomics Annual, 1993.* Cambridge, MA: MIT Press, 1993. pp. 15-74.

Clower, Robert W. and Peter Howitt. "Money, Markets and Coase." In *Is Economics Becoming a Hard Science?* Edited by Antoine d'Autume and Jean Cartelier. Proceedings of conference in Paris, October 1992 (forthcoming).

David, Paul. "Computer and Dynamo: The Modern Productivity Paradox in a Not-Too-Distant Mirror." In *Technology and Productivity.* Paris: Organization for Economic Co-operation and Development, 1991, pp. 315-348.

Dosi, Giovanni. "Sources, Procedures, and Microeconomic Effects of Innovation." *Journal of Economic Literature*. 26, (September 1988): 1120-1171.

Gordon, Robert J. *The Measurement of Durable Goods Prices*. Chicago: University of Chicago Press, 1990.

Griliches, Zvi. "Hedonic Price Indexes for Automobiles: An Econometric Analysis of Quality Change." In *The Price Statistics of the Federal Government*. Washington, DC: National Bureau of Economic Research, 1961, pp. 173-196.

———. "Issues in Assessing the Contribution of Research and Development in Productivity Growth." *Bell Journal of Economics*. 10, (1979): 92-116.

———. "Productivity, R&D, and the Data Constraint." *American Economic Review*. 84, (March 1994): 1-23.

Hayek, F. A. "The Use of Knowledge in Society." *American Economic Review*. 35, (September 1945): 519-530.

Jorgensen, Dale W. and Ralph Landau, eds. *Technology and Capital Formation*. Cambridge, Mass: MIT Press, 1989.

Klenow, Peter J. "New Product Innovations." Unpublished, University of Chicago, January 1994.

Lucas, Robert E. Jr. "On the Mechanics of Economic Development." *Journal of Monetary Economics*. 22, (January 1988): 3-42.

Prescott, Edward C. "Theory Ahead of Business Cycle Measurement." In *Carnegie Rochester Conference Series on Public Policy*. Vol. 25, 1986, pp. 11-66.

Rae, J. *Statement of Some New Principles on the Subject of Political Economy*. Boston: Hilliard, Gray and Co., 1834.

Romer, Paul M. "Increasing Returns and Long-Run Growth." *Journal of Political Economy*. 94, (October 1986): 1002-1037.

———. "Endogenous Technological Change." *Journal of Political Economy*. 98, (October 1990): S71-S102.

Rose, Antoine. "Strategic R&D Alliances." *Service Indicators - 4th Quarter 1994*. Ottawa: Statistics Canada, Cat. No. 63-016, Vol. 1, No. 3, 1995.

Stigler, George. "A Sketch of the History of Truth in Teaching." *Journal of Political Economy*. 81, (March-April 1973): 491-495.

Usher, Dan. *The Measurement of Economic Growth*. New York: Columbia University Press, 1980.

Wallis, John J. and Douglass C. North. "Measuring the Transaction Sector in the American Economy, 1870-1970." In *Long-Term Factors in American Economic Growth*. Edited by Stanley Engerman and Robert Gallman. Chicago: University of Chicago Press, 1986.

Comment

Thomas K. Rymes
Department of Economics
Carleton University

[F]ormal theory is ahead of conceptual clarity. As the Cambridge, United Kingdom side of the Cambridge capital controversy used to insist, the real question is one of meaning, not measurement (Howitt).

INTRODUCTION

IT IS ALWAYS A PLEASURE to read anything by Peter Howitt. Though it is an added pleasure to be able to comment on what he has written, I do so with trepidation, because I disagree with him on a number of points.

The paper essentially deals with measurement problems which Professor Howitt claims yield steady-state measures of the rate of economic growth which are too low. (This translates, in nominal terms, to the argument that our overall measures of the rate of inflation will be too high.) More important, he argues that the measurement problems, when applied to a sequence of temporary equilibria, as the system adjusts from a low to a high rate of growth, will be such that, not only will the level of measured output be too low, but the temporary equilibria growth rates of output and capital will be too low so that "GNP and productivity may appear to be slowing down when in fact they are surging" (Howitt). (In such expansionary temporary equilibria, the overall rate of change of prices, if recorded as rising, may not be rising and may in fact be falling.)

If these measurement errors that stem from the endogenous knowledge growth literature are, in fact, in our current measures of output and total factor productivity (TFP) growth, they would raise serious doubts about their own validity and about our understanding of the processes of economic growth. (They would also raise doubts about the anti-inflationary stance of our monetary authorities and about the welfare costs of steady-state and incipient temporary equilibria inflations on which Professor Howitt has made such important contributions.[1])

The four measurement problems discussed by Professor Howitt are the "knowledge-input problem," the "knowledge-investment problem," the "quality-improvement problem" and the "obsolescence problem." Much of what Professor Howitt sees as problems stems from his theoretical view on endogenous growth and his position that the "underlying problem is that the very conceptual foundations on which national income accounting is based assumes away the mainsprings of long-term economic growth, by taking knowledge as unchanging and freely available" (Howitt).

National accounting does *not* take knowledge as unchanging nor does it record the stock of knowledge, or growth in it, as freely available. Input–output accounts are designed to show the changes and improvements in productive techniques as the blueprints change and the accounts record expenditures on knowledge acquisition as "on-the-job training" or "formal" education. Professor Howitt, drawing on the endogenous growth literature, is really arguing that many expenditures involved in acquiring advances in knowledge are not recorded in the accounts in the same way as expenditures on new capital goods, because of differences between acquiring new capital goods and acquiring new knowledge. The differences arise because of the problems of non-appropriability and increasing returns to scale.

The non-appropriability of advances in knowledge as part of the endogenous growth literature has been abandoned as deeper understanding of the Coasean position takes hold. The astonishing myriad of ways in which returns to expenditures on advancing knowledge are captured militate against Professor Howitt's position.[2] To the extent that individuals pay for their schooling, they capture the benefits. To the extent that costs are paid for collectively, the costs are recorded, while the fact that the benefits are not recorded is precisely why the expenditures are made collectively in the first place. This is not a new problem in national accounting or in the measurement of the level and growth of national output. One might as well argue that, with the rise of government, the level and growth of national product have been understated.

Professor Howitt also argues that the use of knowledge necessarily involves increasing returns to scale. When introducing new lines of product which emerge as a result of its research and development (R&D), a firm may have to replace its plant with capital goods of new design or retrain its labour force, because new goods may be associated with new techniques, and new techniques are associated with different physical capital goods and labour forces requiring new skills. Though such start-up costs do not have to be replicated as the firm considers repeat outputs of the new goods, I fail to see where increasing returns to scale appear. The extent to which technology may exhibit increasing returns to scale in the sense of Smith and Young, depends as Kaldor pointed out, on the rate of expansion for aggregate demand. We may be capturing economies of scale or technical progress, and since higher levels of production will involve different machines (with the newer and different machines being those associated with higher levels of output, picking up Professor Howitt's indivisibilities) which will be associated with the advances in technology, it becomes impossible to separate technical progress and increasing returns to scale as distinct sources of growth. Given that there is a theory indicating what rate aggregate demand is expanding means that the ghost of Keynes hangs over Professor Howitt's neoclassical models of endogenous growth. The rate of expansion of aggregate demand will be a factor determining the rate at which increasing returns or induced technical progress are occurring. That is a theory of endogenous growth, on which Professor Howitt's approach from the supply side alone does not dwell.[3]

MEASUREMENT

I TURN TO PROFESSOR HOWITT'S four measurement problems. The quality-improvement issue comes primarily in the form of problems in the measurement of TFP. Howitt explicitly uses Hicks–Solow residuals. The difficulty with such residuals is that, while they show the increases in the efficiency with which labour and capital are used, they do not consider the increasing efficiency with which these capital inputs are produced. More correctly, the flow of services of the capital goods, is an endogenous input which is increasing partly because the services are being produced with ever-increasing efficiency. One wants Harrod residuals, where it is the increase in the efficiency with which labour and waiting are used that is measured. Waiting – the willingness of agents to postpone consumption involved in carrying, maintaining and augmenting capital goods – is the capital input associated with rates of return. The capital goods are associated with the rentals. The capital goods and their services result from waiting and from increases in the efficiency of waiting. This distinction is the dynamic part of the Cambridge capital controversy, to which Professor Howitt refers but does not "take on board."[4]

Consider a world in which the rate of exogenous technical progress in Harrod's sense is exactly the same in both the consumption good and the capital good sectors of Professor Howitt's basic scheme. In his model, no capital is used to produce capital. Therefore, the calculation of TFP in the production of capital goods is simple: it is the rate of growth of output per unit of labour, a formulation which exacerbates the confusion that Harrod-neutral technical progress is labour, and only labour, augmenting. Since Professor Howitt is assuming that the labour force growth is zero, then this is just the rate of growth of the output of the capital goods sector. In the steady state with Harrod neutrality, the rate of growth of the stock of capital and capital consumption in the production of consumption goods will be equal to the rate of productivity advance in the capital goods sector. Then the TFP measures Professor Howitt works with will show it to be growing less rapidly than the TFP in the capital goods sector. This is the outcome because it has been forgotten that the efficiency with which the growing stock of capital in the production of consumption goods is being produced is also rising. This is captured by the Harrod residuals.

Assume that the old price indexes for consumption and capital goods were showing no relative change. Suppose a statistical agency adopts the view that the technical progress taking place is really not in methods of production but in the models of capital goods being produced. The price index of capital goods is biased upward and a Robert Gordon hedonic price index adjustment is made, so the price index of capital goods will fall relative to that of consumption goods. The rate of TFP growth in the production of capital goods will be greater than before, and the rate of growth of TFP in the production of consumption goods will be correspondingly less.[5] Of course, the Harrod residuals will be unaffected because in the production of consumption goods, they automatically take into account the fact that the services of the capital goods used are now being produced with greater efficiency than before, in the sense of the improved models. If I understand Professor Howitt correctly, he accepts this. If all the estimates are converted back to consumption goods, and the relative quantity changes of new capital goods to consumption goods match the supposed differences in relative price changes, then the overall rate of growth of sustainable consumption and TFP in the Harrod sense remain unchanged, unless the price index of consumption goods is also adjusted for its supposed quality upward bias.[6] (Remember that, if the relative prices of capital goods in terms of consumption goods remain unchanged, this does *not* mean that the Solow and Harrod residuals are the same.[7]) Thus, all that is left to the supposed downward bias in the steady-state growth in net domestic product (NDP) is the upward bias, because of the supposed quality problem in the consumption goods price indexes.[8]

I turn now to the knowledge-input problem. Professor Howitt says that this is not a steady-state problem, but let us start with that case for simplicity. In the production of the consumption goods, I assume that the growth of all purchased R&D, all scientific machines and so forth has been properly recorded as growing capital inputs which are produced elsewhere but are used as capital inputs in the production of consumption goods. I also assume that part of the labour force in the production of consumption goods is engaged in R&D, and rather than treat such inputs along with other production workers, I capitalize their earnings so the R&D used in the production of consumption goods now also reflects this growing stock of human capital. It will have, within it, the labour applied in the past and the learning by doing, because those who have been in the activity longer will be earning higher real wages. In Professor Howitt's model, labour classified as production workers is not growing, but the stock of human capital – a part of the stock of R&D – is growing because the real wages of those who are said to contribute to R&D are growing at the same rate as real wages through the consumption goods sector. The capitalization of their earnings – both past and expected – is how one constructs the human capital addition to the stock of R&D in the industry.

The rate of growth of consumption would not be changed, but the Solow residual in the consumption goods sector would be reduced. One could argue that some of the productivity advance in the production of consumption goods would be accounted for, but that would simply reflect the fact that the Solow residuals are subject to the reclassification of inputs from primary to produced categories. The greater the number of capitalized inputs in a Solow residual that are capitalized, the lower the residuals, and the more you seemingly account for growth in productivity. The underlying Harrod residuals tend to be impervious to this classification of inputs.

Suppose technology, with the R&D knowledge capital as an input, exhibited increasing returns to scale. The R&D knowledge capital is growing and is said to contribute to the observed growth in consumption. Using Solow residuals and not treating knowledge as an input, we have:

$$c - [al + bk] = tc \tag{1}$$

where c is the growth rate of consumption; l and k are the growth rates of labour and capital; a and b are their respective partial elasticities; and tc is the Solow residual. Treating knowledge as an input we would have:

$$c - [a^{**}l + a^*k^* + bk] = tc^* \tag{2}$$

where a^{**} is the partial elasticity of the labour said not to be part of R&D human capital, k^* is the growth rate of the R&D human capital; $a^{**} + a^* = a$; and tc^* is less than tc. Before, if we doubled labour and capital, output would double if tc = 0 and technology exhibited constant returns to scale. If tc is greater than zero and we add knowledge as an input, k^* (and the growth of knowledge as an input, when capitalized, exceeds l), then the Solow residual would be reduced and we could not distinguish between technical progress and human knowledge capital accumulation. Where, however, are the increasing returns to scale?

What of Professor Howitt's argument that the transitions or traverses[9] from one steady state to another would be affected? Suppose part of the labour force classified as engaged in R&D is increased in a transition to a higher rate of growth. Would we then have a better measurement of the growth process? If the observed growth in the production of consumption goods was related to the observed growth in R&D, perhaps. But, within the context of the assumptions, the switch of labour away from production would slow down learning on the job. One could argue that the stock of human R&D had increased, but it is not clear whether the stock of human capital would necessarily do so. In addition, if increased activity in R&D by non-production workers should render obsolete, at a faster rate, the human capital employed by other non-production workers, it is not at all obvious that the growth of net output or sustainable consumption would be necessarily increased in transition states. (As I indicated, Professor Howitt has not incorporated the obsolescence problem seriously into his analysis.) In short, the fact that, in some transition phase, a larger part of the consumption output of the economy would be capitalized does not mean anything, so far as I can tell, with regards to the possible declines in the rate of growth of output being replaced by surges in the rate of growth if only the knowledge-input measurement problem could be resolved.

I turn to the knowledge-investment problem. Here I understand Professor Howitt to be saying that many activities which are concerned with the creation of new knowledge within firms are treated differently than if the activities had been engaged in the creation of capital goods and so were capitalized on the firms' accounts. This may be true, but I cannot see its significance. I have already discussed the problem of accounting for growth in the case of R&D. So I shall discuss the effects on productivity measurement. I believe that, according to Professor Howitt, when firms increase their purchases of capital goods, production workers have to spend time to learn how to use the new machines. Regular production is reduced while the retraining is under way. Professor Howitt argues that the retraining and retooling expenses should be capitalized. If some of these expenses involved intermediate inputs and they were capitalized, it is true that GNP would be higher. This is the old problem of how gross should GDP be. If these expenditures which are normally charged to operating results are capitalized, then the level of GNP would be higher. But would the level of NDP or sustainable consumption be higher? When the facts that such expenditures will be written off quickly and that the argument ignores the cost of the reallocation of the labour force from production (activities which may interrupt, as I have suggested, the returns from learning by doing) are taken into account, it is not clear what weight, if any, should be attached to his point.

All Professor Howitt seems to be suggesting is that, during upswings, we may be understating the amount of gross investment going on, but I do not see why we are necessarily understating the amount of net investment nor the transitions or the traverse rates of change in sustainable consumption.

CONCLUSION

I HAVE RAISED SOME QUESTIONS about Professor Howitt's analysis. His measurement problems amount to no more than the statement that in steady states there may be a downward bias in the rate of growth of sustainable consumption owing to the quality-adjustment problem.[10] I confess to not seeing much significance in his arguments with respect to the other three measurement problems for measures of growth in temporary equilibria.

I conclude on a Keynesian note. I suspect that, if governments were able to operate the economic systems at levels remotely close to what one used to think of as Keynesian efficient equilibria, the recorded rate of growth and productivity advance in the Western World would be higher. To argue this, however, one needs a theory of how advances in aggregate demand can affect productivity growth. In particular, one needs arguments to show that expansionary monetary policy may lead to higher rates of growth, rather than arguments that expansionary monetary policies must necessarily only raise nominal rates of interest and growth, and may lower real rates by bringing about slower endogenous rates of growth associated with higher rates of inflation.

ENDNOTES

1 See Peter Howitt, "Zero inflation as a long term target for monetary policy," *Zero Inflation: The Goal of Price Stability*, edited by Richard Lipsey. (Toronto: C.D. Howe Institute, 1990); and "Money and growth revisited," *Monetary Theory And Thought: Essays in Honour of Don Patinkin*, edited by H. Barkai, S. Fischer and N. Liviatan. (London: Macmillan, 1993).

2 Indeed, the dazzling array of formal and informal ways in which such externalities are eliminated, e.g., payments for learning on the job, trade associations and the like, as outlined in Chris Freeman, "The economics of technical change," *Cambridge Journal of Economics*, XVIII, August 1994, pp. 463-514, would suggest that any simple theoretical or empirical representation of advances in knowledge, at present, escapes economics.

3 My own feeble efforts in that direction are found in "Technical process, research and development," *Joan Robinson And Modern Economic Theory*, edited by F. Feiwel. (London: Macmillan, 1989).

4 An account of the dynamic aspect of that theory and measurement is found in Thomas Rymes, *On Concepts Of Capital And Technical Change*. (Cambridge: Cambridge University Press, 1971); and in Thomas Rymes and Alexandra Cas, *On Concepts And Measures Of Multifactor Productivity In Canada*, 1961-81. (Cambridge: Cambridge University Press, 1991).

5 Let us assume that, before the Gordon adjustments to the price indexes were made, the same Solow residuals were exhibited in the computer and banking industries. After the Gordon adjustment, the residual in the computer industry is increased; in banking, it is decreased. If done in constant consumption good prices or if Harrod residuals are chosen instead, no differential change need be shown. If it is argued that it is not the computers which are "better" but the chips whose hedonic price indexes would show sharp declines, then the Solow residuals in the computer industry would be reduced, when the increased rate of growth of the constant dollar flow of chips as intermediate inputs into the computer industry is considered. The Solow residual in the chip industry would be increased. The Harrod residuals would be unaffected. The Solow residuals collapse into indeterminacy when the fact that the banking industry produces output, which flows as an intermediate input into the computer and chip industries, is taken into account. Again, the Harrod measures are unaffected. The reason for this is that the Solow residuals attempt to allocate productivity advances by the originating industry when the contribution of produced inputs that gets netted out – an attempt which fails when it is realized that the capital inputs are endogenous, and the separation attempted by activity cannot meaningfully be done by Solow residuals in a technologically interdependent economy. See Rymes and Cas (1991) and my statement as part of the panel discussion on the implications of computer price indexes and productivity measurement in Murray F. Foss, Marilyn E. Manser and Allan H. Young, (eds.) *Price Measurements And Their Uses*. (Chicago: University of Chicago Press for the NBER, 1993).

6 I ignore Professor Howitt's observation that, in this case, there may be an effect because of a supposed difference arising for this measurement problem on measures of net versus gross investment. I do this because, if one is talking about the problems resulting from improvements in models rather than methods, his use of an unchanged rate of depreciation of the usual radioactive decay type, rather than a rate of depreciation which reflects the rate of obsolescence of old models, seems to suggest that he does not attach much weight to his own argument.

7 The late Edward Denison, though sympathetic to the consumption goods analysis, continued to think that at the aggregate level, if the relative prices did not diverge, the differences between the Denison and Harrod residuals would be small. See Edward Denison, *Estimates Of Productivity Change By Industry: An Evaluation and an Alternative*. (Washington: The Brookings Institution, 1989), especially Chapter 2 on the new way of measuring production of computers.

8 For an argument that this bias must be small, see Allan Crawford, "Measurement biases in the Canadian CPI," *Bank of Canada Technical Report*, No. 64. (Ottawa: Bank of Canada, September 1993).

9 See John Hicks, *Capital And Time: A neo-Austrian Theory*. (Oxford: Clarendon Press, 1973).

10 One can even quarrel with the Gordon adjustment. See Edward Denison, "Robert J. Gordon's concept of capital" and Robert J. Gordon, "Reply: the Concept of Capital," *The Review of Income and Wealth*, XXXIX, (March 1993): 89-110. This debate deserves more attention than it has received. Denison's point is that Gordon's concept of capital as an

input means that his hedonic price indexes for computers continue to be biased upward, that is, Professor Gordon should show quality-adjusted price indexes for capital inputs showing even more decline than he does. Professor Gordon agrees! Gordon's procedure, carried out to its logical conclusion, would eliminate any record of technical progress and show it all appearing as the growth of capital inputs. Once again, take note that the Harrod residuals would remain impervious, in principle, to how much the hedonic price indexes are said to continue to have an upward bias.

ACKNOWLEDGEMENTS

I WOULD LIKE TO THANK MICHAEL FRANCIS AND RICHARD BRECHER for discussions on matters related to these comments.

Frank C. Lee & Handan Has
Micro-Economic Policy Analysis
Industry Canada

2

A Quantitative Assessment of High-Knowledge Industries Versus Low-Knowledge Industries

ABSTRACT

KNOWLEDGE HAS ALWAYS BEEN THE DRIVING FORCE behind economic growth. In order to formulate a set of micro-economic policies, we first need to understand the role of knowledge in the economy. This paper attempts to understand the impact of knowledge on the Canadian industrial structure by classifying 55 Canadian industries into high-, medium- and low-knowledge sectors on the basis of research and development (R&D), education and occupational data. The paper then examines their economic performance over the 1980s. The high-knowledge sector outperforms both the medium- and low-knowledge sectors in terms of output, employment and wage growth. On the other hand, the high-knowledge sector's labour productivity grew the slowest, and the low-knowledge sector's labour productivity grew the fastest over the 1980s. However, glancing at industry-by-industry economic performance indicates that there is considerable variation even within the same sector. This suggests that it would be difficult for the government to pick future winners and losers.

INTRODUCTION

CANADA IS A RICH COUNTRY by any standards. However, in the last two decades, the real income growth of individual Canadians has slowed, the unemployment rate has risen steadily and earnings have become more unequal. Whether Canada can continue to maintain its high living standards and social fabric is of increasing concern. Solving these economic problems appears to be much more difficult than initially envisaged since Canada is also undergoing waves of changes in its industrial structure spurred by reductions in transportation and communication costs (Harris, 1993). These reductions heighten international competition and allow a faster diffusion of micro-electronic and information-based technologies in the economy. The diffusion of these technologies is fundamentally transforming the way we do business. Some even suggest that a new techno-economic paradigm is taking place (Jensen, 1993; Lipsey, 1993). In any case, this poses new challenges for firms, governments and workers as the economy becomes more knowledge intensive and requires faster adjustments by firms and workers. Traditional fiscal and monetary policies by themselves are not likely to solve Canada's economic problems. The co-ordination and reform of micro-economic polices is needed.

To formulate co-ordinated micro-economic policies, we first need to have a better understanding of the changes that are taking place in the Canadian economy. Many studies have focused on the performance of macro-economic variables. But little has been done in the context of the new economy highlighting the importance of the knowledge component in the Canadian economy. This is because it is fundamentally difficult to measure knowledge statistically, its characteristics often being qualitative rather than quantitative. The aim of this paper is to provide a better understanding of the Canadian industrial structure in the context of the knowledge-based economy by classifying industries according to their knowledge content and then examining their economic performance over the 1980s.

The next section classifies 55 industries into the high-, medium- and low-knowledge sectors using a variety of indicators. Then, we discuss other indicators that could be used to examine the knowledge intensity of an industry. Next, we present the economic performance of these three sectors over the 1980s. Finally, we draw conclusions.

CLASSIFICATION OF HIGH-, MEDIUM- AND LOW-KNOWLEDGE INDUSTRIES

NEW GROWTH THEORIES SUGGEST that advances in knowledge are the driving force behind economic growth. The accumulation of knowledge allows firms to develop more effective production processes as well as new products. It is, however, difficult to assess the impact of knowledge on the economy since knowledge is inherently differentiated and difficult to quantify. There have been many attempts to come up with proxies to measure knowledge, often based on either inputs that go into accumulating more knowledge or outputs of knowledge. Figure 1, a simplified knowledge production process, is helpful in discussing proxies for measuring knowledge.[1] Note that knowledge, in addition to physical capital and labour, is vital for increasing output of an economy. The stock of knowledge, in turn, can be increased by increasing inputs into knowledge. That is, the accumulation process of knowledge is not automatic but requires efforts and investments. Expenditures on education, research and development (R&D), the number of scientists and engineers, machinery and equipment (M&E) investment (to proxy learning-by-doing) may be considered as measures of knowledge input. Patent statistics may be regarded as the outcome of this knowledge-generating process.

As noted above, there are several indicators that can be used to measure the production of knowledge. And the measurement of knowledge may be sensitive to the proxy that is used. To reduce this potential sensitivity, we used more than one indicator to measure the knowledge content of an industry. In this section, we classify Canadian industries into the high-knowledge, medium-knowledge and

FIGURE 1

A SIMPLE PATH DIAGRAM FOR KNOWLEDGE

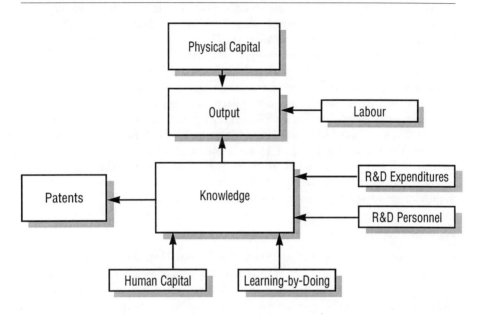

low-knowledge sectors on the basis of several indicators of R&D activity and human capital content. In other words, we are attempting to identify knowledge-producing industries rather than knowledge-using industries.[2] But there appears to be a close relationship between the two as becomes evident in the discussion of the patent activity. Other commonly used indicators of knowledge that could have been used are discussed in the next section.

R&D ACTIVITY

A NATION'S ABILITY TO COMPETE SUCCESSFULLY in a globalized economy is becoming increasingly dependent on its capacity to generate new ideas and innovations. Innovative effort is most commonly measured by expenditures on R&D since data on the latter are readily available. For instance, the Organization for Economic Co-operation and Development (OECD) (1986) classified industries into high-, medium- and low-technology categories based on their R&D intensity[3] across the reference countries. The justification for using R&D as an indicator of knowledge is perhaps best illustrated in the OECD's *Frascati Manual* where it defines R&D as "creative work undertaken on a systematic basis in order to increase the stock of knowledge including knowledge of man, culture and society, and the use of this stock of knowledge to devise new applications" (OECD, 1994a, p. 29).

Although R&D expenditures are small in Canada (1.5 percent of GDP in 1991), they are much more important than the figures indicate. First, they often generate new and improved products and/or processes that enable firms to increase and/or maintain their market shares and contribute to aggregate economic growth. For instance, in a survey by Levin et al. (1989), independent R&D was shown to be a more effective way of learning about rival technology outpacing other methods of learning such as licensing and reverse engineering.[4] Second, R&D expenditures likely generate spillovers of knowledge from one sector of the economy to another or from one country to other countries suggesting that social rates of return on R&D may be higher than private rates of return. Many existing empirical studies show that social rates of return on R&D exceed private rates of return (Bernstein, 1989, 1994; Coe and Helpman, 1993; Mohnen, 1992). R&D activity not only increases the knowledge stock of an economy, it also induces more investment activity as shown by Lach and Shankerman (1989). Since both R&D expenditures and R&D personnel are inputs into R&D activity, we consider both of these inputs to provide an adequate representation of the effort devoted to R&D.[5]

Human Capital

WE ALSO USE THE HUMAN CAPITAL CONTENT of an industry to define high-, medium- and low-knowledge industries. R&D may raise the level of technological knowledge, but it does not automatically transform this new knowledge into new processes and/or products. A skilled work force is required to access, retrieve and adapt this new knowledge to develop new production processes and products.

There are several studies of economic growth, such as those of Becker, Murphy and Tamura (1990) and Lucas (1988, 1993), that stress the importance of human capital in explaining economic growth. Many empirical studies (for example, Barro, 1991; Mankiw, Romer and Weil, 1992) have used educational attainment as a proxy for human capital. By allowing individuals to absorb knowledge much more rapidly, education is likely to increase the productive capacity of individuals. Relying on educational attainment as a measurement of human capital ignores the importance of on-the-job training and presupposes that there is no mismatch between the level of education and employment. This is not likely to be the case in times of rapid technological change when skills tend to become obsolete at a faster rate.

Alternatively, one can also use an occupational mix criterion to identify knowledge-based industries. There are several advantages associated with this approach. First, occupational categories are standardized across industries which facilitates comparisons. Second, it alleviates the problem of mismatch between the level of education and employment. It only focuses on skills that are being used on the job rather than potential skills that could be used.

Defining Knowledge-based Industries

THERE HAVE BEEN MANY ATTEMPTS to define high-technology and knowledge industries. In Canada, Wong (1990) used the ratio of high-technology inputs (for example, computer chips, robots, precision instruments, etc.) to total inputs to define high-technology industry. This approach ignores the human capital aspect and relies entirely on products and not processes. While this definition may be used to define knowledge-using industries, it cannot be used to identify knowledge-producing industries. Rose (1992), on the other hand, relied on the proportion of total weeks worked by individuals with a university degree to define a knowledge-intensive industry. As mentioned above, this approach fails to take into account a possible mismatch between the level of education and employment. Beck (1992) calculated a knowledge ratio for the United States by dividing the number of knowledge workers[6] by total employment. She then used this U.S. knowledge ratio to classify Canadian industries as high-, medium- or low-knowledge industries. Apart from applying the U.S. definition to Canada, the definition is biased toward defining knowledge-using industries rather than knowledge-producing industries.

Before discussing our methodology for defining industries, it is useful to describe the data used in our analysis. The 55 industries were classified in the high-, medium- and low-knowledge sectors on the basis of the 1984 to 1988 R&D data,[7] and 1986 educational and occupational data. The 1984 to 1988 investment, capital stock and patent data were used to analyze the characteristics of the three sectors. We also described the economic performance of the three sectors over the 1980s. In particular, output, employment, wages, labour productivity and the degree of openness of each sector were examined.[8] The data used in the analysis are described in greater detail in the following sections.

Three indicators of R&D activity and three indicators of human capital content were considered in defining high-, medium- and low-knowledge industries. While we focused on knowledge-producing industries rather than knowledge-using industries, our method invariably picked up some knowledge-using industries since the human capital content of an industry is also used for the purpose of classification. For R&D activity, we considered three measures: R&D intensity,[9] the proportion of R&D personnel to total employment and the proportion of professional R&D personnel[10] to total employment.

For the measurement of human capital content, we used three indicators:

- the ratio of workers with post-secondary education[11] to total employment;

- the ratio of knowledge workers[12] to total employment; and

- the ratio of the number of employed scientists and engineers[13] to total employment.

Industries were initially ranked by each of six indicators and divided into three equal groups. We then classified industries on the basis of the following rule: an industry was considered as high knowledge if:

- at least two of its three R&D indicators belonged to the top one third; and

- at least two of its three human capital indicators belonged to the top one third.

Likewise, an industry was defined as low knowledge if:

- at least two of its three R&D indicators belonged to the bottom one third; and
- at least two of its three human capital indicators belonged to the bottom one third.

All remaining industries were classified as medium-knowledge industries.

Table 1 groups industries into the high-, medium- and low-knowledge sectors. Industries in each sector are listed in descending order of R&D intensity, but the order does not necessarily reflect descending order of knowledge intensity. A few industries lacking R&D data are classified purely on the basis of their human capital content and appended at the end of each group. The medium-knowledge sector has the largest number of industries since it includes those industries that are not classified as either high- or low-knowledge industries. However, this sector can be further subdivided into medium-high and medium-low using other criteria, although this was not attempted in our study. Obviously, some medium-knowledge industries also could be classified as high- and low-knowledge industries using other criteria.

TABLE 1

KNOWLEDGE INTENSITY GROUPS

High-Knowledge	Medium-Knowledge	Low-Knowledge
Scientific & professional equipment	Other transportation equipment	Fishing & trapping
Communication & other electronics	Other electrical & electronics	Other manufacturing products
Aircraft & parts	Primary metals (non-ferrous)	Wood
Computer & related services	Textiles	Furniture & fixtures
Business machines	Communication	Logging & forestry
Engineering & scientific services	Paper & allied products	Transportation
Pharmaceutical & medicine	Mining	Storage & warehousing
Electrical power	Rubber	Agriculture
Other chemical products	Plastics	Retail trade
Machinery	Primary metals (ferrous)	Personal services
Refined petroleum & coal products	Non-metallic mineral products	Quarry, sand pits & mining services
Management consulting services	Wholesale trade	Accommodation, food & beverage services
Educational services	Crude petroleum & natural gas	Clothing
Health & social services	Fabricated metal products	Leather
Pipeline transportation	Motor vehicles & parts	
Other business services	Food	
	Beverages	
	Tobacco	
	Finance, insurance & real estate	
	Other utilities	
	Services incidental to mining	
	Other services	
	Printing & publishing	
	Construction	
	Amusement & recreational services	

TABLE 2

R&D ACTIVITY BY INDUSTRY: 1984 TO 1988 AVERAGE

	R&D Intensity		R&D Personnel per Worker		Professional R&D Personnel per Worker	
	%	Rank	%	Rank	%	Rank
Scientific & professional equipment	27.88	1	3.14	9	1.65	9
Communication & other electronics	17.14	2	19.38	1	11.41	1
Aircraft & parts	10.89	3	11.17	3	4.92	3
Computer & related services	9.77	4	6.36	5	3.57	4
Business machines	9.33	5	15.73	2	9.36	2
Engineering & scientific services	8.62	6	4.99	7	2.70	7
Pharmaceutical & medicine	3.54	7	5.39	6	2.88	6
Electrical power	1.21	9	1.98	12	0.91	12
Other chemical products	0.96	10	3.16	8	1.76	8
Machinery	0.95	11	1.68	14	0.64	14
Refined petroleum & coal products	0.85	14	7.94	4	3.41	5
Management consulting services	0.53	17	0.43	27	0.22	24
Other transportation equipment	1.22	8	2.25	11	0.94	11
Other electrical & electronics	0.90	12	1.69	13	0.87	13
Primary metals (non-ferrous)	0.87	13	2.57	10	0.97	10
Textiles	0.60	15	0.84	18	0.38	18
Communication	0.58	16	0.75	19	0.50	16
Paper & allied products	0.43	18	0.89	17	0.38	17
Mining	0.40	19	0.92	16	0.37	19
Rubber	0.30	20	0.59	21	0.31	20
Plastics	0.28	21	0.46	23	0.19	26
Primary metals (ferrous)	0.28	22	0.53	22	0.27	21
Non-metallic mineral products	0.26	23	0.44	24	0.20	25
Wholesale trade	0.25	24	0.25	29	0.12	29
Crude petroleum & natural gas	0.24	25	1.01	15	0.53	15
Fabricated metal products	0.21	27	0.37	28	0.17	28
Motor vehicles & parts	0.20	28	0.65	20	0.24	22
Beverages & tobacco	0.15	31	0.43	26	0.18	27
Finance, insurance & real estate	0.09	34	0.21	32	0.08	33
Other utilities	0.09	35	0.14	36	0.09	32
Services incidental to mining	0.09	36	0.15	34	0.07	35
Other services	0.05	39	0.03	41	0.02	40
Printing & publishing	0.04	41	0.07	38	0.04	38
Construction	0.01	43	0.02	42	0.01	42

(cont'd)

TABLE 2 (cont'd)

	R&D Intensity		R&D Personnel per Worker		Professional R&D Personnel per Worker	
	%	Rank	%	Rank	%	Rank
Fishing & trapping	0.21	26	0.11	37	0.05	37
Other manufacturing industries	0.18	29	0.22	31	0.10	31
Food	0.17	30	0.44	25	0.22	23
Wood	0.13	32	0.24	30	0.11	30
Furniture & fixtures	0.11	33	0.16	33	0.07	36
Logging & forestry	0.08	37	0.14	35	0.08	34
Transportation & storage	0.06	38	0.06	39	0.03	39
Agriculture	0.05	40	0.04	40	0.01	41
Retail trade	0.02	42	0.01	43	0.01	43

Notes: Agriculture, fishing and trapping, and logging and forestry industries, 1985 to 1988 averages.

Here, other manufacturing industries includes clothing and leather, and other manufacturing product industries, and other services includes other business services and personal service industries. 1986 gross ouput and employment are used for the scientific and professional equipment and other manufacturing industries.

Gross output for computer and related services, engineering and scientific services, and management and consulting services is approximated using their employment shares of the business service sector.

Source: Authors' calculations based on Statistics Canada data. Employment data for scientific and professional equipment are from Canadian Occupational Projection System, Human Resources Development Canada.

Table 2 presents R&D activity[14] by industry. For the high-knowledge sector, it turned out that all three R&D indicators exceeded the average of all industries (0.52, 0.56, 0.29 respectively) except for management consulting services. The management consulting service industry has relatively low R&D personnel content to belong to the first group. However, due to its exceptionally high human capital content, we categorized it under the high-knowledge sector. At the same time, all three R&D indicators for low-knowledge industries were below the average of all industries. The reason for this is that all three indicators were highly correlated as shown in the rank correlation matrix of R&D indicators given in Table 3.

TABLE 3

RANK CORRELATION MATRIX OF R&D ACTIVITY

	R&D Intensity	R&D Personnel per Worker	Professional R&D Personnel per Worker
R&D intensity	1.00		
R&D personnel/worker	0.94	1.00	
Professional R&D/worker	0.95	0.99	1.00

Source: Based on Table 2.

Table 4 presents the proportion of workers with post-secondary education and two alternative representations based on occupational mix to indicate the human capital content of industries. As Table 5 shows, the rank correlation coefficient between the proportion of workers with post-secondary education and the proportion of knowledge workers was relatively high (0.85). This suggests that there is a rather close match between the level of education and knowledge-intensive occupations. However, their respective rank correlation coefficients with the proportion of scientists and engineers were lower (0.62, 0.61)[15] suggesting that this occupational category tends to focus on scientific or technological capacity of an industry and, therefore, it may not be particularly adequate to measure the knowledge content of service industries that are not involved in producing new processes or products. Thus, it is not surprising to observe a small number of scientists and engineers for those industries such as educational services and health and social services that rely on other industries for innovations and new products. Generally, high-knowledge industries have above-average human capital content (41.1, 24.6 and 3.6 respectively), and low-knowledge industries have below-average human capital content. There were a few exceptions: the machinery industry's proportion of knowledge workers was below average and the proportion of scientists and engineers for education, health and social service and other business services was lower than average. At the other end of the spectrum, the logging and forestry industry had a higher than average proportion of scientists and engineers. For medium-knowledge industries, the crude petroleum and natural gas industry had higher than average human capital content based on all three human capital measurements. But its R&D activity was too low for the industry to be categorized in the high-knowledge sector.

TABLE 4
HUMAN CAPITAL BY INDUSTRY: 1986

	Proportion of Workers with Post-Secondary Education		Proportion of Knowledge Workers		Proportion of Scientists, Engineers per Worker	
	%	Rank	%	Rank	%	Rank
Scientific & professional equipment	45.3	16	30.7	13	12.6	10
Communication & other electronics	51.4	13	38.7	8	21.9	4
Aircraft & parts	50.5	14	26.1	16	14.8	9
Computer & related services	69.2	3	62.2	3	42.0	2
Business machines	59.6	7	44.6	7	21.2	5
Engineering & scientific services	74.9	2	75.4	1	62.1	1
Pharmaceutical & medicine	51.7	12	34.5	11	10.0	12
Electrical power	59.2	8	29.7	14	18.2	6
Other chemical products	44.6	18	28.0	15	11.2	11
Machinery	45.4	15	22.1	18	8.5	15
Refined petroleum & coal products	53.6	11	33.9	12	15.6	8
Management consulting services	67.4	4	62.0	4	9.1	13
Educational services	76.4	1	69.7	2	2.3	35

(cont'd)

TABLE 4 (cont'd)

	Proportion of Workers with Post-Secondary Education		Proportion of Knowledge Workers		Proportion of Scientists, Engineers per Worker	
	%	Rank	%	Rank	%	Rank
Health & social services	65.6	5	61.8	5	0.7	50
Pipeline transportation	54.9	10	36.1	10	16.0	7
Other business services	57.0	9	37.8	9	1.3	42
Other transportation equipment	45.3	17	15.0	31	6.3	20
Other electrical & electronics	33.9	35	19.0	23	7.9	18
Primary metals (non-ferrous)	40.0	22	16.0	29	8.2	16
Textiles	23.3	49	11.5	42	2.7	31
Communication	37.6	25	17.6	26	5.3	22
Paper & allied products	35.6	29	12.3	40	4.6	25
Mining	40.5	20	14.2	35	7.9	19
Rubber	31.0	37	14.4	32	4.9	24
Plastics	26.2	44	14.0	37	2.9	29
Primary metals (ferrous)	34.5	32	12.5	39	6.3	21
Non-metallic mineral products	28.6	42	14.0	36	3.4	28
Wholesale trade	35.1	30	18.9	24	1.9	39
Crude petroleum & natural gas	61.6	6	46.6	6	24.7	3
Fabricated metal products	38.1	24	14.4	33	4.1	27
Motor vehicles & parts	28.8	41	11.2	43	4.4	26
Food	23.9	47	10.8	44	2.1	37
Beverages	32.0	36	15.8	30	2.8	30
Tobacco	34.5	31	16.5	28	5.2	23
Finance, insurance & real estate	44.0	19	25.2	17	2.6	32
Other utilities	36.6	27	18.6	25	2.1	38
Services incidental to mining	34.4	33	21.3	19	9.0	14
Other services	37.3	26	16.5	27	0.8	49
Printing & publishing	38.4	23	21.0	21	1.3	43
Construction	36.5	28	9.9	47	2.3	34
Amusement & recreational services	34.2	34	14.2	34	0.9	48
Fishing & trapping	19.8	53	4.7	54	2.2	36
Other manufacturing products	29.9	38	20.6	22	1.7	40
Wood	25.3	46	7.2	51	1.2	44
Furniture & fixtures	26.1	45	10.1	46	1.5	41
Logging & forestry	29.6	39	12.3	41	8.0	17
Transportation	29.0	40	8.9	50	2.3	33
Storage & warehousing	23.4	48	21.2	20	1.0	46
Agriculture	21.5	50	10.6	45	0.5	51
Retail trade	28.1	43	13.1	38	0.3	53
Personal services	40.5	21	3.4	55	0.1	55
Quarry, sand pits and mining services	20.6	51	9.3	49	1.0	47
Accommodation, food & beverage services	20.0	52	9.4	48	0.1	54
Clothing	16.2	54	6.7	53	0.4	52
Leather	14.5	55	6.8	52	1.0	45

Source: Authors' calculations based on Canadian Occupational Projection System, Human Resources Development Canada.

TABLE 5

RANK CORRELATION MATRIX OF KNOWLEDGE WORKERS

	Proportion of Workers with Post-Secondary Education	Proportion of Knowledge Workers	Proportion of Scientists, Engineers and Technicians
Proportion of workers with post-secondary education	1.00		
Proportion of knowledge workers	0.85	1.00	
Proportion of scientists, engineers and technicians	0.62	0.61	1.00

Source: Based on Table 4.

OTHER INDICATORS

AS MENTIONED ABOVE, THERE ARE OTHER INDICATORS that are often used to measure the knowledge content of an industry.

INVESTMENT ACTIVITY

IF INVESTMENTS IN PHYSICAL CAPITAL are accompanied by investments in new ideas or knowledge, then physical capital accumulation becomes a powerful engine of economic growth. Romer (1987) estimated a simple Cobb–Douglas production function and found the coefficient of physical capital to be significantly larger than its share of the economy. He interpreted this as evidence of physical embodiment of knowledge. In a subsequent study, Barro (1991) showed no evidence of large externalities generated by capital accumulation based on cross-country regressions. In addition, Hulten (1992) suggested that knowledge embodied in physical capital was not particularly important in explaining output growth in U.S. manufacturing. However, when the analysis was restricted to the impact of machinery and equipment (M&E) investment on economic growth, De Long and Summers (1991) found a strong positive association based on cross-country regressions. Furthermore, they estimated that the social return to investment in M&E was higher than the private return implying externalities stemming from investment in M&E.

Our analysis, however, indicated that the relative standings of industries do not change significantly whether we use gross investment or M&E investment. The rank correlation between the gross investment intensity[16] and the M&E investment intensity was 0.88, and the rank correlation between gross capital stock intensity[17] and M&E capital stock intensity was 0.91. Each industry's investment and capital stock intensity is shown in Table A2 in Appendix A. There was no clear pattern to infer any relationship between knowledge-intensive industries and investment-intensive industries. This becomes more evident in Table 6 where we present investment and capital intensity for the three knowledge sectors. Note that there was no clear distinction among the high-, medium- and low-knowledge sectors on the basis of investment intensity. However, the high-knowledge sector had a significantly higher capital intensity than the medium- and low-knowledge sectors, and the medium-knowledge sector had a higher capital intensity than the low-knowledge sector.[18]

TABLE 6

INVESTMENT ACTIVITY OF HIGH-, MEDIUM- AND LOW-KNOWLEDGE INDUSTRIES

	Gross Investment Intensity	M&E Investment Intensity	Gross Capital Stock Intensity	M&E Capital Stock Intensity
	(%)	(%)	($000)	($000)
High-knowledge	8.4	4.2	281.4	66.3
Medium-knowledge	8.9	5.3	119.4	46.4
Low-knowledge	7.6	4.4	64.1	24.3

Note: Services incidental to mining are in the low-knowledge group as part of the quarry and sand pits and mining services category because investment data are not available separately.

Source: Based on Table A2.

PATENT ACTIVITY

THE R&D STATISTICS APPEAR TO PROVIDE VALUABLE INFORMATION in identifying knowledge-producing industries. They, however, are generally recognized as input measures producing knowledge that has the potential of being economically valuable. (Not all R&D endeavour is known to be successful in producing economically valuable knowledge.) Patent statistics, on the other hand, are often used as indicators of output of innovative effort. However, there are a number of problems associated with using patent statistics as summarized by Ducharme (1991). First, it is difficult to identify which patents are going to be commercialized. The value of patents presumably depends on whether they are going to be used to develop new products or processes. But many patents can sit idle if they are not commercially successful. Furthermore, not all inventions are patented or patentable. Second, they do not measure incremental innovations transferred from publications, personal contacts and licences. Third, the economic value of each invention is treated equally. That is, patent statistics do not have any information about the relative importance of one patent against another.

Despite these shortcomings, patent statistics are repeatedly used as an economic indicator[19] for at least two reasons. First, there is some evidence that there is a strong relationship between R&D and patent statistics across firms and industries (Pakes and Griliches, 1984). Second, patent statistics can yield information on the inter-industry flow of technology[20] that is not available from R&D statistics since a patent can be classified according to the industry that is likely to use it and to the industry that is likely to produce it.

The Canadian patent data base (PATDAT) assigns all patents to the most likely industry of origin and the industry of potential use. A small percentage of single patents may be assigned to two or three different industries of origin and potential use. In addition, if a patent is assigned to more than one industry (say at the four-digit SIC level), these industries generally belong to the same major industrial grouping (i.e., at the three-digit SIC level). Therefore, we arranged patent data by their first industry of origin and potential use as in Ducharme (1991) and Hanel (1994).

Table A3 in Appendix A lists patent characteristics by industry, and the results are summarized in Table 7. The high-knowledge sector had both the highest number of patents granted and in potential use, followed by the medium-knowledge sector. The low-knowledge sector had the lowest number of patents granted and in potential use. The differences among the three sectors became magnified once the size of the sector was considered as shown by the last two columns in the table.[21] If we assume that patent statistics are reliable indicators of knowledge output, then the high-knowledge sector produces the most knowledge and is the most intense user of that knowledge while the low-knowledge sector produces the least amount of knowledge and uses little of it in producing products. This proposition is somewhat reinforced in Table 8 which shows the use of advanced technologies by industry for the manufacturing sector.[22] It shows that high-knowledge industries and some medium-knowledge industries in our study tended to be heavy users of advanced technologies compared to low-knowledge industries. Therefore, as shown by patent statistics and advanced technologies, high-knowledge industries appear to be heavy users of new and advanced products and processes.

TABLE 7

PATENT ACTIVITY OF HIGH-, MEDIUM- AND LOW-KNOWLEDGE
INDUSTRIES: 1984 TO 1988

	Total Patents Granted	Total Patents by Potential Use	Total Patents Granted per Output	Total Patents by Potential Use per Output
	Number	Number	per $ Billion	per $ Billion
High-knowledge	48,053	40,659	58.1	49.1
Medium-knowledge	21,199	31,554	9.0	13.4
Low-knowledge	3,524	5,054	4.2	6.1

Notes: Patents granted refers only to product patents whereas patents use refer to both product and process patents.

Output refers to gross output.

Source: Based on Table A3.

TABLE 8

USE OF ADVANCED TECHNOLOGIES[a] BY MANUFACTURING INDUSTRY: 1989

| | Use of Advanced Technology | | | |
| | At least 1 | | At least 10 | |
	% of Shipments	Rank	% of Shipments	Rank
Scientific & professional equipment	81	17	53	17
Communication & other electronics	97	6	81	4
Aircraft & parts	99	1	93	1
Business machines	99	1	90	2
Pharmaceutical & medicine	99	1	68	10
Other chemical products	93	11	63	13
Machinery	91	13	55	16
Refined petroleum & coal products	90	14	76	6
Other transportation equipment	96	8	74	7
Other electrical & electronics[b]	95	9	68	10
Primary metals (non-ferrous)[b]	93	11	67	12
Textiles	67	25	32	22
Paper & allied products	89	15	69	9
Rubber	97	6	84	3
Plastics	79	18	27	23
Primary metals (ferrous)[b]	98	5	81	4
Non-metallic mineral products	88	16	49	18
Fabricated metal products	75	21	40	19
Food	78	19	40	19
Beverages	94	10	62	14
Tobacco	76	20	57	15
Printing & publishing	72	23	26	24
Motor vehicles & parts[b]	99	1	70	8
Other manufacturing products	63	27	14	28
Wood	75	21	35	21
Furniture & fixtures	65	26	26	24
Clothing	68	24	23	26
Leather	55	28	23	26

Notes: [a]These refer to the use of 22 advanced technologies which can be grouped into seven broad technologies: design and engineering, fabrication and assembly, automated material handling, automated sensor-based inspection and/or testing equipment, communications and control, manufacturing information systems, and integration and control.

[b]Derived from Statistics Canada, Catalogue 88-002, Vol. 2, No. 3, using shipment weights.

Source: Statistics Canada, 1991, Indicators of Science and Technology 1990, Catatogue 88-002,Vol. 2, No. 3, Ottawa.

ECONOMIC PERFORMANCE

THIS SECTION EXAMINES THE OVERALL ECONOMIC PERFORMANCE of high-, medium- and low-knowledge sectors over the 1980s. A detailed industry-by-industry performance is given in Appendix B. Output, employment, wage rate, labour productivity and openness to trade are analyzed and compared for each sector.

Figure 2 plots output growth (GDP at factor cost) from 1980 to 1993 for each group. In our study, the high-knowledge sector exhibited the highest growth, followed by the medium-knowledge and low-knowledge sectors. All three sectors peaked in 1989, after which time each sector experienced a decline due to the recession. Both the high- and medium-knowledge sectors experienced a slight decline while the low-knowledge sector experienced the most decline. All three sectors exhibited increases in output as the recovery began in 1992. As shown in Table 9, the high- and medium-knowledge sectors grew at annual growth rates of 3.6 percent and 3 percent respectively from 1981 to 1990 while the low-knowledge sector had modest annual growth of 2 percent over the same period. Thus, all three sectors exhibited absolute growth over this period.

FIGURE 2

REAL GDP AT FACTOR COST

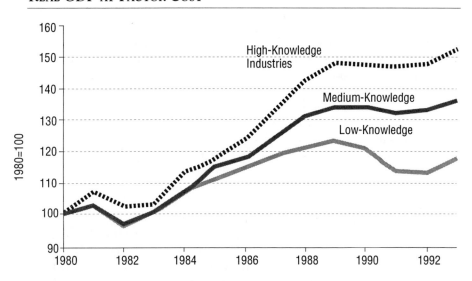

Notes: Annual data for the scientific and professional equipment industry are not separately available. Thus, it is included in the low-knowledge group as a part of other manufacturing in this figure.

The mining service industry is included in the low-knowledge group as a part of quarry and sand pits and mining services.

Source: Based on Statistics Canada data.

TABLE 9

PERFORMANCE OF GROSS OUTPUT AT FACTOR COST: 1981 TO 1990

	Annual Growth Rate	Market Share 1981	Market Share 1990	Point Change in Market Share	Market Share Growth Rate
	%	%	%	%	%
High-knowledge	3.6	16.0	17.1	1.1	6.6
Medium-knowledge	3.0	59.4	60.1	0.7	1.2
Low-knowledge	2.0	24.6	22.8	-1.8	-7.3

Note: Services incidental to mining are in the low-knowledge group as part of the quarry and sand pits and mining services category because investment data are not available separately.

Source: Based on Table B1.

When we examined each sector's relative output performance, we saw that the high-knowledge sector's market share increased from 16 percent to 17.1 percent (1.1 percent). The medium-knowledge sector's market share increased to 60.1 percent from 59.4 percent (0.7 percent). On the other hand, the low-knowledge sector lost market share which decreased from 24.6 percent to 22.8 percent (-1.8 percent).

A similar scenario emerged for employment as shown in Figure 3. Since 1980, the high-knowledge sector has exhibited the highest employment growth followed by the medium- and low-knowledge sectors. In contrast to output growth, employment in the high-knowledge sector continued to grow at a rapid pace. However, employment growth in the medium-knowledge sector slowed down significantly beginning in 1989. The low-knowledge sector's employment growth slowdown began two years earlier, in 1987. Table 10 reveals that employment performance across the three sectors is not significantly different from their respective output performance. The annual growth rate in employment in the high-knowledge sector was 4.2 percent between 1981 and 1990, while the medium- and low-knowledge sectors grew at 1.8 percent and 1.1 percent, respectively. At the same time, the high-knowledge sector increased its relative importance with a 2.9 percent increase in its employment share. Next was the medium-knowledge sector with a decrease of 0.03 percent in employment share. The low-knowledge sector became less important by losing 2.9 percent of its employment share over the same period.

Table 11 presents the wage performance of the three sectors. The high-knowledge sector had the fastest wage growth rate over the 1980s, followed by the low-knowledge sector. The medium-knowledge sector had the slowest wage growth. In other words, the wage rate of the high-knowledge sector, which was lower than that of the medium-knowledge sector in 1981, caught up to the level of the medium-knowledge sector in 1990. On the other hand, the low-knowledge sector consistently had the lowest wage rate in both 1981 and 1990.

FIGURE 3

EMPLOYMENT

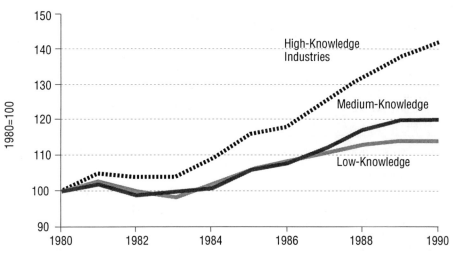

Notes: Annual data for the scientific and professional equipment industry are not separately available. Thus, it is included in the low-knowledge group as a part of other manufacturing in this figure.

The mining service industry is included in the low-knowledge group as a part of quarry and sand pits and mining services.

Source: Based on Statistics Canada data.

TABLE 10

PERFORMANCE OF EMPLOYMENT: 1981 TO 1990

	Annual Growth Rate	Market Share 1981	Market Share 1990	Change in Market Share Growth	Market Share Rate
	%	%	%	%	%
High-knowledge	4.2	12.5	15.4	2.9	23.2
Medium-knowledge	1.8	43.3	44.3	-0.03	-0.1
Low-knowledge	1.1	44.3	41.4	-2.9	-6.5

Note: Services incidental to mining are in the low-knowledge group as part of the quarry and sand pits and mining services category because investment data are not available separately.

Source: Based on Table B2.

TABLE 11

WAGES PER HOUR: 1981 TO 1990

	Wage Rate 1981	Wage Rate 1990	Annual Growth Rate	Relative Wage Rate Ratio 1981	Relative Wage Rate Ratio 1990
	$/Hour	$/Hour	%		
High-knowledge	11.6	20.0	6.3	1.16	1.24
Medium-knowledge	13.1	20.0	4.8	1.31	1.24
Low-knowledge	6.5	10.7	5.7	0.66	0.67

Notes: Services incidental to mining are in the low-knowledge group as part of the quarry and sand pits and mining services category because investment data are not available separately.

Scientific and professional equipment is included in the low-knowledge group.

This table can be derived from Table B3. Wage rates are weighted averages of wages in Table B3 where the weights are total hours worked relative to total hours worked in each sector.

Although the high-knowledge sector is more capital intensive and probably more knowledge intensive than the medium-knowledge sector, the high-knowledge sector's labour productivity was lower than that of the medium-knowledge sector in both 1981 and 1990 as shown in Table 12. This appears to indicate that the medium-knowledge sector may be more resource-intensive than the other two sectors, and high labour productivity is a reflection of resource rents. At the same time, Table 12 shows that the high-knowledge sector, which had the fastest wage growth, had the slowest labour productivity growth (0.7 percent) over the 1980s. There is one possible explanation for this: given that the high-knowledge sector's output growth was much faster than that of the medium-knowledge sector, the high-knowledge sector expanded its employment faster to meet its increased output demand thereby slowing down its labour productivity growth. Since the high-knowledge sector is a newly emerging sector, it may not have had time to reach its equilibrium where workers are paid their marginal productivity. On the other hand, many medium-knowledge industries are likely to be mature and stable industries where workers are likely to be paid according to their marginal productivity.

The low-knowledge sector which has suffered most in terms of output and employment appears to be most successful in shedding its low-performance workers much faster than the other two sectors. This appears to have increased its labour productivity faster than for the other two sectors (although not significantly compared to that of the medium-knowledge sector).

The notion that high-knowledge industries face stiffer international competition is supported in Table 13 where the high-knowledge sector exhibits the greatest degree of openness, followed by the medium- then the low-knowledge sectors.

TABLE 12

LABOUR PRODUCTIVITY: 1981 TO 1990

	Labour Productivity 1981	Labour Productivity 1990	Annual Growth Rate	Relative Productivity Ratio 1981	Relative Productivity Ratio 1990
	$/Hour	$/Hour	%		
High-knowledge	29.90	31.70	0.7	1.33	1.27
Medium-knowledge	30.80	33.60	1.0	1.37	1.35
Low-knowledge	12.40	13.60	1.1	0.55	0.55

Notes: Labour productivity is calculated as value-added per hour.

Scientific and professional equipment is included in the low-knowledge group.

Services incidental to mining are in the low-knowledge group as part of the quarry and sand pits and mining services category because investment data are not available separately.

Source: Based on Table B4.

TABLE 13

DEGREE OF OPENNESS:[a] 1981 AND 1991

	1981	1991
	%	%
High-knowledge	91	133
Medium-knowledge	65	79
Low-knowledge	37	49

Notes: [a] Openness is defined as (exports+imports)/GDP.

Services incidental to mining are in the low-knowledge group as part of the quarry and sand pits and mining services category because investment data are not available separately.

Scientific and professional equipment is included in the low-knowledge group.

Source: Based on Table B5.

Between 1981 and 1991, openness to trade in high-knowledge industries increased from 91 to 133, from 65 to 79 in medium-knowledge industries and from 37 to 49 in low-knowledge industries.

CONCLUSION

THIS PAPER CLASSIFIES 55 CANADIAN INDUSTRIES into the high-, medium- and low-knowledge sectors on the basis of R&D, education and occupational data. The rank coefficients among R&D intensity, the level of education and the proportion of workers in knowledge-intensive occupations indicate that they are highly correlated. This suggests that there could be complementary factors among them.

In terms of the characteristics of the three sectors, the high-knowledge sector was more capital intensive than the other two sectors. The medium-knowledge sector, in turn, was more capital intensive than the low-knowledge sector. At the same time, the high-knowledge sector was granted the largest number of patents and was likely to be the heaviest user of these followed by the medium-knowledge sector, then the low-knowledge sector.

The three sectors' economic performance can be summarized as follows:

1. Output: The share of output for the high-knowledge sector was the smallest, but its growth outperformed those of the medium- and low-knowledge sectors from 1981 to 1990. This was followed by the medium-knowledge sector which had the highest share of the economy. The low-knowledge sector had the second highest output share but its share declined between 1981 and 1990.

2. Employment: The same scenario as output performance emerged in terms of employment share and growth for the three sectors.

3. Wage rate: The high-knowledge sector had the highest wage growth rate followed by the low-knowledge sector and then the medium-knowledge sector. However, the low-knowledge sector had the lowest wage rate in both 1981 and 1990.

4. Labour productivity: The medium-knowledge sector had the highest level of labour productivity followed by the high-knowledge sector and then the low-knowledge sector. In contrast, the low-knowledge sector exhibited the fastest labour productivity growth followed by the medium-knowledge sector and the high-knowledge sector.

5. Openness to trade: The high-knowledge sector exhibited the greatest degree of openness followed by the medium- and low-knowledge sectors.

The high-knowledge sector outperformed the medium- and low-knowledge sectors in terms of output, employment and wage growth. The low-knowledge sector, however, outperformed the high- and medium-knowledge sectors on labour productivity growth. Therefore, it became rather difficult to make a case to target specific sectors since targeted sectors would change depending on the criteria used. Furthermore, glancing at industry-by-industry performance indicates that there was a lot of variation in economic performance of industries even within the same sector. This suggests that it would be even more difficult to pick winners and losers.

An industry which is high-knowledge today may become a medium-knowledge or low-knowledge industry tomorrow. Given that government cannot predict the industry dynamics of tomorrow, it seems almost impossible to target sectors or industries successfully. Despite the difficulty associated with targeting specific sectors or industries, there are things the government can do to encourage innovations in the economy.

- The government can focus on factors that induce the accumulation of more knowledge. For instance, the government can concentrate on human capital development and encourage the accumulation of commercially oriented scientific and technological knowledge.

- The government can become less intrusive in the economy and allow individuals, firms and industries to adapt and respond more quickly to the competitive changes that are taking place in the world.

APPENDIX A
INDICATORS OF KNOWLEDGE

TABLE A1
RANK CORRELATION MATRIX OF R&D ACTIVITY AND KNOWLEDGE WORKERS

	R&D Intensity	R&D Personnel per Worker	Professional R&D per Worker	Proportion of Workers with Post-Secondary Education	Proportion of Knowledge Workers	Proportion of Scientists, Engineers and Technicians
R&D intensity	1.00					
R&D personnel/worker	0.94	1.00				
Professional R&D/worker	0.95	0.99	1.00			
Proportion of workers with post-secondary education	0.59	0.61	0.64	1.00		
Proportion of knowledge workers	0.59	0.60	0.62	0.90	1.00	
Proportion of scientists, engineers and technicians	0.79	0.84	0.84	0.76	0.72	1.00

Note: The rank correlation matrix is for those 43 industries listed in Table 2.
Source: Based on tables 2 and 4.

TABLE A2
INVESTMENT ACTIVITY BY INDUSTRY: 1984 TO 1988 AVERAGE

	Gross Investment Intensity		M&E Investment Intensity		Gross Capital Stock Intensity		M&E Capital Stock Intensity	
	%	Rank	%	Rank	$000	Rank	$000	Rank
Scientific & professional equipment	69.1	2	54.5	1	39.9	35	19.2	37
Communication & other electronics[a]	2.9	38	2.7	34	43.3	32	29.6	28
Aircraft & parts	5.1	26	4.1	24	40.4	34	24.6	32
Business machines	6.8	19	5.2	15	72.8	25	38.4	23
Pharmaceutical & medicine	4.6	29	3.0	30	93.3	22	36.7	25
Electrical power	37.8	5	17.6	5	1,882.7	4	480.9	1
Other chemical products	6.1	21	5.0	16	352.9	8	213.1	2
Machinery	2.2	43	1.8	40	34.8	37	16.3	38
Refined petroleum & coal products	2.8	39	1.0	46	1,048.1	6	178.5	7
Educational services	122.6	1	37.2	2	2,301.6	3	149.7	9
Health & social services	13.4	13	4.7	18	197.5	13	22.9	33
Pipeline transportation	22.1	8	4.0	25	4,304.5	1	201.7	4
Business services	1.5	46	1.4	45	8.6	47	7.3	44
Other transporation equipment & motor vehicles	5.0	28	4.1	23	87.2	23	57.7	19
Other electrical & electronics[a]	3.7	33	3.4	28	39.9	36	21.0	34
Primary metals (non-ferrous)[a]	17.3	10	13.7	6	307.3	9	177.9	8
Textiles	3.9	30	3.5	26	57.4	28	36.3	26
Communication	66.9	3	33.2	3	295.8	10	146.7	10

(cont'd)

TABLE A2 (cont'd)

	Gross Investment Intensity		M&E Investment Intensity		Gross Capital Stock Intensity		M&E Capital Stock Intensity	
	%	Rank	%	Rank	$000	Rank	$000	Rank
Paper & allied products	12.1	14	10.7	7	279.7	11	210.1	3
Mining	21.5	9	6.1	11	617.7	7	126.8	11
Rubber	6.4	20	5.7	12	101.7	21	63.7	17
Plastics	5.3	24	4.3	21	51.2	30	34.2	27
Primary metals (ferrous)[a]	7.4	17	6.8	10	261.7	12	200.1	5
Wholesale trade	3.1	37	2.3	37	21.8	41	9.4	42
Non-metallic mineral products	5.3	25	4.5	20	130.9	19	87.8	13
Crude petroleum & natural gas	27.8	7	2.8	32	2,333.1	2	199.3	6
Fabricated metal products	3.6	34	2.8	33	43.3	33	25.0	31
Food	2.7	40	2.1	38	70.3	26	40.0	22
Beverages	5.4	23	4.5	19	150.8	16	76.7	14
Tobacco	NA	48	NA	48	115.2	20	71.2	16
Finance, insurance & real estate	3.9	32	3.5	27	142.9	17	27.5	29
Other utilities	57.9	4	8.9	9	1,370.4	5	93.0	12
Other services	33.1	6	32.0	4	4.1	49	3.7	48
Printing & publishing	3.2	35	2.9	31	32.0	39	20.0	36
Construction	2.0	44	1.6	42	21.2	43	16.0	39
Amusement & recreational services	8.7	16	3.3	29	46.3	31	7.3	43
Fishing & trapping	7.1	18	4.8	17	53.6	29	45.6	21
Other manufacturing products[a]	2.2	42	1.7	41	24.6	40	12.1	40
Wood	5.1	27	4.3	22	74.0	24	51.9	20
Furniture & fixtures	2.0	45	1.4	44	16.9	44	6.6	45

(cont'd)

HIGH-KNOWLEDGE INDUSTRIES VERSUS LOW-KNOWLEDGE INDUSTRIES

TABLE A2 (cont'd)

	Gross Investment Intensity		M&E Investment Intensity		Gross Capital Stock Intensity		M&E Capital Stock Intensity	
	%	Rank	%	Rank	$000	Rank	$000	Rank
Logging & forestry	3.2	36	1.6	43	67.1	27	20.1	35
Transportation	9.7	15	5.7	13	178.5	14	61.4	18
Storage & warehousing	14.5	11	5.3	14	176.3	15	38.0	24
Agriculture	14.3	12	10.2	8	137.2	18	74.6	15
Retail trade	3.9	31	2.6	35	15.6	46	5.3	46
Personal services	NA	NA	NA	NA	NA	NA	NA	NA
Quarry, sand pits & mining services	2.5	41	2.0	39	33.9	38	27.1	30
Accommodation, food & beverage services	6.0	22	2.4	36	15.7	45	2.8	49
Clothing	1.1	47	0.9	47	7.7	48	4.4	47
Leather	NA	NA	NA	NA	21.4	42	10.0	41

Notes: [a] 1991 investment gross output data and 1990 employment data are used.

Other services includes personal services.

Quarry and sand pits and mining services are combined because investment data are not available separately.

Source: Authors' calculations based on Statistics Canada data. Employment data for scientific and professional equipment are from Canadian Occupational Projection System, Human Resources Development Canada.

TABLE A3

PATENT ACTIVITY BY INDUSTRY: 1984 TO 1988

	Total Patents Granted		Total Patents Used		Total Patents Granted per Output		Total Patents Used per Output		Externally Used Patents	
	Number	Rank	Number	Rank	per $ Billion	Rank	per $ Billion	Rank	%	Rank
Scientific & professional equipment	5,285	5	1,593	13	6,350.0	1	1,914.0	1	74.5	6
Communication & other electronics	10,063	3	8,014	2	372.5	2	296.6	3	33.2	26
Aircraft & parts	117	25	526	32	6.8	19	30.6	18	17.1	29
Computer & related services	1	34	187	44	0.1	33	21.1	24	0.0	35
Business machines	1,928	11	2,436	10	155.6	6	196.5	4	46.0	20
Engineering & scientific services	0	37	1,312	16	0.0	37	71.3	11	NA	35
Pharmaceutical & medicine	2,464	8	4,467	5	179.0	5	324.6	2	83.2	3
Electrical power	0	37	1,183	20	0.0	37	14.5	30	NA	35
Other chemical products	12,112	2	8,538	1	138.8	7	97.8	9	59.5	13
Machinery	15,802	1	6,469	3	370.9	3	151.8	5	68.2	9
Refined petroleum & coal products	281	20	1,652	12	3.0	26	17.4	28	80.4	4
Management consulting services	0	37	52	54	0.0	37	3.6	48	NA	35
Educational services	0	37	332	38	0.0	37	45.9	14	NA	35
Health & social services	0	37	3,356	7	0.0	37	54.3	13	NA	35
Pipeline transportation	0	37	60	53	0.0	37	3.9	46	NA	35
Other business services	0	37	482	33	0.0	37	1.5	54	NA	35
Other transportation equipment	616	15	1,407	14	43.3	11	98.9	8	26.5	27
Other electrical & electronics	7,520	4	4,648	4	188.3	4	116.4	6	49.4	18
Primary metals (non-ferrous)	262	21	1,113	22	4.4	23	18.9	27	62.6	11
Textiles	506	17	863	27	16.9	16	28.8	20	34.2	25
Communication	0	37	284	39	0.0	37	3.2	50	NA	35
Paper & allied products	666	14	990	26	6.3	20	9.4	35	42.2	22
Mining	30	30	608	29	0.5	30	10.9	34	73.3	7

(cont'd)

TABLE A3 (cont'd)

	Total Patents Granted		Total Patents Used		Total Patents Granted per Output		Total Patents Used per Output		Externally Used Patents	
	Number	Rank	Number	Rank	per $ Billion	Rank	per $ Billion	Rank	%	Rank
Rubber	304	19	550	31	21.8	15	39.5	16	59.2	14
Plastics	2,237	9	2,406	11	95.9	8	103.2	7	38.4	24
Primary metals (ferrous)	319	18	1,012	25	6.3	21	19.8	25	79.0	5
Non-metallic mineral products	1,016	12	1,195	19	29.9	12	35.1	17	65.1	10
Wholesale trade	0	37	442	34	0.0	37	2.5	52	NA	35
Crude petroleum & natural gas	1	34	1,071	23	0.0	35	9.3	36	0.0	35
Fabricated metal products	4,522	6	3,450	6	58.3	10	44.5	15	61.6	12
Motor vehicles & parts	2,149	10	3,260	8	11.0	18	16.7	29	10.1	33
Food	727	13	1,250	17	4.1	24	7.1	40	14.6	31
Beverages	32	29	158	47	1.2	28	5.8	43	15.6	30
Tobacco	99	27	229	42	12.0	17	27.7	21	43.4	21
Finance, insurance & real estate	2	33	81	51	0.0	36	0.1	55	50.0	17
Other utilities	0	37	1,203	18	0.0	37	90.3	10	NA	35
Services incidental to mining	9	31	1,147	21	0.4	31	55.7	12	55.6	15
Other services	1	34	271	40	0.0	34	7.1	39	100.0	1
Printing & publishing	101	26	1,013	24	1.9	27	18.9	26	19.8	28
Construction	80	28	2,693	9	0.2	32	7.2	38	55.0	16
Amusement & recreational services	0	37	210	43	0.0	37	6.7	41	NA	35
Fishing & trapping	0	37	176	46	0.0	37	23.3	23	NA	35
Other manufacturing products	2,474	7	835	28	89.2	9	30.1	19	47.4	19
Wood	221	22	395	35	3.4	25	6.2	42	72.4	8
Furniture & fixtures	515	16	248	41	26.2	13	12.6	31	38.8	23
Logging & forestry	0	37	143	48	0.0	37	3.9	47	NA	35
Transportation	0	37	384	36	0.0	37	2.3	53	NA	35
Storage & warehousing	0	37	48	55	0.0	37	8.7	37	NA	35

(cont'd)

TABLE A3 (cont'd)

	Total Patents Granted		Total Patents Used		Total Patents Granted per Output		Total Patents Used per Output		Externally Used Patents	
	Number	Rank	Number	Rank	per $ Billion	Rank	per $ Billion	Rank	%	Rank
Agriculture	0	37	1,394	15	0.0	37	11.8	32	NA	35
Retail trade	0	37	589	30	0.0	37	2.7	51	NA	35
Personal services	0	37	109	50	0.0	37	4.0	45	NA	35
Quarry, sand pits & mining services	3	32	62	52	0.5	29	11.1	33	100.0	1
Accommodation, food & beverage services	0	37	351	37	0.0	37	3.5	49	NA	35
Clothing	152	24	142	49	4.9	22	4.6	44	9.9	34
Leather	159	23	178	45	23.6	14	26.4	22	13.8	32

Notes: Only industries of first manufacture are considered for the analysis.

Patents granted refers to product patents whereas patents used refers to both product and process patents.

Source: Authors' tabulation from PATDAT, Canadian Intellectual Property Office.

APPENDIX B
INDUSTRY ECONOMIC PERFORMANCE

TABLE B1

PERFORMANCE OF GDP AT FACTOR COST BY INDUSTRY: 1981 TO 1990

	Annual Growth Rate	Output Share 1981	Output Share 1990	Absolute Change in Share	Output Share Growth Rate
	%	%	%	%	%
Scientific & professional equipment	-3.9	0.23	0.13	-0.11	-45.6
Communication & other electronics	4.8	0.67	0.79	0.12	18.7
Aircraft & parts	1.9	0.68	0.63	-0.05	-7.9
Computer & related services	8.2	0.31	0.48	0.18	58.1
Business machines	26.6	0.07	0.44	0.37	548.5
Engineering & scientific services	1.5	1.14	1.02	-0.12	-10.8
Pharmaceutical & medicine	5.7	0.31	0.39	0.09	28.7
Electrical power	1.7	3.36	3.05	-0.31	-9.2
Other chemical products	3.1	1.39	1.43	0.04	2.7
Machinery	-1.6	1.30	0.87	-0.43	-32.9
Refined petroleum & coal products	0.8	0.60	0.50	-0.10	-16.2
Management & consulting services	15.7	0.26	0.74	0.48	189.7
Education services	2.5	0.24	0.23	-0.01	-3.1
Health & social services	3.3	2.45	2.54	0.09	3.8
Pipeline transportation	4.9	0.59	0.70	0.12	19.7
Other business services	5.7	2.44	3.13	0.69	28.2
Other transportation equipment	-2.8	0.48	0.29	-0.19	-39.6
Other electrical & electronics	-0.3	0.98	0.74	-0.24	-24.4
Primary metals (non-ferrous)	3.7	0.69	0.74	0.06	8.0
Textiles	-0.3	0.63	0.48	-0.15	-24.4
Communication	5.5	3.44	4.34	0.90	26.2
Paper & allied products	0.3	2.26	1.80	-0.46	-20.3
Mining	4.4	1.27	1.45	0.19	14.8
Rubber	1.9	0.28	0.25	-0.02	-8.1
Plastics	4.6	0.38	0.45	0.07	17.0
Primary metals (ferrous)	-1.0	1.13	0.81	-0.33	-28.8
Non-metallic mineral products	0.3	0.87	0.70	-0.17	-19.7
Wholesale trade	5.2	5.55	6.84	1.29	23.3
Crude petroleum & natural gas	3.1	2.66	2.72	0.06	2.2
Fabricated metal products	0.5	1.91	1.56	-0.35	-18.3
Motor vehicles & parts	8.4	1.42	2.30	0.87	61.5
Food	0.8	2.71	2.27	-0.44	-16.3
Beverages	-1.2	0.81	0.57	-0.24	-30.1
Tobacco	-5.0	0.30	0.15	-0.15	-51.0
Finance, insurance & real estate	3.4	18.45	19.34	0.89	4.8

(cont'd)

TABLE B1 (cont'd)

	Annual Growth Rate	Output Share 1981	Output Share 1990	Absolute Change in Share	Output Share Growth Rate
	%	%	%	%	%
Other utilities	2.6	0.56	0.55	-0.01	-1.9
Other services	1.8	1.71	1.57	-0.15	-8.7
Printing & publishing	1.7	1.53	1.39	-0.15	-9.5
Construction	2.0	8.39	7.79	-0.60	-7.1
Amusement & recreational services	3.6	0.94	1.01	0.06	6.8
Fishing & trapping	3.4	0.26	0.27	0.01	5.4
Other manufacturing products	2.7	0.43	0.43	-0.00	-0.9
Wood	3.4	1.12	1.18	0.06	5.3
Furniture & fixtures	-0.2	0.49	0.38	-0.12	-23.4
Logging & forestry	3.0	0.68	0.69	0.01	1.6
Transportation	2.7	4.49	4.43	-0.06	-1.4
Storage & warehousing	-1.4	0.21	0.14	-0.07	-31.4
Agriculture	1.1	3.04	2.61	-0.43	-14.1
Retail trade	2.8	7.46	7.43	-0.03	-0.4
Personal services	5.7	0.88	1.12	0.25	28.1
Quarry, sand pits & mining services	-2.6	0.87	0.53	-0.34	-38.8
Accommodation, food & beverage services	0.1	3.76	2.94	-0.81	-21.7
Clothing	-0.2	0.78	0.60	-0.18	-23.4
Leather	-3.9	0.18	0.10	-0.08	-45.5

Note: Quarry and sand pits and mining services are combined because investment data are not available separately.

Source: Authors' calculations based on Statistics Canada data.

TABLE B2

PERFORMANCE OF EMPLOYMENT BY INDUSTRY: 1981 TO 1990

	Annual Growth Rate	Employment Share 1981	Employment Share 1990	Absolute Change in Share	Employment Share Growth Rate
	%	%	%	%	%
Scientific & professional equipment	-4.7	0.34	0.18	-0.15	-44.9
Communication & other electronics	2.9	0.57	0.63	0.05	9.4
Aircraft & parts	2.1	0.48	0.49	0.01	1.9
Computer & related services	6.4	0.37	0.55	0.18	48.2
Business machines	-0.3	0.21	0.17	-0.04	-17.1
Engineering & scientific services	-0.2	1.39	1.17	-0.23	-16.3
Pharmaceutical & medicine	2.4	0.20	0.21	0.01	4.9
Electrical power	0.3	0.99	0.87	-0.13	-12.9
Other chemical products	0.1	0.90	0.77	-0.13	-14.7
Machinery	-0.9	1.15	0.89	-0.25	-22.1
Refined petroleum & coal products	-4.6	0.27	0.15	-0.12	-44.2
Management consulting services	13.8	0.31	0.85	0.54	171.7
Education services	5.1	0.25	0.34	0.08	32.5
Health & social services	5.2	1.52	2.03	0.51	33.5
Pipeline transportation	1.0	0.07	0.06	-0.01	-7.5
Other business services	8.4	3.43	6.00	2.56	74.7
Other transportation equipment	-2.7	0.41	0.27	-0.14	-33.8
Other electrical & electronics	-2.5	1.02	0.69	-0.34	-32.7
Primary metals (non-ferrous)	-5.7	0.65	0.32	-0.32	-49.9
Textiles	-1.6	0.80	0.59	-0.21	-26.7
Communication	0.2	2.53	2.18	-0.34	-13.6
Paper & allied products	-1.0	1.55	1.20	-0.35	-22.7
Mining	-3.9	1.02	0.61	-0.42	-40.8
Rubber	-0.8	0.33	0.26	-0.07	-20.8
Plastics	4.9	0.42	0.55	0.13	30.5
Primary metals (ferrous)	-1.1	0.88	0.68	-0.21	-23.4
Non-metallic mineral products	-0.3	0.69	0.57	-0.12	-17.1
Wholesale trade	3.5	6.02	6.93	0.91	15.2
Crude petroleum & natural gas	1.4	0.39	0.37	-0.02	-4.0
Fabricated metal products	0.7	1.95	1.76	-0.19	-9.8
Motor vehicles & parts	3.2	1.45	1.63	0.18	12.2
Food	0.0	2.44	2.08	-0.36	-14.8
Beverages	-3.4	0.41	0.25	-0.15	-38.1
Tobacco	-6.1	0.11	0.05	-0.06	-51.8
Finance, insurance & real estate	2.8	6.61	7.18	0.57	8.6
Other utilities	4.0	0.21	0.26	0.04	20.3
Other services	5.1	2.50	3.31	0.81	32.4
Printing & publishing	2.8	1.38	1.50	0.12	8.7
Construction	2.0	8.61	8.71	0.10	1.1
Amusement & recreational services	6.2	0.89	1.31	0.41	46.2
Fishing & trapping	1.8	0.43	0.43	-0.00	-0.3
Other manufacturing products	1.9	0.63	0.63	0.00	0.4
Wood	0.3	1.40	1.21	-0.18	-13.1

(cont'd)

TABLE B2 (cont'd)

	Annual Growth Rate	Employment Share 1981	Employment Share 1990	Absolute Change in Share	Empolyment Share Growth Rate
	%	%	%	%	%
Furniture & fixtures	2.1	0.61	0.62	0.01	2.0
Logging & forestry	-0.9	0.76	0.60	-0.17	-21.7
Transportation	-0.1	5.61	4.73	-0.88	-15.7
Storage & warehousing	-0.4	0.25	0.20	-0.04	-18.1
Agriculture	-1.1	6.23	4.78	-1.45	-23.3
Retail trade	1.2	16.91	15.90	-1.00	-5.9
Personal services	4.7	1.65	2.13	0.48	28.8
Quarry, sand pits & mining services	-0.9	0.61	0.48	-0.13	-21.5
Accommodation, food & beverage services	3.2	7.44	8.42	0.98	13.1
Clothing	-1.0	1.41	1.09	-0.32	-22.4
Leather	-5.4	0.34	0.17	-0.16	-48.6

Note: Quarry and sand pits and mining services are combined because investment data are not available separately.

Source: Authors' calculations based on Statistics Canada data.

TABLE B3

PERFORMANCE OF WAGE RATE BY INDUSTRY: 1981 TO 1990

	Wage Rate 1981	Wage Rate 1990	Annual Growth Rate	Relative Wage Rate 1981	Relative Wage Rate 1990
	$/Hour	$/Hour	%		
Communication & other electronics	12.85	20.65	5.42	1.29	1.28
Aircraft & parts	14.37	25.74	6.69	1.44	1.60
Business machines	13.13	19.11	4.26	1.32	1.19
Pharmaceutical & medicine	13.55	24.06	6.59	1.36	1.49
Electrical power	15.38	26.55	6.25	1.54	1.65
Other chemical products	14.86	23.66	5.30	1.49	1.47
Machinery	13.30	18.08	3.47	1.34	1.12
Refined petroleum & coal products	20.56	30.83	4.61	2.07	1.91
Educational services	16.41	24.60	4.61	1.65	1.53
Health & social services	9.19	18.19	7.88	0.92	1.13
Pipeline transportation	21.02	34.73	5.74	2.11	2.16
Other business services	9.19	18.27	7.93	0.92	1.13
Other transportation equipment	14.35	19.96	3.74	1.44	1.24
Other electrical & electronics	11.71	17.95	4.87	1.18	1.11
Primary metals (non-ferrous)	17.56	25.23	4.11	1.76	1.57
Textiles	9.75	14.36	4.39	0.98	0.89
Communication	15.05	25.19	5.88	1.51	1.56

(cont'd)

TABLE B3 (cont'd)

	Wage Rate 1981	Wage Rate 1990	Annual Growth Rate	Relative Wage Rate 1981	Relative Wage Rate 1990
	$/Hour	$/Hour	%		
Paper & allied products	15.58	24.81	5.31	1.56	1.54
Mining	16.03	26.90	5.92	1.61	1.67
Rubber	13.92	22.27	5.36	1.40	1.38
Plastics	10.10	15.40	4.80	1.01	0.96
Primary metals (ferrous)	17.09	22.57	3.14	1.72	1.40
Non-metallic mineral products	13.29	18.79	3.93	1.33	1.17
Wholesale trade	12.24	19.95	5.58	1.23	1.24
Crude petroleum & natural gas	22.34	32.91	4.40	2.24	2.04
Fabricated metal products	12.02	16.81	3.80	1.21	1.04
Motor vehicles & parts	14.48	20.22	3.78	1.45	1.25
Food	11.40	17.43	4.84	1.14	1.08
Beverages	14.77	22.27	4.67	1.48	1.38
Tobacco	16.17	34.07	8.63	1.62	2.11
Finance, insurance & real estate	13.85	24.33	6.46	1.39	1.51
Other utilities	12.51	20.46	5.61	1.26	1.27
Other services	7.61	9.21	2.14	0.76	0.57
Printing & publishing	12.40	21.14	6.11	1.25	1.31
Construction	13.79	20.24	4.35	1.39	1.26
Amusement & recreational services	7.00	10.64	4.75	0.70	0.66
Fishing & trapping	2.14	4.31	8.09	0.21	0.27
Other manufacturing products	10.22	15.34	4.61	1.03	0.95
Wood	12.92	17.32	3.31	1.30	1.07
Furniture & fixtures	9.08	13.41	4.43	0.91	0.83
Logging & forestry	13.32	20.62	4.98	1.34	1.28
Transportation	11.18	16.87	4.68	1.12	1.05
Storage & warehousing	10.13	15.08	4.52	1.02	0.94
Agriculture	1.14	2.37	8.45	0.11	0.15
Retail trade	6.39	11.42	6.65	0.64	0.71
Personal services	5.88	11.21	7.42	0.59	0.70
Quarry, sand pits & mining services	11.34	18.56	5.63	1.14	1.15
Accommodation, food & beverage services	5.80	8.59	4.47	0.58	0.53
Clothing	8.00	10.58	3.15	0.80	0.66
Leather	8.02	10.92	3.49	0.81	0.68

Notes: Wage (including supplementary income) rates refer to hourly wages.

Scientific and professional equipment is included in the low-knowledge sector.

Quarry and sand pits and mining services are combined because investment data are not available separately.

Source: Authors' calculations based on Statistics Canada data.

TABLE B4

PERFORMANCE LABOUR PRODUCTIVITY BY INDUSTRY: 1981 TO 1990

	Labour Productivity 1981	Labour Productivity 1990	Annual Growth Rate	Relative Productivity Ratio 1981	Relative Productivity Ratio 1990
	$/Hour	$/Hour	%		
Communication & other electronics	25.46	28.35	1.2	1.14	1.14
Aircraft & parts	30.70	31.02	0.1	1.37	1.24
Business machines	7.24	54.71	25.2	0.32	2.19
Pharmaceutical & medicine	34.92	47.31	3.4	1.56	1.89
Electrical power	74.86	83.61	1.2	3.34	3.35
Other chemical products	34.28	43.08	2.6	1.53	1.72
Machinery	24.67	20.62	-2.0	1.10	0.83
Refined petroleum & coal products	50.72	72.28	4.0	2.26	2.89
Education services	25.16	23.30	-0.9	1.12	0.93
Health & social services	38.18	35.25	-0.9	1.70	1.41
Pipeline transportation	180.32	287.50	5.3	8.05	11.51
Other business services	17.61	20.17	1.5	0.79	0.81
Other transportation equipment	25.44	23.39	-0.9	1.14	0.94
Other electrical & electronics	20.93	23.75	1.4	0.93	0.95
Primary metals (non-ferrous)	24.49	33.98	3.7	1.09	1.36
Textiles	16.91	17.60	0.4	0.75	0.70
Communication	43.79	68.51	5.1	1.95	2.74
Paper & allied products	32.19	34.19	0.7	1.44	1.37
Mining	27.22	52.14	7.5	1.21	2.09
Rubber	18.06	22.22	2.3	0.81	0.89
Plastics	19.76	18.65	-0.6	0.88	0.75
Primary metals (ferrous)	29.88	27.31	-1.0	1.33	1.09
Non-metallic mineral products	27.31	26.35	-0.4	1.22	1.06
Wholesale trade	19.42	23.87	2.3	0.87	0.96
Crude petroleum & natural gas	140.80	155.28	1.1	6.28	6.22
Fabricated metal products	20.80	19.12	-0.9	0.93	0.77
Motor vehicles & parts	21.17	29.18	3.6	0.94	1.17
Food	24.58	25.54	0.4	1.10	1.02
Beverages	44.32	47.52	0.8	1.98	1.90
Tobacco	68.22	75.65	1.2	3.04	3.03
Finance, insurance & real estate	64.05	68.38	0.7	2.86	2.74
Other utilities	84.68	91.89	0.9	3.78	3.68
Other services	16.14	12.71	-2.6	0.72	0.51
Printing & publishing	25.58	23.36	-1.0	1.14	0.94
Construction	20.83	20.96	0.1	0.93	0.84
Amusement & recreational services	25.44	20.40	-2.4	1.14	0.82
Fishing & trapping	11.36	15.02	3.2	0.51	0.60
Other manufacturing products	17.00	16.30	-0.5	0.76	0.65
Wood	17.81	20.73	1.7	0.79	0.83
Furniture & fixtures	16.63	13.44	-2.3	0.74	0.54

(cont'd)

TABLE B4 (cont'd)

	Labour Productivity 1981	Labour Productivity 1990	Annual Growth Rate	Relative Productivity Ratio 1981	Relative Productivity Ratio 1990
	$/Hour	$/Hour	%		
Logging & forestry	19.06	24.47	2.8	0.85	0.98
Transportation	17.51	21.53	2.3	0.78	0.86
Storage & warehousing	19.27	17.44	-1.1	0.86	0.70
Agriculture	8.63	11.01	2.7	0.38	0.44
Retail trade	10.65	12.67	2.0	0.48	0.51
Personal services	12.54	14.04	1.3	0.56	0.56
Quarry, sand pits & mining services	25.40	23.19	-1.0	1.13	0.93
Accommodation, food & beverage services	11.91	9.21	-2.8	0.53	0.37
Clothing	12.60	12.07	-0.5	0.56	0.48
Leather	11.26	11.57	0.3	0.50	0.46

Notes: Labour productivity is defined as value-added per hour.

Scientific and professional equipment is included in the low-knowledge sector.

Quarry and sand pits and mining services are combined because investment data are not available separately.

Source: Authors' calculations based on Statistics Canada data.

TABLE B5

DEGREE OF OPENNESS[a] BY INDUSTRY: 1981 AND 1990

	1981	1990
	%	%
Communication & other electronics	166	394
Aircraft & parts	284	286
Business machines	755	855
Pharmaceutical & medicine	78	76
Electrical power	11	8
Other chemical products	150	214
Machinery	341	454
Refined petroleum & coal products	114	233
Educational services	17	43
Health & social services	2	2
Pipeline transportation	59	52
Other business services	61	88
Other transportation equipment	110	190
Other electrical & electronics	178	316
Primary metals (non-ferrous)	350	347

(cont'd)

TABLE B5 (cont'd)

	1981	1990
	%	%
Textiles	140	208
Communication	7	9
Paper & allied products	154	184
Mining	194	172
Rubber	173	278
Plastics	130	178
Primary metals (ferrous)	140	140
Non-metallic mineral products	71	100
Wholesale trade	21	23
Crude petroleum & natural gas	102	126
Fabricated metal products	127	175
Motor vehicles & parts	820	702
Food	81	114
Beverages	56	91
Tobacco	26	44
Finance, insurance & real estate	5	9
Other utilities	2	4
Printing & publishing	36	62
Construction	0	0
Fishing & trapping	61	44
Other manufacturing industries	293	388
Wood	148	146
Furniture & fixtures	63	153
Logging & forestry	12	15
Transportation	11	31
Storage & warehousing	41	57
Agriculture	62	67
Retail trade	1	1
Quarry, sand pits & mining services	7	12
Clothing	69	154
Leather	181	447

Notes: [a]Openness = (imports + exports)/GDP.

Other services include business services.

Scientific and professional equipment is included in the low-knowledge sector.

Quarry and sand pits and mining services are combined because investment data are not available separately.

Source: Authors' calculations based on Statistics Canada data.

ENDNOTES

1   A similar figure is also used by Pakes and Griliches (1984) and Grupp (1991).

2   Often input–output matrices or patent matrices are used to identify knowledge-using industries.

3   The ratio of R&D expenditures to gross output.

4   Acs and Audretsch (1988) find that the total number of innovations is closely related to R&D expenditures and patented inventions based on U.S. data.

5   R&D expenditures correspond only to an investment flow which is different from the existing R&D capital stock. Perhaps, accumulated spending on R&D would be a more adequate representation of the stock of knowledge. In this paper, we focus on R&D intensity rather than the R&D capital stock since relying on the R&D capital stock would restrict us to a much smaller number of industries. However, for those industries for which we calculated R&D stocks, their rankings (based on the ratio of R&D stock to output) do not change significantly for those based on R&D intensity.

6   She defined knowledge workers as professionals, such as doctors, engineers, lawyers, accountants and actuaries, engineers, scientific and technical workers and senior managers.

7   R&D data were available only for 45 industries. For the purpose of classification, we relied on educational and occupational data for those industries missing R&D data.

8   In some cases, data were not available for the level of aggregation we were interested in. Therefore, a few industries were put in the wrong sector since they were included as part of a broader aggregate industry. For example, investment data on the scientific and professional equipment are not separately available from the other manufacturing product industries. Thus, we categorized the scientific and professional equipment industry under the low-knowledge sector along with the other manufacturing product industries when we examined the investment activity. However, this did not appear to change the results significantly.

9   The ratio of R&D expenditures to gross output is used.

10   R&D personnel with university-level degrees.

11   This included workers with trade-vocational education, post-secondary non-university education and university education.

12   This included those with occupations in natural sciences, engineering and mathematics, in education and related occupations, other managers and administrators, occupations related to management and administration, social sciences, law and jurisprudence, medicine and health, and writing. Their corresponding 1980 standard occupation classifications included 21, 27, 113/114, 117, 231, 234, 31 and 335 respectively.

13   This includes those with occupations in natural sciences, engineering and mathematics.

14   Although many studies suggest that the rate of return on private R&D is higher than publicly funded R&D, we used total R&D expenditures to increase the number of industries for the analysis (since the portion of foreign-financed R&D is not available for some industries).

15   The rank correlation matrix for R&D activity and human capital measurements for those industries listed in Table 2 is given in Table A1 in Appendix A.

16   Gross M&E investment intensity is the ratio of gross M&E investment to gross output.

17   The gross M&E capital stock intensity refers to the ratio of gross M&E capital stock to workers.

18   A crude investigation suggests that there appears to have been some changes in investment intensities in the sample. In particular, the rate of investment in the high-knowledge

sector appears to have slowed down in the 1980s compared to before 1980 whereas the extent of slowdown may not be significant in the other two sectors.

19 For example, Pakes and Griliches (1984), Scherer (1984), Ducharme (1991) and Hanel (1994).

20 See Scherer (1984), Ducharme (1991) and Hanel (1994).

21 Although not presented here, focusing on patents granted to Canadians and their potential use by industry does not change the results significantly.

22 The importance of the manufacturing sector has declined in terms of its share of total output and employment, but its role remains important in the economy since the sector generates a significant proportion of technological innovations which have spillover effects to the rest of the economy.

ACKNOWLEDGEMENTS

THE AUTHORS WISH TO THANK Jeffrey Bernstein, Tereasa Chudy, Denis Gauthier, Peter Howitt, Donald McFetridge, Someshwar Rao, Gary Sawchuk and Hollis Whitehead for their valuable comments and Haider Saiyed for a computer program to construct patent data matrices. Any remaining errors are the sole responsibility of the authors. The views expressed in this paper are those of the authors and do not necessarily reflect those of Industry Canada.

BIBLIOGRAPHY

Acs, Zoltan J. and David B. Audretsch. "Innovation in Large and Small Firms: An Empirical Analysis." *American Economic Review.* 78 (4), (September 1988): 678-690.

Abramovitz, Moses. "The Search for the Sources of Growth: Areas of Ignorance, Old and New." *Journal of Economic History.* 53 (2), (June 1993): 217-243.

Baldwin, John, Brent Diverty and David Sabourin. "Technology Use and Industrial Transformation: Empirical Perspectives." Paper delivered to the conference entitled "Technology, Information, and Public Policy" at the John Deutsch Institute of Economic Policy, Queen's University, 1994.

Baldwin, John and M. Rafiquzaman. "Structural Change in the Canadian Manufacturing Sector (1970-1990)." Statistics Canada Research Paper Series No. 61, 1994.

Barro, Robert. "Economic Growth in a Cross Section of Countries." *Quarterly Journal of Economics.*106 (2), (May 1994): 407-444.

Basberg, Bjørn L. "Patent and the Measurement of Technological Change: A Survey of Literature." *Research Policy.* 16, (1987): 131-141.

Beck, Nuala. *Shifting Gears: Thriving in the New Economy.* Toronto: Harper Collins Publishers Ltd, 1992.

Becker, Gary S., Kevin M. Murphy and Robert Tamura. "Human Capital, Fertility and Economic Growth." *Journal of Political Economy.* 98 (5), (October 1990): 512-537.

Bernstein, Jeffrey. "The Structure of Canadian Interindustry R&D Spillovers, Rates of Return to R&D." *Journal of Industrial Economics.* 37 (3), (May 1989): 315-328.

————. "Price Indexes for Canadian Industrial Research and Development Expenditures." Statistics Canada Working Paper ST-92-01. Ottawa: 1992.

————. "International R&D Spillovers between Industries in Canada and the United States." Industry Canada Working Paper No 3, Ottawa, 1994.

Coe, David T. and Elhanan Helpman. "International R&D Spillovers." IMF Working Paper WP/93/84, Washington, DC, November 1993.

Cohen, Wesley M. and Richard C. Levin. "Empirical Studies of Innovation and Market Structure." In *Handbook of Industrial Organization*. Volume II. Edited by R. Schmalensee and R. D. Willig. North Holland, Amsterdam, 1989, pp. 1059-1107.

De Long, J. Bradford and Lawrence H. Summers. "Equipment Investment and Economic Growth: Reply." *Quarterly Journal of Economics*. 106 (2), (May 1991): 445-502.

Diwan, Romesh and Chandana Chakraborty. *High Technology and International Competitiveness*. New York: Praeger, 1991.

Dollar, David and Edward N. Wolff. *Competitiveness, Convergence, and International Specialization*. Cambridge, MA, MIT Press: 1993.

Ducharme, Louis M. "Inter-industrial Technology Diffusion: A Macro Analysis of Technical Change in the Canadian Economy." Ph.D. dissertation submitted to University of Sussex, 1991.

Griliches, Zvi. "Patent Statistics as Economic Indicators: A Survey." *Journal of Economic Literature*. 28 (4), (December 1990): 1661-1707.

————. "Productivity, R&D, and the Data Constraint." *American Economic Review*. 84 (1), (March 1994): 1-23.

Grupp, H. "Innovation Dynamics in OECD Countries: Towards a Correlated Network of R&D-Intensity, Trade, Patent and Technometric Indicators." *Technology and Productivity*. OECD, (1991): 275-295.

Hanel, Petr. "Interindustry Flows of Technology: An Analysis of the Canadian Patent Matrix and Input–Output Matrix for 1978-1989." *Technovation*. 14, (1994): 529-548.

Harris, Richard. "Presidential Address: Globalization, Trade, and Income." *Canadian Journal of Economics*. 26 (4), (November 1993): 755-776.

Hulten, Charles R. "Growth Accounting When Technical Change Is Embodied in Capital." *American Economic Review*. 82 (4), (September 1992): 964-980.

Jensen, Michael C. "The Modern Industrial Revolutions, Exit, and the Failure of Internal Control Systems." *Journal of Finance*. 48 (3), (July 1993): 831-880.

Lach, Saul and Mark Schankerman. "Dynamics of R&D and Investment in the Scientific Sector." *Journal of Political Economy*. 97 (4), (August 1989): 880-904.

Levin, Richard C., Alvin K. Klevorick, Richard R. Nelson and Sidney G. Winter. "Appropriating the Returns from Industrial Research and Development." Cowles Foundation for Research in Economics at Yale University, Paper No. 714, 1989.

Lipsey, Richard G. "Globalisation, Technological Change and Economic Growth." Paper delivered to Annual Sir Charles Carter Lecture, Northern Ireland Economic Council, Belfast, Northern Ireland, 1993.

Lucas, Robert E., Jr. "On the Mechanics of Economic Development." *Journal of Monetary Economics*. 22, (1988): 3-42.

————. "Making a Miracle." *Econometrica*. 61 (2), (March 1993): 251-272.

Machlup, Fritz. *The Production and Distribution of Knowledge in the United States*. Princeton, NJ: Princeton University Press, 1962.

Mankiw, N. Gregory, David Romer and David N. Weil. "A Contribution to the Empirics of Economic Growth." *Quarterly Journal of Economics*. 107, (May 1992): 407-437.

Markusen, Aann, Peter Hall and Amy Glasmeier. *High Tech America*. Boston: Allen & Unwin, 1986.

Mohnen, Pierre. *The Relationship Between R&D and Productivity Growth in Canada and Other Major Industrialized Countries*. Economic Council of Canada, 1992.

OECD. "Structural Change and Industrial Performance: A Seven Country Growth Decomposition Study." Paris, 1992.

———. *Frascati Manual 1993: The Measurement of Scientific and Technological Activities: Proposed Standard Practice for Surveys of Research and Development*. Paris, 1994a.

———. *Manufacturing Performance: A Scoreboard of Indicators*. Paris, 1994b.

Pakes, Ariel and Zvi Griliches. "Patents and R&D at the Firm Level: A First Look." In *R&D, Patents and Productivity*. Edited by Zvi Griliches. Chicago: University of Chicago Press, 1984.

Romer, Paul A. "Crazy Explanations for the Productivity Slowdown." In *NBER Macroeconomics Annual*. Edited by S. Fischer. Cambridge: MIT Press, 1987, pp. 163-202.

———. "Idea Gaps and Object Gaps in Economic Development." *Journal of Monetary Economics*. 32, (1993a): 543-573.

———. "Two Strategies for Economic Development: Using Ideas and Producing Ideas." *Proceedings of the World Bank Annual Conference on Development Economics 1992*, Washington, DC, 1993b, pp. 63-92.

Rose, Graham. "Employment Growth in High-Tech and Knowledge Industries." Mimeo. Department of Finance, Government of Canada, 1992.

Scherer, Fredrick M. "Using Linked Patent and R&D Data to Measure Interindustry Technology Flows." In *R&D, Patents and Productivity*. Edited by Zvi Griliches. Chicago: University of Chicago Press, 1984, pp. 417-461.

Statistics Canada. "Industrial Research and Development Statistics 1989." Catalogue 88-202, Ottawa, Canada, 1991.

Wong, Fred. "High Technology at Work." *Perspectives*. Statistics Canada, (Spring 1990): 17-28.

Comment

Donald G. McFetridge
Department of Economics
Carleton University

IN THEIR PAPER, FRANK LEE AND HANDAN HAS CLASSIFY 55 Canadian industries according to their knowledge intensity. They use three classes: high-, medium- and low-knowledge intensity. They then investigate whether there are systematic interclass differences in economic performance.

This is an interesting paper that raises some fundamental questions.

- First, why would one wish to distinguish among industries on the basis of their knowledge intensity?

- Second, how do you define a knowledge-intensive industry?

- Third, what is meant by the term "economic performance?"

With respect to the first question, presumably one wishes to distinguish from the less knowledge-intensive industries because knowledge-intensive industries are of special importance. But why are they of special importance? It is not sufficient merely to argue that the accumulation of knowledge is central to the growth process. If knowledge-producing industries are of special importance, it must be because we believe they need encouragement, i.e., that commercial incentives for knowledge accumulation should be reinforced by public policy. Many have argued that public policy measures are indeed required to bring the private rate of return on knowledge production into line with the social rate of return.

What of the intensive users of knowledge? Would they not be among the major beneficiaries of the spillovers emanating from the knowledge producing industries? Why would they need special encouragement? Viewed from a resource allocation perspective, it does not appear to make much sense to lump intensive producers and users of knowledge together in the same category as the authors have done. Presumably, it is the potential *net domestic producers* of knowledge that require the most encouragement.

The intensive knowledge-using industries may also confer spillover benefits of a different nature on the economy. Employees in these industries may acquire transferable skills and knowledge in the course of performing their duties. If, for some reason, they do not "pay" for this knowledge – perhaps by accepting lower wages – they are the recipients of a spillover benefit. The industries conferring this spillover benefit on their employees might require special encouragement. This would depend, again, on whether they are *net providers* or *net recipients* of spillover benefits in general.

It would, of course, be preferable to focus support on the *activities* that result in spillover benefits. These activities may be prevalent in some knowledge-intensive industries but not in others. Thus, some R&D activities may result in spillover benefits and some may not.[1] For example, the pharmaceutical industry may be an important source of new knowledge in the form of new drugs. This does not imply that there is an inadequate commercial incentive to develop new drugs. That would depend on the extent to which inventors of new drugs can make use of intellectual property, secrecy and co-specialized assets to appropriate the returns from their inventions.

With respect to the second question, there are a number of possible ways to define a knowledge-intensive industry. The definition chosen will presumably depend on how the industry classification is being used. Lee and Has have defined knowledge-intensive industries as being either relatively research and development (R&D)-intensive or having a relatively well-educated work force. They associate R&D intensity with knowledge production and human capital intensity with knowledge use. Some industries qualify as both intensive knowledge users and intensive knowledge producers.

As I have argued above, if the goal is to identify and encourage sources of knowledge spillover benefits, *knowledge-producing* industries and *knowledge-using* industries should be treated differently. Moreover, if one is concerned with the amount of knowledge an industry is currently producing, it is the dollar amount of industry R&D rather than R&D intensity that is relevant.

With respect to measures of knowledge use, the authors focus on the proportion of an industry's work force that is well educated or the proportion that has a technical education. Again, it may be the size of the technical work force rather than its relative importance that is relevant if one is interested in current knowledge use.

Knowledge may also be embodied in the physical capital used by an industry. Indeed, knowledge-intensive physical capital may be a substitute for human capital. Some industries may have relatively unskilled labour forces but be intensive users of knowledge embodied in physical capital.

This raises the question of how one measures the knowledge intensity of physical capital. Are so-called advanced manufacturing technologies relatively knowledge intensive? Presumably, more recent vintages of physical capital embody more knowledge than earlier vintages. But the most recent vintage may not be particularly new. For example, the state-of-the-art metallurgical or chemical processes may have been developed some time ago. Does that make them less knowledge intensive?

Lee and Has explore the use of so-called patent flow data as an indicator of knowledge production and use. The limitations of patent data are well known. Patent "flows" are inferred from the most likely industry of use and the most likely industry of manufacture designations entered on patent applications by the patent examiner. These designations reflect the examiner's opinion regarding the industry most likely to manufacture the invention (if it is a product) and the industries most likely to use the invention. The industry of *manufacture* is not necessarily the industry of *invention*. Indeed, the inventor need not be affiliated with *any* industry. Thus, patent flows may or may not correspond to knowledge flows.

With respect to the third question, there are many definitions of industry performance. The appropriate definition depends on the question being asked. If it is economic growth that is at issue, then the appropriate performance measure is total factor productivity growth. If the concern is with employment opportunities, then employment growth is a useful measure of performance. Whether past employment growth can be extrapolated to imply something about future employment opportunities is another question.

Lee and Has use employment, GDP and labour productivity growth over the period 1981 to 1990 as measures of performance. They find that their high- and medium- knowledge intensity sectors do not differ much in terms of labour productivity levels and growth rates. It is not clear what to make of this. There are many factors at play. I have argued that the classification of industries employed by the authors is not particularly meaningful. In addition, labour productivity growth may not mirror total factor productivity growth. It is also the case that, in the presence of spillovers, an industry's own productivity growth does not fully reflect its contribution to aggregate productivity growth.

The policy implications of these results are equally obscure. There is nothing in them that implies that some industries should be more or less favoured by public policy than they presently are. Nor, given the authors' methodology, could there be. If the analysis has another purpose, Lee and Has may wish to clarify what it is.

ENDNOTE

1   The econometric evidence is variable but it appears to imply that some of the more R&D-intensive industries do not generate spillover benefits while some of the less R&D-intensive industries do.

John R. Baldwin & Joanne Johnson
Micro-Economics Analysis Division
Statistics Canada

with the assistance of Michael Pedersen

3

Human Capital Development and Innovation: A Sectoral Analysis

EXECUTIVE SUMMARY

THIS PAPER EXAMINES HOW TRAINING DECISIONS RELATE to the business plan of the firm. The basic hypothesis is that the adoption of a wide variety of innovation strategies, across a variety of firm types and sectors, fosters a need for training. The results are based on a Statistics Canada survey that queried small- and medium-sized firms on their strategies, activities and characteristics. This survey permits training decisions to be analyzed within the broader context of the firm's many activities and developmental strategies, including decisions about products, organizational structure, technological capabilities, financial structure and marketing programs. Furthermore, the results are linked to longitudinal administrative data on assets and employment, and provide a rich set of information on the firms.

MAJOR FINDINGS

Training Activities Are a Concomitant Part of Innovation Strategies

- Firms differ substantially in their training strategies.

- A significant portion of the variation in training strategies can be explained by differences in the innovation strategy of the firm.

The Importance of Innovation to Training Is Evident on a Sectoral as well as a National Basis

- Approximately three quarters of innovative firms in all sectors train, compared to less than half of non-innovative firms in all sectors.

- Innovative firms in manufacturing and dynamic services perform formal training at approximately twice the rate of non-innovative firms. Similarly, about half of innovative firms in these sectors engage in informal training, compared to just under 30 percent of non-innovative manufacturing firms and 37 percent of non-innovative dynamic service firms.

- Innovative firms in the traditional services sector place a greater emphasis on both formal and informal training relative to non-innovative firms. Innovative firms are almost twice as likely to engage in either type of training as non-innovative firms.

The Training–Innovation Relationship Varies Across Sectors

- In manufacturing firms, the decision to train is closely linked with the technological and research and development (R&D) innovation strategy of the firm, and with the growth in capital per worker.
- In firms involved in the dynamic services sector, training is stimulated by each of the three elements of innovation defined here: R&D/technology, quality and human resource strategies.
- In firms engaged in the traditional services sector, an emphasis on human resource or quality strategies stimulates greater training.

Innovation Takes Many Different Forms

- In firms that make extensive use of machinery and equipment, innovation primarily involves developing new technologies and production processes. Human capital development is complementary to this type of innovation, as working with new technologies requires adopting new skills.
- In other areas, such as the services sector, human capital is the dominant form of capital. In these situations, the human capital formation and the innovation system of the firm are one and the same.
- In manufacturing firms, innovation strategy is primarily oriented toward technology and R&D.
- In the dynamic services sector, a technology and R&D innovation strategy is complemented by a human resource and quality strategy.
- In the traditional services sector, the innovation strategy is solely defined by the human resource and quality strategy.

INTRODUCTION

TRAINING HAS INCREASINGLY BEEN HERALDED AS KEY to improving business performance (Betcherman, 1994). As markets become globalized, firms must continually produce higher-quality products at a lower cost. As a consequence, firms require increasingly skilled and adaptable employees. Training is one means of providing these skills.

This argument can be simplistically interpreted to mean that more training is better, in all circumstances. Yet, training has not been consistently linked with success. On reflection, it is more sensible to argue that it is the quality of training rather than just the quantity that matters.

The factors that lead a firm to engage in training have not been thoroughly investigated. Indeed, most studies have relied on employee surveys that examine characteristics of those who have been trained. In summarizing the results of these studies, the Organization for Economic Co-operation and Development (OECD) (1991) concluded that it was generally workers with more education who received training.[1] A few studies (Mincer, 1989; Lillard and Tan, 1986; Bartel, 1991, 1992; and Bartel and Lichtenberg, 1987) examined the relationship between the nature of technological change and training at the industry level. However, an industry-level rather than a firm-level analysis neglects the fact that, in any given industry, some firms will exhibit greater technical skills and need more skilled labour. Furthermore, these studies represent technological change in a uni-dimensional fashion using only one variable and, hence, the importance of innovation, broadly applied, is not examined.

A Statistics Canada survey[2] allowed the factors that influence the training decisions of small- and medium-sized firms to be studied within the broader context of the many strategies and activities followed by a firm, particularly those relating to innovation and technological change. The survey provided both subjective and objective measures of marketing, technology, innovation, finance, input-sourcing and human resource strategies and activities. This permits examination of the relation between innovativeness – defined broadly – and human resource strategies. Moreover, the measures of other strategies, particularly with respect to quality and valuation of labour skills, permit an integrated picture of the firm to be developed and related to the training decision.

Baldwin and Johnson (1994) examined the relationship between firm strategies – in particular, innovation – and training, using the Statistics Canada survey. Innovation was found to be strongly linked to training. Training is therefore complementary to the other forms of capital required by innovative firms. Emphasis on quality and human resources also affects the training decision. While this analysis was useful in examining the typical firm characteristics that lead to training, industry differences were not analyzed in depth. This paper extends the earlier work to examine how the innovation–training relationship varies in three sectors: manufacturing, traditional services and dynamic services.

The paper is divided into six parts. The first section lays out the framework for analyzing training. The second section describes the survey that provided data to test the innovation–human resource complementarity argument. The third section briefly describes the training measures available from the survey and presents an aggregate picture of the incidence and intensity of training. The fourth and fifth sections outline the variables used for multivariate analysis and present this analysis of training at the national, all-industry level. The sixth section investigates sectoral differences in human resource strategies, generally, and training, specifically.

TRAINING IN THE STRATEGIC PLAN OF THE FIRM

MOST KNOWLEDGE THAT MAKES THE DIFFERENCE between success and failure for a firm is tacit, i.e., it is not subject to ready codification. If it were, blueprints for success could be prepared, and firms that were laggards could quickly emulate the most successful. Tacit knowledge is firm-specific and accumulates over time. It resides in the organization, in the collective knowledge possessed by the work force of a firm. Tacit knowledge in its various forms provides the basis for the innovation system of a firm, its organizational structure and its productive capabilities.

Training creates the human skills that, taken together, are the repository in which the tacit knowledge of an organization resides. That knowledge takes many forms. Most of it is learned on the job in both structured and unstructured formats.

A key type of knowledge is the understanding of how to make and use machines. In industries where large amounts of capital are used in conjunction with labour, "technical know-how" is an important component of knowledge. It is essential not only for the production process but also for the innovation system of a firm. Technological know-how often precedes scientific know-how, and it is the key to innovation in many firms (Mowery and Rosenberg, 1989).

In industries where the production process involves less physical capital, training is also important. Knowledge is the product in most service sectors. In many cases, a business service is the knowledge of a specialist. Success in these industries depends on the ability to embody the amount and type of human knowledge required by a client. Product quality and the human capital embodiment of products in these industries are one and the same. Training involves both skill enhancement and problem solving – learning how to package knowledge in the correct form for clients. The latter is as much a critical tacit skill as is the ability to make machines work.

Even in industries where human capital is complementary to physical capital, human capital will also be important in its second role: providing enhancements to meet individual client requirements or differentiating products by providing specific designs or services that have value to a client.

Training, therefore, has two purposes.

- It provides technology-related skills. These include an intimate understanding of specific technical processes in manufacturing or software and computer-related skills in service industries.

- It teaches workers how to embed knowledge in products to provide new services to clients.

When firms choose their innovation strategy, there is an associated training strategy. The adoption of new technologies requires refinement to workers' skills. The choice of an innovation-related stance necessarily involves a simultaneous choice of a more intense training strategy.

But a firm also has to decide whether to embody a knowledge component in its product, even in industries where physical capital and technological strategy usually go hand in hand. This component is directly connected to the training system.

When large amounts of physical capital are required for production, both reasons for training will be found and will be difficult to disentangle. In industries, such as manufacturing, the technological strategy of a firm will, at a minimum, determine its training strategy. As problem solving moves to focus on innovation, firms in these industries may also choose to place an additional emphasis on training as they move from a world where know-how is narrowly focused on making machines work to one where it is more broadly focused on deciding what to make.

In other industries, innovation and the training system are just as intimately linked, though for different reasons. The knowledge base, as opposed to the technology base, is the innovation system of these firms. Creating an ability to solve problems, to differentiate the product on the basis of embedded knowledge and develop an environment for continuous innovation is critically dependent on the knowledge base that is built up by the all-encompassing training system.

Thus, training is just one of the decisions in a chain of strategic choices. That chain proceeds sequentially with complex feedback loops. The most basic decision a firm must make revolves around the product market it chooses to operate in. The nature of the product market – the extent to which it is human or physical capital intensive – determines the type of competition the firm faces and the tools (new technologies, human resources) it uses to compete.

THE GROWING SMALL- AND MEDIUM-SIZE FIRM (GSME) SURVEY

THE GSME SURVEY WAS CONDUCTED IN 1992 using firms that grew over the last half of the 1980s. It was designed to examine firms that were not in decline. Only firms that experienced growth in employment, sales and assets between 1984 and 1988 were included in the sample.[3] Small- and medium-sized firms were defined as having less than 500 employees and less than $100 million in assets in 1984. The sample was drawn from all major sectors with the exception of public administration. The survey of 2157 firms was conducted by mail with telephone follow-up. The response rate was 69 percent. Only those firms that responded to all sections of the survey, amounting to some 1009, were included in this study.

The GSME survey was designed to give a broad description of activities, characteristics and strategies followed by a set of generally successful small- and medium-sized firms. Questions in the survey profiled a firm's region of operation, ownership structure, country of control, its involvement in mergers and strategic alliances, its size and its occupational distribution. The activities investigated included export performance, capital structure, sources of financing, investment intensity of R&D, training, marketing, sources of innovation, number of workers trained by occupational category and training expenditures.

Strategies were investigated with several complementary questions. Firms were asked to rank the importance of different factors explaining the growth of their company including management skills, marketing capability, cost of capital, access to capital, technological capability, R&D capability and labour force skill levels. Another question probed the firms' assessment of their capabilities relative to their competitors with regard to price, cost of production, quality, customer service, spending on R&D, labour climate and skill levels of employees. An additional set of questions examined specific directions pursued in marketing, technology, input utilization, management and human resource strategies.

The strength of the survey is the degree to which training can be compared to the other strategies, characteristics and activities of the firm. Survey answers were linked to administrative data on firm employment, worker turnover, sales, profitability and productivity to provide a rich set of characteristics that were used for analysis.

MEASURES OF TRAINING

SEVERAL MEASURES OF TRAINING ARE AVAILABLE from the survey: whether formal or informal training is performed by a firm, the number of employees given formal or informal training by occupation and the total expenditure on training. Formal training is either on-the-job or off-the-job instruction in a place removed from the production process. Informal training is less structured and is done on the job.[4]

- On average, 59 percent of firms offered their workers some form of training, 44 percent delivered formal training and 40 percent gave informal training.

- On average, 31 percent of the work force in firms offering a formal training program received this form of training.

- Some 41 percent of the work force in firms offering an informal training program received informal training.

- Firms with a training program spent an average of $850 per employee in the firm on all forms of training.

THE DETERMINANTS OF TRAINING

INNOVATION AND TECHNOLOGY

A FIRM'S TRAINING DECISION IS POSITED to be a function of its innovativeness and technological advancement. Innovation and advances in technology require knowledge skills that are difficult to acquire purely from external recruitment. This is due to the specificity of the knowledge in high technology firms and the rapidity of change associated with innovation which necessitates ongoing upgrading of the existing work force.

The connection between technology and training has been confirmed by several studies. Lillard and Tan (1986) and Mincer (1989) tested the effect of technological change by correlating measures of multi-factor productivity with the intensity of training at the industry level. They found a positive relationship. Bartel and Lichtenberg (1987) found that the mean age of capital in an industry was inversely related to the proportion of the labour force with higher education. Bartel (1991) examined firm data on training and found it to be positively related to R&D intensity and to the ratio of capital to labour in the firm. Hum and Simpson (1993) found that the probability of training for individuals depended on the growth of investment in their sector of employment and the prevalence of high technology inputs in that sector.

These previous studies used relatively simple proxies for the complexity of technology in industry. However, these variables cannot capture the range of circumstances for which technological complexity and innovation require training.

A host of both subjective and objective measures of innovative activity are available from the GSME survey. In addition to traditional questions, such as the number of employees in an R&D unit and expenditures on R&D, subjective questions relating to the innovative stance of the firm and the importance of innovation-related strategies were also employed. Firms were asked to rate their R&D spending relative to their competitors on a scale of 0 to 5 (0 corresponding to not applicable, 1 much worse and 5 much better). They were also asked to rate the importance of R&D innovation capability, or the ability to adopt technology, on a scale of 0 to 5 as a factor in past growth. Questions on general development strategies looked at the importance firms attributed to strategies related to developing new technology, improving their own or others' technology and using others' technology. Finally, the stimulus for innovative activity was examined by asking firms to rate a variety of factors – both internal and external – on a scale of 0 to 5, in terms of the importance of that factor as a source of innovation. In total, there were 24 objective and subjective measures of innovation. These are described in Appendix A.

While the data base provides a rich set of variables that can be used to measure the innovative characteristics of firms, many of these innovation variables are interrelated. Consequently, including them all in a regression equation would lead to quite serious multicollinearity. A further problem derives from the frequent criticism that subjective questions are problematic as people may interpret them differently. However, subjective questions are critical to investigating the decision to train: the perceptions and beliefs of managers affect the decision to offer training to employees.

To condense the dimensionality in the innovation variables in order to alleviate the multicollinearity problem, and to overcome the criticism of using subjective responses, the variables are combined. Anderson, et al. (1983) suggested that when various subjective responses are centred on a particular theme, those responses, when combined in a more aggregate form, can reasonably be expected to represent that theme. For example, combining the scores on the importance of strategies related to developing new technology, improving others' technology, improving own technology and using others' technology, and the importance of the ability to adopt technology as a factor in growth, gives a reliable measure of the degree of technological orientation of the firm.

There are several methods for combining variables, ranging from summing the scores across variables to principal component analysis. Principal component analysis creates new variables as weighted averages of the old. These new variables jointly have the same amount of total variation that existed in the original sample of variables, but are independent of one another. The weights for the first component are chosen to maximize the total amount of variation accounted for by this component, i.e., the broadest spread of all the variables. The weights for subsequent components are chosen to maximize the amount of residual variation that each variable accounts for, while maintaining independence with all previous components.

The alternate weighting schemes – the size and sign attached to each of the variables – in each of the components identifies different prototypes of innovators. Some firms are at the cutting edge in an industry. Others are imitators and adapters. Firms in each category stress different aspects of innovation by placing emphasis on new products, technologies, inputs and organizational structures. The innovation principal components delineate patterns of innovative types. Multivariate analysis can then be used to examine how these archetypes affect training.

Four principal components capture the majority of variation in the underlying innovation variables. It is sufficient here to describe just the principal components in a general fashion. Readers who are interested in the exact weighting factors for each of the variables in the components are referred to Appendix A.

The four components are named to capture the prototype that each represents. They are:

- the general innovator (GENINOV);
- the passive adapter (PASINOV);
- the R&D-driven innovator (RDINOV); and
- the outward-oriented innovator (OUTINOV).

These four components are arranged in descending order of the variability in the sample that is accounted for by each. The first component accounts for 41 percent of total sample variability, the other three for 8 percent, 7 percent and 5 percent respectively.

GENINOV weights most of the innovation variables highly, except for R&D investment on product and process innovation. It represents the many strategies that stress innovation (technological capability as a factor behind growth, R&D innovation capability, R&D spending relative to competitors, the development of new technologies, the use of others' technology, reducing energy costs, the use of new materials, just-in-time inventory control, process control and obtaining innovative ideas from a number of sources), marketing, management, the R&D unit and patents.

PASINOV primarily weights innovation that comes from management, marketing, parent companies, Canadian patents, foreign patents and government contracts. However, most of the R&D activity, technological, input and management strategies receive negative weights. The emphasis on outside sources of innovation, such as patents, suggests that the firms represented by this component passively adapt ideas from others.

RDINOV is composed almost entirely of R&D-based factors. More specifically, investment in R&D for product and process innovation, the importance of R&D for growth, a firm's competitive position with regard to R&D spending, the R&D unit as a source of innovation are predominant in this component. Developing new technology is also heavily weighted in this component.

OUTINOV comprises the same R&D variables as RDINOV but also includes dependence on the marketing unit, management, customers and competitors as sources of innovation. It represents situations where innovation in technology, inputs and organization receive negative weights. Innovation is limited here to other areas.

QUALITY

THE DECISION TO TRAIN IS ALSO HYPOTHESIZED to depend on the value that the firm attributes to quality. If firms treat investment in human capital as an opportunity to develop skills that permit high-quality standards to be met, then firms that stress quality, generally, and adherence to quality management programs, in particular, will also emphasize training.

The survey provided three measures of the emphasis placed on quality. Firms were asked to rate their product quality, customer service and range of products relative to their competitors. Together, these three (QUAL) offer an indication of the general quality of the firm's products and services. In this case, these variables were so closely associated that a straight summation of the scores was sufficient to measure them – principal component analysis and the diversification of prototypes was unnecessary. Another variable measuring the importance given to total quality management (TQM) was sufficiently different from the emphasis placed on quality in general that it was used as a separate variable in the analysis.

It is important to recognize that, while innovation strategy often has improving quality at its core, this aspect of innovation is distinct from the innovation variables previously defined. The innovation variables reflect attention to technologies, R&D of products and processes, and innovation in the use of inputs. To the extent that quality is improved through any of these means, quality variables will not contribute any additional explanation to differences in the incidence of training. However, firms may also strive to improve quality in other ways, e.g., improving service or offering greater flexibility in responding to customer needs. Improving the skills of their workers through training is one such way.

HUMAN RESOURCE STRATEGIES

FIRMS THAT PLACE A HIGH VALUE ON THEIR HUMAN RESOURCES can augment them through two routes: by hiring employees with the skills they require and/or by training their existing employees. Previous work stresses the relationship between training and a firm's receptivity to human resource strategies. For example, Bartel (1991) found that firms with active human resource planning were more likely to train.

Simpson (1984) and Hum and Simpson (1993) reported that the probability of being trained depended on whether the worker was in a firm or sector that made use of government training programs.

Although an argument can be made that the attitude expressed toward human resources is endogenously determined by the innovation and quality strategy adopted by the firm, there is likely to be a separate, exogenous component. It is included here to test whether the human resource emphasis has a separate effect on the training decision. As was previously argued, a firm's emphasis on human resources may better capture its innovation strategy than the R&D or technology variables stressed in the innovation variables, particularly in the case of human capital intensive industries. Thus, like the quality variables, the human resource variables are included to capture a dimension of innovation strategy. Should the human resource measures be insignificant, the null hypothesis of independence between human resource and innovation strategies will be rejected.

As in the case of innovation, several subjective human resource measures are available in the survey. Firms were asked to rate both their labour climate and their labour skills relative to their competitors. They were also asked to rate the importance of labour skills as a factor contributing to past growth. Several questions elicited the value that firms attribute to various human resource strategies: incentive-based management compensation schemes, continuous staff training, innovative compensation packages and other means of staff motivation.

Principal component analysis is used to ascertain human resource strategy prototypes. The first labour component represents a firm practising a progressive human resource strategy. The comprehensive human resource firm (HRCOMP) weights all the variables highly, including the strategies related to innovative management and employee compensation programs, the importance of labour skills as a factor in growth and both the skill level of their employees and their labour climate relative to their competitors. The second labour component, the wage innovator (HRWAG), represents firms that value innovative compensation packages highly but do not rate the labour skills and climate variables highly. The third component, the skills modernizer (HRSKL), represents firms that place greater value on the importance of labour skills as a factor contributing to growth, but neither offer innovative compensation packages nor boast a superior labour climate.

OTHER VARIABLES

OTHER VARIABLES ARE INCLUDED IN ORDER TO CAPTURE EFFECTS previously found to be important determinants of the training decision. Size (SIZE) has consistently been found to be positively related to the training decision. It has been argued that large firms have access to cheaper capital to finance the investment in training (Hashimoto, 1979), that large firms can reduce the risk of the investment by pooling risks (Gunderson, 1974) and that large firms have a greater payoff from training because their size and their exploitation of economies of scale have led to task specialization and, thus, to a greater benefit for training (Doeringer and Piore, 1971).

Alternately, it could be that the commonly found firm-size effect stems from an aggregation phenomenon. If each firm has an equal probability of training each of its workers, irrespective of firm size, then large firms are more likely to train someone in any given period simply because they have more workers.

The retention rate of employees (RETENRT) is included because it is seen to affect the need for training in two ways. The retention rate is calculated as the percentage of employees in the firm in year t that remained in year t+1. If the firm reduced the number of employees in total, then the percentage of employees in year t+1 that were there in year t is used. The retention rate is calculated for 1986-87, 1987-88 and 1988-89 and an average across the three periods is used. The greater the retention rate, the more benefits the firm can expect to receive from training. However, a lower retention rate implies greater turnover, a greater proportion of new workers and a greater need to engage in training. Simpson (1984) and Bartel (1989) both found that turnover increased the amount of training given.[5]

Measures of change or complexity have been found to be related to training incidence. Therefore, the investment in capital–labour ratio (ICAPLAB), the investment in the market development–labour ratio (IMKTLAB), the change in the capital–labour ratio (DCAPLAB) and the change in labour productivity (DLABPROD) are included. All are hypothesized to have positive signs.

Occupational structure (OCCUP) is included to test whether the relative size of the managerial class has an impact on the incidence of training. Employee-based surveys have found that professionals have a greater probability of being trained. At issue is whether a firm with a greater percentage of its work force in management will be more likely to have a training program.

Finally, binary variables are used to capture industry and regional effects. Industries are divided into eight major sectors. Canada's 10 provinces are grouped into five major regions.

MULTIVARIATE ANALYSIS

ALL THESE VARIABLES ARE SIGNIFICANTLY CORRELATED with the incidence of training. Consequently, multivariate analysis is used to differentiate trainers from non-trainers. Due to the dichotomous nature of the dependent variable, the incidence of training is estimated using a probit model. (The results of the multivariate analysis are reported in Table 6.)

Incidence of training is strongly affected by innovation. All principal components, with the exception of the PASINOV, have positive and significant coefficients both for the equation using training as a whole and for formal and informal training analyzed separately. Despite the difference in the proto-typical firm represented by each of these components, both formal and informal training are associated with innovation. This confirms the existence of strong complementarity between the human capital that is created by training and other innovative inputs.

When the innovation variables are included individually in the regression (not reported here), many have positive coefficients that are significantly different

TABLE 1

INCIDENCE OF TRAINING – A PROBIT MODEL

	Any Form of Training		Formal Training		Informal Training	
	coefficient	st. error	coefficient	st. error	coefficient	st. error
Log–likelihood	495.66		525.46		540.01	
Intercept	0.2957[c]	0.0471	-0.1698[c]	0.0453	-0.2936[c]	0.0458
Innovation principal components						
RDINOV	0.2129[c]	0.0518	0.1718[c]	0.0472	0.1100[b]	0.0456
OUTINOV	0.1428[c]	0.0483	0.1422[c]	0.0455	0.1382[c]	0.0445
GENINOV	0.2414[c]	0.0720	0.2298[c]	0.0690	0.1156[a]	0.0686
PASINOV	0.0735	0.0498	0.0193	0.0480	0.0903[a]	0.0477
Emphasis on quality						
QUAL	0.1574[c]	0.0563	0.1577[c]	0.0575	0.1307[b]	0.0567
TQM	0.1661[b]	0.0656	0.1570[b]	0.0651	0.0774	0.0649
Human resource principal components						
HRCOMP	0.1104	0.0684	0.0569	0.0677	0.1299[a]	0.0679
HRWAG	0.0062	0.0494	0.0437	0.0489	0.0059	0.0490
HRSKL	0.1046[b]	0.0474	0.0633	0.0472	0.0587	0.0474
Other factors						
SIZE	0.2488[c]	0.0640	0.1914[c]	0.0514	0.0555	0.0476
OCCUP	-0.1476[c]	0.0570	-0.1354[b]	0.0575	-0.2313[c]	0.0636
QUEBEC	-0.1824[c]	0.0483	-0.1399[c]	0.0481	-0.2127[c]	0.0495
DYNAM	0.0272	0.0749	0.1042	0.0738	-0.0117	0.0744
TRADIT	0.0603	0.0709	0.0407	0.0699	0.0103	0.0705
MANUF	-0.1496[b]	0.0764	-0.1238	0.0757	-0.1054	0.0759
OTHER	0.0606	0.0566	0.1273[b]	0.0553	0.0066	0.0566
DCAPLAB	-0.0404	0.0894	-0.0167	0.0712	-0.0941	0.2127
IMKTLAB	0.0134	0.0437	0.0171	0.0432	0.0565	0.0429
ICAPLAB	-0.0245	0.0437	-0.0385	0.0460	0.0248	0.0430
RETENRT	-0.0475	0.0479	-0.0220	0.0475	0.0160	0.0477
DLABPROD	-0.1079	0.0764	-0.0216	0.0431	-0.1362[a]	0.0770

Notes: [a]Significant at the 10 percent level.
[b]Significant at the 5 percent level.
[c]Significant at the 1 percent level.

from zero. One aspect of innovation that is consistently found to be important is R&D activity. The coefficients attached to the percentage of investment devoted to R&D for new processes and the firm's spending on R&D relative to competitors are positive and significant. There are other aspects of innovation that are significant as well. Firms that place greater emphasis on using existing materials more efficiently and reducing energy costs are more likely to do training. Training is also more likely when firms stress just-in-time inventory control and have a large percentage of production workers.

The stress placed on quality is significantly related to both formal and informal training. In addition, total quality management (TQM) is significant for formal training incidence and the incidence of training defined more generally. While it is not included directly in the innovation principal components, the score given to quality is probably indirectly related to the innovative capabilities of a firm. Improvements in quality require attention to improved technologies, new organizational structures and other innovative activities. However, attention to quality clearly exerts an effect separate from these variables.

Two human resource principal components are related to formal training. The first, the comprehensive human resource firm (HRCOMP), is weakly significant for informal training. The skills modernizer (HRSKL) is significantly related to training incidence as a whole, but not to formal or informal training incidence separately. This confirms the hypothesis that human resource emphasis, like quality, has an effect that is separate from the R&D- and technology-based innovation components.

This picture is confirmed when regressions are calculated using the labour variables separately in their original form (not reported here). When the variable that measures the importance the firm gives to innovative compensation packages is entered along with the labour skills variables, its coefficient is positive and significant in the formal training equation. The two variables that measure the importance of labour skills to the firm have positive signs as hypothesized, but are only significant in the informal training incidence equation. Both variables are strongly correlated with the incidence of training. In the multivariate analysis, their significance disappears because of their multicollinearity with other human resource related variables and innovation itself. Innovative firms are those where skilled labour is highly valued and where training programs are implemented.

A small number of firm characteristics are significant. Firm size has a positive and significant coefficient for formal or general training but not for informal training. The percentage of employment in management (OCCUP) has a negative effect on both informal and formal training incidence and is significant in both cases.[6]

While previous studies have found that some measures of technological change are related to the training decision, when measures of technological complexity and change at the firm level are included here, they have only mixed success. The growth in the capital–labour ratio (DCAPLAB) is negatively, although not significantly, related to training. The growth in labour productivity (DLABPROD) is weakly related to informal training but has a negative coefficient. The uneven performance of these firm-level variables stands in marked contrast to the responses for the innovation components and illustrates the importance of collecting more comprehensive measures of innovative activities and strategies at the level of the firm.

Labour force turnover is a measure that has been emphasized elsewhere. It is not always possible to obtain direct measures of turnover, and proxies have often been used. In this study, the retention rate is measured directly using administrative data that track workers over time. Despite having an accurate measure of the degree to which a firm's work force turns over, this variable (RETENRT) is not found to have a significant effect on the probability that a firm will offer either formal or informal training. This may be due to an inability to distinguish between the conflicting effects of a higher incentive to train due to longer tenure (and thus a higher retention rate) versus the greater need to train due to the frequency of introduction of new employees (and thus a lower retention rate).

There are few significant differences across regions after firm characteristics and industry differences are considered. The one exception is Quebec where the incidence of both formal and informal training is significantly less than in other regions after the firm characteristics and strategies are considered.

Differences at the industry level in training intensity are large. Upwards of 60 percent of firms in business services offer either formal or informal training but, in the construction industry, only 40 percent offer training programs. The construction industry is the omitted industry. After firm characteristics are taken into account, industry binary variables are rarely significant. Firms in manufacturing are significantly less likely to offer training. Firms in other industries (primary) are more likely to offer formal training. There are no significant industry differences for informal training.

While the finding that industry dummy variables are not significant is interesting in light of the differences in the incidence of training, it is important to realize that industry effects may still exist. The industry dummy variables only measure whether there is a level effect on the incidence of training due to industry differences assuming that the relationships between all the strategic emphasis variables are constant across industries. It is more likely that the industry effects are to be found in differences in the relationship of strategic emphases to training as discussed in the next section.

SECTORAL ANALYSIS

CHARACTERISTICS

THE PREVIOUS MULTIVARIATE ANALYSIS SUGGESTS that innovativeness and training are closely related across a wide range of firm types. This section serves three major purposes. First, by examining the actual difference in training activities in innovative and non-innovative firms, it illustrates the importance of innovativeness in a way that the coefficients from the multivariate analysis at the all-industry level cannot.

Second, it allows differences in emphases in the three sectors to be examined. Third, it permits investigation of sectoral peculiarities.

Three major sectors are analyzed: manufacturing, traditional services and dynamic services.[7] The traditional services sector encompasses industries such as retail outlets, personal services, education, health services and accommodation. The dynamic services sector consists of finance, communication and utilities, real estate, transportation services, wholesale trade and business services. Previous studies have found substantial differences between these sectors.[8] Data on other sectors, construction and primary industries, which were used for the all-industry analysis, were insufficient to permit sectoral analyses.

The training decisions of firms in different sectors are unlikely to be the same, because the product market and competitive arena within which they operate are not uniform. Some firms will compete through greater production efficiencies, while others will compete by offering greater differentiation in their products. Some sectors will base their innovation strategy around technology decisions; other sectors will make human resource development the key component of their innovation strategy.

The differences in the characteristics of firms across sectors are striking as shown in Table 2. The number of employees in an average firm varies substantially. Manufacturing firms have, on average, the greatest number of employees, followed by firms in the dynamic services sector.

TABLE 2

EMPLOYMENT, SALES AND INVESTMENT BY INDUSTRY SECTOR

Average Across Firms		Sectors	
	Manufacturing	Traditional	Dynamic
Number of employees	64.73	41.25	52.19
Sales in 1991 ($ 000s)	8,321.88	6,603.53	11,424.69
Sales ($ 000s) per employees	128.56	160.09	218.91
Retention rate of employees (%)	75.27	73.68	78.41
Percent of investment devoted to:			
R&D for product innovation (%)	18.86	11.83	12.65
R&D for process innovation (%)	5.69	5.31	2.55
Machinery & equipment (%)	44.60	21.00	36.41
Buildings for production (%)	6.61	3.02	2.57
Market development (%)	16.33	32.64	24.42
Training (%)	5.20	20.56	17.90
Other (%)	2.72	5.64	3.50

Note: All averages are unweighted.

TABLE 3

SECTORAL DIFFERENCES IN THE INCIDENCE OF TRAINING

Percent of Firms Offering		Sectors	
	Manufacturing	Traditional	Dynamic
Any training	58.55	60.00	61.97
Formal training	42.76	41.63	51.06
Informal training	39.14	40.00	43.31

Average sales per firm also show large variations between sectors, ranging from approximately $6.6 million per year in the traditional sector, to $8.3 million and $11.4 million in the manufacturing and dynamic sectors respectively. Dynamic firms sell the most per employee, while manufacturing firms sell the least.

The retention rate of employees is highest in the dynamic services sector and lowest in the traditional services sector.

The share of investment devoted to various functional areas differs markedly across sectors. The bulk of investment in manufacturing firms is devoted to machinery and equipment. Training expenditures rank at the bottom of the list in these firms. Conversely, training expenditures rival those of machinery and equipment in the traditional services sector. Expenditures on market development receive the most emphasis by firms in the traditional services sector. Investment expenditures by firms in the dynamic services sector closely mirror those of the traditional services sector, although investing in machinery and equipment appears to be slightly more important. The percentage of investment devoted to R&D is highest in manufacturing.

These investment figures illustrate the primary direction and emphasis of the firm. Manufacturing firms place greater relative emphasis on introducing new equipment. Service-oriented firms, in both the traditional and dynamic services sectors, place relatively greater emphasis on new products, new markets and enhancing human resources.

The incidence of training varies across these three sectors. Firms in the dynamic sector are the most likely to engage in training – of both a formal and an informal nature – as indicated in Table 3. Firms in the traditional services sector are more likely to perform training than firms in the manufacturing sector (although they are marginally less likely to offer formal training).

DIFFERENCES BETWEEN INNOVATORS AND NON-INNOVATORS

THESE THREE SECTORS CAN BE CLASSIFIED into the two-fold taxonomy presented earlier. Manufacturing firms fit the prototype of a physical capital intensive firm. As such, they focus their innovative efforts on improving their production processes. In the traditional and dynamic services sector, which are human capital intensive, the primary value of the product lies in its intangible aspect – the service of the worker. Firms in the services sector devote a greater proportion of their investment to enhancing the abilities of their workers. Similarly, they devote significant resources to market development, in order to compete successfully by offering highly tailored products.

This suggests that the difference between more innovative and less innovative firms, in the stress placed on human resources, should be greater in the services

TABLE 4			
HUMAN RESOURCE STRATEGIES			
	Manufacturing	Traditional Services	Dynamic Services
Competitive Position of Firms in Terms of			
Labour climate			
innovative firms	3.06	2.94	2.85
non-innovative firms	2.34	1.86	1.95
% difference between firms	31[c]	58[c]	46[c]
Skill levels of employees			
innovative firms	3.43	3.63	3.80
non-innovative firms	3.13	3.11	3.02
% difference between firms	10	17[c]	26[c]
Importance of			
Skilled labour as a factor in growth			
innovative firms	3.06	3.21	3.21
non-innovative firms	2.61	2.01	2.13
% difference between firms	17[b]	57[c]	51[c]
Continuous staff training			
innovative firms	3.40	3.45	3.43
non-innovative firms	2.13	1.89	2.09
% difference between firms	60[c]	84[c]	63[c]
Innovative compensation packages			
innovative firms	2.91	2.93	2.96
non-innovative firms	1.56	1.22	1.50
% difference between firms	87[c]	140[c]	97[c]
Other means of staff motivation			
innovative firms	3.53	3.73	3.58
non-innovative firms	2.36	1.98	2.23
% difference between firms	50[c]	88[c]	61[c]

Notes: [a]Significant at the 10 percent level.
[b]Significant at the 5 percent level.
[c]Significant at the 1 percent level.

sector than in manufacturing. Innovation is more tightly identified with human resource skills in services than in manufacturing, where it is bound up with technology.

To test this, firms in each of the sectors were classified as innovative or non-innovative, and the scores given to a range of human resource strategies were calculated as shown in Table 4. Firms were ranked according to their score on the first innovation principal component (GENINOV). Those in the top half were deemed to be innovative and those in the bottom half were considered non-innovative. The general innovator principal component was used as the classification variable because it captures the greatest amount of variation of all the innovation variables.

Innovative firms in each of the sectors enjoyed a superior labour climate relative to their non-innovative counterparts. However, the differences between innovative and non-innovative firms were most marked in the service sectors. Innovative firms tended to fare better in all three sectors with regard to the skill level of employees. Yet, the difference between innovative and non-innovative firms in the manufacturing sector was sufficiently small that it was not statistically significant. The difference was significant in each of the service sectors. In summary, while innovation was associated with superior human resources, the relationship was strongest in the service sectors.

Not surprisingly, those firms that were most likely to boast a superior labour climate and set of labour skills were more likely to credit their labour skills for their contribution to past growth. Innovative firms in all sectors rated skilled labour more highly as a factor in past growth than non-innovative firms. Once more, the differences were greatest in the traditional and dynamic service sectors.

This pattern of differences in the valuation of human resources by innovative firms was confirmed by their valuation of human resource strategies. Innovative firms attributed greater value to each of the three human resource strategies – continuous staff training, innovative compensation packages and other means of staff motivation – than non-innovative firms. The differences were generally greatest in the service sectors. The strategy where the difference between the two groups of firms was most similar among the three sectors was that of continuous staff training.

Consequently, innovative firms tended to place more emphasis on human resources than non-innovative firms. The relationship between innovation and human resources was stronger in the traditional and dynamic service sectors than in the manufacturing sector. The one exception was the firm's perception of the importance of continuous staff training. Commitment to continuous staff training appeared to be as strongly related to innovation in the manufacturing sector as it was in the service sectors. This suggests that training emerges from the technology strategy in manufacturing and that it is as critical to success as in the services sector. The data on differences in incidence of training substantiate this hypothesis as indicated in Table 5.

Innovative firms exhibited a far higher incidence of training. This was true in each of the three sectors, for formal training, informal training or either type of training. Between 74 percent and 77 percent of innovative firms offered formal or informal training. In contrast, less than 50 percent of non-innovative firms offered

TABLE 5

ACTIVITIES RELATED TO TECHNOLOGY AND HUMAN RESOURCES

	Manufacturing	Traditional Services	Dynamic Services
Technology activities			
Percentage growth in capital–worker (1984 to 1988)			
innovative firms	54.30	50.58	24.50
non-innovative firms	29.02	47.09	37.68
% difference between firms	87[a]	7	-35
Human resource activities			
Training–percent of firms offering any training			
innovative firms	76.97	73.98	75.35
non-innovative firms	40.13	45.90	48.59
% difference between firms	92[c]	61[c]	55[c]
Formal training			
innovative firms	61.18	53.66	66.90
non-innovative firms	24.34	29.51	35.21
% difference between firms	151[c]	82[c]	90[c]
Informal training			
innovative firms	49.34	51.22	49.30
non-innovative firms	28.95	28.69	37.30
% difference between firms	70[c]	79[c]	32[c]

Notes: [a]Significant at the 10 percent level.
[b]Significant at the 5 percent level
[c]Significant at the 1 percent level.

either form of training. The difference in the incidence of training between innovative and non-innovative firms was highest in the manufacturing sector. Some 61 percent of innovative manufacturing firms offered formal training; only 24 percent of non-innovative manufacturing firms did the same. The rate in the innovative group was more than 150 percent of that in the non-innovative group.

The growth in the capital–labour ratio is also included in Table 5 to indicate whether changes in capital intensity distinguish innovative from non-innovative strategies. All industries exhibited growth in the capital–labour ratio. But differences existed in the performance of innovative and non-innovative groups. In manufacturing, the innovative sector had a greater increase in its capital intensity than the non-innovative sector. In the services sector, there was no difference in the changes in capital intensity between the innovative and non-innovative groups of firms.

While innovative manufacturing firms attributed greater value to human resources than non-innovative firms, the differences in the incidence of training and the growth in the capital–labour ratio were larger and more significant. For manufacturing firms, innovation was associated with increasing capital intensity and more training.

Innovative firms in the traditional services sector were not distinguished from non-innovative firms by differences in the growth of capital per worker. Innovation was associated with a greater probability of training – both formally and informally. Thus, innovation in the traditional services sector relied more on augmenting the human, as opposed to the physical, capital of the firm. The increased tendency to train on the part of innovative firms in the traditional services sector can primarily be ascribed to their greater emphasis on human resources as an objective in itself.

Firms in the dynamic services sector were similar to those in the traditional services sector in the sense that they were human capital intensive, and innovation was not accompanied by a higher capital–labour ratio. Innovative firms, similar to those in the traditional services sector, took a balanced approach to their human resources. They possessed a superior labour climate and greater labour skills relative to their competitors than non-innovative firms. Furthermore, they accredited these labour skills with a greater contribution to past growth than non-innovative firms. Innovation was accompanied by a particularly high probability of performing formal training. However, the difference in informal training was much less than for traditional services. The traditional services sector, with its inclusion of the retail sector, has high worker turnover and, thus, a greater requirement for informal training.

Multivariate Analysis at the Sectoral Level

The sectoral differences suggest that the determinants of training vary in importance across the three sectors. Probit analysis was used to investigate these differences as shown in Table 6. The model developed previously for all industries was applied to each of the three sectors.

The importance of innovation was confirmed by the consistently positive coefficient attached to all the innovation principal components in the three sectors. The general innovation component (GENINOV) was significant in both manufacturing and dynamic services, where technology-based innovation strategies are crucial. It was not significant in firms involved in traditional services. R&D-based innovation strategies were also significant in manufacturing and dynamic services, both of which are sectors in which R&D is more important.

The emphasis on quality had a separate and significant positive impact on training in the traditional and dynamic service sectors. In the traditional services sector, it was the emphasis on the general quality variable (which captures the product quality, customer service and range of products of the firm, relative to competitors) that was important. In the dynamic services sector, it was the philosophy of TQM – the commitment to improve quality continuously through ongoing enhancements to all the factors of production, including labour, that was important. Neither of the quality variables were significant determinants of innovation in manufacturing. This indicated that quality was a more distinctive

TABLE 6

A PROBIT ANALYSIS OF THE INCIDENCE OF TRAINING
AT THE SECTORAL LEVEL

	Manufacturing		Traditional Services		Dynamic Services	
	coefficient	st. error	coefficient	st. error	coefficient	st. error
Log–likelihood	140.61		106.77		119.86	
Intercept	0.3402[c]	0.0923	0.3641[c]	0.1094	0.4994[c]	0.1053
Innovation principal components						
RDINOV	0.0626	0.0921	0.1210	0.1146	0.4403[c]	0.1214
OUTINOV	0.1617[a]	0.0901	0.1546	0.1049	0.1375	0.1123
GENINOV	0.3073[b]	0.1366	0.0384	0.1474	0.2984[b]	0.1406
PASINOV	0.1348	0.0976	0.0236	0.1091	0.3039[c]	0.1035
Emphasis on quality						
QUAL	0.1374	0.1045	0.2943[b]	0.1375	0.1365	0.1152
TQM	0.1023	0.1178	0.1848	0.1418	0.2919[b]	0.1343
Human resource principal						
HRCOMP	0.1178	0.1355	0.3641[b]	0.1528	-0.1077	0.1394
HRWAG	0.0813	0.0953	0.0271	0.1145	0.0333	0.1025
HRSKL	0.0409	0.0963	0.1086	0.1041	0.2860[c]	0.0978
Other factors						
SIZE	0.1081	0.1128	0.6024[c]	0.2130	0.4924[c]	0.1888
OCCUP	-0.2796[c]	0.1023	0.1237	0.1224	-0.1757	0.1189
QUEBEC	-0.2215[b]	0.0953	-0.2600[b]	0.1083	-0.3442[c]	0.1057
DCAPLAB	0.2495[b]	0.1129	-0.1391	0.1019	0.1201	0.1080
IMKTLAB	0.3573[a]	0.2121	0.1277	0.1452	-0.1468	0.1312
DICAPLAB	-0.0522	0.0849	-0.0488	0.1073	0.0549	0.0880
RETENRT	0.0878	0.0916	-0.1918[b]	0.1108	-0.0305	0.0972
DLABPROD	-0.0613	0.0845	0.0453	0.1310	-0.1810	0.1662

Notes: [a]Significant at the 10 percent level.
[b]Significant at the 5 percent level.
[c]Significant at the 1 percent level.

All of the independent variables have been standardized to a mean of zero and a standard deviation of 1.

component of innovation (i.e., separate from technology and R&D) in the services sector than in manufacturing.

The probit estimates confirmed the difference in the separate importance of human resource strategies in the services sector. An emphasis on human resources was significantly related to training in the traditional and dynamic services, but not in the manufacturing sector. Thus, technological innovation in the dynamic services sector was complemented by innovation in the form of human capital advancements, in that both are determinants of training. Innovation in the traditional services sector relates almost solely to human resource strategies and quality, since it is these two that affect the training decision.

These observations are reinforced by the fact that the coefficient attached to the growth in the capital–labour ratio was positive and significant in manufacturing, but not in the two service sectors. Manufacturing firms are primarily physical capital intensive, and make their training decisions in response to their physical capital decisions. Conversely, service firms are human capital intensive and focus on human capital decisions.

While the retention rate had an ambiguous effect on training in the all-industry study, the probit analysis at the sectoral level indicated that there were sectoral differences in the relationship. In manufacturing, a higher retention rate was correlated with a higher incidence of training, although the relationship was not significant. In the traditional services sector, a lower retention rate stimulated significantly more training.

Training was positively correlated with firm size in all sectors, but the effect was only significant in the traditional and dynamic service sectors.

CONCLUSION

FIRMS EXPERIMENT WITH A VARIETY OF STRATEGIES as they vie for advantage with their competitors. Foremost among these is a commitment to offering higher-quality products and services and producing them at a lower cost, i.e., innovating both their products and their processes. Employees must acquire new skills in order for firms to develop and integrate new products and processes into the work environment. Consequently, training is a concomitant part of the innovation process. In capital intensive industries, innovation will typically take the form of developing and adopting new technologies. Thus, firms must train their workers in both these areas. In human capital intensive industries, innovation necessarily takes the form of human capital development.

The hypothesized relationship between innovation and training is strongly supported by the firm-level data in this paper. Numerous dimensions of innovativeness and the technological intensity of a firm influence training. All four of the innovative prototypes – the general innovator (GENINOV), the passive adapter (PASINOV), the R&D-driven innovator (RDINOV) and the outward-oriented innovator (OUTINOV) – are more likely to have implemented a training program. Several dimensions of human resource strategies and quality strategies, each of which is either strongly complementary to technological innovation or a form of innovation itself, are also related to training.

The relationship between innovation and training is dependent on the nature of the firm's business. In manufacturing industries, where the investment strategy focuses most heavily on plant and equipment, innovation relies on the technology and R&D strategies and activities. Training is required here both to develop these new technologies and to permit workers to operate them. While human resources and quality strategies are important, it is as a result of the technology/R&D innovation strategy. In this study, they have no independent effect on training.

In the dynamic services sector, which is primarily human capital intensive, all three elements of innovation are important. Enhancements in labour skills, technology, R&D and quality strategies are all sufficiently important by themselves that they each have independent significantly positive effects on training.

In the traditional services sector, the innovation strategy is found to be solely represented by the human resource and quality strategies. An emphasis in either of these areas stimulates the firm to offer more training. The higher turnover rate in these industries makes informal training just as important as formal training.

The results of this paper point to the importance of the firm and industry environment in determining training. Training programs do not appear to be equally useful for all firms. Firms that will be the most receptive to training policies are going to be those where expertise in innovation, human resources and quality management already exists. Consequently, policies which are directed at stimulating the complements to training – innovation and attention to quality – are also likely to be effective in encouraging firms to train. However, focusing on just innovation policy or just training policy, without consideration of the connections between the two, is likely to have a lesser impact than a co-ordinated approach that recognizes the inherent complementarities of both to the firm.

APPENDIX A

INNOVATION VARIABLES

THE 24 INNOVATION VARIABLES CAN BE CATEGORIZED into five groups. Variables in the first group measure various aspects of the importance of research and development.

RDGWTH: the score given to R&D as a factor contributing to growth.

RDCOMP: the degree to which a firm surpasses its competitors in R&D spending.

RDPROD: the percentage of total investment devoted to R&D for new products.

RDPROC: the percentage of total investment devoted to R&D for new processes.

The second group measures technological complexity. These are the scores given by the firm to the importance of three variables.

TECHGWTH: technological capability as a factor explaining growth.

TECHOTH: adopting technology developed by others.

TECHNEW: developing new technology.

Variables in the third group measure the source of innovations for a firm which indicates whether a firm is inward or outward oriented, and whether it is committed to using proprietary information or not. Answers to these questions reveal the scores given by the firm to the importance of the following sources of innovation.

SIMKT: marketing.

SICDNPAT: Canadian patents.

SIFORPAT: foreign patents.

SIRD: the R&D unit.

SICUST: customers.

SISUP: suppliers.

SIMANAG: management.

SIPAR: parent or affiliate.

SIGOVT: government contracts.

SICOMP: competitors.

SIOTHER: other.

The fourth group measures the strategy being followed to improve input efficiency. These are the scores given by the firm to the importance of the following variables.

CSTEN: reducing energy costs.

CSTLAB: reducing labour costs.

CSTMAT: using existing materials more efficiently.

NEWMAT: using new materials.

The fifth group measures the strategy being followed to improve management practices. These are the scores given by the firm to the importance of two variables.

JIT: just-in-time inventory control.

PCONT: process control.

QUALITY VARIABLES

THE IMPORTANCE OF QUALITY is represented by the scores firms give to the following variables.

TQM: the importance attached to total quality management.

QUALPROD: the degree to which firms rank themselves ahead of their competitors with regard to the quality of product.

CUSTSERV: the degree to which firms rank themselves ahead of their competitors with regard to customer service.

RANGPROD: the degree to which firms rank themselves ahead of their competitors with regard to their range of products.

HUMAN RESOURCE VARIABLES

WHETHER A FIRM APPRECIATES THE IMPORTANCE OF LABOUR SKILLS and the emphasis that it places on human resource strategies are represented by the scores given by the firm to these variables.

GWTHSKL: skilled labour as a factor behind growth.

COMPSKL: the skill levels of its employees relative to those of its competitors.

LABCL: the labour climate of the firm relative to its competitors.

COMPENS: the use of innovative compensation packages.

MANREM: management remuneration programs.

TRAIN: the emphasis given to continuous training programs.

GOVT: the value placed on government assistance for training programs.

INDUSTRY DUMMY VARIABLES

DYNAM: dynamic services: finance, communication, utilities, real estate, transportation services, business services and wholesaling.

TRADIT: traditional services: retail outlets, education, health services, accommodation and personal services.

MANUF: manufacturing.

OTHER: primary.

OTHER VARIABLES

THERE ARE OTHER EXPLANATORY VARIABLES.

SIZE: the size of the firm measured in terms of employees in 1991.

SALES: the size of the firm measured in terms of sales in 1991.

TURN: the turnover rate calculated as the percentage of employees in the firm in year t that are still in the firm in year t+1– measured as the average value in 1986-87, 1987-88 and 1988-89.

GROWTH: the rate of change of firm size (employment) between 1984 and 1988.

ICAPLAB: the investment in machinery to labour ratio of the firm in 1991.

IMKTLAB: the investment in market development to labour ratio of the firm in 1991.

DCAPLAB: the change in the capital–labour ratio between 1984 and 1988.

DLABPROD: the change in labour productivity of the firm between 1984 and 1988 relative to the industry.

OCCUP: the occupational structure measured as the percentage of employment accounted for by managers.

TABLE 7

WEIGHTS FOR INNOVATION PRINCIPAL COMPONENTS

Variable	Weight			
	GENINOV	PASINOV	RDINOV	OUTINOV
RDPROD	0.08	-0.02	0.35	0.26
RDPROC	0.07	0.05	0.21	0.18
RDCOMP	0.17	-0.04	0.33	0.26
RDGWTH	0.20	-0.06	0.35	0.22
TECHGWTH	0.22	-0.14	0.06	0.09
TECHNEW	0.25	-0.11	0.21	0.01
TECHOTH	0.22	-0.14	0.01	0.07
NEWMAT	0.26	-0.26	-0.02	-0.14
CSTMAT	0.26	-0.29	-0.09	-0.14
CSTLAB	0.25	-0.27	-0.14	-0.14
CSTEN	0.22	-0.28	-0.20	-0.17
JIT	0.20	-0.15	-0.09	-0.13
PCONT	0.25	-0.18	0.00	-0.02
SIMKT	0.25	0.25	-0.05	0.19
SIMANAG	0.24	0.27	-0.14	0.20
SIPAR	0.12	0.28	0.08	-0.28
SICDNPAT	0.16	0.30	0.21	-0.46
SIFORPAT	0.17	0.25	0.28	-0.46
SIGOV	0.16	0.24	-0.09	-0.09
SICUST	0.24	0.29	-0.25	0.17
SIRD	0.22	0.09	0.23	0.11
SICOMP	0.21	0.18	-0.32	0.16
SISUP	0.22	0.16	-0.31	0.11
SIOTHER	0.01	0.04	0.01	0.05

TABLE 8

WEIGHTS FOR HUMAN RESOURCE PRINCIPAL COMPONENTS

Variable	Weight		
	HRCOMP	HRWAG	HRSKL
LABCL	0.38	-0.52	-0.51
COMPSKL	0.39	-0.54	0.01
GRWTHSKL	0.43	-0.13	0.82
MANREM	0.49	0.50	-0.23
COMPENS	0.52	0.42	-0.10

ENDNOTES

1   See Economic Council of Canada, 1991, pp. 124-126 for a summary of the results of training incidence from other Canadian surveys. The 1991 National Training Survey that was performed for the Canadian Labour Market and Productivity Centre found that about half of firms spent money directly on structured training of employees.

2   A copy of the survey may be obtained by contacting the author in the Micro-Economic Analyses Division at Statistics Canada.

3   While the survey was taken only of growing firms, the training characteristics, the R&D intensity and the occupational distribution of the sampled firms are broadly representative of the population as a whole.

4   A previous study (Baldwin and Johnson, 1994) examined the factors determining the incidence and intensity (number of employees trained and training expenditures per employee) of training. The initial decision to train was strongly affected by the strategies and other activities of the firm. However, once the decision to train had been made, the number of employees trained was primarily a function of the number of employees in the firm, and the expenditures on training were simply a function of the number of employees trained. Consequently, this study will review only the factors affecting the incidence of training.

5   Simpson (1984) used a turnover rate derived from the answers given by personnel directors, while Bartel (1992) used average length of tenure to capture turnover effects. It should ne noted that, in addition to the measurement problem involved in examining the relationship between labour force turnover and training, a simultaneity problem may exist. While higher turnover creates a greater need for training, and longer tenure suggests greater benefits, the causality may operate in the opposite direction. Firms that do not offer training may have a more dissatisfied work force and, subsequently, greater turnover. The authors believe this problem is minimal.

6   This is an interesting result, particularly given previous findings that managers are more likely to receive training than employees in other occupation categories (Hum and Simpson, 1993). Part of the result may be a firm size effect – managers typically account for a greater proportion of workers in smaller firms, and smaller firms are less likely to train employees. However, not all of the effect can be attributed to firm size as both the

firm size and occupation variables are significant. This point merits further investigation with a larger sample to permit investigation of possible industry effects.

7   A total of 433 manufacturing firms responded to the survey, a response rate of 72.7 percent. In the traditional services industry, 344 firms replied, for a response rate of 67.7 percent. Within the dynamic services sector, 411 firms responded to the survey, resulting in a response rate of 55.8 percent.

8   The Economic Council of Canada (1991) noted several sectoral differences in human resource make-up and strategies. Almost three quarters of workers in the manufacturing sector were blue collar workers, compared with just 15 percent of workers in the services sector (p. 93). While wage rates were more favourable in the manufacturing sector than the traditional services sector, they were highest in the dynamics services sector (p. 139). Growth in employment over the 1974 to 1989 period was similar in the dynamic and traditional service sectors, each contributing to about a third of total employment growth in Canada. Conversely, the manufacturing sector was credited with only about 5 percent of employment growth over the period (p. 155).

BIBLIOGRAPHY

Anderson, Andy B., Alexander Basilevsky and Derek P. J. Hum. "Measurement: Theory and Techniques." In *Handbook of Survey Research*. Edited by Peter H. Rossi, James D. Wright and Andy B. Anderson. New York: Academic Press, 1983.

Baldwin, J.R., W. Chandler, C. Le and T. Papailiadis. *Strategies for Success*. Catalogue No. 61-523E. Ottawa: Statistics Canada, 1994.

Baldwin, J.R. and Joanne Johnson. "Human Capital Development and Innovation: The Case of Training in Small and Medium-Sized Enterprises." Statistics Canada, Research Paper Series, No. 74. Ottawa, 1995.

Bartel, A.P. "Employee Training Programs in US Businesses." In *Market Failure in Training? New Economic Analyses and Evidence on Training of Adult Employees*. Edited by D. Stern and J. Ritzen. Springer-Verlag, 1991.

——. "Training, Wage Growth and Job Performance: Evidence from a Company Database." National Bureau of Economic Research Working Paper No. 4027, 1992.

Bartel, A.P. and F. Lichtenberg. "The Comparative Advantage of Educated Workers in Implementing New Technology." *The Review of Economics and Statistics*. (February 1987).

Betcherman, G. "Are Firms Underinvesting in Training?" *Canadian Business Economics*. 1, (1992): 25-33.

——. "Inside the Black Box: Human Resource Management and the Labour Market." Essay prepared for the labour market volume in the C.D. Howe series, The Social Policy Challenge. Second draft, 1994.

Canadian Labour Market and Productivity Centre. *1991 National Training Survey*. Ottawa, 1993.

Doeringer, P. and M. Piore. *Internal Labour Markets and Manpower Analysis*. Lexington, MA: D.C. Heath, 1971.

Economic Council of Canada. *Employment in the Service Economy*. Ottawa: Supply and Services Canada, 1991.

Gunderson, M. "The Case for Government-Supported Training Programs." *Relations Industrielles*. 29, (1974): 709-725.

Hashimoto, M. "Bonus Payments, On-the-Job Training, and Life-Time Employment in Japan." *Journal of Political Economy.* (1979): 1086-1104.

Hum, D. and W. Simpson. "Which Employers Train? Sectoral Evidence on Employer-Based Training in Canada." Unpublished paper prepared for Employment and Immigration Canada, 1993.

Lillard, L. and H. Tan. "Training: Who Gets It and What Are Its Effects." Rand Corp. R-331-DOI, March 1986.

Mincer, J. "Human Capital Responses to Technological Change in the Labor Market." National Bureau of Economic Research Working Paper No. 3207, 1989.

Mowery, David C. and Nathan Rosenberg. *Technology and the pursuit of economic growth.* Cambridge: Cambridge University Press, 1989.

Organization for Economic Co-operation and Development (OECD). "Enterprise-Related Training." In *Employment Outlook.* Paris: OECD, 1991, pp. 135-175.

Picot, G. "The Participation in Training by Women, the Unemployed, and the Educationally Disadvantaged." Analytical Studies Branch, Statistics Canada, Research Paper No. 24, 1986.

Simpson, W. "An Econometric Analysis of Industrial Training in Canada." *The Journal of Human Resources.* (1984): pp. 435-451.

Simpson, W., R. Sproule and D. Hum. "Specification of on-the-job training incidence." Unpublished paper, 1993.

Statistics Canada. *Human Resources and Development Survey, 1987.* Catalogue 81-574E. Ottawa: Statistics Canada, 1990.

Comment

Lewis Alexander
U.S. Department of Commerce

OVER THE LAST TWO YEARS, I have been involved in G-7 and Organization for Economic Co-operation and Development (OECD) discussions on the interaction between technology, firm performance and employment. The use of establishment level data in conjunction with surveys on technology use and innovative activity is, in my judgment, the most promising empirical approach available to advance our understanding of these critical policy-relevant relationships. John Baldwin and his colleagues at Statistics Canada have been pioneers in this area. They have published a long series of interesting studies on the dynamics of industrial competition in Canada and the role of technology and innovation in that process. The paper that Baldwin and Johnson present here is another novel contribution to this growing literature.

After experiencing a downward trend for much of the postwar period, the wage premium for skilled work relative to less-skilled work has increased in a number of countries over the last 15 to 20 years. The causes of this widening skills premium are not well understood. Many authors have concluded that skill-biased technical change is one, perhaps the, critical factor. But only a few researchers have offered direct evidence to support this explanation. Krueger (1993) and Entorf and Kramarz (1995) have shown that workers that use computers have higher earnings, even after other worker characteristics are taken into account. Doms, Dunne and Troske (1995) have shown that plants that use a large number of advanced technologies pay higher wages, even after various characteristics of the plant and work force are taken into account. Baldwin and Johnson relate innovative activity to the demand for training by showing that successful small- and medium-sized firms that undertake a larger amount of innovative activity also provide more training. This is another type of evidence supporting the skill bias of the current wave of technological change. This approach is particularly appealing because it does not rely on wages. Many industrial countries, particularly in Europe, have not experienced the rising wage premium for skilled work that has been observed in the United States presumably because wage-setting institutions behave differently. Results similar to those presented in Baldwin and Johnson for other countries, particularly where the skills premium in wages has not increased, would go a long way toward confirming the skill bias story.

The results of this paper are useful for other reasons as well. Empirical research on Canada and other industrial countries shows that there is no one key to success for individual businesses. Successful firms appear to rely on a complex set of strategies. The Baldwin and Johnson paper has shown that innovative activity and training may be complementary elements of that set of strategies.

The paper uses data from Statistics Canada's Survey of Growing Small- and Medium-Sized Enterprises (GSMEs). This survey, which was conducted in 1992, covered a set of small- and medium-sized firms – defined as having fewer than 500 employees and less than $100 million in assets in 1984 – that grew over the second half of the 1980s. The firms were chosen from a panel covering 1984 and 1988. The GSME survey is extremely valuable because it collected data on a broad range of firm characteristics including management practices, innovative activities, training, financing, marketing, exporting and government assistance. Survey responses were then linked to other data on firm performance. The breadth of the data available through this effort makes it possible to analyze the interaction among a large number of factors that are likely to affect firm performance.

There is a problem with this survey, however. The manner in which the sample was restricted may bias the results. At a minimum, observers must keep in mind that the data only covers a subset of Canadian firms. One issue is the exclusion of large firms. Size has consistently been shown to be an important factor affecting establishment performance. In Baldwin and Johnson's own regressions, the SIZE variable was usually significant. It is true that, unlike the U.S. manufacturing sector, small- and medium-sized enterprises have been shown to account for a disproportionate share of net job creation in Canada. But something is missed by excluding large firms.

Excluding firms that did not grow during the late 1980s, or opened after 1988, could also bias the results. A similar problem often arises in the use of establishment level data due to start-ups and closures. When comparing the performance of a set of plants or firms at two different points in time, there is always the question of how to treat those that close or start up during the intervening period. Excluding them from the analysis can bias the results. For example, Olley and Pakes (1992) estimated production functions for the U.S. telecommunications equipment industry during the period of deregulation in the 1970s and 1980s. The authors used an innovative two-step procedure that considered the sample selection bias generated by the closure of old plants and the entry of new ones. They showed that production function estimates were quite sensitive to this correction.

The underlying thought behind the GSME survey seems to have been that we learn more from success than failure. This is not obvious. For example, in other work, respondents to the GSME survey were split into more- and less-successful firms. Differences in responses to a variety of questions were used as a measure of what contributed to firm performance. I cannot really criticize the authors for using the GSME. It contains a wealth of data that should be thoroughly explored. But, I cannot help wondering how the results might have been different if the sample had not been restricted.

The basic results of the Baldwin and Johnson paper are straight forward and reasonable. The authors show that innovative activities and training are associated in the GSME survey. The survey asked a variety of questions relating to innovative activity, such as various measures of the importance of research and development to the firm, technology, sources of innovation (foreign or domestic patents, etc.), strategies for increasing efficiency, the role of marketing and innovative management practices. Principal component analysis was used to reduce the dimensionality of the data. The indicators of innovative activity were used to construct four variables representing different types of innovative activity:

- a general indicator of innovative activity, the so-called general innovator;
- an indicator reflecting heavy dependence on research and development, the so-called R&D innovator;
- an indicator reflecting a heavy reliance on external sources of innovation, such as patents, the so-called passive adopter; and
- an indicator which puts heavy weights on both R&D and marketing, the so-called outward-oriented R&D innovator.

These four variables, along with a host of other firm characteristics, such as emphasis on quality, human resource policies (also represented by principal component constructs) and a variety of other variables, such as size, capital–labour ratio, productivity and industry dummies, were related to whether or not the firm provided training using probit regression techniques. The R&D innovator, the outward-oriented R&D innovator and the general innovator variables were all shown to be significantly related to the probability that firms will provide training.

The authors then divided the sample into three sectors – manufacturing, traditional services and dynamic services – and compared the relationship between the innovation variables and training using the same approach. In this case, the results were somewhat different. The general innovator variable was significant in the regression for training in both the manufacturing sector and the dynamic service sector. The R&D innovator variable and the passive innovator variables were significant only for training in the dynamic service sector. The authors have argued that this is a reasonable pattern. The manufacturing sector is capital intensive, and so it is not surprising that training does not respond to R&D. In contrast, the dynamic service sector is human capital intensive and, therefore, training is most sensitive to innovative activity in this sector.

In many respects, the most intriguing methodological aspect of this paper is the classification of innovative activities implicit in the principal components breakdown. The fact that these variables seem to provide sensible, or at least interpretable, results at the sectoral level supports the authors' approach. It will be interesting to see whether this classification proves useful in other contexts.

It seems quite reasonable that innovative firms invest more in training. But the question of causality remains unresolved. Baldwin and Johnson argue that their results confirm "the existence of strong complementarity" between skills and other innovative inputs. I think this overstates the case. The authors have shown that innovation and training are associated. They have not demonstrated that they are complements. This points to a broader issue, i.e., causality. This is one of the most important issues in this general field – how to develop better techniques for inferring causality.

Consider the following example. In data for the U.S. manufacturing sector, it has been shown that the usage of advanced technology, measured at a single point in time, i.e., 1988, is strongly related to a variety of measures of plant performance such as growth in employment and output, wages, survival rates and gross margins. However, new work is showing that the adoption of advanced technology by itself does not seem to contribute greatly to plant performance. This calls into question whether technology is causality related to plant performance or whether usage of advance technologies is just a good screening device for successful firms. What seems to be emerging from a variety of studies, including many by Statistics Canada, is that technology and innovative activity are important elements of the strategies of successful firms.

To demonstrate that training and innovation are in fact complements, it will be necessary to show that doing the two things together contributes more to firm performance than they do separately. This could be done using the GSME survey. In earlier work, the respondents to the GSME were divided into two groups based on firm performance. It would be possible to use the same type of probit analysis to determine whether the combination of innovative activity and training contributed to a likelihood that individual firms were in the "more successful" group. Alternatively, it would be possible to estimate the impact of this interaction directly on firm performance.

We hope to be able to use this approach with new data that has just been collected on human resource practices in the United States. This data will be linked to the Census Bureau's Longitudinal Research Database (LRD) as well as the Survey of Manufacturing Technology (SMT) and should allow us to undertake this type of analysis for the U.S. manufacturing sector.

ACKNOWLEDGEMENTS

I WOULD LIKE TO THANK INDUSTRY CANADA and the organizers of the conference this volume is based on for the opportunity to participate. My colleagues and I at the U.S. Department of Commerce have learned a great deal from the broad range of high-quality analytic work, much of it sponsored by Industry Canada, that has been done on private sector performance in Canada.

BIBLIOGRAPHY

Doms, Mark, Timothy Dunne and Ken Troske. "Workers Wages, and Technology." Paper presented at the conference, The Effects of Technology and Innovation on Firm Performance and Employment. Washington DC, May 1-2, 1995.

Entorf, Horst and Francis Kramarz. "The Impact of New Technologies on Wages: Lessons from Matching Panels on Employees and on Their Firms." Paper presented at the conference, The Effects of Technology and Innovation on Firm Performance and Employment. Washington DC, May 1-2, 1995.

Krueger, Alan. "How Computers Changed the Wage Structure: Evidence from Micro Data, 1984-1989." *Quarterly Journal of Economics*. (1993).

Olley, G. Steven and Ariel Pakes. "The Dynamics of Productivity in the Telecommunications Equipment Industry." CES Discussion Paper 92-2, 1992.

*Part II   A Knowledge-Based Approach to
Framework Policy Issues*

Richard G. Harris
Department of Economics
Simon Fraser University
and Canadian Institute for Advanced Research

4

Evidence and Debate on Economic Integration and Economic Growth

INTRODUCTION

THE LITERATURE ON GROWTH EFFECTS OF TRADE AND INTEGRATION has a long history. In Scitovsky's (1958) famous book on the economic integration of Western Europe, he forcefully argued that the dynamic effects of economic integration would dominate all static efficiency effects that traditional trade theory concentrates on. While visionary, such arguments did not translate into any concrete theorizing or quantitative evaluation at the time. By the mid-1970s, the issue was front and centre again as discontent with the import substitution economic development model emerged. A number of scholars began an empirical research program seeking to link national growth rates to export performance and export orientation. The "export-led growth" hypothesis gained substantial credence with the remarkable growth performance of East Asian economies and became the official line of the World Bank. Economic theory, however, lagged in terms of formal theorizing. The emergence of the new growth theory, or endogenous growth theory, quickly led to models in which the connection between trade and growth became more explicit. In some cases, the link was positive (Rivera-Batiz and Romer, 1991), in others negative (Young, 1992) and in still others, it was largely indeterminate depending in complex ways on specific parameter values (Grossman and Helpman, 1991). The engines of growth in these models included international technology spillovers, learning by doing, investment in physical capital, human capital development and research and development (R&D) investment – sometimes all lumped under the term "knowledge-based" source of growth. For the most part, this paper is not about those theories. At this point in time, there is neither enough consensus on the appropriate theory nor the necessary empirical base to implement these models in a useful fashion. There has been progress though over the last decade on the growth of trade links, and the purpose of this paper is to review our knowledge of those links.

    Much of the debate around openness and growth is closely linked to the convergence hypothesis of Abramovitz (1990) and others – the idea that a lot of growth can be explained by "catch-up." While this literature is not directly relevant to the question of endogenous technological change in the advanced countries, it has largely defined the debate on the sources of economic growth over the last 10 years. When talking about the effects of economic integration on growth, a large portion of what we know is drawn from the convergence literature. The other major impetus to the literature was the European Community (EC) 1992 Single Market Program which culminated in the famous Cecchini Report (1988). Within Europe, this research began in the mid-1980s, and a lot of speculation occurred as to the possible dynamic gains which would occur as a result of further European economic integration. Actually, very little quantitative work was done in the context of the type of theories or links stressed in this paper. It did, however, succeed in raising the profile of the issue considerably and in furthering the empirical debate on the growth effects of economic integration.[1]

This paper is not concerned with the wealth of evidence at the level of the firm dealing with technological change and international diffusion of technology – in particular, the role of foreign direct investment. Instead, the focus is at the level of the national economy – its growth and trade performance. The evidence at the level of the firm has yet to be integrated with evidence at the national level on trade, growth and investment.

The paper begins with a brief review of a stripped-down neoclassical growth model and how economic integration might affect growth. Important empirical distinctions between steady states and transition paths are made. The paper then discusses the evidence that has been brought forward at the macro level to address the question of how trade regimes affect growth. This is still an area of considerable controversy despite what you may have heard. The final part of the paper turns from historical evidence to empirically calibrated dynamic general equilibrium models which have been used to look at the link between explicit trade policy changes and growth links. There are a wide variety of such models, and the results are not conclusive. They are, however, quite interesting and serve to isolate probable factors linking trade and integration to growth performance.

The paper concludes by outlining the lessons that can be drawn from this research program and where future developments might occur.

BACKGROUND: SOME THEORY

IN THIS SECTION, SOME THEORETICAL BACKGROUND to the whole issue of integration and growth is provided through a sketch of a couple of simple models. As will be clear when the empirical literature is reviewed, the theory is remarkably weak or simply not very helpful throughout the entire area. There are two reasons for this. First, formulating, estimating and even simulating multisector/multicountry dynamic trade models is still a field which is very much "in progress." While there are now a large number of highly disaggregated trade models which are relatively good at focusing on trade integration questions, these models are typically quite poor at developing any implications regarding growth and investment. Second, and related to the first observation, the dynamic models which have been used tend to be highly aggregated growth models for the same reason. Solving and estimating aggregate growth models is a field which developed rapidly in the late 1980s, but it has not yet been extended to more elaborate disaggregated models which would naturally emphasize trade. For these reasons, there is a very big empty middle which needs to be filled. Consequently, this paper is more of a progress report on where things might be headed than a summing up of a well-developed and mature sub-field.

Much of the recent publicity surrounding the endogenous growth theory stems from the conclusion that growth rates can be influenced by policy variables such as tariffs or trade integration agreements. The set of models presented in the Grossman and Helpman (1991) book is an excellent example of this type of theoretical literature. At the more practical level, however, both in terms of identifying empirically the mechanisms by which trade affects growth and in building models which are useful for analyzing economic integration, the stark contrast between endogenous and exogenous growth is not as useful as one might imagine.

The basic point is that, in looking at medium-term dynamic effects of policy changes, the difference in effects on levels versus growth rates is difficult to determine. This is illustrated in the transition diagram in Figure 1 for a typical Solow–Swan model with fixed saving rates. It illustrates the evolution of the growth in per capita income relative to the level of per capita income. Starting with the equations of the model:

$$y=f(k)$$

$$\dot{k}=sf(k)-(n+\delta)k \tag{1}$$

where y is per capita Gross Domestic Product (GDP); k is capital per worker; and $f(k)$ is the intensive production function giving output per worker as a function of capital per worker. Parameters are s the savings rate, n the population growth rate and δ the depreciation rate on capital. $G(y)$ denotes the growth rate of y. Inverting to express everything in terms of y, the diagram looks as follows with AA denoting the phase transition curve, i.e., how growth rates are related to income levels.

In the absence of exogenous technological progress for y less than y^*, the growth rate is positive, and for y greater than y^*, the growth rate is negative. If the economy starts at $y_o=f(k_o)$ then during the transition, the income level rises and the growth rate in per capita income slows. Within non-endogenous growth models, there are two ways of looking at trade liberalization. One method assumes that, at the date on which the trade liberalization of integration shock occurs, the economy is in a position like y_o, i.e., non-steady state with a growth rate at date 0 of g_A. A change in productivity or economic structure shifts the $f(k)$ function up giving rise to a new transition-phase curve such as BB. This gives rise instantaneously to a higher growth rate, g_B. Over the long run, as the economy moves to a new steady

FIGURE 1

GROWTH RATES RELATED TO RISING INCOME LEVELS

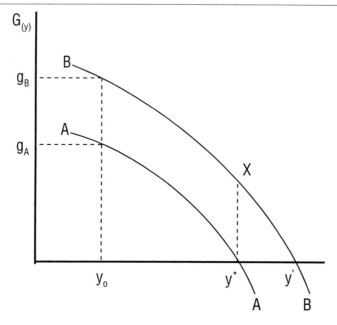

state, the growth rate declines and a new long-run income level y' is approached. There are clearly growth effects but these are in place only during the transition period. In much of the literature, the initial starting point is *assumed* to be a steady position such as y*. The effect of the policy shock is a comparison of y* relative to the new transition from X to y'.

The relevant empirical question is twofold: how long are transitions likely to be and is an assumed initial hypothesis of a steady state a reasonable approximation to reality? To answer the first question, for most models (even the most neoclassical ones), transitions are really quite long. The initial Sato–Atkinson experiments suggested the half-life was anywhere from 30 to 100 years, and this still appears to be the case. For whatever reason, there is a folk-theorem in the literature suggesting these neoclassical transitions are quite rapid which, as far as I can discern, is unjustified by published results. Generally, the more comprehensive the definition of capital or the closer one moves to models with non-malleable capital, the longer these transitions are likely to be. One immediate implication is that a comparative steady-state analysis is clearly not very useful for policy purposes. The second issue is whether an assumed steady state is a reasonable description of an economy before the policy shock. Here, latitude for judgment on the part of the researcher is much wider. For most developing countries, it clearly seems to be a leap of faith. For industrialized countries, it is harder to make the call. There are clear examples in the literature of models in which the empirical judgment is made that forces are at work on either the demand or supply side which preclude assuming an initial steady state.

In almost all models with welfare-based indexes of evaluation which use discounting, the question of growth rates versus levels turns out to be far less important than imagined. For example, BB relative to AA in Figure 1 may give rise, starting at y_o to higher growth rates over the medium term, say the next 20 to 40 years, but the question as to the impact on the value of discounted consumption streams is more closely related to the comparison of medium-term income levels than to a comparison of long-term growth rates.

The possibility of endogenous growth raises the potential for trade liberalization to have an impact on long-term growth rates. Most endogenous growth models depend on some form of social increasing returns to accumulating factors. The simplest possible endogenous growth model is one in which the production function is linear in a single reproducible factor, call it K, so Y=aK, where Y is aggregate output. With this production function, no population growth, a constant depreciation rate δ and a constant savings rate s, the growth rate g(Y) is equal to:

$$g(Y)=sa-\delta \qquad (2)$$

Thus, the growth rate is a direct function of the savings rate – hence the potential for policy to have long-term dynamic effects. Suppose the model is such that the initial growth path of log y(t), as illustrated in Figure 2, is the locus CC. The slope

FIGURE 2

GROWTH RATES RELATED TO DECLINING INCOME LEVELS

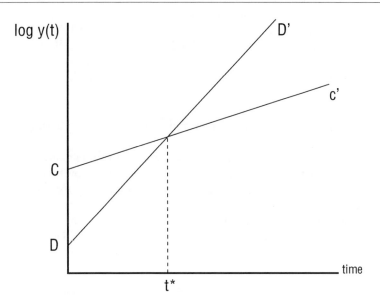

of this curve gives the initial growth rate. Suppose that there is a shift in the trade regime which gives rise to a long-term growth rate which is higher, but at the same time induces a short-term reduction in income at date 0 – the date at which the policy comes into place. Let this income path be represented by DD' in the same figure. As represented, the growth rate is higher but, until date t*, the income level is lower. The fact that the growth rate is higher is certainly very interesting but, if t* is equal to 100 years, it is not a very compelling case for the policy change. Furthermore, the evidence for endogenous growth is actually quite inconclusive.[2]

EMPIRICAL EVIDENCE ON TRADE, GROWTH AND ECONOMIC INTEGRATION

A LARGE PART OF THE DEBATE on the potential effects of trade liberalization and the extent of trade (or openness) on growth is concerned with either historical or statistical analysis which claims to establish such a link. With EC 1992 and NAFTA, this debate has been extended to more general forms of economic integration. As noted in the introduction, the debate goes back to discussions surrounding the formation of the EC in the 1950s. To limit the scope of the survey, the focus is on the more recent evidence and theories which gained momentum in the 1970s.

EXPORTS AND GROWTH

BEGINNING WITH MICHAELY (1977) AND BALASSA (1982), a large number of studies done in the last two decades documented a correlation between exports and economic growth using samples of both developed and undeveloped economies.[3] Generally, these studies found either an association between exports expressed as a percentage of GDP and growth, or between economic growth and the growth in exports. Many authors found evidence of a threshold effect, i.e., growth only occurs after some minimum level of exports occurs. At the theoretical level, there are a number of reasons to suspect a connection running from growth in exports to growth in GDP based on demand side arguments. The endogenous growth and trade literature gives a rationale for the so called dynamic links based on arguments regarding learning by doing and technology transfer that have often been made at a less formal level.

The majority of the studies in the pre-endogenous growth literature derive or appeal to either an explicit or implicit static production function framework. A basic model was first formalized by Feder (1983) who pointed out the logical distinction of export-led growth arising because of a Pigovian externality between export and other sectors, versus growth due to shifting output composition in the presence of a productivity differential between the advanced (export) and informal sectors. Imagine an economy with two sectors – an export sector (X) and a non-export sector (N) with production functions:

$$N = F^n(L_n, K_n; X)$$

$$X = F^x(L_x, K_x) \tag{3}$$

X enters as an output externality in the non-export sector. Depending on the institutional set-up of this economy, marginal products (private) may or may not be equalized across sectors. Suppose, for example, that marginal products are constant between sectors due to unemployed resources and that they are higher by a factor of δ in both factors in the export sector. Taking time differentials growth in the export sector alone and holding the external effect in sector N at zero gives rise to aggregate growth due to the higher productivity of the export sector. Alternatively, if marginal private products are equalized across sectors, then growth in the export sector gives rise to growth if there is a non-zero external effect of X on the N sector.

In principle, estimation of the production functions could distinguish between these hypotheses, but the reduced form literature did not really succeed in making a clear distinction. The lack of a complete general equilibrium model underlying this framework is unfortunate. While a framework such as this can be used to generate transitory effects on aggregate productivity levels due to some exogenous change in exports, it is not clear how changes in the growth rate of per capita income (which are related to export growth) fall out of this framework.

The question of causality is completely open in these studies, most of which are based on cross sections. Some recent time series work by Jung and Marshall (1985) using Granger causality methods, is generally quite sceptical of a causal relationship in the statistical sense from export promotion to growth. Some would argue, for example, that exogenous and high rates of productivity growth in manufacturing will necessarily lead to manufactured exports and to economic growth in a number of trade theories. The root cause of the growth, however, is the productivity improvements – not a policy-induced shift to exports. The export-led growth hypothesis, and the vast number of studies it generated, have now given rise to more micro-economic based studies focusing directly on productivity growth as surveyed, for example, by Havlyshyn (1992). In these studies, the connection between openness and total factor productivity (TFP) growth is also difficult to demonstrate conclusively. But despite the lack of a theoretical foundation and conclusive empirical support, the export-led growth hypothesis undoubtedly stimulated much of the subsequent empirical and theoretical literature on the trade and growth linkages.

Trade Liberalization and Growth

Taking off from the export-led growth hypothesis, another set of studies looks at the connection between trade liberalization and growth, based almost entirely on detailed case studies of specific countries, and much of it directed by the World Bank. Generally, these studies are supportive of the idea that trade reform removed the "anti-export bias" of various forms of protective schemes and thus contributed to export growth. The connection between economic growth and export growth is often invoked. However, there is no clear distinction between this idea and the alternative that static efficiency gains from trade reform should lead to transitory increases in productivity and thus economic growth. The single largest study was that carried out by Choski, Michaely and Papageorgiou (CMP) (1991) on trade liberalization episodes in 19 countries. They estimated the average growth of real exports three years before liberalization at 4.4 percent; for the three years after liberalization, it was 10.5 percent. Average rate of growth of output three years before liberalization was 4.45 percent; three years after it was 5.51 percent. While relatively crude, methodologically, the results are quite suggestive of the causality between liberalization and growth.

Within the basic framework of an assumed relationship between export growth and economic growth, there is the question of how to test for the add-on effect of trade liberalization. One interesting approach is that of Greenaway and Sapsford (1994). They took the sample from CMP and estimated an export growth specification for each of the 19 countries. The basic equation became:

$$\dot{N} = a_1 + a_2 \dot{X} + a_3 \dot{K} + a_4 \dot{L} + u \tag{4}$$

where N is GDP less exports and X is exports. (The dot notation indicates proportionate rates of change.) The measure of output growth is that of the non-export sector reducing the problem of double counting when GDP is used as the output measure. They then included slope and constant dummies corresponding to each of the liberalization episodes documented by CMP. Data constraints cut down the sample to 12 countries. In eight of the 12 cases, it appeared that the liberalization had no impact on the growth–export relationship. In three cases, there was a statistically significant change and, in one case, there was a statistically significant and negative impact. In terms of the slope coefficients, there were no effects in 10 of the 12 cases, with one positive and one negative. With this methodology, there does not appear to be a strong case for arguing that liberalization increases sensitivity of growth to export growth. The real problem, as the authors recognize, may lie in omitted variables such as human capital. Generally, specification (4) is at odds with much of the literature on openness and growth which finds the level of openness or share of exports as a determinant of growth rates. The absence of a tightly specified model makes interpretation of a growth accounting equation difficult.

TRADE LIBERALIZATION, OPENNESS AND GROWTH – CROSS-SECTION EVIDENCE

THE MANY STUDIES USING CROSS-COUNTRY EVIDENCE and done primarily in the 1980s were a major stimulus to the trade and openness growth question. Much of the impetus to these studies came from the increased availability of internationally comparable data for a large number of countries. Of particular note is the Summers and Heston (1988, 1991) data. These cross-section studies have been reviewed extensively elsewhere and criticized on a number of grounds. A large number of explanatory variables have been used and much of the debate has focused on the convergence hypothesis. This section briefly reviews the role of the

TABLE 1

CROSS-COUNTRY AVERAGES, 1960 TO 1989

Variable	Fast Growers	Slow Growers
Share of investment in GDP	0.23	0.17
Secondary school enrolment in 1960	0.30	0.10
Primary school enrolment in 1960	0.90	0.54
Government consumption/GDP	0.16	0.12
Inflation rate	12.34	31.13
Black market exchange rate premia	13.57	57.13
Share of exports to GDP	0.32	0.23

Notes: Mean growth rate =1.92.
   Fast growers are countries with a greater than mean growth rate. Slow growers
   are countries with a less than mean growth rate.
Source: Levine and Renelt (1992).

openness issue in this debate. It draws heavily from the survey by Levine and Renelt (1992).

The message of the Levine and Renelt paper, and others, is that many of the proposed determinants of growth are correlated with growth, but the results are statistically fragile. Using extreme bounds analysis, they found that only a small set of variables were robustly related to growth.

The typical equation that finds fairly strong support in the literature looks as follows:[4]

$$GROWTH_j = a_0 + a_1 INV_j + a_2 SCHOOL_j + a_3 OPEN + \beta INCOME_j + u_j \qquad (5)$$

where GROWTH is growth in per capita income; INV is the share of investment in GDP; SCHOOL is some measure of schooling; OPEN is an index of openness and INCOME is the initial income level. The regression is run across countries for a period, such as 1970 to 1988, using purchasing power parity (PPP) adjusted data. The coefficient β should be negative indicating conditional convergence, i.e., countries which started out poor should subsequently grow faster. A vast literature has emerged proposing variables which are capable of policy manipulation and, therefore, might be added to (5). Some of the more common ones are presented in Table 1.

Levine and Renelt examined a number of indicators of openness and/or trade policy and found that many were correlated with growth. However, many of them were not robust when included with the investment share, partially because many of the openness indexes appeared to be highly correlated with the investment share. For example, in their sample, they found that the export and investment share had a correlation coefficient of 0.50. They interpreted their results as an indication that the relationship between trade and growth may be based on trade contributing to enhanced resource accumulation and not necessarily on improved resource allocation. That is, trade causes growth because it increases investment and not through some independent channel. Many of the theoretical models of trade and growth do not stress this particular link.

The bulk of the export-led growth literature either suffers from the use of subjective indexes of trade orientation, which are not comparable across countries, or assumes that exports are the result of a more liberalized trade regime. Korea is the classic example of differences in interpretation. The World Bank uses Korea as an example of a successful outward-oriented trade regime while many others (Collins and Park, 1988; Sachs, 1987) regard Korea as a prime example of a high-growth country which did not liberalize its trade regime. For these reasons, it is important to get other, hopefully more objective, indexes of the degree of distortion induced by the trade regime. Edwards (1992) is an important example of an attempt to do just that.

His framework starts with an aggregate production function which is identical across countries up to a Hicks-Neutral technological coefficient A. A is assumed to evolve in each country according to the following dynamics:

$$\frac{\dot{A}}{A} = \left\{ \alpha + \delta\left(\frac{W-A}{A}\right) \right\} + \beta\omega \tag{6}$$

where W is the stock of the world's knowledge assumed to evolve at an exogenous rate ω; and β is a parameter between zero and one which measures a nation's ability to absorb inventions in the rest of the world. Note that, in this theoretical formulation, each nation's technical progress is tied to the technology gap (i.e., convergence is at work) and to a catch-up factor which is tied to the growth rate of the world's knowledge capital.

Edwards demonstrated that it was quite possible, depending on parameter values, that an individual country's growth rate may or may not depend on its trade orientation, assuming this affects only the β parameter. In one case, there will be a steady-state knowledge gap and the growth rate of A will be independent of the trade orientation of the economy, i.e., the parameter β. However, the level of GDP will be a function of the degree of trade orientation because the steady-state stock of A depends negatively on the degree of trade distortions. In this case, liberalization episodes will be characterized during transitions by higher rates of knowledge accumulation and thus higher rates of growth.

For other parameter values, the growth rate of A will depend positively on trade policy. Thus, nations with lower trade distortions will have a higher steady-state rate of growth. Here we see again the problem discussed earlier that even quite aggregate-level theorizing does not distinguish between a prediction on steady-state growth rates versus transitional growth effects without strong assumptions on parameter values.

The basic equation, estimated on 51 developed and developing countries, for the average growth experience from 1970 to 1982 is:

$$\text{GROWTH}_j = a_0 + a_1 \text{INV}_j + a_2 \text{GAP}_j + a_3 \text{TRADE}_j + u_j \tag{7}$$

where GAP is a measure of the gap between the national and world stock of knowledge; TRADE is an index of trade intervention; and j indexes countries.[5]

The main strength of this paper is in the focus on a variety of openness and intervention indexes. These indexes are difficult to construct because of the large significance of non-tariff barriers in most developing countries. Due to these problems, Edwards used the Leamer (1988) indexes of openness which are constructed from the difference between predicted and actual trade intensity using an empirical Heckscher–Ohlin (H–O) model to get predicted trade intensity ratios. This difference is interpreted as reflecting the role of trade barriers. The advantage is that the resulting indexes of intervention are objective and come from a well-defined static trade model. In principle, this should not lead to any particular bias toward predictions on growth rates. The disadvantage, of course, is that the trade model itself – the H–O – is subject to numerous qualifications particularly with regard to the basic assumption that all countries share the same technology. This hypothesis is in sharp contrast to the underlying assumption of the Edwards paper on the sources of productivity growth.

Using a variety of indexes, Edwards' results were overwhelmingly supportive of the hypothesis that trade intervention significantly affects growth in the predicted direction. A battery of econometric tests were used to examine the robustness of the results, and the author found they all stood up. Interestingly, two outliers were identified: Hong Kong and Singapore. When these were removed, the results continued to hold up. Edwards also tested three other potential explanatory variables for growth: human capital, political instability and size of government. In each case, the variable added explanatory power to the growth equation but did not reduce the significance or sign of the trade distortion indexes.

Edwards concluded by looking at a number of alternative indicators of the trade regime. However, all were available for only a subset of the initial sample. These indicators included:

- average black market premiums;
- the coefficient of variation of the black market premiums;
- an index of relative price distortions between the commodities that are and are not traded;
- average import tariffs;
- average coverage of non-tariff barriers;
- index of effective protection; and
- the World Bank's subjective index of outward orientation.

In each case, on the reduced samples the variables entered the growth regressions negatively (with the exception of the non-tariff barriers index), but not all significantly. In general, Edwards concluded that the hypothesis that trade intervention reduces growth rates is robust, although his evidence could not necessarily be linked directly to the theories he used to advance the hypothesis.

Convergence and the Timing of Trade Liberalization – a Case Study of the European Community (EC)

A MAJOR PROBLEM WITH MOST OF THE ECONOMETRIC WORK, in particular the cross section studies, is that little evidence is offered on the question of causality and timing in the relationship between trade liberalization and growth. A somewhat indirect approach to this problem was taken in a novel study by Ben-David (1993). Ben-David studied the impact of the formation of the EC on the convergence of income levels in Europe, using the convergence experience before the formation of the EC, the most recent experience of the same countries and the convergence experience of other countries as his basis for comparison. The convergence hypothesis is closely related to the question of the impact of trade on growth. The Ben-David paper, however, focuses on convergence of income levels rather than on growth rates per se. The evidence for the EC is illustrated in Figure 3 which shows the rapid reduction in per capita income divergence among the six original EC countries from 1950 to 1968. The trade liberalization policies which followed the signing of the Treaty of Rome in 1957 included the reduction in internal tariffs, the introduction of non-discriminatory internal quotas in 1959 and the completion of the internal customs union in 1968. The changes in trade patterns of the EC during this period are well known. Intra-EEC (European Economic Community) imports grew from under 4 percent of EC GDP in 1950 to just under 12 percent by 1970. EC external imports were relatively stable at around 11 percent of GDP during the same period.

FIGURE 3

Per Capita Income Divergence For Six Original EC Countries, 1950 to 1968

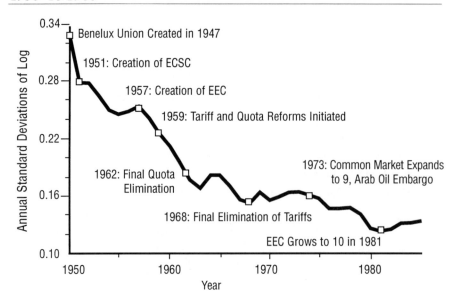

The major point of the study, however, was to make the connection between the trade liberalization and the convergence identified. Ben-David did this in three ways:

- by contrasting the postwar period to the pre-war period;

- by examining the impact on the three countries that joined in 1973; and

- by comparing the EC to other cases, i.e., the world and the United States.

Looking at the pre-war experience, he found that the dispersion index was remarkably stable from 1870 to 1950 and then declined significantly from 1950 to 1970. He argued that this supported the trade liberalization explanation and refuted the alternative explanation that convergence was the consequence of a return to the normal pre-war pattern. The evidence on the three that joined in 1973 (Ireland, Denmark and the United Kingdom) confirmed the convergence hypothesis for the 1970s. However, during the 1980s the EC dispersion index diverged slightly suggesting the forces for convergence had waned.

Ben-David also used a traditional (unconditional) convergence equation to estimate the rate at which per capita income (or GDP per capita) among the EEC countries converged toward the average income in the region during three periods: before the liberalization in the EEC, during a 10-year transition period in which trade barriers were eliminated within the EEC and the years after the transition period. His estimates showed an increase in the rate at which income converges during the period of trade liberalization. The rate of convergence, Φ, was estimated using the equation:

$$(y_i/\bar{y})t = (y_i/\bar{y})^{\Phi}_{t-1} \tag{8}$$

where y_i is per capita income for each country i; and $\bar{y}$ is the average per capita income for the region. The analytical basis for this convergence equation derives from the basic neoclassical growth model with identical technological possibilities across countries.[6] Before World War II, Φ was estimated to be equal to 0.9908 which implied that the per capita income gap was being halved every 75 years. In the postwar period (1951 to 1985) Φ was estimated at 0.9707, implying that the income gap is halved every 23 years. Moreover, in the years immediately following the creation of the EEC (1957 until 1968) when all tariff barriers were removed, the income gap was halved every 13.3 years with Φ equal to 0.9494. The final evidence came from estimating the convergence rate in the world – a very non-integrated region – and in the United States – the benchmark of a highly integrated region. The convergence half-life for the United States (1931 to 1984) was 15.3 years and for the world (107 countries from 1960 to 1985) 93.9 years. Ben-David concluded that the timing of trade liberalization and convergence in the EC was strongly suggestive of causality running from economic integration to income convergence.

Total Factor Productivity and the International Diffusion of Technology: The Helliwell Study

IN A NUMBER OF PAPERS, JOHN HELLIWELL (1992, 1994a, 1994b) has exploited a rich Organization for Economic Co-operation and Development (OECD) data set covering 19 industrial countries from 1963 to 1989. Much of the work emphasized testing for the convergence hypothesis. Helliwell (1994a) turned his attention to the empirical links between trade and technical progress. Specifically, the questions were whether aggregate production possibilities across the OECD countries for the time period 1963 to 1989 tended to equality and whether trade facilitated the international transfer of knowledge that would be necessary for observed identical technical conditions of production. The great strength of this approach is a direct attempt to measure convergence of TFP as it relates to trade rather than to other summary measures of performance such as income per capita or average labour productivity. It also avoids some of the more obvious difficulties of interpreting the cross-section studies by using a linked time-series cross-section data set on the OECD.

Aggregate production in each country was described by an aggregate two-factor Cobb–Douglas production function for country i in time period t:

$$Y_{it} = K_{it}^{\alpha} (A_{it} L_{it})^{1-\alpha} \tag{9}$$

where K is the aggregate capital stock; L is the level of employment; and A is the level of technology. Note that all countries were assumed to have identical share parameters and to differ only in capital and labour endowments, and in the technology or TFP parameter A.[7]

To measure the level of technology, a value of α is chosen and the TFP or Solow residuals are computed in the conventional manner using the production function given observed Y, K and L to solve for A. In general, the A_{it} vary considerably across countries and across time. Helliwell started with the general convergence formula as his starting point:

$$d\ln A_{it} = \beta_{oi,t} + \beta_1 \ln(A_{1,t-1}/A_{i,t-1}) + \beta_2 d\ln A_{i,t-1} + \beta_3 C_i + u_{i,t} \tag{10}$$

where the second term indicates the importance of technological catch-up given the position of the lead country – subscript 1, the United States – relative to the position of the country being analyzed; β_2 reflects the potential persistence in Solow residuals which is central to the whole real business cycle literature; and C_i refers to cyclical variables that reflect capacity utilization effects. This was estimated for the 19 countries. The results showed strong support for convergence of rates of technical progress but the rates varied widely across countries.

Trade was introduced by first estimating a trade intensity equation from a pooled cross-section/time series regression:

$$TI = \log((X+M)/GDP) \tag{11}$$

on time and GDP where trade intensity is defined as the log of the ratio of total trade volume (exports plus imports) divided by GDP; TI is regressed on a constant – time and real GDP. Not surprisingly, time enters positively, and country size is significantly negative in the explanation of trade intensity.

The basic approach is to see whether trade intensity affects the pattern of international convergence of technology. Since Helliwell found little evidence of pooling in looking at (10) as a system of time series equations, he looked at the convergence equations as a set of 27 annual cross sections each with 19 observations with a different constant term for each year. The equation tested was:

$$dlnA_{it} = \beta_{ot} + \beta_1 ln(A_{1,t-1}/A_{i,t-1}) + \beta_2 dlnA_{i,t-1} + \beta_3 TI_{i,t} + \beta_4 lnGDP_{i,t} + u_{i,t} \tag{12}$$

The residuals from the trade intensity equation are used for TI. Therefore, only those trade intensity effects not already explained by country size are presumed to affect the rate of technological convergence.

Both scale and trade intensity effects were found to be significant in most years. The constant term reflects the exogenous movement in global technology common to all countries. The convergence, size and trade intensity coefficients were constrained to be the same across countries and across years. While significant, trade intensity and scale contributed remarkably little to total cumulative technical progress over the period. By far, the bulk of the movement is explained by convergence – less than 10 percent of cumulative technical change is explained by the combined effects of size and openness. Since theory is vague on whether it is level or growth effects that trade is supposed to contribute to, Helliwell also tested (12) by using differences in TI as an additional explanatory variable and found that both level and difference effects appeared to have independent importance in the results. Helliwell concluded:

> Overall the experiments ... suggest that the level of openness may have effects on both the level and the rate of growth of productivity. If confirmed, this in turn suggests that some of the observed positive linkage between openness and growth may relate to the gains from expanding trade rather than to international knowledge transfers (Helliwell, 1994b, pp. 265-266).

This conclusion must be qualified, however, given the large reliance on the maintained convergence hypothesis embodied in the basic equation (10). Much of the theoretical literature can be interpreted in the following way. Openness contributes to the rate at which knowledge diffuses from the less advanced to the most advanced. Thus, in the absence of a gap between the leader and the follower, one would not expect openness to explain any additional TFP growth. A different interpretation of the openness hypothesis would be to consider the convergence parameter on the gap to be a function of the degree of openness and size rather than to have these as independent explanatory variables of TFP growth. The Helliwell study, while suggestive of the contributions of trade as facilitating the transfer of knowledge capital, casts doubt on how significant it is relative to other mechanisms.[8]

INVESTMENT AND CAPITAL IMPORTS

BOTH THE THEORETICAL AND EMPIRICAL LITERATURE ON GROWTH suggest a strong link between investment and growth. At the theoretical level, embodied technological progress via the transfer of new technology through imported capital goods is one of the principal causal channels running from investment to growth. De Long and Summers (1991) noted that there are some strong differences between the prices of machinery and equipment across countries. Rich nations tend to have cheaper investment goods and, at identical savings rates, these nations have high rates of capital accumulation. These observations are the basis for a study by Lee (1994) which looked at the link between capital imports and growth. Lee calculated that, for a sample of poor countries, the national prices of domestic investment goods were relatively more expensive by a factor of 1.55 compared with the United States. He set up a simple model of endogenous growth open to trade that built on a model by Rebello (1991).[9] The model had two sectors: consumption and investment. Investment inputs were differentiated in the less-developed country (LDC) between foreign and domestic sources. There was also a distinction between the developed country (DC) and the LDC. Growth in the DC proceeded exogenously. DCs imported consumption goods and used their own capital goods for export. LDCs used foreign, as well as their own capital goods, and exported consumption goods. In the LDC, foreign capital goods were cheaper than domestic capital goods. Representative households maximized lifetime utility in the conventional way giving rise to optimal savings.

The model has a number of straightforward predictions. In the steady state, the LDC and DC have the same growth rates with a positive steady-state share of imports in LDC investment. The interesting predictions concern the transition phase.

- During the transition, the growth rate of income is higher in an economy with a higher ratio of imports in investment. Thus, if an economy uses imported capital goods relatively more than its own domestic capital goods for accumulation, it grows faster.

- If two LDCs have the same per capita income and trade with the same DC, the country that devotes relatively more of a given portion of its income to the importation of cheap capital goods grows faster than the other country.

The empirical work focuses on the model's prediction for the transition in which the (quantity) ratio of domestically produced to imported capital goods is important for growth. Any trade distortions on capital goods, such as tariffs or quantitative restrictions which affect either the price or quantity of capital imports, become important potential policy variables. The empirical equation, applied to the growth experience of a cross section of 89 countries from 1960 to 1985, is:

$$GROWTH_i = const + aIMPORT_i + bINFO_i + u_i \qquad (13)$$

where GROWTH is growth in per capita income; IMPORT is the ratio of foreign to domestic investment quantities; and INFO is the set of other variables taken to explain growth. These include initial real GDP, the initial secondary school enrolment rate, the rate of population growth and the investment share in GDP.[10]

The results strongly confirm the important effect of imported capital goods. Using ordinary least square (OLS), the estimated coefficient on imported capital implies that an increase of 0.1 in the ratio of imports to investment leads to an increase in the growth of per capita income of 0.3 percent per year. Using two-staged least square (2SLS), the same figure more than doubles to 0.7 percent. The results suggest that imported capital has a much higher productivity than domestically produced goods. Since trade variables often enter significantly in growth regressions, Lee tested the robustness of his specification by including total import ratios. Total imports, conditional on the other variables, including the imported investment ratio, were insignificant.[11]

MODELING THE DYNAMIC EFFECTS OF ECONOMIC INTEGRATION

THIS SECTION TURNS TO THE USE OF COUNTERFACTUAL MODELS to illustrate the dynamic effects of economic integration. In each model, there is an explicit theory of how trade affects the dynamics of accumulation. The models surveyed illustrate the diversity of approaches used by economists and the orders of magnitude of estimated output, employment and welfare effects from changes in trade policy.

THE NEOCLASSICAL BENCHMARK

A GOOD EXAMPLE OF A DYNAMIC MODEL without endogenous growth but in an otherwise fairly conventional neoclassical single country framework is that of Ho and Jorgenson (1994) applied to trade policy changes in the United States. The model has a single infinitely lived utility-maximizing consumer who saves and thus accumulates real capital. There is a 10-industry breakdown with production functions characterized by the typical capital, labour, energy and materials (KLEM) structure inputs. Exogenous technical change is Harrod-Neutral. Labour supply is endogenous. Under the assumption of perfect foresight, consumers' savings decisions are, of course, super-rational. An interesting characteristic of the model is the specification of the trade side. Both import and export demands are treated as non-homothetic and time dependent during transitions. Import shares at constant prices and income are assumed to change in a logistic fashion gradually increasing but then stabilizing at higher levels in the long run. Export demand functions are specified exogenously and have elasticities with respect to foreign income which are different from one. In fact, the majority of all export income elasticities are assumed to exceed one during the transition, but are assumed to equal one in the steady state.[12]

The treatment of the current account is less interesting. Its evolution is treated as exogenous. Thus, changes in trade policy result in changes in the terms of trade to balance the current account much like the old elasticities approach to balance of payments theory. There are some induced changes in savings behaviour but no changes in net borrowing or lending from foreigners. This is unfortunate because it ignores the potentially important endogenous dynamics in the current and capital accounts that would ultimately affect wealth accumulation. Nevertheless, in addition to the usual static effects of trade liberalization, the model captures the accumulation effect usually associated with closed economy models of tax policy effects on savings and investment.

The Ho–Jorgenson model is econometrically estimated and simulated from a given set of initial state variables. No steady-state restrictions are imposed on the base case. Given the assumed non-homotheticity in the trade equations, virtually all the action is in the transition to the steady state. Furthermore, population growth is assumed to go to zero at the end of the 75-year simulation. While this appears to be done for computational purposes, some of the accumulation effects reflect the fact that the transition is toward a trend of zero population growth.

The effects of trade policy in the Ho–Jorgenson model are generally larger than those in the static models. Cutting all tariffs and quotas on the U.S. economy and on the rest of the world beginning in 1980 results in about a 0.5 percent increase in GNP and 1.2 percent increase in consumption by the year 2040. The capital stock increases by 0.8 percent indicating that induced accumulation effects are not trivial. The reason is a fairly significant reduction in the price of capital goods of about 1.2 percent. Unlike many static models of multilateral tariff cuts, the Ho–Jorgenson model predicts a terms-of-trade deterioration for the United States. While these numbers may not appear large, they are much larger than the gains to the United States reported in static models such as Deardorff and Stern (1986) – 0.1 percent of U.S. GNP – or Whalley (1985) – 0.05 percent for a 50 percent multilateral cut.

Not surprisingly, the model gives very small growth effects. Eliminating virtually all trade barriers raises the average annual growth rate of real GNP over the 1980 to 1990 period from 3.47 percent to 3.50 percent. Measured from 1980 to 2000, the same growth rate changes from 2.34 percent to 2.38 percent.[13]

This model raises a couple of interesting points. First, how sensitive are the results to the non-unitary income elasticities in the trade equations? Clearly, the model hinges on a fairly optimistic view of U.S. export growth with respect to the rest of the world. A comparison with a model calibrated to a steady-state assumption would be useful for comparison purposes even if not deemed to be relevant for policy purposes. Finally, the treatment of the capital and current accounts needs further work. All in all, it is an excellent example of how neoclassical models of trade and integration can be dynamized.

Taking the Capital Account Seriously: Goulder–Eichengreen

An interesting multicountry model is that of Goulder and Eichengreen (1992). It is an explicit neoclassical model optimizing consumers and producers. Specification of the consumption, trade and production side is quite similar to Ho–Jorgenson with two important exceptions. First, on the production side there are explicit investment dynamics due to the assumed presence of adjustment costs – unlike the Ho–Jorgenson framework in which savings automatically determine investment with instantaneous stock adjustment. At the industry level, this implies that capital is intersectorally immobile and investment is "sluggish." Second, this is an explicit two-country model, and the current account dynamics are endogenized. Portfolio decisions are incorporated by introducing asset "preferences" over foreign and domestic assets. Specifically, there is a CES aggregator function which defines asset preference over foreign versus domestic assets. The portfolio share of each type of asset depends on relative after tax rates of return to each asset. Consumers/investors are assumed to exhibit a "home bias" in their asset preferences that is consistent with observed portfolio behaviour. Asset preferences introduce an important transmission mechanism from shifts in portfolio preference which affect the capital account and thus current account dynamics that are broadly consistent with the portfolio balance view of modern international finance theory. While purists might object to the method by which asset preferences are introduced to the model, in a world of highly mobile financial capital, this issue is important in analyzing the intertemporal effects of trade liberalization or economic integration.[14]

The multilateral tariff cuts result in an estimated increase in welfare of 2.8 percent – one of the largest numbers I have seen in a neoclassical style model. Most of the effort in the Goulder–Eichengreen paper is directed toward analysis of unilateral U.S. tariff and quota reductions and the role of the international capital market in conditioning the model's response to trade liberalization. Since this is the most novel element of their model, let me focus on that feature.

Reductions in U.S. tariffs lead to an adverse change in the U.S. terms of trade. This effect grows over time as the United States adjusts its capital stock to higher imports. Gould and Eichengreen argue that the principal effect at work here, is largely demand side driven – more weight on imported goods in indexes of demand. Investment declines in import-competing sectors following the tariff cuts lead to a long-run capital stock which is smaller. The evolution of the current account depends critically on the manner in which portfolios adjust to the tariff changes – something virtually all other dynamic trade models ignore. In the model's portfolio adjustment, prices are normalized by fixing nominal wages in both countries. This requires the introduction of an exchange rate. The elimination of tariffs weakens the U.S. dollar which reduces the value of holdings by foreigners of U.S. assets that are below desired levels. To restore portfolio equilibrium, foreigners devote a larger fraction of current savings to accumulating U.S. assets which in turn drives down U.S. interest rates, reduces U.S. savings and increases investment. Thus, the current account goes into deficit.

After a period of nine years, Gould and Eichengreen found that the trade balance eventually moved back into surplus in order to finance the growing foreign debt level. They also reported the approximate speed of adjustment – using the half-life of the capital–output ratio as the yardstick. In the case of unilateral tariff cuts, it took eight years to reach the half-life mark which is relatively fast compared to other models.

They highlight the difference that financial capital mobility assumptions can have on model results by considering the case in which asset trades between countries are prohibited in some fashion, i.e., reduced openness of financial markets. The biggest effect comes through reduced international cross-ownership of assets under one definition of reduced capital mobility. Suppose U.S. residents own most of the U.S. capital stock on the initial date of the tariff cuts. The subsequent capital gains and losses on U.S. assets fall entirely on U.S. residents. Tariff elimination raises the value of infra-marginal firms. This capital gain partially offsets the efficiency and terms-of-trade losses from tariff cuts. If portfolios were internationally diversified, foreigners would share in part of these gains. The general point is that movements in asset price induced by policy changes, in a model with agents of differing income and wealth levels, have implications for the international distribution of wealth and welfare. Modelling the degree of openness of asset markets becomes critical in assessing goods or factor market integration. Gould and Eichengreen also note that while reduced openness implies reduced opportunities for consumption smoothing, this does not seem to play a strong role in the models. They also point out that reducing adjustment costs hastens the arrival of the long run and, therefore, magnifies welfare results. This suggests that static models which ignore adjustment costs overstate both costs and benefits of policy changes.[15]

INVESTMENT, SCALE AND IMPERFECT COMPETITION: MERCENIER–AKITOBY 1993

THIS IS A MULTISECTORAL FULLY GENERAL EQUILIBRIUM MODEL of the European economies modelled in a six-region framework: Great Britain, Germany, France, Italy, the rest of the EC(RE) and the rest of the OECD (ROW). The model is different from neoclassical models in two respects. First, product markets are presumed to be imperfectly competitive subject to markup pricing and characterized by static scale economies. Second, labour markets are characterized by institutional real wage rigidity in the short run. Thus, rather than focus on real wage effects of economic integration, the emphasis is on potential employment gains. Productivity changes, given indexing of wages, fall first on prices.

An important issue in the European trade policy literature of the last decade is how to model the integration effect of 1992. The basic problem is that tariff barriers within Europe are very low, and quantifying non-tariff barriers in the EC has been notoriously difficult. An emerging tradition in the imperfect competition literature on EC 1992 has been to avoid the measurement problem altogether and to treat economic integration as a structural change in the pricing behaviour of oligopolists. Specifically, it is assumed that before integration firms price discriminate between national markets. Post-integration price discrimination between national markets is not feasible due to implicit post-integration arbitrage. This modelling strategy pioneered by Smith and Venables (1988) is easily implemented. The empirical basis for this assumption on the market conduct consequences of integration relies on two observations made in an extensive study done on EC 1992 by the European Commission.[16] First, using fairly disaggregated data, a significant dispersion in prices across regional markets was observed within the EC, and the dispersion was greater on an intra-EC basis than on a national basis. Second, on a cross-sector basis, those sectors with higher non-tariff barriers appear to have large price dispersions. The presumption, therefore, is that, with the elimination of these non-tariff barriers, this price dispersion due to segmentation of national markets will be eliminated.[17]

The dynamics of this model are greatly simplified by a procedure of dynamic aggregation which reduces the infinite future into two periods: the short run and the long run. This allows for a more detailed treatment of the industry structure and the role of entry and exit in response to integration. There are costs, however. Forcing the analysis into two periods results in a dramatic simplification on the description of intertemporal production possibilities. Furthermore, it requires explicit use of a finite horizon; in the empirical implementation the horizon is taken to be 20 years.[18]

The model has nine sectors with a large amount of detail on industry structure which is now standard in the applied general equilibrium (AGE) literature of imperfect competition. Economies of scale and markups are calibrated in the benchmark. In the benchmark, the economies of scale are quite significant. The ratio of marginal to average costs ranges from an EC average of about 0.62 in pharmacy to a high of 0.83 in office machinery. There is also significant price discrimination in the benchmark. In general, the pattern is one of higher markups in the domestic than in the export market with export prices being anywhere from 10 percent to 2 percent lower than the domestic price of the same good.

The great virtue of this model is its ability to handle the dynamics of entry and exit in a non-competitive framework through a clever use of the Marshallian period analysis. Industry structure is assumed fixed in the short run, and abnormal profits or losses are possible. In the long run, the entry and exit of firms occur to ensure zero profits. These types of dynamics are potentially quite different than the dynamics of neoclassical adjustment cost models and may lead to a quite different pattern of capital accumulation.

In general, the quantitative results of this model are supportive of the proposition that EC 1992 is likely to bring significant benefits – although less than the Cecchini Report suggested. All countries experience welfare increases. With the exception of RE, these are in the range of 1.5 percent to 2.4 percent of GDP. In all countries, except RE, there are large improvements in realized economies of scale. The major dynamic (long-run) effect is an increase in investment which adds to the long-run production capacity. This ranges from an increase of 2.6 percent in Germany to a 1.5 percent increase in Italy. Only RE experiences a decrease in investment which is attributed to an adverse terms-of-trade effect. Employment gains are also significant (in the range of 1.1 percent to 0.5 percent). With a fixed real wage, lower prices result in lower wages and thus the improved competitiveness of Europe vis-à-vis ROW.

Given the time aggregation procedures used in this model, it is not clear how these results would differ from the same model without time aggregation. This is clearly a question which deserves further investigation. The results indicate, however, that if the EC 1992 program is about eliminating price discrimination then its effects may not be all that large. The general model used has much wider interest though. It would be interesting to see it applied in a context where more conventional trade barriers are involved.

Capital Stock Externalities – The Baldwin Model

The Baldwin (1992) paper is an important innovation because it is the first to address the issue of dynamic quantitative effects of induced accumulation in the presence of capital externalities. The paper uses a standard single sector representative agent growth model but with a positive externality of physical capital in the production function, i.e., the social marginal product of capital is different than the private marginal product of capital.

The external effect is modelled as follows. Individual firms have "private" production functions given by:

$$y=Ak^\alpha l^{1-\alpha} \tag{14}$$

Total inputs in the economy, K and L, are derived by adding individual k and l across firms. A is total factor productivity which is taken as given by firms. It is assumed that A evolves according to:

$$A(t)=e^{\eta t}K^\theta \tag{15}$$

Thus, the external economies are due to increases in the aggregate capital stock.

Suppose the static output effect of a trade liberalization or economic integration in percentage change is $\hat{\beta}$ given no change in the capital stock. Baldwin shows the dynamic effect on the change in aggregate output at a point in time:

$$\hat{Y}=(\frac{1}{\alpha+\theta}-1)^{-1}\hat{\beta}+\hat{\beta} \tag{16}$$

This formula reflects the critical role of the social capital–output elasticity, $\alpha+\theta$.

There is considerable debate about the exact magnitude of this elasticity. Using a number of studies from the literature, Baldwin estimates this parameter for European countries as ranging from a low of 0.195 to a high of 0.576. Induced capital formation can be thought of as a multiplier of the static effect from (16). Using the estimates of $\alpha+\theta$, the static effect $\hat{\beta}$ underestimates actual output change by anywhere from 30 percent to 136 percent. The larger the capital–output elasticity, the larger the error between the dynamic and static estimates. The impact of this correction to conventional GDP effects is illustrated for a number of EC countries using the Cecchini Report estimates of the static effect of EC 1992. For example, the static GDP effects on Germany are in the range of 3.2 percent to 8.4 percent of GDP. Using Baldwin's dynamic corrections, these translate into dynamic changes of 5.7 percent to 14.9 percent.[19]

Moving to a welfare calculation involves discounting the consumption gains rising from the additional accumulation. The multiplier effect is quite significant ranging from 0.17 to 0.87 for Belgium, for example. Welfare is higher by 17 percent to 87 percent than a conventional static EV or CV measure would indicate.

USING THE CONVERGENCE HYPOTHESIS – HARRIS–ROBERTSON

THE IDEA THAT CONVERGENCE IS RELATED TO TRADE POLICY or economic integration is a theme which underlies much of the discussion thus far. Harris and Robertson (1993) used this theme in an attempt to estimate the potential dynamic gains which might occur as a consequence of the formation of a free trade area in the Western Hemisphere – an extension of NAFTA to include all of Latin America and the Caribbean referred to by the acronym WHFTA. The static gains from a WHFTA are not insignificant with estimates of the gains to Latin America falling in the range of 2 percent to 7 percent of GDP. The total gains are generally estimated to be quite small – in the range of 0.5 percent to 1.5 percent. The Harris–Robertson exercise is motivated by the Ben-David observation that the rate of convergence in levels is affected by the extent of economic integration in the region. The counterfactual question is to ask: what would be the impact on growth and income if WHFTA replicated for Latin America the experience of the original EC economies following the Treaty of Rome? The basic theoretical framework is the Solow–Swan neoclassical growth model used to calibrate steady-state income levels plus a convergence equation presumed to shift with changes in the trade regime.

What do these convergence rates imply for the economies of the Americas, in terms of growth in per capita GDP, if they were to undergo an experience similar to that of European economies following the formation of the EC? The procedure involves using a version of the basic convergence equation together with some assumptions about trend income growth in Canada and the United States, together with assumptions on demographic developments in both regions. The initial values of per capita income in five broad sub-regions of the Western Hemisphere were obtained from the Summers and Heston (1991), Penn World Tables. These and the projected population levels, taken from the World Bank (1991b), are shown in Table 2.

The per capita and total GDP estimates for each region were compared under two scenarios. The first assumes that a hemispheric free trade agreement is signed in 1995, with tariff elimination by 2000. The second scenario assumes that no tariff

TABLE 2

STARTING VALUES FOR CONVERGENCE

	Income per Capita in 1985 ($ PPP)	$\frac{y_i}{\bar{y}}$	Population (millions) 1989	2000	2025
Central America & Caribbean	2,222	0.43	42	54	84
Mexico	5,332	0.77	85	103	142
Brazil	3,995	0.54	147	178	236
Other South American	3,597	0.51	131	173	232
USA & Canada	16,610	1.03	275	301	341

Source: Harris and Robertson (1993).

reduction occurs so incomes converge at the rate consistent with the experience in Europe before the Treaty of Rome, i.e, with a half-life of 75 years. The resulting differences in GDP growth can be seen in the following tables. In Table 3, the per capita income gap between a number of Western Hemisphere countries and the Unites States–Canada region is reported with and without a WHFTA.

In the case where a WHFTA is assumed, the fast and slow columns represent the results at the lower and upper bounds of the standard deviations of Ben-David's estimates. The case presumes that the status quo, circa 1985 persists indefinitely

TABLE 3

PROJECTED INCOME GAP RELATIVE TO THE UNITED STATES–CANADA (%)

Year	Central America & Caribbean			South America (except Brazil & Mexico)			Brazil			Mexico		
	Fast	Slow	Base	Fast	Slow	Base	Fast	Slow	Base	Fast	Slow	Base
1995	85.2	85.2	85.2	77.0	77.0	77.0	74.7	74.7	74.7	67.1	67.1	67.1
2000	78.0	80.7	84.4	69.7	72.4	76.3	67.5	70.2	74.1	60.6	63.0	66.7
2005	69.5	75.5	83.6	61.4	67.2	75.6	59.4	65.1	73.3	53.2	58.4	66.1
2006	67.7	74.4	83.5	59.7	66.1	75.4	57.7	64.0	73.2	51.8	57.5	66.0

Note: Fast Φ = 0.9301; Slow Φ= 0.9597; Base Φ= 0.9908, see text for explanation.
Source: Harris and Robertson (1993).

with respect to trade policy. The Canada–United States Free Trade Agreement (FTA) is assumed to be in effect under all cases. The income gap is defined as $-100(y^i-y^N)/y^N$ for each country/region i where y is per capita GDP; and y^N is per capita GDP in Canada–United States. The average gap over a 10-year period is reduced by about 13 percent in the case of Central America, Brazil and South America. In the case of Mexico, the gap is reduced by approximately 14 percent. Note that even after 10 years, a substantial per capita income gap remains, but clearly the gap is narrowing much faster with a free trade area than without one.

Looking at the income gains expressed relative to each country's GDP, rather than the gap measured against Canada–United States gives fairly dramatic numbers. In the case of Brazil, for example, the results imply that in the year 2006 Brazilian GDP would be 34 percent to 57 percent higher than it would be in the absence of a WHFTA. These numbers no doubt overestimate the impact of a free trade area on the region. Comparison with the European case may be inappropriate as geographic proximity in Europe may play an important role which is not present in South America.[20] Nevertheless, the numbers suggest the overwhelming potential importance of income convergence as a factor in looking at the longer-term benefits of trade liberalization.

HUMAN CAPITAL AND INTERNATIONAL CAPITAL FLOWS

ONE ENGINE OF GROWTH common to both new and old growth theory is human capital. Lucas (1988, 1990) noted that one reason countries remain poor is that capital does not flow from rich to poor countries. These flows may not occur if poor countries have low levels of human capital per worker. The basic theory is fairly straightforward. Suppose production possibilities in all countries are described by an augmented neoclassical aggregate production function:

$$Y=F(K,H,L) \tag{17}$$

with the factors of production being physical capital, K; human capital, H; and raw labour, L. The marginal product of physical capital is a function depending on the ratios k=K/L and h=H/L. The function is denoted by (MPK)(k,h). If F($\cdot$) has the usual neoclassical properties, then a marginal productivity of capital (MPK) iso-value locus is an upward sloping locus as drawn in Figure 4.

Rich countries are those endowed with large amounts of per capita physical and human capital such as point B on the iso-MPK locus. Poor countries have low amounts of per capita human and physical capital denoted by A. If capital is mobile across countries but human capital is not then, as indicated in this graph, there can be a long-run equilibrium with no physical capital flowing because the marginal product of physical capital is equal in both locations, but income per capita differences are large. This basic theoretical framework can go a long way toward accommodating income differences without relying on a priori differences in technological blueprints across countries. Few would argue that all income differences can be attributed

FIGURE 4

PER CAPITA INCOME DISPERSION: BETWEEN SIX ORIGINAL EEC
COUNTRIES, 1950 TO 1985

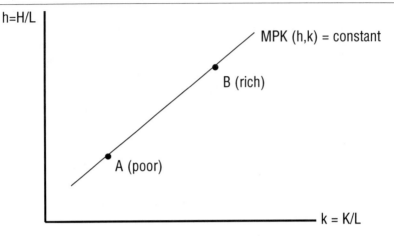

TABLE 4

RELATIVE PER CAPITA INCOMES AND RELATIVE HUMAN CAPITAL
STOCKS, 1980

	Relative Per Capita Income (%)	Percentage Income Differential Explained by Human Capital (%)	Relative Stock of Human Capital Per Person (%)
Bangladesh	4.4	15.2	45.2
Brazil	29.7	55.0	37.8
Cameroon	10.1	19.4	49.6
Canada	85.7	92.9	91.4
Ecuador	21.7	50.6	27.6
Honduras	9.7	22.8	49.4
Japan	63.8	32.5	82.3
New Zealand	61.0	96.7	5.9
Panama	23.3	37.5	54.4
Sri Lanka	10.8	43.5	43.5

Source: Gundlach (1994).

to differences in human capital, but most would accept that a large part of the difference can be explained this way. Gundlach (1994) has recently estimated how much the level of per capita income of a number of countries relative to the United States can be explained by human capital differences. His results for a sample of countries are given in Table 4.

Depending on the country, a fairly significant portion of the income differences can be explained by human capital endowments alone. The implication of these observations for the trade and growth question has been largely untouched. On the other hand, given the large fraction of national income that accrues to labour and, given that much of that income is returns to human capital, a broad policy change, such as economic integration, is bound to affect both the returns to human capital and the subsequent accumulation of human capital.

These issues are taken up in Harris (1994) in an explicit two-country growth model applied to the potential economic integration of North and South America within a WHFTA-type arrangement. The basic features of the model are:

- the international mobility of new investment;

- the immobility of human capital and raw labour;

- human capital formation which is constrained by income;

- differences in demographic patterns of a long-term nature; and

- the assumption that technology is identical across regions.

In this model, the extreme hypothesis is made that all income differences are due to different human and physical capital factor endowments. In addition, given the assumption that new investment is mobile, the model must be calibrated such that, in the initial equilibrium, physical capital is not induced to move between regions. To make the model consistent with observed data, it is necessary to model impediments to capital mobility due to legal restrictions, government controls on foreign investment, capital taxation and potential uncertainty in property rights. These are lumped into an ad valorem capital income tax levied on capital which is foreign-owned but is resident in South America (the South).

It turns out that, when this model is fully calibrated to observed data on the North and South American growth experience over the 1970 to 1988 period and then simulated over a 100-year period, income convergence is remarkably slow. There appears to be two reasons for the slow convergence. First, the speed of convergence in a model with diminishing returns is related to how the marginal productivity of accumulating factors diminished in response to the deepening capital. That is approximately equal to the elasticity of output with respect to the broadly defined capital stock – both physical and human. In this model, that number is approximately 0.60 to 0.65 – much closer to unity than in the usual physical-capital-only model. This implies that convergence is much slower than would otherwise be the case. The half-life of convergence to the steady state in a closed economy model in such a framework is about 30 to 35 years. There is also the presence of non-traded human capital which slows down the rate at which capital–labour ratios converge across countries. Furthermore, as saving rates and population growth rates differ between regions, the potential dynamics of the model are fairly complicated with elastic capital flows. For example, faster growing labour in the South raises the return to capital in the South thus attracting capital, while a lower rate of human capital accumulation tends to slow it down. It appears that, for practical purposes, the transition dynamics are the whole story.

The approximation of the static production gains from trade liberalization is treated as an impact similar to a once-off change in the efficiency of factors of production within a given aggregate GDP function following the procedure pioneered by Baldwin (1992).[21] Thus, trade liberalization can be thought of as enhancing the productivity of all factors (a "neutral" productivity increase) or only one of the factors (a "biased" productivity increase). Consider a general production function:

$$Y=F(\tau_L L, \tau_k K, \tau_H H) \tag{18}$$

The shift parameters τ_f can be thought of as approximating the one-time effects on factor efficiency which are induced by the reducing trade barriers. If the productivity effects are predominantly neutral, then this can be modelled as a proportionate increase in all τ. In this model, factor prices play a crucial role in the transmission process through which trade integration has both long-term effects on accumulation and an induced "growth bonus" effect. Factor prices can be thought of as the derivatives of the respective factors of the aggregate GDP function. Different assumptions as to which τ_f increase in response to trade liberalization are equivalent to assumptions on which factor prices will be affected most by trade liberalization.

Three sets of productivity "bias" in integration shocks are explored. The first is that all productivity changes are factor neutral, so all factor prices increase by the same proportionate amount. Alternatively, trade theories suggest that trade liberalization tends to raise the efficiency of some factors differentially relative to others. A "new trade theory" view of protection, for example, would lead to the prediction that the factors used intensively in the protected sectors are those whose efficiency is raised most by a trade liberalization.[22] In the case of liberalizing trade in the Americas, the pattern of protection is fairly clear. In North America (the North), labour-intensive manufacturing and agricultural products are protected, while in Latin America the long history of import substitution in manufacturing raised protective barriers against capital intensive manufacturing. Harris and Robertson (1993) reported that 77 percent of total static welfare gains to Latin America from a Western Hemispheric free trade area fell on the manufacturing sector. This view of the "inappropriate capital intensity of developing countries" was summarized by Pack (1988). A set of country studies by Kreuger (1983) emphasized the strong potential employment effects of import substitution which tend to encourage the artificial expansion of capital-intensive sectors.[23]

The alternative to the "new trade theory" view is that suggested by a conventional Heckscher–Ohlin two-factor model. Protection tends to reduce productivity of the export sector. Thus, given the pattern of North–South protection in the Western Hemisphere, a WHFTA would raise the productivity of labour-intensive goods in the South and raise the productivity of capital-intensive exports in the North. Via the Stolper–Samuelson theorem, these effects are reflected in factor prices. A WHFTA integration shock in the Heckscher–Ohlin model should raise real wages in the South and raise real returns to capital in the North. This is referred to as the Heckscher–Ohlin bias in the WHFTA integration shocks. Analytically, all increases in labour productivity are attributed to an improvement in the efficiency of unskilled labour rather than to an increase in the returns to human capital.

The major policy counterfactual investigated is a WHFTA beginning in 1995. The assumed static productivity shock, treated as increases in the τ_ρ, are phased in over five years ending in the year 2000. The interesting characteristic of this model is the strong persistence effect of the integration shocks on both factor allocation across regions and factor accumulation. Increased productivity generally raises income which increases human capital stocks which in turn attract further investment. Biased productivity changes affect factor allocation. Assuming a "new trade theory" bias to the integration-induced productivity shocks, the relative returns to capital in the South increase, and this shifts the share of total investment in the region going to the South during the period in which the liberalization occurs. However, this effect is strongly persistent. Once the share increases, it stays high given that the South now has a larger share of regional GDP and capital stock. In the case of the Heckscher–Ohlin bias, the productivity gains in the South fall on wages rather than returns to capital. This tends to slow down the movement of capital to the South. However, in this case the non-steady-state nature of the model is quite important. The labour force is growing much faster in the South than the North – the relative size of the South labour force almost doubles over the period under consideration. But given that the abundant factor in the South also experiences the productivity growth, this tends to raise income in the South more than if it fell on the other slower-growing factors.

In any case, the long-term effects of integration are substantial and different than the short-term static effects. The results on the "dynamic gain multiplier" are reported in Table 5. The multiplier is defined as change in GDP in a given year relative to the assumed static increase in GDP. For example, if the static effect is 2 percent and the multiplier is 2.0 in 2010, then the interpretation is that, in 2010, GDP in the region will be 4 percent higher than it would have been in the absence of the assumed trade integration shocks. The numbers in Table 5 are based on an assumed 6 percent productivity gain from WHFTA in the South and a 1 percent productivity gain in the North. Y_w denotes aggregate GDP in the Western Hemisphere; Y_n GDP in Canada and the United States; and Y_s the rest of the Hemisphere.[24]

There are a number of interesting features in this table. First, looking at the neutral case, all multipliers are in excess of unity – dynamic gains are all significantly greater than static gains although perhaps not on the order of magnitude that a convergence-type model would suggest. Over time, the multiplier for the

TABLE 5

DYNAMIC PRODUCTIVITY MULTIPLIERS

Year	2000	2005	2010	2015	2020	2025
			Neutral Productivity Shock			
Ys	1.25	1.54	1.78	1.97	2.14	2.28
Yn	1.01	1.04	1.10	1.17	1.23	1.29
Yw	1.21	1.47	1.71	1.94	2.15	2.35
		Biased Productivity Shock: Labor in North and Capital in South				
Ys	1.10	1.41	1.64	1.82	1.98	2.11
Yn	0.72	0.58	0.47	0.38	0.28	0.17
Yw	1.01	1.23	1.42	1.59	1.75	1.89
		Biased Productivity Shock: Capital in North and Labour in South				
Ys	1.17	1.40	1.59	1.74	1.87	1.98
Yn	0.99	1.11	1.25	1.40	1.55	1.69
Yw	1.14	1.38	1.61	1.82	2.02	2.20

Source: Harris (1994), tables M1-M3.

North tends to get lower and, in fact, to get very close to unity after 30 years. There are, however, strong distribution effects if the productivity effects are not neutral. In the case in which the productivity gains fall on capital in the South and labour in the North, the North is a significant "loser" relative to the outlook suggested by static estimates. The reason is simple – investment diversion. The South gets a larger share of total investment in the region, and this is at the expense of the North. On the other hand, in the case that the productivity gains fall on labour in the South and capital in the North, both regions' dynamic gains are much larger, increasing over time. For the region as a whole, real GDP is more than 2.2 times that suggested by static calculations. These results indicate that incorporating dynamic accumulation effects can be quantitatively quite important to the assessments of distribution and efficiency consequences of economic integration. The analysis also suggests that we need to know a lot more about the exact nature of the productivity consequences in order to make a correct dynamic evaluation of a policy change.

SUMMARY: EVALUATION OF THE MODELS

THE MODELS SURVEYED PROVIDE A WIDE RANGE of theoretical and quantitative perspectives on the links between trade and growth. None have yet to exploit micro-economic behavioural mechanisms of endogenous technological change. Even without this complication, however, the potential variety of theories and the associated data and parameter requirements are overwhelming. In the mid-1970s, when applied general equilibrium modelling of trade policy took off, there was a reasonably strong consensus in the profession that the static neoclassical general equilibrium model was the appropriate policy "workhorse." It met the joint requirements of:

- coming from a well-understood and plausible theoretical framework;
- providing an accounting framework for data collection; and
- having feasible requirements for most parameters.

These features led to its rapid and widespread adoption. This is certainly not the case in 1995 with respect to growth models. The field is characterized by investigators employing a wide variety of theoretical frameworks in which to address long-term dynamic issues. Until we have a more decisive rejection of some of these theories, or greater consensus on which of the mechanisms for growth are the most important, this state of affairs is unlikely to change.

CONCLUSION

IT IS DIFFICULT TO DRAW STRONG CONCLUSIONS from the body of work surveyed here, however compelling it may seem to resolve these issues. While economists have long argued that the dynamic effects of trade liberalization are much larger than static efficiency effects, the empirical basis for such a claim must be regarded as speculative. It seems that the best that one can say is that, with regard to the medium- and long-term dynamic effects of economic integration, much remains to be learned. This uneasiness reflects the inadequate empirical foundations for existing growth theory and its links to trade and integration issues. Let me catalogue what I think are some tentative conclusions of a field very much in a state of flux.

1. Much of the empirical evidence amassed on growth in the last decade and a half relies on the postwar experience of a large number of present and former developing countries. While many view such evidence as supportive of the basic neoclassical growth model, it is clear that it is inadequate as an appropriate model of productivity growth of countries at the frontier. There is still no strong consensus as to the relative importance of human capital, investment or domestic research and development, nor how they interact with international trade in the determination of growth rates.

2. There is a strong empirical argument for taking the view that increased trade liberalization causes faster economic growth. This is supported by historical, statistical and counterfactual evidence. The exact micro-economic mechanisms by which openness affects growth, however, are not clear. Again, much of the evidence presented in favour of this view comes from countries which started behind the technological frontiers.

3. Analytically, it appears that accommodating the long-term dynamics of factor accumulation into models of economic integration leads inevitably to an explicit analysis of very long transitions between steady states,

often on the order of four to five decades or more. This apparently robust finding puts a much larger burden on modellers' justifications of the dynamic structures used in their models, and the appropriateness of assumed responses of investment, education and wealth to changes in relative prices and income.

4. It appears that dynamic effects are potentially much larger than the typical static efficiency effects derived from existing trade policy models. This is true across a wide class of models, even the most basic neoclassical growth model. However, it is also possible that while efficiency effects of policy are large, so are the distributional consequences. This necessarily makes welfare evaluation of policy that much more difficult, but also both valuable and necessary.

5. The research program on endogenous technological change within multi-country general equilibrium frameworks is still in its infancy. There are a number of highly stylized theoretical models in the literature, but there is no consensus on which of these is the most appropriate, or how they might be usefully calibrated to real world economies. Things are moving fast, and this situation may change within the next few years. In the meantime, the best historical and micro-economic evidence that is available should be used in order to frame policy decisions directed toward economic integration.

ENDNOTES

1 Baldwin (1989) provides a survey of this discussion.

2 Howitt this volume discusses some of this evidence.

3 For recent surveys, see Edwards (1993) and Harrison (1991).

4 Theory also suggests that population growth and resource degradation should appear in this equation (see Brander, 1992). However, the bulk of the literature neither deals with these variables nor finds them to be significant.

5 The knowledge gap is approximated in two ways. In the initial (1970) level of real GDP, the equation looks much like the conventional convergence equation. The other estimate of technological gap is the number of engineers engaged in R&D per thousand inhabitants. The problem, of course, is that it may be a better proxy for the measure of technological absorptive capacity rather than the gap itself.

6 The underlying dynamics of income levels are assumed to be motivated by the slow diffusion of average practice technology. This is slightly different than the hypothesis that best-practice technology diffuses.

7 There is, of course, a great deal presumed in this particular description of technology. It is quite possible, for example, that countries' micro-production structures at the industry level could be identical and yet the aggregate value added functions of different countries, when viewed as Cobb–Douglas approximations, could be quite different for a variety of reasons, e.g., different industry compositions, different relative price structures, different resource and human capital endowments, and so forth. Some corrections are made for basic differences in price levels by using the now standard method of correcting for

PPP differences in measuring real GDP and capital stocks. To be honest, however, this criticism is true of the bulk of the work on international productivity comparisons.

8   It is often argued that investment contributes to convergence through the embodied transfer of knowledge in capital goods. To test this, Helliwell added average gross investment rates to equation (12) and found that it added little to the explanation power. This is in sharp contrast to much of the literature on growth and openness in which investment rates usually figure prominently as the explanatory variable.

9   The Rebelo model generates endogenous growth because the capital goods producing sector is linear in the reproducible factors. In Lee's model, investment goods are produced according to a linear technology I=aK and thus generate endogenous growth. The two-sector trade framework is very close to the famous Oniki–Uzawa (1965) model.

10 To take account of simultaneity between import of capital and other structural characteristics of the economy, (13) is estimated with 2SLS using the following variables for instruments: land size (resources), distance from trade partners (the gravity model) and tariff rates. Imported capital goods are approximated by using OECD export data to individual countries. Domestic investment is computed by subtracting imported investment from total investment adjusting for relative price effects by using the PPP-adjusted current international price in Summers and Heston (1991).

11 When the model is applied to only the OECD countries, the sign on capital imports is negative and insignificant.

12 This model, therefore, is much different than the dynamic general equilibrium models used in the public finance literature. In that literature, all functional forms and benchmarking are done to ensure the existence of a balanced growth steady-state benchmark. See Ballard, Fullerton, Shoven and Whalley (1985), for example.

13 Even though the model relies on a framework involving a single infinitely lived utility-maximizing consumer, no welfare numbers are reported. One suspects that, as in much of the dynamic tax literature, these numbers are extremely small (ratios of equivalent variations to the present value of future consumption or GNP) given the effect of discounting.

14 The equilibrium concept is that of a conventional, perfect foresight, competitive equilibrium under certainty. The model is calibrated under a steady-state assumption. Technological change and population growth are constant and exogenous. All preferences are homothetic, and all production functions are constant returns to scale. The model permits a well-defined balanced growth steady-state solution and is calibrated rather than estimated, which is not surprising given its fairly detailed structure. An unfortunate aspect of the empirical calibration of the model is that parameter values for the rest of the world are completely ad hoc having been generated by using a strong symmetry assumption, i.e., the United States faces a rest of the world that is the same size and structure as itself. This greatly reduces the empirical relevance of the multilateral policy simulations.

15 Unfortunately, Gould and Eichengreen do not report any results on growth rates but, given the relative magnitude of the welfare results, these are not likely to be large.

16 See Emerson, et al. (1991).

17 It is worth pointing out that some of the big gains reported in the Cecchini Report (1988) on EC 1992 were constructed using these types of price dispersion data. If one assumes, for example, that all observed prices would move to the lowest price in the distribution, and real expenditure on each good remains constant, then the estimated "gain" calculated as a reduction in consumer expenditures, comes to as much as

8.3 percent of GDP. This "gain," however, is not a true welfare gain since producer losses are not netted out against consumer gains.

18 Truncating the horizon of a dynamic model is an old trick used by modellers. It always has the problem of requiring a method of valuing the capital stock left at the end of the last period.

19 It is important to note that these percentages are calculated using formula (16) which is, strictly speaking, only a linear approximation. With changes in the capital stock between the benchmark and the shock potentially getting quite large, there is reason to be worried about the accuracy of this type of approximation method.

20 An objection to Ben-David's procedure is that the convergence observed in Europe, post 1955, reflects in part the restoration of pre-World War II capital stocks. Ben-David tested for this and found little evidence for pre-war convergence among the EC countries. The reader should also be cautioned against confusing convergence of one country's income level to another (the sense in which convergence is used in this paper) with convergence toward a higher steady-state level of income, another common use of the term.

21 This procedure can only be justified as an approximation, given that the changes in relative prices which accompany trade reform conditions for exact aggregation across sectors cannot be satisfied. The aggregate production function, however, is useful in that it provides a convenient way of keeping track of both factor price changes in response to changes in aggregate inputs as well as shifts in production possibilities due to trade reform.

22 In models with imperfect competition and economies of scale, import protection tends to reduce the absolute productivity of all factors used in the protected sector. See Harris (1985). The bias assumed here is that the reduction in efficiency falls entirely on the factor used intensively in the protected sector.

23 In a sample of eight countries, for example, Krueger found that, with a fixed capital stock, a shift away from an import substitution strategy could increase employment by an average of 47 percent. In the model described here, employment is viewed as exogenous but clearly, the move away from protection of capital intensive sectors would raise productivity substantially.

24 The multipliers are fairly similar for wide variations in the magnitude of the static gains.

ACKNOWLEDGEMENTS

THE AUTHOR IS GRATEFUL to the conference discussants and audience for comments on an earlier draft. All views expressed and errors are the sole responsibility of the author.

BIBLIOGRAPHY

Abramovitz, M. "The Catch-Up Factor in Postwar Economic Growth." *Economic Inquiry.* Vol. 28, (1990): 1-18.

Balassa, B. "Development strategies and economic performance." In *Developing strategies in semi-industrialized economies.* Edited by B. Balassa. London: Oxford University Press, 1982.

Baldwin, R. "The Growth Effects of 1992." *Economic Policy.* October 1989.

———. "Measurable Dynamic Gains From Trade." *Journal of Political Economy.* Vol. 100, No. 1, (1992): 162-174.

Ballard, C., D. Fullerton, J.B. Shoven and J. Whalley. *A General Equilibrium Model for Tax Policy Evaluation*. Chicago: Chicago University Press, 1985.

Barro, R.J. and X. Sala-i-Martin. "Convergence." *Journal of Political Economy*. 100, (2), (1992): 223.

Ben-David, D. "Equalizing Exchange: Trade Liberalization and Income Convergence." *Quarterly Journal of Economics*. Vol. 108, (1993): 653-679.

Brander, J. "Innis Lecture: Comparative Economic Growth: Evidence and Intrepretation." *Canadian Journal of Economics*. 25, (1992): 792-818.

Cecchini, Paolo, et al. *European Challenge, 1992: The benefits of a single market*. European Community Monograph. Brookfield: Gower Publishing Company, 1988.

Choski, A., Michaely and Papageorgiou. *Trade liberalization episodes*. Oxford: Basil Blackwell, 1991.

Collins, S. and W. Park. "External debt and macroeconomic performance in South Korea." NBER Working Paper No. 2596, Cambridge, MA, 1988.

De Long, J. Bradford and Lawrence H. Summers. "Equipment Investment and Economic Growth." *Quarterly Journal of Economics*. 106, (1991): 445-502.

Deardorff, A and R.M. Stern. *The Michigan Model of World Production and Trade*. Cambridge, MA: MIT Press, 1986.

Edwards, S. "Trade orientation, distortions and growth in developing countries." *Journal of Development Economics*. 39, (1992): 31-57.

——."Openness, Trade Liberalization, and Growth in Developing Countries." *Journal of Economic Literature*. XXI, 3, (1993): 1358-1393.

Emerson, M., et al. *The Economics of 1992*. Oxford: Oxford University Press, 1991.

Feder, G. "On Exports and Economic Growth." *Journal of Development Economics*. (1989): 59-73.

Goulder, L. and B. Eichengreen. "Trade liberalization in general equilibrium: intertemporal and inter-industry effects." *Canadian Journal of Economics*. XXV No. 2, (1992): 253-280.

Greenaway, D. and D. Sapsford. "What Does Liberalisation Do for Exports and Growth." *Weltwirtschaftliches Archiv*. Band 130, Heft 1, (1994): 152-173.

Grossman, G.M. and E. Helpman. *Innovation and Growth in the Global Economy*. Cambridge, MA: MIT Press, 1991.

Gundlach, E. "Accounting for the Stock of Human Capital: Selected Evidence and Potential Implications." *Weltwirtschaftliches Archiv*. Band 130, Heft 2, (1994): 350-371.

Harris, R.G. "Human Capital and the Dynamic Gains from Economic Integration." Discussion Paper 95-3, Department of Economics, Simon Fraser University, Burnaby, B.C., 1994.

——. *Trade, Industrial Policy and Canadian Manufacturing*. Ontario Economic Council, 1985.

Harris, R.G. and P. Robertson. "Free Trade in the Americas: Estimates of the Impact of a Western Hemispheric Free Trade Area." Canadian Institute for Advanced Research Working Paper, Harbour Centre, Simon Fraser University, Vancouver, Canada, 1993.

Harrison, A. "Openness and Growth: A Time-Series, Cross-Country Analysis for Developing Countries." World Bank Policy Research Working Paper WPS809, Washington, 1991.

Havrylyshyn, O. "Trade Policy and Productivity Gains in Developing Countries." *The World Bank Observer*. Vol. 5, No. 1, (1990): 1-24.

Helliwell, John F. and Alan Chung. "Tri-polar Growth and Real Exchange Rates: How Much Can be Explained by Convergence?" In *A Quest for a More Stable World Economic System*. Edited by L.R. Klein, C. Moriguchi and A. Amano. New York: Kluwer, 1992.

Helliwell, John F. "Trade and Technical Progress." In *Economic Growth and the Structure of Long-Term-Development*. Edited by L.L. Pasinetti and R.M. Solow. St. Martin's Press, International Economic Association, 1994a, pp. 253-271.

——. "International Growth Linkages: Evidence From Asia and the OECD." In *Macroeconomic Linkage: Savings, Exchange Rates, and Capital Flows*. Edited by T. Ito and A.O. Krueger. Chicago: University of Chicago Press, 1994b, pp. 7-28.

Ho, M.S. and D.W. Jorgenson. "Trade Policy and U.S. Economic Growth." *Journal of Policy Modeling*. 16 (2), (1994): 119-146.

Jung, W.S. and P.J. Marshall. "Exports, Growth and Causality in Developing Countries." *Journal of Development Economics*. 18 (1), (1985):1-12.

Kreuger, A. *Trade and Employment in Developing Countries: Synthesis and Conclusions*. Chicago: University of Chicago Press, 1983.

Leamer, E.E. "Measures of Openness." In *Trade Policy Issues and Empirical Analysis*. Edited by R.E. Baldwin. Chicago: University of Chicago Press, 1988.

Lee, Jong-Wha. "Capital Goods Imports and Long Run Growth." NBER Working Paper No. 4725, Cambridge, MA, April 1994.

Levine, Ross and David Renelt. "A Sensitivity Analysis of Cross-Country Growth Regressions." *American Economic Review*. 82, (1992): 942-963.

Lucas, R.E. "On the mechanics of economic development." *Journal of Monetary Economics*. 22, (1988): 3-42.

——. "Why Doesn't Capital Flow from Rich to Poor Countries?" *American Economic Review*. Vol. 90, (1990): 92-96.

Mercenier, J. and B Akitoby. "On Intertemporal General-Equilibrium Reallocation Effects of Europe's Move to a Single Market." Institute for Empirical Macroeconomics, Discussion Paper No. 87, Federal Reserve Bank of Minneapolis, 1993.

Michaely, M. "Exports and growth: An empirical investigation." *Journal of Development Economics*. 1, (1993): 49-53.

Mun S. Ho and D.W. Jorgenson. "Trade policy and U.S. economic growth." *Journal of Policy Modeling*. 16, (2), (1994): 119-146.

Oniki, H. and H. Uzawa. "Patterns of Trade and Investment in a Dynamic Model of International Trade." *Review of Economic Studies*. 32, (1965): 15-38.

Pack, H. "Industrialization and Trade." In *Handbook of Development Economics*. Vol. 1. Edited by H. Chenery and T.N. Srinivisan. New York: North Holland, 1988.

Rebelo, Sergio. "Long Run Policy Analysis and Long Run Growth." *Journal of Political Economy*. 98, (1990): 500-521.

Rivera-Batiz, L.A. and P. Romer. "Economic Integration and Endogenous Growth." *Quarterly Journal of Economics*. Vol. CVI (2), (May 1991): 531-556.

Romer, Paul. "Human Capital and Growth: Theory and Evidences." *Carnegie-Rochester Conference Series on Public Policy*. 1990.

Sachs, J. "Trade and exchange rate policies in growth-oriented adjustment programs." In *Growth-oriented adjustment programs*. Edited by V. Corbo, M. Goldstein and M. Khan. Washington, DC: International Monetary Fund and the World Bank, 1987.

Scitovsky, T.D. *Economic Theory and Western European Economic Integration*. Stanford: Stanford University Press, 1958.

Smith, A. and A. J. Venables. "Completing the internal market in the European Community: some industry estimates." *European Economic Review*. 32, (1988): 1501-1525.

Summers, R. and A. Heston. "A New Set of International Comparisons of Real Product and Prices: Estimates for 130 Countries, 1950 to 1985." *Review of Income and Wealth*. Vol. 34, (1988): 1-25.

———. "The Penn World Tables (Mark 5): An Expanded Set of International Comparisons, 1950-1968." *The Quarterly Journal of Economics*. (May 1991): 327-365.

United Nations. *World Demographic Estimates and Projections, 1950-2025*. 1988.

———. *Human Development Report*. Oxford University Press, 1992.

Whalley, J. *Trade Liberalization Among Major World Trading Areas*. Cambridge MA: MIT Press, 1985.

World Bank. *World Development Report*. Washington, DC: World Bank, 1987.

———. *World Development Report*. Washington, DC: World Bank, 1991a.

———. *World Tables*. Washington, DC: World Bank, 1991b.

Young, A.W. "Learning by Doing and the Dynamic Effects of International Trade." *Quarterly Journal of Economics*. Vol. 106, (1991): 369-405.

Comment

James A. Brander
Faculty of Commerce
University of British Columbia

INTRODUCTION

RICHARD HARRIS HAS PROVIDED A VERY VALUABLE SURVEY of recent research on the relationship between economic integration and economic growth. I started my deliberations by asking myself how this paper fit into the overall theme of the conference: "Implications of Knowledge-Based Growth for Micro-Economic Policies." On reflection, it seems to me that the question that links the paper and the conference topic could be expressed as follows: how should our understanding of "knowledge-based growth" affect public policy toward international trade, international investment and international integration?

One inference to be drawn from the Harris paper is that we are not yet in a position to say much about this question, and I must concur. However, there is a good deal of interesting research that seeks to explain the causes of economic growth and to understand the role of international trade and related policies.

SOURCES OF ECONOMIC GROWTH

ONE WAY OF APPROACHING THE STUDY of economic growth is by starting with a production function of the following form:

$$Q = Q(K,L,H,R,A;\mu) \tag{1}$$

where Q is output; K is capital; L is labour; H is human capital; R is natural resources (including land); A is the state of technological progress; and μ is a "catch-all" variable that represents, among other things, various policy instruments and exogenous shocks. Presumably, we are interested in the growth of some measure of real income. Thus, as shown in Brander and Dowrick (1994), we can take derivatives and divide through by population to obtain a representation of changes in per capita income.

Carrying out this exercise yields several factors that might be viewed as explanatory variables for per capita real income growth. These factors are:

1. changes in the state of technology;
2. changes in human capital;
3. changes in capital per worker (investment);
4. changes in labour per capita (changes in participation or dependency);
5. changes in natural resources per worker;
6. returns to scale; and
7. changes in policy variables (including trade policies).

Broadly speaking, items one and two would be viewed as knowledge-based sources of growth, whereas items three through seven would be other sources of growth. However, item three (investment), as measured in any data set, will consist largely of investments that embody improved technology. Therefore, in real data, much of what is attributed to investment would also be reasonably viewed as knowledge-based growth. Including item seven as a direct explanatory variable suggests that policy variables might have a direct impact on growth. What I have in mind is that policy can affect the efficiency with which factors of production are used. In addition, policy variables may have an impact through their effect on other variables. Thus, for example, trade liberalization may speed up technological progress or increase investment. Indeed, presumably the central point of interest of this conference is the indirect effect of policy on growth through its effect on items one, two and three of my list.

One important type of research is cross-country regression analysis. Typically, regression equations similar to equation (5) in the Harris paper are estimated using data contained in the Penn World Tables, as developed by Robert Summers and Alan Heston in conjunction with the U.N. Income Comparison Project. The current version is PWT5.6 (1995), which has just recently been made available.[1]

My view of this cross-country regression analysis is not very different from the views expressed by Harris, but there are a few points I would like to make. First, as Harris indicates (correctly), growth economists tend to emphasize the first three items on the above list and do not pay much attention to items four and five, which are essentially demographic variables. I think that growth economists are making a serious error by not focusing on these factors.

LABOUR FORCE PARTICIPATION

CONSIDER ITEM FOUR, LABOUR FORCE PARTICIPATION. Brander and Dowrick (1994) found that changes in labour force participation (or, more accurately, reductions in the dependency ratio) are highly significant in explaining cross-country variations in per capita real income growth. Young (1994) focused on the postwar growth of Hong Kong, Singapore, South Korea and Taiwan and found that reductions in dependency explained a large part of the rapid economic growth of these countries. For example, GDP per capita in Singapore grew by 6.6 percent per year from 1966 to 1990, but GDP per worker grew by 4 percent per year. Thus, increasing labour force participation accounted for 2.6 percent annualized per capita growth.

In general, in the rapidly growing East Asian countries, there has been a remarkable demographic transition. Between the 1950s and the present, birth rates have fallen from 45 to 50 per 1000 to under 20 per 1000, despite an increase in the relative number of women of childbearing age. As a result, the number of children has been falling relative to the number of workers, giving a sharp boost to per capita real income growth. This is clearly a transitory effect, in that labour force participation will stop increasing at some point in the near future, but it can be important over a 30-year to 40-year period. In sub-Sahara Africa, on the other hand, dependency ratios actually rose during the 1980s, contributing to the decline in per capita income experienced there.

NATURAL RESOURCE DILUTION

ITEM FIVE, CHANGES IN NATURAL RESOURCES PER WORKER, is harder to investigate as we have few reliable aggregate measures of natural resources. However, I suspect that it is likely to be a very important factor in restraining economic growth over the next few decades. As we all know, over the last decade fish stocks per capita have fallen dramatically around the world. I believe the evidence is also very clear that declines in resources per worker have contributed significantly to real income declines in Africa.

For example, the Ivory Coast experienced significant increases in real income during the 1970s as harvesting of hardwood lumber expanded enormously, and unsustainably. As the stock of tropical hardwood declined, harvests eventually fell, and in the early 1990s were about 10 percent of levels in the 1970s. As hardwood exports are the main source of foreign exchange earnings in the Ivory Coast, this has been an important factor in the 50 percent decline in per capita real income that has occurred there since the mid-1970s. Current population growth rates in Africa are certainly the highest that have ever been reliably recorded for any region in the world, and this is clearly putting downward pressure on real incomes.

While discussing resource dilution, I would like to make a related point about the relationship between trade, technological progress and renewable resources. Many renewable resources, such as forests and land, have incomplete property rights. The extreme case is complete open access. Brander and Taylor (1995) have modelled the effect of technological progress and trade liberalization on open-access renewable resources. Improvements in harvesting technology for such a resource normally reduce steady-state welfare. Essentially, the open-access resource is already subject to excessive exploitation and technological progress. Harvesting only magnifies this market failure. Continuing improvements in harvesting technology will eventually cause the resource to be extinguished. This accurately describes what happened to passenger pigeons, blue whales and many specific areas of forest and agricultural land.

One striking point about resource dilution is that it is likely to have its impact relatively quickly. In 1950, there were about 2.5 billion people in the world. The human consumption chain accounted for a relatively small share, perhaps 15 percent, of the world's biomass. Compared to the scope of the natural world, humans could have been viewed as minor in importance. In one sense, the world was "empty." Currently, with a world population approaching six billion, the human consumption chain uses over 40 percent of the world's biomass, and the world is rapidly becoming "full." A naive extrapolation of current population growth rates would imply a world population of about 12 billion halfway through the next century, although it is hard to imagine how such a population could be accommodated without major technological breakthroughs. Thus, while resource dilution effects are hard to observe in past data, they may become very important very soon.

EDUCATION AND HUMAN CAPITAL

IN CROSS-COUNTRY REGRESSIONS, education often emerges as an important variable. However, one must be careful about attributing causality. Education, is in part, a consumption good. Furthermore, it is a good with a high income elasticity. As income rises, people demand more education. If we observe that growth in real income is correlated with increases in education, either cross sectionally or in a time series, some of this correlation is due to the endogeneity of education. Therefore, it is wrong to interpret the coefficient on education in a regression equation like equation (5) in Harris as reflecting a causal effect of education on real income growth. The same problem arises with most of the other variables on the list, including investment and fertility. In order to deal with these endogeneity problems, it is important to exploit the time series dimension of panel data sets like PWT5.6. For example, Brander and Dowrick (1994) were able to establish that declines in fertility precede increases in income growth, which makes us more confident about the direction of causality for this variable.

I would also like to draw attention to the frequently made point that not all types of education are equal. For example, Murphy, Schliefer and Vishny (1991) suggested (using some empirical information) that education in law and humanities is much less effective in contributing to economic growth than education in engineering and sciences. Magee, Brock and Young (1989) went further and suggested that legal education, in particular, has negative effects on growth. Another important distinction is between formal education (e.g., in schools) on the one hand and apprenticeship and on-the-job training on the other. Very probably, there is an "optimal" mix of formal education and on-the-job training, but this will be a difficult problem to solve empirically. Certainly, just putting years of schooling in a cross-country regression is going to miss much of the importance of getting educational policy right.

CONVERGENCE AND TECHNOLOGY TRANSFER

IF TECHNOLOGICAL PROGRESS IS IMPORTANT, then technology transfer should also be important. Anecdotal reports of specific industries, such as the microwave industry in South Korea, suggest, for example, that reverse engineering played an important role in Korean economic growth. If technology transfer is easier than primary innovation, then we might expect to see countries "catching-up" with technological leaders over time. This is the convergence hypothesis. To me, the striking thing about convergence is that it hasn't occurred. As reported in Dowrick (1992), real income in the world has diverged over the last 25 years. This is what Harris would refer to as unconditional divergence (i.e., without correcting for other variables). The stylized fact, of course, is that East Asia has converged on the Organization for Economic Co-operation and Development (OECD) countries, Latin America has grown at approximately the same rate (from a much lower base) as the OECD, and Africa has fallen further behind. Within the OECD, there has been some convergence. As we observe East Asian real income converging on OECD levels, it seems clear that an important part of the story is technology transfer. But why has this been restricted to East Asia? To me, that is the major question. One can "observe" conditional convergence in the data by including enough variables in the regression. In particular, openness has an effect similar to a dummy variable for the rapidly growing East Asian economies, and education has an effect similar to a dummy variable for sub-Sahara Africa.

INTERNATIONAL OPENNESS

THE KEY ISSUE ADDRESSED BY HARRIS is whether international trade, international openness and economic integration affect economic growth. Second, to the extent that these things affect growth, do they work through knowledge-based sources, such as technology transfer, or do they arise from changes in the efficiency of resource allocation of the type normally associated with trade liberalization? Harris reviews this literature very effectively, but I would like to raise a couple of points not emphasized by Harris.

First, there are many different types of international openness, each of which may have different effects on growth in general and knowledge-based growth in particular. It might be useful to list major activities subject to variations in openness:

    i)   international trade
    ii) international (real) investment
    iii) international financial transactions
    iv) international migration
    v)   international communication.

Most analysis has focused on items i) and ii). To assess the role of international trade, the standard empirical approach is to regress some measure of growth on the amount or proportion of international trade. The main point I wish to make here is that I find any monotonic specification (including the usual linear specification) to be hard to understand. Presumably, the best that can be done with international trade is to exhaust all possible gains from trade. This suggests that, conditional on particular values of other variables, there is an amount of trade that is just "right." There could be too little, but there could also be too much. One might argue that, as an empirical matter, there has always been a consistent bias against trade, so that all our observations are in the region where trade is less than it "should" be. However, even if this is true, I think it is important for economists to avoid the more is better trap in their discussions, if not in their econometric specifications.

Also, I might note that Brander and Taylor (1995) showed that countries that export products based on renewable resources tend to experience steady-state losses from trade liberalization if those renewable resources are subject to incomplete property rights. In essence, trade worsens the market failure associated with open access to a resource. Quite a few countries seem to have suffered from this problem, as trade liberalization leads to excessive exploitation of a resource.

Of the other items listed above, the least-studied is almost certainly international communication. I am referring here to private communication (e-mail, telephone, etc.) as well as to broadcast communication (TV). Subjective empiricism (i.e., thinking about what I do) suggests that the effects of international communication links may be very important in influencing knowledge-based growth.

There is an important distinction between international openness and economic integration. Typically, economic integration, as in the European Union (EU), includes increases in openness within the group, but it also includes harmonization and standardization of regulation and various areas of policy. In addition, of course, linkages with the rest of the world may become more or less open, depending on the nature of the integration agreement. The standardization problem is reminiscent of the optimum currency area literature which suggests that there is an optimal geographical range for any given policy instrument. Thus, for example, can the extent of harmonization in the EU go too far in imposing harmonized regulation given underlying heterogeneity?

CONCLUDING REMARKS

IN ECONOMICS, AS IN ALL RESEARCH ACTIVITIES, there are two primary sources of knowledge (or at least educated belief). One source is theoretical: our beliefs about a particular situation are built up from logical inference based on underlying axioms or principles that we take as plausible. The other source is empirical or inductive, and is based on finding empirical regularities in repeated observation of similar situations. Ideally, theoretical and empirical knowledge would coincide, as when we have a theory, derive testable implications of the theory and find that empirical observation is consistent with those implications. Usually, the situation is not so rosy. We may lack sound theoretical-based expectations or we may lack empirical knowledge. Occasionally, we lack both.

I think the area described by the Harris paper is an area where we lack both empirical and theoretical knowledge. First, our theoretically based understanding of the relationship between economic integration and growth is very equivocal, in the sense that basic widely accepted economic models or principles do not give clear predictions. Second, while we have quite a few examples of economic integration to consider, each case is so idiosyncratic that it is hard to assert the existence of reliable stylized facts. At this stage, economists should be modest about claims concerning the effects of economic integration.

To reinforce this point, I would like to draw attention to recent intellectual history. The late 1950s and early 1960s gave rise to the first flowering of growth theory, in which the study of economic growth was a high priority and high prestige activity for a variety of economists ranging from abstract theorists to very applied development economists. Despite this attention, I have encountered no inkling in the literature of this period of the remarkable growth experience that the world was about to embark on. I am referring to the fact that beginning in the 1960s, a number of East Asian economies were beginning a growth trajectory that was completely unprecedented in recorded world history, resulting in real incomes rising by factors of five or six in a single generation (i.e., in 30 years). However, another major part of the world, sub-Sahara Africa, has been in a state of actual economic decline for much of this period. Yet if one goes back to the literature of the early 1960s, there is, if anything, optimism about Africa and pessimism about East Asia.

This caution is not intended to be nihilistic. Economics is a powerful discipline with many successes to its credit. We know some things about growth. Wars retard economic growth; political stability promotes it. Central planning appears to have a negative effect while markets have a positive effect. I would argue that high fertility levels also have a negative impact while fertility declines are positive. However, my overall view is that understanding economic growth in general, and its interaction with economic integration, in particular, is a challenging problem.

I have undoubtedly said too much about my pet areas of interest and less about the details of the Harris paper than I should have. Let me conclude, however, by reiterating my opening comment that the paper is a very valuable and insightful review. I found his review of his own recent work on human capital and the dynamic gains from integration to be particularly interesting and promising as an area of research.

ENDNOTE

1   I might note in passing that it is rare in economics that the collection of a data set serves as the starting point of a major research area, but that has happened in this case. During the 1960s and 1970s, Robert Summers was in the shadow of his famous brother Paul Samuelson and, in the 1980s, was overshadowed by his son, Larry Summers. However, the 1990s have definitely been Robert Summers' decade.

BIBLIOGRAPHY

Brander, J. and S. Dowrick. "The role of fertility and population in economic growth." *Journal of Population Economics*. Vol. 7, (1994): pp. 1-25.

Brander, J. and S. Taylor. "International Trade and Open Access Renewable Resources: the Small Open Economy Case." Discussion Paper No. 5021. Cambridge MA: NBER, 1995.

Dowrick, S. "Technological catch up and diverging incomes: patterns of economic growth 1960-88." *Economic Journal*. 102, (1992): 600-610.

Magee, S., W. Brock and L. Young. *Black Hole Tariffs and Endogenous Policy Theory*. Cambridge: Cambridge University Press, 1989.

Murphy, K., A. Schliefer and R. Vishny. "The allocation of talent: implications for growth." *Quarterly Journal of Economics*. 106, (1991): pp. 503-530.

Summers, R. and A. Heston. *Penn World Tables*. Version 5.6. Cambridge, MA: NBER, 1995.

Young, A. "The Tyranny of Numbers; Confronting the Statistical Realities of the East Asian Growth Experience." Discussion Paper No. 4680. Cambridge MA: NBER, 1994.

John Whalley
Department of Economics
University of Warwick

5

Interprovincial Barriers to Trade and Endogenous Growth Considerations

INTRODUCTION

WITH VARYING DEGREES OF INTENSITY, interprovincial barriers to trade have been an issue of policy focus in Canada for the last 20 years or more. The 1994 Agreement on Internal Trade (Government of Canada, 1994) sought to use a GATT-like mechanism, including general rules and a dispute settlement procedure, to both restrain and lower internal barriers. Claims of significant gains to the Canadian economy – as much as 1 percent of Gross Domestic Product (GDP) or $7 billion annually – accompanied the release of the 1994 agreement.

In 1983, I published two pieces in an Ontario Economic Council volume (Trebilcock, Whalley, Rogerson and Ness, 1983) in which I characterized the internal barriers issue as akin to a tempest in a teacup. I argued that the large majority of manufactured products flow freely across provincial borders in Canada, that provincial barriers tend to be product or instrument concentrated (beer, agriculture, procurement, professional licensing, transportation regulation) and that several of these barriers impinge on a relatively small base. (In the procurement case, for instance, provincial government expenditures are heavily labour intensive.) Theoretically, it is even possible for interprovincial barriers to be welfare improving, if they offset the artificial stimulus to interprovincial trade from national protection, such as the tariff. The range of estimates I suggested for the annual costs of interprovincial barriers were much smaller than the 1994 government estimates, perhaps one tenth to one fifth of 1 percent of GDP, but with high variance since key parameters, such as elasticities in interprovincial trade, were (and still are) not estimated.

In this paper, my goal is to review these earlier calculations in light of developments since the early 1980s but, more important, in light of recent literature on endogenous growth to see if there are arguments explaining why larger effects may be expected for this subsequent agreement. Between the early 1980s and mid-1990s, not that much happened to change either the relative size or composition of interprovincial trade in the national economy or the structure or significance of interprovincial trade barriers. I also suggest that the substance of the 1994 agreement remains to be proven, since in key areas, such as agriculture, it establishes a process for new negotiation rather than for direct agreement.

I also note that some of the endogenous growth literature, such as King and Rebelo (1990) and Perroni (1993), is revising upward, the estimates of the impact of certain policy changes by taking into account knowledge-based spillovers and externalities. However, these are mainly tax policy changes with dynamic distortions involving savings and investment, and are more likely to experience significant upward revisions of their effects than is the case with intercommodity distortions, as typically occur with trade barriers. Indeed, as Young (1991) has argued, endogenous growth-type spillover effects can even provide an argument as to why autarky in some regions may be preferred to free trade. Moreover, there is little evidence to support the notion that significant unappropriated knowledge-based spillovers occur in the key industries or areas affected by interregional barriers (beer, agriculture, professional services, trucking). There seems to be no compelling argument that, on endogenous growth grounds, estimates of the costs of interprovincial barriers should be revised sharply upward,[1] and removing interprovincial barriers could even be undesirable on endogenous growth grounds.

Thus, endogenous growth considerations add noise to the discussion of interregional trade barriers but, for now, it is ill-focused noise – neither large nor small noise, amplifying nor dampening noise, nor even sign-reinforcing noise. Given the uncertainties of elasticities and data in early estimates, we seem to be even less certain of the effects due to such considerations, even though there appears to be no clear presumption that the mean value rather than the variance of previous central case estimates has markedly changed.

INTERREGIONAL BARRIERS AND THEIR EFFECTS

BARRIERS, AS IN INTERREGIONAL (OR INTERPROVINCIAL) TRADE BARRIERS, or just barriers, is an umbrella term used in Canadian policy discussion to capture a variety of regulations used by provincial governments or their agencies which either directly or indirectly affect interprovincial flows of goods, services and factors. It is important, however, to elaborate a little on what the term implies. It does not capture border measures, as with international trade barriers, since no barriers physically exist at the borders between provinces. Instead, most of the barriers at issue rise from various forms of within-province preference, entry impediments or differential regulations which operate as part of provincial policies administered within provincial economies. Insofar as they affect consumption and/or production within a province, most provincial policies have some effects on interprovincial trade flows. For this reason the term, "interprovincial barriers," is usually reserved for those elements of policy which are discriminatory in treating products or suppliers, either from within or outside the province, differently. Finally, the term, as generally used, covers interprovincial flows of goods, services and factors. The impacts of discriminatory provincial policies on both labour and capital flows between provinces is part of the policy debate on interprovincial barriers.

TABLE 1

MAIN INTERPROVINCIAL TRADE BARRIERS

1. Provincial Government Procurement Policies
- Most provinces in the early 1980s gave some form of preference to local suppliers when sourcing government purchases.
- Newfoundland had a local-suppliers-wherever-possible policy; Quebec had a policy of accepting Quebec bids, even if higher, if acceptance promoted Quebec development; Alberta required evidence of maximum use of Albertan inputs; other provinces had related policies.

2. Transport Regulation
- Provinces control activities of trucking firms within-province, even though firms conduct business beyond provincial boundaries.
- Six areas where barriers arise: economic regulation (rates, entry), registration requirements, weights and dimension regulations, safety restrictions, enforcement, fuel taxes.

3. Provincial Liquor Policies
- Preferences to local products through marketing practices of provincial liquor commissions: better advertising support for local products, advantageous positioning of local products in outlets, less-stringent listing requirements, preferential pricing policies.
- Use of unique packaging requirements, making it too costly for out-of-province suppliers to enter local markets.
- Limits on private purchases from other provinces, either through a quota system or by levying taxes on such products.

4. Agricultural Policies
- Three instruments of provincial agricultural policies affect interprovincial trade flows: agricultural marketing boards, agricultural support programs and restrictive product standards or regulations.
- Supply management boards at national level involve market-sharing production quotas. Provincial boards control where and how producers can market their products.
- Direct aid and promotional support to farmers within provinces affect interprovincial trade flows.
- Packaging and labelling standards by province also impede interprovincial trade flows.

5. Provincial Resource Policies
- Controls on in-province processing, different mining taxes and resource royalties within provinces affect rates of provincial resource flows.

6. Preferential Hiring Practices and Labour Market Impediments
- Occupational licensing and certification requirements by province limit interprovincial labour mobility.
- Special problems arise in the professions, which are administered provincially (law, architecture, engineering, accountancy and others).
- Provincial licensing of trades; more than one third of craftspeople in production-process occupations are subject to licensing.
- Portability of employment-related benefits is restricted.
- Some provinces impose local hiring restrictions on the provincial private sector.

7. Capital Market Impediments
- Controls on land ownership by non-provincial residents.
- Restrictive provincial investment policies by provincial government investment funds, pension plan funds, insurance funds.
- Operations of provincial crown corporations.
- Provincial subsidies and financial assistance programs.

Source: Trebilcock, Whalley, Rogerson and Ness (1983).

Table 1, lists the main interprovincial barriers in Canada. It begins with provincial government procurement policies and preferences given to local (within-province) suppliers and continues with trucking regulation and a variety of sub-areas within this broad category in which within-province preference is given. It then moves to provincial liquor commissions and their provincial preference practices in marketing and sourcing. It moves on to agriculture and the practices of agricultural marketing boards and support programs, which combine with product standards and other regulations to retard interprovincial trade in affected products. From there, natural-resource policies within provinces are listed as well as related policy interventions affecting within-province processing. Next, come preferential hiring practices and occupational licensing in the professions and trades. And finally, various capital market impediments are listed.

At first sight, this is a long list which led some commentators at the time, such as Safarian (1980), to talk of the balkanization of Canada and the fragmentation of the Canadian market into 10 separate provincial markets. However, in my earlier piece, I argued that, on reflection, things were probably less extreme than seemed to be the case. First, there were no barriers in the list which directly affected trade in manufactured goods which, seemingly, continued to flow around in Canada relatively unimpeded. Second, several barrier items had features which reduced their effects, such as provincial government expenditures being wage- and salary-intensive. As a result, procurement practices impinged on only a minority of these barriers. Third, depending on the implicit model used, the effects of perceived barriers on interprovincial trade can be sharply reduced even completely eliminated. Thus, if one believes that all provinces interact as part of global capital markets as far as financing and capital flows are concerned, actions in one province have no effect on capital flows into or out of any other province. As small actors in an international capital market, actions of any one province have no effect on flows to or from other provinces.

I then went on to offer some simple calculations, suggesting that the overall effects of interprovincial barriers on trade and welfare would be small. As the basis for this argument, the costs of interprovincial barriers were calculated drawing on unpublished Statistics Canada data for 1974 of interprovincial trade flows for goods and services, compiled as part of the first interprovincial input–output tables for Canada for the same year.

Table 2 lists some of the basic data and shows how, for most provinces, interprovincial trade exceeds international trade by, on average, 50 percent. For smaller provinces and the territories (Newfoundland, Saskatchewan, Yukon and the Northwest Territories), international trade is larger than interprovincial trade but, for the remainder of the provinces, the reverse is true. In turn, the two largest central Canadian provinces (Quebec and Ontario) run deficits in their international trade, but surpluses in their interprovincial trade. The opposite is true of British Columbia, Alberta and Saskatchewan, all resource and/or grain-exporting regions.

The analysis of the effects of interprovincial barriers offered in my earlier work (Whalley, 1983a) and based on this data proceeded along the following lines.

TABLE 2

1974 INTERPROVINCIAL TRADE FLOW DATA

A. Interprovincial and International Trade in Goods and Services by Province ($Billions, 1974)

	Imports from Rest of Canada	Imports from Outside Canada	Exports to the Rest of Canada	Exports to Outside Canada
Newfoundland	1.32	0.61	0.19	0.92
Prince Edward Island	0.32	0.05	0.12	0.02
Nova Scotia	1.79	1.28	1.05	0.55
New Brunswick	1.60	0.90	0.95	0.79
Quebec	10.29	8.85	12.12	5.30
Ontario	11.60	14.54	18.06	12.47
Manitoba	2.50	0.97	1.78	0.89
Saskatchewan	2.26	0.80	1.45	2.17
Alberta	4.68	1.87	5.08	3.42
British Columbia	5.17	3.32	2.16	4.37
Yukon/NWT	0.20	0.04	0.05	0.21
Total	43.01	34.20	43.01	31.11

B. Destination of Production by Province (1974, Percentages of Goods and Services Produced)

	Sold Within Province	Sold to Rest of Canada	Sold Abroad
Newfoundland	61	7	32
Prince Edward Island	75	22	3
Nova Scotia	67	22	11
New Brunswick	61	21	18
Quebec	68	22	10
Ontario	68	19	13
Manitoba	66	23	11
Saskatchewan	52	19	29
Alberta	61	23	16
British Columbia	71	10	19
Yukon/NWT	71	5	24
All Canada	67	19	14

Source: Whalley, 1983.

TABLE 3

ESTIMATE OF INTERPROVINCIAL TRADE AFFECTED BY BARRIERS

Goods and Services Trade (Provincial)	% of Provincial Trade Covered
1. Government Policies (provincial government expenditures approximately 10% of GDP and extremely labour-intensive)	2
2. Transport Regulation (assumed to be 1/4 of interprovincially traded services)	10
3. Provincial Liquor Policies (recorded interprovincial trade in soft drinks and alcoholic beverages)	1
4. Agricultural Policies (recorded interprovincial trade in grains, dairy and fish products)	2.5
5. Provincial Resource Policies	2
Total	17.5

Source: Whalley, 1983.

First, I noted Melvin's argument (1985) that one of the effects of the federal tariff was to stimulate interprovincial trade with potentially significant internal transportation costs. As such, Melvin argued that one of the more pernicious effects of the federal tariff was to generate socially wasteful transportation costs as products were shipped between provinces in Canada behind the protective wall created by the federal tariff. For this reason, interprovincial barriers need not necessarily be bad if, to some degree, they offset the adverse incentive effects of federal policies and mitigate an artificial stimulus to interprovincial trade with associated socially wasteful transportation costs.

Having noted this argument, I moved on to evaluate the potential quantitative significance of barriers, putting the policy offset argument above on one side. I first calculated the amount of trade seemingly affected by interprovincial barriers. My estimates by main product group as a percentage of interprovincial trade are reported in Table 3.

I then noted the difficulties in attributing ad valorem equivalents to the various interprovincial barriers listed in Table 1, but offered the calculation that, if an average barrier rate of 10 percent were assumed, along with interprovincial trade elasticities of unity (a strong assumption made in the absence of any available elasticity estimates for interprovincial trade flows), a partial equilibrium estimate of the welfare gain from eliminating interprovincial trade barriers might be in the region of 0.2 percent of GDP.

I made no calculation of the potential gain from eliminating interprovincial barriers in capital markets, on the grounds that such markets are linked to international capital markets. Hence, barriers do not directly affect interprovincial capital flows. As far as interprovincial labour markets are concerned, I noted the difficulty in inferring barriers from observed interprovincial wage differentials, which reflect not only mobility barriers, but also productivity differentials, locational preferences and other factors. By making various assumptions on the barriers and elasticities of provincial marginal revenue product of labour schedules, I put the additional gain from removal of mobility restrictions at around 0.05 to 0.1 percent of GDP.

This, then, was the basis for the conjecture that the interprovincial barriers issue was akin to a tempest in a teacup.

MULTIPLIERS, MARKUPS AND MAGNIFICATION

ONE REACTION TO SUCH SMALL WELFARE ESTIMATES of the social cost of interprovincial barriers is that something is missing; the implicit model is misspecified to such a degree that the major sources of gain are simply not captured. This is a strong theme in recent numerical literature on the gains from trade liberalization, some (but not all) of which suggests that, with changed model structures, perceived small effects become substantially larger. It is also a theme in much of the recent endogenous growth literature, that externalities and, more specifically, knowledge-based spillovers, have large potential effects on both growth performance and welfare (King and Rebelo, 1990 and Perroni, 1993). This search for missing factors is consistent with much of the direction subsequently taken in endogenous growth literature.

The notion that something is missing from conventional partial or general equilibrium estimates of the gains from trade liberalization has its origins in the work of Bela Balassa (1967) on economic integration in Europe in the 1960s. Following the formation of the European Economic Community (EEC), and the move toward more integrated national markets, Balassa noted that, first, much of the trade growth in Europe after the Treaty of Rome had occurred within manufactures in closely related products. Second, the elevated European growth rates of the time substantially exceeded the *ex ante* estimates of gains by Scitovsky and others which had used conventional partial equilibrium methods. Balassa discussed what he called "dynamic" gains from trade liberalization due to specialization, scale economies and increased competition. He suggested his so-called "X factor" of five – the approximate multiple to be applied to conventional static partial or general equilibrium estimates of gains from trade liberalization. This factor was subsequently used by Cline, et al. (1978) in their work on the Tokyo Round.

Insofar as work on European integration (which seeks to assess either the effects from various steps toward integration which have been taken, or those that might be taken in the future) examines the effects of a removal of internal barriers to trade, there would seem to be parallels to the Canadian interprovincial trade barriers issue. A similar number of countries has been involved to the main group of Canadian provinces and, as with the provincial barriers issue, the original objectives were similar.

Further impetus in Europe subsequently came in the mid-1980s with the ambitious European Commission 1992 program, and a large array of proposed measures to move toward a more integrated European market through barrier removal. This was accompanied by the Cecchini Report (1988) which suggested gains to Europe in the region of 5 percent of GDP from the implementation of the 1992 program. These estimates were in excess of Balassa's multiple of Scitovsky's original calculations, and they involved a conventional partial equilibrium estimate of the benefits of border elimination (customs delays and other border barriers that were not an issue in the Canadian case), along with larger estimates of the gains from scale economies and increased competition.

The latter, in turn, drew heavily on work at the time by Smith and Venables (1988). They had used static, partial equilibrium modelling to evaluate the effects of lowered non-tariff barriers on various EEC sectors. They considered 10 sectors, each of which was modelled with firms having an increasing returns-to-scale technology, with each firm producing a differentiated product, and with the Armington assumption employed. They considered France, Germany, Italy, the United Kingdom, the rest of the EEC and the rest of the world as the trading regions. They evaluated sector-by-sector trade barrier reductions, looking at different cases; and at segmented versus integrated markets, with both Cournot and Bertrand conjectures by firms and with constant and variable numbers of firms. Under Bertrand conjectures, they showed substantially higher welfare effects (by over 50 percent) from reducing barriers under integrated compared to segmented markets, with no significant difference under Bertrand conjectures. Similar results emerged later in Smith, Venables and Gasiorek (1992) for a related general equilibrium formulation.

Similar themes on the size of the gains from trade integration can also be found for Canada in the Harris and Cox (1984) work on Canada–United States trade. In this case, unlike in Balassa, an explicit model was used with optimizing firm and household behaviour. What increased estimated gains was a formulation with fixed and variable costs at firm (and plant) level, and increasing returns to scale with fixed costs met by a "substitutable" mix of capital and labour inputs. With focal-point pricing around the world price gross of the tariff, any tariff reduction would move firms down their average cost curve, reduce the number of firms and achieve rationalization gains by spreading fixed costs over fewer firms. Harris and Cox suggested that rationalization gains would imply gains to Canada from a negotiated free trade arrangement with the United States of around 10 percent of GDP, in contrast to less than 2 percent in models with no rationalization features.

More recently, Baldwin (1992) has argued that dynamic gains will always exceed static gains by a significant factor. He used a small dynamic general equilibrium model to capture dynamic gains, arguing that higher capital stock and, hence, higher long-run income are needed to support estimated static gains along an economy's growth path. Dynamizing the static gains calculated by Cecchini, Catinat and Jacquemin (1988) for the 1992 European program suggests that in Gross National Product (GNP) terms, dynamic gains from trade liberalization would be from 24 percent to 136 percent larger than estimated static gains.

The issue for discussion here is whether any or all of these arguments apply to current estimates of the gains from interprovincial trade and how they relate, if at all, to endogenous growth considerations. The Balassa arguments applied to an

initial observation of increased inter-industry trade and increased trade in manufactures. This observation finds little obvious parallel in the Canadian interprovincial trade experience except, perhaps, for Ontario–Quebec trade. The Harris and
Cox arguments also appeal to collusion around a focal point of the world price gross
of the tariff, which does not seem to be a realistic treatment for the effects of barriers
to interprovincial versus international trade. And the later European arguments all
have the same differences as with the Balassa calculations: interprovincial trade is
less dominated by inter-industry trade and more toward trade in factors than is
European trade. Thus, the transfer of these higher estimates to the case of Canadian
interprovincial trade barriers, while intuitively appealing since all these analyses
relate to trade liberalization, becomes less clear once specific features of potential
interprovincial liberalization are considered.

CHANGES SINCE 1983

IF THE VARIOUS DEVELOPMENTS IN THE TRADE LITERATURE since my 1983 calculations
which potentially revised sharply upward estimates of the gains from liberalization, do not seem directly applicable to the interprovincial barrier issue in Canada,
the natural next question is: have there been other developments in the intervening
years which also change the picture?

The first source of change is ongoing evolution in the Canadian economy.
Real growth and structural change in the underlying economy may somehow have

---

TABLE 4

CHANGES IN INTERPROVINCIAL TRADE FLOWS SINCE 1974

Destination of Production by Province (Percentages of Goods and Services Produced)

	Percentage Sold Within Province		Percentage Sold to Rest of Canada		Percentage Sold Abroad	
	1974	1988	1974	1988	1974	1988
Newfoundland	61	71	7	7	32	22
Prince Edward Island	75	5	22	16	3	9
Nova Scotia	67	73	22	15	11	12
New Brunswick	61	64	21	17	18	19
Quebec	68	72	22	15	10	13
Ontario	68	69	19	14	13	17
Manitoba	66	67	23	20	11	13
Saskatchewan	52	67	19	15	29	18
Alberta	61	70	23	16	16	14
British Columbia	71	72	10	9	19	19
Yukon/NWT	71	61	5	7	24	32

Source: Author's calculations based on Statistics Canada data.

altered both the importance and structure of interprovincial trade patterns either elevating or dampening the significance of barriers. Changes in the composition of interprovincial trade flows between 1974 and 1988 are set out in Table 4. As can be seen, the changes in aggregate are relatively small even though the changes for individual provinces are more substantial. This picture suggests that, at least in terms of trade flows, not much has changed in the intervening years, and probably little which would, on this count, change the underlying argument for small effects from the elimination of interregional barriers, especially since the relative importance of trade within Canada opposed to trade outside Canada, or within a province has, if anything, fallen.

TABLE 5

MAIN FEATURES OF 1994 AGREEMENT ON INTERNAL BARRIERS

- *General Rules*
  - Broad principles are: (i) non-discrimination, (ii) right of entry/exit, (iii) new policies not to create obstacles to trade, (iv) "legitimate objectives" justify deviation from principles (consumer protection, environmental protection, public health and safety), (v) reconciliation (barriers due to differences in standards to be eliminated) and (vi) transparency (publication/notification).

- *Sectoral Chapters*
  - Government procurement – aims to end local price preferences, biased contract specifications and other impediments.
  - Investment – limits residency requirements, use of local content, local purchasing and local sourcing requirements.
  - Labour mobility – restricts use of residency requirements and establishes a process for mutual recognition of qualifications and reconciliation of occupational standards.
  - Consumer-related measures and standards – harmonization of standards and regulations (fees for licensing and registration, location being a condition of certification, harmonized labelling).
  - Agriculture – provincial minister to review agricultural policies; standstill on new trade restrictions, including sanitary and phytosanitary measures.
  - Alcoholic beverages – phased elimination of barriers for wine and beer.
  - Natural resources – prohibition of new barriers affecting processing of forestry, fisheries and mineral resources products.
  - Communications – supports single communications market, non-discrimination provisions in telecommunications.
  - Transport – moves toward harmonization of trucking licensing and inspection.
  - Environmental protection – recognized as a legitimate objective of provincial governments.

- *Institutional Provisions*
  - Ministerial level Committee on Internal Trade (CIT), with secretariat in Winnipeg.
  - Dispute settlement based on panel procedures, public pressure to implement panel findings, with CIT-sanctioned retaliation as a final resort.

Source: Author's own summary.

The second is the Agreement on Internal Barriers concluded between the provinces in 1994 and in effect as of July 1, 1995. At first sight, this seems to be a far-reaching document which moves a substantial distance toward achieving the integration of the internal market and hence, the gains from a unified market. As such, it potentially makes the interprovincial trade barriers issue the issue of yesterday rather than an issue for the future. However, as can be seen from Table 5, many of the key interprovincial barrier issues either remain, or are only dealt with indirectly.

Agriculture is an important example where the agreement only involves further negotiation. Transportation also involves only partial movement toward national standards. Dispute settlement is vague and ill-defined since, unlike the GATT, withdrawal of equivalent concessions has no direct analogue since bound tariffs are not the issue.

Moreover, much of the agreement seeks to move toward provincial harmonization of policy. But as is well known, harmonization and removal of distortions are different things. Imposed harmonization where regional preferences exist on such matters as environmental protection or where safety standards differ can worsen as well as improve things.

Interprovincial barrier issues remain despite these developments since 1985. Interprovincial trade patterns remain largely unchanged. Moreover, the recent Agreement on Internal Barriers goes only part way to resolving the interprovincial barriers issue.

ENDOGENOUS GROWTH CONSIDERATIONS AND INTERPROVINCIAL BARRIERS

I'VE ARGUED IN EARLIER SECTIONS that the effects of interprovincial trade barriers are small, and there is no compelling reason to change this line of reasoning in light of more recent developments either in the literature on measurement of the effects of trade barriers (scale economies, competition) or in the interprovincial structure of the Canadian economy. In this final section, I discuss whether or not considerations from recent endogenous growth literature can change the analysis and, if so, in which ways.

By now, the endogenous growth literature is voluminous, widely disseminated and developed in many directions. However, a few central themes emerge that are clearly relevant to the analysis of interprovincial barriers. Much of the endogenous growth literature is attributed to the work of Romer whose recent survey (1994) traced the evolution of some of this work. An especially influential piece appearing parallel to Romer's initial work, was that of Lucas (1988) on the mechanics of economic development. All this literature stresses the importance of knowledge-based spillovers in affecting growth processes, although Romer's initial work focused on the possibility that increasing returns of scale played a key role in changing the traditional analysis of growth in a Solow–Swan model in which there is an exogenous and fixed growth rate for the labour force.

There has been much debate about the way these knowledge-based spillovers that Lucas and Romer suggest operate in reality and, in an exchange between Lucas and Romer, about whether or not the knowledge-based spillovers themselves are appropriable and, therefore, already representing externalities which are internalized. The heart of the debate focuses on the role that knowledge-based spillovers and externalities of this form can have in accounting for and speeding up growth. As Romer emphasized, much of the endogenous growth literature is devoted to developing lines of reasoning as to why a conventional Solow–Swan model – even with differences in technology between countries – cannot account for various growth phenomena. Related to this is the debate on convergence (see Barro and Sala-i-Martin, 1992).

Because of the voluminous nature of this literature, four key questions on interprovincial barriers emerging from this literature have been identified, and their implications for the analysis of interprovincial barriers discussed, arguing that, to the extent they are relevant, endogenous growth considerations may have impacts which are opposite to those which advocates of larger effects of liberalization of interprovincial barriers might wish to see.

Do Endogenous Growth Considerations Increase the Impacts of Interprovincial Barriers?

Some pieces in the endogenous growth literature (King and Rebelo, 1990 and more recently Perroni, 1993), have used numerical simulation techniques to analyze the effects of distortion in models with endogenous growth features (knowledge-based spillovers). These analyses are forced to use strong assumptions as to how endogenous growth features enter the analysis. For example, in Perroni the assumption is made that four times the value of any development of knowledge accrues to firms other than the firm developing the knowledge. In addition, no appropriability of these added revenues occurs.

With assumptions such as this, it is not surprising that the incorporation of endogenous growth features has a large effect on the impacts of various kinds of distortion on both behaviour and welfare. In King and Rebelo, for instance, the move from an income to a consumption tax (usually analyzed by public finance economists within a numerical framework which generates welfare gains in the region of 2 percent to 3 percent of the national income in discount of present value terms) is translated into a dramatically higher gain – as high as 50 percent of discounted present value of income. Perroni also identifies cases where these gains can be as large as 20 percent. Using these calculations, there seems to be some basis to the contention that endogenous growth considerations increase the impacts of removals of distortions – and substantially so where distortions are related to the endogenous growth considerations themselves.

There is, however, an important distinction between trade-based and intertemporal distortions of the kind considered within this tax literature. With knowledge-based spillovers, when intertemporal distortions are crucial to investment, dramatically larger results follow from any policy which removes intertemporal distortions, such as a move from an income to a consumption tax. In the trade case, when the effects are compositional rather than intertemporal, not only is the presumption that endogenous growth considerations will increase the impacts of policies questionable but, if anything, arguments go the other way. And as Young (1991) pointed out, there could even be an argument that things could be made worse in some regions by liberalization with, in effect, trade barriers in the presence of endogenous growth considerations operating as akin to infant industry protection.

CAN ENDOGENOUS GROWTH CONSIDERATIONS REVERSE THE SIGN OF THE IMPACTS OF INTERPROVINCIAL BARRIERS?

THE ARGUMENT ABOVE ATTRIBUTED TO YOUNG (1991) clearly seems to indicate that this is possible for certain regions, even if not in aggregate. Because of the presence of knowledge-based spillovers and the need to appropriate the benefits of knowledge-based spillovers which accrue to other firms, protection (which provides support to domestic industries) can have effects akin to those of an infant industry tariff in more classical trade literature.

In fact, infant industry debate going back to the turn of the century is similar to the debate associated with endogenous growth. Hence, the interprovincial trade barrier issue in the presence of endogenous growth considerations becomes not only one of whether or not effects for regions are made larger or smaller, but whether their sign can reverse, since welfare losses may be possible with the elimination of interprovincial barriers.

IS THERE ANY EVIDENCE OF KNOWLEDGE-BASED SPILLOVERS IN BARRIER-RELATED INDUSTRIES?

IT IS ON THIS DIMENSION that the introduction of endogenous growth considerations is the weakest in its applicability to interprovincial barriers. It seems difficult to argue that knowledge-based spillovers occur in the beer industry, even though alcoholic beverages are a central product category associated with interprovincial barriers. Perhaps there are some knowledge-based spillovers in agriculture through development of new techniques for higher yield variety seeds and animal husbandry and related techniques but, generally, because the vast majority of manufactured goods flow around Canada relatively free of barriers, the knowledge-based spillover issue is seemingly mute, because interprovincial barriers do not apply directly to these products. As a result, the conjecture seems reasonable that estimates of the costs of interprovincial barriers may be little affected by endogenous growth considerations.

INTERREGIONAL CONVERGENCE AND BARRIER REDUCTION?

IT IS IN THIS COMPONENT OF THE ENDOGENOUS GROWTH LITERATURE that interregional barriers have their largest impact. As noted above, the discussion in Barro and Sala-i-Martin (1992) of convergence between economies has been along the lines of whether or not relatively rapid convergence of differentials in income per capita across U.S. states can be explained in ways consistent with a traditional Solow–Swan endogenous growth model. The conclusion has been that this is not the case. Hence, the presence of such features as knowledge-based spillovers may be crucial in explaining this convergent growth process.

In contrast, the remarkable feature of the Canadian case has been the relative lack of convergence of interregional differentials in income per capita. Differentials between the highest and lowest per capita regions in Canada are still in the region of 2:1, larger than in the United States. These differentials have been relatively slow to adjust over time. It is possible that reductions in interregional trade barriers would have an effect on regional convergence by lowering these differentials. Hence, changes in interregional barriers through time could be a factor in explaining the relative lack of convergence in provincial income per capita, and persistence of the differentials given the slowly changing nature of the barriers themselves. In these ways, endogenous growth considerations may change the picture on the effects of interregional barriers.

CONCLUSION

IN THIS PAPER, I HAVE RETURNED TO EARLIER CALCULATIONS on the effects of interregional barriers in Canada on interregional trade and welfare. This reconsideration has been undertaken in light of recent literature on endogenous growth, other related developments including the agreement on internal trade, implemented in July 1995, and changes in interprovincial trade patterns.

In my earlier work, I argued that the effects of interregional barriers were likely to be small because they applied to only a small portion of interregional trade, and the components to which they applied had further offsetting features, such as provincial procurement applying to expenditures which were heavily labour intensive. Does this earlier evaluation still apply in light of various more recent considerations, including those raised in the endogenous growth literature?

I assessed the implications of developments in the literature on the evaluation of the impact of trade barriers including market structure and related considerations. This re-examination was carved out in light of more recent provincial trade data and endogenous growth considerations including the role of knowledge-based spillovers. I have concluded that, while much added noise is created by these considerations, the noise would seem to go in several directions simultaneously, increasing the variance of estimates but having uncertain impacts on their mean. The tempest in the teacup may spill over onto neighbouring plates, but in uncertain ways and with unpredictable velocity.

ENDNOTE

1   Even if barriers are not directly related to interprovincial distortions, and even if the industries affected are not ones that seem to generate significant knowledge-based spillovers, there are still wealth or income effects that may affect knowledge accumulation and, hence, the permanent growth rate. Too little is known about savings behaviour and how it is influenced by changes in trade barriers to count too much on this effect, but the possibility should be noted. I am grateful to Peter Howitt for making this point.

ACKNOWLEDGEMENTS

I AM GRATEFUL TO ROBIN BOADWAY AND PETER HOWITT for helpful comments, and to Deanna Foell for research assistance.

BIBLIOGRAPHY

Balassa, B. "Trade Creation and Trade Diversion in the European Common Market." *Economic Journal.* 77, (1967): 1-21.

Baldwin, R. "Measurable Dynamic Gains from Trade." *Journal of Political Economy.* 100, No. 1, (1992): 162-174.

Barro, R. and X. Sala-i-Martin. "Convergence." *Journal of Political Economy.* Vol. 100, No. 2, (April 1992): 223-251.

Cecchini, P., M. Catinat and A. Jacquemin. *The European Challenge, 1992. The Benefits of a Single Market.* Aldershot, UK: Wildwood House, 1988.

Cline, W., et al. (eds.). *Trade Negotiations in the Tokyo Round: A Qualitative Assessment.* Washington, DC: The Brookings Institution, 1978.

Government of Canada. *The 1994 Agreement on Internal Trade.* Ottawa, 1994.

Harris, R.G. and D. Cox. *Trade, Industrial Policy, and Canadian Manufacturing.* Ontario Economic Council Research Study, Toronto, 1984.

King, R.G. and S. Rebelo. "Public Policy and Economic Growth: Developing Neoclassical Implications." *Journal of Political Economy.* Vol. 95, (1990): 675-709.

Lucas, R. "On the Mechanics of Economic Development." *Journal of Monetary Economics.* Vol. 22, No. 1, (1988): 3-42.

Melvin, J.R. "The Regional Economic Consequences of Tariffs and Domestic Transportation Costs." *Canadian Journal of Economics.* XVIII, No. 2, (May 1985): 237-257.

Perroni, C. "Endogenous Growth and the Choice of Tax Base." Mimeo, 1993.

Romer, P. "The Origins of Endogenous Growth." *Journal of Economic Perspective.* Vol. 8, No. 1, (1994): 3-22.

Safarian, E. "Ten Markets or One: Regional Barriers to Economic Activity in Canada." Ontario Economic Council Discussion Paper, Toronto, 1980.

Smith, A. and A. Venables. "Completing the Internal Market in the European Community: Some Industry Simulations." *European Economic Review.* 32, (1988): 1501-1525.

Smith, A., A. Venables and M. Gasiorek. "1992: Trade and Welfare – A General Equilibrium Model." Paper presented at the Centre for Economic Policy Research Conference on Trade Flows and Trade Policy, Paris, January 16 to 18, 1992.

Trebilcock, M.J., J. Whalley, C. Rogerson and I. Ness. "Provincially Induced Barriers to Trade in Canada: A Survey." In *Federalism and the Canadian Economic Union*. Edited by M.J. Trebilcock, et al. Ontario Economic Council, 1983.

Whalley, J. "Induced Distortions of Interprovincial Activity: An Overview of Issues." In *Federalism and the Canadian Economic Union*. Edited by M.J. Trebilcock, et al. Ontario Economic Council, 1983a.

———. "The Impact of Federal Policies on Interprovincial Activity." In *Federalism and the Canadian Economic Union*. Edited by M.J. Trebilcock, et al. Ontario Economic Council, 1983b.

Young, A. "Learning by Doing and the Dynamic Effects of International Trade." *Quarterly Journal of Economics*. No. 1106, (1991): 369-405.

Comment

Robin Boadway
Department of Economics
Queen's University

INTRODUCTION

THE TOPIC OF THIS PAPER BY JOHN WHALLEY is, at first sight, a very unlikely one: the assessment of the impact of endogenous growth considerations on the effects of interprovincial barriers to trade. In this borderless country of ours in which barriers to trade are almost bound to be selective and of limited consequence, and in which capital and labour move with relative freedom among the provinces, it is not surprising that Whalley's characteristically careful calculations indicate that the conventional welfare cost of such barriers is trivial. Also, given that endogenous growth is influenced mainly by capital accumulation, including tangible, intangible and human capital, rather than by trade considerations, it would not be surprising to find that the implications of endogenous growth for the costs of interprovincial barriers are small. After all, even the costs of trade barriers between countries are not regarded as being affected by endogenous growth. It is not hard to accept Whalley's considered conclusion that interprovincial barriers to trade remain a quantitative tempest in a teacup.

This makes my job as a discussant relatively easy. I could simply say I agree and leave it at that. However, I shall try and do slightly more than that. After briefly reviewing Whalley's arguments and especially addressing the endogenous growth aspects of them, I shall cast the net more broadly and raise the issue of whether our perspective might change if we interpreted interprovincial barriers to trade also to include the effect of policies in general on the interregional allocation of resources. The purpose is not to provide definitive answers or to present numbers, but to raise questions that might be worth further consideration.

SUMMARY OF WHALLEY'S ARGUMENT

W HALLEY HAS ARGUED CONVINCINGLY THAT:

- the cost of distortions caused by interprovincial barriers to trade in goods and services and factor flows is unlikely to be very large, based on standard static welfare cost measurement;

- these are not likely to have increased in the last decade because the structure of trade and the nature of the barriers have not changed much;

- the recently concluded interprovincial agreement on internal barriers is not likely to have much effect on the cost of barriers;

- considerations based on non-standard assumptions about scale economies, firm and industry rationalization, increased competition and dynamic gains are unlikely to change that view significantly, since the barriers apply largely to non-manufacturing industries, to labour intensive activities and to a small portion of interprovincial trade and since interprovincial trade tends not to be intra-industry; and

- considerations based on endogenous growth theory are unlikely to change our most likely estimates of the costs of barriers to trade since most of these arguments rely on capital market distortions rather than trade distortions, since protection can actually improve welfare by improving the ability of local firms to appropriate knowledge-based externalities and since there is no evidence of knowledge-based externalities applying to the sorts of industries that are subject to interprovincial barriers.

Thus, Whalley maintains that the internal barriers issue is a tempest in a teacup.

I find it hard to take issue with these arguments. Indeed, I would argue that it may be even more of a tempest than his numbers imply, because many of the so-called barriers to trade induced by provincial policies are an inevitable consequence of decentralizing decision making to the provinces. Most economists would argue that this decentralization itself should be efficiency-enhancing because it increases cost-effectiveness and innovation, and improves accountability. As well, lower jurisdictions are likely to be better informed about local needs, costs and preferences. Constraining provinces to abide by codes of common conduct may reduce so-called barriers to trade. But, to the extent that they are enforceable, constraints can also put provinces in a straitjacket and preclude them from responding effectively to the needs of their constituents. As a stark example, it would be understandable if economists were to regard provincial laws stipulating that the language of work in provincial firms be French or that English language films be translated into French as a condition for local distribution as imposing barriers to trade. However, a broader perspective would view such forms of language or cultural protection as having some positive benefits in terms of the preferences of provincial residents.

The benefits of so-called provincial barriers to trade were brought home in a striking manner during the constitutional debate leading up to the Charlottetown

Accord. At the public conference devoted to the internal economic union, much debate surrounded the federal government's proposal to enshrine, in the Constitution, better protection for the free flow of goods, services, labour and capital within the internal common market. This would be done either by strengthening section 121 of the *British North America Act* to allow the courts to enforce free internal trade or by providing the federal government with the responsibility and the power to enforce it (as tends to be the case in the United States). Surprisingly, the consensus of the conference was that such strengthening would not be welcome, because it might be applied in a way that would preclude the provinces from exercising their decentralized responsibility in a way that would serve the interests of their constituents. The alternative route of seeking interprovincial agreements was preferred. We should not be surprised that such agreements do not really affect the measure of the cost of barriers significantly.

Having said this, I find Whalley's reasoning entirely convincing. Static welfare cost measures of distortions in many contexts tend to be very small. When they are made large, as in trade liberalization or tax policy contexts, alternative modelling assumptions that seem important for the context of trade or tax policy have been adopted. These assumptions are less likely to be important for issues of interregional allocation of resources. Examples include the following.

- The incorporation of scale economies and of oligopolistic market structures are likely to be of little relevance for distortions that will probably arise as a result of interprovincial barriers to trade.

- While incorporating equity considerations into welfare cost measurement can lead to results of a different order of magnitude, that is unlikely to be the case here.

- Adding dynamic considerations can also lead to very sizable long-run welfare consequences of policies that affect the rate of capital accumulation. However, I would argue that these are often very misleading because the long-run gain they measure is frequently a consequence not of an efficiency improvement but of an intergenerational redistribution of income. For example, much of the long-run welfare gain attributed to moving to a consumption tax (or eliminating unfunded public pensions or reducing government debt) arises from an increase in the capital stock. This necessarily causes per capita consumption and utility to rise, and the economy to move closer to the Golden Rule growth path, as long as the rate of return on capital is greater than the rate of growth. However, contrary to what many think, this does not represent a gain in efficiency, even in the long run, but a pure redistribution. Long-run gains in efficiency come about only because of reductions in distortions per period, and these are difficult to measure. The distortions may be taxes or they may take the form of externalities associated with the accumulation of capital itself. In any case, none of this seems especially relevant to interprovincial barriers to trade. There is no reason to believe that removing them will have a special effect on capital accumulation.

FURTHER OBSERVATIONS OF ENDOGENOUS GROWTH EFFECTS

WHALLEY NEXT ADDRESSES THE INTERACTION between endogenous growth considerations and the cost of interprovincial barriers to trade. He does so by posing four key questions. Let me briefly remark on these.

DO ENDOGENOUS GROWTH CONSIDERATIONS INCREASE THE IMPACTS OF INTERPROVINCIAL BARRIERS?

I COMPLETELY CONCUR WITH WHALLEY'S ASSESSMENT that the answer to this is largely "no." Endogenous growth considerations might increase the welfare cost of capital market distortions because the engine of endogenous growth is capital accumulation. Unless one can argue that interprovincial barriers to trade tend to reduce relevant forms of capital accumulation – physical capital accumulation embodying new knowledge or learning by doing, intangible capital accumulation [including knowledge acquired by research and development (R&D)] or human capital accumulation – endogenous growth would not seem to be especially relevant. One might argue that interprovincial beggar-thy-neighbour competition induces too little capital accumulation in the end. We return to that below.

CAN ENDOGENOUS GROWTH CONSIDERATIONS REVERSE THE SIGN OF THE IMPACTS OF INTERPROVINCIAL BARRIERS?

THE ANSWER GIVEN HERE IS "MAYBE." The idea, based on Young (1991), is that interprovincial barriers might function like infant-industry protection that could increase the extent to which knowledge-based spillovers are appropriated. I find these second-best arguments a bit dangerous in the absence of further quantitative information. It could go either way. It seems to me that if the "wrong" industries are being protected, infant-industry protection can reduce the extent to which such externalities are both created and appropriated.

IS THERE ANY EVIDENCE OF KNOWLEDGE-BASED SPILLOVERS IN BARRIER-RELATED INDUSTRIES?

I AGREE WITH WHALLEY'S ASSESSMENT that the answer to this is a clear "no." The sorts of goods to which barriers apply are not those associated with knowledge-based spillovers. On the other hand, since much knowledge in endogenous growth models is said to be introduced and spread by human capital and physical capital accumulation, perhaps if one included barriers to labour and capital flows as part of what is at stake (and Whalley's own work seems to do that), one might be somewhat less decisive about the answer to this question.

INTERREGIONAL CONVERGENCE AND BARRIER REDUCTION?

I MUST CONFESS TO NOT BEING SURE OF THE POINT BEING MADE in this section, since no real question is posed. The argument seems to be that the persistence of interregional differences in income per capita, which are compatible with the endogenous growth perspective, might indicate that interprovincial barriers to trade do balkanize the Canadian economy and prevent the spread of knowledge-based externalities across regions. I am unclear about the nature of this argument for a couple of reasons. First, I had thought that endogenous growth theory was trying to explain differences in the rate of growth of income across countries (regions) rather than differences in per capita income levels. The fact that per capita income differentials have been persistent across provinces is an indication that their rates of growth are the same, which would be incompatible with the endogenous growth argument. Second, I would argue that differences in per capita income across regions are not incompatible with standard neoclassical theory. Moreover, such differences probably have much more to do with things other than interprovincial barriers to trade such as resource endowments, preferences and general government policies.

Nonetheless, although I might address these four questions differently than Whalley, my conclusions concerning the impact of interprovincial barriers to trade would differ little. Thus, Whalley is able to give a short answer to his assignment, which was to reassess the conclusion from his earlier calculations that the cost of barriers to trade were relatively small in light of recent changes and of the insights of endogenous growth theory. I am not constrained by this assignment. A natural question to ask is whether there are any other issues of an endogenous growth type that are likely to arise in a large regionally diversified economy, especially one that has a relatively decentralized federal structure.

CASTING THE NET WIDER

SUPPOSE WE EXTEND THE NOTION OF BARRIERS to include anything that can cause an interregional misallocation of resources. Then, in addition to the standard interprovincial barriers to trade, we would include the following sorts of things.

- Provincial policies are likely to influence the regional allocation of resources in ways that lead to inefficiencies. They may also affect capital accumulation. They include:
    - tax policies (especially capital taxes);
    - transfer policies (including welfare payments);
    - expenditure policies on social programs (health, education);
    - goods and services expenditures including those that can have a regional impact within provinces (infrastructure, etc.);
    - resource management and environmental policies;
    - public and quasi-public corporations (e.g., provincial hydro corporations); and
    - transfers to local governments.

- Federal policies can actually improve the efficiency of resource allocation across regions. For example, a properly designed equalization system that removes net fiscal benefit differentials across provinces can eliminate fiscally induced migration. Some measures can be efficiency reducing from a regional perspective. Others can reduce capital accumulation thereby reducing the level of income per capita in the long run and possibly reducing the rate of growth. Moreover, some of them can also enhance the inefficiencies of the internal common market of the sort suggested by Melvin (1985) for tariff policy. For example, to the extent that unemployment insurance or regional development policies induce more interregional trade, they will also incur inefficient east–west transportation costs. These policies can include:

- transfers to persons, especially those that are regionally differen-tiated through such programs as Unemployment Insurance;
- transfers to businesses (those affecting agriculture, declining industries, slow growth areas, etc.);
- transfers to the provinces and territories (equalization, financing for established programs, the Canada Assistance Plan);
- expenditures on goods and services, especially those that have a regional focus, such as defence expenditures;
- policies governing public and quasi-public corporations (e.g., transportation facilities, communications, postal service);
- tax policies, especially those that have regional implications (regional tax credits, R&D incentives); and
- regulation in areas such as communications, transportation and environment.

- In regional economies, there is plenty of scope for inefficiency of resource allocation among regions. This does not occur in a more compact economy. For example, it is well known that free migration of labour can result in an inefficient allocation of resources in an economy with efficiently functioning local jurisdictions. As well, there are many non-convexities that are likely to arise in regional economies due to economies of scale in transportation facilities and in basic services.

The magnitude of these additional sources of inefficiency is difficult to know for sure. Presumably, some are offsetting in the aggregate. Others might be small, such as the inefficiency of labour allocation across regions caused by fiscally induced migration. Naturally, estimating the welfare costs of these distortions is not likely to be an easy task, and is likely to give rise to great differences depending on the modelling features adopted. Nonetheless, I suspect that they would swamp the inefficiencies due to interprovincial barriers to trade. Much research needs to be done in this area. In that sense, the tendency to focus on barriers to trade in a fed-eration is somewhat surprising to an economist who is steeped in the economics of regional and federal economies.

The above considerations have to do with conventional static inefficiencies in a regional economy when we broaden the scope of sources to include more than provincially induced barriers to interprovincial trade. Following Whalley's presen-tation, the next question to ask is whether considerations of endogenous growth are likely to make matters worse. As with interprovincial barriers to trade, there are no particular reasons to think that endogenous growth problems are of particular relevance to a regional economy. However, there are some considerations that are worth drawing to your attention.

1. To the extent that growth is enhanced by human capital considerations, the more integrated the national markets become for more trained and educated labour, the more opportunity there will be for the knowledge embedded in labour to be passed on to others. Anything that restricts labour mobility across provinces or across firms will reduce the size of the knowledge externality, and anything that facilitates human capital investment will enhance it. In a decentralized federation in which labour markets are regulated provincially and in which education is locally supplied, this could be an issue. For example, during the last round of constitutional negotiations, some prominent economists adopted the view that one of the most important features of maintaining an efficient internal common market in Canada was the knowledge and skill externalities generated by the mobility of highly trained persons across Canada. In their view, the federal government could be assigned the responsibility for maintaining the efficient internal common market. Thus, while it may be efficient to decentralize the provision of education, labour market training and labour market regulation to the provinces, if this action reduces the mobility that would otherwise occur among highly skilled and entrepreneurial labour across provinces, national efficiency is compromised.

2. A special issue that has recently arisen in the trade literature that is closely related to the endogenous growth literature concerns the benefits of agglomeration: the way in which knowledge-based externalities are transmitted involves interpersonal contact and highly integrated local labour and financial markets. This is more likely to occur if industries employing highly skilled workers are situated near one another in agglomerated communities. To the extent that the decentralization of responsibilities to the provinces or the use of regional policies by the federal government militates against agglomeration (migration of workers and businesses to core areas), some of the benefits of knowledge-base externalities will be foregone. The sorts of policies one has in mind are those that prevent market forces from operating, such as regionally differentiated unemployment insurance, regional development policies, federal goods and services expenditures (e.g., on defence) based on regional considerations, infrastructure provisions and transportation policies.

3. One interesting feature of the Canadian federation concerns provincial responsibility for the regulation of capital markets – at least the non-bank financial sector. Economists conventionally argue that capital market regulation should be centralized because of the mobility of capital and the possibility that decentralized regulation will induce an inefficient allocation

of capital across regions. However, there is another perspective: the very mobility of capital should discipline provincial regulators from trying to interfere with the allocation of capital. At the same time, decentralized regulation may enhance the efficiency of local capital markets for the same sorts of reasons that decentralization more generally leads to enhanced efficiency. Local regulators may be more knowledgeable of, and responsive to, local conditions, more accountable to the government and the public, and more innovative and cost-effective because of the greater competition they face. This improves the way information is transmitted on capital markets and the ability of capital markets to provide capital to new enterprises and to those that are involved in innovation, entrepreneurship and the creation of knowledge. These improvements are of obvious relevance for economic efficiency and knowledge-based growth.

4. The ability of provinces to tax capital and capital incomes is related to provincial regulatory powers in capital markets. In this case, the decentralization of powers to the provinces can have obvious deleterious effects on the capital accumulation process, not only making its allocation across provinces inefficient, but also reducing the aggregate amount of investment that takes place. As Whalley mentions, given the openness of Canadian capital markets, this may be an unimportant issue. However, there is certainly some evidence that the sorts of firms that are likely to generate knowledge-based externalities, such as high-tech firms, are very footloose and responsive to local policies. It is not hard to imagine inefficiencies in the location of these firms induced by provincial policies.

5. Finally, R&D is extremely important to the growth process and generates knowledge that is often difficult to appropriate. It would be interesting to know whether the sort of decentralization that exists in our federal system of government militates against maintaining a high level of R&D.

All these considerations go beyond the mandate presented to Whalley. Nonetheless, they are important dimensions to the interaction between federalism and the growth process.

BIBLIOGRAPHY

Melvin, J. R. "The Regional Economic Consequences of Tariffs and Domestic Transportation Costs." *Canadian Journal of Economics*. XVIII, No. 2, (May 1985): 237-257.

Young, A. "Learning by Doing and the Dynamic Effects of International Trade." *Quarterly Journal of Economics*. No. 1106, (1991): 369-405.

A.L. Keith Acheson & Donald G. McFetridge
Department of Economics
Carleton University

with the assistance of M.P. Francis

6

Intellectual Property and Endogenous Growth

INTRODUCTION

ENDOGENOUS GROWTH LITERATURE began with a simple purpose but, as it evolved, it developed some far-reaching implications. This paper examines those implications for public policy toward intellectual property.

The simple purpose was to develop models in which savings and investment decisions of individuals responding to market incentives could result in sustained growth. In the received neoclassical model, output per head could be increased by increasing capital per head, but diminishing marginal productivity ultimately sets in, capital accumulation is no longer profitable and growth (increases in output per head) ceases. Sustained growth is generated by adding exogenous technical change (the Solow residual).

The new models of endogenous growth solve the variable proportions problem in a variety of ways. These solutions rely, in one way or another, on the accumulation of knowledge. While the accumulation of knowledge is central to these models, intellectual property is not. Intellectual property can play a role, but its presence is not essential.

The endogenous growth literature has, however, led economists to look at intellectual property from another perspective. The historic emphasis in the economics of intellectual property has been on the tension – the "intellectual property bargain" – between creators and users. With its emphasis on the accumulation of knowledge, the endogenous growth literature has focused attention on relationships among innovators, in particular, on the interdependence between current and past innovative activity. The institutions for co-ordinating the pioneering and improvement innovations have been brought to the fore.

While the emphasis on the cumulative aspect of innovation is novel from the perspective of economic theory, the issues it presents will be familiar to practitioners. Indeed, there is much in the administrative and judicial interpretation of intellectual property statutes that reflects a concern with the allocation of surplus resulting from cumulative improvements in technology.

With the study of successive improvements in knowledge, has come an appreciation of the hazards facing market relationships between innovators and both their predecessors and successors. These relationships have sometimes been made more hazardous than is necessary by antitrust authorities. Given the natural and contrived barriers to market co-ordination of knowledge accumulation, it is not surprising that there has also been renewed interest in non-market co-ordination mechanisms particularly in non-proprietary or "open" science.

The institutions of open science do not appear to have been subject to the relentless and sceptical scrutiny historically accorded intellectual property. They have an internal logic and an intuitive appeal in situations in which potential follow-on innovators are not identifiable. Whether the respective domains of open and proprietary science should be changed is another question.

This paper begins with a comparison of open and proprietary science. It then turns to a description of the features of the intellectual property rights most relevant to technological innovation. This is followed by a discussion of endogenous growth models and the role of intellectual property in them. The implications of a cumulative innovative process for the welfare analysis of intellectual property and for patent and licensing policy are then explored.

The Nature of Intellectual Property

Alternative Means of Encouraging the Production of Public Goods

Scientific and technological knowledge has the characteristics of a public good. It is non-rivalrous. Access and variations in the intensity of use by one individual do not affect the productive opportunities available to other users of the knowledge base. Exclusion is often costly. Production of increments to the base generally involves initial fixed costs. David (1993) suggested that the three general classes of institutional arrangements under which knowledge is produced are *patronage*, *procurement* and *property*.

He defined patronage as: "the system of awarding publicly financed prizes, research grants based on the submission of competitive proposals, and other subsidies to private individuals and organizations engaging in scientific discovery and invention in exchange for full public disclosure of their findings" (David, 1993, p. 226).

Procurement was defined as: "governmental contracting for intellectual work generally and for scientific research performance in particular" (David, 1993, p. 226).

Contracts may be internal, e.g., in-house research and development (R&D), or external, e.g., contracting-out. Information produced under contract may or may not be disclosed to the public.

The procurement and patronage regimes are collapsed into a "community of open science" or "republic of science" by Dasgupta and David (1994). The incentive system in open science hastens discovery and disclosure. The reward system depends on priority in obtaining results. Success is signalled by being first to disclose new results in a manner that permits others in the community to verify by reproduction.

This "winner take almost all" system disproportionately rewards the first to report the solution of important scientific problems: "Priority creates a privately owned asset from the very act of relinquishing exclusive possession of the new knowledge. To put it dramatically, priority in science *is* the prize" (Dasgupta and David, 1994, p. 500).

The third institutional alternative is to create a property right in knowledge. A patent essentially grants the right to require payment for the use of knowledge and to exclude those who do not pay from its use. Copyright protects the owners of an expression of knowledge or work from unsanctioned reproduction and dissemination. Trade secrecy law adds legal processes and sanctions to the strategies available to an owner of information for preventing trespass by others. Specific laws protect the knowledge in integrated circuits and plant breeding. Such intellectual property rights enhance the commercial value of knowledge either through protecting its use as an input into the production of goods and services or through the sale or licence of the knowledge to others. The ability to sell innovative products or copies of new expressions or to license this right to others encourages inventive and creative activity.

THE INTERFACE OF OPEN AND PROPRIETARY SCIENCE

THE REGIMES OF OPEN AND PROPRIETARY SCIENCE differ in the incentives they provide for engaging in inventive activity. Open science relies on rewards based on priority of discovery and peer evaluation. This reward system encourages early discovery, full disclosure and some sharing of results.

By basing rewards on priority of discovery, the system encourages "racing." Winning depends on disclosing a result that is sufficiently novel to warrant publication in a journal of reputation in science. The value of winning depends on the expected value to society of the innovation. In the traditional sciences, the validity of a result is subject to experimental confirmation. However, the race remains imprecisely defined because participants must conjecture what the value attributed by the scientific community to the result will be.

Only in a subset of instances is the significance of the discovery clear at the time of announcement. For instance, the current interest in the science of cold fusion and logical devices based on optics derives from the ease in perceiving the benefits for energy provision and computing that breakthroughs in these areas will generate. In the discovery process, the difficulty of establishing priorities depends on the costs as well as the benefits of an area of research. Even when the benefits are clear, the costs of achieving the objective are not. In most instances, neither are clear. Little is known about the positive process by which the effective priorities for supporting research are determined in the world of open science.

Given the priorities, optimal search requires a breadth of approach, some *ex ante* duplication with different researchers independently going over the same ground, and a narrowing of focus as information improves. As compared to an ideal incentive system, racing typically generates excessive duplication of effort and a relative neglect of some avenues of inquiry.

Frequently, the most effective unit of search is a team rather than an individual. The efficacy of a team depends not only on the characteristics of its members but on its internal governance structure. An open science organization may do well in a race because of the quality of its processes for forming effective teams and motivating them through well-crafted rules for sharing effort and reward. Since the scientists and equipment are highly mobile resources, persistent success by particular university and government laboratories reflects either the importance of such governance structures or barriers to entry based on reputation.

While the priority reward system discourages the sharing of information within the scientific community, this tendency is partly offset by the advantages of participating in collaborative networks. Teams from universities, from non-educational but publicly funded laboratories and from some commercial R&D units form a net of informal alliances and associations that result in the sharing of some, but not all, information while the race proceeds. These alliances are constantly changing, and a team can participate in more than one at a time, with each involving different implicit obligations to exchange information. The effectiveness of such alliances in shortening the race will be enhanced if there are repeated interactions, a member's defection from the expected sharing can be measured and ostracism from participating in networks in the future is a sufficiently large penalty.

The structure of financing in open science also encourages a degree of early information sharing. Grants are typically allocated depending on appraisal by other scientists. Submissions by applicants provide precompetition information about specific research programs to the scientific community at large. Once a project is funded, success is registered by being the first to report results. Disclosure must be sufficiently detailed to allow replication. This emphasis on disclosure (hence free use) is suitable for inventions that do not have a well-defined body of potential users (market niche) and for which the economic value is highly uncertain.

The combining of teaching and research in universities also aids in the dissemination of research techniques, achievements and norms of open science. Science faculties are providing a joint product of research, teaching and training of researchers. Career risks from the racing environment are reduced by this portfolio of interests, if teaching and training play some role in acquiring a tenured position.

Proprietary science also relies on a race with the rewards based on priority of filing (inventing in the United States) for patents, on "publishing" an expression for copyright and on commercial exploitation of products based on knowledge protected by secrecy laws. All the intellectual property laws encourage early creativity. Each regime provides for a different degree and mode of disclosure. By the design of patent law, public disclosure is part of the patenting process and inherently part of copyright, unless an author suppresses publication. Trade secrecy obviously protects against public disclosure by some routes, for example, disclosure or exploitation by former employees, while permitting it along other dimensions, for example, reverse engineering. As with open science, the economic literature generally regards the racing as producing some wasteful duplication of effort.

In commercial innovation, research teams are often more productive than more fragmented searches. Each firm arranges the conditions for internal co-operation or controlled competition and decides to exchange certain information with subsets of other firms. Since profit plays a significant role in deciding how the partial co-operation among commercial R&D concerns will be defined, these alliances differ from those in open science and may have different stability properties.

Several features distinguish open science from proprietary science. Some of these distinctions involve subtle variations on the same mechanisms. For example, both systems encourage rivalry through establishing an ongoing series of tournaments with disproportionate gains to the winners. Both also encourage co-operation within competing teams and some restricted co-operation among alliances of competing players. The "culture" and expectations of behaviour of open science are also said to differ from that of proprietary science and to support more co-operation. The extent of the actual difference in culture as compared to the rhetorical difference is difficult to measure. Open science claims to be more collegial and less tainted by opportunistic behaviour than proprietary science. Neither is a world on to its own. There is a significant migration of researchers between the two communities, and achievements in one enhance the value of a researcher in the other.

An important distinction between open and proprietary science is the manner in which the reward to successful inventors is determined. In the case of proprietary science, commercial prospects for the invention determine the reward. In open science, the reward is based on peer evaluation of the contribution the invention is likely to make to ongoing research. This raises the question of the circumstances under which prizes are superior to property rights as an incentive to innovate.

Wright (1983) compared patents, prizes and contracts when innovators have better information of the value of the innovation and its costs than is available to policy setters. The patent is the most effective of the instruments in motivating economical use of the information about benefits. Both the patent and the prize provide incentives for cost information to be used. Both also encourage dissipation of wealth from racing while contracting controls dissipation from excessive entry.

It has long been understood that the outputs of open science are inputs to proprietary science. This has become known as the linear model of innovation. It has also been stressed by Rosenberg (1982) and others that open science benefits in many ways from developments in proprietary science. This is known as the feedback model.

Feedback occurs on many levels. Results of applied, commercially motivated research have, on occasion, opened up entire new fields of "basic" research. Solutions to technological problems obtained through trial and error in commercial establishments have pointed the way to theoretical explanations of the phenomena involved.

At another level, the discoveries made in a university laboratory would be significantly reduced without access to equipment – the production and finance of which depends on patent protection. Similarly, the dissemination of the results of laboratory work to students would be less effective without textbooks – the production and finance of which depends on copyright protection.

Increasingly, work done in the university setting is being patented. Procedures for licensing access to patents held by universities and sharing the revenue with the creative personnel, the science program and the universities' other departments are in an early stage of development. The boundaries between open and proprietary science are fuzzy and shifting.

Commercial R&D is motivated by the prospect of contracting with the potential users of the knowledge that is created. The economic purpose of intellectual property laws is to make the revenue-generating contracts and sales more economical to arrange. Some of the revenue potential is realized by selling products embodying the result of the quality-improving or cost-reducing innovation. However, others involve information transactions that allow a better or cheaper product to be made. The dissemination of the fruits of proprietary science is more complicated than setting a simple monopoly price during a period of protection. Many clever licensing and organizational mechanisms have been developed to reduce the well-known costs of making transactions based on new knowledge. In many instances, these contracting innovations both increase revenue and widen the market or audience reached.

The effectiveness and subtlety of these private responses are often underestimated. Nevertheless, there may be important potential gains from serving some users that cannot be realized by private arrangements. Some aspects of intellectual property law, for example, exemptions of coverage and compulsory licensing, can be viewed as responses to this contracting problem.

With respect to science, recent developments in the economics of growth and research have focused attention on the difficulty of arranging, through private means, the transfer of valuable information from inventors to a variety of follow-on inventors who can create additional value by building on the information base created by their predecessors. Before returning to this concern, we briefly describe the nature of rights and obligations conferred by different intellectual property regimes.

Characteristics of Intellectual Property Rights

All the intellectual property right regimes that we address – patents, integrated circuit design, plant breeders' rights, copyright and trade secrecy – are based on national laws or common law. In general, intellectual property right regimes can be described in terms of the following characteristics:

- eligibility for the right
- the duration of the right
- the breadth of the right
- the novelty requirement
- the disclosure requirement
- access requirements.

In briefly discussing how these characteristics differ across regimes, we use the specifics of Canadian practice unless otherwise noted. Although important international agreements constrain regime options of member countries, particularly for patent and copyright laws, national laws vary both in the letter and in enforcement.

The Patent Right

A patent is a property right in a new invention. It allows its owner (the patentee) to exclude others from making, using or selling the patented invention in the country granting the patent for up to 20 years from the date the application is filed.

In return for the *right to exclude*, the patentee must *disclose his or her invention*. Disclosure involves the provision of a clear and complete description of the invention on the patent application. The description must be sufficient to enable anyone with average skill in the technology to make or use the invention. Patent applications are published 18 months after they are filed.

New biotechnological inventions cannot be reproduced on the basis of a written description of the invention alone. A sample of the life form described in the patent application is also required. Samples must be deposited in a recognized depository and kept viable for the duration of the patent. They are available to anyone attempting to reproduce the invention.

Patents are for new (novel) technologies. Novelty implies an improvement on existing technologies. The improvement must be non-obvious. To meet the novelty requirement, an applicant must be the first to apply (file), except in the United States where the patent is granted to the first to invent. A patent will not be granted on an invention that has been in the public domain for more than a year.

Breadth and novelty are related. The broader the patent right, the less competition the patentee has from substitute inventions. That is, the broader the patent, the more distant the substitutes that would infringe the existing patent. A broader patent right implies greater horizontal differentiation.

The stronger the novelty requirement, the less competition the patentee has from improvement inventions. That is, the stronger the novelty requirement, the more significant is the improvement that would infringe the existing patent. A stronger novelty requirement implies greater vertical differentiation.

To qualify for a patent, an invention must be useful and operational. Patents can be granted on a new product, a new apparatus, a new chemical composition or a new process. Patents are not granted on ideas, scientific principles, theorems, organizational forms or methods, mathematical formulas or medical treatments. Algorithms in computer programs are patentable in the United States provided they are part of a process in which there are other steps (Carstens, 1994). The same is true in Canada.[1] Patents are also issued for *combinations* of hardware (communications, measurement devices) and software that derive their novelty from the mathematical algorithm they employ. It is the combination that is protected, however, not the algorithm itself.[2]

Patents are granted on microbial life forms including bacteria, yeast, moulds, fungi, actinomycetes, algae, cell lines, viruses and protozoa provided that the usual standards of novelty, utility and non-obviousness are met. Processes for manipulating or using micro-organisms may also be patentable. Micro-organisms that are found in nature are also patentable, but patent protection does not extend to the naturally occurring form of the micro-organism.

To date, the Canadian Patent Office has not allowed patent claims for new plants and animals (such as the Leder and Stewart genetically altered "Harvard" mouse) as has been the case in the United States and Japan. Processes for producing plants and animals which require significant human intervention may be patentable in Canada. Traditional biological breeding processes (cross-breeding) used for the production of plants and animals are considered to be natural processes and, as such, not patentable. New plant varieties developed by cross-breeding are covered by plant breeders' rights (see below).

The patentee's right to exclude is limited in a number of respects. First, there are provisions for the free use of patented inventions under some circumstances. For example, a patented invention may be used for research purposes.[3] This right is qualified. On the basis of cases decided in the United States, a research use defence does not appear to be available when the defendant's research is motivated by a commercial purpose (Eisenberg, 1989, p. 1023). Eisenberg also suggested that it is reasonable to infer that the potential research exemption may be broader than this:

> [T]he timing of the disclosure requirement suggests that there are limits to the patent holder's exclusive rights even during the patent term. If the public had absolutely no right to use the disclosure without the patent holder's consent until after the patent expired, it would make little sense to require that the disclosure be made freely available to the public at the outset of the patent term. The fact that the patent statute so plainly facilitates unauthorized use of the invention while the patent is in effect suggests that some such uses are to be permitted (Eisenberg, 1989, p. 1022).

Second, a patent may be subject to a compulsory licence on concessionary terms. Canadian patent law (section 66 of the *Patent Act*) provides for compulsory licences in cases of patent abuse. Patent abuse is defined (in section 65) to have occurred under the following circumstances.[4]

- Working in Canada is being hindered by the importation of the patented article from abroad.

- Demand for the patented article in Canada is not being met to an adequate extent and on reasonable terms.

- A trade or industry in Canada is unfairly prejudiced by the refusal of the patentee to grant a licence.

- A trade or industry in Canada is unfairly prejudiced by the terms of purchase of a patented article or the terms on which a patented process may be worked or the terms on which a licence is granted.

- Production or use in Canada of materials produced by a process covered by a patent is unfairly prejudiced.

As of 1993, patented medicines are exempted from the working in Canada provisions of section 65.

From 1923 to 1993, the *Patent Act* also provided for compulsory licensing of inventions for the preparation or production of food or medicine. During the period 1969 to 1993, the *Patent Act* permitted the issue of compulsory licences to manufacture, import, use or sell patented medicines or preparations for patented medicines or medicines made with a patented process. The power of the Commissioner of Patents to award compulsory licences to import patented medicines was qualified in the 1987 amendments to the *Patent Act*. These amendments had the effect of guaranteeing pharmaceutical patentees a period of exclusivity of seven to 10 years during which compulsory licences could not be awarded.

Compulsory licensing of patents, copyrights and registered integrated circuit topographies may also be ordered by the Federal Court of Canada under section 32 of the *Competition Act*, if the Court finds that the right in question has been used to restrict competition unduly. The statute also provides for other remedies including voiding a licence or other agreement relating to the use of intellectual property, enjoining the execution of a licence or other agreement, revoking a patent and expunging a trademark or an integrated circuit topography.

Third, a patentee's ability to make use of various forms of non-linear pricing is limited by national competition law. For example, it may be possible to expand the use of a patented invention while covering the costs of invention by engaging in price discrimination. Ideally, under discriminatory pricing, the marginal user pays marginal cost. Thus, price discrimination can maintain the incentive to innovate while also achieving efficient diffusion. Price discrimination can take a variety of forms including multi-part pricing and forcing, tying and bundling provisions. These are subject to national competition (antitrust) law. In some countries, such as the United States, antitrust law has been hostile to attempts of patentees to practise price discrimination. There have been fewer limitations in Canada (see below).

Copyright

Copyright grants an owner of an expression the exclusive right to reproduce his or her work and authorize its distribution. The "copy" can be transmitted to the public through a performance, an exhibition, a broadcast, a telecommunication signal, a sale or a rental. Copyrighted material includes books, artistic and musical works, records and tapes, films and audio-visual works, data bases and computer programs.

No formal procedure is required for obtaining a copyright. There is no initial screening process, as is the case for patents. Copyright attaches to a work automatically when it is embedded in some physical medium. Registration of a copyright facilitates its commercial exploitation and may aid in proving ownership in the case of an infringement.

The duration of copyright depends on the work that is protected and whether copyright is generated by a natural person or a corporation.[5] Copyright of a work created in the course of employment, belongs to the employer if the employment contract so stipulates. The legality of such clauses is important for certain copy-right-based industries, such as computer software production and advertising. For a written work, the length of copyright is the life of the author plus 50 years. For a movie, photograph or record, the duration of the right is 50 years. Over the last decade, the trend has been to extend the length of copyright.

Only the particular expression in a work, not the ideas incorporated in it, is protected by copyright. There is no bright line marking the boundary between idea and expression. Court decisions provide markers indicating where the boundary might be for each type of work. With a young technology, there are few markers and there is considerable uncertainty about what will and will not be protected.

That any expression "stands on the shoulders of" previous creators is obvious, although it is often denied by those who hold a romantic view of the author as an isolated genius. What Northrop Frye noted in discussing poetry is generally true.

> To demonstrate the debt of A to B may get C his doctorate if A is dead, but may land him in a libel suit if A is alive. This state of things makes it diffi-cult to appraise a literature that includes Chaucer, much of whose poetry is translated or paraphrased from others; Shakespeare, whose plays sometimes follow their sources almost verbatim; and Milton, who asked for nothing better than to copy as much as possible out of the Bible. It is not only the inexperienced reader who looks for a *residual* originality in such works: most of us tend to think of a poet's real achievement as distinct from, or even contrasted with, the achievement present in what he stole. But the central greatness of, for instance, *Paradise Regained* is not the greatness of the rhetorical decorations added to his source but the greatness of the theme itself, which Milton *passes on* to the reader from his source (Frye, 1960, pp. 43-44).

The breadth of protection granted by copyright is difficult to determine. Copyright does not generally require originality in expression. Unlike the patent, an identical expression does not infringe if it is created independently. One dimen-sion of the breadth of copyright is the minimum changes which would make an expression not infringe on an existing copyrighted work. This "distance" is deter-mined by the courts. A recent American court case, *Feist Publications, Inc. v. Rural Telephone Service, Co. Inc.* has made explicit a "novelty" requirement for copyright in a factual compilation such as a telephone directory or a data base. The work must exhibit a minimal level of creative selection, co-ordination or management. The breadth of copyright is also determined by the scope of rights to develop derivative material based on a copyrighted expression. For example, the author of a novel has the right to publish a translation and to develop a play or screenplay or television program based on that novel. Again, the courts are left with the difficult task of determining when a play or movie infringes on a novel telling a similar story.

From the perspective of science, the most important works protected by copyright are articles, books, photographs and computer programs. The distinction between idea and expression is currently being explored and mapped with respect to the copyrighting of software. The test for copyright occurs not in obtaining it, but in enforcing against infringement in a court. With a patent, an investigation and delineation of the property that can be protected occurs in obtaining the patent. What can be protected in a copyrighted work is determined only in an infringement action. The costs of definition are reduced, but there is more uncertainty for the rights holder. The software industry is currently waiting for a critical mass of court cases that will decide which copyrights claimed by companies in the industry are valid and which are not.

That the expression and not the idea is protected aids the dissemination of scientific knowledge. Authors of textbooks can access any aspect of science and compete to write better and clearer explanations of fundamental ideas. For those involved in the races of open science, publication of results is a means of obtaining other rewards and is not seen as a source of revenue. Indeed, the researcher typically pays a journal that has accepted his or her work for the right to publish the piece. Copyright plays no or little role in providing an incentive for the work to be written. As Arnold Plant remarked in 1934:

> There is ... an important group of authors who desire simply free publication; they may welcome, but they certainly do not live in expectation of, direct monetary reward. Some of the most valuable literature that we possess has seen the light in this way. The writings of scientific and other academic authors have always bulked large in this class (Plant, 1934, p. 169).

Plant continued: "For such writers copyright has few charms. Like public speakers who hope for a good press, they welcome the spread of their ideas" (Plant, 1934, p. 169). Nonetheless, the providers of the medium, the publishers, need to be remunerated for their efforts whether the supply price of their works is zero or negative. Copyright in journals presumably does this and may contribute to effective distribution.

Electronic networks provide an ideal way of disseminating working papers and preliminary research to interested individuals and institutions. How copyright will be defined and enforced on electronic bulletin boards is currently being addressed. There seems little doubt that the new technologies will dramatically alter the costs of disseminating codified information.

Copyright is a legal framework designed to make a contract effective in distributing a work widely while generating sufficient revenue to reward the creator. Copyright legislation also regulates the contracting of the rights created through listing exceptions, usually purposes for which copies can be made without paying the copyright owner, and provision of a fair dealing defence against charges of infringement.[6] In Canadian law, a copyright can be accessed without charge if the purpose is for private study or research, and the use is fair.

Whether scientific scholarship is included in research is an open question. In a draft report, the Copyright Subcommittee to the Working Group on Canadian Content and Culture states that "there is probably not much distinction between 'scholarship' on the one hand and 'private study' or 'research' on the other hand" (Copyright Subcommittee to the Working Group on Canadian Content and Culture, 1994, p. 25). The American fair use defence applies explicitly to scholarship and covers teaching which is not listed as subject to fair dealing in the Canadian Act. However, in a 1992 class action suit, *American Geophysical Union, et al. v. Texaco Inc.*, an American court ruled that unauthorized copying of articles from scientific and technical journals used by a for profit company's researchers was not a fair use (Banner, 1993, p. 32).

The Canadian courts have provided little guidance on what is fair except that the reproduction of all of a work is unfair and the fairness defence cannot be applied to an infringement of an unpublished work. In the United States, an unpublished work is covered by fair use.

The use of unpublished material, without acknowledgement, in scientific research obviously raises ethical and economic issues but may not represent infringement of copyright. The economic issue is whether the ideas in an unpublished work should be a common property right or a private one. To claim them as his or her own, the researcher must publish them, perhaps mixed in with other results. The ease with which a researcher can paraphrase and avoid copyright infringement depends on how the courts decide when an expression becomes original. What is clear is that fair dealing could not be used as a defence by a researcher deemed to be reproducing a substantial part of an unpublished work in Canada while an American researcher could employ such a defence. The infinite duration of copyright in unpublished work in Canada augments its inaccessibility.

Canadian copyright law allows the government to issue a compulsory licence for a book to be printed in Canada when that book is not reasonably available. A royalty set by the relevant minister has to be paid to the owner of the copyright. If for some reason, some scientific texts under copyright were not available in Canada they could be made available under these circumstances.

In Canada, copyright legislation provides explicitly for a rental right with respect to software and recordings. The rental right on software allows a copyright holder to deny a buyer the right to rent the software to others. By exercising this right and preventing rentals, piracy is made more costly and the revenue potential of the copyrighted work is enhanced. The rental right on software is particularly significant for the protection provided proprietary science by copyright.

Canadian copyright law also establishes a compulsory licence allowing copyrighted works carried on distant signals to be retransmitted by cable television systems. The royalty rates paid by the cable companies are set by the Copyright Board of Canada. Collectives, representing the owners of the copyrighted material carried on the retransmitted television signals, receive a share of the pool and disperse it to their members. In a similar manner, the Copyright Board sets rates for public performance, mainly through broadcasts, of the musical works of composers and lyricists. The funds collected are paid to a collective representing the creators, which in turn distributes the money collected to its members. Compulsory licences, collectives and rates set after hearings by a regulatory board are presumably a collective response to the costs of individual bargaining and contracting.

Consider the parallel between the music industry–broadcasters and that between open science–proprietary science. The interactions between the recording industry and broadcasters are complex with each creating value for the other. The law requires the broadcaster to pay the record company a royalty, and in many instances this may reflect the "shadow price" of the exchange. However, the recurrent "scandal" of payola indicates that, in some instances, the recording industry will pay substantial sums to have its products aired.

This complicated and uneven interaction in terms of value creation is similar to the relationship between open and proprietary science. Individual contracts between each composer and each programmer or record owner would be prohibitively costly as would be such contracts between each open scientist and a proprietary scientist. The broadcast public performance royalty is costly to administer. A conservative estimate is that the administrative costs of the collectives absorb about 15 percent to 20 percent of the funds collected. Despite this cost and the crudeness with which the scheme rewards suppliers and taxes users, it has survived. No clearly superior alternative systems have been proposed. Given the similarity of the measurement problems, it will be difficult to develop a system that is more subtle than taxing consumers and industry to create a fund which is then distributed by some collective procedure to inventors in place of an exclusive right.

The copyright law is permissive of price discrimination. Such discrimination can be efficient in distributing a public good or in allocating a levy (entry fee) to cover the difference in average cost and marginal cost for a declining-cost industry. Canadian copyright holders have greater scope to practise price discrimination than their counterparts in the United States, because the Canadian copyright law makes the first sale principle inapplicable in situations in which it is applicable in the United States (Copyright Subcommittee to the Working Group on Canadian Content and Culture, 1994, p. 22). In both Canada and the United States, copyright law provides for the legal prevention of imports of competing products that are not licensed for sale in the domestic market. For example, article 45.(1) of the Canadian Copyright Act states that, with some minor exceptions, it is illegal to import into Canada copies of books, if the right to reproduce the book in Canada has been licensed by the copyright holder.

Trade Secrecy

Information is protected as a trade secret under the following conditions.

- The information is useful and valuable in the trade or business.

- It is not generally known in the trade.

- Reasonable measures to protect it have been introduced.

The law of trade secrecy grants the right to take legal action against someone who has received information of this type in confidence and makes unauthorized use of it that damages the original holder of the information. An action can also be taken against the person who acquires the information by improper means. Ideas that spring from the information contained in a trade secret are also protected.

Trade secrecy is not part of property law. If the information is imparted to others through, for example, carelessness or reverse engineering, no action can be taken against those who obtain it. Trade secrecy law is not easily classified within the usual categories of law. Vaver (1981) provided this description: "Perhaps it should be straightforwardly recognized that the modern action for wrongful acquisition or use of trade secrets and confidential information is best treated as an action *sui generis*, using the most applicable features of equity and common law to serve functions and policies furthering a competitive market" (Vaver, 1981, p. 262).

An employment contract may contain a clause prohibiting disclosure of information gained from the employment. If this obligation is not met, the employer can sue for breach of contract. In many countries that do not explicitly have trade secrecy legislation, protection of confidences can be realized through contract law.

In providing redress, the courts generally consider the commercial damages caused by the unauthorized use of the information. Exemplary damages can and have been granted. Injunctions will be issued, if the situation warrants. The courts may also regulate the future use of the secret information by either one or both of the parties in an action.

The duration of protection provided by trade secrecy is, in principle, infinite. In practice, it depends on the difficulties of others obtaining the information by unprotected means or through their own innovative efforts. Protection against independent discovery is not granted by this body of law. Secrecy encourages more duplication than the patent when the costs of innovation are constant over time or not falling very rapidly. However, when costs are falling rapidly over time and inventing early is socially costly, trade secrecy provides lower rewards for being first thereby encouraging less costly racing than does the patent (Friedman, Landes and Posner, 1991, pp. 65-66).

Information that is well known in the industry or commercial circles cannot be protected by trade secret law. This requirement acts as the equivalent of a novelty requirement.

Trade secrecy can protect an innovation that is not patentable. When innovators with the lowest costs differ from those with a commercial advantage in developing the innovation, realizing the gains from specialization requires a mechanism for economically transferring an unprotected discovery from one party to the other. Commissions to pursue specified research are relatively common. Post-discovery agreements to share information are more problematic. Although information protected by trade secrecy can be and is licensed, Cheung concluded that "trade secret diffusion through contracts is difficult" (Cheung, 1982, p. 45). He based this conclusion on his finding that only 10 percent of a sample of over 150 contracts he investigated involved trade secrets. Interestingly, many development firms require an inventor to sign a waiver of any confidentiality before examining the idea. They do so to protect themselves from later claims under trade secrecy law.

A puzzle that remains is how independent innovation continues in the face of the obvious contracting problem. Anton and Yao (1994) provided some insights into conditions which permit an innovator to capture a substantial part of the commercial potential from a developer through a cleverly constructed contract. For example, they described competitive circumstances in the product market in which an innovator can divulge the nature of an unpatented technological advance to a potential developer without fear that the developer will exploit the innovation without compensation rather than agreeing to a contract with the innovator. The developer is prevented from developing the idea without compensation by the threat that the innovator will divulge the advance to a competitor in retaliation. Conversely, as long as the innovator continues to share in the developer's monopoly profit, the innovator has no incentive to divulge the idea to rival developers.

Trade secrecy also augments patent protection by keeping secret tacit information that is part of the innovation. Even when an innovation can be patented, an innovator may prefer trade secrecy as a mode of protection. Secrecy may be less costly than obtaining a patent, or it may offer stronger protection. Offering legal protection of some secrets may pre-empt the use of more costly private means of protecting information that would be adopted in the absence of legal sanctions. The Institute of Law Reform of Alberta listed the following consequences of an absence of trade secrecy law.

> Security precautions within companies would have to increase, and salary patterns to employees would probably change. Companies would have to make very sure that it was not worthwhile to decamp. Smaller companies would be at a disadvantage in these respects. The increased costs would be passed on to consumers. Innovative entrepreneurs would narrow the circle of those who they could trust. Ultimately, organized scientific and technological research could become fragmented. If there is no, or not sufficient, legal protection for trade secrets, there would be no way of licensing others to exploit them. If a trade secret holder could not utilize licences, either he would have to limit his utilization of the invention, or build manufacturing and marketing facilities for himself. Whether the trade secret holder can do

this more efficiently than a possible licensee depends upon the particular circumstances of the trade secret holder and his licensee. Some degree of economic inefficiency is likely (Institute of Law Reform of Alberta, 1986, pp. 115-116).

Obviously no written disclosure occurs when trade secrecy is chosen as compared to taking out a patent. David and Foray argued that "... trade secrecy and the various forms of access restriction (within the firms and scientific institutions, in the case of military research, at the international level) are important obstacles that impede knowledge distribution" (David and Foray, 1994, p. 30).

However, in the absence of a contract stipulating otherwise, finding out a secret by reverse engineering is legal. By choosing which disclosing actions will be legally protected and which will not, trade secrecy law influences where private expenditures to protect and uncover secrets will be focused. Friedman, et al. (1991) argued that the exemption for reverse engineering channels discovery efforts into an activity that generates more useful knowledge than required to reproduce the secret. This is also the rationale for permitting the reverse engineering of chip topographies (see below). The process of reverse engineering itself generates additional knowledge.

A defence in a trade secrecy action is that disclosure serves a public interest. However, this defence does not appreciably weaken protection since public interest is narrowly restricted to disclosures making the public aware of an offence committed or revealing information that affects public safety or health.

The *Integrated Circuit Topography Act*

An integrated circuit is a miniature electronic circuit. It is also called a microchip or semiconductor chip. The circuits on a chip are embodied in a three-dimensional hill and valley configuration called a topography. The original design of a chip topography is protected by the *Integrated Circuit Topography Act* which came into force in Canada in 1993. Similar legislation has been in force in the United States since 1984.

Programs stored on microchips may be protected under the *Copyright Act*. Chip manufacturing processes and circuit diagrams may be protected under the *Patent Act*.

The *Integrated Circuit Topography Act* provides the owners of registered topographies with the exclusive right to:

- reproduce the topography;
- manufacture a product incorporating the topography; and
- import or sell the topography or any product embodying it.

The right has a 10-year term. It is deemed to be exhausted after legitimate first sale. That is, the right holder cannot control resale of the topography. Copying for research, evaluation or teaching is permitted.

Reverse engineering of a topography is also permitted. A reverse-engineered topography is defined as one which has been copied but also improved in terms of size, speed or thermal output. A pirated chip, on the other hand, is one that is copied without testing, analysis or improvement. The degree of novelty required for the reverse-engineered product not to infringe can and does vary among the laws of different countries (Knopf, 1989, n. 44).

Plant Breeders' Rights

The *Plant Breeders' Rights Act* was passed in 1990. It provides for an exclusive right to sell and produce in Canada propagating material (seeds) of a new plant variety. It also provides an exclusive right to make repeated use of propagating material of a new plant variety in order to produce another plant variety. A variety is new if it is clearly distinguishable from all commonly known varieties as of the date of application.

The right is transferable and has a term of 18 years from the date of grant. Priority is given to the first to file. Applications and grants are published.

The right is subject to compulsory licensing in order to ensure that the plant variety in question is made available to the public "at reasonable prices." In the event of infringement, the holder of the right is entitled to sue for damages and injunctive relief. For an infringement defence:

- the variety in question cannot be new;

- the variety was being sold before the grant of the right; and

- the right holder has not maintained a sufficient supply of propagating material.

The United Kingdom and the United States have provided a property right in new plant varieties since 1964 and 1970 respectively. An international union of countries with plant breeders' rights legislation has existed since 1961.

The Choice of Intellectual Property Regimes

Patent and Copyright versus Trade Secrecy

Law makers can choose to place a creative activity under patent or copyright law. Alternatively, the creator can be given the right to protect the fruits of his or her labour through trade secrecy law. Of course, the government can choose to grant open access to a particular type of creative work or to works for a particular purpose. In some instances, the government may allow the owners of the creative work to choose among alternative modes of legal protection. To assess this option, the government has to predict which of the available alternatives the creators will choose under different circumstances.

Although they have the same economic function of providing incentives for creative acts, copyright and patent law differ considerably. The first copyright act, the Statute of Anne of 1710, was in part a response to the demands of publishing interests in England for protection from pirated works from Scotland and Ireland. As copyright has evolved to accommodate different technologies of "fixing" literary, musical, visual or dramatic works, the impact of copying on creative activity and the viability of the commercial distribution system serving each new media have been important influences on policy. Unauthorized production of patented goods has sometimes been a significant issue for patent policy, but it has not dominated the course of its history, as illegal copying has for copyright.

Illegal copying impacts differently on the book publishing, recording, film, television and software industries. Contract stipulations embodied in copyright law, such as a rental right for a particular medium, address the idiosyncratic piracy problems of that medium. The Canadian *Copyright Act* contains detailed sections on civil remedies concerning infringement and criminal penalties for commercial piracy of copyright. The copyright-based industries have put considerable pressure on the government to enforce the criminal provisions against piracy. In some instances, they finance private security investigations to aid in that enforcement.

The industries involved with mass distribution of copyrighted material also face considerable transaction costs. Transacting difficulties are exacerbated by piracy but would exist even in its absence. Presumably, to reduce transaction costs, copyright legislation affecting these industries contains detailed provisions for compulsory licensing and for adjudicating, among collectives, the terms for granting access to copyrighted material. For the copyright industries, policy often includes photocopying levies, blank tape levies and funds from video rental income that are set aside and redistributed to performers, creators and producers to augment the income they receive by contract. The fair dealing defence against infringement and various specific exemptions provide many more individuals with freedom to reproduce copyrighted material than are allowed to access patent rights on terms not acceptable to the owner. Such features are generally absent for industries depending on patents.

Wiley (1991, pp. 380-383) argued that the disclosure and search processes required to obtain a patent are particularly supportive of innovation for activities in which a number of contributors provide incremental advances of the state of the art (standing on the shoulders of predecessors of ordinary stature). For this reason, he endorsed the American decision to provide patent protection and deny copyright protection for systems and processes.

Designing and writing software is an example of a creative activity in which a choice of protective regimes exists. For example, in the United States software can be protected by patent, copyright or trade secrecy. To receive a patent, the developer of software must establish that it is a novel and useful process or a patentable apparatus while demonstrating that it does not foreclose general use of the algorithms being employed.[7]

The last factor reflects the principle that a law of nature or abstract idea cannot be patented. This rule is of the same level of generality as the copyright guideline that an idea cannot be protected. Unfortunately, it provides as little help to a patent examiner as the patent maxim does to judges. A further difficulty is the determination of prior art. Prior art is determined by reference to existing patents.

Until the last decade, little software was patented. It was protected instead by trade secrecy. As a result, existing software patents give an imprecise picture of the state of software technology. This has given rise to concern that patent examiners in the United States are granting patents to software that does not meet the novelty requirement.

The creator of software can also protect it by copyright. Copyright grants a longer period of protection than a patent but does not protect against an independent development of what otherwise would be an infringing program. There is also considerable uncertainty as to the protection software copyright grants to non-literal infringement (i.e., minor variations on the copyrighted work) (Carstens, 1994, p. 74). A patent can protect a piece of software as an entity on the basis of its function. This is not true of copyright.

Software can also be protected under trade secrecy law. Protection depends on the software being in use, being valuable, being secret and the owner taking precautions to safeguard it against theft. In the United States, trade secrecy law is mainly state law and varies among states. Trade secrecy protection is not limited in duration. However, no protection is provided against reverse engineering. If the trade secret has been licensed, the contract may restrict the scope of reverse engineering. For example, software is often delivered in object or machine code under a contract prohibiting the customer from reverse-compiling it to a language that is more amenable to structural analysis. In addition, if the software can be copyrighted, it cannot be protected by trade secrecy law.

In deciding which regime to use, a software owner presumably assesses the strength of protection, its breadth, the impact of disclosure or reverse engineering on "appropriability" and the expected enforcement against trespass.

Patent and Copyright versus *Sui Generis* Legislation

Both patent and copyright have adapted to rapidly changing technologies. This accommodation is particularly clear with respect to copyright. The interpretation of concepts, such as what constitutes a copy, whether a work was being delivered to the public, breadth of coverage and fair dealing, differ with the mode of fixation and the technology of dissemination. Copyright impacts on the music industry in a different way than on print publishing. A knowledge of the details of the law in one area is of little guidance in the other. Collectives, royalty funds, compulsory licensing, contractual stipulations and concerns with piracy occur in each, but the incidence is markedly different. In cases where the principles of patent and copyright protection are appropriate to the development of the technology, the courts and legislators have been able to frame decisions and the regulations applying them.

With some technologies, new "property" legislation is adopted either because the principles of patent or copyright are not suited to the situation or the processes of applying these principles are sufficiently idiosyncratic to warrant a distinct act. The cost of not adapting an existing intellectual property regime to the new technology is the loss of predictability due to the absence of both legal precedents and an established international treaty framework.

Margins are often instructive in economics. Copyright protection, for example, provides an alternative to separate chip legislation. A chip topography is constructed from a series of masks that can conceivably be protected as designs under copyright law. It is more profitable for the creator of the mask to sell the chip topography rather than the mask. If the mask was protected by copyright, it would be infringed by imitators of the chip. In this instance, copyright protection would inhibit reverse engineering while chip topography protection explicitly allows for it.

Chip protection is an area of creativity for which a separate law has been deemed superior to providing coverage under the elastic tent of copyright. The semiconductor industry has generally supported legislation providing less durable protection and requiring more disclosure than copyright. We place the music industry at the margin of idiosyncratic structures that can coexist with the prior body of copyright law.

The different contracting problems faced by the music industry, compared to the book publishing and film industries, are reflected in the existence of two international conventions, distinct from the main copyright conventions, that address the international co-ordination of laws. These are the International Convention for the Protection of Performers, Producers of Phonograms and Broadcasting Organisations, adopted at Rome in 1961, and the Convention for the Protection of Producers of Phonograms against Unauthorized Duplication of Their Phonograms, adopted at Geneva in 1971. The Rome convention governs the complex relationship between composers, performers, record companies and broadcasters. It co-ordinates laws and regulations implementing an interconnected set of rights and obligations for each of these parties and sanctions a neighbouring right – a public performance right in broadcast of works for performers and record companies.

The traditional neighbouring-rights initiative collects funds from broadcasters and disperses them to record companies and performers of recorded music. This right is similar in effect to that exercised under copyright by composers. Recently, some countries have augmented this approach with levies charged on blank tapes or recording machines. These programs are often enabled by separate national legislation. The funds collected from these taxes have been dispersed to the same groups according to prescribed formulas. An economic reason for the wider use of such levies in the music industry is that new copying technologies have reduced the ability of a contract to provide adequate remuneration for record companies, performers and composers.

THE IMPORTANCE OF ENDOGENOUS GROWTH MODELS

FROM EXOGENOUS TO ENDOGENOUS GROWTH

IN THE EARLY 1960S, economists from the two Cambridges engaged in a spirited debate on the modelling of economic growth. Differences of opinion were expressed on the nature of the capital input, the process for setting wages, the representation of technology by a production function, the savings relation and stability properties of different models. Although little attention was paid to research and development and organizational issues, one can discern some of the roots of recent work in endogenous growth in that debate.

In particular, on the neoclassical side of the debate, output was related to capital and labour inputs by a constant returns-to-scale production function. In this framework, the generation of a positive equilibrium rate of growth depends on exogenous improvements in technology. Nature lifted her skirts by a predictable amount each year revealing a superior set of technological alternatives. These improvements are assumed to be labour augmenting. Under these circumstances, the capital-to-raw labour ratio can continue to increase without reducing capital productivity, as long as the ratio of capital to efficiency units of labour does not fall. Nature's contribution, a costlessly generated increment in knowledge capital, interacts with raw labour units to produce efficiency units of labour. The impact of knowledge capital on the effectiveness of raw labour depends only on the increment in its stock and not on its level.

This last aspect of knowledge capital has been preserved in recent work that has endogenized technical change. What nature was earlier assumed to bestow in a mysterious fashion is now produced within the economy. In some of the endogenous growth models, nature's role was replaced, at least in part, by an externality, generated by the R&D process or by human capital accumulation (cf. Lucas, 1993). To focus our discussion, we concentrate on the R&D-based models. In this case, the externality is an unpriced and therefore unmanaged by-product of the innovative activities of firms. An externality is not needed for sustained endogenous growth. Without an externality, investment in R&D takes into account all the different impacts on value at the margin. We are agnostic about whether a model with or without externalities better describes the growth phenomenon. We concentrate on the models with spillovers, since they pose the more interesting challenges to intellectual property regimes.

With respect to models that focus on externalities generated by the accumulation of knowledge capital, a sceptic might argue that we have just renamed our ignorance, substituting externality for nature within the old narrative. The difference is, however, marked. For an endogenous effect, we can make and test hypotheses concerning its roots and alter its impact through better-crafted policies. This agenda includes understanding the private arrangements that reflect the often uncodified understanding participants in the economy have of the consequences of their actions and their genius in devising remedies. Similarly, it includes understanding the interactions of the relevant private parties with the government as they devise and formulate policies that reduce the wealth dissipation from the externality.

INTELLECTUAL PROPERTY IN ENDOGENOUS GROWTH MODELS

TO CAPTURE THE FLAVOUR of the aggregated endogenous growth literature, we provide a capsule summary of two variants, the variety model and the quality ladder model.

The Variety Model

The variety model presented by Grossman and Helpman (1991) is based on the Dixit–Stiglitz (1977) model of monopolistic competition. In the variety model, both the elasticity of demand for, and the profitability of, any one variety depend on the number of varieties. The more varieties there are, the higher is the elasticity of demand for any one variety and the lower is its profitability. Entry continues until the flow of monopoly profit is just sufficient to cover the fixed cost of entry. In this model, the fixed cost of entry is the R&D cost of developing a new variety.

Imitation, that is, the introduction of a variety that is identical to one of the existing varieties, is ruled out in either of two ways. The first assumption is that the costs of innovation and imitation are assumed to be sunk, and competition between firms producing the same variety is assumed to be undifferentiated Bertrand. In this case, a potential imitator knows that competition with the innovator will drive the price to marginal cost leaving no prospect of recovering the cost of imitation. As a consequence, there is no imitation and innovators can expect an infinite stream of monopoly profits.

The alternative assumption is that each inventor receives a costlessly enforceable, infinitely lived patent. The number of varieties in existence depends solely on the R&D cost of inventing another variety. The lower the cost, the more varieties there will be. All varieties in existence, regardless of when they were introduced, are equally novel, equally good substitutes for each other and non-infringing. Infringing varieties are never introduced.

The growth process in this model involves the continuous expansion of the number of varieties available. This generates greater utility or, if the good involved is an intermediate good, greater total factor productivity (TFP). Left as we have described it, however, the growth process would grind to a halt. The expansion of the number of varieties available would reduce anticipated monopoly profit and, eventually, entry would cease. That is, no more R&D would be done.

To get continuous growth in this model, it is assumed that there is a learning curve for R&D and that the learning involved is available to any firm contemplating the invention of a new variety. More precisely, the productivity of the R&D effort of any one inventor and, hence the cost of inventing, depend on the cumulative R&D effort of all the inventors in the economy. If the decline in R&D cost is sufficient to offset the decline in the profitability of each variety, the introduction of new varieties will continue indefinitely.

In essence, continuing growth is generated by assuming that the productivity of R&D depends on cumulative R&D effort and that this accumulated knowledge spills over in its entirety to all potential inventors. While the inventor receives an ironclad patent on his or her invention and can exclude others from imitating the good for sale or use in the factor or product market, the patent owner cannot appropriate the value of the knowledge increment caused by the invention. This knowledge increment is available without cost to anyone wishing to invent a new variety. This means that there is no trade secrecy, and reverse engineering is costless or that all relevant knowledge ("blueprints") is revealed in the patent.

The learning externality occurs at the industry level and is not internalized by the firm. Each research firm acts as if it has constant marginal (average) cost and its size is indeterminate. The Grossman–Helpman specification also has the feature that entry by a new research firm or expansion by an existing one does not affect the productivity of resources already committed to the industry through crowding, i.e., there is no racing or common property right effect generated by free entry.

Without a spillover, a firm making an innovation has an advantage over rivals in making the next innovation. Rivals that have not experienced as many successes begin the race from an inferior knowledge base. As that advantage affects further innovation, the lead of the best firm in the economy expands. When the lead reaches a critical level, no rival firm will do R&D because of the extent of the leading firm's know-how advantage. This monopoly firm innovates at a pace dictated by the interests of its shareholders. Unlike the competitive spillover process, the monopoly innovator takes learning into account. The economy faces a potential monopoly problem but not an R&D spillover problem. In a later section, we discuss how adjustments in ownership may resolve the monopoly problem.

The Quality Ladder Model

The quality ladder model assumes that there are a fixed number of products or industries in the economy. The quality of each product can be varied (in discrete steps) up to the quality of the variant defining the state of the art at the moment. Higher-quality products generate a greater flow of services to their users and thus command a higher price. In the Grossman–Helpman version, the equilibrium price in each sector is equal to the marginal cost (equal average production cost) of the second-best variant less epsilon.[8] Therefore, only the best variant is produced.

The state of the art can be improved by R&D. A firm that is successful in inventing a higher quality product earns "monopoly" profits dependent on the quality improvement achieved. The size of this improvement, the distance between rungs on the ladder, is determined endogenously in the model. This monopoly continues until another advance in the state of the art occurs at which time profits go to zero.

Imitation of the state-of-the-art quality is precluded by either of two assumptions. The first assumption is that invention and imitation costs are sunk and that competition between the inventor and the imitator is undifferentiated Bertrand. Under these circumstances, there will be no imitation, and monopoly profits are secure until the next quality improvement occurs. The alternative assumption is that infinitely lived and costlessly enforceable patents are granted for improvements in the state of the art. The patent becomes redundant once a further improvement in the state of the art occurs.

The growth process in the quality ladder model involves continual improvements in product quality. This results in greater utility, in the case of final goods and services, or higher TFP, in the case of intermediate goods and services. The spillover makes every potential inventor as knowledgable of the state of the art as the developer of that state. Introducing the most recent innovation in an industry does not create an advantage over others in terms of the mapping of resources expended into the probability distribution of making the next innovation.

The spillover mechanism in the quality ladder model can be perceived as full disclosure or costless reverse engineering. With this spillover, outsiders compete on equal terms for an improvement in the state of the art. Although the temporarily incumbent monopolist and outsiders face the same technical opportunities for improving the state of the art, the incumbent would rather spend R&D funds in an industry in which it does not currently operate. The incumbent would have the same expectation of obtaining a new temporary monopoly position in an outside industry as in its home industry but would not hasten the demise of its existing monopoly. As a result, a firm is a state-of-the-art-leader in a particular sector for only one period. There is no continuity of technical dominance of any industry by a particular firm in this model.

Grossman and Helpman described the spillover in their version of the quality ladder model as implying that "newcomers can attempt to develop innovative products without having themselves taken all of the steps in creating the technologies for previous generation products" (Grossman and Helpman, 1991, p. 92). This industry orientation has significant consequences, if the knowledge spillover is blocked. In this situation, a firm making an innovation has an advantage over rivals in making the next innovation. Rivals would begin the race from a knowledge base for that industry that is at least one rung inferior to the quality leader. As that advantage affects further innovation, the lead of the best firm in the industry will widen. At some point, this lead will be such that no rival will compete against the leader. Each leading firm stands on its own shoulders as far as stepping to the next rung. The leader is a monopolist in both the product market and R&D.

On the new equilibrium path, a single firm that is technologically dominant eventually dominates the industry. The industrial make-up of the economy is very different from that of the spillover case in which no firm is the market leader for successive steps in the quality ladder. Rivalrous R&D is replaced by monopoly R&D. The pace of innovation depends on the decisions of the leading firm.

IMPLICATIONS FOR INTELLECTUAL PROPERTY

The Variety Model

The variety model of endogenous growth can function without any intellectual property. Barriers to entry can provide the incentive to invent. Disclosure of all knowledge underlying an invention is costless and unavoidable. The expanding pool of public knowledge is a by-product of "commercial" R&D. Because R&D costs are continuously reduced by the expansion of the pool, continuous growth in income per capita can occur. There is no basic applied research distinction and no non-profit research sector.

Intellectual property in the form of an infinitely lived costlessly enforceable patent is a substitute for barriers to entry (imitation) as an incentive to invent. If there is no barrier to imitation, then intellectual property is essential for growth. With no barrier to imitation and no intellectual property, the economy in the variety model presented in Grossman and Helpman (1991) would continue to produce some assumed initial number of varieties forever.

Under the Grossman–Helpman intellectual property regime for this model, the patent awarded to the inventor of a new variety is infinitely lived. The consequences of shortening its term would be to reduce the number of varieties available at any point in time. The value of a firm with the right to produce a variant would fall. With a sufficient reduction in the patent length, sustained growth would not be possible, assuming it was possible with an infinite duration of patent.

While the duration of this patent is specified, the breadth of it is not. Products are not defined over a metric space, and the partitioning of the product space into groups that are close to each other cannot be done. There are only two meaningful choices – to grant separate patents for each variant or make a single patent cover the whole product space. Grossman and Helpman chose the first option. If the second option had been chosen, the first inventor would control the field and any new variant would be an infringement. The knowledge externality would be internalized and the only issue would be the monopoly control of technical change. The very broad patent envisaged in this framework is similar to that advocated by Kitch (1977) and discussed in more detail below.

With the Grossman and Helpman assumption of a separate patent for each variant, all varieties are equally close substitutes, and the number of varieties is continuously increasing over time. The patentee's degree of monopoly is also decreasing over time. There is no explicit novelty requirement in this patenting framework, although one is defined implicitly by the amount of R&D that is required to invent a new variety.

The following observations hold for both the variant and the quality ladder models. With the Bertrand assumption and imitation costs providing protection, there is no obvious mechanism by which the knowledge is disseminated from current inventors to their future rivals. As the patent requires disclosure, the assumption that patenting provides the product protection makes the assumption of costless disclosure and absorption of information more credible. Since all knowledge embodied in the state-of-the-art quality is costlessly observable to other inventors, disclosure is complete and instantaneous. Secrets are revealed costlessly. Their revelation cannot be a source of legal action.

The Quality Ladder Model

Like the variety model, the Grossman and Helpman (1991) quality ladder model can function without any intellectual property. If the state-of-the-art quality is protected by barriers to imitation (sunk costs, undifferentiated Bertrand intra-quality level competition), there is an incentive to invent higher quality products. The knowledge embodied in these inventions is available to all other inventors and thus constitutes the stock of public knowledge. As is the case with the variety model, the "science base" is a by-product of commercial R&D activities.

If there are no barriers to imitation, an infinitely lived patent is necessary to provide an incentive to make quality-improving inventions which are, in turn, the source of TFP growth in the model. The effective patent term is less than infinite in that the current state of the art is rendered obsolete within a finite period by further quality improvements. The speed at which obsolescence occurs depends on the cost of inventing an improved product and other parameters. The lower this cost, the shorter the effective patent term. If the statutory patent term were finite, the expected profitability of quality improvements would be inversely related to the chosen duration of protection. With a lower patent term, there would be fewer quality-improving inventions and, by definition, slower growth. At some critical duration, the growth rate would go to zero.

Since innovation can only occur in terms of improving the quality of any of the fixed number of products, an inventor cannot invent closer to any one variety. This model is similar to the variety model in not having a metric of closeness among products. The indexing of the products from 1 to n is arbitrary. Each bears the same relationship to the others.

The breadth options for patent policy are limited to protecting each product separately, to the Grossman and Helpman assumption or to providing a patent for the whole field of n products. The broad patent would allow its owner to manage the R&D development to fill out the protected rung of the economy-wide ladder. The firm holding the patent for one level of technology would be informed by the developments at other levels. It would be as efficient at developing new product innovations within that technology as any other firm. The probabilities of a better generation of technology being patented and subsequently "filled out" restrict the profit potential from patenting an earlier technology level.

Novelty can be measured by the length of the minimum distance between rungs on the ladder that an innovation must attain to receive a patent. This novelty requirement is a policy parameter. If this threshold is set above the rate of quality improvement that is privately optimal for inventors, fewer quality improvements may occur but the ones that do occur will be larger.

WELFARE ANALYSIS OF INTELLECTUAL PROPERTY

THE THREE EXTERNALITIES

THERE ARE THREE EXTERNALITIES or potential externalities in the endogenous growth models described above:

- the consumers surplus (Nordhaus) externality;
- the Schumpeterian creative destruction externality; and
- the shoulders of giants externality.

There will be a consumers surplus externality if some of the benefits of a new innovation accrue to users. This is a positive externality. It occurs if innovations are subject to competition from imitations or potential imitations or if innovators are not able to engage in discriminatory pricing. A consumers surplus externality occurs in the endogenous growth models described above because the owners of firms do not recognize that they are also consumers.

A creative destruction externality occurs if an innovation reduces profits or rents on existing products or inputs. This is a negative externality. For this to happen, prices of the products or inputs involved must exceed their respective opportunity costs. A creative destruction externality occurs in the endogenous growth models described above because the shareholders of the innovating firms do not realize that, given the assumption that all individuals hold diversified investment portfolios, they also own the firms which produce existing varieties or qualities of products.

A shoulders of giants or follow-on innovation externality occurs when a current invention facilitates or otherwise reduces the cost of subsequent inventions and the initial innovator is not compensated for this contribution. This occurs in the endogenous growth models described above because future consumers are assumed to be unable to make contracts with current inventors. We return below to the issue of the consistency of these externalities with the saving and portfolio assumptions of the endogenous growth models.

DIFFUSION OF KNOWLEDGE

INTELLECTUAL PROPERTY MAY ALSO FACILITATE the diffusion and application of knowledge. This goes beyond the mere disclosure of the knowledge in a patent application. Intellectual property rights can reduce the cost of transactions involving knowledge. The principal barrier to the sale of knowledge, as explained by Arrow (1962), is that it must be disclosed to a potential buyer if it is to be evaluated. But once it has been disclosed, the buyer may no longer have any reason to pay for it. If the knowledge involved is protected by an intellectual property right, the buyer can be enjoined from using it until he has paid for it. Further guarantees against opportunism on the part of either the buyer (contingent or running royalties, post-expiry royalties) or the seller (field of use restrictions, grantbacks, best-effort clauses) can be embedded in licensing agreements. The importance of these licensing provisions in facilitating follow-on innovation is discussed below.

Intellectual property rights may also facilitate the transfer of tacit or uncodified knowledge. It is argued that the provision of assistance (tacit knowledge) can be bundled with the licensing of the use of codified knowledge such as patents or copyrights for purposes of transfer. It has been argued that the willingness of an inventor to transfer both codified and complementary tacit knowledge to others is an increasing function of the strength of both the intellectual property and trade secrecy protection available (David, 1993, pp. 242-243).

PERSPECTIVES FOR WELFARE ANALYSIS

THE WELFARE ANALYSIS OF INTELLECTUAL PROPERTY can take either a national or a global perspective. The two may differ depending on the relative size of the national economy involved and on the importance of indigenous innovative activity.

The welfare analysis of intellectual property can be conducted under a variety of assumptions regarding the nature of innovative effort. It can be assumed to be:

- either responsive or unresponsive to prospects for financial gain; and
- unique in that only one individual or group has the capacity to make a specific innovation, differentiated in that innovative capacities differ or are homogeneous.

If there is free entry into innovative activity and innovative capabilities differ, inframarginal inventors will earn rents. With free entry and homogeneous inventors, innovative activity yields no rents *ex ante*.

THE CONSUMERS SURPLUS EXTERNALITY

THE CONSUMERS SURPLUS EXTERNALITY is the focal point of Nordhaus' (1969) pioneering optimal patent term model illustrated in Figure 1. The model assumes a (non-drastic) process invention that reduces the cost of production in the using industry from c_0 to c_1. The maximum royalty income of the inventor is $A per period during the life of the patent. After the patent expires, the invention becomes freely

FIGURE 1

THE CONSUMER EXTERNALITY — THE NORDHAUS MODEL

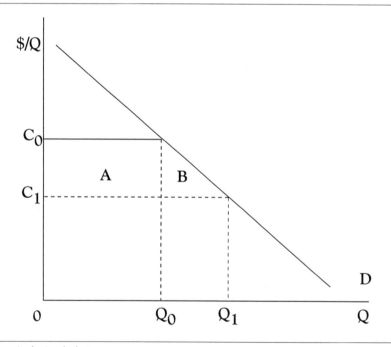

Source: Author's calculations.

available, production cost in the using industry falls to c_1, output expands to Q_1, and an additional consumers surplus in the amount of $(A+B) per period is realized. The externality is the present value of the difference between the inventor's income of $A per period during the life of the patent and the social value of the invention ($A per period forever plus $B per period after the expiry of the patent).

In the Nordhaus model, a longer patent term generates a social benefit by attracting more resources to inventive activity through increasing the present value of the promised royalty stream. The increased research effort results in more quality or greater cost reductions in using industries. The social cost of a longer patent term is that it postpones the free availability of the cost-reducing technology, hence the realization of triangle B in Figure 1. The socially optimal patent term is such that the gain in surplus from the additional inventive activity induced by a longer patent term is equal to the loss in surplus resulting from the further postponement of the expansion of output in the using industry. The more elastic the demand for the using industry's product and the less responsive inventive activity is to an increase in the expected income of inventors, the shorter the optimal patent term will be.

The optimal patent term also depends on the assumption made about entry into inventive activity. There are two alternatives. The first is the unique inventor assumption. The second is the rival inventors assumption. Rivalry may occur before the granting of the patent (rivalry for the patent) or after the granting of the patent (inventing around the patent) or both. The most extreme form of the rival inventors assumption is that there is free entry into inventing. In this case, the *ex ante* profit from inventing is zero and the optimal patent term is shorter than is implied in the discussion above.[9] The social cost of a longer patent term becomes the postponement of the realization of both rectangle A and triangle B in Figure 1 as opposed to B alone in the unique inventor case.

Another factor influencing optimal duration is what motivates inventive activity. The traditional approach stresses commercial incentives, but non-pecuniary factors are likely to be significant in cultures, such as ours, that place a high status on discovery. The commercial incentives to innovate may also be understated by area A if the innovator can benefit from relative price changes generated by the discovery (Hirshleifer, 1971). In addition, the attitude to risk will change the calculation of the best duration (Rafiquzzaman, 1987) while moral hazard and adverse selection problems raise the costs of transferring risk through financial markets.

The optimal patent term also depends on whether a national or a global perspective is taken. From a technology-importing country's perspective, the optimal patent term may be shorter than from a technology-producing country's perspective. In the case of a country that imports all its technology, rectangle A is transferred abroad for the life of the patent and the cost of extending the patent term is, again, the postponement of the realization of both A and B in Figure 1. With side payments, countries could agree on a patent system that maximized joint wealth. Presumably the broadening of trade agreements to incorporate intellectual property results in beneficial political exchange. In situations where a country may adopt more or less protective intellectual property laws in return for changes in trade or investment regimes, the patent duration must be judged in the context of the overall set of policies and not in isolation.

The Nordhaus model assumes that the other sectors of the economy are characterized by marginal cost pricing. As a consequence, the expansion of the innovation-using sector results in a net increase in surplus. Innovation does not result in a destruction of rents elsewhere in the economy. Nor is there an intertemporal externality in the model. A longer patent term does imply a greater cost reduction in the using industry, but this does not make subsequent cost reductions less costly or more attractive.

In addition to the optimal duration of patent protection, the Nordhaus model can be used to analyze the consequences of compulsory licensing. Tandon (1982) and others have shown that the welfare cost of a given incentive to invent could be reduced by a policy of lengthening the patent term while imposing compulsory licensing at concessionary royalty rates. This point can readily be demonstrated using Figure 1. The inventor's maximum royalty income is $(c_0 - c_1)Q_0$ or ρQ_0 per period. The inventor's flow of royalty income could be maintained by cutting the royalty rate in half and doubling the number of periods over which royalties are collected (assuming, for simplicity, a discount rate of zero). The deadweight loss per period from output foregone in the using industry (triangle B in Figure 1) can be written as $1/2\rho^2\eta$ where η is the elasticity of demand for the product of the using industry. Doubling the patent term and cutting the royalty rate in half cuts the deadweight loss in half to $(\rho/2)^2\eta$ or $1/4\rho^2\eta$. The deadweight loss is endured for a longer period, but its magnitude is proportionally smaller. The limiting case is that of an infinite patent term with compulsory licences at infinitesimal royalty rates.

SCHUMPETERIEN CREATIVE DESTRUCTION

THE CREATIVE DESTRUCTION EXTERNALITY is illustrated in figures 2A and 2B. The creative component is illustrated in Figure 2A. A new product A is invented. The inventor receives P_A in profit (gross of the cost of invention) per period during the term of the patent. Consumers surplus in the amount of S_A per period is also realized. As a consequence, there is a positive externality in the amount of S_A per period during the term of the patent and $S_A+P_A+W_A$ after the expiry of the patent. By itself, this results in an under-allocation of resources to invention in that new products, with an R&D cost in excess of the present value of the flow of gross profit, P_A, but less than the social benefit of the invention $[P_A+S_A$ (indefinitely) $+W_A$ (after the expiry of the patent)], will not be invented.

The destructive component is illustrated in Figure 2B. Product B is an existing substitute for new invention A. Product B is priced above production cost and is yielding a flow of monopoly profits which were expected to cover the R&D cost of inventing it. The appearance of product A on the market reduces the demand for product B. The producer of B loses S_B per period (during the life of the patent or other source of monopoly power). This is a negative externality. If this is greater than the positive externality, $S_A + W_A$ (after the expiry of the patent), there will be an over-allocation of resources to invention.

FIGURE 2

CREATIVE DESTRUCTION

FIGURE 2A

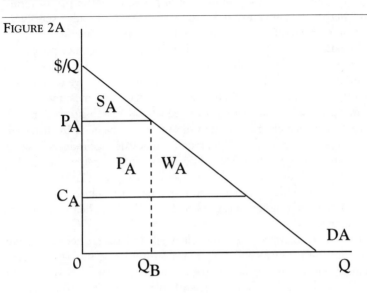

FIGURE 2B

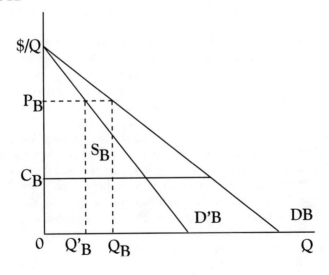

Source: Author's calculations.

A longer patent term extends the period over which P_A is realized by the patentee thereby increasing the incentive to invent. It also postpones the realization of W_A on inventions that would have occurred with shorter patent terms. Depending on whether the amount of new product R&D was initially excessive, a longer patent term may be either surplus-increasing or surplus-reducing.

A more broadly defined patent right would rule out the development of close substitutes for patented products. Whether this is surplus increasing, depends on whether the initial number of varieties was too low or too high. As we have noted, the concepts of close and distant "substitutability" have no meaning in the Dixit–Stiglitz model in which all varieties are equally close substitutes for each other. A distinction between close and distant substitutes can be made in an address model. Maintaining symmetry in this model requires that existing products "change addresses" as new products enter the market. The issue of optimal patent breadth has been considered in the context of an address model by Klemperer (1990).

The determination of the optimal breadth of a patent is subject to the same considerations as the determination of the optimal term. Indeed, the two should be determined simultaneously.

Given the term, the narrower the patent claim allowed, the greater the amount of competition that the patentee will face from non-infringing substitute inventions. With closer non-infringing substitutes available, the value of the patent monopoly is reduced. If the patent has a sufficiently narrow definition, the inventor has no monopoly power and the patent provides no incentive to invent.

The more narrowly defined the patent claim, the longer the term required to provide a given incentive to invent. This raises the question of whether a broad claim with a short term is socially preferable to a narrow claim with a long term. The answer depends on the assumptions made regarding the nature of the interaction between the patentee and potential imitators.

In Klemperer's model, the breadth–duration issue turns on the different distortions associated with narrow and broad claims. With a narrow claim, the distortion is the result of substitution by those preferring the patented brand in favour of lower-priced close substitutes.[10] With a broad claim, a patentee who finds it profitable to provide several varieties will also find it profitable to price them so the users' choice is not distorted. The only distortion will be from substitution outside the broad class covered by the patent. A narrow, long-lived patent is preferred if the deadweight loss from substitution in favour of distant substitutes exceeds the deadweight loss from substitution in favour of close substitutes.[11]

Gallini (1992) analyzed a different situation. In her model, a broader patent right prevents socially wasteful duplicative inventing and increases the maximum rent the patentee can expect to earn. Gallini finds that the optimal policy is to make the patent broad enough in scope to deter all inventing around. This returns her to the Nordhaus situation (described above) in which the patent term is set to trade off additional innovative effort from a unique inventor against the additional deadweight loss (triangle B in Figure 1) from restricting the use of the innovation for a longer period.

There is no follow-on or improvement innovation in the models described above. Imitators may enter the market but these new entrants do not build on the knowledge embodied in existing varieties. There is no cumulative sequence of innovations in these models. While the benefits of innovation are shared with imitators as well as consumers, they are not shared with future generations of innovators. Indeed, in Gallini's model the disclosure of an invention serves no useful purpose.

The Shoulders of Giants Externality

The third externality occurs as a result of benefits conferred on follow-on inventors by pioneering inventors. A positive externality occurs when one invention makes subsequent inventions less costly (and follow-on inventors do not compensate their benefactors). Scotchmer elaborates.

> Part of the first innovation's social value is the boost it gives to later innovators, which can take at least three forms. If the second generation could not be developed without the first, then the social value of the first innovation includes the incremental social surplus provided by the second generation products. If the first innovation merely reduces the cost of achieving the second innovation, then the cost reduction is part of the social surplus provided by the first innovation. And if the first innovation accelerates the development of the second, then its social value includes the value of getting the second innovation sooner.

> Because of these externalities provided to later innovators, developing the first innovation may be efficient even if its expected cost exceeds its value as a stand-alone product. First innovators will have the correct incentives to invest only if they receive some of the social surplus provided by the second generation products. But at the same time, enough profit must be left for the second innovators so that they will invest if investing is efficient (Scotchmer, 1991, p. 31).

The follow-on invention externality is the focal point of the endogenous growth models described above. These models recognize that knowledge is accumulated and that current efforts at horizontal and vertical product differentiation build on the results of earlier R&D.

The existence of the follow-on invention externality increases the likelihood that the market mechanism will allocate too few resources to R&D. The Grossman–Helpman variety model has the unambiguous implication that there is too little new product R&D and that growth is slower than is socially optimal as a consequence. This striking result is obtained because the creative and destructive externalities offset each other leaving only the follow-on invention externality to consider. Because inventors do not consider the effects of their efforts on the productivity of future inventors, they do too little R&D from a social perspective, and the growth rate is slower than that which would maximize the present value of national income. Grossman and Helpman also demonstrate that this could be remedied, in theory, by an R&D subsidy.

In the Grossman–Helpman quality ladder model, the net effect of the three externalities is ambiguous. Quality improvements benefit consumers but only after the next quality improvement appears. Thus, the follow-on and consumers surplus externalities are combined. The producers of products superseded by better-quality products lose profits. This is a negative externality. Grossman and Helpman concluded that this externality may be greater or less than the consumers surplus externality. As a consequence, there may be too much or too little R&D and growth may be either too fast or too slow. Remedial policy in this selectively teflon-like world involves the setting of an optimal novelty requirement in the patent legislation and subsidizing or taxing R&D depending on the configuration of parameters.

In the presence of a follow-on externality, disclosure and novelty requirements become important issues. A weak novelty requirement implies that relatively minor improvements will not infringe existing patents. Modest improvements could then be patented and sold in competition with the original invention. This reduces the return on the original invention but it has the compensating virtues of encouraging the development and disclosure of follow-on inventions.

In the endogenous growth models examined above, the existence of a follow-on externality does not affect the decision making of the inventing firms that generate it. In contrast, where the inventing firm realizes that disclosure helps rivals and that the disclosure decisions of rivals affect success, a weak novelty provision permits patenting and the accompanying disclosure of more minor innovations but does not ensure it.

In a game theoretic context such as this, the externality is partly internalized by inducing changes in the strategic behaviour of the maker of the early discovery. In the absence of a contract and with a weak novelty requirement, the innovator can capture part of the benefit of the early discovery by suppressing it. The innovating firm foregoes an immediate profit flow from not commercially exploiting the early discovery but increases its chances, relative to those of its rivals, of making a second related profitable discovery. Scotchmer and Green (1990) investigated the equilibrium in such a game and explored its welfare properties. The welfare assessments depended on two aspects of choosing not to disclose. Suppression delays the attainment of significant breakthroughs but also reduces the negative externality on profit of creative destruction. The latter effect influences *ex ante* profits and the amount of resources committed to R&D.

With a weaker novelty requirement, follow-on inventors do not have to obtain a licence from the original inventor in order to market their improvements. With a weak novelty requirement, the original inventor may not be compensated for facilitating follow-on inventions and there will, as a consequence, be too little incentive to make original inventions. In addition, the incentive to engage in follow-on invention is excessive since part of the follow-on inventor's profit may be at the expense of the original invention.

With a stronger novelty requirement, relatively minor improvements would infringe on the existing patent. On the other hand, strong protection may induce more

R&D investment. With the Scotchmer and Green model, if patenting a subsequent innovation under a weak regime erodes profits significantly and affects initial investment, the firm will choose not to patent under a weak novelty requirement. This feature drives their conclusion that weak patent protection is generally more attractive than strong.

Scotchmer and Green conceded that the virtues of a weak novelty requirement fade if disclosure is not meaningful. In the case of uninformative disclosure, patenting a minor improvement reduces the return earned by the owner of the pioneering technology without assisting future inventors. Similarly, they conceded that if reverse engineering is not possible, a modest improvement may be marketed without being disclosed. This also reduces the profit of the inventor of the pioneering technology without helping follow-on inventors.

Disclosure is important if original and follow-on inventors cannot contract for the transfer of information, and follow-on inventors learn about the state of the art only to the extent that it is disclosed in patent applications. This raises the question of whether information disclosed in patent applications is actually meaningful. It also raises the question of whether original and follow-on inventors can contract with each other and thus internalize the follow-on invention externality.

CONTRACTS BETWEEN PIONEERING AND FOLLOW-ON INVENTORS

FOR POLICY PURPOSES, an externality exists when there is a potential government action that will generate a Pareto improvement. From this perspective, the more successful private actions are in providing remedies, the less need there is for government action. Private actions include contracting, which will be the main focus of this section, and institutional responses such as a merger. If one holds a contractual view of institutions, the two blend.

The first step in exploring the consequences of an alleged externality is to explore the efficacy of private institutions that would credibly operate in the informational setting. For example, in the quality ladder model, are there credible responses by the actors in the model that would capture some or all of the loss in wealth generated by the R&D externality? In that model, Grossman and Helpman avoided issues of risk, because diversification by wealth holders dissipates the idiosyncratic risk associated with R&D projects. These shareholders are "unanimous in their demands that the entrepreneur maximize the expected net gain from research" (Grossman and Helpman, 1991, p. 92).

In this rational expectations model, individuals have the same dynastic utility functions and the same views about probabilities, and would, therefore, choose portfolios of the same composition. They would also be unanimous in giving instructions to the entrepreneurs in each of the n activities that they should coordinate their R&D decisions to take into account the knowledge externality. The same line of reasoning that was used to avoid dealing with thorny issues of risk would also make it unnecessary for the government to take remedial measures. There would be no residual policy problem.

One can also observe the rich mix of practice by owners of intellectual property in granting others access. The general view that the fences are high and enforced with great rigour may fit many instances but certainly not all. Nelson observed: "It is interesting, however, that in some cases, firms take positive action to make their proprietary knowledge more public. They engage in patent licensing and in many cases are members of patent pools. In a number of industries patents are not vigorously enforced by their possessors" (Nelson, 1991, p. 78).

Patent pools and arrangements among a group of firms to provide each other with relatively free access are more likely to occur among active innovators. Nelson noted that these firms have "worked out arrangements to mutually exploit the gains of making technological knowledge public" (Nelson, 1991, p. 79).

Much tacit knowledge about how to address different technological challenges and the information gleaned from past failures are passed on within the cultures of firms dependent on proprietary science and in the universities and laboratories of open science. This transmission process represents an institutionalization of cruder processes, such as kinship relationships that passed on information to follow-on inventors in an earlier era.[12]

Another principle in assessing policy implications is that remedial government actions should be judged under the same information assumptions used to determine the effectiveness of private measures. It is not persuasive to claim that information has measurement problems and public good attributes that make licensing prohibitively costly and a few pages later to discuss a policy of R&D subsidization in which the government knows exactly what the R&D stock is and which actions claimed by taxpayers represent bone fide increments in that stock. The experience with tax credits and subsidies for R&D has been a creative struggle to define better what should be subsidized and what not and to develop measures assessing the effects of these policies on subsequent innovation.

Many policies, in addition to intellectual property initiatives, affect innovation. Large economic entities, such as the United States, Japan and the European Community have undertaken a number of pre-competitive research projects that have required co-ordination of both private and public organizations. Projects such as the Japanese very large scale integrated (VLSI) circuit initiative, the American SEMATECH project and the development of the research consortium, Microelectronics and Computer Technology Corporation (MCC) by American firms other than AT&T and IBM required complex governance structures, some assurance of antitrust exemption and some explicit governmental support. These projects have been examined by Katz and Ordover (1990) who commented that the MCC consortium:

> has been well able to appropriate the benefits of its research; otherwise, it would have found it difficult to license the fruits of its research, particularly to third parties, who could be expected to free-ride if spillovers were substantial. It follows that in the absence of the MCC, firms that undertook R&D programs similar to the MCC's would also have been able to appropriate their results. The social justification for the MCC, then, must turn on its ability

to generate knowledge for its member more cheaply than they could generate it themselves. The current strategies of the MCC for delivering its R&D well illustrates the proposition that joint ventures and research consortiums are in part a substitute for *ex post* co-operation through licensing. (Katz and Ordover, 1990, p. 190).

The recent process for developing digital high-definition television and the proposed flat panel initiative indicate that American policy may be shifting to *sui generis* innovation development regimes for specific technologies. These regimes raise important issues for the scientific community in small countries that tend to be assigned peripheral roles.

The nature of interactions between proprietary and open science is also changing. Universities have been actively developing linkages with single firms or a consortium of firms whereby they receive funds, and the firm (or firms) receives privileged access to the results of the research. Firms in the pharmaceutical and semiconductor business have found such arrangements to be particularly attractive. In addition, universities are taking out many more patents on the research done by their employees. The integration of these new initiatives with the traditional norms and practices of open science has created frictions.[13]

These initiatives are important. Nevertheless, judgments about the efficacy of contract in linking an innovating firm with those who derive value from its efforts remains a critical determinant in assessing science and R&D policy.

Ex Ante Versus Ex Post Contracting

THE ROLE OF INTELLECTUAL PROPERTY in providing appropriate incentives for both original and follow-on invention has been analyzed under a variety of assumptions about the arrangements that might be made between original and follow-on inventors. One of the many possible distinctions is between agreements reached before the commitment of resources to follow-on invention (*ex ante* or prior agreements) and agreements negotiated after resources have been committed to follow-on invention (*ex post* agreements). Scotchmer (1991) used the term "licensing" to describe *ex post* agreements.

Scotchmer argued that if, having committed resources to R&D, follow-on inventors are obliged to obtain licences from the original inventor (strong novelty requirement), the outcome of the bargaining process will be such that some welfare-increasing follow-on inventions will not be profitable.

A second innovator who cannot market the next generation product without a license has a very weak bargaining position. If the second innovator does not get all the surplus bargained over, he will earn only a fraction of the new product's market value and presumably only a fraction of its social value, and this fraction may be less than the cost of developing it. Hence the incentive for an outside firm to develop second generation products can be too weak (Scotchmer, 1991, p. 32).

The situation Scotchmer had in mind is one in which the investment in follow-on invention has already been sunk at the time the follow-on inventor approaches the original inventor for a licence. In this case, an original inventor with a broadly defined patent (strong novelty requirement) may be able to appropriate all the quasi-rents to the follow-on invention. Anticipating this, potential follow-on inventors may not invest resources in R&D before reaching an agreement with the original inventor on the division of surplus. Thus, in the absence of prior agreements, a broad patent (strong novelty requirement) discourages follow-on innovation and may over-compensate original inventors. On the other hand, with a weak novelty requirement, follow-on inventors with modest, but patentable improvements, can impose damages on the prior inventor and thereby reduce the incentive for the pioneering innovation to occur.

With a strong novelty requirement, allowing follow-on inventors to contract with pioneering inventors before they have committed resources to follow-on R&D changes matters considerably. Potential follow-on inventors have an incentive to enter any arrangement with the pioneering inventor that promises to yield returns in excess of follow-on R&D costs. It is also in the interest of the pioneering inventor to agree to any follow-on invention that increases his or her profits. Thus, there is an incentive for the pioneering and potential follow-on inventors to agree to undertake any follow-on invention that promises to increase their combined income by more than the cost of follow-on R&D. Any invention that is jointly profitable for the pioneering and follow-on inventors is also welfare-increasing. This does not imply, however, that original and potential follow-on inventors have an incentive to undertake all welfare-increasing inventions. To the extent that the benefits of follow-on innovations are shared with "consumers," some welfare-increasing inventions will not be undertaken.[14]

The case for a strong novelty requirement (broad patent claim) is stronger when the possibility of prior agreements exists. That Scotchmer and Green generally favour a weak novelty requirement reflects their assumption that such agreements are prohibitively expensive to enter. With a strong novelty requirement, potential follow-on inventors are obliged to enter into a prior agreement with the original inventor but the original inventor has an interest in facilitating any follow-on invention that increases their combined profits. Follow-on inventions that are profitable only because they shift profits from the original inventor or from other follow-on inventors would be ruled out. If the original and follow-on inventors are able to capture all the surplus from their inventions, then, given a strong novelty requirement, they would have an incentive to enter into prior agreements to pursue any welfare-increasing invention.

PROSPECT THEORY

KITCH (1977) ARGUED THAT THE PATENT RIGHT has prospect features that allow the owner of a patent on a pioneering invention to co-ordinate follow-on research. Given a broad patent (i.e., a strong novelty requirement), a patentee would have effective control over follow-on research. That is, follow-on inventors could not exploit their inventions without making some accommodation with the owner of the patent for the original invention.

The prospect features of the patent right include its being awarded to the first to file and the liberal interpretation of the "reduction to practise" requirement. Thus, a regime of exclusivity is established early in the process of commercialization. This provides a framework for transactions between the pioneering inventor and follow-on inventors. Kitch assumed that the original and follow-on inventors would recognize their mutual interest in allowing any improvement that increased their total surplus. The only follow-on inventions that would be ruled out would be those that reduce the combined surplus of the original and the follow-on inventor. These would be "me too" inventions which redistribute rather than increase inventors' surplus.

There have been three types of criticisms of the prospect theory. The first [see McFetridge and Smith (1980)] is that the patent prospect does not eliminate duplicative rivalry, it merely pushes it to an earlier stage in the inventive process. The second criticism [see Beck (1983)] is that the patent right does not allow for the type of control over subsequent inventions that Kitch has assumed.

Third, and most relevant to the concerns of this paper, it is argued that all potential gains from exchange between the original and follow-on inventors will not be realized. The essential point here is that transactions between the original and follow-on inventors can be very costly. Efficiency dictates that, when assigning rights in the presence of high transaction costs, the right be assigned to the party who would buy it if a transaction could be arranged. Critics of the prospect theory and, more generally, of a strong novelty requirement are of the view that the holder of the patent on the original invention is not likely to be the high-valued user of the right to engage in follow-on innovation and that transaction costs may preclude the transfer of that right in a significant number of cases. For this reason, they maintain that the right to make use of the original invention for follow-on inventions be assigned to potential follow-on inventors.

Among the authors who state this proposition in transaction cost terms are Merges and Nelson (1990, 1991) and Eisenberg (1989) who stated:

> One might object that if subsequent research is truly valuable, the parties ought to be able to agree on license terms that would be profitable for both of them. But there are a number of reasons to believe that private bargaining between the parties would not lead to an efficient outcome. First, uncertainty or disagreement as to the value of the patented invention, the likely outcome of the research project, and the validity and scope of the patent claims might make it difficult for the parties to agree on the price of a license.... Second, if the subsequent researcher and the patent holder are research rivals, the subsequent researcher might be reluctant to disclose valuable research plans to the patent holder in the course of negotiations for fear that the patent holder will pursue the research plans herself rather than extend a license to the researcher (Eisenberg, 1989, p. 1074).

Merges and Nelson argued from an evolutionary perspective that the original inventor may not know enough to determine which follow-on inventions are surplus-increasing and which are surplus-dissipating. The evolutionary theory assumes that decision makers consider only a small subset of the choices actually available to them. The set they consider may not contain the best possible choice. If they face a given choice situation often enough, decision makers may ultimately come to make the best possible choice. In situations that are new to them, however, decision makers are unlikely to make the best possible choice, and different actors would make different choices. According to Merges and Nelson, exploring a new "prospect" is exactly this kind of situation. Granting a broad prospect patent "would substitute one myopic decision maker for a plurality of them" (Merges and Nelson, 1991, p. 11). This would reduce the choice set actually explored and would not necessarily be more orderly when viewed from the perspective of the choices actually available.

Merges and Nelson further maintained that contracts between the prospect holder and a multiplicity of follow-on researchers would be costly to negotiate, perhaps prohibitively so.

> [E]volutionary theory would lead one to expect strong differences of opinion among persons and firms, in this case between [the] principal owner and potential explorers of parts of the prospect, regarding the promise of different parts of the prospect, about the significance of the prospect holder's accomplishments, and about what that patent ought to cover. This would suggest that, at the least, fine-grained contracting would be difficult and costly. Transaction costs would be high. Indeed, such complex contracts might be impossible to achieve (Merges and Nelson, 1991, p. 11).

Merges and Nelson went on to consider the circumstances under which the award of a broad right (strong novelty requirement) might be productive. They defined several types of inventions. The first is the "discrete" invention which neither builds on past inventions nor contributes to future inventions. In this case, there is no interdependence between current and follow-on inventors hence, no externality to internalize.

A second category of invention is also discrete but is capable of improvement and variation.

> For many follow-ons, the original inventor is likely to be better positioned than anyone else to see the opportunities and the solutions. For some, users or customers may be better positioned, but in such cases the relationships between those that see the needs or opportunities and the prospect owner are likely to be cooperative, not rivalrous (Merges and Nelson, 1991, p. 14).

A third category of invention involves a new process or principle that has the potential to produce perhaps many new classes of products. In this case, the question is whether the patent grant should cover all applications of the principle or a limited number of applications. The prospect owner may not be well-placed either to apply or to contract efficiently for the application of the principle when significant modification is required. Similar considerations arise when there are a number of alternative processes for making a particular product. The question is, again, whether to define a process patent broadly to include all alternative processes for producing the same product or narrowly to include only individual processes.[15] The inventor of one process may be at a disadvantage in developing or contracting for the development of the others.

A fourth category of invention involves "systems" inventions. Systems technologies have a number of components. The question arising in this case is whether the patent right on individual components should be defined in a manner that gives component patentees control over the development of the systems in which their components are installed. Mechanical and electronic equipment have systems characteristics. Conferring a broad prospect on the inventors of individual components of systems technologies may result in each component patentee being able to block the development of the system and thus each has an incentive to hold out in order to appropriate all the potential rents to the system as a whole.

The essential point made by critics of the prospect approach is that initial inventors may co-ordinate follow-on invention so poorly and the cost of co-ordination may be so high that it is preferable, from a social point of view, to allow open access to follow-on invention. This reduces the incentive to make the initial invention. The assumption of those making this argument is that the increased return from better follow-on exploitation of initial inventions more than compensates for the reduction in the supply of initial inventions.

The breadth of a patent claim and the strength of the novelty requirement are determined by national patent offices and by the courts. There are several ways these institutions can narrow patent claims and weaken novelty requirements. Merges and Nelson (1990, pp. 909-916) suggested narrowing the definitions of enablement and equivalents in infringement suits. Follow-on inventions should, in their view, be regarded as infringing on a pioneering patent only if they were specifically enabled by a disclosure in the pioneering patent.[16] Merges and Nelson also suggested a more liberal interpretation of the doctrine of reverse equivalents under which a follow-on invention is regarded as being sufficiently advanced over a pioneering invention to merit a non-subservient patent and, as a consequence, not require a licence under the pioneering patent.

Ko (1992) noted that the courts (in the United States) have traditionally granted a narrower scope to chemical patents than to mechanical patents. This is consistent with the argument that, because follow-on mechanical inventions are more predictable than follow-on chemical inventions, a mechanical patent "teaches" or enables more in the way of follow-on invention than a chemical patent. Those taking the evolutionary view would also argue that a pioneering mechanical patentee would be in a better position than a pioneering chemical patentee to conduct or at least co-ordinate follow-on research and that, for this reason, a broader prospect may be more efficient for mechanical inventions than for chemical inventions. Ko concluded that, given the unpredictability of follow-on biotechnology research, limiting the scope of biotechnology patents to what they actually teach or enable would result in much narrower patent claims than are presently being allowed. Biotechnology patent claims would also be narrowed, in Ko's view, if the courts recognized that follow-on inventions that perform the same function as a pioneering invention frequently do so in much different ways and thus do not meet the test for equivalents.[17]

Eisenberg (1989) has suggested a modest expansion of the experimental use exemption in patent infringement suits. She argues that the original inventor should not have the right to enjoin the use of his or her invention in follow-on research. However, the original inventor would continue to have the right to enjoin infringing follow-on commercialization and to collect royalties.

Ordover (1991) cited several characteristics of the Japanese patent system that improve the access of potential follow-on inventors to patented inventions. First, the Japanese system requires disclosure of the invention at the time a patent application is filed rather than at the time a patent is granted.[18] Second, the Japanese system allows rivals to oppose the granting of a patent at the time of application rather than after it is granted. This increases the incentive of potential patentees to enter into licensing agreements. Third, Japanese patent examiners define patent claims very narrowly (weak novelty requirement). Follow-on inventors can reverse engineer an original invention during the application period, improve it slightly and apply for an improvement patent. This may block improved versions of the original invention and may create an incentive for cross-licensing. Ordover conceded that this system favours follow-on invention at the expense of pioneering invention and is no longer suited to the needs of Japan or of other countries that are in a position of technological leadership.

LICENSING PRACTICES

CONTRACTS BETWEEN ORIGINAL AND POTENTIAL FOLLOW-ON INVENTORS provide for the transfer of knowledge from the original to follow-on inventors and for the compensation of the original inventor by follow-on inventors. A variety of licensing practices assist in the distribution of surplus from cumulative inventive activity. Merges and Nelson maintained that it is too costly to craft a licence to the requirements of individual follow-on inventors (Merges and Nelson, 1990, pp. 874-875). Nevertheless, many licensing practices do just that. There is increasing appreciation of the importance of licensing terms as incentives to accumulate and disseminate knowledge (Lewis and Yao, 1995; United States Department of Justice and Federal Trade Commission, 1995).

Licensing practices are governed by national competition (antitrust) statutes rather than intellectual property statutes. In the United States, judicial interpretation of the *Sherman Act* has limited the flexibility of licensing practices especially as they relate to tying arrangements and post-expiry royalties.

Under section 32 of the *Competition Act*, licensing arrangements that lessen competition unduly can be declared void or their execution enjoined in whole or in part. There are no reported cases under section 32. Two cases brought under earlier legislation were settled.[19] These cases, both of which involved Union Carbide, illustrate the problems that competition policy can pose for efficient licensing. The Union Carbide cases involved two sets of patents: extrusion patents and printing patents. With regard to the printing patents, the licensing patents at issue were: royalty rates that decreased as volume increased, field of use restrictions, no challenge clauses and post-expiry restrictions on licensees. The practices at issue with respect to the licensing of the extrusion patents were the imposition of higher royalties on licensees not purchasing resin from the patentee or his nominee and post-expiry restrictions on licensees.

U.S. antitrust decisions have also been hostile to post-expiry restrictions on licensees. They have interpreted them as an unlawful extension of the patent beyond its statutory term. From another perspective, post-expiry licensing provisions merely stretch out, to the mutual benefit of the patentee and licensee, the royalty payments that a patented invention would otherwise command during its statutory term.

Royalty rates that decrease as volume increases were regarded as abusive by the Director of Investigation mainly because they placed small licensees at a disadvantage. It is also the case, however, that decreasing block rates can result in higher welfare (surplus) than a uniform royalty rate. Indeed, the tension between invention and diffusion can be reduced by discriminating in this manner. Tying, block booking and package licensing arrangements can have the same effect.

Field of use restrictions confine a licensee to a particular application of a patented invention. This may facilitate discriminatory pricing which, in turn, can increase the use of a patented invention. Field of use restrictions may also facilitate the sharing of surplus between a patentee and a licensee where the two would otherwise be rivals. That is, field of use restrictions can facilitate the very type of arrangements between original and follow-on inventors that are cited as being desirable but prohibitively costly to negotiate.

No challenge clauses and grantback provisions increase the willingness of the patentee to share information with a licensee. A no challenge clause provides a licensee with a means of assuring a patentee that the information he or she is seeking is to make better use of or improve the licensed invention rather than to challenge the validity of the patent on it. A grantback is a means of sharing the benefits of improvements. With a unilateral grantback, a licensee can assure a patentee that the license is not for developing a competing improvement invention.[20] The alternative to a grantback may be no licence, a delayed licence or a licence at a higher royalty rate.

Another means by which pioneering and follow-on inventors can co-ordinate their R&D is cross-licensing. The virtues of cross-licensing as a means of encouraging both pioneering and follow-on inventing can be illustrated with reference to Figure 2. As drawn, the figures reflect the assumption that both the pioneering and the follow-on inventor set monopoly prices. If they act in a more competitive manner, say as differentiated Bertrand duopolists, the prices of inventions A and B could be bid down to the point at which the profits on the two inventions do not earn sufficient to cover their respective R&D costs. If this situation is anticipated, the pioneering and the follow-on inventions may not occur. One way of forestalling this possibility is for the pioneering and follow-on inventors to cross-license each other and set royalty rates at a level that results in monopoly prices even with non-co-operative behaviour. This would run afoul of section 1 of the *Sherman Act* in the United States and section 45 of the *Competition Act* in Canada as they are currently interpreted. Proper application of these two statutes requires a change in the benchmark. The relevant comparison is not between monopoly and competitive prices for inventions A and B but between the monopoly prices of A and B and the absence or delayed appearance of one or both inventions.[21]

SOME CONCLUSIONS

ENDOGENOUS GROWTH MODELS emphasize the importance of the accumulation of knowledge and of the widespread diffusion of knowledge for growth. Within the rational expectations and costless transacting worlds of these models, institutional adaptation coupled with broad patent definitions would, in our opinion, solve the problem. In a world in which seeking out the highest-valued users of a patent right and making effective transactions with them is costly, the effectiveness of licensing versus weaker patent protection and the domains of proprietary science and open science are important and difficult policy issues. In these circumstances, the policy framework must be adaptive and must modify the application of regimes to the imperatives of different technologies with different developmental potentials. The polarized world of the endogenous growth models, with zero transactions in most dimensions and prohibitive ones in a selected few, demonstrates the interconnections between sectors in a dynamic economy. If the mix of teflon and sandpaper is judicious, it can provide an effective overall guide to policy.

Students that have focused more on the complexity and subtlety of the innovative process have also observed that an increasing proportion of innovative activity is in fact cumulative, that is, dependent on knowledge embodied in previous inventions as endogenous growth models assume. Current and follow-on inventions are both complements and substitutes. This has resulted in considerable scepticism as to whether current and follow-on inventors can successfully contract to share the surplus which their co-operation would bring. With this has come a concern that the access of follow-on inventors to the stock of knowledge is likely to fall well short of the ideal.

This new emphasis on access to, and distribution of, knowledge has led one group of writers to advocate two broad types of policies:

- increasing or resisting intrusions into the domain of open science; and

- making proprietary science more open by weakening intellectual property protection and making trade secrecy less attractive.[22]

A typical policy prescription from this school of thought is:

Intellectual property rights are not themselves a natural obstacle to the distribution of knowledge. They can be designed to induce the agents to enter into cooperative arrangements. To do this it is necessary to reduce the private value of individual increments to the privately owned knowledge base by restricting the duration and especially the scope of patent protection; by introducing *sui generis* legislation adapting property rights specifically to meet the needs of sectors where the recombination model of innovation is particularly important; by extending the principles of compulsory patent and copyright licensing at "a reasonable cost," especially for research uses, and so forth.... On the other hand, trade secrecy and the various forms of access restriction ... are important obstacles that impede knowledge distribution. Two strategies are possible to address this problem: one approach is to make the forms of intellectual property protection that require detailed disclosure more attractive ... the other is to promote collective forms of precompetitive R&D (David and Foray, 1994, pp. 45-46).

The alternate view is not so convinced of the optimality of the incentive system in the regime of open science and is less pessimistic regarding the ability of the institutions of proprietary and open science to interact productively. It would not necessarily oppose the patenting and licensing on commercial terms of university and government inventions.

The alternate view is also less sceptical as to the ability of pioneering and follow-on inventors to contract with one another and thus to exploit fully the opportunities embodied in the knowledge stock. Those holding this view would find some virtue both in strong novelty requirements and in licensing practices to which antitrust authorities in some countries have historically been hostile.

Endnotes

1 See "Guidelines on the Patenting of Computer-related Inventions," *Patent Office Gazette*. (June 15, 1993): 10.

2 It has been argued that a properly drafted patent claim on a process that includes an algorithm can protect the algorithm itself: "Depending on how carefully claims are constructed, the computational logic and processes – even the algorithm itself – can be protected" (United States Congress, Office of Technology Assessment, 1990, p. 22).

3 Section 55.2 (6) of the *Patent Act Amendment Act*, 1992, R.S. 1993 c. 2; confirms a similar exception to the patentee's exclusive rights in Canadian law for acts done privately and on a non-commercial scale, or for a non-commercial purpose or for experiments relating solely to the subject matter of the patent.

4 Failure to work an invention on a commercial scale in Canada when this invention is capable of being worked in Canada was eliminated as grounds for compulsory licensing under the *NAFTA Implementation Act* of 1993.

5 Canadian law makes no distinction between a natural person and a corporation. One surmise is that, in any dispute concerning a corporate-owned copyright, the work would be treated as a collective work. The right would then extend to 50 years plus the life of the last employee involved. We were unable to obtain any opinions on what would happen if the set of employees responsible could not be identified.

6 Exceptions vary widely. They range from the right to make a backup copy of a computer program to the playing of music in public places for charitable purposes. New exceptions for schools and people with special needs are expected to be included in the revision of the Canadian *Copyright Act* expected in 1995.

7 The Internet Patent News Service reports 4569 software patents issued in the United States during 1994. Of this total, IBM obtained the most patents (396) – more than twice as many as the next most prolific patenting company, Hitachi. The cumulative total since 1970 is over 15 000 patents. There is some concern that the search of prior art for the software patent applications has often been incomplete.

8 The Grossman–Helpman quality ladder model is a simplified version of a model by Aghion and Howitt (1992).

9 Gallini (1992) analyzed a case in which there was no rivalry for the patent but there was free entry into *non-infringing* imitation (inventing around) at a fixed cost of $K per imitator. In this case, the most the patent can do is to promise the patentee profits of $K by precluding *infringing* imitation (direct copying). An attempt to increase the patentee's profits above $K by lengthening the patent term, merely increases inventing around. In terms of Figure 1, the optimal patent term τ is such that the present discounted value of $A per period over τ periods is equal to $K.

10 Lerner (1994) found that the market value of biotechnology firms is an increasing function of the breadth of their patent claims but that this relationship is weaker among firms with more unique patents. Thus, a broader patent claim increases the patentee's profitability in cases where the invention of close substitutes would otherwise be possible.

11 Klemperer conceded that his case for a narrow patent was in part a result of his assumption that consumers prefer the same product variety. Faced with the choice of selling to all or none, the patentee prices to sell to all. Thus, the social costs association with a narrow patent are ruled out. That is, there is no migration to close substitute brands and no dissipation of surplus due to entry of close substitutes.

12 In his interesting historical account of the social context of innovation, Wallace examined the iron industry and commented that kinship was:

> the only way in which, in the iron industry at that time, a stable cadre of mechanicians and managers could be assembled and perpetuated over several generations, passing on the paradigm from one cohort to the next. In the close and intimate setting of the family firm, father could pass on to son, or son-in-law, the principles, the techniques and the awareness of unsolved problems, by that combination of visual and tactile communication that is crucial in technological thinking and communication (Wallace, 1982, p. 101).

13 Among the more contentious issues that has arisen is whether university and government inventions should be patented. There are two questions here. First, should some inventive activities be transferred from the domain of open science to the domain of proprietary science? Second, is there a role for intellectual property rights within the domain of open science? This issue was discussed by Dasgupta and David (1994) who argued, in

effect, that the introduction and enforcement of intellectual property will be detrimental in a variety of ways to the institutions of open science.

14 In Figure 2, a follow-on invention A is mutually beneficial for pioneering inventor B and follow-on inventor A if $P_A - S_B$ exceeds follow-on R&D cost (in present value terms). Any follow-on invention for which this condition holds is welfare-increasing. There can, however, be welfare-increasing inventions for which this condition does not hold (e.g., $S_A + P_A - S_B > R\&D\ Cost > P_A - S_B$).

15 Eisenberg (1989, pp. 1079-1082) and Ko (1992, pp. 786-789) cited the example of the blood clotting factor patents issued to Scripps Clinic and Research Foundation. The patent claim covered a process (using monoclonal antibodies) for producing clotting Factor VIII:C as well as the product Factor VIII:C however prepared. When Genentech used recombinant DNA technology to produce Factor VIII:C, Scripps sued for infringement. The Courts upheld Scripps claim of infringement although the suit ultimately failed for other reasons.

16 The extent to which one patent enables another is a matter of judgment. Merges and Nelson cited a case of an International Nickel patent on nodular iron which involved the addition of *a minimum of* 0.04 percent magnesium to molten iron. Ford produced nodular iron with 0.02 percent magnesium. Ford was held to be infringing on the Inco patent in that the two products were equivalent. In essence, Ford benefited from Inco's idea even though its process was outside Inco's patent claim.

17 For example, Wellcome's version of t-PA, an anti-clotting drug, was found to be equivalent to Genentech's version even though it did not work in the same way and was not administered in the same manner (Ko, 1992, p. 790).

18 The European Patent Office also publishes applications at the time they are filed. The United States Patent and Trademark Office publishes applications at the time they are granted. The Canadian Intellectual Property Office publishes applications 18 months after they have been filed. This is, on average, 18 months before the patent is granted.

19 For an historical survey of the treatment of intellectual property under competition legislation in Canada, see Anderson, Khosla and Ronayne (1991).

20 With a unilateral grantback, all rights to improvements made by the licensee accrue to the licensor. The *Working Paper on Patent Law Reform* (CCAC, 1976) recommended that unilateral grantbacks be prohibited.

21 This issue is analyzed in the context of merger policy by Ordover and Willig (1985).

22 This may also involve resistance to the strengthening of intellectual property rights. Concern has been expressed, for example, over the breadth of patents awarded in the area of biotechnology. See Lerner (1994) and Merges and Nelson (1990).

BIBLIOGRAPHY

Aghion, P. and P. Howitt. "A model of growth through creative destruction." *Econometrica.* 60, (1992): 323-351.

Anderson, R.D., S.D. Khosla and M.F. Ronayne. "The Competition Policy Treatment of Intellectual Property Rights in Canada: Retrospect and Prospect." In *Canadian Competition Law and Policy at the Centenary.* Edited by R.S. Khemani and W.T. Stanbury. Halifax, Institute for Research on Public Policy, 1991, pp. 497-538.

Anton, James J. and Dennis A. Yao. "Expropriation and Inventions: Appropriable Rents in the Absence of Property Rights." *American Economic Review*. 84, (1994): 190-209.

Arrow, Kenneth J. "Economic Welfare and the Allocation of Resources for Invention." In *The Rate and Direction of Inventive Activity: Economic and Social Factors*. Edited by Richard R. Nelson. Princeton: Princeton University Press, 1962.

Banner, D. "Selected Intellectual Property Developments in the United States of America." *LAW/Technology*. 26, (1993): 1-34.

Beck, Roger. "The Prospect Theory of the Patent System and Unproductive Competition." *Research in Law and Economics*. 5, (1983): 193-201.

Canadian Intellectual Property Office. "Guidelines on the Patenting of Computer-Related Inventions." *Patent Office Gazette*. (June 15, 1993).

Carstens, David W. "Legal Protection of Computer Software: Patents, Copyrights, and Trade Secrets." *Journal of Contemporary Law*. 20, (1994): 13-75.

Cheung, Stephen S. "Property Rights in Trade Secrets." *Economic Inquiry*. XX, (1982): 40-53.

Consumer and Corporate Affairs Canada. *Working Paper on Patent Law Reform*. Ottawa, Supply and Services, 1976.

Copyright Subcommittee to the Working Group on Canadian Content and Culture. "Draft Report." Ottawa, December 1994.

Dasgupta, Partha and Paul A. David. "Towards a New Economics of Science." *Research Policy*. 23, (1994): 487-522.

David, Paul A. "Knowledge, Property and the System Dynamics of Technological Change." *Proceedings of the World Bank Annual Conference on Development Economics 1992*. Washington, International Bank for Reconstruction and Development, 1993, pp. 215-248.

David, Paul and Dominique Foray. *Accessing and Expanding the Science and Technology Knowledge Base*. Organization for Economic Co-operation and Development, DSTI/STP/TIP(94)4, 1994.

Dixit, A. K. and J. E. Stiglitz. "Monopolistic Competition and Optimum Product Diversity." *American Economic Review*. 67, (1977): 297-308.

Eisenberg, Rebecca S. "Patents and the Progress of Science: Exclusive Rights and Experimental Use." *The University of Chicago Law Review*. 56, (1989): 1017-1086.

Friedman, David D., William M. Landes and Richard A. Posner. "Some Economics of Trade Secret Law." *Economic Perspectives*. 5, (1991): 61-72.

Frye, Northrop. "The Language of Poetry." In *Explorations in Communication*. Edited by Edmund Carpenter and Marshall McLuhan. Boston: Beacon Press, 1960.

Gallini, N. "Patent Policy and Costly Imitation." *Rand Journal of Economics*. 23, (1992): 52-63.

Grossman, Gene M. and Elhanan Helpman. *Innovation and Growth in the Global Economy*. Cambridge: MIT Press, 1991.

Hirshleifer, Jack. "The Private and Social Value of Information and the Reward to Inventive Activity." *American Economic Review*. (1971): 561-574.

Institute of Law Research and Reform. *Report on Trade Secrets*. Edmonton, Alberta, 1986.

Katz, Michael L. and Janusz A. Ordover. "R&D Co-operation and Competition." *Brookings Papers: Microeconomics*. (1990): 137-203.

Kitch, Edmund. "The Nature and Function of the Patent System." *Journal of Law and Economics*. 20, (1977): 265-290.

Klemperer, P. "How Broad Should the Scope of Patent Protection Be?" *Rand Journal of Economics*. 21, (1990): 113-120.

Knopf and P. Howard. "New Forms and Fora of Intellectual Property." *Canadian Intellectual Property Review*. 5, (1989): 247-274.

Ko, Yusing. "An Economic Analysis of Biotechnology Patent Protection." *The Yale Law Journal*. 102, (1992): 777-804.

Kotowitz, Y. "Issues in Patent Policy with Respect to the Pharmaceutical Industry." Commission of Inquiry into the Pharmaceutical Industry, Ottawa, Supply and Services, 1986.

Lerner, J. "The Importance of Patent Scope: An Empirical Analysis." *Rand Journal of Economics*. 25, (1994): 319-333.

Lewis, T. and D. Yao. "Some Reflections on the Antitrust Treatment of Intellectual Property." *Antitrust Law Journal*. 63, (1995): 603-620.

Lucas, R. "Making a Miracle." *Econometrica*. 61, (1993): 251-272.

McFetridge, Donald G. and Douglas A. Smith. "Patents, Prospects and Economic Surplus: A Comment on Kitch." *Journal of Law and Economics*. 23, (1980): 197-203.

Merges, Robert P. and Richard R. Nelson. "On the Complex Economics of Patent Scope." *Columbia Law Review*. 90, (1990): 839-916.

———. "On Limiting or Encouraging Rivalry in Technical Programs: The Effect of Patent Scope Decisions." Working Paper, 1991.

Miller, E. "Antitrust Restrictions on Trade Secret Licensing: A Legal Review and Economic Analysis." *Law and Contemporary Problems*. 52, (1989): 183-209.

Nelson, Richard R. *Understanding Technical Change as an Evolutionary Process*. Amsterdam: North Holland, 1991.

Nordhaus, W. *Invention, Growth and Welfare*. Cambridge: MIT Press, 1969.

Ordover, Janusz A. "A Patent System for Both Diffusion and Exclusion." *Economic Perspectives*. 5, (1991): 43-60.

Ordover, Janusz A. and Robert D. Willig. "Antitrust for High-Technology Industries: Assessing Research Joint Ventures and Mergers." *Journal of Law & Economics*. 28, (1985): 311-333.

Plant, A. "The Economic Aspects of Copyright in Books." *Economica*. 1, (1934): 167-195.

Rafiquzzaman, M. "The Optimal Patent Under Uncertainty." *International Journal of Industrial Organization*. 5, (1987): 233-246.

Romer, P. M. "Endogenous Technological Change." *Journal of Political Economy*. 97, 1990.

Rosenberg, N. *Inside the Black Box: Technology and Economics*. New York: Cambridge University Press, 1982.

Scotchmer, Suzanne. "Standing on the Shoulders of Giants." *Economic Perspectives*. 5, (1991): 29-41.

Scotchmer, Suzanne and Jerry Green. "Novelty and Disclosure in Patent Law." *Rand Journal of Economics*. 21, (1990): 131-146.

Tandon, P. "Optimal Patents with Compulsory Licensing." *Journal of Political Economy*. 90, (1982): 470-486.

United States Congress, Office of Technology Assessment. *Computer Software and Intellectual Property*. Washington, D.C, 1990.

United States Department of Justice and Federal Trade Commission. 26 Stat. 209 (1890): 15 U.S.C., Sec. 1-7. 1995.

Vaver, David. "Civil Liability for Taking or Using Trade Secrets in Canada." *The Canadian Business Law Journal*. 5, (1981): 253-301.

Wallace, Anthony F.C. *The Social Context of Innovation*. Princeton: Princeton University Press, 1982.

Wiley, John Shepard Jr. "Copyright at the School of Patent." *University of Chicago Law Review.* 58, (1991): 119-185.

Wright, Brian D. "The Economics of Invention Incentives: Patents, Prizes, and Research Contracts." *American Economic Review.* 83, (1983): 691-707.

Comment

Jock Langford
Senior Policy Analyst
Industry Canada

THE ACHESON–MCFETRIDGE (A–M) PAPER provides an overview of how endogenous growth theory, and in particular, formal models, can be applied to the economics of intellectual property rights (IPRs). A–M correctly identify that endogenous growth theory, "[w]ith its emphasis on the accumulation of knowledge ... has focused attention on relationships among innovators, in particular, on the interdependence between current and past innovative activity." In contrast, the historical emphasis in the economics of intellectual property (IP) has been on the bargain between creators and users. Unfortunately, there is too much emphasis in this paper on traditional IP appropriability issues relating to the monopoly control over technology and not enough emphasis on the potential economic effects of knowledge spillovers as they relate to IPRs. That being said, the paper should be viewed as a pioneering treatment of endogenous growth–intellectual property linkages which will act as a precursor to a more involved policy debate on spillovers and externalities arising from IPRs.

A–M's survey of the literature covers a wide range of seminal papers on IPRs, and I refer interested readers to their references as an important source of theoretical perspectives on the economics of IPRs. One could not reasonably expect the authors to be able to reconcile the divergent views on IPRs found among leading economists throughout history. This lack of consensus would also seem to be reflected in the divergent conclusions, of the different schools of endogenous growth theorists, about the role, importance and implications of IPRs.

A–M conclude that, in an IP world of high transaction costs which interface with open science, "the policy framework must be adaptive and must modify the application of regimes to the imperatives of different technologies with different developmental potentials." Given the limitations for discriminating against specific technologies under the General Agreement on Tariffs and Trade–Trade-Related Intellectual Property (GATT–TRIP) agreements, it would seem that the only practical method to achieve this policy goal would be to increase the use of *sui generis* IP regimes. If this is the conclusion of the authors, then pursuing the *sui generis* IP option is an issue that warrants further analysis.

The authors conclude that, within the costless transacting worlds of endogenous growth models, broad patent protection coupled with more flexible judicial interpretations of IP licensing practices under antitrust law would produce an optimal outcome. Key to the two models presented by A–M (the variety model and the quality ladder model) is that imitation is precluded by either of two assumptions.

- Invention/imitation costs are sunk coupled with undifferentiated Bertrand competition.

- Or, there is an infinitely lived, costlessly enforceable patent.

Both models have spillover mechanisms based on costless reverse engineering and full disclosure of the invention in the patent. In evaluating the validity of policy prescriptions flowing from formal endogenous growth theory models, one should consider the applicability to markets of models with zero transactions in most dimensions and prohibitive ones in a selected few. From my experience as an IP policy advisor, the economic analysis of IP policy issues tends to be in the details of a particular case rather than in generalized models.

In the variety model, based on a model of monopolistic competition, growth consists of a continuous expansion of the number of varieties available. The growth process is not sustainable since the introduction of new varieties reduces anticipated monopoly profit, entry ceases and no more research and development (R&D) would be done. Continuing growth is only achieved by assuming that the productivity of R&D effort depends on cumulative R&D effort and that this accumulated knowledge spills over in its entirety to all potential inventors. Growth will continue if the decline in R&D costs is sufficient to offset the decline in the profitability of new varieties.

In the quality ladder model, successful inventors of higher-quality products earn monopoly profits dependent on the quality of the improvement. The growth process consists of continual improvements in products. Spillovers enable outsiders to compete on equal terms for an improvement in the state of the art since all firms face the same technical opportunities for improving the state of the art. As a result, there is no continuity of technical dominance of any industry by a particular firm.

The authors consider the implications of a firm establishing leadership over a product/variety. The spillover assumptions, in both models, are violated by a firm blocking knowledge spillovers to obtain an advantage over rivals. Using this superior knowledge base, the firm's lead widens and, at some point, no rival will compete against the leader. In the quality ladder model, rivalrous R&D is replaced by monopoly R&D. Each leading firm then stands on its own shoulders to create new innovation. In the variety model, A–M conclude that the economy will not face an R&D spillover problem since the knowledge externality is being internalized, and the only issue would be the monopoly control of technical change.

The welfare analysis of IPRs in the paper highlights the endogenous growth theory approach that innovation endogenous to the innovative firm is the key determinant of economic growth (Fagerberg, 1994). The A–M analysis argues that the optimal levels of investment in private sector R&D will only be met by limiting externalities which diminish an innovative firm's ability to appropriate rents. The authors suggest that Kitch's prospect theory in which the patentee of a pioneering invention is provided with broad claims to appropriate higher returns and to co-ordinate follow-on research, provides a theoretical model for minimizing these externalities to a firm's inventive activities. Innovative licensing strategies between pioneer and follow-on inventors are proposed by A–M as a solution to the concerns about high transaction costs raised by evolutionary theory economists.

Evolutionary economics would seem to suggest that there are potentially significant spillover effects related to firms pursuing strategies to block spillovers to establish technological leadership. The principal themes of evolutionary economics are that processes determine the variety or range of actual innovations introduced into the economy, and processes alter the selection or relative economic importance of the competing alternatives. These processes are dynamic and are related to the nature of competition as a process of endogenous change – variety drives selection, and feedback processes result in the development of variety shaping the process of selection (Metcalfe, 1994). If innovation is a dynamic process within a system, then the authors' concerns with appropriability issues related to externalities seem misplaced. Not only is innovation both exogenous and endogenous to the firm but firms may consider both as part of the same innovation process. Support for the existence of this relationship is provided by Stoneman and Diederen (1994) who suggest that a firm's own R&D program generates the knowledge required internally for the monitoring, evaluation and adaption of exogenous sources of innovation. Thus, the potential effects on the evolution of innovation by allowing pioneer inventors more control over the rate and nature of follow-on innovation is a key factor that needs to be considered in assessing the welfare effects. A–M have not adequately addressed these concerns.

It is essential for micro-economists to assess the impacts of marketplace framework policies on the firm. However, the authors have focused solely on the firm, particularly innovation endogenous to the firm, to the exclusion of other institutions. In contrast, the patent system has evolved to reflect the fact that there are various sources of innovation – both endogenous and exogenous – to the firm. The patent system recognizes that some innovation is endogenous to inventive firms by providing for a period of market exclusivity. Public disclosure and dissemination of patent information support the notion that some knowledge creation is exogenous to the firm by encouraging inter-firm spillovers as a means of promoting innovation. The patent system also recognizes the importance of publicly financed basic research as another source of innovation since research institutions have traditionally been afforded a degree of intellectual freedom by the courts to perform basic research.

A–M identified the interface of open and proprietary science as an important issue for endogenous growth theory. However, the two formal models do not include spillovers between the open and proprietary science. There are some recent IP trends affecting publicly funded research that should be raised. Public research institutes facing budgetary cuts have aggressively sought to create new revenue streams through the licensing of "proprietary" technology protected by intellectual property rights. In this case, it would seem that fiscal restraints rather than IPRs are the primary causal factor behind this trend. The end result is that public research institutions are disseminating publicly funded knowledge to achieve both public and agency goals, and this has resulted in a blurring of the public and private research sectors. Government research institutions and universities are competing directly with private firms or, in some cases, competing indirectly through their participation in a strategic alliance with another firm. There are examples of potential spillover effects of this blurring of roles.

- Hoffman-LaRoche's patent suit against academic and government biotechnology research institutions for infringing its patents for polymerise chain reaction technology, if successful, will increase the cost of basic research (Carlton, 1995).

- The U.S. National Institutes of Health's applications for patents on human gene sequences of unknown function adversely affected international co-operation among members of the Human Genome Project.

In summary, the key criticism of the A–M paper is that the emphasis on firms to explain knowledge accumulation fails to consider fully the endogenous growth literature on spillovers between open and proprietary science and systems approaches including evolutionary economics, national systems of innovation and endogenous growth theory explanations of technological spillovers between countries.

INTELLECTUAL PROPERTY RIGHTS IN A GLOBAL, KNOWLEDGE-BASED ECONOMY

THE OBJECTIVE OF THE CONFERENCE this volume is based on was to understand the impact of knowledge-based growth on the Canadian economy and the microeconomic policy implications that arise. There are some indications that, in a global, knowledge-based economy, the role IPRs play in encouraging innovation is fundamentally changing. The ongoing shift toward a global, knowledge-based economy has resulted in the law and economics of intellectual property rights changing more in the last five years than in the last two centuries. Some of the main structural changes affecting the evolving economics of IPRs include GATT–TRIPs, international trade liberalization, rapid technological change and powerful information technologies. Metcalfe states that one of the facts of modern growth is that there are "structural changes at all levels from the microeconomic to the macroeconomic." (Metcalfe, 1994). Thus, the new economics of IPRs must consider not only the firm but also the national economy within a global trading system.

The Organization for Economic Co-operation and Development (OECD) report entitled, *Economic Arguments for Protecting Intellectual Property Rights Effectively* supports the notion that there are now a wider range of impacts of IPRs on firm behaviour that government policy makers must consider in their welfare analyses. The OECD found that IPRs can encourage international trade, support the innovation process, encourage technology transfers, promote foreign and domestic investment, improve prospects for competition and have positive effects on national creativity (OECD, 1989).

Endogenous growth theory suggests that IP policy makers need to understand the effects of IPRs on trade, investment and innovation and recognize the need to understand better the knowledge spillovers both within a national economy and internationally. To contribute to this discussion, two perspectives of the potential welfare effects of IPRs on spillovers in two systems are presented: national innovation systems and the global trading system.

Patel and Pavitt define "national system of innovation" as "the national institutions, their incentive structures and their competencies, that determine the rate and direction of technological learning." Four types of institutions that engage in a variety of activities are central to a national system of innovation (Patel and Pavitt, 1994).

- Firms invest to create innovation.

- Universities provide basic research and related training.

- Educational institutions provide education and vocational training.

- Governments promote and regulate technology.

In a national system of innovation, there are two areas of learning of particular significance to endogenous growth theory–intellectual property – information flows and human capital. IPRs may exert potentially significant impacts on these two areas in terms of innovation and knowledge spillovers. IPRs may affect levels of spillovers resulting from the information highway indirectly through their impact on the adoption of technical standards (i.e., highway infrastructure) and directly through the enforcement of IPRs on knowledge flows in cyberspace. IPRs may also have some negative impacts on knowledge accumulation if they are used to restrict, excessively, human capital mobility between firms and former employees starting up competing firms.

Within the context of a national innovation system, there is a greater need for policy co-ordination between IP strategy and other trade, investment and innovation policies affecting economic growth. Increasingly, patents seem to provide more than incentives for companies to invest in R&D to create technology (i.e., new products and processes). More and more IPRs also seem to affect what Lipsey and Carlaw call the "facilitating structure" at the firm, industry and economy-wide levels. In the knowledge economy, IPRs accelerate innovation by enabling innovators to organize into the most effective market arrangements and by facilitating knowledge-based transactions. For example, patents are often necessary for the formation of strategic alliances between multinational enterprises (MNEs) and small biotech firms and seem to be an important condition in the efficient functioning of high technology capital markets. It is also possible that IPRs may be an important influence of business culture, i.e., the way in which firms compete domestically and globally. Ruttan and Hayami's theory of induced institutional change suggests that institutions, such as property rights, can have significant effects on culture as well as resource, technological and institutional endowments (Ruttan and Hayami, 1984). In conclusion, IPRs may have a role in shaping structural and cultural aspects of the innovative capacity of the Canadian economy.

Ostry has suggested that in the post GATT–TRIPs environment, "deeper integration" of national economies will redefine the concept of market access and blur the boundary between the international and domestic domains. She concluded that the focus of international trade negotiations is shifting away from traditional border barriers to other national structural impediments for market access. For MNEs, effective market access involves trade, investment and access to technology (Ostry, 1995). There is some evidence that governments and firms are increasing their use of IPRs in trade, investment and innovation strategies. In a global economy, national marketplace frameworks compete with each other for investments and jobs. In this environment, governments which use more sophisticated economic strategies to achieve first-mover advantages in IP policy have the potential to realize significantly greater economic growth than laggard countries. Additionally, IP policies may have a direct impact on the rate of global spillovers since they affect the level of access to markets, technology and investment.

It is proposed that "too weak" and "too strong" IP regimes can be used to create trade barriers. The United States has recognized that inadequate IP protection was a trade barrier affecting the ability of U.S. firms to compete and increase market shares in foreign countries. Historically, protectionist IP measures, such as compulsory licensing and working requirements, have been used by smaller, technology-importing countries to support domestic generic industries. Embedded in these IP policies is a spillover strategy. In a global, knowledge-based economy, preventing infringement and copying of IP in foreign markets protects the investments necessary for global marketers to expand their markets successfully for innovative, branded and media products and services. Obviously, global marketing changes the nature of expected spillovers. "Too strong" IP protection may also act as a trade barrier. By using a first-mover strategy consisting of adopting the highest IP standards, extending the scope of protection (e.g., patents on software, higher life forms) and vigorous border enforcement, the United States may be creating significant barriers to entry into their domestic market. This strategy may ultimately force laggards to harmonize to higher U.S. standards of protection in selected areas.

Where tariff and non-tariff barriers to trade have been replaced by trade barriers erected by firms, IPRs become a more important factor in attracting foreign direct investment. The United States currently supports MNEs' use of IPRs to segment and price discriminate in national markets by prohibiting parallel imports and by enforcing IP border measures. During NAFTA negotiations the United States opposed a Mexican proposal for North American exhaustion of IPRs. In the context of segmented national markets, many OECD countries negotiated with MNEs for increased foreign direct investment in return for strengthened pharmaceutical patent protection (e.g., Bill C-22 in Canada) and corresponding higher levels of profitability. There is some risk to smaller countries, such as Canada, that IP standards will be "ratcheted up" as countries compete with one another for MNE investments and jobs using "IP subsidies."

Foreign governments have implemented techno-nationalistic policies designed to encourage domestic innovation while limiting outward spillovers of knowledge across borders. In some cases, IPRs are used as an alternative form of government subsidy to strategic industries such as informatics and biotechnology. Additionally, governments are competing with each other using patents to protect publicly financed research from foreign competitors. Access to government patents is already an important spillover issue. In 1993, the U.S. Patent and Trademark Office reported that the U.S. government was granted 1165 patents ranking it as the largest inventor. One example of techno-nationalistic IP policies is the effort by the U.S. government to restrict foreign access to human genome project research findings through the National Institutes of Health gene patent applications.

A key question raised by the implications of endogenous growth theory is: what is the optimal national spillover strategy in a global, knowledge-based economy with higher international standards of IP protection? Coe and Helpman's research on international spillovers is presented because their findings may have important implications for IP-induced technological spillovers. They suggest that in an economy in which there is an international exchange of information and dissemination of knowledge, a country's productivity depends on its own R&D as well as on the R&D efforts of its trading partners. An important concept is that its own R&D enables a country to capture spillovers from foreign technological advances. Additionally, foreign R&D affects a country's productivity directly through learning about new technologies and materials, production processes or organizational methods and indirectly from imports of goods and services. Coe and Helpman concluded that R&D spillovers from big countries are large with U.S. spillovers affecting Canada the most (Coe and Helpman, 1994). These findings may be an interesting starting point for considering an IP policy based on spillovers. For example, do we need to understand the economic effects of higher global standards of IPRs on both the rate of Canadian innovation and inward spillovers from the United States and other countries?

IPRs inherently create a policy conflict between the objective of providing an incentive to technological innovation and the objective of encouraging the rapid diffusion of new technology and the accumulation of technological knowledge. Each nation has established national IP systems which attempt to balance competing objectives that are deemed appropriate for its national economic, political and social context (National Research Council, 1993). The centre of gravity of this balance will shift with changes in the state of the technology, the market or social values (USOTA, 1992). Canada has traditionally been a net importer of IP-embodying goods and services – high technology, culture and brand name products – and as a result Canadian policy has attempted to achieve multiple economic and social objectives. In Canada, the historical lack of domestic innovative firms and sectors has contributed to a domestic IP culture where the tendency has been to focus on the redistributive effects of IPRs. As we continue to build a more innovative economy, the IP debate must focus on the innovation, investment and trade implications of a knowledge economy as well as on the implications of knowledge spillovers at the institutional, national and global levels.

BIBLIOGRAPHY

Carlton, Jim. "Right to Use Patented Products In University Research Threatened." *Wall Street Journal.* (May 25, 1995): B12.

Coe, David T. and Elhanan Helpman. *International R&D Spillovers.* National Bureau of Economic Research Working Paper No. 4444, Cambridge, MA, August 1993.

Fagerberg, Jan. "Technology and International Differences in Growth Rates." *Journal of Economic Literature.* XXXII, (September 1994): 1147-1172.

Lipsey, Richard G. and Ken Carlaw. "A Structural View of Innovation Policy." This volume.

Metcalfe, J.S. "Evolutionary Economics and Technology." *The Economic Journal.* (July 1994).

National Research Council. *Global Dimensions of Intellectual Property Rights in Science and Technology.* Edited by Mitchell B. Wallerstein, Mary Ellen Mogee and Roberta A. Schoen. Washington, DC: National Academy Press, 1993.

Organization for Economic Co-operation and Development (OECD). *Economic Arguments For Protecting Intellectual Property Rights Effectively.* Paris: OECD, 1989.

Ostry, Sylvia. *The Post Uruguay Trading System: Major Challenges.* Industry Canada Distinguished Speakers Series, May 12, 1995.

Patel, Parimal and Keith Pavitt. "National Innovation Systems: Why They Are Important, and How They Might be Measured and Compared." *Economics of Innovation and New Technology.* 3, (1994): 77-95.

Ruttan, Vernon W. and Yujiro Hayami. "Toward a Theory of Induced Institutional Innovation." *Journal of Development Studies.* 20, 4, (July 1984): 203-223.

Stoneman, Paul and Paul Diederen. "Technology Diffusion and Public Policy." *The Economic Journal.* (July 1994).

U.S. Congress, Office of Technology Assessment (USOTA). *Finding a Balance: Computer Software, Intellectual Property, and the Challenge of Technological Change.* OTA Report No. 052-003-01278-2, Washington, DC, April 1992.

Part III   Dinner Speech

Luc Soete
Faculty of Economics
University of Limburg

7

Economic and Social Implications of a Knowledge-Based Society

I WOULD LIKE TO RAISE SOME OF THE BROADER SOCIAL ECONOMIC ISSUES of the knowledge-based economy. To put this into perspective, I would like to take you back in time and give you an overview of how these issues have evolved and emerged into the forefront today. I will do so by drawing on some of my own work which I have been involved in since the early 1980s on the "radical," sometimes destructive, changing nature of technology.

In more recent years, Richard Lipsey has presented a much more elaborate view of these issues. As in other areas of science, there has been substantial progress in our understanding of old and new concepts, particularly those in relation to the nature of technological "change." In the 1980s, these ideas, often referred to as Schumpeterian, were unacceptable to the economics profession, even those economists working on the economics of technological change, because of the lack of factual evidence. The 1982 book by Chris Freeman and John Clark, did its best to present a variety of historical aggregate and sectoral data to support our views but could not compete with the large number of traditional applied growth studies and macro-economic modelling exercises, which didn't point to anything radical in most economic performance indicators. But neither could we, like many other businesspeople, technology specialists and social scientists, become convinced by the "business as usual" or oil shock stories coming out of international organizations such as the Organization for Economic Co-operation and Development (OECD). So we further refined our analysis, trying to escape the empirical debate by pointing to the institutional mismatches and the long "learning" lags involved in agents adjusting to such new radical technological change.

Despite the many empirical breakthroughs of the last 10 years, it is not really surprising that we still face basically the same problem. We, and if I may, I would group all the participants in this conference in this category of "convinced," are still having difficulty illustrating empirically the radical nature of present day technological change, associated with the convergence of information and computer technology. It remains very difficult to convince traditional macro-economists that there is strong evidence in terms of one or other traditional macro indicators. But clearly, there is a growing belief among economists of the importance of some of the present new, general purpose technologies and the overall emergence of what could be called a knowledge-based economy.

Of course, there are obvious features of today's information and communications technology we could not have foreseen 15 years ago. Viewed historically, information and communications technology appear more and more as the first truly global technology. These features have been emphasized in papers in this volume. Information and communications technology have an impact which is not localized in the traditional sense to a particular region or country, but have a much wider global impact. Furthermore, information and communication technologies are characterized by a particularly important feature which has also been mentioned at this conference – codification. Information and communication technologies are really technologies which codify knowledge. It is still an open debate whether this increase in the codification of knowledge allows for the more rapid diffusion and international transfer of technology or whether the firm-specific, tacit knowledge is still essential for productivity growth and effective technology transfer. But, there is little doubt that codification of knowledge is at the core of the new technologies.

Let me continue by focusing on some of the social aspects of the new information and communication technologies. A couple of weeks before the Brussels G-7 Summit on the Information Society, I received a copy of a recent article by David Noble, "The truth about the information highway" and I quote:

> The propaganda never mentions the road kill of course. But that is the future for many. Most people in Canada instinctively know this already. According to a 1993 gallop poll, 41% of those currently employed believe they will lose their jobs. But despite this intuition, people have been terrorized into a hopeless fatalism. It's inevitable. Or else they have been seduced by an exciting array of new tools and diversions of the information society. Home shopping, home videos, home learning, home entertainment, home communication, the operative word is home. Because home is where people without jobs are. If they still have a home. The focus is on leisure because there will be a lot more of it in the form of mass unemployment. Some lucky few will get homework as their job takes over their home in the sweatshops of the future.

What I wanted to illustrate by quoting these "Noble" concerns, is that there is, I believe, a growing gap between the economists, policy makers, businesspeople and technologists on one hand and the public at large on the other, concerning the importance of those technologies and their likely impact on society. The public seems to be more fearful of the insecurities associated with those technologies, in particular, the impact on the stability of their employment, possibly even the loss of their jobs. One really has to go back in history to see the fundamental nature of those previous radical technology waves and to see how they shifted society in new, sometimes totally different directions. A lot has been written on this subject by economists in attendance at this conference. Let me, therefore, be brief.

One could say that the first real information technology was printing. Printing technology has been studied by many scholars, particularly with respect to why printing technology diffused and spread across the world in such a different way. One of the major factors explaining the differences in diffusion across countries was religion. Indeed, the printing of the Bible became the "tool" for the reform movement to get its message across in Europe in the Middle Ages in its fight against the Roman church. By contrast, in the culturally more advanced Arab world, the basic principle of printing technology had been known for centuries, but did not diffuse because religion forbade the printing of Arab characters. As a result, the first Koran was printed around 1876 in Cairo, nearly 400 years later. The result, in terms of the spreading of libraries, universities and knowledge, is still with us today. In other words, some features we would think of as being elements of social integration led, in some countries, to a more rapid diffusion and adaptation of the new radical technology. In others, they prevented the rapid diffusion of the new technology. I would argue that we might well be confronted with a similar potentially radical, new technology which will again lead to differences in the capacity of our societies to integrate such fundamental change. And as before, some countries will be more capable than others in adjusting, adapting and integrating the new technologies.

This is probably one of the main reasons why I'm so interested and keen on the so-called G-7 project I'm co-ordinating at the OECD. The aim of the exercise is nothing less than to analyze, in greater detail, the social integration of the new trend our societies are witnessing as they move toward a knowledge-based economy. So far, we have addressed four different issues.

First and foremost, there is growing concern about the nature of the jobs being created and destroyed following the introduction of new technologies and about the accompanying remuneration – who benefits and who loses. This issue is raised to some extent by David Noble in the paper I just quoted. Recent literature suggests that the question of how technology affects the volume of unemployment in a country has extended to questions about the skill and distributional aspects of employment growth and decline. I think this issue is at the core of the present debate in the United States and, increasingly, in Europe. Why do we observe so clearly, in the case of the United States, the evidence of some form of skill-biased technical change closely associated with the use of computers? Why is there so little evidence of this bias in countries such as Germany or Japan? The evidence collected so far suggests that the increasing use of new information technologies has reduced the relative demand for unskilled workers and has increased the relative demand for skilled workers. Technological change has increased the mismatch between the skills workers have and the skills employers demand. The most pertinent policy issues relating to skill demand centre on human capital development. Changes in the skill mix of the labour force across the different OECD countries have undoubtedly been significant, and different countries have had different experiences with their changes in the relative wages between skilled and unskilled workers. Overall, there are no clear, single lines of change in training and education policies across countries – as yet. Instead, there is considerable experimentation aimed at shifting education and learning closer to work requirements, while attempting to provide wider skills to underpin continuous learning. There is a strong recognition in all countries of a need to accelerate the shift toward continuous lifelong learning and to adopt new teaching and learning approaches. These include "just-in-time" learning, wider training options, expanded opportunities for work-based learning and education, and training to encourage entrepreneurship.

Second, there are also questions about the actual (measurable) productivity gains associated with the introduction of new technologies. Such gains have been small and slow to materialize despite substantial investments in new technologies. Again, the evidence suggests that the productivity and growth impact of new technologies, and in particular information and communication technologies, depend crucially not only on "knowledge generation" but also on the way technology/knowledge is being accessed both nationally and internationally and distributed across all layers of the economy. At present, technology policy still focuses on the generation (rather than diffusion) of industrial technology (rather than knowledge) in large (rather than small) manufacturing (rather than service) firms. A "rebalancing" of technology policy would make its objectives more coherent with those of other policies and more closely aligned with changing priorities and framework conditions. This would require, in my view:

- a widening of the range of options considered in policy formulation through a greater and earlier involvement of all the actors concerned including business firms of all sizes and sectors, research centres, universities, the financial sector and technology users;

- adapting policies to some of the systemic features of innovation – success is determined more by the weakest link than by the strongest; and

- reconsidering the respective roles of support for strengthening market mechanisms and, especially, competition in product markets.

Third, there is increasing doubt, particularly in Europe, about the actual "new demand" creation arising from the use of new technologies, particularly in areas where markets seem to fail or appear "wrongly" regulated. For example, it is commonly agreed that telecommunications technology changes more rapidly than the accompanying regulatory frameworks. There is a need to speed up the process of regulatory reform in this area given that it is essential for the development of "information highways" and associated services which are widely regarded as major sources of new demand and output growth. The actual effect on employment of information infrastructure applications or the general impact on the economy is difficult to project. On this point, but only this point, I have some sympathy with David Noble. The net balance will, in any case, depend on the time frame under consideration. In the short term, the employment balance might well be negative. In the long term, it will depend on a number of interrelated factors:

- on the speed and extent of take up of new consumer/business applications;
- on pricing structures for use of, and access to, applications which will influence usage rates and diffusion;
- on the speed and extent to which new applications are developed; and
- on the existence of proper market incentives for the development of applications and their diffusion.

Fourth, there are questions about the required organizational changes within firms. New technologies raise issues with respect to the organization of work (e.g., flexibility, multi-skilling and job security), the organization of production (e.g., "lean" production, downsizing and flexible specialization) and the learning capacity of firms (e.g., knowledge acquisition and the role of complementary assets). There is also the question of employment creation – actual and potential – of small- and medium-sized enterprises, (SMEs) particularly of new technology-based firms. Internal structures of firms are being organized along the lines of decentralizing tasks, reducing hierarchies, shifting responsibilities to production activities and reducing the size of operating units. External features include technology partnerships to develop new products, processes and services; out-sourcing of production, component supply and service inputs; and new kinds of marketing arrangements. Policy should focus on decreasing the costs and increasing the benefits from such organizational change. This includes decreasing transition costs and dealing with market failures as well as decreasing the costs associated with long learning phases involved in the introduction of new technologies and organizations. Three policy areas are of particular importance:

- changing qualification requirements (e.g., training and skill formation for excluded people and groups);
- regulation, competition and organizational change (e.g., labour regulations, the balance between competition and co-operation, role for public procurement); and
- improving the business infrastructure (e.g., diffusion of information on best practice, especially to SMEs, human capital accounting).

Let me conclude by saying that this whole analysis really brings to the forefront the broadness of the many challenges we face. These challenges are not restricted to science and technology, knowledge generation in the narrow sense nor to policy issues. They involve issues of macro-economics, the influence of high real interest rates, for instance, on the diffusion of technology and on investments – not just physical investments but also knowledge investments. They relate to education, to the fact that large parts of our education system are in need of fundamental change, again as a result of the trend toward a more knowledge-based economy. And they relate to the many other policy areas I mentioned before.

This whole area is a typical illustration of why, when confronted with relatively radical changes, both policy makers and the way policies are organized are in need of radical change. And, of course, we are stuck, to some extent, in a framework of discussing policies based on the past – nicely departmentalized and focusing on issues as we perceive them from the past which may no longer correspond to the new challenges associated with the knowledge-based economy.

Part IV   Facilitating Knowledge-Based Growth

Richard G. Lipsey & Ken Carlaw
Department of Economics
Simon Fraser University

8

A *Structuralist View of Innovation Policy*

INTRODUCTION

IN THIS PAPER, WE USE THE APPROACH provided by a structuralist theory of growth to assess policies designed to encourage innovation.[1] The first part outlines the basic elements of the structuralist theory which distinguish technology from the facilitating structure within which it operates. The discussion draws heavily on Lipsey and Bekar (1995). Three key results are needed:

- first, the distinction between the economy's technology, its facilitating structure and its performance;

- second, some important generalizations about the characteristics of innovation and technological change; and

- third, some implications of these empirical generalizations, the most important of which is that innovation inevitably involves a substantial exposure to uncertainty.

Significant uncertainty in turn implies that, given current theory, it is impossible to derive:

- an optimal amount of research and development (R&D) and innovation;

- optimal directions in which innovations are to be attempted;

- optimal cutoff points when attempted innovations yield disappointing results; and

- optimal government policies for supporting innovation.

Instead, of providing optimal conditions for determining policy decisions, economists can provide only informed judgment.

The second part of this paper deals with the criteria for judging the success of an innovation policy and our scheme for classifying the 30 cases we studied.

The third part reports on a few of our case studies of innovation policies. The majority of the studies are reported in Appendix A, and the text is only intended to illustrate the kinds of cases we have studied and the kinds of policy lessons we have derived.[2] These discussions drastically condense the information we have built up on most of the cases.

The final part looks at the general policy lessons that can be derived from our case studies. We do not regard these lessons as proven. They are merely suggested by our observations and the theory we have developed. As such, they are candidates for further, more detailed, study.

SOME ELEMENTS OF A STRUCTURALIST THEORY

THE MATERIAL IN THIS SECTION, adapted from Lipsey and Bekar (1995), gives those elements of a structuralist approach to innovation and technical change that we need for our present purposes.

TECHNOLOGY, STRUCTURE AND PERFORMANCE

IN THE LIPSEY–BEKAR STRUCTURAL-HISTORICAL VIEW, growth is primarily driven by changes in techniques of production: the things we produce and how we produce them.[3] These techniques operate within a complex facilitating structure to produce economic performance. Knowledge lies behind this technology, structure and performance. Without knowledge, there would be none of the other things.

Technology

The *techniques of production*, loosely referred to as *technology*, are divided into product or process technologies.

T-1 *Product technologies*: the specifications of the goods and services that are produced.

T-2 *Process technologies*: the specifications of the processes that are employed to produce these goods and services (and to produce research results).[4]

Behind technology, lies *technological knowledge* which consists of applied knowledge of existing production and process technologies, and fundamental principles. Knowledge of existing technologies consists partly of codifiable knowledge and partly of tacit knowledge in the sense that the ability to produce and operate capital equipment cannot be learned completely from blueprints and manuals. What cannot be codified is called tacit knowledge and is acquired slowly by individual producers through learning by doing and learning by using. Lipsey and Bekar refer to these specifications as "blueprints+" to indicate both the codifiable and the tacit part of the knowledge. The more fundamental an innovation, the greater the tacit knowledge involved in successfully using it, i.e., the bigger the difference between the blueprint, as given say in a patent application, and the blueprint+ which is sufficient knowledge to allow the innovation to be used successfully.

As its definition of technology, neoclassical theory assumes the existence of a production function which describes a continuum of blueprints, any one of which can be costlessly selected and then installed and operated at known costs. In other words, the firm can move from one point on the existing production function to another with known new capital and operating costs.

In contrast, according to the structuralist view, the only things that are certain are what has already been done. Fundamental knowledge suggests that we could do other things, but the development of the technology to do so is a costly and uncertain business. Until we undertake the task, we do not know what the costs associated with these yet-to-be developed technologies will be. Thus, existing fundamental knowledge does not tell us exactly what we could create, nor exactly what it would cost to do so. Instead, it gives us some idea of what we could do that we are not now doing and of what it might cost. These ideas carry with them a significant degree of uncertainty, and the greater the departure from the blueprints now in use and the facilitating structure in which they operate, the greater the exposure to uncertainty when putting these ideas into practice – partly because of the increasing number of new elements of technology that will have to be generated and partly because of the number of new structural linkages required. (The concept of exposure to uncertainty is further explained in a later section.)

The stock of existing technological knowledge (both applied and fundamental) resides in firms, universities, government research laboratories and other similar production and research institutions.

Facilitating Structure

In our structural theory, technology operates within the larger concept of a facilitating structure, and much of the action that links technology to outputs takes place in the interrelationship.. s between technology and this structure. The *facilitating structure* includes variables at the firm, industry and economy levels.

Firm Level

S-1 The existing stock of producers' (and researchers') capital goods that (partially) embody the techniques of production.

S-2 The existing stock of durable consumers' goods (used to produce a future flow of consumption services).

S-3 The layout of the capital goods within productive units and the allocation of particular jobs to particular people.

S-4 The geographical location of physical capital.

S-5 The financial and institutional organization of the production unit.

Industry Level

S-6   The industrial structure, including the degree of concentration and the amount of co-operation or competition among legally separate units.

Economy Level

S-7   The economy's infrastructure that facilitates the production of goods and services, such as roads and rails, power and phone lines, air and shipping ports, traffic control facilities; and that helps to train humans, such as elementary schools, trade schools, universities and all forms of on-the-job training.

S-8   Private sector institutions which assist in financing productive activity such as banks, insurance companies, trust companies, and savings and loan institutions, plus the instruments they create, such as bills of exchange, credit cards and negotiable certificates of deposit.

S-9   Public sector institutions such as private property.

S-10   Local, national and super national public sector activity designed to facilitate and/or control economic activity.

Note several things about this facilitating structure.

- Although the existence of a unique, optimal structure for any given set of product and process technologies is an open question, various structures are well or poorly adapted to the existing set of technologies.

- Changes in technologies cause changes in the specifications of the structure that would be best adapted to the technologies. This, in turn, causes lagged changes in the actual structure.

- There are significant inertias in the adaptation of various parts of this structure to changing technologies. For example, two of the many sources of lags are the durability of capital goods and the slow speed with which governments typically change laws, rules and regulations. Thus, we would always expect some degree of mismatch between the existing structure and the current techniques of production.

Behind the facilitating structure lies two bodies of knowledge. The first is policy knowledge. The stock of this knowledge resides in policy-making and policy-analyzing institutions. It is a body of theory and experience that provides guidance in choosing policies that are effective in achieving given goals. The second is the knowledge that goes into the making, the functioning and the altering of the non-public policy parts of the facilitating structure, for example, how to set up a firm or organize a particular type of on-the-job education. This knowledge resides in all the agents which take part in the facilitating structure.

In this paper we are concerned with how policy knowledge can be used to cause changes in technological knowledge and hence in technologies.

Economic Performance

The techniques of production operating within the economy's facilitating structure produce *economic performance*.

P-1 Gross Domestic Product (GDP), its growth rate and its breakdown among sectors and among such broadly defined groupings as goods production and service production.

P-2 Total national income and its distribution among size and functional classes.

P-3 Total employment and unemployment, and its distribution among such sub-groups as sectors and skill classes.

Since our emphasis is on technology and structure, we can suppress further detail concerning the performance variables.

Innovation

The terms research, development, innovation and diffusion are all used rather loosely in many discussions of technological change. For present purposes, it will be sufficient to use the following distinctions.

- Pre-commercial R&D: This is R&D whose results are *de jure* non-appropriable. It is mainly research and is conducted in non-profit institutions as well as in firms (which can often temporarily appropriate it *de facto* through secrecy).

- Commercial R&D: This is R&D whose results are *de jure* (although often not *de facto*) appropriable. It is mainly development and is conducted by firms and by non-profit organizations.

- Commercialization: This is successfully marketing a new product or a new process technology. It is the generic definition: what is "successful" will depend on the particular case at hand, e.g., a firm will not take externalities into account while a public body may.

One obvious direction of the innovation process is "downstream" from pre-commercial R&D, to commercial R&D to commercialization. However, problems that arise in development can give rise to further pre-commercial research, while problems that arise in commercialization can give rise to further development and/or to further pre-commercial research. (Indeed, many fundamental discoveries in pure science have been made in an attempt to understand why some established technology really worked.)

We define the term "innovation" as *the process of developing and bringing to market, or otherwise into use, in places where it had not been used or marketed before, the result of any change in technology.* This process includes both the direct flows from pre-competitive to competitive R&D to commercialization and the necessary feedbacks from "downstream" to "upstream" stages. The qualification "where it had not been used or marketed before" allows us to include both leading edge developments and the so-called diffusion of existing technologies in our definition (following the empirical generalization concerning slow and costly diffusion given below).

Empirical Generalizations Concerning Innovations

WE LIST HERE A FEW OF THE KEY EMPIRICAL GENERALIZATIONS that are critical for understanding the behaviour of technological change and evaluating innovation policies. These generalizations are based on a wealth of detailed studies of technology made over the last four decades by researchers on both sides of the Atlantic.[5]

1. Endogenous R&D: Because R&D is an expensive activity which is often undertaken by firms in search of profit, innovation is partly endogenous to the economic system altering in response to changes in perceived profit opportunities.

2. Pre-commercial and commercial R&D: Firms doing pre-commercial research often keep the results as closely guarded secrets hoping to be able to develop commercially viable applications in advance of competitors. As a result, competing firms may all be doing similar pre-commercial research at the same time or, if they feel they cannot guard the results, they may be doing much less than they would if they were all co-operating as one decision unit. Furthermore, commercial research is only appropriable in principle. In many types of products, patents give limited or negligible protection.

3. Competition in innovation: Innovation is a major strategic variable for firms competing in manufacturing and service production. (These industries have market structures that do not remotely approach perfect competition.) Constant successful innovation is needed just to maintain market share. *Ceteris paribus*, a market served by a few competing oligopolists usually produces more innovation than either a market served by a monopolist or one served by price-taking firms which cover no more than their full cost of production.

4. Continuous innovation: Changes in both product and process technologies occur continuously and cover the whole range from incremental improvements in existing technologies to those that are revolutionary in conception and effect.[6] A high proportion of all technical change takes the form of incremental changes to existing product and process technologies. (Points 9, 10 and 17 to 20 help to explain why these incremental changes are more pervasive than a casual observation of new products over a decade would suggest.)

5. Current decisions constrained by past decisions: Because technological change takes place within an existing facilitating structure – including institutions, organizational structures, and the nature and location of the

physical and human capital that embody established technologies – there is no pure long run in which decisions take place in an environment unconstrained by the past decisions of any agent.

6. A range of induced effects on structure and performance: Some major innovations have effects on economic structure and performance that are relatively small in magnitude and scope of application, such as the introduction of rayon. Others are fundamental in the magnitude and scope of their technical changes and effects. Examples include the introduction of iron, steam-powered machinery, electricity, the transistor and the computer. Lipsey and Bekar (1995) used the term "enabling technologies" to refer to technologies that are widely used as inputs across most, or all, of the economy. Changes in these technologies induce a broad range of adjustments in the facilitating structure and economic performance. There is a sub-class of these enabling technologies, changes which cause adjustments that are not only wide in scope but large in magnitude – what Lipsey and Bekar call "deep structural adjustments (DSAs)."

7. Changes in structure required for efficient working of new technologies: When new fundamental technologies are fitted into the old structure, they often operate well below their full potential which can only be achieved when they operate within a structure that has evolved to fit them. [David's study of the electricity industry (1992) provides a classic illustration of this phenomenon.]

8. Changes in structure can cause changes in technology: There is a feedback from changes in structure to changes in technology. For example, in the aftermath of some fundamental new innovation, there is usually a series of derivative innovations some of which can be quite profound. A rigid structure that is slow to adapt can slow this process of related innovations while a flexible structure can speed it up. Furthermore, arbitrary changes in the structure, such as those imposed by government policy, can cause reactive changes in technology. For example, government-imposed constraints on location, factor use or emissions, can induce profit-seeking firms to innovate around these constraints.

9. Evolution of new technologies from crude beginnings: Major radical innovations never bring new technologies into the world in fully developed form. Instead, these technologies first appear in a crude embryonic state with only a few specific uses. Improvements and diffusion then occur simultaneously as the technology is made more efficient and is adapted for use over an increasingly wide range of applications. The more fundamental the innovation (running up to major innovations in enabling technologies) the more marked will be the long, slow evolutionary process (from crude prototypes with narrow uses, to highly efficient products with a vast range of applications). New products often require new machinery, while new processes often make possible, or require, the design of new products.

10. Technological convergence: Major innovations in product technologies, such as the introduction of completely new products, often require only incremental changes in production technologies. Thus, in a process that Rosenberg (1976) calls technological convergence, technologies that produce such widely separated products as sewing machines, bicycles and automobiles may come to share common production technologies. It follows that radical innovations occurring in both products and production processes are less common than one would think by studying products only.

11. Externalities: Innovations are vertically and horizontally linked to other innovations, often occurring in a related cluster of changes in several branches of the economy. The total set of these innovations produces much more additional value than would be produced if each were introduced in isolation. Major innovations, particularly in enabling technologies, confer massive externalities, since they apply across much of the economy and bring many gains that cannot be reaped by the original innovators.

12. Slow and costly diffusion: The diffusion of knowledge about successful innovations is a slow and costly business. Just to discover what is currently in use throughout the world is a daunting task, particularly for small firms. That activity at best only provides the blueprint; learning the blueprint+ implies acquiring all the tacit knowledge that goes with successfully adopting something new that is in use elsewhere. It follows that the existing set of technologies does not provide a freely available knowledge pool for existing firms. Learning about what is in use elsewhere and adapting it to one's own uses is a slow and costly process that typically requires innovation in its own right. (Thus, innovation and diffusion are not clearly distinct activities.)

13. Path dependency: For reasons given in points 5 to 12, technological change is highly path dependent.

14. Source of innovations: The source of innovations is sometimes found among suppliers, sometimes among producers and sometimes among users. The different locations across different industries can often be explained by which type of firm can most easily appropriate the rents from innovation.

15. Commercialization: Commercialization is an important part of the innovative process. Many marvelous technological advances were commercial flops. A country that successfully commercializes fundamental developments made elsewhere can have an excellent growth record, while a country that makes fundamental developments that its firms are unable to commercialize will have a poor growth record.

16. Innovation involves uncertainty: Because innovation means doing something not done before, there is an element of uncertainty [in Frank Knight's sense of the term (1964)] in all innovation. It is often impossible even to enumerate in advance the possible outcomes of a particular line

of research. Time and money are spent investigating specific avenues of research to discover if they are blind alleys or full of immensely rich pots of gold. As a result, massive sums are sometimes spent with no positive results while trivial expenditures sometimes produce results of great value. Furthermore, the search for one objective often produces results of value for quite different objectives. All this implies that agents will not be able to assign probabilities to different occurrences in order to conduct risk analysis as conventionally defined.

17. Uncertainty with respect to range of applications: There is enormous uncertainty with respect to the range of applications that some new technology may have. The steam engine, electricity, the telephone, radio, the laser, the computer, the VCR and fibre optics are examples of technologies that were initially thought to have very limited potential, and that did have very limited actual applications during the first decades of their life. Most development expenditure is on product not process development largely because, as we have observed above, new technologies come into the world in crude form, after which they are slowly developed and their range of applications is expanded in ways that seem impossible to predict in advance.

18. Exposure to uncertainty varies with the magnitude of the attempted technological advance: Attempts at big technological leaps involve a greater exposure to uncertainty than do attempts at small technological changes. Large leaps require more changes in the product and process blueprint+s. Smaller technology leaps require fewer such changes.

19. Exposure to uncertainty varies with the changes required in the facilitating structure: The more (in terms of number) and greater (in terms of magnitude) the structural changes required to accommodate some technological change, the greater will be the exposure to the uncertainty attached to that technological change.

20. Successful innovation requires flexibility: Because firms grope in an uncertain world toward better lines of innovative activity as experience accumulates, successful innovators must stay flexible. Successful firms, learn from their experience and constantly alter their courses of action.

UNCERTAINTY FURTHER CONSIDERED[7]

IN THE ABOVE LIST, ONE OF THE MOST IMPORTANT SETS of generalizations concerns the place of uncertainty in the innovative process. Economists have produced much valuable theory about decision taking under conditions of risk because risk is amenable to treatment with standard analytical tools. There are fewer positive results on uncertainty because it is difficult to theorize about uncertainty beyond explaining, in the tradition of Frank Knight (1964), that there is a trade off between some degree of exposure to uncertainty and the profits associated with success (or what might be called the rents of innovation).

The Nature of Uncertainty

In the uncertain world the innovator may be thought of as deciding at the outset on where he or she wants to end up (with some given product or process innovation) and the maximum amount it is worth paying to get there. Over time, experience accumulates as to what can be done, and the cost at which it can be done. The flow of costs actually incurred will differ from the estimate, and the goals may have to be changed as more is learned about what is feasible. On the cost side, the innovator cannot say, at the outset, how much is at risk – unless he or she sets some arbitrary cutoff which may not be a credible commitment when he or she reaches the cutoff point and must then decide, in light of what has been learned, whether or not to continue the project. On the payoff side, there is no telling in advance what may be discovered, nor what the demand response will be to some particular new piece of technology.

Because, under uncertainty, the range of the costs and benefits of some endeavour cannot be determined, it does not make sense to talk about increasing or decreasing the *amount of uncertainty* to which an innovator is exposed. Nonetheless, one can say something about uncertainty comparisons. To do this, we define our concept of *the degree of exposure to uncertainty*.

First, consider extreme cases. At one extreme, someone who seeks to make a small change in one component of an existing technology, such as a new aereolon for a one-engine aircraft, faces relatively low exposure to uncertainty. There is uncertainty about the payoff because, for example, the innovator may discover something that is widely applicable to all aircraft, or even to such non-flying vehicles as speedboats. But because the successful innovation will require few changes to the current blueprint+ and the existing firm-level structure of aircraft design and production, the number of things about which the innovator can be surprised is quite small. At the other extreme, consider an innovator seeking to create a wholly new technology such as harnessing atomic power for civilian purposes in the 1940s and early 1950s. In this case, the blueprint cannot be adapted from a similar predecessor. Many related innovations are needed, any one of which may require quite unexpected costs or yield quite unexpected applications. Much new knowledge will also be needed, and creating it will require changes in the existing economy-level, structural network of physical and human capital whose richness and adaptability will influence the outcome of the attempted innovation. The degree of exposure to uncertainty is much larger than for the first innovator.

Different innovations require a different number and direction of supporting technological advances and different changes in the facilitating structure. The more fundamental the desired innovation, the more the number and variety of related innovations and structural changes that will be needed – each subject to its own uncertainties. So the degree of exposure to uncertainty refers to the number of separate technological advances that are needed and the number of innovative changes in the facilitating structure that are required, in order to complete a projected innovation. Each supporting advance is subject to its own uncertainty regarding costs and benefits. Incurring higher cost does not imply higher returns.

Modelling Uncertainty

In this section, we describe formalizations meant to capture the generalizations about technological change discussed above. Our purpose is merely to show that the problems facing an innovator are vastly more complex than is assumed in the conventional theory of maximization under conditions of risk.

Let the innovation problem be described by making drawings from a set of urns each one containing a finite but unknown number, b of blue balls, r of red balls and y of yellow balls: $0 \le b,r,y$; $b+r+y = n$. The innovator never knows how many blue, red and yellow balls are in any one urn, and the number for any one colour may be zero.

Attempts at innovations are represented by drawing balls from one or more urns at a given cost per draw. Blue balls indicate success in solving the technological problem under investigation; red balls represent unexpected knowledge that is useful in other contexts but not for the problem being addressed; yellow balls represent failure.

The balls that represent failed experiments are not replaced indicating that successive failed attempts do provide learning that increases the chances of solving the problem. In this case, each drawing increases the odds of getting a blue ball on the next drawing, unless there are no blue balls in the urn. Since n is unknown, the amount by which the odds change is itself uncertain.

Success

A successful innovation is made when a blue ball is drawn from each of the prescribed urns.

Exposure to Uncertainty

Uncertainty takes many forms. The most obvious is in not knowing n, b, r or y, or the number of urns from which drawings must be made. The simplest form of the innovation attempt, with a low exposure to uncertainty, is to have only one urn from which to draw. A complex innovation attempt, with higher exposure to uncertainty, requires one blue ball to be drawn from each of m urns.

Another dimension of uncertainty is that nasty surprises often occur when unforeseen obstacles arise in the course of a research effort. This is modelled by having some of the balls in the urns carry the label: "You must now get a successful drawing from x more urns, the existence of which you had no previous knowledge."

Cutting Edge versus Duplication

If no one has done what is being attempted, the innovator is operating at the cutting edge of technological advance. Most important, one or more of the urns may have zero blue balls which means that the attempt *must* fail, although this cannot be known in advance. In contrast, if others have succeeded before, an important element of uncertainty is removed: it is known that there are no urns with no blue balls.

Qualitative Knowledge

Qualitative knowledge can be viewed as the bridge that connects risk and uncertainty. At one extreme, qualitative knowledge may be complete in the sense that the innovator is able to attach objective or subjective probabilities to the experiment. At the other extreme, the innovator may have no qualitative knowledge about the experiment, i.e., the uncertainty is complete. There are many intermediate cases, for example, the person may have some idea of the proportion of blue balls in some of the urns. One also may have some idea of how many balls there are in total, e.g., $n<x$. He or she then has some idea of how the odds change when an unsuccessful drawing removes one unfavourable ball. This captures the idea of the innovator having some idea of how big an advance is being tried and of how difficult it is.

Alternative Technical Solutions

Usually, there are several alternative technical solutions for one generic technological problem (e.g., gas-cooled or heavy-water-cooled methods of nuclear fission). A successful innovation then requires drawing blue balls from a subset, r, of m available urns. However, the would be innovator must choose a set of urns in advance from which drawings are to be made, i.e., the innovator must decide which version of the technology he or she is going to try to develop.

Implications of Uncertainty

In this section we mention only the few implications of uncertainty that are relevant to assessing policies to encourage innovation.

The Firm

Neoclassical analysis is based on firms which make choices under conditions of either certainty, or under the type of risk that can be reduced either to an expected value or to some other certainty equivalent, measured in either the point or the set sense. Firms can, therefore, survey the expected value of the outcome of each line of action, then set a strategy and stick to it (as is typically assumed in many types of game theory).

In non-neoclassical theory, particularly the evolutionary branch pioneered by Nelson and Winter (1982), innovation is not the result of a decision-making process that can be described as rational, profit maximization in the neoclassical sense. Nonetheless, the firms' innovative activities can be described as profit-seeking. They care about profits and consciously seek out the lines of activity that seem to offer the best chance of profits. They do this by groping toward more profitable courses of action in an uncertain world, using their own and others' past experiences to help in guessing about the best courses of action.

The Price System

This behaviour has important implications for the function played by the market mechanism. In neoclassical hidden hand theory, the price system provides the set of relative prices that reflect national scarcities, and the firms do the maximizing themselves, after scanning all possible lines of activity and calculating the expected value of each line's outcome. Thus, optimization takes place within black boxes called firms, using information about relative scarcities fed to them by the price system. Things that are done are maximizing activities for those firms, while things that are not done are not maximizing activities.

In the contrasting structuralist-evolutionary theory, firms grope toward better courses of action under uncertainty, trying new lines of activity in situations in which no one knows the precise values of the probable outcomes. Firms that choose the better lines of activity are rewarded by profits, and those that choose worse lines are punished by losses and possible insolvency. This evolutionary hand theory gives the price system more importance than does the neoclassical, hidden hand theory. Firms grope as best they can in an uncertain world, and it is the price–profit system, not the maximizing firm, that ensures that the more successful lines of activity survive while the less successful fail.

Alleged Underproduction of R&D

In the neoclassical world, any output characterized by positive externalities will be underproduced. Arrow (1964) extended this argument to R&D: since its results often create massive externalities, the maximizing firm will produce too little R&D and its production should, therefore, be subsidized.

However, once we accept that major uncertainties are attached to innovation, this argument no longer holds. Agents seeking to make major inventions and innovations are in the position we modelled with our urn analogy. The market economy encourages innovation by giving rewards to successful innovators, and huge rewards to the few who are really successful, while the unsuccessful suffer losses. We cannot predict from some well-articulated theory how people will react to such uncertain possibilities. Since we cannot define an optimal amount of R&D, and since we do not know how people behave when they are faced with this type of situation (observation tells us that different people behave very differently), there is no way to say, scientifically, that there will be too much or too little R&D. In summary, whether the unaided market produces too much or too little R&D depends on two judgments, neither of which can be established scientifically. First, we must know what is the socially optimal amount of R&D and, second, we must be able to predict how much R&D the free market will produce relative to that social optimum.

By rejecting Arrow's argument (1964), we are not rejecting the possibility that R&D may be underproduced by some agreed criterion. Most economists, the authors included, believe that innovation and economic growth improve human welfare on average, so innovation is correctly judged to be socially valuable. But what we cannot do is determine the amount of innovation that is too much or too little by comparing the actual amount against some criteria of optimality.

Economists do not like to be told that some policy decisions are a matter of judgment rather than scientific generalization. They often cling to models that provide precise policy recommendations even though the models are obviously inapplicable to the world of our experience. Our view is that, rather than using models of risk that give precise answers for situations that do not apply, it is better to face the reality that there is no generalization about whether the market produces too much or too little R&D, and accept that we must decide this question with informed judgment based on the details of each individual case.

No Optimal Cutoff Point

Just as there is no optimal amount of innovation, there is no optimal cutoff point when the process of groping toward some specific innovative goal seems to be producing disappointing results. Some decision has to be taken about when to cut the losses by stopping the search, but it is always possible that spectacular success may be just around the next corner. Since, if the project is abandoned, that next corner is never turned, one can never know for sure whether or not the decision to stop was a good one, let alone the "optimal" one.

POLICIES TO ENCOURAGE INNOVATION

WE HAVE ALREADY OBSERVED that one cannot determine an optimal innovation policy when decisions are taken under uncertainty. This does not imply that any policy is as good as any other policy. Policy makers can be informed by economic reasoning even if, in the end, an element of judgment is needed.

CRITERIA OF SUCCESS

CONSIDER AN IMAGINARY INNOVATION which offers some profit if successful but affects none but those directly involved. There would seem to be no case for the government to second guess private decision takers on whether or not to attempt the innovation. Successful innovations almost always confer both positive and negative externalities. The usual case for policy support makes the implicit assumption that there are positive net externalities, although we doubt it is true of every case and see no way to establish that it is true when averaged over all cases.

A policy to encourage the development and use of some specific technological advance has costs measured by the development and operating costs, and benefits measured by the operating revenues and the net externalities. For the activity to pass a cost-benefit test, the net externalities have to be at least equal to the development costs plus any operating subsidy or minus any operating profits (everything stated in suitable dimensions). Although we cannot measure the externalities in the cases we study, we can say what they would have to be to make the activity pass such a test: the value of the externalities must be more or less than the development cost by the net operating loss or profit on using the new technology.

In this study, we take a twofold criteria for success of a policy directed at commercial innovations.

Level One Success

The policy succeeded in creating a commercially viable innovation in the sense that a technology (T-1 and/or T-2) was created for which private sector firms would voluntarily create the facilitating structure needed to put it into production. This assumes that the externality equals the full development cost. If it is more or less than that amount, the criterion of success can be correspondingly adjusted.

Level Two Success

The attempted technological development offered what seemed like reasonable chances of success at the outset but the activity was ended when the prospects for success seemed too low. If there were no externalities and no uncertainty, the criteria would be: did the government drop the attempt at the time that the private sector would have done? Given uncertainty and externalities, however, we must be less precise than that. First, as we observed above, in a world of uncertainty, we cannot say precisely when a firm should, or would, drop some line of attempted technological advance. Second, when there are externalities, the government's criteria of when to drop an attempted line should be different from a private firm's even if no uncertainty (i.e., only risk) were involved.

It may seem odd that we call an attempted innovation that failed to produce acceptable results but was dropped at what seemed a reasonable time a success. Given the uncertainties of innovation, however, any successful agent who continually innovates will have failures as well as successes. Since failures are as much a part of a successful innovation policy as are successes, the criteria of a good policy is not the impossible one of no failures, but that failures are recognized as such and the activity cut off before further funds are wasted.

Finally, we need to mention another type of policy – one that is directed at non-commercial goals but which creates spinoffs in the form of commercially viable innovations. Military procurement and space research are important examples. Such policies must be assessed primarily on whether or not they achieve their non-commercial ends. They can, however, also be evaluated on whether or not, *ceteris paribus*, they achieved the maximum possible spinoffs of commercially viable innovations.

CLASSIFICATION OF CASES

WE HAVE CLASSIFIED OUR CASES ALONG TWO DIMENSIONS relating to the magnitude of the changes that are required in technology (T) and structure (S). The technological change refers to the number of changes needed in the elements of existing product and process specifications to effect the desired overall technological change. Making this measure operational, in a detailed way, and relating the required changes in product and in process specifications is an important part of our ongoing theorizing about technological change. For present purposes, however, we rely on an impressionistic metric of incremental and large-leap technological advances. Within each of these categories, we find it useful to distinguish whether the policy was to catch up or to push the leading edge forward. Studies of technological change show that the vast bulk of R&D activity is to accomplish incremental changes in technology. So our incremental category must not be taken to mean unimportant. Although governments frequently attempt big leaps, these are much less common in private sector innovative activity.

A fully operational treatment of the structural dimension, would require consideration of both the type and the magnitude of the structural change entailed by the attempted innovation: small, medium and large changes in each of the firm level, industry level and economy level of the facilitating structure. In the preliminary treatment of this paper, we give an impressionistic classification of the structural changes required by each policy as merely small, medium or large. Large changes are usually felt at the industry and firm levels, while medium and small changes may be felt only at the firm level. While some changes would require changes in the economy-wide facilitating structure, these are not important for the analysis we need to make here. This classification scheme gives us the 12 possible cases shown in Table 1 which is presented later in this paper.

Technology policies come in two broadly different forms. First, they may target specific technologies, encouraging them in a number of different ways, ranging from the promotion of a single national champion to encouragement to all the firms in the industry that produce the targeted technology. Second, they may change the facilitating structure in the hope that this will feed back to more technological dynamism without targeting specific technologies. In this paper, we devote most of our space to studying the first type of policy. The second type is briefly considered but a full treatment must await a book-length study elaborating on our basic approach.

EXAMPLES OF CASES: DATA AND LESSONS

IN THIS SECTION, WE OUTLINE A FEW OF OUR CASE STUDIES that illustrate the policy conclusions drawn from the more than 30 cases we studied. The remainder are presented in Appendix A which contains much of the real meat of our work. The treatments are brief due to space considerations. We hope the general reader will follow the text's illustrative cases while specialists will either read Appendix A in its entirety, or refer to it as necessary. Each set of cases in both the text and Appendix A concludes with suggested policy lessons which we regard as generalizations to be tested against further evidence. The first time a generalization occurs, whether in the text or Appendix A, it is stated in full. Every time it recurs, only the short, bold-faced form is given. Since each application is context specific, a different discussion surrounds the generalization each time it reappears.

FOUR AIRCRAFT EXAMPLES

THE FIRST TWO OF THESE EXAMPLES are of attempted large, leading edge, technological leaps which entailed medium industry-level structural changes.

The Anglo–French Concorde[8] (Failure)

By pioneering the world's first supersonic commercial airliner, the British wanted to leapfrog the Americans whose Boeing 707 had made them the world's leaders in sub-sonic commercial jet aircraft. The U.K. government's Supersonic Transport Committee was formed in 1956, significantly, without any representation from the Treasury Department. In 1959, the Committee recommended the initiation of design work on two new supersonic airliners. The recently formed British Aircraft Corporation (BAC) produced a short, commissioned report that formed the basis of the 1962 Supersonic Aircraft Agreement between France and Great Britain. The Agreement contained no provisions for limiting costs (initially estimated at £150 to £170 million) or for reviewing or cancelling the project.

At the time of the agreement, BAC estimated the potential market at between 300 and 500 units. As time passed, development costs grew massively. In 1973, the project's costs had reached £1065 million. Over half of the cost increases were due either to revisions in the costs of meeting foreseen development problems or to additional, unforeseen technical problems. Much of the unexpected expenditure was devoted to unsuccessful attempts to reduce the sonic boom – a technological advance that still eludes today's researchers. Before production began, some key countries passed sub-sonic speed limits for commercial airliners passing through their airspace. The massive gamble to beat the sonic boom failed, and this led to a drastic curtailment of the market that would have existed if all other conditions had been favourable.

During the development, it also became apparent that the aircraft's running costs would be very high. As a result, no airlines were willing to take the aircraft *even as a gift*. In 1977, British Airways suffered an operating loss of £17 million on the operation of five Concordes over one year. The final realized sales of nine were to the captive markets of the national airlines in Britain and France. (Sixteen were built in all.)

Spinoffs from the Concorde were useful in other aircraft projects including the Airbus. Some Europeans argue that these were sufficient to justify the project. We find this implausible for two reasons. First, the net spinoffs would have to have been massive to justify the cost. Second, both the direct payoffs and the spinoffs would have been much higher if the same money had been spent on supporting the successful sub-sonic Caravelle, rather than an unsuccessful attempt to commercialize supersonic transport.

The SST in the United States[9] (Type 1 Failure; Type 2 Success)

In 1962, the U.S. government entered the race to develop a supersonic civilian aircraft and, from 1962 to 1970, spent US$1 billion on related research. The project was then cancelled. In reaching this decision, the Americans had the advantage of the U.K. experience as well as their own. By that time, many U.S. observers had concluded that the first generation of commercial supersonic aircraft was not going to be a commercial success. Others who still thought that success was possible, realized that there would be little room for a second competitor in the small market that would exist unless the sonic boom could be overcome by hypersonic aircraft.

Caravelle[10] (Success Turned into Failure)

Caravelle is an example of incremental, leading edge, technological advance combined with small, firm-level changes in structure.

Following on the heals of the British Comet's technical failure in the 1950s, the French Caravelle emerged as both the technical leader and the top commercial contender in the short- and medium-haul jet aircraft market. The Caravelle was a 120 to 150 seat passenger airliner, similar in size and range to the Comet but produced after the problem of metal fatigue had been solved.

In 1960, the Caravelle was the only short- or medium-haul commercial jet aircraft in operation and, more important, there were no other such aircraft on competitors' drawing boards! Caravelle's existing competitors were turboprop aircraft, such as the successful British Viscount and the U.S. Convaire. These aircraft were superior to those powered with internal combustion engines, but were slower than jets and, in retrospect, were a transitionary generation except in the very short-haul range where they continue to be competitive.

In that same year (1960), Northwestern Airlines decided to purchase the Caravelle for its short- and medium- haul needs, indicating a vast, unexploited U.S. market for commercial jets.

The history of the MacDonald Douglas DC-9 and Boeing's 727 and 737 illustrate one of the important generalizations given in a previous section: products have a trajectory in which they are improved, usually incrementally and occasionally somewhat more dramatically. They sell over decades, during which time the employed technology is fairly stable, only to be interrupted by occasional major technological advances (that are much rarer than aircraft producers typically predict).

Although the French were in possession of a world leader, their decision to go for the Concorde, caused them to redirect much of their available R&D and technological support to the prestigious Concorde project. As a result, Caravelle lost its significant technological edge and, subsequently, its market lead, to the DC-9 and the 727 and 737 produced in the 1960s. Caravelle had its share of problems but, as the first successful commercial jet aircraft, the R&D effort to keep it in its front-running position would have been small relative to the massive R&D effort that went into the Concorde.

In 1959, the French had sole possession of a working technology for sub-sonic commercial short- and medium-haul aircraft that has been the dominant commercial technology to the present day. Yet they abandoned that advantage to pursue a technological breakthrough that is still unrealized 36 years later!

The Airbus[11] (Marginal Success)

This case is an example of a large, catch-up, technological leap followed by continued, incremental, leading edge improvements as competition in technology between Airbus and Boeing continued over the decades. At the outset, medium-level structural changes were required in the industry.

Airbus Industrie (AI) was set up in 1970 as a French–German collaboration. The arrangement provides a legal framework for co-operation on individual projects without the participants having to tie up large capital sums in a joint company or merger. The consortium's 1400 partners and subsidiary members can be roughly divided into two tiers. The top tier is dominated by a few large national (sometimes nationalized) companies (which are also the main shareholders) and subcontractors. The second tier is made up of many competing associate and subsidiary members who are second-stage subcontractors.

The shareholder arrangement has enabled member firms to make credible commitments to a co-operative strategy with other members of the consortium in other countries. Since all shareholders are joint beneficiaries of innovation, the members can credibly commit to performing both basic and commercial research knowing that any commercial application resulting from it will bring benefit to all members.

The governments provide low-cost loans to help cover development and production costs. Only new designs are eligible for support. The payment schedule for the loans is contingent on the revenue stream generated by a member company. However, many of the major national firms that make up AI are either nationalized firms or are tied up with such firms as subsidiaries. For example, in 1990, 93 percent of the share capital of Aerospatiale, the main French firm, was held by the state, and the remainder was held by a heavily subsidized agency. Governments have also provided funds for lease contracts to Eastern Airlines and emergency funds for some consortium members. The United States views these as direct subsidies to production.

AI's R&D activities are divided into two levels. Tier one R&D is the most sensitive and complicated and is conducted solely within the large national firms, mostly Aerospatiale. In principle, tier one R&D is the sole right of the firm providing it. In practice, this R&D is disseminated throughout the consortium. This R&D guides the subsequent selection of equipment contractors.

The subsidiary members of AI compete with each other during design and development of the component-specific, tier two R&D. Based on this competition, work is subcontracted to the partners. This organizational structure allows AI to internalize some of the uncertainty surrounding the innovative process. The consortium itself is unhurt if a given member firm fails to bring a development idea to market. The consortium structure allows spillovers to be more fully captured and facilitates the transfer of tacit knowledge.[12]

The consortium required massive government subsidies to start up and continues to require support for the development of subsequent generations. "In general terms the French and their partners readily concede that without government help in the early 1970s, the project would have died." (Hayward, 1986, p. 166). Although its beginnings were heavily influenced by government, it has steadily become a more industry-driven program. AI has managed to capture market share in highly competitive international markets and has introduced several design innovations. For example, it pioneered the prefabrication of large sub-assemblies so they could be moved to various sites.

Many U.S. observers have been critical of the program. Boeing developed a cost analysis of the project, based on its own production costs, and projected that initial government outlays to the program could never be recovered. In contrast, by internal costing analysis, Airbus predicts a better than break even record before the end of two existing production runs. Europeans believe the project has allowed them to re-establish a competitive position in the international market for full-sized commercial aircraft.

There is no doubt that great technological achievements have occurred. The A320 can be expected to cover at least its current production costs and to be a success on our criteria. However, many observers feel that AI failed to cover production costs of the earlier generations. (It is difficult to pin down AI's financial situation because of national ownership and no legal requirement to disclose its finances). Whether it will ever cover its full development costs on the total of all the A300, A310 and A320 iterations is an open question. It is also probable that Airbus has received more unpaid help in the form of subsidies to meet development costs than did Boeing in the form of military contracts that covered a significant part of the development costs of its successful commercial jet transports, the 707 and the engines for the 747 (which we discuss in Appendix A).

Over the next few years, competition between the new designs for the A330 and A340 and similar designs by Boeing will tell much of the remaining story. If Airbus is to continue to be a qualified success, these models will have to sell well. To do so, AI will have to keep pace with Boeing's changes in design and production that are speeding up the whole process of producing a new model of aircraft. Many observers worry that AI's national-champion structure will not prove flexible enough to do so (at least without a permanent government subsidy).

Policy Lessons

These cases offer some important policy lessons that are listed below, followed by supporting observations.

> **Large technological leaps are dangerous.** Attempts at large technological leaps involve major exposures to uncertainty because:
>
> - they require many changes in the blueprints+ for technology;
>
> - the technologies are initially produced in a crude embryonic form; and
>
> - they require many changes in the facilitating structure.
>
> If policy makers pursue these leaps, they need to be patient.

No one could have foreseen the acceleration of Concorde's development costs and the high running costs of supersonic aircraft until much money had been spent on early development. Furthermore, large sums were spent on what turned out to be a futile attempt to reduce the sonic boom. The unfortunate effects of this unavoidable uncertainty seem to have been compounded on the demand side by some non-professional wishful thinking. Surely, a high degree of scepticism would have been realized if military aircraft had been used to conduct tests of supersonic flights over populated areas. Recognition of the likelihood of prohibition of such overland flights would have led to a drastic downward revision of the estimated market. The developers of both the Concorde and the SST spent much money discovering that the alley of 20th century, commercially viable, supersonic transport was blind.

In supersonic transport, the new technology was so far removed from the existing facilitating structure that the changes required in structure implied much higher costs. Higher costs, in turn required a higher expected return for success. The expected return was actually revised downward in this case.

Airbus has required patience from its funders (in most cases government) in order to develop its technology and establish itself in the market. The dilemma is that one must be patient when such a big leap is attempted but, sooner or later, one must become impatient with the lack of payoff. *Ex ante*, it is hard to know which quality is required in any particular set of circumstances.

Technological development follows a trajectory. Policy makers are well advised to exploit the potential within an established trajectory.

The French would have been better off developing their lead in the Caravelle rather than diverting their R&D effort into the uncharted territory of supersonics. They could have reduced their exposure to uncertainty by limiting the number of required changes in both structural and technical blueprints and would have exploited an already successful venture into a market that became massive in the 1960s and remained so through the 1990s. In contrast, they are now following a technological trajectory with successive versions of the airbus.

Exploit established trajectories. Policy makers should realize that competitors are likely to continue through an established development trajectory because firms face the constant threat of being innovated out of a market by competitors.

The policy of directing R&D resources away for Caravelle and into Concorde choked off Caravelle's lead in short- and medium-haul jet aircraft. As a result of not continuing through the aircraft's development trajectory, the French were surpassed by subsequent American designs.

Policy needs to be flexible. Coping with uncertainty requires learning from experience so policy must be able to change course or cancel the venture as experience accumulates.

The Anglo–French experience illustrates the ability and willingness of governments with no bottom line to continue long after any privately financed commercial venture would have ended. The Concorde venture had built in inflexibilities with no mechanism to check expenditures and no escape clause in the agreement between the two countries.

The Americans were able to cut off their SST venture when it seemed unlikely to succeed commercially. This experience is often cited as a policy failure because large sums were spent with little return. But, in the uncertain environment of innovation, many alleys that initially seem worth investigating turn out to be empty. The Americans recognized the dead end, and Congress cut off the project on a close vote in spite of the administration's continued support for the SST.[13]

Before such ventures are committed, thought needs to be given to creating effective review and cancellation mechanisms which will induce flexibility in the policy. (Possibly an independent review body could hold the initial recommendation to continue or to terminate from political considerations, although the final decision cannot be so shielded.)

> **Multiple objectives are dangerous.** One of our major policy lessons is that when governments have multiple objectives, the uncertainties of innovation decisions make it likely that the other objectives will predominate, *and the prediction about the future commercial viability of the innovation will be whatever is needed to justify the decision to proceed.* The implication is that successful innovation policies must be single-objective policies. Mixing them with political prestige, regional development, redistribution, employment maintenance (or any other of our P variables), is almost to guarantee that the innovation objectives will be perverted to the other ends – given the uncertainty surrounding any prediction of the commercial viability of current attempts at developing innovations.

All three governments (French, British and American) entered the supersonic race with multiple objectives of creating new fundamental technology, commercial viability and employment in the aerospace industries, and generating political prestige. The French and British decisions, and the U.S. administration's support, illustrate the wishful thinking that often occurs when governments contemplate major innovations and are concerned with considerations of national prestige and short-term political gain connected with employment in specific areas and industries.

> **Policy should be aware of the interrelation between technology and structure.** Change in one causes change in the other. If policy makers target only technology or structure, there will be induced consequences in the other which will affect the overall performance of the policy, e.g., by imposing unforeseen costs or by retarding the changes that are being targeted.

Although Airbus required a great leap forward in domestic technology, Europeans did have a significant existing structure in the form of several major aircraft firms, many component manufacturers and much human capital. Airbus had all the experience from Concorde and other European aircraft manufacturing programs such as the Comet and Caravelle.

Airbus is an example of how policy innovation in industry structure (in this case allowing for credible commitments to share the results of pre-commercial research) can lead to innovation in technology. It has allowed for inter-firm idea exchanges, credible commitments to pre-commercial research, flexibility, commercial objectives to be central and the exploitation of feedback among innovations and between innovation and the facilitating structure. In spite of all this, Airbus is probably *the* marginal case between success and failure of a technology-specific policy.

> **Policy intervention can be useful if guided by private sector knowledge**. Policy makers can aid innovators through market intervention provided commercial and competitive objectives guide the intervention. This implies that market concentration and protection must be balanced by competition in innovation, and policy must tie itself to commercial signals reflecting viability. Policy makers are ill-advised to dictate business decisions.

The consortium structure invented for Airbus has partially avoided many of the problems, such as lack of innovative competition and high exposures to uncertainty, that beset single national champions serving protected markets. The consortium has integrated a number of national champions operating in a European market. It has also induced competition in level-two R&D. However, the European national champion ethos has remained in place within the consortium.

> **Because innovation is uncertain, policy should encourage many diverse experiments.**

The tier-two R&D conducted by Airbus allows many firms to bring their diverse expertise to any given innovation problem. However, the tier-one R&D conducted by Airbus is concentrated within a single experiment by a national champion.

> **Policy can play a useful role, inducing and co-ordinating pre-commercial R&D efforts and encouraging competition in innovation.** Policies that gather and disseminate non-appropriable technical information and provide a mechanism through which firms can credibly commit to conducting joint pre-commercial R&D help to level firms' non-appropriable technical knowledge, to reduce hoarding of such knowledge, to minimize costly duplication and to induce innovation.

It is not clear whether using national champions to produce pre-commercial research is the most efficient production technique. However, Airbus did create a structure which induces firms to commit credibly to such R&D. The structure also allows for the diffusion of the pre-commercial knowledge developed within the large national champions, thus levelling the playing field for all members.

The tier-two R&D conducted by Airbus induces firms to compete in innovation since design contracts are awarded on the basis of this competition.

JAPANESE POLICY TOWARD SEMICONDUCTORS[14] (Successes and Failures)

THE MINISTRY OF INTERNATIONAL TRADE AND INDUSTRY (MITI) is the Japanese government's major institution for operating its innovation policies. As early as the 1950s, MITI targeted the semiconductor industry as a key industry. The goals were to catch up with American technology and, later, to forge ahead. Japan has used several mechanisms of technology-push, demand-pull and information co-ordination and transfer, thus avoiding the shortcomings of each when applied individually.

The policy structure relevant to the Japanese semiconductor industry is as follows.

- Central co-ordination (MITI):
  - industry-wide goals;
  - formulation of a "vision" for the industry;
  - co-ordination of subsidies for large-scale projects;
  - basic research shared by government and industry; and
  - co-ordination of information for basic and applied research.

- Supply-side incentives:
  - tax incentives; and
  - Japanese development bank and other public and semi-public institutions granting preferential loans.

- Demand-side guarantees:
  - Nippon Telephone Telegraph (NTT) and other public procurement policies; and
  - a general focus on economic growth to foster the growth of domestic demand.

- Infant industry protection:
  - import duties;
  - control over, and restriction of, foreign direct investment; and
  - control over technology purchases and licensing.

- Legislation:
  - interpretations of the anti-monopoly act; and
  - promotion of key industries.

Early Development (Success)

This is a case of incremental, catch-up, technological changes combined with medium, structural changes. Early Japanese policy targeted technology catch-up. MITI's control of licensing agreements allowed it to choose proven technological winners, developed by companies such as IBM, and to seek licensing agreements with them. The policy was successful but, sometimes, overly conservative. For example, the firm of Tokyo Tsushin Kogyo sought permission to purchase Western Electric's transistor technology in 1953. MITI was reluctant to approve the purchase because the technology had uncertain commercial applicability. The company persisted with the deal in spite of MITI's disapproval and went on to become the Sony Corporation.

The licensing of proven technologies allowed technological followers to exploit niche markets and products that the originators of the technology inevitably left behind as they progressed through the development trajectory the first time.

Policy Lessons

> **Successful policies often pursue incremental innovation and (where possible) aid in the acquisition of tacit knowledge.** Policy makers can reduce exposure to uncertainty by pursuing incremental innovation, by acquiring the tacit knowledge in established foreign technology and by targeting niche developments based on that technology.

MITI's strategy of adopting proven technologies reduced exposure to uncertainty by:

- foregoing the uncertainty of creating new innovations;
- foregoing the ancillary innovations required to set up a new production system for such innovation;
- allowing policy makers to fit the adopted technology into both the existing structure and the policy vision for how the structure is to change; and
- allowing tacitness to be reduced in the technology transfer by seeking licensing partnerships with the originators of the technology.

Catch-up policies provide room for secondary innovations that adapt and develop niche innovations from known technologies while acquiring tacit knowledge already known elsewhere.

> **Policy needs to be flexible.**

MITI's policy of only licensing proven technologies nearly cost them the huge commercial success of the Sony Corporation.

Contemporary Policy Framework

These are policies that look for small leading edge technological and economy-wide structural changes.

Supporting Network (Success)

The critical role for MITI has always been to act as information co-ordinator. "Vast amounts of information, much of it quite sensitive, are exchanged between MITI and industry through formal and informal channels" (Okimoto, Sugano and Weinstein, 1984, p. 101).

By fostering a relationship of trust, MITI has been able to induce industry leaders to share pre-commercial information that would normally be guarded in order to extract transitional rents. MITI has built a network capable of gathering and disseminating information that is useful to all members of the industry. The construction costs of this communication network were high but the system paid off in many subsequent projects.

MITI has created social value by assisting the rapid dissemination of pre-commercial research results. This has forced firms to compete on commercial research that generates appropriable results. Thus, needless duplication of effort has been reduced by encouraging firms to share technical knowledge that is not commercially exploitable. One of the major Japanese hardware firms "commented that without the [very large scale integrated circuits] VLSI program Japanese manufacturers would have spent five times as much on R&D in the development of electron beam technology [a non-appropriable technology]" (Langlois, et al., 1985).

Before setting up a national project, MITI uses its information network to discover the targets of firms in their own R&D labs. "Out of the countless hours of discussion emerges a 'vision' for the semiconductor industry, including a fairly concrete agenda of national research priorities" (Okimoto, 1989, p. 101). "The national research agenda is based on an assessment of technological needs and prospects, commercial opportunities, foreign competition, long-term trends and desired directions" (Okimoto, 1989, p. 101).

It is worth noting that this method has not been restricted to the semiconductor industry. For example, in 1981, MITI initiated national research projects in six specific materials after it had consulted closely with industry, research institutes and other experts (Gregory in Forester, 1988, pp. 121-122). In both cases, the national research project undertook "basic" research to aid the industry in the commercial development of applications based on this research.

Research Labs (Success)

Japan maintains a network of public research laboratories that were established jointly with many of the national research projects the country adopted. The labs provide facilities in which firms may conduct joint, pre-commercial research.

The innovations produced out of the public research labs help to level the stock of non-rivalrous, technical knowledge held by each firm in a key industry. Firms that use public research for commercial applications are restricted from patenting this technology. Thus, they must produce commercial innovations in order to exploit it. Japan's ability to penetrate so deeply into the memory chip market has been, at least partially, attributed to the research conducted in these and other laboratories.

Finance (Success)

MITI prefers to finance only a portion of national projects – an amount that makes the project feasible but requires industry to supply its own capital. Subsidies are regarded as "seed money," sufficient to aid industry but not to dampen its incentives to be efficient. Seed money financing has been successful for national projects designed to catch up.

Two Attempted Big Leaps

VLSI Circuits Project (Marginal Success)

An example of Japanese policy in leading edge development is the VLSI Project started in 1976. It targeted pre-commercial research and sought to develop leading edge breakthroughs in semiconductors. MITI initially adopted the role of partial funder and information co-ordinator, but ended up in a leadership role and, in some cases, had to resort to coercion to obtain industry participation. The ministry facilitated the transfer of information between firms whose internal application of the research would be in direct competition with each other. A central feature of the program was MITI's ability to maintain a pre-commercial focus of obtaining inter-firm co-operation and information dissemination.

In terms of its major goal of creating leading edge breakthroughs, the VLSI Project was a failure. At most, it hastened the development of many technologies, and provided some limited advances in the use of liquid crystal. In spite of the small degree of technical progress, however, the Project succeeded in generating many commercial successes that were critical in helping Japanese firms establish a market lead over U.S. firms. These were spinoffs from the central objective that were made possible by the rich structure of firm co-operation, information sharing and idea nurturing that MITI has created.

The Fifth Generation Computer Project (5G) (Type 1 Failure; Type 2 Success)

This was an attempt at a large, leading edge advance combined with significant structural changes. The 5G Project followed closely on the heels of VLSI, and much of the research conducted under VLSI continued under 5G. The Project's main objective was to produce intelligent computers capable of problem solving and knowledge management. Pre-commercial R&D was conducted under a central agency, the Institute for New Generation Computer Technology (ICOT), by eight computer and micro-electronic companies and two national research labs.

At the outset, the project had difficulty getting participation from firms. MITI wanted a 50:50 split in financing between industry and itself, but industry refused to risk the funds. MITI settled for adopting the leadership role of 100 percent financier for the first three years of the project after which the funding arrangement was to be reviewed. The project generated much private sector interest over its life time. Besides the big five Japanese producers who were involved in the VLSI (Fujitsu, Hitachi, Mitsubishi, NEC and Toshiba), several smaller firms joined the Project. Private interest was apparently spurred by the success of VLSI. The 5G program was a failure, and massive R&D investments were written off. Since it did not persist long after it looked like a failure, it must be rated a type 2 success.

Japan failed to create a packaged software industry to parallel its successful hardware industry, and the 5G Project did not help. It can be argued that MITI's attempts at co-ordination were more appropriate to catching up than to frontier research, the latter being better conducted in the U.S. model of decentralized unfocused research efforts by independent firms. The VLSI and 5G experiences support this view, although evidence is not yet conclusive.

Policy Lessons

Japan's post-catch-up policies have had a mixed record and suggest a number of lessons.

Policy needs to be flexible.

Japanese project financing is a study in flexibility. The time horizon to commercial payoff is longer, and the co-ordination effort between firms is larger than in the United States. MITI has set up a formal interface through which it learns what industry experts think is important. Rather than trying to dictate courses of action, it seeks to aid the development of research based on this information. After it decided on appropriate directions for R&D efforts, MITI was able to stay the course long enough to check the viability of the technology and to demonstrate credible commitment to private innovators.

Policy can play a useful role, inducing and co-ordinating pre-commercial research and encouraging competition in innovation.

The provision of pre-commercial R&D by public research labs and the co-ordinating and disseminating roles played by MITI reduce needless duplication of effort and allow firms to share and exploit the same non-appropriable technical knowledge.

The creation of a credible commitment mechanism which equalizes firms' non-appropriable technical knowledge, pushes inter-firm competitive efforts into commercial innovations, instead of into shielding the results of their pre-commercial research in order to gain an advantage by exploiting it themselves.

MITI has been instrumental in inducing competition in innovation via this levelling mechanism. The innovations produced by firms, while not spectacular technical marvels, have had much commercial success. Furthermore, the scope for commercial innovation is large because there is a wide spectrum of not completely rivalrous commercial innovations that are producible from a given pre-commercial, technical knowledge base, i.e., innovation breeds further innovation.

Policy that has multiple objectives must use several, separate policy tools to accomplish them.

MITI has developed a policy structure that acts as an interface between innovation and the facilitating structure, mobilizing knowledge and capital resources, producing supporting innovation, reducing industrial and economy-wide exposure to uncertainty and forcing flexibility in the facilitating structure. Thus, Japan is well positioned to exploit innovations that extend from the very small to fundamental and that originate anywhere in the world. For example, the VLSI Project failed to generate the fundamental breakthroughs it sought yet it was successful in commercially exploiting the incremental innovations it produced.

Policy should be aware of the interrelation between technology and structure.

MITI has adopted a mechanism for inducing the sharing of, and co-operation in, the production of non-appropriable technical knowledge. The information network collects and disseminates this knowledge, and the public research labs and national projects are facilities within which it is produced. This is in contrast with policies such as Alvey, (the British program for developing computer software) where not only were pre-commercial mechanisms missing, but several conflicting policy objectives were sought. (Alvey is discussed in more detail in Appendix A.)

The Japanese policy structure explains how many of Japan's national projects have been successful in catching up (and not succumbing to overly ambitious schemes), in making many smaller commercially viable innovations, in successfully accomplishing some fundamental technological leaps and in producing large commercial gains out of small improvements in technology that spun off from failures at larger leaps. (This last is dramatic in comparison with the absence of positive spin-offs from the failures of fundamental leaps in France and the United Kingdom.)

The value of MITI's approach in pushing leading edge advances is still being debated. The case against it is that MITI tried for a large leap forward in its 5G program, which failed, while U.S. firms, which were not prodded by any government agency, went for the more incremental step of multi-tasking software which succeeded. Furthermore, MITI forced unwilling firms into the 5G Project and funded it fully at the outset. This conflicted with the lesson we have drawn from other experiences (including MITI's) that when firms and public sector bodies find unresolvable differences about the desirable course of future technological change, private sector judgment should be deferred to.

TWO COMPUTER INDUSTRY EXAMPLES

French Micro-Electronics Policy[15] (Failure)

French policy has typically targeted high-profile technology meant to make France a world technology leader. The most widely used method has been the establishment of a national champion in the targeted industry. These champions are either private monopolies supported through government R&D funding or state-owned operations.

The micro-electronics industry provides a good example of French innovation policy which has repeatedly attempted to set French producers on an equal competitive footing with American firms. In 1967, the Plan Calcul created a state-owned flagship in micro-electronics designed to close the Franco–American gap in a single stroke. CII (Compagnie Internationale de l'Informatique) was established with subsidies of US$40 million to US$50 million per year. Its first product was to be a large computer, based on a central processing unit of French design which would be in direct competition with IBM's "bread and butter" product line.

The main supplier of components to CII was the U.S. firm, Texas Instruments. However, a small French semiconductor firm, SESCOSEM, was linked directly to CII and required by the policy to duplicate Texas Instruments' entire range of components to realize the "made-in-France" nature of the project. SESCOSEM was too small to satisfy the sourcing needs of CII, and it was overwhelmed by the requirement that a firm of its size maintain such a large catalogue of components. This requirement eventually eroded its competitive position in the domestic market. The final result was less made-in-France technology than before the policy intervention.

The policy was abandoned when CII set up a joint venture with a U.S. producer in the late 1970s. At the time, it was estimated that, to be internationally competitive, a firm needed to control 5 percent of the world market which was about equal to the entire French market. CII never obtained more than 5 percent of the French market!

The French tried several further policies to support the micro-electronics industry. There were two between 1970 and 1980, and a further plan was established in 1983 to support the computer and data processing industries. Total funding amounted to 4.5 billion francs. None of the initiatives experienced significant success.

British Support of the Computer Industry[16] (Failure)

In the early 1960s, the U.K. government sought to establish a world-class industry that could compete with IBM. Since the U.K. industry was relatively small, the method adopted was merger and protection of the domestic market. The Ministry of Technology insisted on merging a number of competing private companies creating a national champion called International Computers (Holdings) Limited. ICL was given substantial assistance and a protected home market through public sector procurement. The main technical contributor to the merger, International Computers and Tabulators (ICT), had developed a computer that was technically competitive with IBM, but the company lacked sufficient internal cash flow to conduct long-term R&D and compete effectively in lease financing. The government reneged on its initial monetary commitment to the merger when economic recession hit the U.K. economy. A cash-rich, third party sought to join the merger. While the government's commitment was to have been for long-term pre-commercial R&D, the third party sought immediate return on investment. This restricted the company's ability to conduct the necessary R&D. It was left permanently cash poor.

The policy failed. Although ICT's computers had been significant technical achievements, after the merger, the technology fell behind IBM products and could not compete on the open market.

Policy Lessons

Large leaps are dangerous.

In both cases, governments sought to make a single large leap in technology to put them on equal footing with the United States. Each required significant and sometimes inappropriate structural changes. They both failed.

Policy should be aware of the interrelation between technology and structure.

The U.K. and French facilitating structures were suited to supporting small niche-market firms rather than large firms in direct competition with IBM. The British policy of forced merger was in direct conflict with the existing structure. In France, inappropriate policy intervention in the market forced a competitive firm into an impossible role and eroded its competitiveness.

By not understanding and working within their own facilitating structures, these policies increased the exposure to uncertainty. They ignored vital parts of their own structure and forced the creation of new structures.

Because innovation is uncertain, policy should encourage many diverse experiments.

The policy of a single national champion limited the number of experiments and increased the exposure to uncertainty for both policies.

Policy can play a useful role, inducing and co-ordinating pre-commercial R&D efforts and competition in innovation.

Britain's forced merger and subsequent market protection removed any incentive to compete in innovation in the domestic market. The details of the merger limited ICL's ability to conduct pre-commercial R&D.

Prestige should be an outcome not an objective of policy. Going for prestige projects rather than ones chosen for potential commercial viability is a likely road to failure. Such policies tend to bring the opposite of international prestige and commercially viable innovation. In the end, these projects actually impair technical progress because they introduce inferior technologies, making it a mystery why governments persist in them.[17]

As these cases show, the negative externalities can be enormous since many other industries rely on the technology. These other industries suffered losses of competitive advantage because they were forced to use equipment inferior to that available to their foreign competitors.

Multiple objectives are dangerous.

The national champion approach of each country highlights the need to avoid combining political and other objectives with the objective of producing commercially successful innovations. Both policies mixed the desire for prestige with objectives of inducing successful technical change. The prestige objective ruled out the possibility of successful technology change.

Successful policies often pursue incremental innovation and (where possible) aid in the acquisition of tacit knowledge.

CII was more successful when it formed an alliance with a successful U.S. firm.

POLICY LESSONS

THIS SECTION PUTS THE POLICY LESSONS derived from the cases outlined in the previous section and in Appendix A into a more general setting. The classification matrix described above and shown in Table 1 is used to organize our case material and draw out the general lessons.

TABLE 1

POLICY LESSONS

STRUCTURE	TECHNOLOGY[a]			
	INCREMENTAL		LARGE LEAP	
	Catch-up	Leading Edge	Catch-up	Leading Edge
Large	Korean electronics Taiwanese electronics	U.S. military software procurement	*Japanese commercial aircraft phase I*	Japanese automobiles AGR
Medium	Japanese commercial aircraft phase 2 Early Japanese semiconductors	SEMATECH(M) U.S. military semiconductor procurement NACA ←	Airbus(M) *French microelectronics* *British computers* Korean industrial policy ← *Indian industrial policy*	*Concorde* *SST*[b] *Alvey*
Small	Indian trading companies Canadian IRAP West German SME	Stoves in Kenya, boats in India, electricity in Nepal MITI: Supporting networks, research labs, finance *Consolidated computers* *Caravelle*		VLSI U.S. aircraft procurement *Japanese 5G*[b]

Failure = *Italic*   Success = **Bold**   Marginal success = **M**

Notes: [a] Entries with arrows belong primarily in the cell where they are cited but have major applications in the cell to which the arrow points.

[b] These programs were type 1 failures in that they did not achieve the new technologies they were aiming for. They were, however, type 2 successes in that the programs were halted when they appeared to be failing.

GENERAL LESSONS

Lessons from the Matrix

Our theory suggests that large leaps in technology are likely to be more difficult to accomplish than incremental changes. They require more alterations in technology blueprints, the acquisition of more tacit knowledge, often gained by making mistakes and more associated adjustments in related technologies. We would also expect that big technological changes that can be fitted into the existing structure with little adjustment would be easier to accomplish than those that required major changes in the facilitating structure. The combination least likely to succeed, therefore, would be large leaps accompanied by large changes in structure. The most likely to succeed would be incremental change that fits into the existing structure.

The cases in our matrix are in broad conformity with these expectations. The successes tend to be in the incremental columns but spread through small, medium and large structural adjustments. The failures tend to be in the large-leap columns and tending toward large structural adjustments. Now, consider those cases that do not fit into these expectations.

Prefer Incremental Changes to Large Leaps

The two failures in the incremental columns are special cases. In both instances, government agencies starved a successful private concern of R&D support and dissipated an early lead. In the Canadian case of Consolidated Computer Incorporated (CCI) which is discussed in Appendix A, the public body actually thought it could run an entrepreneurial firm and substitute money for innovative talent with predictably disastrous results. With the French Caravelle, R&D money and talent that could have gone into maintaining the lead in sub-sonic commercial transport went to the Concorde instead. Although the Caravelle had problems with its competitive position, it would have been strongly placed for further incremental improvement if a significant portion of the R&D effort that went to Concorde had gone into Caravelle's successors instead.

Although the successes are mainly in the incremental columns, there are several in the large-leap columns that need explaining.

As discussed in Appendix A, U.S. procurement policy, with respect to aircraft, was well designed to create spinoffs from its main defence purposes, and it required few changes in the existing structure.

Although judgments about the industrial policy of Korea, and the other newly industrialized countries (NICs) which are discussed in Appendix A are contentious, early experiences show that, if handled flexibly and with good criteria for cutting off failures, some strategies that require significant interventions can work. As the economy develops and more industries get closer to the leading edge, the balance of decision power needs to move from government to firms – even though, as MITI shows, a successful symbiotic relation can still be maintained between the public and the private sectors.

The Airbus is a specific technology pushed largely through national champions. It has not had as rigid a structure as some of the national champions such as the British Alvey and the British advanced gas-cooled reactor (AGR) which is discussed in Appendix A. It is a genuine marginal case and can be argued as a success or a failure depending on how the many imponderables (caused by gaps in information and an inability to predict the competitive outcome over the next five years) are judged.

The Japanese VLSI was a failure in its primary objective of creating a large technological leap forward. It was a commercial success, generating numerous spinoffs from the central effort – something MITI's structure is well designed to accomplish.

The Japanese automobile industry case, discussed in Appendix A, stands as a magnificent illustration of two points: nothing is certain in the uncertain world of innovation policy, and Japan is the exception to many generalizations about the economy and economic policy. Setting up an industry with an enormous scale disadvantage compared to U.S. automakers and leaving the firms to compete in the protected home market should, by all precedent, have been a recipe for creating a weak home industry that never grew up. Indeed, MITI showed it did not understand what was needed for success when it tried to promote industrial concentration in Japan and the production of a mass produced "people's car." The firms resisted MITI's own mistakes and innovated themselves out of their market disadvantage. Lean production allowed the Japanese to become efficient in their home market and then go on to defeat the U.S. car industry on its own home turf. No one can be sure of the extent of the Japanese victory in the U.S. automobile market if free trade had been maintained. We do know, however, that the Japanese penetration would have been much higher if the Japanese had not been forced to accept voluntary export agreements (VERs). The Japanese success was based on a remarkable burst of endogenous innovation that changed not only the Japanese car industry but the whole world as flexible manufacturing spread abroad.[18]

Of these big leap successes, only Airbus represents a success in a specific, targeted product and its accompanying technology. The Japanese automobile industry success derives from a policy that created nurturing industrial conditions and significant general assistance within which several private sector firms could compete, innovate and prosper.

No Doctrinaire Advice

Two doctrinaire positions are commonly met on innovation policy. According to the interventionist position, substantial government assistance is needed for many of a nation's firms to remain competitive in the tough world of international competition. The laissez-faire position holds that government assistance to private sector innovation is always counter-productive. We do not believe that either of these positions can be maintained in light of the rich empirical evidence, a sample of which we have studied. Some policies work and some fail. The same policy works well in some structures and poorly in others. A policy that works well at some stages of the development of a particular technology or a whole economy may not work at others, and so on. There seems to be no substitute for making an informed judgment, policy by policy, guided by the details of the case at hand and by any available general lessons such as those derived from our cases.

Picking Winners

A long debate concerns a government's ability to pick winners. This debate seems to miss many of the real issues highlighted by our analysis.

First, there is enough uncertainty in the innovative process that anyone can pick the occasional winner, and almost everyone will, sooner or later, pick some spectacular failures.

Second, even more important than picking winners is the ability to get rid of losers. In the private sector, the bottom line is a ruthless eliminator of losers. In contrast, public sector bodies find it difficult to admit mistakes and back away from them. Successful government interventions have almost always had good substitutes for the private sector's bottom line. For example, the export orientation of the NICs in the 1960s and 1970s, in contrast with the inward-looking policies of most of the other less-developed countries, allowed them to get away with significant interventions.

Third, the image of bureaucrats generating their own knowledge and using it to pick winners is wide of the mark in many cases. Bureaucratized decision processes have led to some massive failures in such programs as Alvey and the AGR. Success is more common when the public sector "picks" winners in close and sustained consultation with the private sector, backing and assisting those efforts that the private sector is willing to back for itself, and giving final veto power to the private sector.

Fourth, picking winners is much easier in catch-up than in leading edge development. The major uncertainty that there may be no blue balls in some of the urns is eliminated when one is trying to accomplish variations on what others have done already. Creating a catch-up technology that is new to the domestic economy is no easy task – as several of our failure cases attest – but it is much easier than doing so with a leading edge technology.

Fifth, it is much easier to create a catch-up winner in a niche technology in which there are many different products and producers than in an oligopolistic technology in which there are only two or three competing products and producers against which the new entrant must come into direct competition.

Sixth, going for a winner that requires a large leap in both technology and facilitating structure is courting disaster. It necessarily increases the costs associated with exposure to uncertainty without necessarily increasing the potential payoff to the venture.

Typically, policy makers decide to push some technology and do not concern themselves with the structure. The above argument suggests, however, that chances of success are increased if policy makers look for a likely structure. It might be better to look for a segment of a global structure that is easy to enter and a good match to the economy's domestic structure in that area. Then let structural considerations determine the technology that is to be pushed.

Be Flexible

The need to be flexible under conditions of uncertainty is a recurring theme in our studies. We met it in the last of our empirical generalizations in the section on making choices under uncertainty and in several lessons associated with particular policy successes and failures.

To generalize what we have learned, we distinguish between the choices of original strategies and the alteration of these strategies as experience accumulates. First, in any attempt at technological advance, a choice must be made regarding the ends and the means: where to try to go and how to try to get there. Second, as time passes, experience accumulates and re-thinking of both ends and means is often needed.

We can distinguish three pure-case models for making the necessary choices. The first is the bureaucratic model in which bureaucrats make the major decisions, as commonly happens with technological initiatives in France and the United Kingdom. The second is the laissez faire model in which a large number of firms compete in the market to establish their vision of the lines along which the technological path should develop. Some U.S. industries come close to this model. The third is a model in which the private and public sectors have some symbiotic relation in which the private sector is driven mainly by market forces. The two sectors form a joint vision, and the public sector assists the private sector to fulfil that vision with pre-commercial research, development funding, protection of the home market and a number of other devices. Japan comes close to this model.

It is clear that the highly bureaucratized model has many defects. In an either/or choice, the private sector must surely be the one that is better suited to making decisions on where to go technologically and how to get there. Furthermore, the bureaucratic model has difficulty reacting flexibly to what is learned as experience accumulates. It also seems clear that the other two models each have strengths and weaknesses that preclude one being judged unambiguously superior to the other.

The U.S. model has the advantage of diversity in exploring many avenues and not risking excessive investment in any one. Also, it is highly flexible in reacting to new experience since, if one firm does not do so, others will and those that choose the best reactions will be rewarded with profits. This model is often criticized for being shortsighted especially because of the takeover threat that is absent in Japan and much of continental Europe.

The Japanese model is best at choosing ends and means with a high degree of private sector input and then backing the private sector with targeted public assistance of many sorts. It suffers from heavy concentration when a technological direction is chosen for the R&D push no matter how diffuse the decision-making process. It is also capable of taking a long view since public funding is not motivated by short-term considerations, and firms are insulated from short-term pressures by their ownership structures. When MITI has been inflexible and gone against the strong views of the private sector, it has often made mistakes. The model also seems to be excellently adjusted to catch up or to take advantage of leading edge developments elsewhere. It is not clear, however, how well it compares with the U.S. model in genuine leading edge developments.

There are many intermediate models. For example, firms may choose the direction for technological developments, but the public sector may assist with such things as pre-competitive research and funding. The main lesson is that, whatever the precise model used, sensitivity to private sector ideas on ends and means, and the flexibility to alter direction as experience accumulates are important conditions leading to success. In contrast, lack of sensitivity to private sector assessments and rigidity in the face of changing experience tend to cause failure.

In the rest of this section, we classify the lessons suggested by individual cases into the cells of the matrix shown in Table 1. For each, we consider common lessons and those that apply specifically to leading edge and to catch-up technological changes.

Lessons From Large Leaps in Technology

Common Elements

There are many reasons why attempts at large technological leaps are fraught with uncertainties. Here are a few which we relate to our earlier urn analogy.

- Some version of the technology must prove technologically viable, which can only be discovered by investing money and time. (All the urns must contain some blue balls.)

- A series of supporting innovations is required, each of which is subject to its own risks and uncertainties. (A successful drawing must be made from each urn in a set of urns.)

- Large changes in the facilitating structure are often needed.

- A guess usually needs to be made on the best bet from several competing versions of the basic technology. (The choice must be made as to which of several subsets of urns to draw from.)

- As experience accumulates, flexibility is required to alter course – changing means, changing final objectives or even abandoning the whole project. These are decisions that governments, which often have multiple objectives, find difficult to make. (At any point in the process, a ball may be drawn stating that some alternative set of urns may be substituted for the remaining urns in the set currently being drawn from.)

- A technological breakthrough is not enough; commercial viability is also needed, and this often requires the invention of a complex facilitating structure to exploit the basic innovations. (Successful drawings must also be made from a subset of urns labelled "commercial success.")

- Subsequent experience with the technology must continue to show it to be technologically and commercially viable. In the world of technological uncertainty, surprises can occur long after a technology appears to be successfully commercialized. (Even after successful commercialization, periodic successful drawings must be made from an urn labelled "market conditions.")

The Anglo–French Concorde and the Boeing SST attempted a fundamental technological leap. In retrospect, there was no successful technological choice available in the 1960s (i.e., the urn relating to the sonic boom probably contained no blue balls). The United States correctly pulled back as experience showed that the SST was unlikely to be a commercial success. The French and British persevered. They made a massive technological leap but failed in the supporting technological developments that would have made it a commercial success. Notice that in its failed attempt, French policy was perverse because it withdrew funds and effort from the development trajectory of a less prestigious, but more commercially successful technology embodied in the Caravelle.

In nuclear energy, the British chose gas-cooled reactors which turned out to be an inferior version of the technology. They selected a poorer subset of urns from which to make their drawings than did several other nations. They stuck to their project far longer than any commercial venture would have and therefore failed in a really big way.

The Canadians chose better than the British with the CANDU technology which is detailed in Appendix A. They produced a reactor that was a technological success. However, the commercial market did not materialize sufficiently to make the project worthwhile. Thus, the project failed as a commercial venture. Also in retrospect, this generation of nuclear-powered electricity plants has been judged inadequate, which is all part of the enormous uncertainty when the project began. The general reaction against nuclear power and the technical difficulties that became apparent only after years of operation caused revisions of estimated costs and benefits long after the technology was in full operation. The Canadians succeeded in choosing a good set of urns from which to draw, succeeded only marginally (at best) on the urn of commercialization and failed on the urn of continued favourable market conditions.

Catch-up Projects

Stated in terms of our urn analogy, catch-ups have two advantages over leading edge developments. First, followers know that there are no urns without any blue balls since others have already succeeded. Second, followers have fewer urns from which to draw because they can use some of the knowledge developed by those companies already in the market.

In Alvey, a fundamental catch-up leap in software was attempted using inappropriate methods and without a supporting facilitating structure. Under these circumstances, the attempt was bound to fail, even without the large number of subsidiary errors that were made.

As discussed in Appendix A, the Japanese tried a fundamental leap forward when they sought to establish a civilian, Japanese-only commercial aircraft industry that existed elsewhere but had little supporting structure in Japan. The absence of the facilitating structure contributed greatly to the failure of all attempts.

In micro-electronics, the French and British tried fundamental leaps in hardware. This failed when, among other things, both forced changes on their structures that were inappropriate, and the British choked off R&D money and the successful development trajectory of a viable technology, ICT's 1900 series. These hardware firms never reached U.S. competitive levels, and supporting firms were harmed, so the industry became more foreign dominated than it would have been without the policy, making it a double failure.

The European Airbus tried a big leap forward in technology, but one which others (Boeing) had already made. This was combined with modest changes in structure. Unlike the Japanese aircraft and the European hardware cases, European commercial aircraft could draw on a well-developed facilitating structure of specific human capital and experienced parts manufacturers. They successfully innovated in a component of the structure and eventually achieved an apparently viable industry producing a marginal success. It is not clear whether they will recover their full development costs, but neither was Boeing required to do so with the military versions that pioneered the way for the 707 and helped with the engines of the 747.

We have seen that large-leap catch-up policies almost universally fail when they attempt to leap from far behind to far ahead of the pack in one giant step. This is because these industries are complex, with many component producers, and drastic changes or additions to the facilitating structure are required by the large leaps. The large number of required changes, each involving its own costs and uncertainties, makes the single leap forward difficult, if not impossible.

Even if a large-leap catch-up project is a technological and commercial success, in the sense that it can be sold in the existing market, there are further problems. If the market being entered is an oligopoly dominated by a small number of firms, the product is likely to run head on into competition with the leading products already produced in other nations. This may lead to destructive price competition. Even if the newly entering product becomes established, large rents are unlikely to be earned by such head on competition with already established products. So success requires large externalities connected with national ownership of the technology (since the product will always be available from other countries' firms.) Unfortunately, governments that attempt big leaps usually also design their policy to run into head on competition. For example, French and British hardware policies, and Alvey expressly sought to compete head to head with American oligopolists.

If the market is one in which there are many medium- or small-sized competing firms, there is greater scope for entry of a new product that is similar but different and possibly better than existing competitors. In such a market, a new product can occupy one of the many available niches rather than run head on into competition with the few market leaders that define an oligopolistic industry. Japan's experience in the commercial aircraft industry exemplifies both sides of this point. In its first phase, the Japanese policy ran into direct competition with the established airframe assemblers such as Boeing and Airbus. In its second phase, the policy tried niche developments in the fragmented market for parts. Other similar successes include Korean and Taiwanese electronics policies (discussed in Appendix A) and Japanese electronics policies, (discussed above) all of which targeted niche developments in their incremental catch-up policies.

Leading Edge Projects

Commercialization

Even when a successful technological leap is made, many problems must be solved before successful commercialization can occur. Some examples follow.

There is much uncertainty related to demand for a new product. The product may prove to be suitable only for a small market niche with small demand as, for example, was the Anglo–French Concorde.

The 5G Project was a successful large technology leap which demonstrates the difficulty such projects face in terms of commercialization. MITI forced reluctant Japanese firms into a large leap, whereas U.S. firms went for smaller incremental software developments targeting multi-tasking. The end result was that the multi-tasking software had a price advantage and performed adequately for user needs. The intelligent software sought by Japan was more expensive and required users to learn new techniques. Thus, 5G failed to commercialize its technology successfully.

Production or operating costs may prove too high. The technically successful British VC10, which competed with the Boeing 707, was an excellent aircraft which gained high approval ratings from passengers but its slightly higher operating costs (which could not have been predicted in advance) caused it to be a commercial failure.

In a race for some new technology, several firms may get to the market at about the same time. They may then conduct head on competition in a market that would have produced high profits if one of them had clearly been the first to succeed (as occurred with nuclear energy).

Procurement may prove a problem because of political motivation for some purchase decisions, as has happened with the sales of nuclear reactors.

The Relevance of the New Trade Theory

Because of all the issues raised above, leading edge, large leaps beg the question of whether or not it is better to be first in or a follower in such speculative ventures. (We emphasize that we are discussing large leaps not the incremental innovations which must be made by any firm that continues to hold its own in an innovative industry.)

New trade theory emphasizes the value of being first into a market that will eventually only support a few producers because of scale effects and, as a result, will sustain substantial oligopolistic profits. This advice begs the question: how does one know which technology to push in order to be the first successful entrant into some emerging, totally new market that really will become established? New trade theory looks only at the results of being one of the first into a venture that does succeed. It says nothing about the process that results in some markets materializing while others do not, and some early entrants losing while others win.

Ex post facto, it is, of course, easy to say that it would have been a good idea to be first into some particular new industry or new technology that has become a winner. Before the event, however, no such judgment is possible. Innovation is an uncertain activity and so, with major attempted breakthroughs, there is no rule about whether it is better to be first or a follower. If no really nasty surprises occur, the first unit to develop the new technology may establish a market position that is difficult to dislodge. Followers can learn from any nasty surprises the first entrant has encountered and, consequently, may be the first to become entrenched in the market. Comet and Concorde show the hazards of being first into a new technology. Boeing reaped the advantages of being behind deHaviland and being able to learn about the totally new problem of metal fatigue as a follower. As second in, Boeing became market leader with the 707. Boeing also reaped the advantages in being behind the Anglo–French consortium on the Concorde. In this instance, it was able to learn that the venture was not going to be a commercial winner and to stay out of the market. In retrospect, both decisions were good ones and reflected the advantages of not being first in when really unexpected things happen with a new technology.

Another issue not faced in the new trade literature is the empirical generalization that radically new technologies that could give rise to the new oligopolistic industries envisioned by the theory usually come into the world in crude form and go through a long period of evolution before they become established across much of the economy. The arguments for first in are most cogent when applied to what appears to be the empirically empty theoretical box of a new technology that comes into the world more or less full blown.

LESSONS FROM INCREMENTAL CHANGES IN TECHNOLOGY

Common Elements

As noted in the "continuous innovation" empirical generalization, incremental changes in technology account for a significant portion of all technological change and economic growth. They carry much less exposure to uncertainty than do large leaps because they work within, and usually require only small changes in, the existing facilitating structure. Their commercial viability is less uncertain because, for example, they often work within established markets. These and many other similar propositions are illustrated by the incremental innovations we have considered in our case studies.

Catch-up Projects

Going for incremental innovations based on a core of imported technology is a more viable catch-up strategy than a single great leap forward. It can significantly reduce the exposure to uncertainty, increase the transmission of tacit knowledge and allow the development of those niche technologies that the technological leader inevitably leaves unexploited. Examples are the Japanese aircraft industry after "Japan-only" was abandoned, Japanese semiconductors, Japanese automobile "tie-ups," and Taiwanese and Korean electronics.

Leading Edge Projects

All too often, governments of industrially developed countries are mesmerized by large technological advances. They forget that many of the world's millionaires made their fortunes on very prosaic products. Anecdotal evidence from our research makes us suspect that some Canadian policies in support of individual attempts at innovation are overly focused on "hi-tech" and are reluctant to support more mundane innovations that carry less uncertainty and greater prospect for gain. It is important to realize the general lesson that hi-tech is not synonymous with high potential for commercially successful innovations. Policies that encourage innovations must be willing to look at quite minor advances in some very low-tech industries. To do otherwise is to duplicate the French mistake – only on incremental technologies instead of on attempted large leaps.

Examples of successes reported in Appendix A include stoves in Kenya, boat building in India and micro hydro power plants in Nepal. These are illustrative of a large number of cases in which governments have successfully encouraged small technological advances that produced large payoffs working within a country's existing facilitating structure.

In more general policies, both the Canadian Industrial Research Advisory Program (IRAP) which fulfils all the conditions for making small improvements, and the German Small and Medium Enterprise (SME) policy are discussed in Appendix A.

LESSONS FROM STRUCTURE

Private Sector

A large number of lessons about the private sector are implicit in our discussion of various policies. We only mention a few that relate to the subsequent discussion of policies.

Because competition in innovation is an important strategic variable in inter-firm rivalry, competition (in the sense of rivalrous behaviour among firms but not the economist's concept of perfect competition) is more conducive to technological innovation than is monopoly.

Pre-commercial R&D is difficult to manage effectively in rivalrous multi-firm situations.

Because of the many uncertainties in R&D, which firms can only learn about by doing, successful firms must stay flexible.

There is a large unresolved issue about domestic ownership of multinationals versus domestic location. We are inclined to the view that, faced with a choice between a head office and all the production facilities, it would be better to have the production function rather than the head office located domestically. We realize, however, that the choice is seldom as stark as this, and the issue of ownership versus location is still hotly debated.

Government Policy

Change in either technology or structure causes change in the other. If policy makers target only one of these, there will be induced consequences in the other which will affect the overall performance of the policy, e.g., by imposing unforeseen costs or by retarding the changes that are being targeted. If policy makers target both in ignorance of the interrelation, they may target an inconsistent set of changes that will retard attainment of their main goals. If they are aware of the interrelations, they may target a consistent set of changes that will assist in achieving their main goals.

To create effective policy, governments must consult with, and be guided by, industry expertise. When conflicts on where to direct R&D financed by public and private sector money are unresolvable, the private sector should be allowed to make the final decision. MITI has been excellent at this type of consultation and in the few times when disagreements with private sector opinions have been unresolvable, the private sector seems to have been right more often than wrong. Japanese examples are provided by the proposed people's car and the amalgamation of Japanese car producers. In both cases, MITI gave in to private sector opinion which proved to be correct. In the 5G case, MITI did not give in and was proved wrong. Other examples include the Canadian experience with CCI, the British experiment with ICL and the Plan Calcul in France.

We have stressed the need for governments to be flexible. This in turn requires that they have good tools for self-evaluation to identify mistakes and successes. Potentially good policies, such as IRAP, often have not been subject to the penetrating external evaluations needed to determine if there is sufficient payoff in terms of projects that meet the test of additionality. Governments must be ready to learn from mistakes and alter course or eliminate projects. Many projects did not meet this criterion. Concorde is a good example of a project that was continued long after it was an obvious failure. The U.S.-only policy of the Semiconductor Manufacturing (SEMATECH) program which is discussed in Appendix A, the Japan-only aircraft and the French-only computer are all examples of rigid objectives that limit the flexibility of private firms. The export orientation of Japan and the NICs provided an external market test of success without which many of the fairly interventionist projects would probably have failed to result in efficient producers in the way that inward-looking policies often did.

Governments also need to work within the existing facilitating structure or to require feasible changes in it. Many big projects failed on this count. For example, the Plan Calcul, ICL and Alvey, phase 1 of the Japanese aircraft case and MITI's mistakes in the automobile industry tried to impose rigid, and sometimes inappropriate, structure on industry.

Governments which get involved in attempted technological advances need to have single-minded objectives. Multiple objectives will usually result in a loss of needed flexibility in evaluating the innovation objective. India's industrial policy, which is discussed in Appendix A, is a case study in inflexibility due to the imposition of several conflicting policy objectives. National prestige is best seen as a by-product of technological success not as an end in itself. AGR, CANDU, Alvey, Plan Calcul, ICL and Concorde provide examples of failures in this respect, while MITI and many of the NICs provide examples of successes.

Even if the goal is to catch up on a broad front in some whole industry (which is attempted in both developed and developing countries), there is much to be said for attempting to do so incrementally rather than in one large leap.

If the catch-up is to be accomplished by home-based firms, there are advantages in protecting the home market to provide domestic firms with a market in which to learn. The Japanese automobile industry is the classic example of initial success within a protected home market. The industrial policies of Taiwan and Korea (discussed in Appendix A) also exemplify success to some degree. However, protecting the home market is dangerous if a national champion is chosen to make the domestic advances. A protected, perpetual infant is the all too likely result, as was the case in the French and British electronics policies, and in the SEMATECH case for lithography equipment producers. It is better, therefore, to have several firms competing fiercely in the protected domestic market using innovation as their main competitive tool.

Government tends to make big pushes in industries that create widely used technologies, which Lipsey and Bekar (1995) call enabling technologies. The very externalities that are often seen as a source of added gain, if a technological leap in an enabling technology succeeds, make failure more serious than when a technology is more or less specific to the industry being fostered. Failure to succeed in a large leap with an enabling technology affects not only the industry in question but all others that use that technology. For example, Concorde helped shorten the life of the Caravelle, and ICL, Plan Calcul and AGR forced government and industry to adopt inferior technologies.

Governments have important roles to play in creating and changing the facilitating structure to suit new technologies. Antitrust and education provide obvious examples. Airbus made small but important changes in structure as did several U.S. procurement policies. U.S. procurement has sometimes created a whole facilitating structure in an industry. More generally, MITI has created a structure that allows Japanese firms to exploit inventions made both in Japan and abroad.

Another important role for the government is to encourage and co-ordinate pre-commercial research leaving firms to compete in commercial research.

Although government can fail here as elsewhere, e.g., SEMATECH, there is great potential for success. Pre-commercial research is subject to the many market failures discussed earlier. Governments have been successful in assisting this research either in their own facilities or merely by creating the climate of trust and co-operation in which the results can be shared and sometimes jointly created, e.g., MITI, Airbus and NACA.

Finally, we note that spinoffs from public sector activity directed to other goals have been important in product, process and structural changes. Although such spinoffs are not usually sufficient to justify the expenditure in the first place, they are important enough that policies with high potential spinoffs should be designed with the maximization of these spinoffs as one of their objectives. U.S. procurement policy is designed to foster competition in innovation, exploit user–producer feedback, set up a facilitating structure in research and education and target technologies in the early, generic stages of their development when spinoffs are most common.

Our structuralist theory and the lessons we have derived from our case studies suggest that there is no one best model of innovation policy. It is more useful to ask if a country has an innovation policy regime that is suited to that economy's facilitating structure than to ask if it has the world's best regime. An innovation policy will work well or poorly depending on how well adapted it is to such elements of the structure as:

- the pattern of industrial concentration;

- the structure and behaviour of financial institutions;

- the mobility of labour;

- the way in which the political system brokers regional interests; and

- the ability of special interest groups to capture particular policies and public bodies.

It is useful to ask how well adapted a country's policies are to its structure. Do other countries have elements of their innovation policy that work well and could be easily transferred to one's own structure? It is not useful to think of copying, completely, another country's set of innovation policies, especially when their structures are as radically different as are, say, those of Japan and Canada or the United States.

APPENDIX A
CASE STUDIES – SPECIFIC AND GENERAL POLICIES

THIS APPENDIX REPORTS BRIEFLY ON OUR CASE STUDIES that were not outlined in the text. As in the text, we conclude most of the brief sections with policy lessons suggested by the cases in question – lessons that we regard as generalizations to be tested against further evidence. We divide our cases into those that seek to promote firms and industries in particular technologies, which we call specific encouragement, and those that seek to encourage a class of technological changes without favouring a particular technology firm or industry which we call general encouragement. We then classify the cases according to Table 1: policies may seek cutting edge or catch-up technological changes that are either large leaps or incremental changes, and that may entail large, medium or small changes in the facilitating structure. To provide a complete arrangement of our cases, we place the headings for the cases discussed in the text in the appropriate place in the appendix.

SPECIFIC ENCOURAGEMENT – TECHNOLOGY: LEADING EDGE, LARGE LEAP; STRUCTURAL: LARGE

The Japanese Automobile Industry[19] (Success)

The enormous success of the Japanese automobile industry is the result of innovative behaviour by Japanese firms, particularly Toyota, combined with a few key government policies. It is a result that few would have predicted given the objective data circa 1950 and, as such, it is a classic example of the uncertainties facing innovation policy.

The first critical government intervention was the military procurement arrangements established between 1936 and 1939. These eventually caused General Motors and Ford to abandon production in Japan while providing increased sales for Toyota, Nissan and Isuzu.

A second key intervention was to prevent the return to Japan of U.S. firms following World War II. This, combined with domestic market protection, guaranteed the small but rapidly growing domestic market to domestic producers. There seems little doubt that if U.S. firms had been allowed to re-establish themselves in Japan after World War II, the Japanese industry would have closely resembled the U.S. industry in the way that the Canadian industry did.

The Japan development bank provided low-interest loans to domestic automobile firms while MITI targeted R&D and technology diffusion. Its motor vehicle technology institute carried out research on engines, transmissions and other parts. It encouraged "tie-ups" with foreign producers, e.g., Nissan–Austin, Isuzu–Rootes and Hino–Renault.

MITI then made its first misjudgment. In line with the view prevailing at that time that scale economies called for, at most, a few large firms in each manufacturing industry (a view that led to the establishment of many nationalized monopolies in countries such as the United Kingdom), MITI tried to limit the number of manufacturers in the industry to two major industrial groups: Toyota and Nissan. Fortunately for the Japanese industry, the firms refused to follow MITI's lead. Protection of the domestic market created rents for producers, which attracted more producers. The nature of competition in this industry is such that the entry game is played through innovation. The entry of these independents ensured a high degree of innovative competition in the industry.

In a second mistaken policy, MITI pushed for a cheap, mass-produced people's car. MITI was to approve the design and then subsidize its production. The people's car concept was exactly opposite to the concept that allowed Japanese auto producers to succeed – the lean production developed by Toyota through the 1950s.

Policy Lessons

Policy can play a useful role, inducing and co-ordinating pre-commercial R&D efforts and competition in innovation.

MITI's pre-commercial R&D helped to bring the technical capability of each firm in the industry to roughly the same level. Combined with protection of the domestic market, this channelled rivalries into commercial research and reduced exposure to uncertainty, providing both the incentives and the revenues for innovation, and avoiding the lack of incentives that beset a national champion with a monopoly in the home market.

Successful policies often pursue incremental innovation and (where possible) aid the acquisition of tacit knowledge.

The policy of seeking tie-ups limits exposure to uncertainty and allows for faster diffusion of tacit knowledge.

Policy intervention can be useful if guided by private sector knowledge.

The policies of specific market concentration and the people's car illustrate this point. In the end, MITI gave in to producer resistance to its mistaken policies. In other countries, the firms might have been ordered to do what the government thought best, and the necessary funding would have been found either through unlimited subsidies or nationalization to tap into the public purse.

Policy should be aware of the interrelation between technology and structure.

The protected Japanese market was too small to produce world leaders in the context of the U.S. structure. The only possible route to success was to restructure the whole industry to make it competitive at world prices in the small Japanese market. No one could know in advance how this would happen. However, if it had succeeded in imposing U.S. market concentration (which would have prohibited innovative entry) and a mass-production car (which would have prevented the development of lean production), MITI would have guaranteed that the necessary adjustments in structure did not happen. MITI created a situation in which a change in structure was necessary for commercial success and then tried to impose two critical characteristics of the old structure. The inconsistency would have created defeat whatever else had happened.

Policy needs to be flexible.

MITI backed off its people's car and attempts at mass production while Toyota developed lean production which allowed the Japanese automobile industry to become a world leader based on new methods of design and production that suited Japanese conditions.

The British AGR Program[20] (Failure)

The establishment of the Atomic Energy Authority (AEA) in 1954 marked the beginnings of the British nuclear energy program. The AEA was a centralized agency for conducting R&D as well as producing nuclear reactors. It was a monopoly closely connected to the Ministry of Energy. Its decision-making process for the development of prototypes and subsequent commercial applications was "top down" and highly political.

The chosen technology for nuclear reactors was a gas-cooled (CO_2) design which had been developed to produce plutonium for military uses. The production of energy was a spinoff of that development. At the time, the British were world leaders in nuclear technology and thought the CO_2 reactor was superior to the water-cooled technology being developed elsewhere.

Almost from the outset, questions were raised within the AEA as to the superiority of gas-cooled reactors relative to light water, heavy water and fast breeder reactors. However, the agenda for gas cooled reactor research was entrenched within the mandate of the AEA and the project continued. In 1955, the AEA set out its plan to build a 1500 to 2000 MW nuclear-powered generation capacity for the Central Electric Generating Board (CEGB). By 1957, the planned capacity base was tripled to 5000 MW to 6000 MW. In the same year, the AEA began to construct its first accelerated gas-cooled reactor prototype, a 30 MW reactor which came on line in 1963. By then, U.S. firms had demonstrated the commercial viability of light water reactors capable of producing 600+ MW, and the British CEGB was considering purchasing some. The AEA conducted a cost comparison between the light water reactor and its own proposed advanced gas-cooled reactor (AGR), finding the latter to be a low-cost option. Unfortunately, cost estimates were based on the existing 30 MW reactor and not the unbuilt 650 MW reactor (whose costs turned out to be much more than could be expected from the experience of the smaller reactor, demonstrating the uncertain nature of innovation). In 1976, the first of the promised British reactors began production at 200 MW capacity. By that time, it was clear that nuclear energy programs in general were suffering from cost overruns and environmental questions. It was also clear that the decision to pursue gas-cooled technology in Britain had been a mistake. The total cost of the program was £3800 million in 1975 values. The capital cost of the program was no where near covered, making the return on the investment a large negative amount.

This case is classified as a failure by our criteria because the CEGB would have bought the light water reactor made in the United States if they had not been forced to buy the AGR. No market existed for AGR where private firms would have voluntarily created the necessary structure.

The Canadian CANDU[21] (Uncertain)

Compared with the United Kingdom, Canada chose what turned out to be the superior technology. The Canadian policy experience in the high-technology venture of CANDU nuclear energy appears to have been at least as successful as the national nuclear programs of West Germany and the United States. However, nuclear fission turned out to be an unsatisfactory technology, at least with current knowledge.

The CANDU, heavy water reactor design has several technological and economic advantages over other designs. In spite of these technical achievements, it is not clear whether the project, which began in 1952 and by 1986 had cost in direct expenditures C$5.4 billion 1986 dollars, has reached the break even point. As well as the direct costs, there are also several other forms of support including:

- carrying charges on inventories;
- losses on subsidized export sales;
- subsidies to the uranium industry; and
- the cost of waste storage and disposal that is yet to be determined.

Against these costs, there have been nearly 40 years of energy production, as well as sales of CANDU technology abroad. When everything is considered, a strong case can be made that the nuclear energy program in Canada has been, at best, a break even venture, and that the best case scenario is unlikely.

On our criteria, CANDU is ranked a success since producers are prepared to purchase it. The qualifications are that the sale price should not contain concealed subsidies to cover part of the reactors' production costs, and the four concealed costs mentioned above should not exceed the operating profits on the production and sale of reactors. Also, CANDU got a nasty surprise when the durability of nuclear powered plants proved less, and the environmental hazards more, than were expected. Since there are so many aspects of CANDU on which we have not been able to get adequate information, we have not tried to grade it as a success or failure. We suspect, however, that which ever way a more informed judgment went, the failure or success would be marginal.

Policy Lessons

Large leaps are difficult.

Faced with enormous uncertainty at the beginning of a radically new type of energy, the British chose what turned out to be the wrong technology, the AGR.

The Canadian case illustrates that, even when a good technological choice is made, the massive uncertainties associated with a major technological leap forward make commercial success very much a gamble. There seems little doubt that, if the funds involved had been invested more conservatively in proven ways, the return would have been higher.

Policy needs to be flexible.

The need for flexibility in the face of uncertainty is amply illustrated by the rigidity of the British experiment. Counter-productive rigidity was exhibited at all stages, from the original mandate of the AEA, through the lack of commercial assessments, to the continuation long after large amounts of unfavourable experience had accumulated.

Multiple objectives are dangerous.

The AEA's internal mandate regarding the gas-cooled reactor and its desire to obtain political prestige were in conflict with the objective of producing a successful innovation.

Procurement policy needs to be wary of political pressure. Investing in innovation where governments heavily influence the sale and purchase of the product increases the exposure to uncertainty, due to a lack of bottom line cost considerations and political pressures which may result in the selection of inferior products.

The market for nuclear reactors is dominated by government procurement decisions in almost every country except the United States, and, even there, governments exert some influence on purchase decisions. The variable costs of production in nuclear energy are small compared with the fixed costs of development, so when two or more producers come into competition to sell their versions, something close to Bertrand price competition ensues. Prices may then be driven close to variable costs since any sale above that amount is better than no sale. Commercial viability is even more unlikely in these circumstances of high fixed costs and government procurement.

SPECIFIC ENCOURAGEMENT – TECHNOLOGY: LEADING EDGE, LARGE LEAP; STRUCTURAL: MEDIUM

The British Alvey Program[22] (Failure)

Fear over emerging Japanese dominance of the computer hardware and software manufacturing sector led to the initiation of the United Kingdom's Alvey Program in 1982. The focus was collaborative, pre-competitive R&D in software, by industry, government and academia, designed to "strengthen the technology base and create a software industry able to compete in domestic and export markets" (Grindley, 1994, p. 25).

The program sought to establish British world leadership within five years. It was, in part, a response to the Japanese 5G program and was supposed to be built on that model of industrial policy. However, Alvey omitted a critical element of 5G: the co-development of software technology alongside hardware technology. The British sought to develop their software industry independent of a well-established hardware sector. Langlois and Mowery (1994) considered the co-development of these two sectors to be a necessary (but not a sufficient) condition for the success of Japan in this industry.[23]

The program was politically motivated and created in a top down fashion. There was little detailed analysis of the problems of the industry or of realistic goals. The program was administered by bureaucrats rather than industrial experts while foreign interests (and expertise) were excluded. It was based on a "technology push" approach which let technology rather than market considerations dictate the path of development. As a result, it created over-automation and over-capitalization which were inconsistent with successful commercialization.

Alvey was targeted at the pre-competitive R&D stage while simultaneously pursuing market objectives – all within a very short time frame and using a single policy instrument. It had no reward mechanism for performance. Over its five-year life, the program tended to favour large projects designed to achieve fundamental innovations. Most of them did so, but lacked commercial applicability. Only 10 of the 200 industrial projects generated any marketable products, and these were predominantly military applications.

Policy Lessons

Alvey is a composite study of most of the things that should not be done in any technology policy.

Large leaps are dangerous.

British policy makers were mesmerized by the prestige of leading edge science, and blindly followed the Japanese into a large leap project. The British were not as advanced as the Japanese in the software industry, yet they sought to out perform the 5G Project in a five-year time frame.

Policy can play a useful role, inducing and co-ordinating pre-commercial R&D efforts and encouraging competition in innovation.

Alvey sought out large national champions to do both pre-commercial and commercial R&D simultaneously. This reduced competition in commercial innovation.

Multiple objectives are dangerous.

By trying for both pre-competitive breakthroughs and commercial viability, Alvey failed to recognize that the motivations of firms differ for pre-competitive and commercial innovation. The public good is served by inducing firms to share non-appropriable technical knowledge and to compete in creating commercial innovations. The project would have been better served if different policy mechanisms were employed to accomplish each objective.

Flexibility is essential to policy success.

The technology push approach ignored issues of commercial viability. Although pre-competitive research is, by definition, not commercially saleable, it needs to be directed at commercial prospects, not just at technology for its own sake.[24]

Policies should exploit as much expertise as possible.

Alvey's technology push approach ignored the user–producer interface that U.S. and Japanese semiconductor policies have managed to exploit. (The U.S. case is detailed below and the Japanese case is in the text.)

Policy should be aware of the interrelation between technology and structure.

Ignoring the link between hardware and pre-commercial software was a recipe for disaster. Alvey blindly pursued technology for its own sake, ignoring the structural costs imposed on firms and industry.

The Anglo–French Concorde (Failure)

The U.S. SST Program (Failure)

See text for a full discussion of the above two cases.

SPECIFIC ENCOURAGEMENT – TECHNOLOGY: LEADING EDGE, LARGE LEAP; STRUCTURAL: SMALL

United States Aircraft Procurement Policy[25] (Success)

Procurement policy with respect to the U.S. aircraft industry has not been designed to support commercial innovation. Commercial applications and successes have been spinoffs generated by military policy objectives.

Defence procurement has provided important civilian spinoffs in the past, not just in the United States but in Europe as well. One of the most important examples is in the design of the military transport KC-135 which bore a major share of the development cost for the Boeing 707. This helped to give Boeing the edge needed to establish a lead in the world long-haul jet market. When deHaviland's earlier lead was destroyed by the unexpected metal fatigue phenomenon in the world's first operational commercial jet transport, the Comet (a lead that was in turn built up by defence contracts in World War II), Boeing captured the long-haul market and the French Caravelle made great inroads into the short- and medium-haul markets. The knowledge that Boeing obtained in the design of the KC-135 and the 707 was directly applied in subsequent designs.

The spinoff from military to commercially successful innovation is a common theme in U.S. policy support for innovation, particularly in the aircraft industry. The U.S. system of letting procurement contracts involves direct support for firms which compete to satisfy Department of Defense (DoD) design and use requirements. The R&D efforts of each firm are at least partially (sometimes fully) subsidized by the DoD, with the reward for success being the long-term contract to produce the winning design. The Boeing 747 resulted from competition between Boeing and Lockheed to provide the military with a jumbo jet for transport. Boeing lost the race, but was able to use the research in the design of the 747's engines for the commercial industry.

Today, defence procurement does not appear to be providing significant support for innovation in the commercial aircraft industry. "Increasing divergences between civilian and military aircraft technology, as well as the absence of major defense procurement and development programs in large transports since the late 1960's, have reduced the amount and significance of military–civilian technology spill-over" (Mowery and Rosenberg, 1989, p. 185).

Policy Lessons

Competition-inducing mechanisms are essential for policy success. Policies designed to produce competition in innovation increase the likelihood of commercial success and reduce exposure to uncertainty.

The military's method of letting procurement contracts directly induces competition in innovation, which increases the potential for successful innovations. For example, the competition between Boeing and Lockheed for the contract to produce large-scale military transports induced sufficient competition and quality in innovation that both companies benefited even though Boeing lost the contract. Competition for procurement is an effective way of inducing innovation as contrasted, for example, with the national champion approach.

Policies should understand and exploit innovation spillovers. Support for fundamental innovation induces innovative spillovers. However, as applications of a specific technology become more specialized, the spillovers become more limited.

Technical spillovers from military research to the commercial sector have historically been large in this industry. But, they have diminished as the technology and the military's demands have become more specialized through successive generations of design evolution.

Policy can reduce exposure to uncertainty by exploiting the interrelation between users and producers.

Military procurement exploits the technical expertise of both users and producers. Military users define performance characteristics, while producers create innovations to meet military demand.

Japanese VLSI Program (Success)

Japanese 5G Program (Failure)

See text for discussion of the above two cases.

SPECIFIC ENCOURAGEMENT – TECHNOLOGY: CATCH-UP, LARGE LEAP; STRUCTURAL: LARGE

Japanese Commercial Aircraft, Phase 1[26] (Failure)

The Japanese targeting of the aircraft industry began in the defence sector and resulted in several costly false starts. In 1954, support changed to include the commercial side of the industry. Private firms required enormous financial assistance from MITI before they were willing to enter the industry and, between 1954 and 1965, MITI established several non-profit corporations to conduct a series of projects designed to gather information and channel funds to industry consortia conducting preliminary R&D.

By the late 1960s, MITI became convinced that aircraft were one of the strategic industries of the near future. It decided to support a project to produce an airplane made entirely in and by Japan – the YS-11. It was a "modest technical achievement, ... [but] a commercial flop" (Woronoff 1992, p. 183). All subsequent Japan-only projects have been commercial failures. One of the problems in getting a Japan-only industry off the ground was that, unlike automobiles, the domestic market was too small to support competing aircraft firms operating efficiently, and there was virtually no industry-facilitating structure.

Policy Lessons

Large leaps are dangerous.

The decision to create a commercial aircraft industry when none had previously existed exposed the firms MITI was targeting to a great deal of uncertainty. The entire facilitating structure had to be created, virtually from scratch, along with the development of commercial innovation. This proved to be impossible.

SPECIFIC ENCOURAGEMENT – TECHNOLOGY: CATCH-UP, LARGE LEAP AND LEADING EDGE, INCREMENTAL; STRUCTURAL: MEDIUM

Early Industrial Policies in Korea (Success) and India[27] (Failure)

These are the overall development strategies, which are distinct from several types of more specific policies which include pushing specific activities by means, such as

R&D tax credits, pushing particular industries, such as automobiles, and pushing specific technologies such as integrated circuits or photocopiers. They typically seek both catch-up and leading edge encouragement and are targeted in one way or another. Although what we can say about something as complex as a full development strategy must be brief and superficial, it seems worthwhile to include some comments on such policies since they illustrate one generic type of innovation policy.

Korea's early industrial policy had two main objectives: export promotion and infant industry development. Although biased toward exports and sometimes pushing particular industries, the policy was mainly neutral among firms.

First, in an otherwise regulated economy, the export promotion policy was free trade for exports. Capital and intermediate inputs could be imported with neither tariffs, quotas nor indirect taxes, provided that the production was export oriented. A single realistic exchange rate was established, and exporters were allowed to borrow from state-controlled banks in proportion to their export activity. Quarterly export targets were set, and producers were encouraged (and aided) to meet them: a government "export situation room" expedited the resolution of problems and the highest export achievements received awards and other material benefits.

Infant industry protection helped to create large-scale establishments with temporary monopoly power in the domestic market that could compete freely in the export market. Continued protection in the home market was contingent on a firm meeting quarterly export sales targets which required that infant firms sell a growing proportion of their output at world prices.

The assessment of this policy is still controversial but it did, without doubt, assist in propelling South Korea from poverty to relative affluence in a single generation while many other countries remained stagnant. There might have been better policies but, as the rest of the underdeveloped world reveals, there were many worse ones.

Datta-Chaudhui compares this Korean experience with India's from 1950, when the two countries were at similar levels of development, to 1980, when they were very different. He notes three critical differences between the two sets of policies.

First, India, began with a well-established bureaucracy inherited from the colonial period through which the industrial plans were implemented. Industry and academic expertise did not play a large role in its formulation. In contrast, Korea's bureaucracy was new and was drawn from the emerging business elite.

Second, Indian industrial policy had several, sometimes opposing, objectives such as growth, employment, interregional equity, self-reliance and control of monopolies. Coping with all these objectives through a bureaucracy required heavy control on the activities of firms and not always in a consistent fashion. In contrast, Korean objectives were narrowly defined and instituted at the industry or firm level, allowing firms more autonomy in implementation.

Third, India's industrial policy did not include a mechanism for rewarding good performance, and losses were absorbed by the public sector. Korean industrial support had strong rewards and penalties tied to export performance.

Although public funds were poured into the Indian program over the period studied, India's economic growth performance was poor and in some years negative while Korea's exploded.

Korea's later development policies have been more questionable. In the last years of the rule of Park Chung Hee, development was pushed into heavy industries such as metals, machinery and chemicals. Concentration was encouraged as existing chaebols expanded with the help of massive government-encouraged borrowing. This created a form of moral hazard since the government could not afford to let these massive firms fail which in turn encouraged them into sometimes reckless expansion. In spite of moving toward a more market-oriented economy, the present democratic government is still backing winners, currently in the form of the aerospace industry, a new consortium of car producers and the telephone industry. In the telephone sector, the government backed a big technological leap into digital standards for mobile phones which seems to be losing out to firms in other countries which were left free to chose their standards and which chose more incremental polices for technological advance. The judgment on the success of the attempt to move from a more interventionist to a more fully market-oriented economy remains in the future.

Policy Lessons

The comparison between Indian and early Korean policies suggests a number of policy lessons.

Policy needs to be flexible.

The early Korean model sought to reduce the exposure of companies in targeted industries to uncertainty by allowing flexibility in factor sourcing and providing domestic market security. It also sought to force competitive commercial innovation by exposing targeted firms to international competition. The two policies illustrate the advantages of working through the flexibility of the price system and avoiding the inflexibilities of command economies.

Multiple objectives are dangerous.

India's policy actually reduced firm flexibility by imposing many, sometimes conflicting, objectives on targeted industries. It had no mechanism to induce competitive commercial innovation.

Policy can play a useful role, inducing and co-ordinating pre-commercial R&D efforts and encouraging competition in innovation.

Reduction of price competition can be productive as long as basic rivalries remain and are channelled into competition in innovation. Intervention that removes basic rivalries by rigid control of firm behaviour is almost sure to be counterproductive. Cutoffs for failures are essential. In Korea's case, they were provided by the export orientation of its industrial policy. This did not happen with India's inward-looking policies.

Policy intervention can be useful if guided by private sector knowledge.

The amount of apparently successful interference in Korea shows that it is not an either/or choice between laissez faire and a centrally planned economy. There is room in a market-oriented economy for substantial government intervention, provided it is focused toward, and administered within, the confines of a market orientation. In contrast, bureaucratic control, with little discretion for firms to respond flexibly to market signals and to compete in innovations, produces poor results, particularly when innovation is being sought.

The European Airbus (Marginal Success)

French Microelectronics Policy (Failure)

British Support of the Computer Industry (Failure)

See the discussion in the text for the details of these three cases.

SPECIFIC ENCOURAGEMENT – TECHNOLOGY: LEADING EDGE, INCREMENTAL; STRUCTURAL: LARGE

Military Procurement in the U.S. Software Industry[28] (Success)

The federal government's activities in the software industry, which began in 1950 with a Bureau of Standards project, have been broadly similar to its role in the development of other postwar, high-technology industries such as semiconductors, computer hardware and commercial aircraft. The policy has been motivated primarily by cold war defence concerns. The government's role is interesting for the analysis of this paper because of two major spinoffs to the commercial sector: an infrastructure of academic experts built largely with government funding, and high industry standards arising from rigorous standards set by the U.S. DoD. Both are changes in the facilitating structure. One contrast with other postwar U.S. procurement programs is that the software development programs had few if any direct spinoffs into new civilian products.

Many of the early university research and development activities in software were funded under DoD projects. These created a valuable industrial structure of expertise that other high-technology industries already had in place. Some of this expertise moved into the commercial sector and into private research labs, motivated in part by the high rewards for innovation.

The strict software requirements imposed by the DoD-set standards had many commercial benefits. Standardization allows software makers to build upgrading capacity into programs to accommodate subsequent refinements. Coherent integration of different producers' software is also more feasible with standardized practices. Both features are marketable directly to consumers of final products because this reduces the uncertainty associated with the possibility of having to buy new packages and undergo new learning costs by reassuring consumers that existing software can be upgraded.[29] (These are the subtle relations that heavy-handed bureaucrats often miss when they dictate from on high to an industry – unlike MITI which seldom issues an edict that it has not tested in detailed industry consultations.)

DoD contracts are awarded on prototypes designed by firms to meet DoD needs. The R&D activities of unsuccessful bidders are at least partially covered. The real prize for innovation, however, is the guaranteed production run for the successful bidder.

Success in reaching defence policy objectives with regard to software was illustrated in the effectiveness of the sophisticated software guided weaponry employed in the Gulf War. It is also estimated that much of the United States' early commercial lead in this industry has resulted from the policy of defence procurement.

Policy Lessons

Policy should be aware of the interrelation between technology and structure.

In this case, policy created an academic infrastructure and supported a production structure with a device that allowed an incubation period for innovations that were not sufficiently evolved to be commercially viable.

Policy can reduce exposure to uncertainty by exploiting the interrelation between users and producers.

In this case, policy makers are better informed about the direction innovation should take because they are also the users of the innovation. They detail the desired standards and use characteristics thus reducing the exposure of firms to uncertainty. They also provide exact information to firms about demand for the innovation, which also reduces uncertainty.

Competition-inducing mechanisms are essential for policy success.

The method of letting procurement contracts induces much competition in innovation.

Policy should exploit innovation spillovers.

The policy also inadvertently exploited the spillover nature of innovation by providing pre-commercial innovation and human capital that was adapted to the commercial side of the market. In examinations of several postwar U.S. industries, Mowery and Rosenberg (1989) pointed out that the procurement tool seems to work well (in terms of the spillovers generated) in the early generic stages of new technologies and less well as these technologies mature and become highly specialized.

SPECIFIC ENCOURAGEMENT – TECHNOLOGY: LEADING EDGE,
INCREMENTAL; STRUCTURAL: MEDIUM

SEMATECH[30] (Marginal Success)

Semiconductor Manufacturing Technology (SEMATECH) is a non-profit research consortium established in 1987 in response to flagging U.S. competitiveness in the semiconductor industry. Funding for the consortium is shared between the federal government and the members from private industry. Each private firm pays an amount proportional to its sales, and the government's contribution cannot exceed 50 percent of the annual operating budget. Government representatives sit on the governing board, but the agenda is set by the industrial members.

The original objective of the program was to improve the competitive position of the industry by producing pre-commercial R&D. It was meant to demonstrate the feasibility of manufacturing new, leading edge semiconductors using only equipment made in the United States. Equipment was purchased from the members and used to establish a pre-commercial wafer processing facility. Information obtained from the experiment was to be fed back to the membership and subsequently to the industry at large.

After two years, the program's objective was changed from pre-commercial research to a commercial orientation. With the goal of improving the competitiveness of U.S. firms relative to Japanese companies, the program sought to facilitate the acquisition of new equipment and technological capacity in flagging firms. Between 1987 and 1992, US$371 million (37 percent of the total operating budget for SEMATECH) was allocated to direct support for such firms. Two lithography companies, Perkin Elmer and GCA, world-leading manufacturers in 1980 had, by 1990, been displaced by two Japanese firms, Canon and Nikon. SEMATECH's attempt to support these firms within its own structure failed when one went out of business and the other formed an alliance with a Japanese firm. Two of the original SEMATECH members have quit the arrangement, and 10 of the remaining 12 have indicated they are unwilling to increase funding for the program.

In other ways, SEMATECH appears to have been somewhat successful in meeting its revised objectives. The decline in U.S. market share of the industry has been halted and reversed slightly. Inter-firm partnerships have been established among equipment producers and semiconductor manufacturers, a relationship that previously was fractious. SEMATECH has demonstrated the viability of 0.35 micron line-width integrated circuits, an innovation which has brought the level of American technology roughly even with the Japanese.

Policy Lessons

Policy can play a useful role, inducing and co-ordinating pre-commercial R&D efforts and encouraging competition in innovation.

SEMATECH's switch in objectives, which abandoned the pre-commercial R&D support, suggests that these bodies may need government direction to keep them focused on socially useful lines.

Flexibility is essential for policy success.

Limiting innovators to domestic-content-only products has not been successful, either in SEMATECH or in the other cases we studied. In the uncertain environment of innovation, it seems sensible to use any proven or useful innovation no matter where it originates.

Competition inducing mechanisms are essential for policy success.

SEMATECH's failure to rescue lithography equipment producers illustrates once again that short-term measures to support specific firms that are failing to compete in innovation are not an efficient way to induce innovation. Evidently governments are not alone in being prone to follow this misguided policy. The terms of reference of such bodies should be designed to keep them from wasting money on bailouts of faltering firms.

Military Procurement in the U.S. Semiconductor Industry[31] (Success)

Over the years, support for the U.S. semiconductor industry has come from military procurement designed to produce innovation to solve performance problems but with little concern for cost. In many cases, procurement has provided an important incubation for innovations that were not yet commercially viable: while supplying the military market, innovations were refined and costs were reduced sufficiently to achieve commercial viability.

Between 1955 and 1968, military demand accounted for between one fourth and one half of the semiconductor market. The military imposed rigid standards and quality controls which helped to standardize practices and diffuse technical knowledge.

The policy provided a major catalyst for entry and innovation in the industry. The defence market has been particularly important for new firms. Procurement contracts were (and are) awarded by having firms compete to produce a prototype and then rewarding the best design with a long-term supply contract. This fostered competition in innovation for the contracts and provided a secure market for the successful innovators.

R&D sponsored by recent defence procurement has yielded few commercial spinoffs. "The largest amount of government R&D funds has gone to the development of radiation-hardened integrated circuits, which are used almost exclusively for military and space applications" (Angel, 1994, p. 167). This is another case of spinoffs being concentrated at the generic stage of the development of new technologies.

Mowery and Rosenberg (1989) also made the point that cost-plus military contracts, and the associated lack of concern with costs, inculcates a poor corporate attitude to commercial viability among firms that depend on military procurement for the bulk of their revenues.

Policy Lessons

Policy should exploit innovation spillovers.

As with the U.S. aircraft and software industries, this case demonstrates the benefits of exploiting the spillover nature of innovations. It also demonstrates that this type of policy tool has limits in producing commercial benefits – limits that appear to be specific to each technology.

Policy can reduce exposure to uncertainty by exploiting the interrelation between users and producers.

In this case, the policy maker is also the direct user of the innovation. Military demands for innovation tend to define specific technical problems for innovators to solve. Allowing users to help define the research agenda reduces exposure to uncertainty in market demand and helps innovators locate and exploit relevant knowledge sets.

Policy should be aware of the interrelation between technology and structure.

The procurement market established a production structure in which innovation could be developed and tested for usefulness, without inventors facing high degrees of exposure to uncertainty while at the same time inducing competition in new designs.

National Advisory Committee on Aeronautics (NACA)[32] (Success)

A major source of government assistance in the U.S. commercial aircraft industry, NACA supported aviation innovation by providing it directly, through its government-operated experimental facilities. It helped to develop pre-competitive research that had many applications in both the commercial and military sectors. NACA pioneered the construction and use of large wind tunnels and provided essential test data that led to the development of such innovations as the "NACA cowl," and demonstrated the superiority of airframes designed with a retractable landing gear. In 1958, NACA was absorbed by the National Aeronautics and Space Administration (NASA), and the pre-commercial research function disappeared.

Policy Lessons

Policy can play a useful role, inducing and co-ordinating pre-commercial R&D efforts and encouraging competition in innovation.

NACA played an important supporting role by freely providing pre-commercial research. It levelled the non-appropriable technical knowledge of firms and forced them to compete in generating commercially viable innovations. This provision of technical knowledge reduced duplication of costly research and allowed firms to produce incremental, commercially oriented innovation. Thus, it reduced exposure to uncertainty.

SPECIFIC ENCOURAGEMENT – TECHNOLOGY: LEADING EDGE, INCREMENTAL; STRUCTURAL: SMALL

Stoves in Kenya[33] (Success)

In the 1980s, Kenya faced a problem of dwindling wood supplies – the major source of both commercial and non-commercial energy. The Kenya Renewable Energy Development Project (KREDP) was instituted to address the problems of efficient fuel consumption, alternative fuels and afforestation.

KREDP studied existing energy sources, production techniques, household energy consumption and the ability to adopt new technologies. As one response, KREDP developed the new stove technology that used oil and chemical drums to produce stoves with greatly increased energy efficiency but which did not require changes in household use patterns. The technology was diffused to the artisans who were already producing the old form of the stoves. This was assisted by a further innovation: a mobile training facility which was able to reach the widely dispersed artisan labour force.

As a result, consumption of wood has fallen and, with it, the environmental threat. The program has successfully retrained those required for the growing industry that produces the stoves.

Boat Building In India[34] (Success)

The boat building technology of the Kottur region of India relies heavily on the light wood of the mango tree. Between 1978 and 1983, boat prices doubled due to an acute shortage of wood supplies.

The Centre for Appropriate Technology (CAT) and a private firm, Mutton Boat Building Centre (MBBC), developed and diffused the technology for building plywood boats which use fewer trees per boat than the traditional technology. CAT and MBBC had to overcome several design problems and made several refinements as they received feedback from fishermen using the new boats. The program has successfully overcome the materials shortage while improving productivity and profitability in the region's boat building industry. MBBC has subcontracted to several boat building firms, and the industry has grown under healthy competition.

Electricity in Nepal[35] (Success)

Nepal's micro hydro project was initiated in the early 1960s, partly in response to the growing rural demand for automated crop processing and partly in response to the government's desire to electrify the rural portions of the country. At the time, the main technology for milling was either diesel- or water-powered mills.

The project designed and diffused a technology for micro hydro mills. The technology was developed to meet the varying characteristics of the landscape, and it relied mainly on a cross-flow turbine that could be used as a dedicated mill, as an electricity generator or be adapted to switch among several activities (such as a mill for wheat and maize, an oil expeller for mustard seed or electricity generation). Several small companies now produce these turbines and 450 have been installed. A further 700 new sites have been designated for new installations.

The program has met its objectives of providing crop processing based on water power and assisting rural electrification.

Policy Lessons

These three cases illustrate a large body of experience attesting to the value of small, leading edge innovations that work within a country's existing facilitating structure.

Policy should be aware of the interrelation between technology and structure.

By targeting incremental innovation in technologies that were already integrated into the facilitating structure of their respective economies, policy makers were able to maximize the commercial and social benefits of new technologies while minimizing the exposure to uncertainty. The policies minimized the dislocations that occur between existing structure and new technology and thus minimized the number of supporting technical and structural innovations that were required.

Large leaps are dangerous.

These policies adopted an incremental approach to introducing innovation and change into their facilitating structure. By targeting incremental changes in technologies they reduced exposure to uncertainty.

Consolidated Computer Incorporated (CCI)[36] (Failure)

While the stove, boat building and electricity projects were all successes, this next one was a spectacular failure.

In 1967, Mers Kutt, former sales chief for Honeywell's eastern Canada region and Queen's University professor, established CCI to market his data processing invention Key-Edit. The company's product faced direct competition with IBM whose customers were attracted by the low outlay for a one-year lease for the product. CCI knew that customers were captured through the cost required to learn to use a new machine effectively. IBM was able to finance the lease contracts internally; Kutt needed external funds if he was to compete on the same terms.

By 1969, the company had gone public, employed 200 people and had sales of $650,000. Kutt applied to the General Adjustment Assistance Board (GAAB) for a loan guarantee to secure financing for the leases. GAAB agreed.

The secured financing allowed CCI sales to explode causing cash flow problems. Kutt sought to solve these with a stock issue for which the underwriters required a loan guarantee from GAAB. While the demand for CCI's product was strong, its balance sheet looked weak because of the one-year term of the leases. Although the users of Key-Edit were committed by their learning costs to a long time horizon, GAAB insisted that Kutt improve the appearance of CCI's balance sheet, and surrender control of the company, as the price of providing the guarantee. Kutt felt that effort was better spent on R&D and attracting new sales. These differing views resulted in the stock issue being aborted. Kutt made some accusatory comments in an interview and the GAAB-controlled board of directors fired him.

At that point (1971), the government had put $7 million into the firm. Fearing that a write-off would be an admission of mistakes, GAAB kept CCI in business. By now, the company had lost its technological lead and was unable to maintain a competitive position in spite of large R&D investments. Ten years later, the government ended its involvement with losses of $120 million.

Policy Lessons

Policy intervention can be useful if guided by private sector knowledge.

A major government mistake was attempting to intervene in the detailed operation of CCI. The entrepreneur was much better positioned, by virtue of industrial background and innovative abilities, to manage. In this case, the government did not understand the feedback relationship between users and producers of innovations – specifically, the lock in due to users' learning costs and the secured revenue streams firms could obtain as a result. Nor did it understand that the innovator could not simply be replaced by R&D money. It should have provided the loan guarantee while leaving Kutt the flexibility he needed to solve CCI's problems.

Policy needs to be flexible.

Public sector officials compounded their first mistake by not admitting it. They persisted in the management of a private company and lost $120 million of taxpayers' money instead of the $7 million that had been lost by the time the first mistake was evident.

Caravelle (Success Turned into Failure)

MITI's Supporting Networks, Research Labs and Finance (Successes)

See text for details of the above cases.

Specific Encouragement – Technology: Catchup, Incremental; Structural: Large

The Taiwan Electronics and Information Industry[37] (Success)

Taiwan is an interesting case study in innovation policy due in part to its recent emergence as a NIC. Taiwan was one of the first Asian countries to adopt market-oriented, outward-looking economic policies which resulted in rapid and sustained economic growth. Although market oriented, there has been substantial government presence in the economy. Taiwanese industrial policy has established upstream industries – often single factories – then has either handed them off to private entrepreneurs or run them as public enterprises.

Since the early 1970s, Taiwan has been targeting the electronics and information industry with a set of policies that have three key features: use of government agencies, direction of the industry into particular niches and awareness of, and working within, the natural structure of the industry.

The first feature is the deliberate attempt to create the industry through government agencies, rather than government support of private industries. This part of the policy was designed to create an electronics industry from the ground up and foster its development until it was commercially viable. Some parts of the industry were then handed off to private entrepreneurs. The policy was also designed to generate spillovers private firms could use.

The policy evolved over several years and through several different "plans." In 1972, state officials developed a plan to acquire semiconductor design and production capability. In 1974, a government-owned company, Electronic Research Service Organization (ERSO), was formed. In 1976, ERSO set up the first model shop for wafer fabrication and signed a technology transfer agreement for integrated circuit design with RCA. In the late 1970s, the Taiwan government formed a vision for an integrated information industry which linked semiconductors, computers, computer software and telecommunications. A policy task force formulated the information industry development plan to be implemented between 1980 and 1989.

The leadership for the plan was vested in already existing public research organizations such as ERSO. Commercialization of the innovations produced in the public research labs was undertaken by United Microelectronics (a subsidiary of ERSO). The ownership was 55 percent public and 45 percent private which was consistent with the strategy to develop domestic technical capacity and hand activities off to private firms.

The industrial development plan also targeted the development of human capital within the domestic labour force. ERSO trained personnel and then encouraged them to move to the private sector.

One final aspect of this part of the policy is that ERSO licenses foreign technologies to itself. It then sub-licenses these technologies to industry. In this way, it integrates its industrial development vision with proven technologies developed elsewhere and gives small firms access to a worldwide technology pool they could not afford by themselves.

The second feature of Taiwan's policy is the specific direction it gives to the industry. Taiwan's government recognized that the industry was not in a position to compete head to head with the United States, Japan and Korea. Taiwanese firms do not have the financial resources needed for such competition. Therefore, the government emphasized building capacity in custom-tailored integrated circuits [i.e., application-specific integrated circuits (ASICs)]. This capacity provided many horizontal spinoffs across the industry.

The third feature of Taiwan's policy is illustrated by efforts to attract a multinational to make VLSI circuits. Phillips agreed to the joint venture with several small Taiwanese manufacturing firms pulled together by the government into the Taiwan Semi Conductor Manufacturing Corporation, which concentrates on made-to-order, application-specific integrated circuits. The Corporation's strategy exploits the innovative ideas of clients and allows the company to gain insight into a wider set of these ideas. It also helps the corporation determine its research agenda and removes some of the exposure to demand uncertainty that innovative products face.

The policy of targeting the electronics and information industry has been successful. Taiwan has developed the largest pool of chip design talent in Asia outside of Japan. "No where else in Asia has the personal computer revolution spun off such a frenzy of activity." For example, Taiwan has over 100 computer design manufacturers, while Korea has less than 60 (Wade 1990, pp. 106).

Policy Lessons

Successful policies often pursue incremental innovation and (where possible) aid the acquisition of tacit knowledge.

Along with the Japanese semiconductor industry, this case highlights the advantages of licensing proven technologies for further local development. This strategy allows the policy to choose technologies appropriate for the existing facilitating structure, obtain tacit knowledge and limit exposure to uncertainty: the production structure has been created elsewhere, and competing domestic firms can create innovative dynamism in exploiting the niches that are inevitably left behind by the technology leaders. The case also demonstrates the role policy can play in helping to overcome some of the costs and uncertainties involved in technology transfer.

Policy can reduce exposure to uncertainty by exploiting the interrelation between users and producers.

Taiwan's custom-designed chip policy explicitly exploits the user–producer relationship. By guaranteeing the protection of industrial secrets and providing only customized work, Taiwan is able to exploit the niche markets.

Policy intervention can be useful if guided by private sector knowledge.

Taiwan's policy has often been quite interventionist. In this industry, the government created the industrial structure and then parcelled pieces out to private industry. It has single-mindedly maintained the objective of commercial success through export promotion.

Policy needs to be flexible.

Taiwan's policy toward this industry has evolved through several layers of plans and over several years. While the principal objective of commercially viable innovation has remained at the fore, the means and subsidiary objectives of the plans have adjusted to the uncertain innovation environment.

Korean Electronics Industry[38] (Success)

In 1969, Korea enacted its electronic industry promotion law requiring: the formulation of an electronics sector plan by the Ministry of Commerce and Industry, the registration of all producers in the industry, the establishment of an industry promotion fund, the promotion of overseas investment in the industry and the formulation of industry complexes. The policy was characterized by what Kang calls "superaggresive" technology acquisition through licensing arrangements with established electronics manufacturers. These licences have been for technologies that fit into the existing Korean industrial structure, not for leading edge technologies. The policy lets Korean firms exploit their comparative advantage in labour intensive manufacturing while also accumulating human capital. The abundance of downstream technologies has allowed Korean firms to exploit licensing arrangements continuously while developing the flexibility to change over technologies in their production systems.

The industrial policy has been directed at specific outcomes: increasing export potential, minimizing material dependency, increasing value added potential and targeting niche developments (which minimize international trade friction and maximize technology spinoffs) (Kang, 1989, pp. 87-88). The industry's annual sales rose from $10 million in 1960 to $10 billion in 1987. During the 1970s, production grew at 44 percent and exports at 54 percent per year!

Policy Lessons

Successful policies often pursue incremental innovation and (where possible) aid in the acquisition of tacit knowledge.

Along with the Japanese semiconductor industry, this case highlights the advantages of licensing proven technologies for further local development. This strategy allows the policy to choose technologies appropriate for the existing facilitating structure, obtain tacit knowledge and limit exposure to uncertainty because:

- the production structure has been created elsewhere; and
- few innovations are required to exploit the niches left behind in the prior development of the technology.

A large number of competing firms then create innovative dynamism in exploiting the niches inevitably left behind by the technology leaders. The case also demonstrates the role policy can play in helping to overcome some of the uncertainties involved in technology transfer.

Policy intervention can be useful if guided by private sector knowledge.

Korea has a history of extensive government intervention in the market. But, the overriding objective of commercial viability and export promotion has allowed this intervention to stay flexible and meet the structural demands of innovation.

SPECIFIC ENCOURAGEMENT – TECHNOLOGY: CATCH-UP, INCREMENTAL; STRUCTURAL: MEDIUM

Japanese Commercial Aircraft, Phase 2 (Success)

MITI's response to the failure of its phase 1 plans (see earlier discussion) was to drop the idea of a Japan-only industry and look for foreign partners with Japanese firms playing a smaller role, first in engine design and later in airframes. The joint ventures have succeeded, but Japan still lacks a "complete" large commercial aircraft industry.

Policy Lessons

> **Successful policies often pursue incremental innovation and (where possible) aid in the acquisition of tacit knowledge.**

This can be done, for example, by forming partnerships (as MITI did), or other arrangements, that import technological knowledge and tacit experience, allowing the newly entering country to concentrate on niches where it may develop a focused comparative advantage more easily.

> **Policy needs to be flexible.**

MITI once again illustrated the importance of flexibility in the face of learning by experience when it was able to back off its Japan-only policy.

Early Japanese Catch-up in Semiconductors (Success)

See the discussion of this case in the text.

GENERAL POLICIES

THE POLICIES PRESENTED IN THIS SECTION target specific activities and support projects covering a wide range of structural and technological changes. Most of them support incremental catch-up or leading edge activities that cause small structural changes (mainly because this is where the bulk of private sector activity is).

The European Union's (EU's) EUREKA Program[39] (Not Assessed)

EUREKA was initiated in 1985 and evolved from several earlier programs designed to support innovation in the European Community. Its purpose is to foster economic growth through improvements in technical capabilities by acting as a "public funder" and a "marriage bureau."

As a public funder, EUREKA provides funding for qualified projects. The qualification criteria, and the form and size of funding support, are determined by the member state in which the project originates.

As a marriage bureau, EUREKA provides information and co-ordinating services. It encourages collaborative links between firms and institutions that have the same research interests. It also provides information about developments that public research institutions and private firms produce which may have applicability to other firms. The style and degree of support is determined by the sponsoring member state.

The details of what firms and specific activities can be assisted (and how) are purposely not spelled out in the program's mandate. The hope is that the heterogeneity of the allowed projects will encourage innovation. Policy flexibility is also needed because the member states of the EU have different visions of innovation policy. French projects are mainly industry led and targeted at commercial development; German projects are generally initiated by government and target infrastructure and pre-competitive R&D; and British projects appear to be highly bureaucratized (Peterson, 1993, pp. 90-97, 154-158).

Peterson provides a preliminary evaluation of the program based on what he calls an "additionality" criteria (i.e., would the project have proceeded without the support of EUREKA).[40] Forty percent of the total projects undertaken appear to be truly additional. Of the two main functions EUREKA performs, the marriage bureau role seems more important than the public funding role but both roles are likely to come into play on a given project.

Large projects tend to perform pre-competitive R&D. Projects led by small- and medium-sized enterprises tend to perform "near market" R&D specifically targeting commercial applications. Peterson does not clarify if large projects are merely projects led by large firms or if these projects have some kind of joint leadership in government. If it is the latter, the story fits the policy generalizations suggested elsewhere in our analysis: projects that are not closely tied to the bottom line tend to target large leaps in technology that often do not produce commercially viable results. The projects undertaken by small- and medium-sized enterprises tend to be more careful about cost efficiency and thus to target commercial innovation.

We attempt no assessment of EUREKA because it needs to be assessed program by program, and individual results are hard to come by. We include it because it is an important initiative which seems to avoid at least some of the conditions that have led to failure elsewhere.

Indian Public Trading Companies (Success)

One successful aspect of India's industrial policy (failures in the policy were considered above) is its public trading companies which were designed to exploit gains from spillover externalities. They are horizontally integrated across several industries and provide a mechanism for importing inputs, disseminating technology and exporting manufactured goods. These agencies appear to have been successful in diffusing technology and disseminating information that would otherwise have been unavailable to Indian firms.

Canadian Industrial Research Assistance Program (IRAP)[41] (Success)

IRAP was established in 1962 with the objectives of (1) "assisting the Canadian firm to improve its internal capability and competence in developing and managing technology effectively; and (2) facilitating the process of development, access, acquisition, and exploitation of technology by the firm" (NRC, 1990, p. 1). The means are threefold.

- IRAP pays staff salary costs of selected research projects likely to initiate significant technical advance through commercial development and application in Canada.

- IRAP makes available R&D out of its own laboratory.

- IRAP consults and advises in an information dissemination and co-ordination role.

The program's regional and national elements account for over 5000 assisted projects. The regional elements of the program are small scale, firm-specific projects. The national elements are "relatively large, technically significant, industrial R&D projects involving collaboration with universities and, or other Canadian or international laboratories" (NRC, 1990, p. 6).

In 1990, IRAP had an annual budget of $90 million of which $60 million was allocated to financial assistance to firms.

IRAP seeks to develop technology acquisition in firms. It allows access to the technology produced in IRAP labs which, in turn, allows firms to select technology that is suitable to their individual technology problem. The provision of support for R&D staff by IRAP allows the firm to engage in proximate development that will have relatively secure commercial payoffs.

As well, government agents operating within the program have discretion to make small grants to firms without going through bureaucratic red tape. This allows firms to adapt technology available elsewhere to their own uses.

In 1990, the National Research Council conducted an IRAP user survey. The findings indicated that a majority of users felt that IRAP support was "fairly" or "absolutely" essential to their undertaking a project.

West German Small and Medium Enterprise (SME) R&D Policy[42] (Success)

In 1978, the West German government instituted a program designed to support R&D activity in SMEs by widening the diffusion of innovations, increasing human capital and enhancing the innovative capacity of firms. The support was provided by subsidizing the salaries of R&D personnel within firms that applied to the program. Over its five-year existence, the policy attracted about half of the eligible firms (i.e., those with employment between 20 and 999).

Meher-Krahmer (1990) used an econometric evaluation technique to demonstrate that the program successfully induced commercial innovation but not pre-commercial research. According to this evaluation, 60 percent of the program's activity created "additional" R&D. It also raised the amount and use of R&D personnel in West Germany and created innovative capacity in the firms it affected.

The policy reduced tacitness and facilitated diffusion by providing a means for small- and medium-sized enterprises that did not have large profits to support fundamental R&D to exploit knowledge sets of well trained R&D personnel. The firms used the program's support for incremental innovation with commercial payoff.

Policy Lessons

The four cases just considered suggest a number of policy lessons.

> **Information co-ordination and dissemination is important**. Policy can play a useful role in providing information and co-ordinating infrastructure for firms, as well as diffusing technological knowledge to firms that do not have the resources to discover superior practices being used elsewhere. Such diffusion can have significant payoffs without creating a high exposure to uncertainty.

The Indian trading companies successfully provide many of the above functions. West German policy has induced small- and medium-sized firms to adopt new technologies by providing them with personnel skilled in the use and creation of these policies. All the above schemes operate, to some extent, as information co-ordinators and disseminators. The Korean case considered earlier also illustrates this point.

> **Policy needs to be flexible.**

The range of discretion given to individual IRAP agents who contact firms, and the lack of red tape in making small grants, gives a flexible administration as does the German policy of providing support for firms to hire R&D personnel yet allowing the firms to direct the R&D activities.

A preliminary assessment of what we have been able to discover so far about EUREKA suggests that some member countries do not seem to have learned from their past experiences. The large projects under EUREKA seem to continue the quest for big science, especially in France – often without the necessary support for fundamental innovations in terms of preparing and organizing the facilitating structure of its economy. British projects still seem to be excessively bureaucratized, inflexible and lacking in commercialization.

Inducing technology for its own sake is not sufficient to justify policy.

Many blanket policies use the additionality criteria for internal evaluations. This criteria is problematic in light of our theory and evaluative criteria. Our theory suggests that the interrelation between technology and structure, as well as commercial viability, are essential for successful policy. In the absence of a fully developed evaluative study, there is no way to tell if the funded projects would have happened anyway or whether they would have been successful. However, our theory suggests that IRAP has the potential for great benefit. It can induce diffusion and adaptation by calling the attention of small firms to technologies in use elsewhere and assisting them in adapting these technologies to their own use.[43]

R&D Tax Credits[44] (Not Assessed)

Many governments allow tax credits on R&D, and Canadian policy is particularly generous in this respect. These credits provide tax relief for capital equipment used for R&D activities. They also provide generous capital cost allowances for machinery that is considered to be high-tech. A number of provinces provide tax credits for capital devoted to R&D. For example, Quebec offers a 100 percent write-off of such capital costs. The federal government and some provinces also offer tax credits for current R&D expenditures. Analysis of the tax expenditures associated with the federal tax credits conducted by the several agencies of the federal government indicate that the foregone revenue for investment tax credits was $759 million in 1986, $1 billion in 1992 and over $1.2 billion in 1994. As much as 80 percent is accounted for by Science Research and Experiment Development tax credits.

The underpinning of such general R&D support policies is the argument, due originally to Arrow, that the price system will tend to underproduce R&D because of its positive externalities. We have already pointed out that this case does not carry over in any simple fashion to decisions characterized by heavy exposure to uncertainty. So the support has to be based on some more general judgment that it is desirable to encourage more R&D than firms would normally engage in. This raises two questions: is this so, and are tax credits a good way to achieve the objective? The second question involves additionality. How much of the R&D activity being subsidized under this policy would be conducted without the support, and how much is induced by it?

Studies by Switzer (1986) and Bernstein (1986) indicated that for every dollar of tax revenue foregone, R&D expenditures increase by between $0.29 and $0.80.

Policy Lessons

Too little is known (by us) to draw policy lessons from the experience of schemes that give tax relief on R&D expenses. However, there does seem to be an empirically testable question raised in the above studies: what is the magnitude of positive spillovers from R&D induced by tax credits? To break even on this expenditure by tax payers, the externalities would have to be between $0.20 and $0.71 for every dollar of R&D expenditure.

Direct R&D Expenditures (Not Assessed)

Many governments support R&D through direct expenditures. Some examples are provided in the case material above (e.g., Concorde, nuclear energy and the SST). Switzer's 1986 analysis indicated that in Quebec one dollar of direct government R&D expenditure produced between $0.70 and $2.31 in direct and indirect R&D spinoffs. Again the problem in analyzing these direct expenditures is additionality. Canada has several programs which perform this direct supporting role, and it is important to evaluate the effectiveness of these policies in the context of the lessons provided above. A more comprehensive project than ours would allow scope for such an assessment. We hope, in the near future, to extend our study to cover this and other similar cases.

ENDNOTES

1 This is a job whose full execution would require a monograph-length treatment and a year of full-time research. Since neither time nor finance was available for such a treatment, this paper is only a beginning, but one that, we hope, establishes a template for further work.

2 The only criterion for selection was that we could obtain reliable data on the case in the small amount of time we had to do the research. In light of this, we find it remarkable how many general issues seem to be raised and illustrated by this small sample of policies.

3 Of course, capital accumulation (Solovian growth) and expansion of markets (Smithian growth) – the terms are due to Mokyr (1990) – also affect growth. As historians of technology attest, technological change is the dominant determinant of long-term economic growth.

4 Notice that we cannot specify in advance what results will be produced by research so the specification of research results does not occur in product technologies. We do, however, have an array of research technologies that are an important part of process technologies.

5 The list partially overlaps the one in Lipsey and Bekar (1995). Each list is chosen for relevance to the problem at hand – in the present case, to evaluate policies designed to influence technological change. Each list provides a subset of the full set of empirical generalizations.

6 This is true at least over the time and geographical spans covered by Rosenberg and Birdzall (1986). At other times and places, periods of technological dynamism have been interspersed with long periods of technological stagnation.

7 The points we make in this section are not without controversy. Our concern is to make contact with facts established by detailed studies of technological change and to avoid theorizing in an empirical vacuum about situations involving uncertainty.

8 This section is based mainly on Hall (1980) and Feldman (1985).

9 The material in this section is drawn mainly from Lambright, Crow and Shangraw (1988), Chathan and Huddle (1971) and the United States Joint Economic Committee, Subcommittee on Priorities and Economy in Government (1973).

10 The material for this section is drawn mainly from Mansfield (1966) and Todd and Simpson (1986).

11 This account is drawn mainly from Hayward (1986), Peterson (1993), Dertouzos, Lester and Solow (1989) and McIntyre (1992).

12 This raises the question of the relation between Boeing and its component suppliers. One presumes that the Euro–U.S. comparison in aircraft will not be as unfavourable to the United States as is the Japanese–U.S. comparison in auto parts. [See Womack, et al. (1990)].

13 We call the policy a type 2 success for being flexible enough to be cancelled after unfavourable evidence accumulated. It is arguable, however, that there was enough unfavourable evidence to condemn President Kennedy's original decision to commit the United States, largely for what appears to be reasons of national prestige. In this view the SST is a type 2, as well as a type 1 failure because it should not have been attempted in the first place.

14 The material in this section comes mainly from Okimoto (1989), Okimoto, Sugano and Weinstein (1984), Langlois, et al. (1985) and Angel (1994).

15 This account is drawn mainly from Zysman (1977, 1983) and Nelson (1984, 1993).

16 The material for this section is drawn primarily from Kelly (1987) and Campbell-Kelly (1989).

17 The persistence of these policies can be rationalized within public choice theory rather than as persistent mistakes. The value of the prestige that accrues at the early stages of the policy, while it still has great expectations, must exceed the present value of the loss of prestige that will accrue when the project fails during the term of a subsequent government.

18 Dertouzos, Lester and Solow (1989) remains the best study of the Japanese endogenous technological response to the conditions that MITI created in the postwar Japanese automobile industry.

19 This section is based on Otagiri and Goto (1993), Woronoff (1992) and Womack, et al. (1990).

20 The material in this section is drawn mainly from Burn (1978) and Cowan (1990).

21 The material in this section is largely drawn from Palda (1993) and Berg (1993).

22 The material in this section is drawn mainly from Grindley (1994).

23 This generalization may seem to conflict with the considerable success of Canadian software firms which do not have a supporting Canadian hardware industry. The major difference between the failed U.K. program and the successful Canadian industry seems to be that, as outsiders, Canadians go for market niches in which close association with hardware producers is not necessary, whereas Alvey was looking for fundamental software innovations in operating systems which are closely linked with hardware producers.

24 Grindley (1994) notes that some observers argue that the program had some intangible benefits in the form of changing institutional attitudes toward collaboration. Although this could be a useful side effect, it could have been achieved at much less cost by operating on that facilitating structure directly.

25 The material in this section is based mainly on Mowery and Rosenberg (1982, 1989).

26 The material in this section and the next is based mainly on Woronoff (1992).

27 The material in this section is based mainly on Westphal (1990), Datta-Chaudhui (1990) and the "Survey of South Korea," The Economist, June 3-9, 1995.

28 The material in this section comes mainly from Langlois and Mowery (1994).

29 Former producers of military software now enjoy a comparative advantage in meeting software standards. Soviet software theorists have this advantage because the lack of computers in the former Soviet Union forced them to do formal theory which is the basis

of the new high-quality software. Russia, India and Pakistan are all enjoying software industry booms because of an increased demand for "formal methods" and the availability of surplus educated labour forces (Gibbs, 1994).

30 This discussion is drawn mainly from Angel (1994), Grindley, Mowery and Silverman (1994).

31 The material in this section is based primarily on Tilton (1971), Angel (1994) and Grindley, Mowery and Silverman (1994).

32 The material for this section comes mainly form Mowery and Rosenberg (1989).

33 The material in this section comes mainly from Opole (1988).

34 The material in this section comes mainly from Kurien (1988).

35 The material in this section comes mainly from Hislop (1988).

36 The material for this case is drawn from Borins (1986).

37 The material in this section comes from Wade (1989) and Rosenberg, Landau and Mowery (1992).

38 The material in this section comes mainly from Kang (1989) and Pack and Westphal (1986).

39 The material in this section is drawn mainly from Peterson (1993). We do not believe we have sufficient information to understand fully the policy nor to evaluate its success but we include it here because of its obvious importance. More research is needed.

40 (Peterson, 1993, p. 10). His analysis does not take the further step of asking if the "additional" projects were commercially worthwhile although he illustrates the importance of this step by observing that "most British-led projects appear to be truly 'additional,' but seem to cause more trouble than they are worth to [the firms that lead them]" (p. 157).

41 The material for this section is drawn from the National Research Council (1990) and Palda (1993).

42 The material in this section is drawn mainly from Meher-Krahmer (1990). The policy is merely typical of a succession of German policies with similar objectives.

43 When suggesting that IRAP may be a good thing, neoclassical friends often say that all it does is give money to people who would have done the same thing anyway. According to that view, knowledge must be freely available to all producers. Massive amounts of research on innovation show that this is not true. It is impossible for a small producer in Saint John or Kelowna to know what is best practice elsewhere. IRAP inspectors can tell the producing company of things that are done elsewhere and then help the company adopt it to its own uses.

44 The material for this section is drawn mainly from the Department of Finance and Revenue Canada (1994), Department of Finance (1994) and the Library of Parliament Research Branch (1994).

ACKNOWLEDGEMENTS

FOR FINANCIAL ASSISTANCE, we are indebted to Industry Canada, the Canadian Institute for Advanced Research and the SSHRC. For comments and suggestions, we thank Cliff Bekar, Peter Howitt, David Mowery, Gilles Paquet, Nate Rosenberg, Rick Harris, Ed Safarian and Russell Wills.

BIBLIOGRAPHY

Alchian, A. "Uncertainty, Evolution and Economics Theory." *Journal of Political Economy*. Vol. 58 (1950): 211-221.

Angel, D.P. *Restructuring For Innovation: The Remaking of the United States Semiconductor Industry*. New York: The Guilford Press, 1994.

Arrow, Kenneth. "Economic Welfare and the Allocation of Resources for Invention." *The Rate and Direction of Economic Activity: Economic and Social Factors*. Princeton: NBER, 1962.

Berg, P. *Nuclear Power Production: The Financial Costs*. Ottawa: Library of Parliament, Research Branch, 1993.

Bernstein, J.I. "The Effect of Direct and Indirect Tax Incentives on Canadian Industrial R&D Expenditures." *Canadian Public Policy*. Vol. 12, (1986): 438-448.

Booth, R.A., et al. and Resource Management Consultants. *Cost Analysis of Supersonic Transport in Airline Operation*. Springfield VA: Clearinghouse for Federal Scientific and Technical Information, 1967.

Borins, S. *Investments in Failure: Five Government Enterprises that Cost the Taxpayer Billions*. Toronto: Methuen, 1986.

Burn, D. *Nuclear Power and the Energy Crisis*. London: MacMillan, 1978.

Campbell-Kelly, M. *ICL, A Business and Technical History*. Oxford: Clarendon Press, 1989.

Carr, M. (ed.). *Sustainable Industrial Development: Seven Case Studies*. New York: Intermediate Technology Development Group of North America, 1988.

Chathan, G.N. and F.P. Huddle. *The Supersonic Transport*. Washington DC: Library of Congress, Congressional Research Service; National Technical Information Service, 1971.

Cowan, R. "Nuclear Power Reactors: A Study in Technological Lock-in." *The Journal of Economic History*. Vol. L, (1990): 541-569.

Crandall, R.W. "The Effects of U.S. Trade Protection for Autos and Steel." *Brookings Papers on Economic Activity*. Vol. 2, Washington DC: Brookings Institution, 1987, pp. 271-288.

Dasgupta, P. and P. Stoneman (eds.). *Economic Policies and Technological Performance*. Cambridge: Cambridge University Press, 1987.

Datta-Chaudhui, M. "Market Failure and Government Failure." *Journal of Economic Perspectives*. (1990): 25-39.

David, P. "Computer and Dynamo: The Modern Productivity Paradox in a Not-too-Distant Mirror." *Technology and Productivity: The Challenge for Economic Policy*. Paris: OECD, 1992.

Department of Finance Canada. "Government of Canada Tax Expenditures." 1994.

Department of Finance and Revenue Canada. "Income Tax Incentives for Research and Development; Report of the Auditor General of Canada to the House of Commons 1994." Vol. 16, 1994.

Dertouzos M.L., R.K. Lester and R.M. Solow. *Made in America: Regaining the Productivity Edge*. Cambridge MA: MIT Press, 1989.

Ergas, H. "Does Technology Policy Matter?" In *Technology and Global Industry: Companies and Nations in the World Economy*. Edited by B.R. Guil and H. Brook. Washington DC: National Academy Press, 1987.

Feldman, E.J. *Concorde and Dissent: Explaining High Technology Project Failure in Britain and France*. Cambridge: Cambridge University Press, 1985.

Forester, T. *The Materials Revolution*. Cambridge MA: MIT Press, 1988.

Gerstenfeld, A. and R. Brainard (eds.). *Technological Innovation; Government/Industry Cooperation*. New York: John Wiley and Sons, 1979.

Gibbs, W.W. "Software's Chronic Crisis." *Scientific American*. (September 1994): 86-95.

Grindly, P. "The Future of the UK Software Industry." In *The International Computer Software Industry: A Comparative Study of Industry Evolution and Structure*. Edited by D. Mowery. Oxford: Oxford University Press, 1994.

Grindly, P., D. Mowery and B. Silverman. "The Design of High-Technology Consortia: Lessons From SEMATEC." *Journal of Policy Analysis and Management*. (1994).

Hall, P. *Great Planning Disasters*. Berkley and Los Angeles: University of California Press, 1980.

Hayward, K. *International Collaboration in Civil Aerospace*. London: Pinter, 1986.

Heiduk, G. and K. Yammamura (eds.). *Technological Competition and Interdependence: The Search for Policy in the United States, West Germany, and Japan*. Seattle: University of Washington Press, 1990.

Hislop, D. "The Micro-Hydro Program in Nepal." In *Sustainable Industrial Development: Seven Case Studies*. Edited by M. Carr. New York: Intermediate Technology Development Group of North America, 1988.

Howell, T.R., W.A. Noellert, J.H. Maclaughlin and A.H. Wolf. *The Microelectronics Race: The Impact of Government Policy on International Competition*. Boulder: Westview Press, 1988.

Kang, T.W. *Is Korea the Next Japan?: Understanding the Structure, Strategy, and Tactics of America's Next Competitor*. New York: The Free Press. 1989.

Kelly, T. *The British Computer Industry: Crisis and Development*. London: Croom Helm, 1987.

Knight, F. *Risk, Uncertainty and Profit*. New York: Augustus M. Kelly, 1964.

Kurien, J. "The Introduction of Plywood Boats in South India." In *Sustainable Industrial Development: Seven Case Studies*. Edited by M. Carr. New York: Intermediate Technology Development Group of North America, 1988.

Lambright, H.W., M. Crow and R. Shangraw. "National Projects in Civilian Technology." In *Government Innovation Policy; Design Implementation, Evolution*. Edited by D.J. Roessner. London: MacMillan Press, 1986.

Langlois, R.N., T.A. Puzel, C.S. Halisck, R.R. Nelson and W.G. Egelhoff. *Microelectronics: An Industry in Transition*. Boston: Unwin Hyman, 1985.

Langlois, R. and D.C. Mowery. "The Federal Government's Role in the U.S. Software Industry's Development." In *The International Computer Software Industry: A Comparative Study of Industry Evolution and Structure*. Edited by D.C. Mowery. Oxford: Oxford University Press, 1994.

Library of Parliament Research Branch. "Scientific Research and Experimental Development: Tax Policy." Canada: Minister of Supply and Services, 1994.

Lipsey, R.G. and C. Bekar. "A Structuralist View of Technical Change and Economic Growth." In the proceedings of the Bell Conference. Kingston: John Deutsch Institute, 1995.

Mansfield, H. Vision: *The Story of Boeing, A Saga of the Sky and the New Horizons of Space*. New York: Duell Sloan and Pearce, 1966.

McIntyre, I. *Dogfight: The Transatlantic Battle over Airbus*. Westport: Prager, 1992.

Meher-Krammer, F. "The Determinants of Investment in R&D and the Role of Public Policies." In *Technology and Investment*. Edited by E. Deiaco, E. Hornell and G. Vickery. London: Pinter, 1990.

Mokyr, J. *The Lever of Riches*. New York: Oxford University Press, 1990.

Mowery, D.C. and N. Rosenberg (eds.). *Technology and the Pursuit of Economic Growth*. Cambridge: Cambridge University Press, 1989.

National Research Council of Canada. *IRAP Evaluation Study: Final Report*. Ottawa, 1990.

Nelson, R.R. (ed.). *Government and Technical Progress: A Cross-Industry Analysis*. New York: Pergamon Press, 1982.

Nelson, R.R. *High-Technology Policies: A Five Nation Comparison*. Washington and London: American Institute for Public Policy Research, 1984.

Nelson, R.R. (ed.). *National Innovation Systems: A Comparative Analysis*. Oxford: Oxford University Press, 1993.

Nelson, R.R. and S. Winter. *An Evolutionary Theory of Economic Change*. Cambridge: Harvard University Press, 1982.

Okimoto, D.I. *Between MITI and the Market: Japanese Industrial Policy for High Technology*. Stanford: Stanford University Press, 1989.

Okimoto, D.I., T. Sugano and F.B. Weinstein (eds.). *Competitive Edge: The Semiconductor Industry in the U.S. and Japan*. Stanford: Stanford University Press, 1984.

Opole, M. "The Introduction of the Kenya Jiko Stove." In *Sustainable Industrial Development: Seven Case Studies*. Edited by M. Carr. New York: Intermediate Technology Development Group of North America, 1988.

Otagiri, H. and A. Goto. "The Japanese System of Innovation." In *National Innovation Systems: A Comparative Analysis*. Edited by Nelson. Oxford: Oxford University Press, 1993.

Pack, H. and L.E. Westphal. "Industrial Strategy and Technological Change: Theory versus Reality." *Journal of Development Economics*. Vol. 22, (1986): 87-128.

Palda, K. *Innovation Policy and Canada's Competitiveness*. Vancouver: The Fraser Institute, 1993.

Patrick, H. *Japan's High Technology Industries: Lessons and Limitations of Industrial Policy*. Seattle: University of Washington Press, 1986.

Peterson, J. *High Technology and the Competition State: An Analysis of the EUREKA Initiative*. London: Routledge, 1993.

Reich, R. and C. Donahue. *New Deals: The Chrysler Revival and The American System*. New York: Time Books, 1985.

Rosenberg, N. *Perspectives on Technology*. New York: Cambridge University Press, 1976.

Rosenberg, N. and L.E. Birdzall. *How the West Grew Rich*. New York: Basic Books, 1986.

Rosenberg, N., R. Landau and D.C. Mowery (eds.). *Technology and The Wealth of Nations*. Stanford: Stanford University Press, 1992.

Shackle, G.L.S. *Uncertainty in Economics and Other Reflections*. New York: Cambridge University Press, 1955.

Sharpe, M. (ed.). *Europe and the New Technologies: Six Case Studies in Innovation and Adjustment*. London: Pinter Publishers, 1983.

Stoneman, P. *The Economic Analysis of Technology Policy*. Oxford: Clarendon Press, 1987.

"Survey of South Korea." *The Economist*. June 3-9, 1995.

Sweeny, G. (ed.). *Innovation Policies: An International Perspective*. London: Pinter Publishers, 1985.

Switzer, L. "Etude des répercussions des mesures fiscal et des dépenses publiques sur les investissements du secteur privé en recherche et développement." Quebec: Government of Quebec, MESS, 1986.

Tilton, J.E. *International Diffusion of Technology: The Case of Semiconductors*. Washington DC: The Brookings Institution, 1971.

Todd, D. and J. Simpson. *The World Aircraft Industry*. Massachussetts: Auburn House Publishing Company, 1986.

United States Joint Economic Committee, Subcommittee on Priorities and Economy in Government. *The Supersonic Transport: Hearing Before the Subcommittee on Priorities and Economy in Government of the Joint Economic Committee, Congress of the United States, Ninety Second Congress, Second Session*. Washington DC: United States Government Print Office, 1973.

Vestal, J.E. *Planning for Change: Industrial Policy and Japanese Economic Development 1945-90*. Oxford: Clarendon Press, 1993.

vonHippel, E. *The Sources of Innovation*. New York: Oxford University Press, 1988.

Wade, R. *Governing the Market: Economic Theory and the Role of Government in East Asian Industrialization*. Princeton: Princeton University Press, 1990.

Warda, J. "International Competitiveness of Canadian Tax Incentives: An Update." Ottawa: Conference Board of Canada, 1990.

Westphal, L.E. "Industrial Policy in an Export-Propelled Economy: Lessons from South Korea's Experience." *Journal of Economic Perspectives*. Vol. 4, No. 3, (1990): 41-60.

Womack, J.P., D.J. Jones and D. Roos. *The Machine that Changed the World*. New York: Rawson Associates, 1990.

Woronoff, J. *Japanese Targeting: Successes, Failures, Lessons*. London: MacMillan Press, 1992.

Zysman, J. *Political Strategies for Industrial Order*. Los Angeles: University of California Press, 1977.

———. *Governments, Markets and Growth: Financial Systems and the Politics of Industrial Change*. Ithica NY: Cornell University Press, 1983.

Comment

Gilles Paquet
PRIME, Faculty of Administration
University of Ottawa

RICHARD LIPSEY AND KEN CARLAW HAVE PRESENTED A PAPER which deals, in an exploratory way, with a most important problem. The problems posed to economists by innovation policy in knowledge-based economies are daunting, and there is no agreement in the profession on a satisfactory analytical framework capable of guiding an effective research program in this area. Whether the exploratory uses principal components on massive survey data or a sample of case studies, the objective is the same: to find ways to stylize, in a provisional way, a map of the innovation process, in order to intervene effectively to catalyze it. Not all explorations are successful, but most expeditions add to our information base. And if at times the pickings appear slim, Industry Canada should find consolation in Thomas Aquinas who used to say that "the slenderest knowledge that may be obtained of the highest things is more desirable than the most certain knowledge obtained of lesser things" (*Summa Theologica*, I, 1, 5 ad 1).

For Lipsey and Carlaw, this is clearly the first phase of a project that will require some additional work. Consequently, what is important is to ensure that the most interesting lessons emerging from this initial work do not get lost. Suggestions on how the authors might want to proceed might also be helpful.

THE STRUCTURALIST APPROACH, TECHNOLOGY AND INNOVATION

L IPSEY AND CARLAW USE THE LABEL "STRUCTURALIST" to define a broad approach to economic growth based on micro-level technological change (i.e., individual technologies and their interlinkages). Since these depend on historical time and institutions, economic growth is defined as a path-dependent, and often irreversible, historical process. The authors' approach is inductive and bottom-up, and the paper is mainly an ethnographic report, enriched by a number of carefully worded empirical generalizations derived from the case studies, and by some careful "appreciative theorizing" (in the sense of Richard Nelson) to explain the stylized facts they have encountered.

In the structuralist world, technology operates within a milieu of facilitating structures to generate performance. Lipsey and Carlaw define technology in a very restrictive way: it pertains only to product and process. On the other hand, they are all-encompassing in their definition of facilitating structures: these cover a broad range of private and public contextual organizations and institutions. When defining performance, the authors are again extremely restrictive: there is little place for anything more than profit, growth and employment.

The authors do not provide their own stylization of the innovation process ex ante. For this, the reader must be thankful. At this stage of our knowledge of the innovation process, they could only have added the view of a seventh blind man to the old Indian tale of the six blind men and the elephant. Lipsey and Carlaw simply recognize that the innovation process is complex, that it is at times continuous and at other times discontinuous, and that it ranges from minor improvements to radical innovations in which enabling technologies trigger deep structural adjustments. Moreover, Lipsey and Carlaw accept the views, in good currency, that the innovation process is path-dependent, that it is an expensive multi-stage evolutionary process plagued with uncertainty and that it is driven by competition.

The complexity of the process entails important consequences, the main one being that the firm faces an extremely important exposure to uncertainty in this profit-driven venture. As a result, firms can only grope and learn, and no optimality is ever assured.

The authors provide a way of thinking about the problem derived from close observations of the micro-terrain, a language of problem definition, a loose statement of plausible relationships and an invitation to discuss issues in a pre-theoretical mode.

POLICIES TO ENCOURAGE INNOVATION

BEFORE EMBARKING ON THEIR SURVEY OF CASE STUDIES, Lipsey and Carlaw chose two criteria of success for innovation: commercial viability and reasonable expectations. The first one is self-explanatory; the second considers a process as successful if the decisions taken can be regarded as "reasonable," given the information available when they were taken. This is a clever way for the authors to free themselves from the stricture of a rigid commercial success criterion. It might have been useful to stylize this second criterion a bit further to ensure that it is not restricted to the decision process and that it can take into account the broader context and all the externalities related to innovations. This might be possible in the second phase of research.

Lipsey and Carlaw have also categorized the nature of the type of assistance and the nature of the target for assistance in policies geared to promote innovation. Their categorizations are as follows.

NATURE OF ASSISTANCE	NATURE OF TARGET
General	Single firms
Specific technology	Selected firms
Specific activity	All firms of an industry
Infrastructure	Subsets of firms
Macroclimate	Group of industries

One may construct a two-dimensional matrix of 25 cells corresponding to each pair of type of assistance and type of target. Not all those cells have been examined by Lipsey and Carlaw. They have surveyed only some 30 cases, and many of them very casually. A large number of the cases pertain to a specific technology or to a specific activity, but many deal with different groupings of firms.

After examining the cases and reporting on them in a sketchy way, Lipsey and Carlaw ventured a success/failure diagnosis and tried to derive some policy lessons. Roughly two thirds of the cases proved successful and one third were deemed to be failures.

Success and failure are ominous categories. Even though the authors introduce all sorts of shades of meaning (e.g., apparently successful, quasi-successful, successful at first and then failing), it is clear that, in the next stage of their research, there must be some refinement of their criteria based on the experience from their initial work.

A GENERAL WORD OF CAUTION

A WARNING MIGHT BE IN ORDER before proceeding to policy lessons. While it pertains to the Lipsey and Carlaw paper only in an oblique way, it would appear to be a major issue in the ensemble of studies trying to make sense of what we know about the innovation process. It has to do with causality.

In the sort of exploratory work that is in good currency in the innovation policy world these days, many different techniques are used, in a first stage, to sort out the information and to identify categories or prototypes in order to reduce the degree of complexity of the field. Even those who have massaged hard empirical data were forced to do so (e.g., the high- and low-knowledge industries of Lee and Has, or the prototypes of Baldwin and Johnson). The temptation is strong, in a second stage, to ascribe some causality to the principle of classification that has just been invented. This is akin to those studies of unemployment rates by regions which end up ascribing differentials in unemployment rates to the regional factor. If my memory serves me right, this is the old logical fault that my teachers used to call *ignoratio elenchi*.

It is unlikely that any of the economists who attended this conference will even come close to falling into this sort of trap. Indeed, when the problem was raised by discussants, everyone implicated quickly reassured the critics that correlation was never confused in their mind with causation. But there is a great danger that what is clear in the analyst's mind might not be equally apparent after the authors' carefully worded conclusions have been distilled and condensed into one of those famous two-page memos that are purported to be at the source of many public policy decisions. Consequently, an extraordinary amount of caution must be exercised.

POLICY LESSONS

L IPSEY AND CARLAW REFER TO POLICY OBJECTIVES and to policy tools in a very general way (in keeping with the categories of events they have examined). Moreover, they recognize openly that each policy case is plagued with much idiosyncrasy. So the policy lessons learned from the material produced in this phase of their project can only be tentative. The authors anticipate that a more complete review of policy cases, here and elsewhere, might help to reach firmer conclusions in identifying answers to the key questions posed by the evolutionary economists about the process of innovation.

- What is the relevant unit of analysis or selection (e.g., firm, technology, development block, network)?

- What are the relevant criteria and mechanisms of selection (e.g., profit, organizational fitness)?

- What process of interaction among economic agents will promote the most effective selection (e.g., competition, a mix of competition and co-operation)?

- What sort of adaptation and learning process is likely to prove most effective in promoting innovativeness?

Lipsey and Carlaw have proceeded with extreme care, and they have recognized that case studies are always, of necessity, incomplete and chatty. They also recognize that the notion of success or failure is somewhat elusive. Nowhere have they found robust patterns on which they could build robust policy lessons. Yet their natural caution or fear of academic and bureaucratic abuse in the face of adventurous conjectures may have led them to be overly conservative in exploiting this material. A discussant has more freedom. So allow me to suggest that already, from this preliminary analysis of a small number of cases, one can see some patterns emerging.

For instance, in four of the five cases where policy was directed to a specific technology, the policy failed. In three more cases, out of five directed toward a specific technology and a single firm, the policy failed. This would appear to suggest that maybe single firm and specific technology might not be the natural focus of the most effective innovation policies.

On the other hand, when the policy focus is a specific activity involving selected firms or all firms in an industry, the rate of success is surprisingly high. This may suggest that meso-level analysis and policies directed at networks of firms might be a more promising lever for innovation policy than either targeting single firms or national systems of innovation.

Indeed, this is one of the merits of this case-by-case approach that it already suggests, to one adventurous researcher at least, plausible workable answers to the four basic questions. Maybe the network is the relevant unit of analysis; maybe capacity to transform is a more relevant criterion of success than profit; maybe a mix of co-operation and competition is a more suitable mechanism than unimpeded competition; and maybe networks learn better.

Evidence from firm-level analysis (along the lines pursued by John Baldwin) suggests that it is not single-instrument policies that are likely to work but "baskets" of co-ordinated interventions. This dovetails nicely with some of the findings in the Lipsey–Carlaw paper: a "basket" of incentives is more likely to be effective if other policy instruments have ensured that the facilitating structures are such that the target group already has a capacity to work cohesively and is instituted in a way that reduces the cost of co-operation.

Finally, the conclusions of the Lipsey–Carlaw paper may lead one to believe that there is a more important source of innovation and learning in networks and clusters than in individual units or in a singularly narrow technology band. This confirms much of my own "appreciative theorizing" and the results of my limited work on economic blocks and local systems of innovation in North America and Europe.

Zoltan Acs
Department of Economics
and Finance
University of Baltimore

& John de la Mothe
Faculty of Management
University of Ottawa

& Gilles Paquet
PRIME
Faculty of Administration
University of Ottawa

9

Local Systems of Innovation: In Search of an Enabling Strategy

INTRODUCTION

IN THE INTRODUCTORY CHAPTER of Nelson's *National Innovation Systems* (1993), a central hypothesis is formulated about "a new spirit of what might be called 'techno-nationalism' … combining a strong belief that the technological capabilities of a nation's firms are a key source of their competitive prowess, with a belief that these capabilities are in a sense national, and can be built by national action" (Nelson, 1993, p. 3). While Richard Nelson and Nathan Rosenberg are careful to explain that one of the central concerns of their 15-country study was to establish "whether, and if so in what ways, the concept of a 'national' system made any sense today," they also add that *de facto* "national governments act as if it did" (Nelson, 1993, p. 5).

Our objective is to raise some questions about this hypothesis and to provide some evidence in support of the "local" systems of innovation as an alternative hypothesis likely to underpin a more effective set of public policies.

In the first section, we deal with the process of *globalization* of economic activities and its impact on the national production and governance systems. This forces a confrontation both with what John Naisbitt has called the "global paradox" and with what we have called the "dispersive revolution" (Naisbitt, 1994; de la Mothe and Paquet, 1994a). In the second section, we suggest that the *innovation process* rarely encompasses the national scene but would appear to be congruent with meso-level, regional or sectoral realities that are the genuine source of synergies and social learning. In the third section, we review the main features of *network dynamics* and the way they are stalled by the phenomenon of *centralized mindset*: a strong attachment to "centralized ways of thinking, assuming that every pattern must have a single cause, an ultimate controlling factor" (Resnick, 1994), and a tendency to bet on centralized means of problem solving that almost inevitably lead to compulsive centralization and misguided approaches. In the fourth section, we review a portion of the literature on innovation to provide some *evidence* in support of our local systems of innovation hypothesis. In the fifth section, we sketch the *new directions for policy* that flow from our argument.

THE PARADOXICAL CONSEQUENCES OF GLOBALIZATION

R EAL LIFE ECONOMIES ARE INSTITUTED PROCESSES, that is, sets of rules and conventions that vest the wealth-creation process with relative unity and stability
by harmonizing the geo-technical constraints that are imposed by the environment
with the values and plans found in decision makers (Polanyi, 1968). Modern
economies have evolved substantially over the last century. The wealth-creation
process of the late 19th century was mainly instituted as a "social armistice"
between fairly rigid constraints imposed by technology, geography and natural
resource endowments, on the one hand, and the less than perfectly co-ordinated
plans of private and public decision makers, on the other hand. As both constraints
and preferences evolved, national economies came to be instituted differently.
They evolved, often quite differently, because of the degrees of freedom afforded
them by the extent to which they were protected from the rest of the world by relatively high transportation costs, transaction costs and tariff walls.

In the recent past, the wealth-creation process has changed dramatically. It
has become increasingly dematerialized as its mainsprings ceased to be natural
resources and material production and became knowledge and information activities. Transportation costs, transaction costs and tariff walls tumbled. And, as a result
of important information economies and of growing organizational flexibility,
transnational firms have become capable of organizing production globally and
escaping, to a great extent, the constraints nation-states might wish to impose on
them. Therefore, economic activity has become less constrained by geography and
has even, in many instances, become truly "deterritorialized."

Globalization cannot be characterized as a simple process of trade liberalization. To be sure, there has been much liberalization, but firms and nations which
have become more exposed internationally have also become increasingly dependent
on intangibles such as know-how, synergies and untraded interdependencies. This
new techno-economic world has required important changes in the managerial,
strategic and political rules of the game.

First, the terms "firm," "government" and "third-sector organization" have
become rather fuzzy concepts. Often, it is no longer possible to distinguish the
inside and the outside of the complex web of networks and alliances that enmesh
them. Second, the knowledge/information fabric of the new economy has led to the
development of a large number of non-market institutions as information and
knowledge prove to be poorly handled by the market. Finally, the traditional and
narrow economic notion of competition has been replaced by the broader and more
socio-politico-economic notion of competitiveness as a benchmark for assessing the
process of wealth creation and as a guide in designing the requisite web of explicit
and organic co-operative links among all stakeholders (Paquet, 1990).

As a result, private and public organizations have become more "footloose" and,
as such, they have become more compatible with a variety of locations, technologies and organizational structures (de la Mothe and Paquet, 1994b). They have also
been potentially affected to a much greater extent by the synergies, interdependencies,

socio-cultural bonds and trust relationships that are capable of producing comparative advantages. Indeed, the central challenge of the new economy has been to find ways to create an environment in which knowledge workers do as much learning as possible – from their experience, but also from each other, from partners, clients, suppliers and so on. This means that, for learning to occur, there must be *conversations* among partners. But working conversations that create new knowledge can only emerge when there is trust and proximity. These have proved to be essential inputs (Webber, 1993).

Two very significant transformations in our modern political economies in the last decades can be attributed, to a large extent, to the challenges posed by the new socio-economy: a fragmentation/balkanization of existing national economies *and* a concurrent massive devolution in the governance system of both private and public organizations.

FRAGMENTATION/BALKANIZATION

THERE ARE MANY REASONS for balkanization to proceed as globalization sets in.

First, global competitiveness has led advanced industrial nations to specialize in the export of products in which they have technological or absolute advantages, and since those export-oriented absolute-advantage industries tend to be found in sub-national regions, this has led to the emergence of a mosaic of sub-national geographical agglomerations and regional "worlds of production" characterized by *product-based technological learning systems* resting, in important ways, on conventions rooted in the cultures of local economic actors (Storper, 1992, 1993).

Second, the pressures of globalization have put so much strain on the nation-state that sub-national regions and communities have strongly felt a need for roots and anchors in local/regional bonds of ethnicity, language and culture. This *tribalism* (to use Naisbitt's term) has been reinforced by the fact that it often proved to be the source of a robust entrepreneurial culture and, therefore, of competitive advantage in the new context (Stoffaes, 1987).

Third, the dysfunctionality of the nation-state has triggered the emergence of the genuine shared community of economic interests at the regional level, and the dynamics of collective action have led to the *rise of the region-state* when sub-national governments or loose alliances among local authorities have become active as partners of foreign investors and providers of the requisite infrastructure to leverage regional policies capable of making the region an active participant in the global economy (Ohmae, 1993; Welcome, 1994).

Fourth, as the region-state emerged, it has provided support for the sub-national development blocs through the nurturing of complementarities, interdependencies and externalities via infrastructure, networking of economic and business competence, etc. and has dynamized the transformation process at the meso-economic level (Dahmen, 1988; de la Mothe and Paquet, 1994c). This, in turn, has reinforced the separate internal dynamics and the resilience of the sub-national systems.

GLOBAL COMPETITIVENESS

GLOBAL COMPETITIVENESS HAS ALSO TRIGGERED a massive devolution in the governance systems of both public and private organizations.

First, the search for speed of adjustment, variety, flexibility and innovation generated by global competitiveness has forced corporations to adapt ever faster, and this has led them to "deconstruct" themselves into networks of quasi-autonomous units capable of taking action as they see fit in the face of local circumstances. Managers ceased to be "drivers of people" and became "drivers of learning" (Wriston, 1992). This required a shift from hierarchical structures of governance to networking structures that were conducive to innovative conversations.

Second, the same process has been witnessed in the governance of public organizations where the need to do more with less and the growing pressure for more sub-national states to co-operate actively with private organizations to ensure success on the global scene has led governments into massive privatizations or the devolution of power to lower-order public authorities (Rivlin, 1992; Osborne and Gaebler, 1992; Paquet, 1994).

Third, this has led to general praise for the flexibility and genuine adaptability of the federal system as a system of governance for both private and public organizations, and to a general celebration of bottom-up management (O'Toole and Bennis, 1992; Handy, 1992, 1994).

Fourth, in transforming the governance of economic, social and political organizations, the growing search for flexibility has not stopped at decentralization and privatization strategies. There has been a growing pressure to dissolve permanent organizations to allow a maximum open use of all the possibilities of networking. This has led to the proposal that virtual enterprises and governments might provide the ultimate flexibility (Davidow and Malone, 1992; de la Mothe and Paquet, 1994a). This form of dissolution of governance systems has not only proved to be dynamically efficient but has also led to a reinforcement of community bonds as private and public organizations ceased to be the main source of identification.

MESO-SYSTEMS OF INNOVATION

IN AN ECONOMY DYNAMIZED BY INFORMATION, KNOWLEDGE AND COMPETENCE, and consequently balkanized and decentralized, the new relevant units of analysis have to be those that serve as the basis for understanding and nurturing innovation. Focusing on either the firm or the national economy would appear to be equally misguided. Under the microscope, too much is idiosyncratic, and white noise is bound to run high. Under the macroscope, much of the innovation and restructuring going on is bound to be missed. One may argue, we think persuasively, that the most useful perspective point is the Schumpeterian/Dahmenian meso-perspective focusing on development blocks, technology districts, sub-national forums, etc. where the learning is really occurring (de la Mothe and Paquet, 1994b).

In an evolutionary model, this process of learning and discovery is only one blade of the pair of scissors. The other blade is the interactive mechanism with the context or environment through which selection occurs. Whether the unit of analysis is the technology or the firm, this interactive mechanism is fitness-driven, and search processes of the firm "both provide the source of differential fitness – firms whose R&D turn up more profitable processes of production or products will grow relative to their competitors – and also tend to bind them together as a community" (Dosi and Nelson, 1994, p. 162).

The central tenet to those interactive mechanisms is that they are fueled by dynamic increasing returns to agglomeration. In most cases, these agglomeration economies are bounded and, therefore, do not give rise to monopoly by a single region or location, but they generate increasing returns that snowball (Arthur, 1990).

We do not know as much as we should about the innovation process, the process of learning and discovery, and the process of diffusion of technical and organizational innovations. But as Nelson and Winter (1977) suggested, at the core of these processes is the notion of "selection environment" which is defined as the context that "determines how relative use of different technologies changes over time" (Nelson and Winter, 1977, p. 61). This context is shaped by market and non-market components, conventions, socio-cultural factors and by the broader institutional structure. This selection environment constitutes the relevant milieu which may be broader or narrower and may be more or less important in explaining the innovative capacity of a country and a sector/region.

The notion of milieu has been defined as "a territorial system made of integrated networks of material and immaterial resources dominated by a historically nurtured culture, a vehicle of knowledge and know-how, supported by a relational matrix based on a model of co-operation/competition between localized players [translation]"(Lecoq, 1989). Consequently, the notion of milieu connotes three sets of forces:

- the contours of a particular spatial set vested with a certain unity and tonus;

- the organizational logic of a network of interdependent actors engaged in co-operative innovative activity; and

- organizational learning based on the dialectics between *adapting actors* and the *adopting milieu* (Maillat, 1992).

While there are innovations and much learning even in the absence of a dynamic milieu, such a milieu is more likely to bring forth innovation networks. These innovation networks are hybrid forms of organization that are better adapted to conditions of technological and appropriation uncertainty than markets or hierarchies. They are more likely to kick start the innovation process (DeBresson and Amesse, 1991). At the core of the dynamic milieu and of the innovation network, are a number of intermingled dimensions (economic, historical, cognitive and normative) but they all depend, to a certain degree, on *trust and confidence* and, therefore, on a host of cultural and sociological factors that have a tendency to be found mainly in localized networks and to be more likely to emerge on a background of shared experiences, regional loyalties, etc. This is social capital in Coleman's sense, and such social and cultural capital plays a central role in both the dynamics and the capacity to learn and transform meso-systems (Coleman, 1988; Saxenian, 1994).

The innovation process depends on the features of a selection environment or milieu. First, innovation is all about continuous learning, and learning does not occur in a socio-cultural vacuum. The innovation network is more likely to blossom in a restricted localized milieu where all the socio-cultural characteristics of a dynamic milieu are likely to be found. Moreover, it is most unlikely that this sort of milieu will correspond to the national territory. Therefore, if dynamic milieux or "milieux porteurs" are identified as likely systems for stimulating innovation, they are likely to be local or regional systems of innovation.

Second, some geo-technical forces would appear to generate meso-level units where learning proceeds faster and better. As Storper argues:

> [I]n technologically dynamic production complexes ... there is a strong reason for the existence of regional clusters or agglomerations. Agglomeration appears to be a principal geographical form in which the trade-off between lock-in technological flexibility (and the search for quasi-rents), and cost minimization can be most effectively managed, because it facilitates efficient operations of a cooperative production network. Agglomeration in these cases, is not simply the result of standard localization economies (which are based on the notion of allocative efficiency in minimizing costs), but of Schumpeterian efficiencies (Storper, 1992, p. 84).

Third, the deconstruction of national economies, the dispersive revolution in governance, the rise of region-states and the growth of the new tribalism tend to provide a greater potential for dynamism at the meso level. But Storper has argued that "codes, channels of interaction, and ways of organizing and coordinating behaviors" are what make learning possible (Storper, 1992, p. 85). He feels that the confluence of issues (learning, networks, lock-in, conventions and types of knowledge) must be rooted in political-economic cultures, rules and institutions and that, in many countries, these are highly differentiated at the regional level. Therefore, a region may trigger technological learning and innovation networks in one subnational area much faster than in others. In Canada, the United States and Mexico, one may reasonably detect a mosaic of political-economic cultures, rules and conventions with differential innovative potential (Maddox and Gee, 1994). Consequently, one may say that there is a genuine "territorialization of learning" in such a Schumpeterian world.

NETWORK DYNAMICS AND CENTRALIZED MINDSET

SUB-NATIONAL AREAS HAVE PROVED to be better loci for "conversations" likely to foster fast learning. Indeed, it is argued by the defenders of the notion of local systems of innovation that such sub-national areas are a more supportive underground for the development of multi-stakeholder networks and new forms of co-operation and relational exchange. But this has not deterred those who have a strong taste for national across-the-broad interventions. The techno-nationalists emphasize the importance of the national network of institutions, acting as a system and providing the foundations and the underpinnings of the innovation system. This leads them to bet on policies designed to act on the national institutions to stimulate innovations.

The opposition between local and national systems of innovation is rooted in the contrast between two dynamics: the bottom-up dynamics of networks and the top-down dynamics built on the centralized mindset.

BOTTOM-UP NETWORK DYNAMICS

THE PARADOXICAL CONSEQUENCES OF GLOBALIZATION have been not only to generate balkanization but also to create the need for new forms of organizations. Hierarchies have limited learning abilities and markets have limited capacities to process information effectively. Networks and alliances are ways to counter these failures and to combine the benefits of being large and small at the same time.

The network is not, as is usually assumed, a mixed form of organization existing halfway on a continuum ranging from market to hierarchy. Rather, it is a generic name for a third type of arrangement built on very different integrating mechanisms: consensus/inducement-oriented organizations and institutions. This suggests that instead of the market–hierarchy dichotomy, one should bet on a partition of institutions and organizations according to three principles of integration:

- those associated with threat/coercion;
- those associated with exchange; and
- those associated with consensus and inducement-oriented systems.

This more useful way of classifying institutions has been used by Karl Polanyi [1968 (orig. 1957)], François Perroux (1960), Kenneth Boulding (1970) and more recently by Shumpei Kumon (1992).

Networks have two sets of characteristics: those derived from their dominant logic (consensus and inducement-oriented systems) and those derived from the dominant intelligence that emerges from their structure.

The consensus dominant logic does not abolish power but it does mean that power is distributed. A central and critical feature of networks is the emphasis on voluntary adherence to norms. While this *voluntary* adherence does not necessarily appear to generate constraints *per se* on the size of the organization, it is not always easy for a set of shared values to spread over massive disjointed transnational communities. Free riding, high transaction costs, problems of accountability, etc. impose extra work. So the benefits, in terms of leanness, agility and flexibility, are such that many important multinationals have chosen not to manage their affairs as a global production engine, but as a multitude of smaller quasi-independent units co-ordinated by a loose federal structure, because of the organizational diseconomies of scale in building a clan-type organization (O'Toole and Bennis, 1992; Handy, 1992).

The structural characteristics of the network, complement nicely the dominant logic for networked intelligence as embodied, for instance, in a company or an organization. The network will be distributed, decentralized, collaborative and adaptive (Kelly, 1994, p. 189). This network structure, based on reciprocity and trust, is a self-reinforcing mechanism that breeds trust and reciprocity thereby increasing the social capital and generating increasing returns. In that sense, reciprocity based on voluntary adherence generates lower costs of co-operation and stimulates more networking as social capital accumulates with trust. The experiences in Emilia-Romagna described by Putnam (1993), echo effects in Denmark or parallel developments in the Silicon Valley described by Saxenian (1994). They all point in the same direction. The site of a dense concentration of overlapping networks of solidarity generates wealth creation on a surprising scale.

Some have argued that new technologies might well generate "cyberhoods" that would be as potent as neighbourhoods and could be the "local" setting for networks of solidarity or for a cultural milieu that would likely generate much innovation. These "cyberhoods" could become truly "deterritorialized" and completely "virtual." But even network enthusiasts are not quite ready to consider the "virtual community" as anything more than a poor simulacrum of the real community and, consequently, see it as unlikely to generate the requisite degree of passion and commitment needed to fuel social capital accumulation on the appropriate scale (Rheingold, 1993).

The growth of network markets in a number of sectors where mass customization is important has generated a new form of externalities that has yielded important increasing returns, some snowballing effects and some possibilities of lock-in. This is the logic of network economies. But the network externalities and spillovers are not spreading in a frictionless world. Networking casts more of a local shadow than is usually presumed: "[S]pace becomes ever more variegated, heterogeneous and finely textured in part because the processes of spatial reorganization ... have the power to exploit relatively minute spatial differences to good effect" (Harvey, 1988). Consequently, a network does not extend boundlessly but tends to crystallize around a unifying purpose, mobilizing independent members through voluntary links, around multiple leaders in integrated levels of overlapping and superimposed webs of solidarity. This underscores the enormous importance of "regional business cultures" and explains the relative importance of the small- and medium-sized enterprise networks in generating new ideas (Lipnack and Stamps, 1994).

Not only are networks generating social capital and wealth, they have also been closely associated with a greater degree of economic "progressivity," that is, with a higher degree of innovativeness and the capacity to transform, because networks cross boundaries. Indeed, boundary-crossing networks are likely to ignite much innovativeness, because they provide an opportunity for reframing and recasting perspectives and for questioning the assumptions that have been in good currency. One might suggest a parallel between boundary crossing and migration into another world in which one's home experience serves as a useful contrast to the new realities. Much of the buoyant immigrant entrepreneurship is rooted in this dual capacity to see things differently and to network within and across boundaries. In the face of placeless power in a globalized economy, seemingly powerless places with their own communication code on a historically specific territory are fitful terrains for local collaborative networks.

TOP-DOWN CENTRALIZED MINDSET

IN THE FACE OF STRONG PRESUMPTIONS regarding the existence of meso-innovation systems, it is surprising to find that so little has been done to escape the mindset of national systems of innovation. The reason for this bias is, however, not very difficult to understand. Since the cost of thinking is not zero, humans adopt paradigms and mindsets to make their thinking routine. Techno-nationalism's appeal is of this sort.

According to Mitchel Resnick, in an era of decentralization in every domain, centralized thinking remains prevalent in our theories of knowledge, in our ways of analyzing problems and in our search for policy responses. "Politicians, managers and scientists are working with blinders on, focusing on centralized solutions even when decentralized approaches might be more appropriate, robust, or reliable" (Resnick, 1994, p. 36). As Resnick went on to explain: "the centralized mindset is not just a misconception of the scientifically naive." There is ample evidence that in science and in governance, there is a strong resistance to the idea of complexity being formed from a decentralized process. The resistance to evolutionary theory is of that ilk. It is more reassuring to presume that every pattern must have a single cause and, therefore, an ultimate controlling factor.

This explains the opposition to a bottom-up explanation when this alternative cosmology has been suggested (Science Council of Canada, 1984, 1990) even when documentary evidence showed that such an approach was not only promising but *de facto* building on already impressive accomplishments in a number of metropolitan areas (Davis, 1991). More than a decade after the suggestion by the Science Council that metropolitan technology councils might be the appropriate lever to energize local systems of innovation, the idea is still in limbo. The centralized national system of innovations continues to dominate the policy scene, and the view of a fragmented and localized set of systems of innovation that could only be nurtured from the periphery is still not in good currency (Paquet, 1992; de la Mothe and Paquet, 1994d; Paquet and Roy, 1995).

CORROBORATIVE EVIDENCE: SOME COMPARATIVE VIGNETTES

WE DRAW FROM THREE SETS of corroborative evidence. First, recent exploratory work on network economies has underlined the importance of local spillovers or externalities, but the extent to which these spillover effects are localized has not been sufficiently emphasized. Second, a body of observations and descriptive/ ethnographical and empirical studies using alternative data bases on innovative activities would appear to provide collateral evidence. Finally, the existing literature of the historical and case study variety shows that innovation systems have blossomed locally.

The "evidence" provided through these three routes supports our hypothesis in a limited and oblique way. However, *in toto*, we feel that a persuasive argument may be constructed out of these less than fully reliable parts.

NETWORK ECONOMIES

A FIRST ELEMENT OF SUPPORT has emerged in a somewhat oblique way from recent work on network economies. The economic literature on networks has rekindled interest in the role of externalities in supply after decades of neglect. At the core of this renewal is the explosion of the new information and communication technologies. These technologies are at the core of a wave of innovations generated and diffused over the last decades. They underpin the new centrality of increasing returns and economies of scale. It is to the increased centrality of communication networks that one may ascribe the new emphasis on the basic characteristics of information: interdependence, inappropriability and externality (Antonelli, 1992, p. 6).

The analysis of telecommunication networks has served as a *révélateur*. The networks represent a sector with a particularly high degree of heterogeneity of components, technical interrelatedness and complexity of technological change, and they are exemplars of a sector with much irreversibility in investment, important scale economies, increasing returns and a broad array of externalities. Indeed, in the "paradigmatic network industry the market demand schedule slopes *upward* (due to demand externalities) and the market supply schedule slopes *downward* (due to indivisibilities and supply externalities)" (David, 1992, p. 104). But the most crucial aspect of this literature is the component suggesting that "these features apply not only to the increasing number of sectors affected by the spreading of information and communication technologies, but more generally to all the processes of growth and change" (Antonelli, 1992, p. 15).

If such is the case, some interesting results are emerging in six major areas (Antonelli, 1992).

- The rate of introduction of innovations by a firm would appear to be more and more influenced by its capacity to co-operate with other firms.

- The success of a new technology depends on adoption externalities.

- Network externalities are determinant in the selection of a technology.

- Key sectors are the providers of externalities through an array of untraded interdependencies and linkages.

- Proximity is a strong necessary condition to take advantage of externalities generated by others.

- Network firms are the result of attempts by firms to internalize externalities.

A critical examination of this new world reveals that three factors will be central to the new dynamics.

- Networks represent an intermediate solution between the dynamic efficiency and innovativeness of market specialization and the static efficiency, coherence and compatibility effected by hierarchical integrated organizations.

- Selective co-operation is the new pivotal tool for economic agents to internalize externalities.

- Any change is likely to have a strong local character (Piore, 1992, p. 443; Antonelli, 1992, p. 23).

These factors may vary from sector to sector but are at the source of the various clusterings that lead to social learning and to the dynamic reinforcement of the cluster (Porter, 1990).

EMPERICAL EVIDENCE

IN A SERIES OF MONOGRAPHS AND PAPERS (Acs, 1990; Acs and Audretsch, 1990, 1992; Acs, Audretsch and Feldman, 1992, 1994a, 1994b; Acs, FitzRoy and Smith, 1994), Acs and his associates have developed new sources of data on innovative activity in the United States beyond the traditional measure using patents. They have critically analyzed new data developed by others, in an effort to provide extensive evidence of the important innovative activity of small firms and to throw some light on the important sectoral/locational/organizational factors that explain the different dynamics of innovative activity of large and small firms in different types of industries and locations. These studies have suggested that small firms are the recipients of important spillovers from knowledge generated in larger centres and in firms and universities. These external effects differ from industry to industry but depend on organizational and locational factors. These studies have provided important new evidence to help us understand the texture of local systems of innovation and the potential levers that might be used to design a new generation of public policies.

An important result generated by these studies is the detailed documentation that research and development (R&D) spillovers which are one of the sources of externalities are greatly facilitated by the "geographical coincidence" of the different partners (universities, research labs, firms) within the state. Not only does innovative activity increase as a result of high private corporate expenditures on R&D, but it increases as a result of research undertaken by universities within the area.

While it is difficult to generalize because the patterns of innovative activity vary greatly from industry to industry and because local embedding is often intermingled with global networks, it is clear from the literature that the local milieu can often be regarded as the collective entrepreneur and innovator rather than the firm. Obviously, the capacity for collective entrepreneurship depends on socio-cultural factors resulting from the history of the region as Putnam has shown for Italy. But much can be gained from the creation of a robust and decentralized system of institutional support to ensure that technical and commercial knowledge is diffused fast and as widely as possible thereby catalyzing the process of social learning (Best, 1990; Todtling, 1994; Cooke and Morgan, 1994).

Bernstein (1986) has produced important work over the last decade demonstrating the importance of R&D spillovers in Canada but, to our knowledge, there has been little done in Canada to organize, systematically, data collection on the innovative process (expenditures, output, etc.) in order to calibrate the local nature of these external effects.

There has been a bit more systematic work on the landscape of innovative activity in the United States using both traditional R&D expenditures and direct measures of innovative activity such as the number of commercially introduced innovations that have derived from a score of technology, engineering and trade journals listing

TABLE 1

INNOVATIVE OUTPUT IN LARGE AND SMALL FIRMS AND R&D INPUTS BY STATE[a]

State	Total Innovations	Large Firm Innovations	Small Firm Innovations	Industry R&D Expenditures	University Research
California	974	315	659	3,883	710.4
New York	456	180	276	1,859	371.0
New Jersey	426	162	264	1,361	70.8
Massachusetts	360	148	212	954	245.3
Pennsylvania	245	104	141	1,293	139.2
Illinois	231	100	131	894	254.9
Ohio	188	76	112	926	76.2
Connecticut	132	77	55	650	54.7
Michigan	112	61	51	1,815	103.2
Minnesota	110	64	46	399	55.7
Wisconsin	86	33	53	224	65.0
Florida	66	21	45	375	70.1
Georgia	53	20	33	78	57.8
Indiana	49	20	29	398	51.3
Colorado	42	13	29	167	77.2
Arizona	41	23	18	201	37.4
Virginia	38	19	19	207	45.9
North Carolina	38	16	22	193	64.6
Rhode Island	24	4	20	32	14.9
Oklahoma	20	12	8	93	19.9
Iowa	20	12	8	135	46.4
Kansas	15	3	12	66	26.6
Utah	11	2	9	72	32.5
Nebraska	9	1	8	9	20.4
Kentucky	9	6	3	72	17.5
Louisiana	5	0	5	65	33.4
Arkansas	5	5	0	9	12.0
Alabama	5	0	5	54	28.3
Mississippi	4	1	3	420	61.4

Note: [a]Industry R&D and university research expenditures are in millions of 1972 U.S. dollars and are taken from Jaffe (1989).

TABLE 2

NUMBER OF INNOVATIONS BY COUNTY (TOP 26 COUNTIES), 1982

No.	County	County Code	State	State Code	Innovation
1	Santa Clara	085	CA	06	386
2	Los Angeles	037	CA	06	178
3	Cook	031	IL	17	155
4	Middlesex	017	MA	25	145
5	Norfolk	021	MA	25	121
6	Orange	059	CA	06	117
7	Bergen	003	NJ	34	90
8	New York	061	NY	36	82
9	Fairfield	001	CT	09	76
10	Nassau	059	NY	36	73
11	Dallas	113	TX	48	64
12	San Diego	073	CA	06	63
13	Suffolk	103	NY	36	62
14	Cuiahoga	035	OH	39	62
15	Essex	013	NJ	34	57
16	Westchester	119	NY	36	54
17	Ramsey	123	MN	27	49
18	Montgomery	091	PA	42	45
19	Philadelphia	101	PA	42	44
20	Hennepin	053	MN	27	42
21	Morris	027	NJ	34	42
22	Alameda	001	CA	06	39
23	Middlesex	023	NJ	34	36
24	Harris	201	TX	48	35
25	Somerset	035	NJ	34	34
26	Monroe	055	NY	36	34

Source: Data from WORKMSA. Analysis by University of Baltimore.

innovations and new products. The work has shown that innovative activity is not evenly spread over the territory. R&D expenditures by industry and by universities are clustered, and they have important spatial spillovers that "territorialize" innovative activity. While small or large firms may dominate the scene, the clustering effect is quite clear in the data presented in Table 1 for individual states within the United States.

This sort of clustering activity is even more evident at the county level. Table 2 shows the number of innovations for the 26 most innovative counties in the United States. As the table clearly indicates, most of the innovations in 1982 were clustered in a few counties. For instance, five counties in California accounted for 80 percent of the innovations in that state.

None of this is robust proof that local systems of innovation exist or that public policy should be directed to the local level. We only suggest that there are undeniably important spatial spillovers and that, in an oblique way, the available data on state and county innovative activity would appear to corroborate the local systems of innovation hypothesis.

CASE STUDIES

THE DOSSIER OF CASE STUDIES showing evidence that local systems of innovation exist and have a dynamic of their own is very extensive. It ranges from commemorative and "boosterism" writings, to carefully documented cases in monographs and books, to anecdotal evidence quoted on the occasion of a paper covering a broader territory, to tentative syntheses on the basis of all the above. While it is difficult to derive precise general propositions from this variegated material, it provides a rich file documenting the ways in which local systems of innovation emerge and evolve.

There is no unanimity in this dossier. One does find strident critics and vehement apologists, but the vast majority of the case work strongly supports the existence and importance of local systems of innovation. Much can be learned from these documents about the types of policies that have had determining impacts on the success of these ventures.

To mention only a few samples of such material, one may cite Putnam's work on the civic communities of Italy (1993), Saxenian's work comparing Route 128 and the Silicon Valley (1994), the work of economic geographers such as Storper (1992, 1993) and the work of Davis (1991), Andrew, et al. (1993), and Voyer and Ryan (1994) for the Canadian scene. They all document the importance of proximity and the centrality of community, linguistic and related dimensions as the fabric of the socio-cultural underground on which sub-national systems of innovation are built. Yet it must be recognized that there has been a lag in the recognition of the bottom-up dynamics in Canada vis-à-vis what one may observe in Europe.

From these case studies, one may derive three commonalities.

1. **The way in which relationships develop between private concerns and both the community and the public actors, and the way in which "enabling agencies" foster collaboration.** Whether these agencies have materialized in formal mechanisms of governance, such as metropolitan technology councils, or have simply crystallized in the form of an ethos, the instruments of collective co-ordination based on appeals to the local values, vision and culture that reflect community solidarity are of central import (Hollingsworth, 1993).

2. **The importance of leadership.** It is "what enables the complex interinstitutional and intersectoral partnerships to develop and become operational" and it would appear that the ability of communities to shape their future depends more on social than on technological processes (Davis, 1991, p. 12).

3. **The great fragility of many local systems of innovation because they are "weakly institutionalized."** This is the sort of weakness that suggests the way in which senior governments might be of most help in getting the local communities to help themselves, i.e., in providing the enabling support to get the communities to

invent new instruments and design new policy approaches. But there is also evidence of very robust local systems of innovation (Cooke and Morgan, 1994; Saxenian, 1994).

POLICY IMPLICATIONS

THE CANADIAN LANDSCAPE is sharply differentiated from region to region. National and provincial institutions, such as research laboratories and universities and colleges, have important and differential local impacts that are very much shaped by proximity as well as by industrial, legal and cultural backgrounds. This very diversified industrial landscape requires a thorough sub-national analysis to expose the real causes and sources of innovation and competitiveness. The same point can be made about the United States with the extraordinary diversity of its regional/sectoral landscape, its various sub-cultures, its very different state strategies and its network of state universities. The same may be said of Mexico where the 32 states may not weigh equally in the innovation equation, but where a certain degree of differentiation is already obvious. A recent survey of science in Mexico has revealed that there is a much greater variety on the innovation system front in Mexico than one might gather from the superficial press coverage in the rest of North America (Maddox and Gee, 1994).

We know that much of the progress of wealth creation in the three countries can be attributed to the innovation system and is rooted in product-based technology-learning à la Storper. We also know that these innovativeness/competitiveness capabilities are based, to a great extent, on what Storper has called "conventions of identity and participation" (Storper, 1993, p. 450). This remains an unexplored corner in the new literature on economic development.

There is a strong presumption that the regional worlds of production may not have been sufficiently recognized as the source/cause of innovation and that a better use of the "conventions of identity and participation" as a lever for policy makers might pay off handsome dividends. Some have even argued that the federal policies in the post-World War II period in the United States have "displaced the role of state governments as actors in this innovation system and contributed to some weakening in the informal ties that linked many corporate and academic research institutions" (Nelson, 1993, pp. 61-62).

If this is reasonably accurate, one must look at the implications of this new centrality of networks, selective co-operation and local character in systems of innovation for the policy agenda. This would require a redefinition of the policy framework.

First, the new policy world would need to be redefined away from the old centralized scheme of goals-cum-guidance control mechanisms toward a new framework based on intelligence and innovation. This, in turn, requires that the appropriate discursive communities be identified and that *adequate forums* be generated or constructed in order for the local system to jell.

Second, there will be a need for determining the sort of *new instruments* likely to trigger effective selective co-operation, i.e., Storper's "conventions of identity and participation" necessary for a bottom-up policy to work.

Finally, if the local system of innovations is to crystallize, there must be a recognition of the need for the *cognitive and learning infrastructures* necessary at the sub-national level and the need to harmonize differently the layers of governance characterizing the policy world.

TOWARD A NETWORK POLICY

THE ROUNDTABLE CONCEPT CONSTITUTES a loose ongoing consultation process that is quite satisfactory at the national level. But nothing more than general guiding principles or, more probably, a sense of the limits or the boundaries defining what is unacceptable can be generated through the roundtable vehicle. It can also help delineate the zone of potential interventions and the least undesirable action plans likely to foster the emergence of robust bottom-up strategies.

This calls for ongoing discussions with all the meaningful stakeholders in meso-forums capable of focusing the strategic search at the middle-range level where synergies and interactions are most visible and the interventions most likely to be effective. Clusters and networks are the new units of analysis, and the most useful meso-forums are likely to be provided by the sort of metropolitan technology councils that the Science Council of Canada proposed in 1984 or through an active strategy of support for business networks.

Already, the Canadian government has put forward its National Business Networks Demonstration program built on wide information dissemination on networks and roundtables to promote the concept of network and network broker training. This will support 30 sectorally and regionally balanced networks. This concept can easily be extended to stimulating networks of innovators (Bianchi and Bellini, 1991). These interventions can take many forms – from encouraging agents to see themselves as part of networks, to the promotion of "collective agents" or service centres aimed at minimizing the costs of co-ordination and enabling greater specialization.

TOWARD CONVENTIONS OF IDENTITY AND PARTICIPATION

THESE FORA WILL NEED TO DEVELOP CONVENTIONS based on local values that might serve as pillars of the local systems of innovation. While these may vary considerably from Quebec to Saskatoon, from Route 128 to the Silicon Valley, they will provide the foundations for the local systems of innovation. Only detailed case studies of the different milieux can provide information about the nature of workable conventions and the relative valence of the different players in the sort of evolving contract likely to lead to innovativeness and progressiveness.

Government may play an important role in shaping those conventions, in an oblique way, through networking strategies and through action aimed at encouraging the creation of "promotional networks" and associations likely to provide the underpinnings for the development of relational contracting, alliances and joint ventures in related areas (Hollingsworth, 1993).

There have been a sufficient number of experiments in Canada and elsewhere to define the contours of what might be the framework for conventions capable of weaving the network together. While local intervention is essential in this bottom-up strategy, there is much that can be done at other levels to help design the sorts of "moral contract" capable of generating the requisite degree of co-operation to stimulate innovation (Acs, 1990; Davis, 1991).

TOWARD A DISTRIBUTED GOVERNANCE SYSTEM

IT WILL BE IMPORTANT FOR GOVERNMENTS to provide the necessary social overhead, capital and the techno-economic infrastructure for the requisite co-ordination to be realized. Such infrastructure is meant to be part of an enabling strategy and should be directed at the meso-level where the requisite amount of trust may be generated and the most effective alliances evolve.

But, governments cannot be simply suppliers of infrastructure. They must actively promote (jointly and transversally through negotiated arrangements to cross-jurisdictional boundaries), the integration of all the various sources of existing infrastructure (industry, academics, consortia and so on), and this must be part of a multi-staged strategy in which local clusters and industrial corridors are leveraged and facilitated (and thus integrated) by technology infrastructure (Tassey, 1992). More important, the choice of governance structure must be geared to reducing both transaction costs and transition costs from one technological situation to another through learning (Ciborra, 1992).

CONCLUSION

A PRESUMPTION, put forward very cautiously and tentatively by scholars a few years ago, suggested that the most effective way to analyze the innovation system and to intervene strategically in it was to tackle the problem at the national level. Yet, much recent work has raised serious questions about this hypothesis. Too many forces at work in the world economy would appear to suggest that, as globalization proceeds, national disintegration occurs, and sub-national components gain more importance. Consequently, focusing on sub-national units of analysis would, in all likelihood, provide better insights into the workings of the "real worlds of production" and better levers for policy interventions on the innovation front.

One might have expected that observers, researchers and policy makers would have focused more of their work and analyses on meso-innovation systems. However, this would be discounting unduly the power of the centralized mindset at work in so many sectors of politics, management and science. This mindset has maintained the dominium of the centralized machine-model of the socio-economy in place and has kept the decentralized garden model at bay. The result is a rather misguided pursuit and concatenation of ethereal national systems when there are only regional/sectoral systems.

Chasing *êtres de raison* can, however, be a most successful national sport as long as one works hard at promoting them and as long as nobody dares, whatever the body of evidence, to question the very existence of the national system.

Consequently, the literature on national systems of innovation has become a cottage industry and is in danger of evolving into a compass in the hands of federal policy makers determined to intervene centrally to catalyze the innovation systems and to make our socio-economies more innovative and more effective engines of wealth creation. The conjectures one can reasonably utter about the features of government policy to promote innovation in Canada, Mexico and the United States in the next decade would appear to point to the continuation of these centralized initiatives.

Yet the costs of such national strategies are likely to be very high if, as we surmise, what is called for is a bottom-up policy. Consequently, it may be important to call for a return to the drawing board before it is too late:

- a return to the cautious and tentative language used by Richard Nelson and to the realization that the hypothesis of national systems of innovation has not been validated yet; and

- a plea for a more serious and careful examination of the alternative hypothesis suggested by the new paradigms of economic geography and clearly spelled out in the work referred to above (Benko and Lipietz, 1992).

BIBLIOGRAPHY

Acs, Z.J. "High Technology Networks in Maryland: A Case Study." *Science and Public Policy*. 17, 5, (1990): 315-325.

Acs, Z.J. and D.B. Audretsch. *Innovation and Small Firms*. Cambridge: MIT Press, 1990.

———. *Innovation and Technological Change: The New Learning*. FS IV 92-5, WZB - Research Unit on Market Processes and Corporate Development, Berlin, 1992.

Acs, Z.J., D.B. Audretsch and M.P. Feldman. "Real Effects of Academic Research." *The American Economic Review*. 82, 1, (1992): 363-367.

———. "R&D Spillovers and Innovative Activity." *Managerial and Decision Economics*. 15, (1994a): 131-138.

———. "R&D Spillovers and Recipient Firm Size." *The Review of Economics and Statistics*. 76, (1994b): 336-340.

Acs, Z., F. Fitzroy and I. Smith. *High Technology Employment and University R&D Spillovers: Evidence from U.S. Cities*. CIBER, Occasional Paper No. 50, 1994.

Andrew, C., et al. "New Local Actors: High Technology Development and the Recomposition of Social Action." In *Production, Space, Identity*. Edited by J. Jenson, et al. Toronto: Canadian Scholars' Press, 1993, pp. 327-346.

Antonelli, C. (ed.). *The Economics of Information Networks*. Amsterdam: North Holland, 1992.

Arthur, W.B. "Silicon Valley's Locational Clusters: When Do Increasing Returns Imply Monopoly?" *Mathematical Social Sciences*. 19, (1990): 235-251.

Benko, G. and A. Lipietz. (eds.) *Les régions qui gagnent*. Paris: Presses Universitaires de France, 1992.

Bernstein, J.I. "Issues in the Determinants and Returns to R&D Capital in Canada." Mimeo, February 1986.

Best, M. *The New Competition*. Cambridge: Harvard University Press, 1990.

Bianchi, P. and N. Bellini. "Public Policies for Local Networks of Innovators." *Research Policy*. 20, 5, (1991): 487-497.

Boulding, K.E. *A Primer on Social Dynamics*. New York: Free Press, 1970.

Ciborra, C.U. "Innovation, Networks and Organizational Learning." In *The Economics of Information Networks*. Edited by C. Antonelli. Amsterdam: North Holland, 1992, pp. 91-102.

Coleman, J.S. "Social Capital and the Creation of Human Capital." *American Journal of Sociology*. 94, Supplement, (1988): 95-120.

Cooke, P. and K. Morgan. "Growth Regions Under Duress: Renewal Strategies in Baden Wurttemberg and Emilia-Romagna." In *Globalization, Institutions and Regional Development in Europe*. Edited by A. Amin and N. Thrift. Oxford: Oxford University Press, 1994, pp. 91-117.

Dahmen, E. "Development Blocks in Industrial Economics." *Scandinavian Economic History Review*. 36, (1988): 3-14.

David, P.A. "Information Network Economics." In *The Economics of Information Networks*. Edited by C. Antonelli. Amsterdam: North Holland, 1992, pp. 103-105.

Davidow, W.H. and M.S. Malone. *The Virtual Corporation*. New York: HarperCollins, 1992.

Davis, C.H. *Local Initiatives to Promote Technological Innovation in Canada: Eight Case Studies*. Ottawa: The Science Council of Canada, 1991.

Debresson, C. and F. Amesse. "Networks of Innovators: A Review and Introduction to the Issue." *Research Policy*. 20, 5, (1991): 363-379.

De la Mothe, J. and G. Paquet. "The Dispersive Revolution." *Optimum*. 25, 1, (1994a): 42-48.

————."The Technology-Trade Nexus: Liberalization, Warring Blocs, or Negotiated Access?" *Technology in Society*. 16, 1, (1994b): 97-118.

————. "The Shock of the New: A Techno-Economic Paradigm for Small Economies." In *The Entry into New Economic Communities: Swedish and Canadian Perspectives on the European Economic Community and North American Free Trade Accord*. Edited by M. Stevenson. Toronto: Swedish-Canadian Academic Foundation, 1994c, pp. 13-27.

————. "Circumstantial Evidence: A Note on Science Policy in Canada." *Science and Public Policy*. 21, 4, (1994d): 261-268.

Dose, G. and R.R. Nelson. "An Introduction to Evolutionary Theories in Economics." *Journal of Evolutionary Economics*. 4, 3, (1994): 153-172.

Handy, C. "Balancing Corporate Power: A New Federalist Paper." *Harvard Business Review*. 70, 6, (1992): 59-72.

————. *The Age of Paradox*. Boston: Harvard Business School Press, 1994.

Harvey, D. "Urban Places in the Global Village: Reflections on the Urban Condition in Late 20th Century." In *World Cities and the Future of the Metropolis*. Edited by L. Mazza. Milan: Electra, 1988.

Hollingsworth, R. "Variation Among Nations in the Logic of Manufacturing Sectors and International Competitiveness." In *Technology and the Wealth of Nations*. Edited by D. Foray and C. Freeman. London: Pinter, 1993, pp. 301-321.

Jaffe, A.B. "Real Effects of Academic Research." *American Economic Review*. 79, (1989): 957-970.

Kelly, K. *Out of Control*. Reading, MA: Addison-Wesley, 1994.

Kumon, S. "Japan as a Network Society." In *The Political Economy of Japan*. Vol. 3. Edited by S. Kumon and H. Rosovsky. Stanford: Stanford University Press, 1992, pp. 109-141.

Lecoq, B. *Réseau et système productif régional*. Dossiers de l'IRER, 23, 1989.

Lipnack, J. and J. Stamps. *The Age of the Network*. Essex Junction, VT: Omneo, 1994.

Maddox, J. and H. Gee. "Mexico's Bid to Join the World." *NATURE*. (April 28, 1994): 789-804.

Maillat, D. "Milieux et dynamique territoriale de l'innovation." *Canadian Journal of Regional Science*. XV, 2, (1992).

Naisbitt, J. *Global Paradox*. New York: William Morrow & Company, 1994.

Nelson, R.R. (ed.) *National Innovation Systems*. New York: Oxford University Press, 1993.

Nelson, R.R. and S.G. Winter. "In Search of A Useful Theory of Innovation." *Research Policy*. 6, 1, (1977): 36-76.

Ohmae, K. "The Rise of the Region State." *Foreign Affairs*. 72, (Spring 1993): 78-87.

Osborne, D. and T. Gaebler. *Reinventing Government*. New York: Addison-Wesley, 1992.

O'Toole, J. and W. Bennis. "Our Federalist Future." *California Management Review*. 34, 4, (1992): 73-90.

Paquet, G. "The Internationalization of Domestic Firms and Governments: Anamorphosis of a Palaver." *Science and Public Policy*. 17, 5, (1990): 327-332.

———. "The Strategic State." In *Finding Common Ground*. Edited by J. Chrétien. Hull: Voyageur Publishing, 1992, pp. 85-101. For a longer version see Prime Working Paper 94-16, Ottawa.

———. "Reinventing Governance." *Opinion Canada*. 2, 2, (1994): 1-5.

Paquet, G. and J. Roy. "Prosperity Through Networks: The Bottom-Up Strategy That Might Have Been." In *How Ottawa Spends 1995-96*. Edited by Susan Phillips. Ottawa: Carleton University Press, 1995, pp. 137-158.

Perroux, F. *Economie et société*. Paris: Presses Universitaires de France, 1960.

Piore, M.J. "Fragments of a Cognitive Theory of Technological Change and Organizational Structure." In *Networks and Organizations*. Edited by N. Nohria and R.G. Eccles. Boston: Harvard Business School, 1992, pp. 430-444.

Polanyi, K. "The Economy as Instituted Process." *Primitive, Archaic and Modern Economies*. New York: Anchor Books, 1968, pp. 139-174.

Porter, M.E. *The Competitive Advantage of Nations*. New York: The Free Press, 1990.

Putnam, R.D. *Making Democracy Work*. Princeton: Princeton University Press, 1993.

Resnick, M. "Changing the Centralized Mind." *Technology Review*. 97, 5, (1994): 32-40.

Rheingold, H. *The Virtual Community*. Reading, MA: Addison-Wesley, 1993.

Rivlin, A.M. *Reviving the American Dream*. Washington: The Brookings Institution, 1992.

Saxenian, A. *Regional Advantage*. Cambridge: Harvard University Press, 1994.

Science Council of Canada. *Canadian Industrial Development: Some Policy Directions*. Ottawa: Supply and Services Canada, 1994.

Science Council of Canada, et al. *Grassroots Initiatives, Global Success: Report of the 1989 National Technology Policy Roundtable*. Ottawa: Science Council of Canada, 1990.

Stoffaes, C. 1987. *Fins de mondes*. Paris: Editions Odile Jacob, 1987.

Storper, M. "The Limits of Globalization: Technology Districts and International Trade." *Economic Geography*. 68, 1, (1992): 60-93.

———. "Regional Worlds of Production: Learning and Innovation in the Technology Districts of France, Italy and the USA." *Regional Studies*. 27, 5, (1993): 433-455.

Tassey, G. *Technology Infrastructure and Competitive Position*. Norwell: Kluwer, 1992.

Todtling, F. "The Uneven Landscape of Innovation Poles: Local Embeddedness and Global Networks." In *Globalization, Institutions and Regional Development in Europe*. Edited by A. Amin and N. Thrift. Oxford: Oxford University Press, 1994, pp. 68-90.

Voyer, R. and P. Ryan. *The New Innovators*. Toronto: Lorimer, 1994.

Webber, A.M. "What's So New About the New Economy?" *Harvard Business Review*. 71, 1, (1993): 24-42.

"Welcome to Cascadia." *The Economist*. (May 21, 1994): 52.

Wriston, W.B. *The Twilight of Sovereignty*. New York: Charles Scribner's Sons, 1992.

Comment

John Burbidge
Department of Economics
McMaster University

THIS PAPER MAKES A CASE against national systems of innovation by suggesting that intermediate-level information networks are in fact much more successful at developing new technology. The authors argue for something like the metropolitan technology councils suggested by the Science Council of Canada in 1984. Their thesis is that "as globalization proceeds, national disintegration occurs, and sub-national components gain more importance" (Acs, et al.). While middle-level units may indeed foster economic growth, undue encouragement of sub-national governance systems may be quite counterproductive. Let me suggest some reasons why this may be the case.

A great deal has been written on models of competing regions. In these models, regions are endowed with land, labour and capital, and regional governments adopt tax and transfer policies that maximize some measure of well-being in each region. While there are special cases where the Nash equilibrium of these competing regions is efficient, there are more realistic settings in which interregional competition wastes resources. There are substantial gains to be had by some national authority intervening to place limits on the ways in which the regions compete. In the present context, I suspect that metropolitan technology councils would not be innocent creatures. They would inevitably play some sort of strategic game against each other (and other organizations outside Canada) that very likely would lead to an inefficient equilibrium just as, say, games of capital tax competition or tariff wars lead to inefficient equilibria. Without some sort of model of how these technology councils (or whatever organization is to be the spur to local innovation) would function, it's difficult to know what outcomes to anticipate.

The thesis that globalization necessarily leads to national disintegration seems to be contradicted by the formation of federations in Europe and in other parts of the world, e.g., Canada's participation in the North American Free Trade Agreement (NAFTA). I think of confederation and deconfederation as components of a process that might be illustrated by a pendulum. Unrestricted strategic competition between regions eventually leads to outcomes that are clearly unappealing to most citizens. Regional governments come to realize that some degree of policy co-ordination would be in their mutual interest. The process of confederation begins and, as time goes by, the centralization of power in the federation grows. Perhaps, for bureaucratic reasons or other reasons, the "national" government eventually becomes ineffective. Pressure mounts in the regions to take power back from the centre and restore it to regional governments. The process of deconfederation begins and, soon enough, the pendulum swings back toward the competing regional model. To summarize, it's not clear to me that there is any particular causal relationship between globalization and federation formation or dissolution. Since the benefits of innovation are larger, one might guess that the larger the potential market, the more "globalization" encourages the formation of a federation.

As we witness provinces and municipalities competing for high-tech firms, perhaps some of the following sorts of actions are required by the national government.

- Put limits on interprovincial and intraprovincial competition so high-tech companies or any other firms can choose to locate for reasons other than special deals with local authorities. Get rid of interprovincial and intraprovincial barriers to trade.

- Improve the quality of the education system so firms from Canada and elsewhere will be encouraged to employ well-trained Canadian workers and to locate their operations in Canada.

- Ensure that the communication and transportation infrastructures are good. It is difficult to imagine many high-tech firms locating where either the transportation or communication infrastructure is poor or even mediocre.

*Part V Canada and the Global
Telecommunications Revolution*

Lars-Hendrik Röller
Research, Competitiveness and Industrial Change
Wissenschaftszentrum, Berlin
Industrial Economics, Humboldt University, Berlin
and
Centre of Economic Policy Research, London

& Leonard Waverman
Department of Economics and
Centre for International Studies
University of Toronto
and
Centre de Recherche en Economie
et Statistique, Paris

10

The Impact of Telecommunications Infrastructure on Economic Development

INTRODUCTION

AMONG THE MOST SIGNIFICANT ISSUES that economists examine are the sources of economic growth. Romer's work (1986) began a set of theoretical and empirical analyses focusing on the endogeneity of the growth process as compared to Solow-type (1956) neoclassical growth models which use an aggregate production function approach and exogenous technical changes. Numerous papers since then have attempted to disentangle those elements of a national economy which create growth. Many have examined whether economic growth (income per capita) is converging relative to the United States and what the forces are that may lead to convergence (Barro and Sala-i-Martin, 1992; Mankiw, Romer and Weil, 1992; DeLong and Summers, 1991, 1992).

Grossman and Helpman (1994) surveyed the recent literature on the determinants of economic growth and divided these works into three types. One set considered the accumulation of "broad" capital, including human capital (Mankiw, Romer and Weil, 1992) and different types of physical capital (equipment in DeLong and Summers, 1991, 1992). A second set used spillovers or external economies (Romer, 1986; Lucas, 1988). The third set "cast industrial innovation as the engine of growth" (Grossman and Helpman, 1994, p. 24). Quah (1993a, 1993b, 1995) criticized the entire set of empirical studies which examine whether long-term growth is converging for a number of countries. Quah argued that these studies which examine a cross section of growth rates cannot shed light on the issue of convergence since the growth process is not studied. In essence, a single cross section of growth rates is consistent with any changing distribution of growth rates over time.

There is also an emerging literature on the returns to public infrastructure investments [see, for example, Munell (1992)]. The debate regarding the elasticity of infrastructure investment on growth has attracted new attention since the study by Aschauer (1989), who found a significant and large effect (elasticity of 0.39) of public infrastructure investment on growth. The Aschauer model constitutes a classical production function approach and has been criticized as not accounting for the appropriate causalities and econometric problems of non-stationariness in the data [see Hulten and Schwab (1991); Jorgensen (1991)].

In this paper we are concerned with how the telecommunications infrastructure affects economic growth. This issue is important for several reasons. Much press these days concerns the information superhighway and its proposed impacts on the economy. Globerman in this volume examines a set of issues in order to forecast what impacts these developments may have. In this paper, we turn to the last 20 years to examine the impacts of telecommunication developments, specifically, the impacts of telecom investments on aggregate economic growth. However, it must be kept in mind that the effects of the "information revolution" are much more general than its impacts on such areas as the methods of production or inventory control. We do not attempt to measure the societal changes such as the emergence of the "virtual corporation."

In suggesting that a country's telecommunications infrastructure affects economic growth, we are suggesting that telecommunication investments have spillovers and create externalities.

It is a common concept that a modern communications system is essential to development. Studies by the United Nations Economic Commission for Europe (1987), by the International Telecommunications Union (1986) and by Saunders, Warford and Wellenius (1983) for the World Bank all attest to the need to have a modern efficient telecommunications sector as part of a nation's basic infrastructure and as a precursor to economic growth.

Telecom infrastructure investment can lead to spillovers to national economic growth in several ways. Where the state of the telephone system is rudimentary, communications between firms is limited, and the transaction costs of ordering, gathering information and searching for services are high.

Wellenius (1977) argues:

> With telecommunications, some of the physical constraints on organizational communication can be removed in all sectors of the economy, permitting increased productivity through better management and administration, making it possible to adopt different structure and locations, and contributing to the evolution of increasingly complex and large organizations. Markets gain in effectiveness from telecommunications; fast responses to market signals become possible, and coverage can be extended at city, regional, national and world-wide levels. The efficiency of household operation rises as telecommunications allows improved access to goods and services. Forms of work are supported in which complete segregation of work place and residence is not desirable [Quoted in Hardy (1980), p. 237].

As the telephone system improves, the costs of doing business fall, and output increases for individual firms in individual sectors of the economy. "If the telephone does have an impact on a nation's economy, it will be through the improvement of the capabilities of managers to communicate with each other rapidly over increased distances" (Hardy, 1980, p. 279). Thus, telecom infrastructure investment and the derived services provide significant externalities; their presence allows productive units to improve their output. The importance of externalities increases as the information intensity of the production process increases. Investing in telecom infrastructure leads to growth because its products (e.g., cable and switches) lead to increases in the demand for the goods and services used in their production. This effect is common to all investments and is not the externality or spillover which is unique to a small set of infrastructure activities (e.g., telecommunications, highways, health and education). A nation's communications infrastructure is available to all firms and to all industries; it has aspects of a public good. The ability to communicate at will increases the ability of firms to engage in new productive activities.

Economics literature shows high returns to innovation and social returns that are well above private returns. The impact of improved communications infrastructure on the economy is similar to the impact of increased innovation – an improvement in the telecommunications sector is, to firms using telecom services, akin to a shift out of their production function. In addition, the social returns to telecom infrastructure investment are much greater than the returns just on the telecom investment itself. Many of the benefits of telecom investment are not appropriable to the firm or to the sector, i.e., the lowering of transaction costs, the ability to search widely or the ability to control a greater span of productive activities. Thus, telecom investments lead to spillovers – improvements in other industries.

Leff (1984) argued that telecommunications lowers the fixed and variable costs of information acquisition. An expansion of the telecommunications network generates cost-saving externalities to other markets. These externalities involve lower search costs, increased arbitrage abilities and more information on the distribution of prices and services. This all leads to lower transaction costs and more efficient operation of the telecommunication-using markets. Leff showed that firms can have more physically dispersed activities as telecommunications increases, and the X-inefficiency of production will be lower.

Telecommunications infrastructure can act as "a boost" to national productivity, leading to higher and accelerating national aggregate economic growth. In a sense, telecommunications is a form of knowledge spillover (Romer, 1990) and has public good aspects (i.e., is non-rivalrous) since all its benefits cannot be appropriated. Moreover, unlike other forms of capital, such as equipment, introduced into growth or aggregate production function models, a telecom infrastructure is clearly country-specific and its costs are sunk.

Several papers empirically examine the role a telecommunications infrastructure plays in economic growth and development. The central problem is to distinguish three effects.

- There is an increase in economic growth attributable to telecom infrastructure and service development that is not income to telecom operators (the externality effect of telecom development).

- Since telecom demand has an income elasticity, as income or gross national product (GNP) increases, more telecom services are demanded.

- It is necessary to distinguish between the impact of an enhanced telecom infrastructure and the many inputs that simultaneously improve telecommunications as well as other goods and services. Simultaneous with the enhancement of telecommunications in the last decades has been the entire electronics/computer revolution. One must be careful not to attribute any spillovers or externalities of computer investment to telecommunications.

It is difficult to distinguish between these three effects and, indeed, the few existing studies of the spillovers from investment in telecommunications infrastructure have not always attempted to make this distinction.

Generally, these studies use simple single-equation models. However, causality problems mar any single-equation model, especially one linking growth and telecom infrastructure The causation clearly works both ways and unless the endogeneity of telecommunications infrastructure investment is introduced, the measured effect on growth will be biased upward. In addition, empirical models of endogenous growth require explicit endogenous elements so the differences from Solow-type models can be observed.

Any attempt to measure the impact of a specific form of capital, such as the telecommunications infrastructure, on economic growth must also consider several problems. First, there is the issue of causality as addressed above. Second is the issue of endogeneity – the process of investment in telecommunications infrastructure is an endogenous process. There is a demand for, and supply of, this investment and this must be modelled. Third, the work of Quah (1993a,b) casts severe doubt on the ability of simple cross-sectional empirical analyses where the left side in the regression is an average growth rate over a lengthy time period. It appears to be superior methodologically to model the process of growth instead. Fourth, one must be careful to avoid spurious correlations. As we suggested above, the improvement in telecommunications technology over the last several decades is due to improvements in electronics and the entire communications revolution. It would be incorrect to attribute, to telecommunication developments, any spillovers resulting from research and development (R&D) in electronics. In addition, it is imperative to disentangle the many forces simultaneously generating growth; otherwise one will attribute to telecom, what should be attributed to other developments.

Next, we examine previous studies before turning to the available data, a set of correlations and a feasible model that could assist in sorting out the various effects.

TELECOMMUNICATIONS AND GROWTH: PREVIOUS ANALYSIS

ONE OF THE FIRST PUBLISHED STUDIES of the potential impacts of telecommunication on growth was Hardy (1980). For 15 developed and 45 developing nations for the 1960 to 1973 period, Hardy regressed gross domestic product (GDP) per capita on GDP per capita lagged one year as well as on both telephones per capita and radios lagged one year. Telephones per capita had a significant impact on GDP; the spread of radio did not. However, when the regression was attempted for developed and developing economies separately, no significant effects occurred. Hardy attributed this to the smaller sample size but it might also be due to fitting a regression across the two different populations. This likely resulted in a regression "fallacy." Hardy did not discuss the reverse causation of GDP on telecommunications demand. He also regressed, for nine countries, growth in telephones per capita with advances in knowledge, improved resource allocation and economies of scale as measured by Dennison (1974). Hardy characterized the significant positive correlation found here incorrectly. "If telephone growth between 1950 and 1955 has a significant correlation with the variables contributing to income growth between 1955 and 1962 ... then there is some evidence telephone growth *leads* [emphasis added] these variables" (Hardy, 1980, p. 284). Correlation is not causality, and the Hardy results contain both the effect of telecommunications on growth and the simultaneous effect of growth on the demand for telecommunication services.

FIGURE 1

GROWTH IN TELECOMMUNICATIONS OUTPUT AND GNP COMPARED

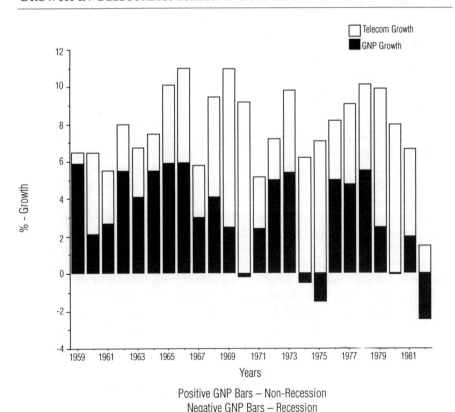

Positive GNP Bars – Non-Recession
Negative GNP Bars – Recession

FIGURE 2

ANNUAL GROWTH IN TOTAL FACTOR EFFICIENCY IN SELECTED
INDUSTRIES, 1963 TO 1982

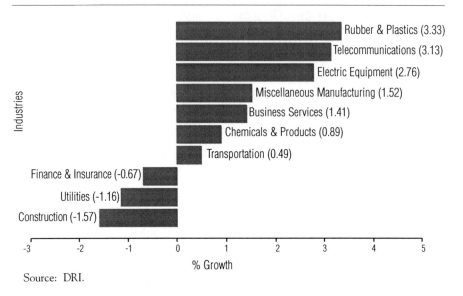

% Growth

Source: DRI.

DRI/McGraw-Hill (1991) argued that the overall efficiency gains for the
U.S. economy, since the 1960s were in part due to an improved telecom infrastructure. Figure 1 shows the growth in telecommunications output and the growth
in GNP for the United States. The correlation in the movement of the two series
is apparent. Figure 2 provides data on the high rate of growth of total factor efficiency in the telecom sector itself. Note that this efficiency, a falling price of
telecommunication services relative to other prices of goods and services, and an
income elasticity greater than one would lead to the correlation shown in Figure 1.
All this correlation may show are the impacts of the business cycle on the demand
for telecommunications. While we examine a number of significant correlations
below, we emphasize that such relationships are not causal.

The DRI study attempted to measure the positive effects of telecom in two
ways: a direct three-part estimate of the gains in efficiency of the U.S. economy
attributable to telecommunications and an indirect examination of the two-way
causality between GNP growth and telecom output.

The direct study involved determining the two-digit sectoral and economy-
wide efficiency gains attributable to increases in both the production and consumption of telecommunications services as well as their combined effects. First, for
29 two-digit industries (such as food or textiles) a production relationship was estimated econometrically. The production of food, for example, was related to the use
of capital, labour and materials as well as to telecom inputs for the 1963 to 1982

TABLE 1

SAVINGS IN TOTAL REQUIREMENTS DUE TO ENHANCEMENTS IN
TELECOMMUNICATIONS USAGE AND PRODUCTION (MILLIONS OF 1990
DOLLARS)

This table shows the total amount of labour and capital saved by the 1982 economy, at 1990 prices, as a result of improved telecommunications production and consumption. It also shows the breakdown of the total savings into the portions caused by improved production and increased consumption. The first column shows the total savings; the second shows savings realized via increased telecommunications production technology; the third shows the savings caused by increased consumption of telecommunications. A positive number for a given industry means that telecommunications caused the economy to consume less of that industry's labour and capital to produce the actual level and composition of 1982 GNP. Similarly, a negative number means that it caused the economy to use more of that industry's labour and capital to produce GNP.

	Total Savings	Savings Due to More Efficient TC Production	Savings Due to Increased TC Consumption
Wholesale and retail trade	18,026	480	17,545
Construction	9,631	766	8,865
Miscellaneous services	4,381	25	4,357
Personal services	3,938	-92	4,030
Finance and insurance	2,702	218	2,483
Electric & electronic equipment	2,498	-284	2,782
Business services	2,425	75	2,350
Real estate	1,814	63	1,751
Automotive repair	1,441	337	1,104
Transportation and warehousing	1,336	-11	1,348
Utilities	1,283	392	891
Food	589	7	582
Printing and publishing	577	-154	730
Non-electrical machinery	488	-43	531
Chemicals and products	488	-9	497
Amusements	475	-4	479
Agriculture, forestry and fisheries	395	48	347
Other transportation equipment	349	-9	358
Miscellaneous manufacturing	260	-24	284
Paper and paperboard	251	-18	269
Fabricated metals	230	24	206
Rubber & plastics	146	3	143
Instruments	116	-8	124
Tobacco	24	0	24
Leather	21	0	22
Furniture	21	0	20
Textiles	-51	-2	-49
Motor vehicles and equipment	-157	-40	-118
Non-telecommunications Subtotal	53,696	1,738	51,958
Telecommunications	27,590	44,754	-17,165[a]
ECONOMY WIDE	81,286	46,493	34,793

Note: [a] The large negative number for telecommunications indicates that the economy greatly increased its requirements of telecommunications from 1963 through 1982.

Source: DRI.

period.[1] Then, the 1982 production of food was hypothetically produced using the 1963 telecom inputs. The resulting changes in production costs were estimated. The input–output tables for 1963 and 1982 were used to estimate the change in the technology that produced the telecom services itself (e.g., less wire and more fibre-optic cable affects the production of other goods and services) and to estimate the change in inputs other than telecom from the econometric cost function for the countries. This also affects the indirect industry production profile. Combining these two effects yields a hypothetical 1982 world that uses the 1963 mix of inputs and telecommunications. Finally, comparing this hypothetical world and the actual 1982 data, the authors concluded that an extra $52 billion in expenditures on labour and capital would have been required in 1982 had the 1963 input of telecommunications with the 1982 mix of labour, capital and materials been used. The telecom sector itself used an additional $17 billion in resources in 1982 compared to 1963. Hence, DRI concluded that the U.S. economy was $35 billion "better off" due to the telecom developments which occurred over the 1963 to 1982 period. (see Table 1).[2]

As a second test, the DRI study examined the degree of causality between real investment in telecommunications[3] and real GNP since, with an income elasticity of more than one, the richer U.S. economy of 1982 would have consumed more telecom inputs than in 1963.[4] Is telecom really an engine of growth? The study examined the two-way causality between annual aggregate U.S. GNP and annual telecommunications investment over the 1955 to 1988 period. The analysis did not use a model of the two-way interaction but a statistical test of two-way causality (the Granger, Sims and modified Sims tests). The results showed "a feedback process in which telecommunication investment enhances economic activity and growth while economic activity and growth stimulate demands for telecommunications infrastructure investment" (DRI, 1991, p. F.5). The results provided no evidence of either the magnitude of the feedback or the structure of the relationship. The DRI study has been criticized for not distinguishing between telecom investment and other sources of growth, [National Telecommunications and Information Administration (NTIA) of the U.S. Government] and for its econometrics [TEKNIBANK (TB),1993]. NTIA showed that other sources of growth – R&D, in general, or industry-specific effects – could account for the efficiency effects that DRI attributed to telecommunications. TB criticized the causality analysis used by DRI.

A 1993 study by TB for the European Commission built on a 1992 U.S. study by the Economic Strategy Institute (ESI). TB attempted to estimate the incremental growth which would be caused by adapting new advanced communication infrastructures in Europe. The ESI and TB studies also used an econometric format. The TB study examined the causality between telecom investment, GDP and output per employee. TB, having criticized the particular econometric approach of DRI (the Granger and modified Sims tests), used a different approach (the Error Correction Representation). Is there a two-way causality between telecom investment on the one hand and both GNP and productivity on the other? While DRI examined aggregate U.S. data, TB examined these links for 32 industries in five countries. Their analysis did not "suggest a strong causal link between telecommunications investment and sectoral GDP or productivity" (TEKNIBANK, 1993, p. 52). However, the link TB attempted to find was, for example, between telecom investment and output growth in the food industry. Surely, this is too limited a test. As our introduction suggests, it is the national telecom infrastructure which is crucial. The impact of telecom on growth is an economy-wide phenomenon. It is the impact of a basic infrastructure investment on the ability, in general, to produce. It is the impact of telecom investments outside the food industry which generate the externality – the incremental impact that is greater than the contribution of telecom investment itself to growth. Thus, the TB analysis is unnecessarily limited by investigating the relationship between telecom and growth at the industry level. Moreover, simply examining causality, while interesting, is not in itself a sufficient analysis of this complex issue.

Norton (1992) provided the most complete analysis to date of the telecom–economy interface. Norton relied on Leff's (1984) arguments that an improvement in the telecommunications infrastructure reduced transaction costs. He estimated the following equation over the 1957 to 1977 period:

$$MDY_i = a_0 + a_1 \, YPC + a_2 \, MDPOP + a_3 \, SDY$$

$$+ \, a_4 \, SRM + a_5 \, MDEXX + a_6 \, MIDINF$$

$$+ \, a_7 \, TELPOP57 + A_8 \, AVTELPOP + a_9 \, MIX + a_{10} \, CLD \qquad (1)$$

where MDY_i is the mean annual growth rate of domestic or national product for the sample years; YPC_i is the initial year per capita income for country I in thousands of US\$ at international prices for the beginning of the period; $MDPOP_i$ refers to the mean annual population growth for country I; SDY_i is the standard deviation of real output for country I; SRM_i equals standard deviation of money supply stocks for country I; MDM_i is the mean money supply growth for country I; $MDGX_i$ is the mean growth of the ratio of government spending to output; $MDEXX_i$ equals the mean growth of exports as proportion of output; $MDINF_i$ is the mean growth in the rate of inflation; TELPOP57 refers to the stock of telephones per hundred population in 1957; AVTELPOP is the average stock of telephones between 1957 and 1977; MIX equals the mean investment to GDP ratio 1957 to 1977; and CLD is a dummy variable for a high degree of national freedom.

Data for 47 countries were used. The paper added telephone variables to an earlier study by Kormendi and Megire (1985) which examined how money supply variables affected growth.

Norton found that either telecom variable was positive and significant and concluded that "the existence of telecommunications infrastructure reduces transactions costs" since output rises "when the infrastructure is present" (Norton, 1992,

p. 184). Since the beginning period telephone stock is significant, Norton argued that the relationship "is clearly not due to reverse causality" (Norton, 1992, p. 184). "The inclusion of the telephone variable also makes the convergence hypothesis stronger (at least among richer countries), and reduced the effect on SRM (monetary instability)" (Norton, 1992, p. 188). "One interpretation is that telecommunications increase growth by reducing macroeconomic uncertainty" (Norton, 1992, p. 186).

Norton also estimated a simpler equation for 78 countries in the Summers and Heston data base for the 1970 to 1980 and 1960 to 1980 periods. Only four right-side variables are included: initial year income per capita, the standard deviation of real output, the stock of telephones per hundred population (TELPOP) and a dummy variable for centrally planned economies. Again, the coefficient on TELPOP is positive and significant. This is "consistent with the view that the stock of telecommunications lowers transaction costs and stimulates economic growth" (Norton, 1992, p. 184).

Norton then estimated the higher growth rates that Burma, Honduras, Sri Lanka and Bolivia would have had given the estimated coefficients and either Mexico's or Canada's telephone penetration rates. He found extremely high impacts and felt it was "implausible that Burma could or would have increased its investment-income rate by 55.5% and its growth rate by roughly the same amount simply by increasing its stock of telephones to a level comparable with Mexico's stock" (Norton, 1992, p. 190). Norton concluded that this occurred because there were many growth effects being captured by the telecom variables including the growth of all the industries that telecommunications encourage.[5]

The very large impact Norton ascribed to telephone penetration was likely due to a number of problems in the analysis. An endogenous model of how telephone penetration increased was not constructed. The problem of causality cannot be adequately addressed by including some past period's level of penetration rate since it is the process of increasing the penetration rate which, in an aggregate production function, will generate growth. Simultaneously, it is the increase in per capita incomes which generates an increased demand for telephones. In addition, the Norton model, while it includes many monetary variables, does not include such factors as the increase in the labour force, increased education and country R&D.

These studies provide some evidence that telecommunications investment has externality effects, but the idea that a modern telecommunications network is of value to economic growth appears inconvertible. If France still had its antiquated telephone system of 1970, where only 12 percent of households had telephone service, and where only analogue voice signals could be carried, the ability to communicate between head offices and factories, or between branches of banks, to use credit cards and automatic tellers, could not be at today's levels. The existing studies, however, do not adequately disentangle the various ways in which a specific infrastructure investment, such as telecommunications, can affect growth.

Telecommunication Investments and Growth: Data and Correlations

WE USED DATA FOR 35 COUNTRIES OVER A 20-YEAR PERIOD from 1970 to 1990. The 35 countries included 21 members of the Organization for Economic Co-operation and Development (OECD) and 14 developing or newly industrialized economics.[6] The 35 countries are listed in Table 2. Generally, data were more prevalent for the developed OECD economies than for the other economies.

The data included general economic variables and country characteristics: GDP, GDP deflator, population, CPI, gross domestic investment, gross domestic savings, government deficit (or surplus), geographic area, population density, labour force, unemployment rate and the percentage of school-age children in primary and secondary schools. Most data are from the Summers and Heston 1991 data base, a set of data commonly used to test empirically the various hypotheses of endogenous growth theory. Data were also gathered on a number of characteristics of telecom developments: main lines, residential main lines, the waiting list for main lines, national and international trunk traffic, income from telephone services, national and international telex traffic, income from telex services, the number of data terminals, circuit ends connected to automatic switching exchanges, machines equipped for direct dialling and investment in telecom. Much of these data (e.g., number of data terminals) were available for only a few years and for only a few of the countries.

TABLE 2

COUNTRIES

OECD Countries	Developing or Newly Industrialized Countries
Austria	Algeria
Australia	Argentina
Belgium	Brazil
Canada	Chile
Denmark	Costa Rica
Finland	Egypt
France	India
Germany	Indonesia
Greece	Korea
Ireland	Malaysia
Italy	Mauritius
Japan	Mexico
The Netherlands	Morocco
New Zealand	Tunisia
Norway	
Portugal	
Spain	
Sweden	
Turkey	
United Kingdom	
United States	

TABLE 3

DEVELOPMENT OF GDP PER CAPITA AND MAIN LINE PENETRATION
RATES IN OECD MEMBER COUNTRIES, 1971 TO 1990

	GDP per Capita (in US$)		CAGR (%)	Main Lines per 100 Inhabitants		CAGR (%)
	1971	1990	1971-90	1971	1990	1971-90
Australia	9,513	12,575	1.48	22.08	47.09	4.07
Austria	10,230	16,991	2.71	14.19	41.76	5.85
Belgium	10,739	16,013	2.13	14.83	39.26	5.26
Canada	10,985	16,472	2.16	31.38	57.46	3.24
Denmark	14,708	20,496	1.76	26.50	56.63	4.08
Finland	10,860	20,135	3.30	20.49	53.54	5.18
France	11,359	17,399	2.27	9.02	49.78	9.41
Germany	12,850	19,799	2.30	15.76	47.41	5.97
Greece	3,750	4,896	1.41	11.90	38.94	6.44
Iceland	11,648	19,724	2.81	28.99	51.37	3.06
Ireland	5,764	9,921	2.90	8.23	28.06	6.67
Italy	7,834	14,718	3.37	12.90	38.77	5.96
Japan	13,383	22,443	2.76	15.39	43.60	5.62
Luxembourg	11,251	18,783	2.73	25.36	48.17	3.43
The Netherlands	11,685	16,080	1.69	18.24	46.42	5.04
New Zealand	9,409	10,490	0.57	29.37	43.47	2.10
Norway	12,767	19,962	2.38	19.75	50.28	5.04
Portugal	2,689	4,378	2.60	6.68	24.13	6.99
Spain	5,390	8,713	2.56	9.52	32.35	6.65
Sweden	13,676	20,001	2.02	45.90	68.33	2.12
Switzerland	20,998	27,831	1.49	32.59	58.02	3.08
Turkey	723	1,201	2.71	1.16	12.38	13.26
United Kingdom	8,490	12,625	2.11	16.51	44.25	5.32
United States	14,719	18,656	1.26	34.06	45.34	1.52
OECD Average	11,297	16,321	1.96	20.38	42.58	3.96

Note: GDP per capita is expressed in US$ at 1987 exchange rates and prices; CAGR
stands for Compound Annual Growth Rate.

Source: OECD Communications Outlook 1993, ITU.

FIGURE 3

MAIN LINES VERSUS GDP

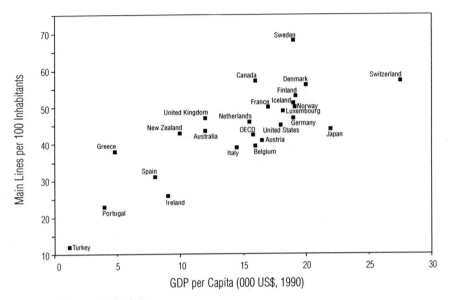

Source: OECD/DRI

In analyzing the data, we calculated broad averages and examined the simple correlations among a number of variables. We do not report the entire set of correlation coefficients but single out the most important or most interesting. As we stress, however, correlations do not show causality.

Table 3 provides estimates of the average growth rates of real GDP per capita and main lines per 100 inhabitants, over the 1971 to 1990 period. The OECD average growth rate for GDP per capita was 1.96 percent and for main lines 3.96 percent. Figure 3 shows the relationship for the OECD for one year, 1990, between main lines per 100 inhabitants and real GDP per capita. It is evident that there is a positive correlation between GDP per capita and the penetration rates, and that the growth in main lines has been double that of GDP.

Tables 4 and 5 provide a set of correlations for 10 variables for the 21 OECD countries and the 14 developing and newly industrialized countries. These correlations portray the following interesting facts, first for the OECD.

- Real GDP (GDPD) is very positively associated with the number of main lines (correlation is 0.99). However, there is less of a relationship between real GDP per capita and the number of main lines (0.42). The penetration rate (main lines per capita) is not correlated with GDP (0.19) but strongly correlated with GDP per capita (0.84).

TABLE 4

CORRELATIONS 1970 TO 1990, 21 OECD COUNTRIES (N = 257)

	GDPD	GDPDP	TELP	GERS	PEN	MAIN	ITXSD	TLF	GDID	TTID	GDD
GDPD	1.000[b]	0.405[b]	0.300[b]	0.128[a]	0.194[b]	0.991[b]	0.727[b]	0.968[b]	0.968[b]	0.855[b]	-0.833[b]
GDPDP	0.405[b]	1.000[b]	-0.134[b]	0.636[b]	0.841[b]	0.423[b]	0.310[b]	0.284[b]	0.393[b]	0.330[b]	-0.233[b]
TELP	0.300[b]	-0.134[b]	1.000[b]	-0.330[b]	-0.447[b]	0.236[b]	0.225[b]	0.275[b]	0.225[b]	0.312[b]	-0.229[b]
GERS	0.128[a]	0.636[b]	-0.330[b]	1.000[b]	0.654[b]	0.169[b]	0.039	0.032	0.146[a]	0.021	-0.029
PEN	0.194[b]	0.841[b]	-0.447[b]	0.654[b]	1.000[b]	0.248[b]	0.130[a]	0.099	0.194[b]	0.117[a]	-0.049
MAIN	0.991[b]	0.423[b]	0.236[b]	0.169[b]	0.248[b]	1.000[b]	0.743[b]	0.973[b]	0.975[b]	0.846[b]	-0.824[b]
ITXSD	0.727[b]	0.310[b]	0.225[b]	0.039	0.130[a]	0.743[b]	1.000[b]	0.760[b]	0.678[b]	0.726[b]	-0.721[b]
TLF	0.968[b]	0.284[b]	0.275[b]	0.032	0.099	0.973[b]	0.760[b]	1.000[b]	0.969[b]	0.858[b]	-0.854[b]
GDID	0.968[b]	0.393[b]	0.225[b]	0.146[a]	0.194[b]	0.975[b]	0.678[b]	0.969[b]	1.000[b]	0.838[b]	-0.813[b]
TTID	0.855[b]	0.330[b]	0.312[b]	0.021	0.117[b]	0.846[b]	0.726[b]	0.858[b]	0.838[b]	1.000[b]	-0.754[b]
GDD	-0.833[b]	-0.233[b]	-0.229[b]	-0.029	-0.049	-0.824[b]	-0.721[b]	-0.854[b]	-0.813[b]	-0.754[b]	1.000[b]

Notes: [a] Significant at the 10 percent level.
[b] Significant at the 1 percent level.

Variables: GDPD: real GDP in millions 1985 US$
TELP: real price of telephone service (1985 US$) total real service revenue per main line
GERS: percentage of school-aged children in secondary school
PEN: penetration rate, main lines per capita
MAIN: number of main lines
ITXSD: real telex revenue
TLF: total labour force multiplied by primary school enrolment ratio
GDID: real total government investments
TTID: real investment in telecom infrastructure 1985 US$
GDD: real government surplus (deficit) millions 1985 US$

The correlation between the penetration rate (main lines per capita) and GDP per capita is what needs to be explained. This correlation is two-way, endogenous and itself due to correlations between each of the two variables and other factors, (e.g., R&D).

Given the near total correlation (0.99) between the number of main lines and real GDP across the OECD, it is not surprising that regressions of GDP on main lines find substantial effects. However, the causality story is crucial since there is likely near total correlation between real GDP and meat consumption but no one would argue that increased meat consumption caused GDP.

- Real GDP (GDPD) is positively correlated with total real telecom investment. The relationship drops significantly (but is still positive) when real GDP is per capita.

The correlation of 0.33 between real GDP per capita and real telecom investment may be due to several factors. First, if telecom investment is correlated with economy-wide investment, such a correlation may indicate the initial investment/growth cycle. Second, the coefficient may be biased downward since, in most OECD countries, investment in telecommunications infrastructure is undertaken by a government-owned firm. Therefore, market signals may not be a major motivation for such investment.

- There is a positive correlation between real GDP and real telephone revenue per main line (0.3) but a negative relationship between real GDP per capita and the real telephone revenue per main line.

- There is a strong relationship between per capita real GDP and real telex income (ITXSD).

- There is a strong positive relationship between the penetration rate and the percentage of school-aged children in secondary school (0.65).

This correlation shows, in stark terms, why one must be careful in constructing explanatory models and in interpreting correlations. An increase in the penetration rate, *ceteris paribus*, is unlikely to cause the percentage of children in school to increase, nor is an increase in the percentage of school-aged children likely, *ceteris paribus*, to generate increased demand for telephones. This correlation is due to the correlations of both variables with GDP and is part of a complex process by which advanced economies are a product of increased human skills and increased capital, one of which is the stock of telephones.

- There is a negative relationship between real telephone income per main line and the percentage of school-aged children in secondary school (-0.33). Here, the correlation is likely spurious.

- There is a negative relationship between real telephone income per main line and the penetration rate (-0.45); there is a small positive relationship

TABLE 5
CORRELATIONS 1970 TO 1990, 14 DEVELOPING COUNTRIES (N = 115)

	GDPD	GDPDP	TELP	GERS	PEN	MAIN	ITXSD	TLF	GDID	TTID	GDD
GDPD	1.000[b]	-0.231[a]	0.227[a]	-0.154	-0.124	0.441[b]	0.302[b]	0.897[b]	0.932[b]	0.304[b]	-0.285[b]
GDPDP	-0.231[a]	1.000[b]	0.435[b]	0.526[b]	0.625[b]	0.372[b]	0.509[b]	-0.506[b]	-0.111	0.509[b]	-0.458[b]
TELP	0.227[a]	0.435[b]	1.000[b]	-0.080	-0.009	0.125	0.756[b]	-0.063	0.271[b]	0.729[b]	-0.541[b]
GERS	-0.154	0.526[b]	-0.080	1.000[b]	0.717[b]	0.571[b]	-0.028	-0.303[b]	-0.015	-0.022	-0.019
PEN	-0.124	0.625[b]	-0.009	0.717[b]	1.000[b]	0.785[b]	0.023	-0.274[b]	0.064	0.028	-0.036
MAIN	0.441[b]	0.372[b]	0.125	0.571[b]	0.785[b]	1.000[b]	0.229[b]	0.212[a]	0.577[b]	0.241[b]	-0.240[b]
ITXSD	0.302[b]	0.509[b]	0.756[b]	-0.028	0.023	0.229[b]	1.000[b]	-0.063	0.298[b]	0.968[b]	-0.802[b]
TLF	0.897[b]	-0.506[b]	-0.063	-0.303[b]	-0.274[b]	0.212[a]	-0.063	1.000[b]	0.770[b]	-0.065	0.053
GDID	0.932[b]	-0.111	0.271[b]	-0.015	0.064	0.577[b]	0.298[b]	0.770[b]	1.000[b]	0.287[b]	-0.254[b]
TTID	0.304[b]	0.509[b]	0.729[b]	-0.022	0.028	0.241[b]	0.968[b]	-0.065	0.287[b]	1.000[b]	-0.876[b]
GDD	-0.285[b]	-0.458[b]	-0.541[b]	-0.019	-0.036	-0.240[b]	-0.802[b]	0.053	-0.254[b]	-0.876[b]	1.000[b]

Notes: [a] Significant at the 10 percent level.
          [b] Significant at the 1 percent level.

Variables: GDPD: real GDP in millions 1985 US$
           TELP: real price of telephone service (1985 US$) total real service revenue per main line
           GERS: percentage of school-aged children in secondary school
           PEN: penetration rate, main lines per capita
           MAIN: number of main lines
           ITXSD: real telex revenue
           TLF: total labour force multiplied by primary school enrolment ratio
           GDID: real total government investments
           TTID: real investment in telecom infrastructure 1985 US$
           GDD: real government surplus (deficit) millions 1985 US$

between the absolute number of main lines and real telephone income per main line.

- The penetration rate is *not* strongly associated with GDP (but it is with GDP per capita), the size of the total labour force, investment in telephone infrastructure, the level of real telex revenue and the number of main lines.

- Real telex revenue is strongly associated with real GDP (but not so much with real GDP per capita) and a number of other variables, such as number of main lines, but this is accounted for by not adjusting for the size of the country.

- The number of main lines is strongly, but negatively, related to the size of the government deficit.

In the developing and newly industrialized countries a number of the correlations between variables for these economies are of interest as are the differences with the OECD grouping.

- Real GDP (GDPD) is much less related to the number of main lines than in OECD countries.

- The number of main lines is more related to the percentage of school-aged children in secondary school in the developing countries compared to the OECD countries, but far less related to real telecom investment.

- There is a strong negative correlation between real GDP per capita and the size of the labour force (TLF) in developing economies; in the OECD the relationship is positive.

- The strong negative relationship between real GDP and real government surplus in the OECD is absent in the developing economies.

- The telephone price (TELP) is positively associated with GDP per capita in the developing countries but negatively related in OECD countries.

- The significant negative relationship between telephone price and the penetration rate in the OECD does not hold across these developing economies.

- Real telex revenues (ITXSD) are strongly associated with telephone revenues per main line (TELP) in developing countries but not in the OECD countries.

- The strong correlation between real telex revenues and the labour force in the OECD does not hold in these 14 developing countries.

- Real investment in telecom is very highly correlated with TELP in the developing countries but not in the OECD.

- Real investment in telecom is very highly correlated with the number of main lines and the labour force in the OECD economies but not in the developing countries.

TABLE 6

CORRELATIONS, 21 OECD COUNTRIES

	Y70	Y80	Y90	GDP7-9	GDP7-8	GDP8-9	PEN70	PEN80	PEN90	PEN7-9	PEN7-8	PEN8-9
Y70	1.00^b											
Y80	0.99^b	1.00^b										
Y90	0.99^b	0.99^b	1.00^b									
GDP7-9	-0.10	-0.07	-0.04	1.00^b								
GDP7-8	-0.18	-0.15	-0.13	0.92^b	1.00^b							
GDP8-9	0.02	0.04	0.07	0.88^b	0.62^b	1.00^b						
PEN70	0.28	0.27	0.26	-0.56^b	-0.56^b	-0.44^a	1.00^b					
PEN80	0.24	0.24	0.23	-0.69^b	-0.67^b	-0.57^b	0.90^b	1.00^b				
PEN90	0.08	0.07	0.06	-0.66^b	-0.58^b	-0.62^b	0.80^b	0.95^b	1.00^b			
PEN7-9	-0.30	-0.29	-0.28	0.58^b	0.52^b	0.52^b	-0.87^b	-0.79^b	-0.70^b	1.00^b		
PEN7-8	-0.16	-0.14	-0.13	0.18	0.19	0.14	-0.74^b	-0.42^a	-0.31	0.79^b	1.00^b	
PEN8-9	-0.33	-0.32	-0.32	0.73^b	0.64^b	0.67^b	-0.69^b	-0.84^b	-0.79^b	0.85^b	0.34	1.00^b

Notes: [a] Significant at the 10 percent level.
          [b] Significant at the 1 percent level.

Variables: Y70, Y80 and Y90 are real GDP in 1970, 1980 and 1990 respectively.
            PEN70, PEN80 and PEN90 are the main line penetration rates, per 100 population, in 1970, 1980 and 1990 respectively (for telephones).
            GDP7-9, GDP7-8 and GDP8-9 are the growth rates of GDP from 1970 to 1990, from 1970 to 1980 and from 1980 to 1990 respectively.
            PEN7-9, PEN7-8 and PEN8-9 are the growth rates of the penetration rate between 1970 and 1990, 1970 and 1980, and 1980 and 1990 respectively.

TABLE 7

CORRELATIONS, 14 DEVELOPING AND NEWLY INDUSTRIALIZED COUNTRIES

	Y70	Y80	Y90	GDP7-9	GDP7-8	GDP8-9	PEN70	PEN80	PEN90	PEN7-9	PEN7-8	PEN8-9
Y70	1.00[b]											
Y80	0.98[b]	1.00[b]										
Y90	0.98[b]	0.98[b]	1.00[b]									
GDP7-9	-0.17	-0.11	0.001	1.00[b]								
GDP7-8	-0.41	-0.30	-0.30	0.81[b]	1.00[b]							
GDP8-9	0.12	0.11	0.28	0.84[b]	0.36	1.00[b]						
PEN70	-0.36	-0.36	-0.42	-0.44	-0.34	-0.38	1.00[b]					
PEN80	0.03	-0.02	-0.14	-0.58	-0.43	-0.61[a]	0.83[b]	1.00[b]				
PEN90	-0.20	-0.16	-0.10	0.49	0.26	0.54[a]	0.43	0.87[b]	1.00[b]			
PEN7-9	-0.11	0.05	0.04	0.82[b]	0.59[a]	0.75[b]	-0.02	0.002	0.84[b]	1.00[b]		
PEN7-8	0.14	0.18	0.18	0.32	0.52	-0.01	-0.06	0.45	0.47	0.78[a]	1.00[b]	
PEN7-9	-0.20	-0.16	-0.05	0.72[a]	0.46	0.84[b]	-0.48	-0.57	-0.11	0.61[a]	-0.02	1.00[b]

Notes: [a] Significant at the 10 percent level.
[b] Significant at the 1 percent level.

Variables: Y70, Y80 and Y90 are real GDP in 1970, 1980 and 1990 respectively.
PEN70, PEN80 and PEN90 are the main line penetration rates, per 100 population, in 1970, 1980 and 1990 respectively (for telephones).
GDP7-9, GDP7-8 and GDP8-9 are the growth rates of GDP from 1970 to 1990, from 1970 to 1980 and from 1980 to 1990 respectively.
PEN7-9, PEN7-8 and PEN8-9 are the growth rates of the penetration rate between 1970 and 1990, 1970 and 1980, and 1980 and 1990 respectively.

- The size of the real government surplus is negatively related to the number of main lines and total labour force and total real investment in the OECD countries; these relationships are much weaker across the developing economies.

In tables 6 and 7, we provide a second set of correlations including growth rates of several key variables: GDP and the penetration rates. For the 21 OECD economies examined, there is a (moderate) positive correlation between the penetration rate in any one year, and the GDP in that year. However, there is a highly *negative* relationship between the penetration rate in a year and the GDP growth in any 10-year period. Thus, the correlation coefficient between the penetration rate in 1970 and growth over the 1970 to 1989 period is -0.56. It is also -0.56 for the 1970 to 1979 period and -0.44 for the 1980 to 1989 period. The correlation is also highly negative between the penetration rate in any one year and the growth in the penetration rate in a 10-year period. Thus, the penetration rate in 1970 is correlated at a -0.87 level with the change in the penetration rate over the 1970 to 1979 period. Note that income in any one year, say 1970, has a low degree of correlation with income growth over the periods. There is, however, a high degree of positive correlation between the growth in the penetration rate over any period and the change in income for that period.

It is important to realize that this does not mean that a high penetration rate in 1970 *caused* negative GDP growth over the next 20 years! What this set of correlations suggests is that those countries with a more developed telephone system in 1970 were those where GDP growth rates subsequently fell. The period 1973 to 1990 has been characterized as the period of slower growth and the so-called productivity slowdown.

It is odd that across this set of countries, the correlation between the number of phones per capita and subsequent growth is negative. Note the highly positive correlation between GDP growth and the growth in the penetration rate. Again, we put little stock in these correlations as proof of any causality.

For the smaller sample of developing countries, somewhat different relationships hold. While the change in the penetration rate is associated positively with income change (except for 1980 to 1989 and 1970 to 1980), the level of GDP and the change in penetration rate have little relationship, and that relationship is not uniformly negative as it is in the OECD economies.

A POSSIBLE MODEL OF ENDOGENOUS TELECOMMUNICATION INVESTMENT AND GROWTH

EXISTING LITERATURE USES EITHER SIMPLE CORRELATIONS, simple causality tests or ad hoc regressions. Most of these studies can be dismissed as insufficiently rigorous, providing little real insight into the specific linkages between developments in the telecommunications sector and economic growth, and little evidence of the degree to which telecommunication investments provide spillovers. The Norton (1992) paper is the only one which uses an explicit model and the only one which provides a measure of the spillover effect. However, it has certain defects. The model links annual GNP growth to a set of determinants which do not include the usual "sources" of economic growth, i.e., labour and capital accumulation. Thus, the Norton model is seriously misspecified. It includes exports, the money supply and population growth (a proxy for labour), and inflation but not capital or labour. In only one regression is investment included, but here it is the investment to income rates (MIX) and in this regression, the 1957 telephone penetration rate is insignificant while the average penetration rate is significant. In examining the determinants of MIX, the penetration rate is included and is significant. However, a two-stage estimation is not used and, therefore, the model results are not necessarily correct.

There are two possible approaches to examining the two-way interaction between telecom developments and economic growth. In addition to the endogenous growth approach, there is a variant of the production function approach. Endogenous growth models examine the process by which economies accumulate capital, labour and innovation in the long run, and link this process to economic growth. Central to this approach is the desire to make the accumulation process endogenous so the long-run growth of an economy can be explained. However, empirical validations of such long-term growth models are suspect (Quah, 1993a, 1993b). The second approach begins with a production function specification for the aggregate economy (in order to account for the crucial spillovers across various sectors). In contrast to the macro-growth approach above, this method does not assume that the economy is in steady state equilibrium.

In a more structured analysis than has occurred in the past, we used a hybrid production function framework, which endogenizes telecom investment. In order to endogenize the telecom sector into the aggregate economy, a micro-model of supply and demand was specified jointly with the macro-growth equation. In this way, telecom investment is endogenized and the causal effects discussed above can be controlled.[7] Such an approach is crucial to sorting out the two-way causality between GNP and telephone demand.

We relate national *aggregate* economic activity to the stock of capital (K), the stock of human capital (HK), the level of telecommunications infrastructure represented here by the penetration rate (TELECOM) and an exogenous time trend (T). Telecommunications infrastructure is incorporated in equation (2) as the penetration rate rather than telecom investment since consumers demand main lines not telecom investment per se and a measure of telecom demand is required in order to model both the demand for and the supply of telecom itself.

GROWTH

OUR AGGREGATE GROWTH/PRODUCTION FUNCTION EQUATION is as follows:

$$GDPD_{it} = f(K_{it}, HK_{it}, TELECOM_{it}, T) \qquad (2)$$

The coefficient on TELECOM in equation (2) estimates the *one-way causal* relationship flowing from telecom developments to economic growth. In order to differentiate between the two effects, i.e., the income elasticity of telecommunications infrastructure and the impact of TELECOM on GDP, we specify three other equations which endogenize the demand and supply of telecommunications infrastructure and its investments.

DEMAND FOR TELECOMMUNICATIONS INFRASTRUCTURE

$$TELECOM_{it} = h(GDPD_{it}, TELP_{it}) \tag{3}$$

SUPPLY OF TELECOMMUNICATIONS INVESTMENT

$$TTID_{it} = g(GA_{it}, WL_{it}, GDD_{it}, TELP_{it}) \tag{4}$$

where TTID is real telecom investment; GA refers to the geographic area of the country; WL is the waiting list for a main line; and GDD is the real government deficit (or surplus).

TELECOMMUNICATIONS INVESTMENT

$$TELECOM_{it} = z(TTID_{it}) \tag{5}$$

For the OECD countries, we attempted to estimate empirically very simple models which capture the main elements of equations (2) and (4). We specified a Cobb–Douglas aggregate production function including capital, labour adjusted for schooling, the penetration rate and a time trend, along with simple demand and supply equations for telecommunications differentiating between the United States and Canada on one hand, because of their private telecom sectors, and the remainder of the OECD countries on the other hand.

While the statistical properties of the equations were good, and most coefficients were significant and had the correct sign, our results showed a number of anomalies requiring further research. The key variable is the coefficient on the penetration rate in equation (2). We used a quadratic specification to allow for either a declining impact of the penetration rate on economic growth or a "critical mass" effect, allowing the penetration rate to affect growth but only after some critical level of penetration occurred. This latter supposition suggests that, where too few individuals and firms are in the system, telecom does little to add to growth.

We did find the "critical mass" hypothesis to hold, but our initial preliminary results provided for too great an effect of the penetration rate on the economy. As Norton had done in 1992, we estimated that an increased penetration rate, by itself, would explain much actual economic growth. These preliminary results bear out the importance of a true endogenous model, since we were able to identify an income elasticity of demand in equation (3) ostensibly separate from the impact of main lines per capita on growth in equation (2). However, these initial results and the subsequent discussion showed us that more work is required to identify any spillovers from telecommunications infrastructure investments.

Thus, we are left with a few tantalizing morsels. It appears correct, on a fundamental basis that a modern telecommunications infrastructure is important to economic growth, yet it is difficult to provide estimates of the degree to which economic growth is generated by investments in telecommunications.

ENDNOTES

1   Actually, the cost function in relation to the production function is estimated.
2   Table 2 also shows that the breakdown of this $35 billion into production and consumption effects (the former reflecting improvements in telecom industry efficiency alone) is small.
3   This investment is measured as the investment in telecommunication structures estimated by the U.S. Bureau of Economic Analysis plus the non-consumer goods output of telecommunications equipment manufacturers adjusted for net imports.
4   This part of the DRI study was also published as Cronin, et al, 1991.
5   Our third form of potential bias in empirical studies of growth alluded to above.
6   Four of the OECD countries were developing or newly industrialized over part or all of the 1970 to 1990 period: Greece, Portugal, Spain and Turkey.
7   The DRI paper had such a framework on an industry-by-industry basis in the United States. DRI utilized a three-input model relating output in an industry to the capital, labour and telecom services consumed. As we stressed above, we do not find these industry-by-industry modelling efforts appealing.

ACKNOWLEDGEMENTS

THE ORIGINAL VERSION OF THIS PAPER was written for the OECD, STI/STCP. We would like to thank Dimitri Ypsalanti and Paul Wijdicks for their comments and support. Paul was able to acquire much of the data we needed for our study, for which we are deeply indebted. An earlier version was presented at a conference of the Ecole Nationale de la Statistique et de l'Administration Economique in June 1994, and we thank the participants for their comments which have greatly assisted this revision. We are presently refining the model we present in this paper to take into account the comments of a number of academics, principally David Aschauer, our discussant and John Helliwell the rapporteur for the conference this volume is based on.

BIBLIOGRAPHY

Aschauer, David Alan. "Is Public Expenditure Productive." *Journal of Monetary Economics.* (March 1989).

Barro, Robert J. and Xavier Sala-i-Martin. "Convergence." *Journal of Political Economy.* Vol. 120, No. 21, (1992).

Cronin, Francis J., Edwin B. Parker, Elizabeth K. Colleran and Mark A. Gold. "Telecommunications Infrastructure and Economic Growth." *Telecommunications Policy.* (December 1991).

DeLong, J. Bradford and Lawrence H. Summers. "Equipment Investments and Economic Growth." *Quarterly Journal of Economics.* (May 1991).

Denison, E. *Why Growth Rates Differ: Postwar Experience in Nine Western Countries.* Washington: Brookings Institution, 1974.

DRI/McGraw-Hill. *The Contribution of Telecommunications Infrastructure to Aggregate and Sectoral Efficiency.* 1991.

Economic Strategy Institute. *The Impact of Broadband Communications in the US Economy and on Competitiveness.* 1992.

Greenstein S. and Pablo T. Spiller. "Modern Telecommunication Infrastructure and Economic Activity: An Empirical Investigation." Working paper, 1995.

Grossman, Gene M. and Elhan Helpman. "Endogenous Innovation in the Theory of Growth." *Journal of Economic Perspectives.* (Winter 1994).

Hardy, A.P. "The Role of the Telephone in Economic Development." *Telecommunications Policy.* (December 1980): 278-286.

Hulten, Charles and Robert M. Schwab. "Is There Too Little Public Capital? Infrastructure and Economic Growth." Paper presented at the AEI Conference, February 1991.

International Telecommunications Union. *Information, Telecommunications and Development.* Geneva: 1986.

Jorgensen, Dale W. "Fragile Statistical Foundations: The Macroeconomics of Public Infrastructure Investment." Paper presented at the AEI Conference, February 1991.

Karlsson, Yan. "Telecommunications: The Dynamics of Economic Growth." 1992.

Kormendi, R.C. and P.C. Meguire. "Macroeconomic Determinants of Growth." *Journal of Monetary Economics.* (1985): 141, 163.

Leff, V.H. "Externalities, Information Costs and Social Benefit-Cost Analysis for Economic Development: An Example from Telecommunications." *Economic Development and Cultural Change.* (1984): 255-276.

Lucas, Robert E., Jr. "On the Mechanics of Economic Development." *Journal of Monetary Economics.* 22:1 (July 1988).

Mankiw, N.G., D. Romer and D. Weil. "A Contribution to the Empirics of Economic Growth." *Quarterly Journal of Economics.* (May 1992).

Munell, Alicia H. "Infrastructure Investment and Economic Growth." *Journal of Economic Perspectives.* (Fall 1992).

Norton, S.W. "Transaction Costs, Telecommunications, and the Microeconomics of Macroeconomic Growth." *Economic Development and Cultural Change.* (1992): 175-196.

Pack, Howard. "Endogenous Growth Theory: Intellectual Appeal and Empirical Shortcomings." *Journal of Economic Perspectives.* (Winter 1994).

Quah, Danny. "Galton's Fallacy and Tests of the Convergence Hypothesis." *Scandinavian Journal of Economics.* 95(4), (1993a): 429-443.

———. "Empirical Cross-Section Dynamics in Economic Growth." *European Economics Review.* 37 (1993b): 289-297.

Röller, Lars-Hendrik and Leonard Waverman. "The Impact of Telecommunication Infrastructure and Economic Growth." WZB working paper. (forthcoming, 1995).

Romer, Paul M. "Increasing Returns and Long-Run Growth." *Journal of Political Economy.* 94:5, (October 1986): 1002-1037.

———. "Endogenous Technological Change." *Journal of Political Economy.* 98, (1990): 71-102.

———. "The Origins of Endogenous Growth." *Journal of Economic Perspectives.* (Winter 1994).

Saunders, R.J., J.J. Warford and B. Wellenius. *Telecommunications and Economic Development*. World Bank. Baltimore: Johns Hopkins University Press, 1983.

Solow, Robert. "Technical Change and the Aggregate Production Function." *Review of Economics and Statistics*, 39, (August 1957): 312-320.

———. "Perspectives on Growth Theory." *Journal of Economic Perspectives*. (Winter 1994).

Summers, R. and A. Heston. "Improved International Comparisons of Real Product and Its Composition: 1950-1980." *Review of Income and Wealth*. (June 30, 1984):207-262.

———. "The Penn World Table (Mark 5): An Expanded Set of International Comparisons, 1950-1988." *Quarterly Journal of Economics*. 106, No. 2. (1991): 327-368.

TEKNIBANK. Study for the European Commission. 1993.

United Nations Economic Commission for Europe. *The Telecommunication Industry: Growth and Structural Change*. New York, 1987.

Wellenius, B. "Telecommunications in Developing Countries." *Telecommunications Policy*. Vol. 1, No. 4, (1977): 289-297.

Comment

David Alan Aschauer
Bates College
Lewiston, Maine

RÖLLER AND WAVERMAN HAVE WRITTEN A USEFUL, INSIGHTFUL PAPER on telecommunications infrastructure and its potential impact on economic growth and development. I am tempted to entitle my comments "déjà vu all over again" since this topic is quite close to that which has guided my own research over the last decade – that of the effect of physical infrastructure on productivity and economic performance [see for instance, Aschauer (1994)].

Röller and Waverman's paper consists of three substantive sections. First, the authors review previous studies linking telecommunications investment and economic development. Second, they analyze simple correlations between telecommunications investment and aggregate output for 21 Organization for Economic Co-operation and Development (OECD) countries and 14 developing countries from 1970 to 1990. Third, in response to their declared need for improved empirical modelling strategies, the authors sketch the beginnings of a more structured analysis in order to provide a tighter connection with growth models and the endogenous growth literature.

The model the authors sketch consists of the following four equations. First, the level of real output, GDPD, is related to capital, K, human capital, HK, the level of telecommunications capital, TELECOM, and an exogenous time trend, T, as in

$$GDPD = f(K, HK, TELECOM, T) \tag{1}$$

where $f(.)$ is termed an aggregate growth/production function. As a key concern is to disentangle the effects of telecommunications capacity on economic growth from the effects of income on telecommunications investment, the authors attempt to endogenize the demand for and supply of telecommunications capacity and investment therein:

$$TELECOM = h(GDPD, TELP) \tag{2}$$

$$TTID = g(GA, WL, GDD, TELP) \tag{3}$$

$$TELECOM = z(TTID) \tag{4}$$

The demand for telecommunications capacity in equation (2) is a function of income and telephone revenue per main line, TELP, as a measure of the telephone service price. The level of investment in telecommunications, TTID in equation (3), is a function of geographic area, GA, the waiting list for telephones, WL, the size of the government deficit, GDD, and telephone revenue. Finally, the stock of telecommunications capacity is related to flow investment in equation (4).

My specific comments relate to the ability of this model to achieve the authors' goal to link telecommunications capacity to economic growth. My first point is that it is a substantial conceptual leap from estimates of the relationship between telecommunications infrastructure capital and output – as in equation (1) – to valid statements about the growth effects of telecommunications infrastructure investment. Specifically, a positive, statistically significant estimate of the output elasticity of telecommunications capital is neither necessary nor sufficient for significant effects of telecommunications investment on long-run economic growth.

First, telecommunications investment may have only transitory effects on economic growth – with no long run or permanent effects – if the economy is best modelled in a neoclassical fashion. The opinion was offered at the conference this volume is based on that, from a policy perspective, the distinction between endogenous and neoclassical growth may not be too important. But if we are really interested in isolating the conceptual, theoretical link between telecom investments and long-run growth, then it is essential to determine if we are estimating relationships in an economy best described in an endogenous or neoclassical growth fashion.

Following this line of reasoning, it would be helpful if Röller and Waverman would develop a model linking telecommunications investment to *economic growth* rather than to the *level of output* and, within that model structure, try to nest hypotheses in terms of endogenous or neoclassical growth. Indeed, there is a related literature which has been fairly successful in accomplishing a similar task.

Kocherlakota and Yi (1992) found permanent effects of infrastructure investment and education expenditures (or human capital investment) on economic growth, a result consistent with an endogenous growth framework. Flores de Frutos and Pereira (1993) also found permanent effects of infrastructure investment on economic growth within a vector, autoregressive, moving-average, modelling structure.

Second, the authors are careful to endogenize the level of telecommunications capacity but fail to control for the possible, indeed likely, endogeneity of private tangible and intangible capital. It is of critical importance to determine the extent to which an increase in telecommunications investment will crowd out investment in other types of physical and intellectual capital. For instance, if an increase in telecommunications capital is matched by an equal-sized decrease in other forms of capital, the effect of the telecommunications investment is likely to be rather small. So, while I applaud the authors for their concern for the endogeneity of telecommunications capital, I urge them to go further than they have in the sketch of their model.

Next, there is a question of the optimality of the stock of publicly supplied telecommunications capital. It is simply not enough that the output elasticity of telecommunications capital is positive in equation (1). Rather, arguing along the lines of Barro (1990) within an endogenous growth framework, an increase in telecommunications capacity will raise economic growth only if the return to telecommunications capital exceeds the after-tax return to private capital. This, would indicate that the output elasticity of telecommunications capital need not be positive, but *sufficiently* positive.

Finally, it is important to take into account possible spillover effects of telecommunications capacity across geographical boundaries. It may well be the case that the marginal product of telecommunications capital within a country is rather small (e.g., less than the estimated net of tax marginal product of private capital) and yet the regional (or even worldwide) marginal product of telecommunications infrastructure is quite high. Indeed, using the Heston and Summers data set, Chua (1993) estimated that the spillover effects of private capital account for as much as 15 percent of growth in neighbouring countries.

In summary, Röller and Waverman's work represents an important first look at the data and a solid first step in understanding the effect of telecommunications on economic performance. With some additional modelling structure, I believe there is much to be learned in this area of research, and I look forward to meaningful results as they travel along this path.

BIBLIOGRAPHY

Aschauer, David A. "Public Capital, Productivity, and Macroeconomic Performance: A Literature Review." In *Infrastructure in the 21st Century Economy*. Federal Infrastructure Strategy Program, 1994.

Barro, Robert J. "Government Spending in a Simple Model of Endogenous Growth." *Journal of Political Economy*. 23 (1990): S103-125.

Chua, Hak B. "Regional Spillovers and Economic Growth." Mimeograph, Harvard University, 1993.

Flores de Frutos, Rafael and Alfredo M. Pereira. "Public Capital and Aggregate Growth in the United States: Is Public Capital Productive?" Discussion Paper 93-31, University of California-San Diego, 1993.

Kocherlakota, Narayana R. and Kei-Mu Yi. "The Long Run Effects of Government Policy on Growth Rates in the United States." Mimeograph, University of Iowa, 1992.

Jeffrey I. Bernstein
Department of Economics
Carleton University
and National Bureau of Economic Research, Cambridge, MA

11

The Canadian Communication Equipment Industry as a Source of R&D Spillovers and Productivity Growth

INTRODUCTION

GROWTH IN THE FACTORS OF PRODUCTION AND PRODUCTIVITY are the two sources of output growth in an economy. Productivity growth generally arises from technological change, scale economies and other sources of production efficiency gains over time. Indeed, these are the gains that lead to improvements in a society's standard of living.

Advances in the state of knowledge through technological change are primarily what determine productivity growth over long periods, and research and development (R&D) investment directly contributes to knowledge accumulation. Investment in R&D activities generates new products and production processes, and thereby productivity improvements. A distinctive feature of R&D investment is that the benefits from these activities spill over to other firms and organizations. Thus, productivity growth of an industry depends on its own R&D activities, as well as on the R&D efforts of other knowledge-generating producers. This fact implies that joint cumulative R&D investment influences knowledge accumulation and, consequently, productivity growth.

The significance of R&D spillovers in generating productivity growth has created an interest in the sources of such spillovers. In fact, it has been observed that high-tech industries exhibit relatively high rates of productivity growth and are important sources of R&D spillovers.[1] Consequently, it is important to understand how knowledge-based industries generate productivity gains throughout the economy and to determine the social rates of return to their R&D capital.

Firms operating in the Canadian communication and other electronic equipment industries [Standard Industrial Classification (SIC) 335] are centres of knowledge-based activities.[2] Northern Telecom, Mitel and Newbridge Networks are highly involved in providing products that emanate from intensive R&D efforts. Therefore, this industry provides an excellent scenario for considering the general role of R&D investment as a source of spillovers.

This paper considers the Canadian manufacturing sector as a user or receiver of R&D spillovers from the Canadian communication equipment industry. Production in manufacturing is carried out using four factors of production and two technology indicators. The four production inputs are labour, intermediate inputs, and physical and R&D capital. One technology indicator is the spillover from the U.S. manufacturing sector. Bernstein (1995) has shown that international spillovers from the United States to Canada are important sources of productivity gains. The second technology indicator is the R&D spillover from the Canadian communication equipment industry.

In our framework, cost per unit of output and factor intensities (i.e., input–output ratios) are simultaneously determined and are functions of factor prices, output quantities and the two spillover variables. Thus, in the model there are two types of R&D capital. The first type is the sector's own R&D capital. It is a factor of production and thereby generates output growth. The second type is the R&D capital from the spillover sources: U.S. manufacturing and the Canadian communication equipment industry. R&D spillovers affect factor intensities and productivity growth for Canadian manufacturing and, consequently, for manufacturing output growth.

Three major issues are addressed in this paper. The first is to determine the effects of R&D spillovers from the communication equipment industry and U.S. manufacturing on the average cost of production, labour, intermediate inputs, and physical and R&D capital intensities for the Canadian manufacturing sector (this sector is to be understood as net of the communication equipment industry).

The second issue relates to the contribution of R&D spillovers to productivity growth. Productivity growth for Canadian manufacturing is measured and decomposed so we can determine the sources of growth and, especially, the contribution of spillovers from the communication equipment industry and the U.S. manufacturing sector. These issues consider the effects of R&D spillovers from the viewpoint of the spillover user or receiver.

The third issue relates to the source of spillovers and pertains to the estimation of the private and social rates of return to the R&D capital of the communication equipment industry. Private rates of return measure the benefits that accrue to the performers of R&D activities, while social returns measure the benefits that accrue to the users of the investment. In most forms of investment, such as plant and equipment, the same firm undertakes and uses the investment. However, in the case of R&D investment, there are externalities or spillovers. Individuals or groups in society can use R&D investment that they have not undertaken. Spillovers are the source of the difference between social and private returns. The existence of these spillovers provides the necessary, but not sufficient, conditions for government action in stimulating R&D activities. In general, there is under investment in R&D when social returns exceed private returns. This deficiency can be overcome through private and public sector actions.

This paper is organized into sections. The next section contains a general discussion of productivity growth and R&D capital. It is followed by a description of the effects of R&D spillovers on average cost and factor intensities or, in other words, an estimation of spillover elasticities. This is followed by a discussion on the measurement and decomposition of productivity growth, and the private and social rates of return. The concluding section addresses policy issues.

OUTPUT, R&D CAPITAL AND PRODUCTIVITY GROWTH

IN THIS SECTION, we develop a simple framework that shows the role of R&D capital as a factor of production and as a spillover source in determining output and productivity growth. The simplest way to understand the mechanism is to consider an output determination and productivity growth in the absence of R&D spillovers.

In most empirical research, output is produced by means of three inputs: labour, capital and intermediate inputs (sometimes referred to as materials), and an indicator of technology which is usually measured as a time trend.[3] Thus, production can be represented as:

$$Y = F(L,M,K,t) \tag{1}$$

where the quantities of output, labour, intermediate inputs and capital are denoted by Y, L, M and K; t is the time trend; and F represents the production function.

To develop a measure of productivity growth, the production function can be written in terms of growth rates:

$$y - (\alpha l + \beta m + \gamma k) = (\rho_y - 1)(\alpha l + \beta m + \gamma k) + \Phi_t \tag{2}$$

where lower case letters represent growth rates in output and inputs; α, β and γ are the output elasticities with respect to the three factors of production; ρ_y is the degree of returns to scale; and Φ_t is the rate of technological change. The left side of equation (2) represents the rate of total factor productivity (TFP) growth, i.e., output growth net of input growth. The right side of the equation shows that TFP growth can be decomposed into a scale term and a technological change term.

If there are constant returns to scale, then $\rho_y = 1$ and TFP growth represents technological change. If $\Phi_t = 0$, then there is no technological change, and TFP growth represents deviations from constant returns to scale. It is important to note that the degree of returns to scale, and the rate of technological change are not generally constant. These variables depend on the same elements that determine input demands such as factor prices and technology indicators.

Next, consider the role of R&D capital and spillovers. The production function becomes:

$$Y = F(L,M,K,R,t,S) \tag{3}$$

where R and S denote R&D capital and R&D spillovers. From the viewpoint of the representative producer whose production process is specified by equation (3), the R&D capital of this producer is a factor of production. Thus, decisions regarding its use and rate of change are governed by the same decision calculus as other inputs. However, unlike other inputs, there are spillovers associated with R&D capital. It is beyond the scope of this paper to enter into a detailed discussion of the measurement issues associated with R&D spillovers [see Bernstein (1991), Griliches (1991) and Nadiri (1993)]. R&D spillovers used by the representative producer arise from the accumulated R&D investment of other producers. Spillovers consist of R&D capital stocks that are endogenously determined through the production decisions of spillover sources or senders. However, spillovers are exogenous variables from the viewpoint of the spillover user or receiver.

Now, if the extended production function is converted into a growth equation by subtracting, from output growth, the same set of inputs (as in the case in which R&D and spillovers are absent), the growth equation becomes:

$$y - (\alpha l + \beta m + \gamma k) = (\rho_y - 1)(\alpha l + \beta m + \gamma k) + \Phi_t + \mu r + \psi s \qquad (4)$$

where r and s are the growth rates of R&D capital and the spillover variable; and μ and ψ are the elasticities of output with respect to R&D capital and spillover. Therefore, TFP growth is decomposed into scale and technological change terms, but the latter contains three elements due to the time trend, R&D capital and the spillover.[4]

If we consider the growth equation in the two cases [i.e., equations (4) and (2), with and without R&D capital], TFP growth appears to be defined in the same way. However, measured rates of TFP growth actually differ. In the TFP growth framework that does not explicitly account for R&D [equation (2)], the costs associated with R&D are, in fact, embedded in the costs of the traditional factors of production. For example, the labour input includes scientists and engineers, while the capital input includes laboratories and machinery used in the development of new products and processes. Next, when R&D is explicitly considered in the production framework [equation (4)], the costs associated with the components of R&D are subtracted out of the relevant traditional inputs in order to avoid double counting.[5] We then find ourselves with a problem: measured TFP growth rates differ in the two cases. The first measure implicitly contains R&D cost in the inputs, and this cost is netted out from output growth to arrive at TFP growth. The second measure does not contain R&D cost in the inputs. With a positive R&D elasticity of output and growth rate for R&D capital ($\mu > 0$, $r > 0$), the second measure of TFP growth always exceeds the first.

Another problem with equation (4) occurs because a producer's own R&D capital is treated differently from other factors of production in the equation. This mistakenly gives the impression that the decision calculus regarding R&D capital differs from other factors of production. In fact, the demand for R&D capital depends on its own factor price as well as on the prices of labour, intermediate inputs, physical capital and the quantity of R&D spillovers [see Bernstein (1991) and Nadiri (1993)]. Thus, although R&D capital generates spillovers to other producers, the demand for R&D capital by a producer depends on the same set of variables that governs the demands for other factors of production.[6]

To preserve the consistency of measured TFP growth rates in the cases when R&D costs are either implicitly or explicitly considered, we can include R&D capital as part of the set of inputs whose growth rates are subtracted from output growth. Now the growth equation becomes:

$$y - (\alpha l + \beta m + \gamma k + \mu r) = (\rho_y - 1)(\alpha l + \beta m + \gamma k + \mu r) + \Phi_t + \psi s \qquad (5)$$

TFP growth is denoted by the left side of the equation, which is compatible with TFP growth when R&D capital is embedded in the other factors of production, i.e., equation (2). TFP growth is still decomposed into a scale term and a technology term. However, scale is now defined over all inputs, including R&D capital, while the technology term contains only two components: the time trend and the spillover variable.[7]

We now have a different view of the role of R&D capital. It generates output growth like other factors of production. In addition, R&D spillovers affect productivity growth. Thus, R&D capital accumulation of a producer causes its own output to grow and, through spillovers, influences the productivity growth of other producers and thereby their output growth rates.[8] This is the view adopted in this paper.

SPILLOVER ELASTICITIES

THIS SECTION INVESTIGATES a particular high-tech industry (communication equipment) as a source of R&D spillover to the Canadian manufacturing sector. Naturally, because communication equipment is considered a spillover source, this three-digit SIC industry is netted out of the manufacturing sector.

The Canadian communication equipment industry is heavily involved in R&D activities. We can observe this by comparing the ratio of R&D expenditure to revenue (or sales) in communication equipment to the ratios found in Canadian and U.S. manufacturing. This ratio is referred to as the R&D propensity, since it measures the average propensity to spend on R&D activities in relation to the income of a producer. We also compare the ratios of R&D capital stock to output for communication equipment and for Canadian and U.S. manufacturing.[9]

Figure 1 shows the R&D propensity for the Canadian communication equipment industry and for the Canadian and U.S. manufacturing sectors. The R&D propensity in communication equipment is substantially higher than for the manufacturing sectors in both Canada and the United States. In addition, U.S. manufacturing has a higher spending propensity than in Canada. It is interesting to note that, although there was a dip in the R&D to sales ratio in 1974 (the time when productivity growth slowed in North America) for communication equipment [see Griliches (1994)], the R&D propensity recovered, at least partially, within two years.

FIGURE 1

R&D PROPENSITY

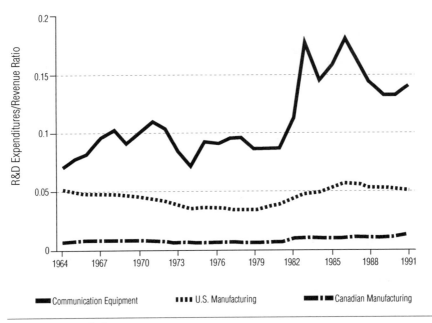

Source: Author's calculations.

Figure 2 shows the R&D intensity for communication equipment and for Canadian and U.S. manufacturing sectors. This ratio is more meaningful with respect to an analysis of productivity and output growth than is the R&D propensity. Knowledge does not depreciate in a single period. One should look at the stock of existing R&D capital, and not just current expenditures, since it is accumulated and undepreciated R&D capital that affects output. Moreover, since output and R&D capital prices do not change at the same rate, ratios denominated in current dollars convolve the underlying trend in R&D intensity with price changes.

Figure 2 shows that the R&D intensity for Canadian communication equipment was higher and grew faster than the R&D intensities for the Canadian and U.S. manufacturing sectors. Although R&D intensity for communication equipment fell over the periods of general decline in productivity growth (1971 to 1974 and 1978 to 1981), in each case, R&D intensity recovered within a couple of years. The R&D intensity for Canadian manufacturing was lower than the intensity for U.S. manufacturing. However, the Canadian intensity was constant over the 28-year period, while the U.S. intensity fell from 1964 until 1988, at which point it began to increase.

Enormous measurement problems must be faced in the construction of R&D capital. R&D expenditures must be deflated by some price index. These deflated R&D expenditures must then be accumulated and depreciated at some rate. Therefore, we need R&D capital price indexes and depreciation rates. Unfortunately, these data are not produced by government agencies or departments.[10] In constructing R&D capital, we assumed a 10 percent depreciation rate. [Recent work by Nadiri and Prucha (1993) has estimated rates that are close to 10 percent.] In addition, for Canadian R&D price indexes we used Bernstein (1992) for the period 1964 to 1987. We extrapolated from 1988 to 1991 using the percentage change in the gross domestic product deflator. The U.S. R&D price index was obtained from Jankowski (1993) for the period from 1969 to 1988, and we extrapolated back to 1964 and forward to 1991 using the percentage change in the U.S. gross domestic product deflator.

The model used to analyze spillover effects is presented in the appendix to this paper.[11] In the model, manufacturing output is produced by four factors of production: labour, intermediate inputs, physical and R&D capital. There are also two sources of technological change: R&D spillovers from communication equipment

FIGURE 2

R&D INTENSITY

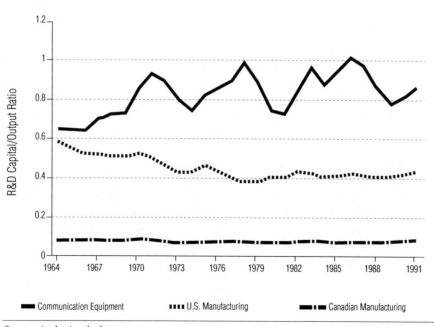

Source: Author's calculations.

and from the U.S. manufacturing sector. Bernstein (1995) has shown that there are significant international spillovers between Canadian and U.S. two-digit manufacturing industries. These results imply that international trade, foreign direct investment and the migration of scientists and engineers are important channels of knowledge transmission. This is especially true of Canadian industries, where spillovers from the United States can generate important structural changes in Canadian production. In light of these results, we include R&D spillovers from U.S. manufacturing to Canadian manufacturing.

It is beyond the scope of this paper to enter into a detailed discussion of alternative ways to measure R&D spillovers [see Bernstein (1991), Griliches (1991) and Nadiri (1993)]. In this paper, R&D spillovers are measured by one-period lagged R&D capital stocks. Since R&D does not depreciate in a single year, R&D expenditures (or deflated R&D expenditures) would not be the appropriate variable to use in a time series context for R&D spillovers. R&D capital is a source of externalities. The benefits from R&D investment cannot be completely appropriated in the present or in the near future and, therefore, spillovers occur. These spillovers have an intertemporal dimension. This means that R&D investment undertaken in the present period provides a source of spillovers in future periods for as long as the R&D capital arising from this investment has not fully depreciated.

In the manufacturing sector, production is assumed to be carried out according to the minimization of production costs. This means that a cost function contains all the available information about production in the sector. We are interested in determining the effects of spillovers on input–output ratios or factor intensities so, for estimation purposes, we specified a function representing variable cost per unit of output or average variable cost. This function represents the costs of labour and intermediate inputs per unit of output and depends on non-capital input prices, output quantity, physical and R&D capital intensities, and R&D spillovers. From the average variable cost function, we obtained factor intensities of labour, intermediate inputs, physical and R&D capital. The intensities associated with labour and intermediate inputs depend on their factor prices, output quantity, physical and R&D capital intensities, and R&D spillovers. The physical and R&D capital intensities depend on the labour and intermediate input prices, the input prices of physical and R&D capital, output quantity and the R&D spillovers.

We estimated an average variable cost function, (as opposed to an average total cost function) because spillovers and capital intensities both affect average variable cost. There are two effects of spillovers on variable cost: one directly through the spillovers and an indirect effect that operates through capital intensities. Physical and R&D capital intensities depend on spillovers, and these intensities affect variable cost.

Another feature of the average variable cost function is that the non-capital input intensities depend on spillovers and physical and R&D capital intensities. Thus, there is both a direct effect of spillovers on non-capital intensities and an indirect effect of the spillovers through the capital intensities. This means that an average variable cost function admits the possibility that there may be a direct link

TABLE 1

SPILLOVER ELASTICITIES: CANADIAN MANUFACTURING

	Spillover from Communication Equipment		Spillover from U.S. Manufacturing	
	Mean[a]	Standard Deviation	Mean	Standard Deviation
Labour/output	-0.0103	0.0085	-0.3310	0.1244
Intermediate/output	-0.0112	0.0066	-0.3920	0.0534
Physical capital/output	-0.0223	0.0127	0.2022	0.0215
R&D capital/output	0.1490	0.0934	-0.5164	0.0842
Average variable cost	-0.0109	0.0070	-0.3759	0.0699
Direct average variable cost	-0.0060	0.0037	-0.2140	0.0399

Note: [a]The elasticities are percentages based on a 1 percent increase in R&D spillover. The mean value of the vector of each of the elasticities is presented along with the sample standard deviation.

between a producer's own R&D capital and R&D spillovers, and this link, through the R&D intensity, can then generate indirect effects on non-capital intensities.[12]

This section focuses on the effects of R&D spillovers on factor intensities for Canadian manufacturing as shown in Table 1.

The direct effect of the spillovers on average variable cost is a result of the interaction between R&D spillovers and the factor prices of labour and intermediate inputs. Thus, the direct effect is synonymous with changes in the non-capital input intensities arising from the spillover. R&D spillovers can lead to either increases or decreases in the non-capital input intensities. Therefore, spillovers can be unit variable cost increasing or decreasing. For example, if the spillover is process-oriented then, at existing output levels, efficiency improvements can reduce labour and intermediate input requirements, and thereby average variable cost. If the spillover is product-oriented, then it is possible for average variable cost to increase as a result of the spillover. In this case, we would expect an increase in the product price, at existing output levels, or an increase in output at existing product price levels. The revenue gain would then outweigh the higher cost.[13]

The effects of R&D spillovers become more complicated in the case of multiple spillover sources (such as models with domestic and foreign spillovers). Suppose there are two process-oriented spillovers, and both spillovers are jointly used in the production process. In this case, it is possible for one of the spillovers to generate cost increases, but simultaneous cost decreases associated with the other spillover can lead to joint cost reductions. An example would be spillovers that relate to hardware and software developments. Clearly, upgrading hardware based on new information obtained via R&D spillovers with existing software may be more costly than using old hardware. However, with new software developments used with the hardware upgrade, the joint spillover effect is to reduce costs.[14]

In the last row of Table 1, we find the direct effect of spillovers on average variable cost. A 1 percent increase in R&D capital in the communication industry leads to a direct reduction in the manufacturing unit variable cost by 0.006 percent. There are a number of channels through which this cost reduction occurs. Spillovers occur through intermediate input or physical capital input purchases of firms directly from the communication equipment industry, indirectly through input purchases from telecommunication carriers which purchase inputs from the communication equipment industry, through joint ventures between firms in communication equipment and other manufacturing industries, as a result of the mobility of scientists and engineers, and from the diffusion of information (through conferences, scientific and engineering publications).[15]

The effect, on average variable cost for Canadian manufacturing, of a 1 percent increase in the R&D spillover from communication equipment is to lower unit variable costs by 0.011 percent. This includes the direct and the indirect effects that operate through the capital intensities. Our results imply that the indirect effect of the spillover reduces average variable cost, since the combined direct and indirect effects outweigh the direct effect. Clearly, although in this case average variable cost declined, it is possible for it to increase. For example, even if the direct effect is to reduce costs, both capital intensities may fall as a result of the spillover. In other words, physical and R&D capital are substitutes to the spillover. If the capital intensity effect dominates the direct effect then, in this example, the average variable cost rises.

In terms of the factor intensities, the spillover from communication equipment reduces labour, intermediate input and physical capital intensities, while it increases R&D capital intensity. Thus, the spillover makes manufacturing production techniques more knowledge intensive, although, in all cases the elasticities are highly inelastic. Moreover, since the indirect effect of the spillover is to reduce average variable cost and because increases in capital intensities decrease average variable cost, then the cost reduction from increases in R&D intensity dominates the cost expansion from decreases in physical capital intensity.

The spillover from the U.S. manufacturing sector also generates direct cost reductions. Not surprisingly, these cost reductions are substantially greater than those arising from the communication equipment spillover. A 1 percent increase in U.S. manufacturing R&D capital leads to a direct unit variable cost reduction of 0.21 percent. The spillover from the United States also reduces the labour and intermediate input intensities, but increases the physical capital intensity. Moreover, R&D capital from the United States is a substitute for Canadian manufacturing R&D capital. As a result of the spillover from the United States, Canadian manufacturing production becomes more physical capital intensive.

PRODUCTIVITY GROWTH AND SOCIAL RATE OF RETURN

IN THIS SECTION, we are interested in determining the contribution of spillovers from the communication equipment industry to productivity growth for Canadian manufacturing. First, it is instructive to compare productivity growth rates in manufacturing with communication equipment. Denny, Bernstein, Fuss, Nakamura and Waverman (1992) computed productivity growth rates for high-tech industries and for other two-digit manufacturing industries. They found that although the productivity slowdown that appeared in the early 1970s was common across the United States, Japan and Canada, high-tech industries either did not exhibit any slowdown, or the slowdown was not as pronounced as for other industries. In each country, electrical products had the highest TFP growth rates before and after the 1973 turning point. More significantly, in the electrical products industry in the three countries, productivity growth actually increased in the post-1973 period. Behind electrical products were textiles, transportation equipment, chemical products and non-electrical machinery. The lowest productivity performers were food, paper, petroleum and primary metals.[16]

The productivity success of electrical products at the two-digit level was extended to communication equipment at the three-digit level. Table 2 shows the TFP growth rates for the communication equipment industry and for the manufacturing sector (net of communication equipment).[17] As the table indicates, over the period from 1966 to 1991 the average annual rate of productivity growth for communication equipment was 1.24 percent, while for manufacturing the rate was 0.5 percent. Communication equipment outperformed the manufacturing sector by 150 percent on an average annual basis. In addition, except for the first five years of the sample, communication equipment outperformed the manufacturing sector in every sub-period. The rates in the pre- and post-1973 periods, when the worldwide productivity slowdown is said to have occurred, shows that there was a slowdown for Canadian manufacturing, but not for communication equipment. Indeed, for communication equipment we found that productivity growth actually increased in the post-1973 period, by about 46 percent on an average annual basis.

Next, we considered the decomposition of productivity growth for Canadian manufacturing.[18] TFP growth was decomposed into two general components: returns to scale and technological change. Within technological change, there were two variables that affected productivity growth: the R&D spillover from communication equipment and the spillover from U.S. manufacturing. Since we were comparing a decomposition of TFP growth from the econometric model to a measured rate of productivity growth, there was also a residual element associated with measured productivity that was not captured by the model. The two spillover variables (deviations from constant returns to scale and the residual) exhausted the decomposition of measured productivity growth.

Table 3 shows that the R&D spillover from communication equipment lead to productivity gains for the Canadian manufacturing sector. Over the sample period from 1966 to 1991, about 8.5 percent of annual TFP growth for manufacturing was accounted for by R&D spillovers from communication equipment. Moreover, the importance of the communication equipment industry grew in the post-slowdown era. From 1966 to 1973, around 2 percent of annual TFP growth was contributed by the spillover from communication equipment. The contribution increased to about 22 percent from 1974 to 1991.

TABLE 2

AVERAGE ANNUAL TFP GROWTH RATES

	Canadian Manufacturing	Communication Equipment
	Percent	
Five-Year Period		
1966-1970	0.660	-1.594
1971-1975	0.842	3.931
1976-1980	0.523	2.451
1981-1985	0.866	1.156
1986-1991	-0.267	0.412
Pre- and Post-Slowdown Period		
1966-1973	1.083	0.940
1974-1991	0.233	1.371
Overall Sample Period		
1966-1991	0.495	1.238

Generally, the major component of TFP growth arose from the U.S. R&D spillover. This result is consistent with Bernstein (1995). Over the sample period, the U.S. spillover accounted for about 76 percent of TFP growth in Canadian manufacturing.[19] Table 3 also shows that R&D spillovers from both communication equipment and U.S. manufacturing mitigated the productivity slowdown in Canadian manufacturing. The slowdown was not caused by a decrease in R&D spillovers.

High-tech industries are important sources of R&D spillovers. For U.S. high-tech industries, Bernstein and Nadiri (1988) estimated that the social rates of return ranged from about two to 10 times the private rate of return. For Canada, Bernstein (1988, 1989) estimated a similar range of magnitude.[20] These high social rates of return imply that high-tech industries are important sources of productivity gains to other producers.

We now turn to an analysis of R&D spillovers from the vantage point of the spillover source – communication equipment. Productivity gains associated with spillovers imply that there are extra-private returns to the R&D capital of industries which are spillover sources. The social rate of return to R&D capital consists of the private return, and the extra-private return due to the spillover.

In the long run, the private return is the marginal product of R&D capital per dollar of R&D investment. Thus, the private return is the before tax rental rate of R&D capital divided by the R&D deflator. The private return is the gross of depreciation before tax rate of return. Over the sample period from 1966 to 1991, the mean value of the private rate of return was calculated to be 17 percent.[21]

TABLE 3

DECOMPOSITION OF THE AVERAGE ANNUAL TFP GROWTH RATES

Canadian Manufacturing

Percent

Five-Year Period	Total Factor Productivity Growth Rate	Scale	Spillover from Communication Equipment	Spillover from U.S. Manufacturing	Residual
1966-1970	0.660	0.222	0.025	0.420	0.007
1971-1975	0.842	0.211	0.021	-0.034	0.644
1976-1980	0.523	0.188	0.016	0.073	0.246
1981-1985	0.866	0.109	0.063	0.503	0.191
1986-1991	-0.267	0.051	0.077	0.822	-1.217
Pre- and Post-Slowdown Period					
1966-1973	1.083	0.286	0.024	0.242	0.531
1974-1991	0.233	0.093	0.050	0.433	-0.343
Overall Sample Period					
1966-1991	0.495	0.152	0.042	0.375	-0.074

The extra-private return to R&D capital from the communication equipment industry is the direct cost reduction in Canadian manufacturing due to the spillover from communication equipment per dollar of R&D investment.[22] We estimated that the extra-private return to R&D capital over the sample period averaged 38 percent.[23] Thus, the mean value of the social rate of return was 55 percent.

The magnitude of the social rate of return is consistent with the spillover literature [see Griliches (1991) and Nadiri (1993)]. Generally, intra-industry spillovers generate smaller returns relative to inter-industry spillovers (where industries are defined at the same SIC aggregation level). This paper considers spillovers from a three-digit industry to a sector or single-digit level industry. Our spillover results are greater than those obtained from intra-industry cases, but less than the magnitudes from two-digit inter-industry spillovers. There are substantial extra-private returns to R&D capital from the communication equipment industry, such that the social rate of return is more than three times the private return.

CONCLUSION

HIGH-TECH INDUSTRIES are important sources of spillovers that generate productivity gains in other industries. In addition, high-tech industries tend to exhibit relatively superior productivity performance. Indeed, in some cases, notably electrical equipment, there was no evidence of the productivity slowdown that affected most industries in North America, Japan and other G-7 countries.

This paper measured productivity growth rates for the Canadian communication equipment industry (which consists of important high-tech firms such as Northern Telecom) and for the manufacturing sector. It also investigated the role of the communication equipment industry as a source of R&D spillovers and productivity gains to Canadian manufacturing. Over the period from 1966 to 1991, average annual productivity growth for communication equipment was 150 percent greater than the annual rate for manufacturing. Moreover, unlike manufacturing which suffered a productivity slowdown in the post-1973 period, average annual productivity growth in the communication equipment industry increased by 46 percent.

The communication equipment industry, as a spillover source, affects the production structure, i.e., factor intensities, of the manufacturing sector. Indeed, an expansion of R&D capital in communication equipment leads to an increase in knowledge intensity for manufacturing. Thus, R&D capital inputs are complementary, although the effect is not large. In terms of relative importance, the R&D spillover from U.S. manufacturing generates greater effects on Canadian manufacturing factor intensities. It is interesting to note that the R&D capital inputs between the two North American manufacturing sectors are substitutes. An increase in U.S. R&D capital leads to a reduction in the domestic knowledge intensity in Canadian manufacturing.

The communication equipment industry is an important source of productivity gains to Canadian manufacturing. Over the period from 1966 to 1991, about 8.5 percent of the average annual productivity growth rate for manufacturing was accounted for by spillovers from communication equipment. Moreover, this contribution increased in the post-1973 period when the productivity slowdown occurred. Thus, the spillover was a mitigating influence in the further erosion of manufacturing productivity performance. However, it should be recognized that the spillover from U.S. manufacturing was the major contributor to Canadian productivity growth. This spillover accounted for 76 percent of the average annual productivity growth rate.

The fact that communication equipment is a source of productivity gains implies that there are extra-private returns to its R&D capital. We estimate that the social rate of return to R&D capital is 55 percent or 225 percent greater than the private rate of return. This difference points to under investment in R&D. However, this does not mean that governments should target this industry for special status. Although high annual productivity growth rates and high social rate of return distinguish this industry, there are other manufacturing industries whose social rates of return to R&D capital exceed the private returns.

R&D investment should be encouraged through policy instruments that focus on R&D capital formation, but these policies should not focus on particular industries. There are a number of policies. The government could provide information that facilitates joint ventures to develop new products and joint research or "laboratory" ventures. Legislation and regulation could be amended to reduce the transaction costs in undertaking these joint ventures. Moreover, reducing the legislative/regulatory burden would also help in encouraging other more indirect means of internalizing the spillovers associated with R&D. One example would be licensing agreements.

Tax expenditures or subsidies are further policy instruments that are and can be directed toward R&D capital formation. It is important to recognize that any analysis of the relative costs and benefits of government tax policies concerning R&D investment must include R&D spillovers. Otherwise, there will be an underestimation of the benefits associated with these policies, not only in the encouragement of R&D investment, but in improving living standards through higher productivity growth rates.

APPENDIX
ESTIMATION MODEL

IN THIS MODEL, producers use labour, intermediate inputs, and physical and R&D capital to produce output. There are also R&D spillovers and a time trend representing dynamic efficiency effects that do not emanate from R&D capital.

In order to estimate the model, we specify a variable cost function or, more precisely, an average variable cost function:

$$c_t^v/y_t = (\Sigma_{i=1}^2 \beta_i w_{it} + 0.5\Sigma_{i=1}^2\Sigma_{j=1}^2 \beta_{ij} w_{it} w_{jt} W_t^{-1} + \Sigma_{i=1}^2\Sigma_{j=1}^2 \Phi_{ij} w_{it} S_{jt-1}$$

$$+ \Sigma_{i=1}^2 \Phi_i w_{it} t) y_t^{\vartheta-1} + [\Sigma_{i=1}^2 \alpha_i k_{it} + 0.5\Sigma_{i=1}^2\Sigma_{j=1}^2 \alpha_{ij} k_{it} k_{jt}/y_t^{\vartheta-1}$$

$$+ \Sigma_{i=1}^2\Sigma_{j=1}^2 \eta_{ij} k_{it} S_{jt-1} + \Sigma_{i=1}^2 \eta_i k_{it} t] W_t \qquad (6)$$

where the parameters to be estimated are given by β_i, β_{ij}, Φ_{ij}, Φ_i, α_i, α_{ij}, η_{ij}, η_i; $i,j = 1,2$; and ϑ is the inverse of the degree of returns to scale. The non-capital factor prices are denoted as w_i; $i=1$ is the labour price; and $i=2$ is the price of intermediate inputs. Capital intensities are $k_i = K_i/y$ where K_i is the capital input, $i=1$ is physical capital; $i=2$ is R&D capital; y is output; and t is the time trend. $W = \Sigma_{i=1}^2 a_i w_i$ where $a_i, i = 1,2$ are fixed coefficients. W can be defined as a Laspeyres index of non-capital input prices. By defining W in this manner, we do not have to normalize the cost function by any one non-capital input price, but rather by a weighted average of both prices. The attractive feature of this average variable cost function is that we are able to impose the curvature conditions on the function. R&D spillovers are denoted by S_{1t} as the domestic spillover from communication equipment and S_{2t} as the spillover from U.S. manufacturing.

Using the average variable cost function and cost minimization conditions, non-capital input equilibrium is given by:

$$v_{it} = (\beta_t + \Sigma_{j=1}^2 \beta_{ij} w_{jt} W_t^{-1} - 0.5\Sigma_{h=1}^2\Sigma_{j=1}^2 \beta_{hj} w_{ht} w_{jt} W_t^{-2} a_i + \Sigma_{j=1}^2 \Phi_{ij} S_{jt-1}$$

$$+ \Phi_i t) y_t^{\vartheta-1} + [\Sigma_{j=1}^2 \alpha_j k_{jt} + 0.5\Sigma_{h=1}^2\Sigma_{j=1}^2 \alpha_{hj} k_{ht} k_{jt}/y_t^{\vartheta-1}$$

$$+ \Sigma_{h=1}^2\Sigma_{j=1}^2 \eta_{hj} k_{ht} S_{jt-1} + \Sigma_{i=1}^2 \eta_i k_{it} t] a_i, \quad i = 1,2 \qquad (7)$$

where non-capital input intensities are $v_i = v_i/y$, $i = 1,2$; v_1 is labour input; and v_2 is intermediate input. Based on the average variable cost function and cost minimization, the demands for the physical and R&D capital inputs are:

$$k_{it} = (\alpha_{jj} A_{it} - \alpha_{ij} A_{jt})/A, \quad i \neq j, \ i,j = 1,2 \qquad (8)$$

where $A_{it} = (-\alpha_i - \Sigma_{j=1}^2 \eta_{ij} S_{jt-1} - \eta_i t - \omega_{it} W_t^{-1}) y_t^{\vartheta-1}$; $i = 1,2$; where ω_i is the factor price of the ith capital input and $A = (\alpha_{11}\alpha_{22} - \alpha_{12}^2)$. Equation sets (7) and (8) define the model that is to be estimated.

This framework enables us to investigate the impact of R&D spillovers on factor intensities, on the decomposition of productivity growth, and to measure the private and social rates of return to R&D capital.

SPILLOVER ELASTICITIES

THE EFFECTS OF SPILLOVERS on average variable cost and the factor intensities can be determined by differentiating equations (6), (7) and (8) with respect to S_1 and S_2. First, in terms of the capital intensities, we have:

$$ek_cS_j = S_jy^{\vartheta-1}(\alpha_{12}\eta_{dj} - \alpha_{dd}\eta_{cj})/Ak_c, \ j = 1,2, \ c{\neq}d, \ c,d = 1,2 \tag{9}$$

where ek_cS_j is the jth spillover elasticity of the cth capital intensity. Second, turning to the non-capital input demands we have:

$$ev_iS_h = [\Phi_{ih}y^{\vartheta-1} + (\eta_{hh}k_h + \eta_{gh}k_g)a_i + (\partial k_1/\partial S_h)(\alpha_1 + \Sigma_{j=1}^2\alpha_{1j}k_jy^{\vartheta-1}$$

$$+ \Sigma_{j=1}^2\eta_{1j}S_j + \eta_1 t)a_i + (\partial k_1/\partial S_h)(\alpha_1 + \Sigma_{j=1}^2\alpha_{j2}k_jy^{\vartheta-1}$$

$$+ \Sigma_{j=1}^2\eta_{2j}S_j + \eta_2 t)a_i]S_h/v_i, \ i=1,2, \ g{\neq}h, \ g,h=1,2 \tag{10}$$

where ev_iS_h is the hth spillover elasticity of the ith non-capital input demand. There are two effects of the spillovers on the non-capital intensities. The first is the direct effect arising from the fact that the non-capital input price interacts with the spillovers. The second is the indirect effect that arises because the non-capital input intensities are affected by the capital intensities.

The last set of elasticities shows the effects of the spillovers on average variable cost. They are:

$$ec_y^vS_h = [\Phi_{1h}w_1 + \Phi_{2h}w_2 + [\eta_{hh}k_h + \eta_{gh}k_g + (\partial k_1/\partial S_h)(\alpha_1$$

$$+ \Sigma_{j=1}^2\alpha_{1j}k_jy^{\vartheta-1} + \Sigma_{j=1}^2\eta_{1j}S_j + \eta_1 t)$$

$$+ (\partial k_2/\partial S_h)(\alpha_2 + \Sigma_{j=1}^2\alpha_{j2}k_jy^{\vartheta-1}$$

$$+ \Sigma_{j=1}^2\eta_{2j}S_j + \eta_2 t)]W]S_h/(c^v/y), \ g{\neq}h \ g,h = 1,2 \tag{11}$$

where $ec_y^vS_h$ is the hth spillover elasticity of average variable cost. There are also two effects of the spillovers on average variable cost: the direct effect and the second is the indirect effect which operates through capital intensities.

PRODUCTIVITY GROWTH AND SOCIAL RATES OF RETURN

TFP GROWTH can be measured as:

$$TFPG(t,s) = (y_t - y_s)/y_m - s_{vm}^T(v_t - v_s)/v_m - s_{km}^T(K_t - K_s)/K_m \tag{12}$$

where the subscript t represents the current period; s represents the past period; the subscript m designates the mean value of a variable (for example, where

$y_m = (y_t + y_s)/2)$; s_v is the vector of non-capital cost shares; s_k is the vector of capital cost shares; and the mean values of the cost shares for the non-capital inputs are defined as $s_{im} = (w_{im} v_{im})/((c/y)_m y_m)$ where c is the sum of variable and capital costs. The mean values of the cost shares of the capital inputs are defined in a similar fashion.

We are able to decompose TFP growth rates by using the estimated variable cost function. The difference in cost between time periods is:

$$c_t^v - c_s^v = .5[\Sigma_{i=1}^n(v_{it} + v_{is})(w_{it} - w_{is})$$

$$+ ((\partial c^v/\partial y)_t + (\partial c^v/\partial y)_s)(y_t - y_s)$$

$$+ \Sigma_{k=1}^m((\partial c^v/\partial K_k)_t + (\partial c^v/\partial K_k)_s)(K_{kt} - K_{ks})$$

$$+ \Sigma_{j=1}^o((\partial c^v/\partial S_j)_t + (\partial c^v/\partial S_j)_s)(S_{jt} - S_{js})$$

$$+ ((\partial c^v/\partial t)_t + (\partial c^v/\partial t)_s)(t - s)] \tag{13}$$

Cost differences are attributable to the variable factor prices, output quantity, capital stocks, R&D spillovers and time trend. In addition, by definition of variable cost, the change over two periods is given by:

$$c_t^v - c_s^v = \Sigma_{i=1}^n (w_{is} (v_{it} - v_{is}) + v_{it} (w_{it} - w_{is})) \tag{14}$$

Using this result with (12) and (13) yields:

$$TFPG(t,s) = ((y_t - y_s)/y_m)[1 - (\partial c^v/\partial y)_m(y/c)_m]$$

$$- \Sigma_{j=1}^o(\partial c^v/\partial S_j)_m(S_{jm}/y_m)(y/c)_m)(S_{jt} - S_{js})/S_{jm},$$

$$- (\partial c^v/\partial t)_m(t - s)(y/c)_m/y_m \tag{15}$$

The decomposition of TFP growth, as shown by the right side of equation (15), consists of three elements. The first is the scale effect. If there are constant returns to scale in long-run equilibrium, then the term inside the square brackets is zero. The second element relates to the R&D spillover effects. (There are two spillover effects.) The third element is the one associated with the time trend.

Next, we examine the rates of return. The social rates of return to R&D capital equal the private rates of return plus the returns associated with the spillovers. These latter returns can be calculated by considering a situation where the spillovers have been internalized. In this regard, we define joint costs to be:

$$\Omega_\tau = \Sigma_{j=1}^2(C^{vj}(w_\tau^j, y_\tau^j, K_\tau^j, S_{\tau-1}^j, t^j) + \omega_\tau^j K_\tau^j) \tag{16}$$

The superscript j refers to the producer; j=1 is manufacturing; and j=2 is communication equipment.

Consider the right side of equation (16) to be evaluated at the equilibrium input–output ratios. In equilibrium, the cost for each producer is at a minimum. However, joint cost is not minimized relative to the case where the spillovers are internalized. With the internalization of the R&D spillovers, there is additional profit (through cost reductions) to be earned from each of the R&D capital stocks. The additional profit is the reduction in joint cost. Using the average variable cost function, the reduction in joint cost in equilibrium from an increase in the R&D capital from communication equipment is:

$$\partial \Omega_t / \partial K^2_{2t-1} = \sum_{i=1}^{2} \Phi^1_{il} w^1_{it} (y^1_t)^{\vartheta 1} + \sum_{h=1}^{2} = k_{ht} \eta_{h1}^{1} W^1_t y^1_t \qquad (17)$$

Equation (17) shows the spillover wedge between the social and private rates of return evaluated in equilibrium that arises from R&D capital from the communication equipment industry.

The private rate of return to R&D capital in long-run equilibrium is the marginal product of R&D capital per dollar of R&D investment. This return is defined gross of depreciation and before tax. The private return is the before tax rental rate deflated by the R&D capital price index.

Let us define ρ^2_{2t} to be the private rate of return to R&D capital in period t for the communication equipment industry. Let the extra-private return to R&D capital for this industry be ι^2_{2t}, which is the right side of (17) divided by the R&D price deflator in the communication equipment industry. Thus the social rate of return to R&D capital is:

$$\gamma^2_{2t} = \rho_{2t} + \iota^2_{2t} \qquad (18)$$

ENDNOTES

1 Denny, Bernstein, Fuss, Nakamura and Waverman (1992) found that the electrical products industry in Canada, the United States and Japan had the highest productivity growth rates from the mid 1960s to the mid 1980s compared to the other manufacturing industries. Bernstein and Nadiri (1988) estimated, for U.S. high-tech industries, that the social rate of return to R&D was two to 10 times the private returns.

2 In this paper we use the terms high-tech and knowledge-based industries interchangeably when referring to communication equipment. In fact, activities can be knowledge-based and not high-tech, such as educational services. Moreover, an industry can be high-tech, but not command a substantial knowledge base from its workers.

3 We can add more outputs and inputs, but we are only using this framework for illustrative purposes.

4 It is important to note that Φ, μ and ψ could be zero in particular empirical applications. The three components of the technology term do not have to be present. In addition, the time trend represents technological change that is not attributable to R&D capital and spillovers.

5 This problem arises for other inputs as well. In the case of the explicit treatment of energy as a distinct factor of production, all related energy costs must be subtracted out of the set of the traditional inputs. One such factor of production would be intermediate inputs.

6 It should also be noted that the definition of returns to scale differs in the two models. In the first case, returns to scale is defined over all inputs, i.e., capital, labour and intermediate inputs, each of which include the relevant components of R&D capital. In the second case, where R&D cost is subtracted from the cost of the traditional factors, returns to scale is defined over capital, labour and intermediate inputs net of the R&D capital components.

7 In most analyses of TFP growth, technological change is only represented by a time trend. This variable is a catch-all that can reflect both productivity gains and losses. Indeed, it seems more appropriate to view changes in the trend variable as an indicator of dynamic production efficiency gains or losses, as opposed to a strict measure of the rate of technological change. The reason is that under constant returns to scale, long-run equilibrium and no spillovers, productivity growth is synonymous with the effect of changes in the trend variable. Since it is difficult to imagine technological regression occurring from a variable that is costless to change, productivity slowdowns should not be observed in this context. Intuitively, one should accept a more circumspect role for the trend variable.

8 If there are deviations from long-run equilibrium because of adjustment costs associated with some factors of production, and the appropriate shadow values are used to construct measured TFP growth rates, our analysis stands. If we use market prices to compute measured rates, the deviation between market price and shadow value appears as a component of TFP growth. This deviation operates in a similar fashion to returns to scale and rates of technological change. In this case, predetermined input quantities affect the components of TFP growth, along with factor prices and other exogenous variables.

9 R&D intensity is often defined by the ratio of R&D expenditure to sales. However, this terminology is inconsistent with the usual definition of intensity that refers to an input–output ratio. Since it is R&D capital, and not R&D expenditures, that appears in a production function showing the link between inputs and outputs, the R&D capital to output ratio is the appropriate measure of R&D intensity.

10 Given the importance of R&D capital formation for technological progress, productivity and output growth, a proper accounting of inflation and depreciation of R&D capital is needed to formulate, conduct and evaluate policies aimed at encouraging long-term growth.

11 The full details of the model including the data are presented in the forthcoming Industry Canada working paper by the author.

12 Because our interest lies in the measurement and decomposition of TFP growth, along with the determination of social rates of return to R&D capital, we abstract from the dynamics arising from adjustment costs. Adjustment costs generally do not account for a great deal of TFP growth over long periods of time. In addition, although short-run, private rates of return to R&D capital can be twice long-run returns, because of adjustment costs, they are each usually swamped by the social rates of return.

13 We do not model the product demand side, but we are conditioning on output, so our estimates capture output increases over time from the spillovers. These effects are also accounted for in our measure of TFP growth which reflects output growth net of input growth. However, our formula for the social rate of return does not include the revenue gain explicitly and may actually be biased in a downward direction. The social rate of return reflects cost changes due to the spillover, and since these changes depend on output, then our actual measure of the return implicitly includes output changes.

14 Another way that process-oriented (and also product-oriented) spillovers can increase costs is if they lead to future cost reductions. Thus, in present value terms, the spillovers are cost-reducing. To the extent that future cost reductions are omitted from the calculation of the social rate of return, there is a possible downward bias in the magnitude. However, since social rates of return are cost-dependent these future reductions are reflected implicitly in the time path of cost, and in the measure of the social rates of return.

15 It is important to note that spillover networks do not have to coincide with the flows of intermediate inputs, as represented by input–output tables. For example, in the United States, in a relative sense, industries purchase little from scientific instruments, but this industry is an important source of R&D spillovers [see Bernstein and Nadiri (1988)].

16 The high-tech/low-tech distinction is not without exception, as petroleum and paper were poor productivity performers, while textiles showed relatively higher productivity growth. The low ranking of petroleum products provides evidence of the severity of the energy crisis, as manifested by higher prices and the ensuing decrease in capacity utilization.

17 The calculation of TFP growth is based on equation (12) in the appendix to this chapter.

18 The decomposition of productivity growth is based on equation (15) in the appendix to this chapter.

19 There was only one period (1971 to 1975) where the spillover from the United States caused productivity growth to decline. As Figure 1 shows, this was due to the decline in R&D expenditures over this period. Our econometric results show that the direct effect on average variable cost from an increase in the U.S. spillover is cost-reducing at every point in the sample.

20 These results and others are summarized in Griliches (1991) and Nadiri (1993).

21 With a depreciation rate of 10 percent and a corporate tax rate of 46 percent, the net of depreciation, after tax rate of return is about 4 percent. Also based on a mean value of 0.17 for the rate of return, the sample standard deviation is 0.015.

22 The derivation of the extra-private return to R&D capital is derived in the appendix to this chapter as equation (17).

23 The sample standard deviation based on the extra-private return of 0.38 is 0.04.

ACKNOWLEDGEMENTS

THE AUTHOR WOULD LIKE TO THANK DAN MALONEY for his excellent research assistance, Mike Denny and Peter Howitt for their comments and suggestions, and personnel in the Services, Science and Technology Division of Statistics Canada for their help with the R&D expenditure data.

BIBLIOGRAPHY

Bernstein, J.I. "Costs of Production, Intraindustry and Interindustry R&D Spillovers: Canadian Evidence." *Canadian Journal of Economics.* 21(2), (1988): 324-347.
———. "The Structure of Canadian Industrial R&D Spillovers and the Rates of Return to R&D." *Journal of Industrial Economics.* 37(3), (1989): 315-328.

———. "R&D Capital, Spillovers, and Foreign Affiliates in Canada." *Foreign Investment, Technology and Economic Growth*. The Investment Canada Research Series. Edited by D. McFetridge. Calgary: University of Calgary Press, 1991, pp. 111-130.

———. *Price Indexes for Canadian Industrial Research and Development Expenditures*. Statistics Canada, Services, Science and Technology Division, Working Paper No. 92-01, 1992.

———. "International R&D Spillovers Between Industries in Canada and the United States, Social Rates of Return, and Productivity Growth." *Canadian Journal of Economics, Papers and Proceedings*. (forthcoming).

Bernstein, J.I. and M.I. Nadiri. "Interindustry R&D Spillovers, Rates of Return, and Production in High-Tech Industries." *American Economic Review Papers and Proceedings*. (May 1988): 429-434.

Denny, M., J. Bernstein, M. Fuss, S. Nakamura and L. Waverman. "Productivity in Manufacturing Industries, Canada, Japan, and the United States, 1953-1986: Was the 'Productivity Slowdown' Reversed?" *Canadian Journal of Economics*. 25(3), (1992): 584-603.

Griliches, Z. "Productivity Puzzles and R&D: Another Nonexplanation." *Journal of Economic Perspectives*. 2, (1988): 9-21.

———. "The Search for R&D Spillovers." *Scandinavian Journal of Economics*. Supplement. 94, (1991): 29-47.

———. "Productivity, R&D, and the Data Constraint." *American Economic Review*. 84(1), (1994): 1-23.

Jankowski, J. "Do We Need a Price Index for Industrial R&D?" *Research Policy*. 22, (1993): 195-205.

Jorgenson, D. "Productivity and Postwar U.S. Economic Growth." *Journal of Economic Perspectives*. 2, (1988): 23-41.

Nadiri, M.I. "Innovations and Technological Spillovers." NBER Working Paper No. 4423, 1993.

Nadiri, M.I, and I. Prucha. "Estimation of the Depreciation Rate of Physical and R&D Capital in the U.S. Total Manufacturing Sector." NBER Working Paper No. 4591, 1993.

Comment

Michael Denny
Department of Economics
University of Toronto

INTRODUCTION

PROFESSOR BERNSTEIN'S PAPER BRINGS TOGETHER several strands of his important research on the links between research and development (R&D) and productivity. This is only a small sample of a much larger body of important research on the underpinnings of productivity growth. On the one hand, we still understand too little about the direct links between R&D and productivity in a given industry. On the other, we know even less about the consequences for other industries, and of the spillovers, of both R&D and productivity growth in a given industry. In the first case, we are interested in the role of measurable R&D in a particular industry, in promoting productivity growth within the industry. Is the R&D done specifically by a given industry an important source of productivity growth in that industry? If so, just how important is it?

We also recognize that R&D done in other industries and in other types of institutions may be an important source of productivity growth for a particular industry and for all industries in general. These are the spillovers from the R&D activity and from the productivity growth in one industry. But, just how important are they?

THE CURRENT PAPER

IN THE BERNSTEIN PAPER, the focus is on the contributions of research and development in one Canadian high-tech industry (communications equipment) and in American manufacturing to the productivity growth in the remainder of the Canadian manufacturing sector. The contributions are developed from three perspectives. Table 1 shows the impacts of R&D on costs and input demands in Canadian manufacturing from communications equipment and U.S. manufacturing. Table 3 provides evidence on the relative importance of these spillover sources on total productivity growth. These are different ways of displaying the impacts of the same spillovers. Finally, the spillovers from the communications equipment industry only, are discussed as the difference between the social rate of return, which includes the spillovers, and the private rate of return which does not. These are parts of the endogenous growth story although there are other parts that are not included in this paper.

The econometric methods in the paper are relatively standard but not particularly easy for the non-specialist to understand. Intuitively, the technique attempts to sort out the impacts on firm costs of a wide variety of possible sources. This is required so one does not attribute reductions in costs to spillovers when, in fact, they are due to other factors. Statistical techniques, econometric or otherwise, will be necessary in the long-run research strategy. These are the only techniques that will ensure that descriptive case studies or path-dependent explanations do not mislead us. Non-statistical techniques are very useful to develop hypotheses and to ensure that we do not miss important factors due to inappropriate measurement. The latter have grown in popularity in recent years but both types of research will be necessary in the long-run.

TRANSMISSION LINKS IN THE ENDOGENOUS GROWTH STORY

IN THE LAST DECADE, growth theory has been actively revived as a research topic. Rather ingenious models have been developed to tell about the use of current resources to promote future growth. This is not simply a case of savings and investment leading to a higher capital stock which implies higher future per capita income. Rather, the models are trying to isolate features of the process of generating growth that cannot be adequately explained by physical capital accumulation. Productivity growth has been called a measure of our ignorance, and the endogenous growth literature can be viewed as an attempt to place some new structure on this ignorance.

The creation and transmission of new knowledge and the acquisition of old knowledge are important aspects of growth. Bernstein's paper is a very important part of this puzzle.

PROBLEMS

WE HAVE ONLY INCOMPLETE INFORMATION about what mechanisms link knowledge creation and acquisition with economic growth. Moreover, it is necessary to learn about the mechanisms before policy can be formulated. The direct and indirect consequences of R&D expenditure are one of the more obvious links.

As several papers have mentioned, measurement problems are severe in all areas of knowledge. There are major problems in measuring R&D, and I would echo Bernstein's emphasis on the problem and his call for further work by Statistics Canada.

In Bernstein's paper and all the aggregate level research on R&D, aggregate measures of R&D inputs have to be used as a substitute for outputs. There is simply little or no evidence on outputs, and attempts to use patent data have not been very successful. The situation is more serious because data on expenditure must be deflated, and reasonable price series for inputs are not available. These data problems will always lead to some degree of concern about the usefulness of the statistical results based on limited evidence.

The measurement of spillovers creates more complex problems. How much knowledge is transmitted from one industry to another and at what cost? It is more complex than measuring the size of the spillovers by lagged R&D. At this time, we need some discussion about how to measure knowledge received in contrast with knowledge produced. This will be crucial for understanding spillovers.

CURRENT ESTIMATES

THE DECOMPOSITION OF PRODUCTIVITY GROWTH in Table 3 provides the clearest picture of the importance of spillovers. Over the complete period 1966 to 1991, Canadian manufacturing total factor productivity growth equalled roughly 0.5 percent a year. Almost 10 percent of this growth arose from spillovers from communications equipment. A further 76 percent arose from spillovers from the United States. These estimates attribute a major role to spillovers in creating growth. My intuitive feeling is that these are too high. However, they do present a serious challenge for Bernstein and others to confirm in other ways that these estimates are sound or need some revision. As Bernstein notes, they are not widely different from estimates from other studies.

There has been less emphasis on the consequences of spillovers on the individual factors including recipient industry R&D. This is the real value of the details provided in Table 1. The results in this table are complex because there are two spillover sources, and the model is only a short-run cost model, but the results are long-run results. For both spillovers, the reduction in direct variable costs is about 55 percent of the total reduction in variable costs. The relative impacts on labour compared to materials are similar from both sources. In both cases, there is little change in the relative demands for variable inputs. However, there are sharply different impacts on the two types of capital from the two sources. Spillovers from communications equipment decrease the marginal value of physical capital and enhance the value of R&D capital. The reverse is true for spillovers from U.S. manufacturing. While this is puzzling, it would be useful to have further research analyze why this occurs.

POLICY IMPLICATIONS

THERE IS A LOGICAL AND USEFUL TENSION – sometimes contempt – between policy makers and academics. The latter always see the need to acquire more information through further study. The former know that there is neither money nor time for this delaying activity unless it is for good political reasons. Good policies have to balance the necessity for action with the uncertainties of consequences. Risks are necessary if action is to be undertaken, and some of these actions will later be proven wrong. Nevertheless, I will describe a small number of implications from Bernstein's research.

A. Better measurement and data are needed if we are to:

- unravel the interconnections between activities in one sector, for example R&D and productivity growth, and activities in other sectors; and

- understand the impacts of policies on these interactions.

B. Monitoring of current government programs that support R&D should be improved, and the results of that monitoring should be made more widely available. This is a serious current failure. At various times, governments have used a wide variety of policies to stimulate productivity growth. These efforts could provide useful information, but programs do not collect sufficient information. It is also necessary that the data be made available to a wide variety of researchers. This will permit a wider set of analytic results from the same data. Outside individuals may have skills and resources to analyze programs which are not available to those who design and implement government policies.

C. Bernstein's research results (and those of others) suggest that there are significant R&D externalities. However, because of problems with the data, these results must be viewed as preliminary. It is not possible to move rapidly to an increased direct role for government.

Steven Globerman
College of Business and Economics
Western Washington University
and Department of Economics
Simon Fraser University

The Information Highway and the Economy

INTRODUCTION

INCREASINGLY, ONE READS IN THE POPULAR BUSINESS PRESS about how changes in communications technology are fundamentally altering "best practice" production and distribution techniques. Indeed, a number of observers are equating these changes to the industrial revolution in terms of the sweeping impact they will have on society and the dramatic stimulus they will provide to economic growth.

Several quotations are illustrative.

> The enabling effects of the information highway will be felt in all industry sectors and all regions of Canada. It will stimulate research and development (R&D) in leading-edge technologies; it will facilitate the diffusion of innovative technologies and information-based services; it will strengthen the competitiveness of large and small Canadian businesses; and it will provide cost-effective access to high-quality health care, educational and social services (Industry Canada, 1994, p. 1).

> When companies are linked the way telephones are linked, we shall create entirely new computer-mediated markets, new ways of doing business, new social patterns, new opportunities and new forms and definitions of work (Denton, 1994, p. 6).

The potential importance of new communication media and services to national economic performance is suggested by the U.S. Office of Technology Assessment.

> An advanced communication and information infrastructure, such as that embodied in the concept of a National Information Infrastructure, could greatly enhance new management and production tools and improve overall US economic performance (U.S. Office of Technology Assessment, 1994, p. 1).

The broad purposes of this paper are to identify, more precisely, the potential economic impacts of technological changes that are summarized under the heading of "information highway" and to assess the likely consequences of those changes for Canada's economic performance. A related purpose is to evaluate whether technological and economic developments associated with the information highway require changes in public policy, either to mitigate new or more substantive sources of market failure or to address adverse distributional consequences.

This paper proceeds as follows. In the next section, a relatively non-technical discussion is provided of recent and emerging changes in telecommunications technology that underlie the explosion of interest surrounding the information highway. Then, some major hypotheses about the likely economic consequences of the information highway are identified and evaluated. The next section, provides a more detailed assessment of the potential economic effects of the information highway. In the final two sections, policy issues are identified, discussed and summarized, and conclusions are presented.

DESCRIPTION OF THE TECHNOLOGY

THERE ARE INNUMERABLE DESCRIPTIONS of the information highway. Perhaps the most straightforward and useful is provided by Stentor: "It is a system of interconnected electronic networks providing universal access to basic and advanced communications and information services. It is a network of many networks, owned and operated by different service providers offering connections to a variety of services, applications and content sources" (Stentor, 1993, pp. 6-7).[1]

The increasing ability of different communications media, such as wired and wireless telephony, cable, satellite and computer networks, to share and exchange electronic traffic reflects a technological phenomenon referred to as convergence. In effect, communication networks are functioning more and more like computer networks in terms of the way they code, store and forward information. In particular, electronic signals are transmitted and switched as digitized bits rather than analogue waves. As a consequence, alternative communication networks are capable of offering the same sets of services, either as substitutes for, or complements to, existing networks.[2]

Digitization, data compression and packeting, and related developments facilitate the proliferation of new services on public, as well as private, communication networks. They also allow data to move at faster speeds over telephone lines. Digital compression techniques are effectively expanding the capacity of existing media to carry more channels of traffic, while multiplexing and packet switching allow more traffic to be carried on any given number of channels. New media such as fibre-optic cable directly expand the transmission capacity of communication carriers, while continuing advances in integrated circuitry and related computer technology enable central office switches and subscriber terminal equipment to process bits of information both more quickly and in multimedia formats.

Techniques that expand the capacity of transmission media lead to new services, such as video conferencing, which require relatively large amounts of transmission capacity. Digitization also allows switching equipment to handle all types of traffic including voice, data, enhanced text, graphics, sound and video. This facilitates the provision of new interactive services including multimedia services, such as video on demand, computer games on demand and graphical product information.

The first major application of digitized communication networks was for high-speed data transmission and exchange. Private corporate networks were (and still are) the main highways. However, the digitization of the public network combined with advances in packaging and switching data are bringing data communication capabilities to users of the public network.[3]

In a similar fashion, the transmission of pictures and images, as well as video teleconferencing, have been possible for some time using leased wideband transmission lines. Large public and private sector organizations have been the users of such services. Increased throughput rates (modem speed), digital compression and multimedia hardware and software for personal computers have made it technically possible for virtually any telephone subscriber to send and receive pictures and other (still) visual images, as well as sound. It is possible to transmit relatively poor quality video signals over the public switched telephone network, although the emergence of high-quality full-motion video as a service on the public switched telephone network awaits one or more of the following developments:

- major breakthroughs in the technology which permit video signals to be transmitted through paired copper wires;

- installation of broadband transmission capacity (i.e., fibre-optic cable) into subscribers' residences;

- use by the telephone companies of the cable companies' coaxial cable that runs into subscribers' homes or the evolution of the cable network into a ubiquitous telephone network; or

- emergence of a digital wireless public network.

It is conceivable that the cable networks will emerge as the first interactive public network capable of providing a full range of services from voice through full-motion video signals.[4] Wireless technology, e.g., wireless cable, is evolving and may emerge as the dominant medium for transmitting the full range of audio, textual and video signals travelling the information highway. While it is impossible to predict with confidence, which networks will carry what traffic, it is possible to predict that the "average" user of the traditional telephone and cable networks will have an ever-increasing range of new services available through those networks, as well as through new networks. At the same time, technically sophisticated large private and public sector organizations should see prices decline for existing services. They will also benefit from increased speed and quality of data transmission and improved video services. Nevertheless, it is likely to be smaller residential and business subscribers

TABLE 1		
GROWTH OF DATA BASES		
Year	Number of Data Bases	On-line Services
1979-1980	400	59
1980-1981	600	93
1981-1982	915	170
1982-1983	1,350	213
1983-1984	1,878	272
1984-1985	2,453	362
1986	2,901	454
1989	4,062	600
1990	4,465	645
1991	6,200	4,700

Source: Huber, Kellogg and Thorne (1992, p. 563).

who will be the largest beneficiaries of the emergence of a public network information highway, since they are unable to afford private network services capable of supplying technologically sophisticated communication services.

Increasingly, people are coming to equate the information highway with ubiquitous computer networks such as the Internet. While the Internet is, perhaps, the most rapidly growing international computer network, it is only one of many networks capable of providing services such as electronic mail, bulletin boards, data bases and other textual material, as well as pictures, graphics and sound.[5] A perspective on the number of available on-line networks and data bases (for North America) is provided by data reported in Table 1. The number of large commercial on-line computer networks (e.g., CompuServe Inc., America Online, Prodigy) is relatively small. However, there are literally thousands of "producers" of information and services available on those networks.

Recent estimates place the number of subscribers to the three large commercial on-line networks (CompuServe Inc., America Online and Prodigy) at around 4.5 million households.[6] Numbers of users of the Internet are not directly available. Indirect estimates from the number of Internet hosts place total usage at between 20 million and 30 million people. Various data discussed in a later section document the extraordinary recent growth of this "networked network."

Some estimates are available on the nature of the services demanded on computer networks. While the claim cannot be objectively validated, it has been suggested that sex "chatlines" constitute the single most popular service available through commercial on-line computer networks (Rowan, 1995). MacKie-Mason and Varian (1994, p. 76) distinguished between type of service and volume of traffic.

According to their research, the most frequent use of the Internet is electronic mail followed by file transfer (moving data from one computer to another) and remote login (logging into a computer that is running somewhere else on the Internet). In terms of traffic, about 37 percent of total traffic is file transfer, 16 percent is electronic mail and discussion groups, and 38 percent is from the information retrieval programs Gopher and World Wide Web browsers (e.g., Mosaic, Netscape).

The uses to which the information highway infrastructure is dedicated will presumably condition the economic impacts of that infrastructure. Existing patterns of use suggest that public computer networks are being used, in many instances, as substitutes for more expensive voice or fax communications. In many other cases, they are being used by researchers to transfer data and text files. Early commercial applications (primarily by computer hardware and software manufacturers) involved the substitution of electronic information for printed information including product updates to customers, completing files for warranties, manuals and so forth.

While there are undoubtedly real cost savings associated with using computer networks for such purposes, there are also pecuniary economies for some users associated with not being explicitly charged for network usage, or being charged a flat rate for essentially unlimited usage. In principle, computer networks, such as Internet, permit cost savings to the extent that they substitute for voice or fax communications, since packets of data require less transmission capacity than the "equivalent" amount of information transmitted as analogue signals. For the Internet, the realization of these cost savings is being compromised, as noted by MacKie-Mason and Varian (1994), by inefficient pricing.

With respect to other new interactive services offered by telephone and cable companies, it is widely believed that entertainment services (e.g., video-on-demand) will be important product offerings. To be sure, surveys of the broad population of potential users report interest in information and educational applications of video-on-demand, as well as entertainment uses. Nevertheless, the ability to offer entertainment programming on demand is seen by the telephone companies as underpinning the economic viability of investments in information highway infrastructure for residential subscribers.

While surveys may be unreliable indicators of future demand, actual usage patterns for 900-number telephone calls offer insights into possible uses of new video-on-demand services. The data reported in Table 2 suggest that information and commercial services may represent important new uses of interactive broadband technologies. Certainly, discussions lauding the potential economic benefits of the information highway anticipate a substantial demand for non-entertainment-type services. However, video signals are arguably much more important for entertainment services than for non-entertainment services. As well, there are probably a greater range of good substitutes to entertainment services delivered by 900 numbers than there are for information services delivered by 900 numbers. Hence, the data in Table 2 likely understate, perhaps substantially, the relative demand for entertainment programming on the information highway.[7]

TABLE 2

900 NUMBER CALLS BY TYPE OF CALL

Type of Call	Number of Calls (Millions)	Minutes of Calls (Millions)	% of Calls
Entertainment	55	157	20.1
Information	98	278	35.6
Fund raising	15	42	5.4
Ordering	19	55	7.1
Polling/surveying	10	27	3.5
Dealer locators	4	12	1.6
Lead generation	8	23	2.9
Sweepstakes	16	46	5.9
Couponing	6	16	2.1
Customer services	2	7	0.9
Messaging	32	90	11.6
Others (including fax)	9	26	3.3
Total	274	779	100.0

Source: Mitchell and Donyo (1994, p. 31).

In summary, the various technological changes outlined in the preceding section have several basic attributes.

- They are providing for electronic communication of information that hitherto has required embodiment in a physical form such as a blueprint, engineering sketch, magnetic medium or even an individual. The ability to communicate pictures (still and moving), diagrams, sound and some video with acceptable speed, detail and accuracy is the major development.

- They are facilitating the ever-faster and more reliable communication of electronic signals, particularly for data traffic.

- They are lowering the costs of communication for "traditional" services, most notably long-distance telephony.

In the following section, the potential economic effects of these developments are identified and discussed.

POTENTIAL ECONOMIC CONSEQUENCES

MOST DISCUSSIONS OF THE INFORMATION HIGHWAY fail to distinguish between marginal and average effects. In particular, they tend to ignore considerations of how new communication technologies will affect the marginal products of earlier (and still installed) vintages of capital, as well as the required complementary investments that may have to be made to realize the full benefits of the new technology. Nevertheless, wide-ranging potential impacts of information highway developments have been identified. These suggest a number of potential economic impacts.

ECONOMIES OF SCALE AND SCOPE

THERE IS SUBSTANTIAL SPECULATION about the likely impacts on optimal size and scope at both the plant and firm levels. However, there is some disagreement among observers which, in part, reflects differences in the precise technological changes being considered. For example, Antonelli (1989/90) seemed to consider implicitly the use of private networks by manufacturing companies when he reached the following conclusions.

- Economies of scale in the provision of on-line services are being accentuated.

- It is increasingly economical to customize large-scale production.

- It is increasingly economical to specialize production at the level of the plant.

The main anticipated implications are increases in product economies of scale at the level of the plant and increased economies of scope at the level of the firm.

More recent observations tend to argue that innovations in information technology are enhancing economies of scope at the plant level, while diminishing the potential importance of traditional economies of product specialization. This claim is buttressed by assertions that product differentiation is becoming an increasingly important focus of competitive strategies at the business-unit level.[8] Orr and Hirshhorn (1994), among others, have made the argument that traditional scale economies at the plant level are becoming less important: new production technologies are allowing short production runs to be economical. As well, they suggest that the greater integration and control of production processes made possible by broadband telecommunications facilitates better monitoring and control of output quality. This development further enhances the prominence of product differentiation, i.e., quality as a differentiator, as an element of competitive strategy.

Anecdotes about mass customization abound. The paradigm of agile manufacturing envisages making customized products as quickly and as cheaply as mass-produced items. Communications technology facilitates agile manufacturing by linking customers, suppliers and manufacturers together in a computer network so factories produce to retail orders received on-line in real time. Manufacturers, in turn, dump their orders directly into the computers of their parts and components suppliers. These on-line linkages significantly reduce time lags between changes in demand and changes in production, thereby making it more economical to respond to "idiosyncratic" demand patterns, i.e., demand patterns that may not be highly repetitive and are, therefore, less predictable across both time and space.

The agile manufacturing model ultimately anticipates the extension of the communications web to individual machines on the factory floor. Computers will calculate which combination of machines would most efficiently carry out the necessary work.[9] In effect, computer communication networks reduce both "outside" and "inside" lags associated with customized production. Outside lags might be time delays and other costs associated with altering transactions in a vertically linked value chain, and inside lags are the time delays and costs associated with reconfiguring inputs within production units in response to the altered transactions.

With respect to economies of scale, the most prevalent claim is that new communication technologies, especially interconnected computer networks, such as the Internet, are reducing the optimal size of firms across a range of industries. In particular, costs of "overhead" functions, such as administration and marketing, are becoming more divisible through the use of new technology. As an example, small- and medium-sized firms are able to access legal data bases for up-to-date summaries and interpretations of cases. This, arguably, allows a more efficient sharing of legal expertise than would be the case using the direct services of legal professionals who presumably would need to be hired on a firm-by-firm basis.[10]

As another example, the Internet is being used more and more for private electronic data exchange including the automatic posting of orders by customers in their subcontractors' computers. Private computer networks have existed in the past to accomplish such activities. However, the Internet is cheaper for smaller firms, since it is a shared computer network, albeit one that allows specific point-to-point communications. The ability to share sophisticated computer communication networks contributes to a reduction in economies of scale at the firm level, with all other things being constant.[11] Along similar lines and as discussed below, the Internet also reduces fixed costs associated with marketing and advertising.

To be sure, new technologies may also enhance the advantages of larger firm size in certain dimensions. For example, Blank, et al. (1994), among others, argued that improved global communication links allow multinational enterprises (MNEs) to accelerate their product development cycles and better tailor products for individual markets. To the extent that the underlying technological or marketing advantage of a firm (e.g., a patent or a trademark) is exploitable in foreign markets, Blank, et al. effectively suggested that, in so doing, MNEs have an advantage in the new communications technologies and services.

MNEs may also find it increasingly possible to extend services geographically at relatively low cost using electronic communication networks. An example is the banking industry. In "virtual banking," bank branches become automated teller machines and telephones with computer screens. Activities, such as withdrawing or transferring funds, making payments or buying equities, can be done on-line, eliminating the need for investments in "bricks and mortar" that may have been required previously. Banks enjoying internationally recognized brand names, such as Barclays or Citibank, may be better positioned than smaller banks to take advantage of the new technology, since they presumably do not have to make the same investments in complementary assets that create consumer acceptance and good will. On the other hand, large multinational banks may already have substantial sunk cost investments in bricks and mortar.[12]

In summary, the recent literature tends to argue that new communication technologies are enhancing economies of scope at both the plant and firm levels, while mitigating conventional economies of firm size and product economies of scale at the plant level. The assessment of plant level changes is largely motivated by the constantly improving economics of microcomputer-based distributed processing. Since the mid-1980s, computing horsepower measured in millions of instructions per second (MIPS) has increased about 20 percent annually for mainframe computers and about 50 percent annually for microcomputers (Gunn, 1992, p. 151). The expectation is that the horsepower of microcomputers will continue to increase faster than that of mainframes which should continue to promote the use of local area networks (LANs) which are essentially local distributed processing networks.

The assessment that traditional economies of scale will decline at the firm level is premised on the perspective that the ever-increasing capacity of microcomputers combined with the growth of public computer networks such as the Internet, are making it more feasible for smaller companies to operate the sophisticated data networks that larger firms traditionally constructed using leased private transmission lines connected to mainframe computers. This development will enable smaller firms to enjoy the same quality of administrative and other "staff" services that larger firms enjoy.

Changes in optimal plant and firm-level scale and scope have potentially important implications for both domestic and international patterns of competition. Harris (1985) identified the potential implications for patterns of international trade and investment:

> In products for which scale economies are not important ... the transfer of technology should be fairly rapid and the ultimate location of production will probably be dictated in many cases on grounds of cost and labour market conditions. In other cases, production location will be dictated by the need to be near the customer. In some industries characterized by product differentiation, small-scale flexible manufacturing systems are likely to prove best suited to local markets. In products such as these, technological innovation may actually reduce trade in final goods. Instead, production will be suited to local markets; the trade in goods will be replaced by trade in technology (Harris, 1985, p. 31).

An implication of this argument is that trade in technology may become increasingly important relative to trade in physical goods. A related implication is that contributions to Canada's economic growth associated with international trade will (for a set of industries) increasingly emphasize technology-based sources of long-run comparative advantage rather than more traditional sources such as product economies of scale. This assessment supports the government's preoccupation with improving innovation and new technology adoption by Canadian firms.

An increased competitive emphasis on product differentiation, customization and quality implies an enhanced strategic role for closer linkages between domestic producers and "leading edge" consumers. For Canadian producers, this may imply a need for closer linkages to the U.S. marketplace. Strengthening the ability of small- and medium-sized firms to market abroad might, therefore, be a complementary strategy to promoting the capacity of these firms to innovate.[13] With regard to non-customized product markets, reductions in economies of scale suggest the attenuation of any advantages associated with having headquarters in a large country, along with the greater influence of "conventional" cost and labour market determinants of production location (Harris, 1985, p. 31).

The direct implication of a reduction in optimal firm size is a decrease, over time, in domestic industrial concentration levels. This, in turn, should be associated with an increase in competition. As will be discussed in the next section, information highway developments may also lower barriers to entry into a range of activities for small- and medium-sized enterprises. This should further stimulate increased levels of domestic competition.

Integration of Product Markets

A frequently made claim has new communication technologies breaking down barriers to the flow of goods and services across geographic markets. An extreme version of this claim is provided by the following quote: "With the Internet, the whole globe is one marketplace."[14] The basic notion is that computer networks, such as Internet, will lower search costs and other transactions costs for consumers, especially as interactive, multimedia features allow prospective buyers to see products and negotiate terms and conditions of sale on-line.

In this context, the Internet is seen as a cheaper and possibly more effective means than catalogues for stay-at-home shopping. An increasing number of companies are using the Internet as an additional marketing channel, although early experience indicates that electronic shopping has not been an immediate success.[15] In fact, industrial companies seem more inclined to use computer networks for buying supplies than do households, perhaps reflecting the fact that the goods purchased by industrial companies are more standardized and, hence, more likely to fall into the category of search goods.[16]

The growth of electronic marketing should contribute to increased competition and contestability in regionally segmented markets:

- by reducing the relevance of transportation costs as a barrier to inter-regional and international trade; and

- by reducing information and other transactions costs that are a function of distance.

Telecommunications has always been seen as an important contributor to the integration of markets within and between countries, and this integrating role has been identified as an important source of the linkage between investments in communication infrastructure and economic growth (Norton, 1992). It is important to stress that the impact of the information highway on market integration is incremental to that of the existing infrastructure which, in North America, already permits quite extensive search and purchase behaviour, especially by commercial enterprises.

The Internet and other public communication networks also contribute to a substantial reduction in fixed and sunk costs associated with marketing and promotion activities. As a case in point, it costs as little as US$1000 a year to open an "electronic storefront" on the Internet which is currently accessible by as many as 20 million people (Solomon, 1995).[17] The reduction in barriers to entry associated with marketing and promotion, in turn, is expected to enhance the contestability of specific markets, presumably contributing to improvements in productivity by suppliers in those markets.

Integration of Labour Markets

The anticipated increased integration of labour markets runs parallel to further increased integration of product markets. The relevant notion here is that advanced communication systems permit a more efficient and effective use of foreign labour services. In particular, they facilitate the indirect importation of labour services. Hong Kong's Electric Holdings Ltd., illustrates this point. It is a producer of micromotors that power hair dryers, blenders and auto features such as door locks, windshield wipers and automatic windows. With factories in South China and an R&D base in a Hong Kong industrial park, the company has, nevertheless, been able to win a relatively large market share among the Big Three U.S. auto makers.

The firm makes extensive use of video conferencing to facilitate design team "meetings" with customers in the United States and Europe. Concepts are transmitted from R&D centres in North America and Europe to Hong Kong. The firm is currently investing in advanced telecommunication facilities to link its production facilities in South China to its Hong Kong facilities.[18] In effect, advanced communication techniques facilitate the substitution of design services in Hong Kong for more locally based services by reducing transportation and information costs traditionally associated with greater geographic distances.

In principle, advanced communication techniques should promote a more complete geographical specialization of labour along the lines of comparative advantage, thereby enhancing this traditional source of increased incomes through international trade. Traditional differences in comparative advantage based on relative supplies of skilled and unskilled labour are still relevant. Specifically, many of the labour services electronically exported to developed countries from developing countries involve relatively unskilled activities such as scanning, coding and retransmitting information, and simple programming. Conversely, North American and European firms are apparently taking advantage of cheaper access to data and video networks to export engineering, software design and related services to Asian manufacturers.[19]

To be sure, relatively low-wage and low-skill areas of the world, such as India, Russia and China, have substantial numbers of skilled engineers, computer specialists and the like. The integration of labour markets through electronic networks means the services of these skilled professionals can be increasingly substituted for those of their higher (in both relative and absolute terms) wage counterparts in developed countries. Moreover, international competition, for what are currently considered skilled labour activities, might be expected to increase as average levels of formal education rise in developing parts of the world relative to levels in the developed North American and European countries.

The implications of an indirect increase in the mobility of labour services for trade flows and terms of trade are potentially quite complex. Presumably, the influence of differences in the prices of relatively immobile factors of production, e.g., natural resources or tangible infrastructure, on production location decisions will become more important compared to differences in labour costs. Furthermore, differences in government policies encompassing tax rates, regulation, security of property rights and so forth may become more important influences on production location decisions than in the past.[20] External economies of scale and scope may also become less important determinants of the international competitiveness of different geographic regions. Specifically, physical proximity to specialists, research institutions, universities and so forth should become less advantageous as electronic access to centres of information becomes cheaper and more effective.

It is useful to put this suggested development into context. Multinational enterprises currently account for the bulk of international trade, and much of this trade is intra-firm. Furthermore, large multinational enterprises already possess relatively sophisticated communication linkages among their affiliates in many parts of the world. Moreover, the intra-firm nature of the relevant transactions makes search costs less relevant than they would be in the case of arm's length purchases of labour services. Again, the contribution of the information highway to the integration of labour markets must be seen as incremental to the integration promoted by the activities of multinationals already using private and virtual private communication networks.

Increased Relative Demand for Skilled Labour

According to the "conventional wisdom," the information highway will place an increased premium on the services of skilled workers. Orr and Hirshhorn (1994) noted that the building of the highway and the provision of software inputs (broadly defined to include content services) to the highway will generate increased demand for a range of creative and technical skills. They also argued that the "knowledge intensity" of many jobs will increase as decision-making responsibility is pushed out from centralized management to workers on the production line and in the field.

There are several implications of this scenario. First, the productivity-enhancing effects of the information highway may be incompletely realized if complementary investments in human capital are not made. Second, disparities in the distribution of income based on educational and related achievements may increase, especially if the demand for skilled relative to unskilled labour is enhanced by an improved ability to export the services of skilled workers and import the services of unskilled workers through global communication networks. Third, an improved ability to import labour services electronically should encourage increased long-run competition in labour markets, especially where domestic supply is relatively inelastic, either because of licensing restrictions, professional cartels or other reasons. This development should have productivity-enhancing effects similar to those associated with closer integration of product markets.

Productivity Growth

The various potential economic effects described in this section suggest that several direct and indirect influences will be exerted on aggregate productivity levels and (possibly) productivity growth rates. Since the impact of communications technology on the behaviour of productivity and, ultimately, real incomes, is arguably of greatest overall concern to policy makers, it is worth explicitly identifying the main potential linkages between productivity and information highway developments as they have been discussed in the literature.

More Efficient Communications

Increased efficiency in the transmission and switching of communication signals directly increases productivity to the extent that it reduces the resource requirements associated with carrying out any given set of communication activities.[21] For example, the ability to share transmission facilities more effectively through data compression and packet switching reduces the resource requirements to supply transmission capacity. As will be discussed more fully in the following section, this is unlikely to be a major contributor to productivity, since communication services are a relatively small input into the production process.

Closer Integration of Output and Factor Input Markets

Reductions in transaction and information costs will contribute to reduced geographical segmentation of markets. This, in turn, should promote efficiency by encouraging greater specialization in those markets, as well as reductions in inefficiency associated with uneconomic methods of production by promoting increased competition. In advanced market economies already subject to substantial international competition, it is questionable whether these integration benefits will be large, at the margin.

Faster Rate of Introduction and Adoption of New Technology

New production and management techniques are, arguably, more advantageous to adopt as a result of the increased speed, accuracy and functionality of new communications technology. Examples include just-in-time production and distribution, flexible manufacturing, contracting out and decentralized organizational decision making. More widespread adoption and the intensive use of these techniques is therefore expected to improve productivity across a wide range of industries. The point is: most large firms already enjoy access to the types of communications infra-structure that facilitate computerized information management networks. Hence, information highway developments, per se, may have a relatively small impact on the adoption of new production and management innovations by these firms.

Increased Efficiency of the Innovation and Technology Adoption Process

Whereas the preceding impacts are related to the level of productivity, this impact potentially affects the rate of growth of productivity. Specifically, it has been sug-gested that the information highway will permanently increase the "yield" of R&D expenditures and increase the speed at which new innovations are adopted. It will also improve educational and training techniques which should accelerate the rate of accumulation of human capital (OECD, 1992).

Various potential reasons are offered to support this optimism. One is that more effective collaboration among communities of researchers will be possible through public networks such as the Internet. A second is that the productivity of individual researchers or groups of researchers will be improved by faster, cheaper and more comprehensive access to information and data with a bearing on their research. A third is that increased specialization of labour in the research process will be possible through more effective and efficient "sharing" of information across research groups. Finally, education and training can be provided electronically by the leading experts in any given field, presumably increasing the effective rate of human capital accumulation. These broad potential links to productivity growth are, perhaps, the most provocative implications of the information highway and also, perhaps, the most difficult to assess.

ASSESSING THE POTENTIAL ECONOMIC EFFECTS

AS NOTED ABOVE, TECHNOLOGICAL CHANGE in the telecommunications industry has been ongoing for some time. Moreover, the consequences of earlier vin-tages are similar to those now identified with the information highway. For example, technological changes in telecommunications have promoted a closer integration of product and labour markets and have contributed to an increased international specialization of production, in part by making the multinational enterprise a more viable organizational form. Indeed, several studies of the productivity impacts of telecommunications infrastructure ascribe the identified impacts to the resulting closer integration of markets, especially capital markets.[22]

Characterizations of the information highway as a new "techno-economic" paradigm presumably anticipate that social returns to future investments in new telecommunications infrastructure will be significantly greater than historical returns to such investments. As well, proponents of a "partnership" between busi-ness and government to develop the information highway presumably see the potential for market failure to be significantly greater in the future than in the more recent past. An assessment (largely qualitative) of these perspectives is offered in this section.

INCREASED EFFICIENCY IN THE COMMUNICATIONS SECTOR

THE RELATIVELY LOW SHARE OF TOTAL BUSINESS COSTS representing telecommunications suggests that the major economic potential of the information highway resides in new uses of communications infrastructure rather than in lower costs for existing services. Table 3 reports several service industry outputs required (directly and indirectly) to produce $100 of final output in four broadly defined economic sectors. One service industry output reported for all four sectors is communication. While this category is broader than telecommunications, it is still relevant since telecommunication services, such as facsimile and electronic mail, can substitute for some of the services included in the communications sector, e.g., postal services. Table 3 reports the largest and smallest service sector inputs to each of the four main sectors, as well as the input coefficient for communications. It is not surprising that communications are more important (as a share of output) in the service sector than in the agricultural, mining and manufacturing sectors. However, even in services, communications are a relatively small input to the production process.

Fuss (1994) estimated that the annual rate of growth in TFP for Bell Canada averaged close to 3 percent over the 1980s, slightly below the averages of between 3.3 percent and 3.5 percent for the 1960s and 1970s. Even assuming that unit costs decline at a commensurate rate to the increase in TFP, this will not have a substantial impact on the rate of productivity growth for communication users, most of which are characterized by communication costs that average less than 2 percent of total costs.

Denny, et al. (1981) identified the cost-reducing impact of the two most important telecommunication innovations which occurred during the period 1952 to 1976: the introduction of direct distance dialling and the change-over to modern switching equipment. They showed that the cost-reducing effects of

---

TABLE 3

SERVICE INDUSTRY OUTPUTS REQUIRED TO PRODUCE $100 OF FINAL OUTPUT, 1986 TO 1987

Service Output	Agriculture	Mining	Manufacturing	Services
1. Wholesale trade	$6.8		$10.1	
2. Business services		$8.9		$16.1
3. Retail trade	$1.1			
4. Services to transportation		$1.0		
5. Rail transport			$1.0	
6. Education, libraries				$4.0
7. Communication	$1.30	$1.5	$1.9	$5.8

Source: Bureau of Industry Economics (1992, various tables).

these innovations (for telephone companies) were modest compared to the TFP estimates of Fuss. Specifically, Denny, et al. found that a 1 percent increase in access (at the mean, a change in direct distance dial use from 53 percent to 53.5 percent) reduced total costs by 0.03 percent. Labour services were reduced by 0.24 percent and materials by 0.1 percent. Capital services increased by 0.14 percent. A 1 percent increase in the "switch" variable (at the mean, an increase from 19.8 percent to 20 percent in the percentage of telephones connected to modern switching facilities) reduced total costs by 0.04 percent. Labour services were reduced by 0.013 percent, capital services by 0.07 percent and materials by 0.03 percent. Furthermore, the cost-reducing effects of access to direct distance dialling and connection to modern switching facilities reached their peaks in 1958 to 1962 and 1963 to 1966 respectively, and declined thereafter.

This is not meant to deny that efficiency improvements by communication suppliers can have substantial impacts on the absolute expenditures required to carry out different production and distribution activities in both the private and public sectors. For example, Cronin, et al. (1994) calculated cost savings to the educational service sector due to advances in telecommunications production and the educational sector's consumption of telecommunications for each year from 1963 to 1991. Cumulative cost savings totalled approximately US$77 billion in 1991 dollars. This absolute savings represented less than 1 percent of total government expenditures on education in the United States over that period.

To the extent that rates of TFP growth among communication carriers accelerate and/or that communication expenditures as a share of total costs grow significantly, the impact of improved carrier efficiency on aggregate productivity will become more important. Based on historical experience, there is no reason to predict the former development. As Fuss (1994) noted, TFP growth in Canadian telecommunications accelerated in the later 1980s, but was still no greater than the average growth rate for the 1960s and 1970s. The latter development might be anticipated given the continued relative growth of the service sector and the increased international, relative to domestic, transactions. However, the price inelasticity of most communication services, especially local distribution, will mitigate these structural impacts.

Facilitating the Adoption of New Production and Management Techniques and the Integration of Markets

A more promising linkage between the information highway and aggregate productivity changes is related to the potential for new communications infrastructure to facilitate the adoption of production and organizational innovations. Unfortunately, the "hard" evidence on this linkage, to date, consists almost exclusively of selected anecdotes and superficial case studies.[23]

Many of the projected changes in production and distribution techniques are associated with the use of high speed, ubiquitous computer networks. In particular, a much broader and more intensive use of electronic data interchange (EDI) is seen as facilitating faster and more reliable transactions in vertical production and distribution "chains" throughout the economy. Some observers have suggested that the need for wholesalers and other intermediaries might ultimately be eliminated both for producers and final consumers.[24] According to one available estimate, EDI currently accounts for no more than 5 percent of daily business transactions (Katsaros, 1994). This relatively small volume takes place largely on private networks. The emergence of the Internet and other public computer communication networks might accelerate the adoption of EDI and related techniques to improve the efficiency of inter- and intra-firm transactions.

Growth of the Internet

The Internet seems to be emerging as an important component of the public information highway. Available information points to an extremely rapid rate of growth in its usage. For example, one source estimates that there were over two million computers connected through the Internet as of May 1994. A more recent estimate for February 1995 identified the core Internet – computers that are fully linked to the Internet – at eight million computers.[25] As of May 1994, over 20 million people were estimated to have access to electronic mail and other resources via the Internet. As of February 1995, this number was closer to 28 million.

Figure 1 reports the number of Internet hosts by geographic region as of July 1994 and October 1994. It indicates that the bulk of Internet users are in North America, and that the next most active region, Western Europe, has only about one third the number of Internet hosts as does North America.[26] As well, between July 1994 and October 1994, most of the growth in Internet hosts was in North America. Nevertheless, the absolute number of host computers connected to the

FIGURE 1

NUMBER OF HOST CONNECTIONS

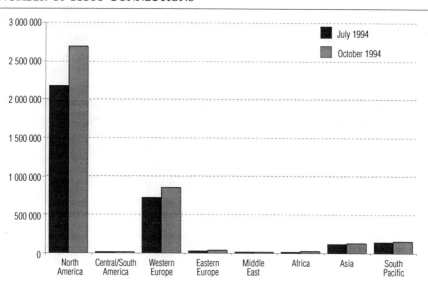

Internet is small. Moreover, many of the host computers are owned by non-commercial enterprises. For example, in the United States, as of July 1994, around 37 percent of host computers were identified by code as commercial.[27] Fully 42 percent were identified as educational and another 15 percent were either government or military.[28] The residual category includes non-profit organizations, professional societies and so forth.

In short, if the Internet is to emerge as a major new communications infrastructure facilitating the adoption of new production and managerial processes, commercial use of the Internet will have to continue to grow dramatically for an extended period of time. Moreover, growth in usage will need to spread to other regions of the world outside of North America if this network is to have significant impacts on international business transactions.

In the absence of a reliable identification of the factors determining the commercial usage of the Internet, one can only speculate about whether recent rapid rates of growth (from very low initial levels) will continue for an extended period of time. It might be relevant to note the significant geographical concentration of commercial domains in North America.[29]

Table 4 reports the number of commercial domains associated with a specific area code for the 15 area codes with the largest absolute number of commercial domains. The associated cities are meant to provide a more accessible geographic reference for the reader than is provided by the area code. It should be noted that the area code frequently identifies a region larger than the individual city or cities mentioned.

Slightly over 18 percent of commercial Internet domains are located in the San Francisco Bay area and Silicon Valley (San Jose and suburbs). Somewhat over 6 percent are located in the Boston area and regions just outside of Boston. In essence, almost one quarter of all commercial Internet domains are located in major centres of computer electronics. While it is not surprising that the computer industry should be an early user of the Internet, it is possible to infer that growth of usage outside this area of commerce might be significantly slower, either because both suppliers and customers in the computer electronics sector are relatively sophisticated about the underlying technology or because transactions in the computer electronics domain lend themselves more readily to electronic mediation.

Almost 50 percent of all commercial domains are located in the 15 regions cited in Table 4. As further testimony to the likely concentration of commercial users in the computer electronics industry (broadly defined), California accounts for almost 26 percent of all commercial domains. Another observation is suggestive. The total number of commercial domains in the computer-intensive regions of Ottawa and southeast Ontario (156) are comparable to the total number in Toronto (297).[30] This latter distribution is striking given the concentration of commercial enterprises in Toronto and the much larger absolute population of potential users in Toronto.

By way of background, Table 5 reports the number of commercial domains for major cities in Canada. Estimates are provided for the following area codes: 416

TABLE 4

COMMERCIAL DOMAINS BY AREA CODE – JULY 15, 1994

Area Code	City	Commercial Domains	% of Total
415	San Francisco (CA)	1,460	8.6
408	San Jose/Sunnyvale (CA)	1,158	6.8
303	Boulder/Denver (CO)	942	5.5
617	Boston (MA)	739	4.4
212	New York City (NY)	532	3.1
703	Arlington/Fairfax (VA)	527	3.1
510	Oakland (CA)	497	2.9
619	San Diego (CA)	375	2.2
508	Worcester/Framingham (MA)	330	1.9
708	Aurora/Evanston (IL)	318	1.9
206	Seattle/Tacoma (WA)	314	1.9
612	Minneapolis/St. Paul (MN)	314	1.9
416	Toronto (ON)	297	1.8
301	Silver Spring/Frederick (MD)	285	1.7
310	Los Angeles (CA)	285	1.7

Source: Internet Info, Falls Church, VA, 1994.

TABLE 5

COMMERCIAL DOMAINS BY AREA CODE FOR CANADA – JULY 15, 1994

Area Code	City	Commercial Domains
416	Toronto (ON)	297
604	Vancouver (BC)	115
613	Ottawa (ON)	87
519	London (ON)	69
514	Montreal (QC)	60

Source: Internet Info, Falls Church, VA, 1994.

TABLE 6

INTERNET HOSTS AND GNP/HOSTS FOR SELECTED COUNTRIES – JULY 1994

Country	Hosts	GNP/Hosts
Iceland	3,268	1.67
Australia	127,514	2.28
Norway	38,759	2.53
Finland	49,598	2.62
United States	2,044,716	2.79
New Zealand	14,830	3.12
Sweden	53,294	3.80
Netherlands	59,729	4.18
Canada	127,516	4.54
Switzerland	47,401	5.02
United Kingdom	155,706	5.93
Denmark	12,107	7.52
Hong Kong	9,141	7.80
Austria	20,130	8.15
Germany	149,193	10.03
Singapore	4,014	10.76
Belgium	12,107	14.19
Taiwan	10,314	14.62
France	71,899	15.30
South Korea	12,109	22.55
Spain	21,147	23.05
Japan	72,409	43.38
Italy	23,616	46.16

Source: Mark Lottor, Network Wizards.

(Toronto and south central Ontario), 604 (Vancouver and the rest of British Columbia), 613 (Ottawa and southeast Ontario), 519 (London and southwest Ontario) and 514 (Montreal and southern Quebec).

The total number of commercial domains listed for Canada (628) is approximately 4 percent of the total number of commercial domains identified. This seeming "under representation" of Canadian domains might reflect biases in the data collection process. Alternatively, it might further attest to the prominence of the computer electronics industry as the major early commercial adopter of the Internet. Canada's small computer electronics sector would, therefore, result in a relatively small number of commercial domains.

Additional insight into the determinants of early Internet usage is provided by data in Table 6, which reports the number of Internet computer hosts and the ratio of GNP (in U.S. dollars) to the number of Internet hosts for July 1994. A lower ratio of GNP to Internet hosts reflects a more intensive adoption of the Internet. It can be concluded, that while Canada has been somewhat slower to adopt the Internet, it has moved rapidly compared to many other developed countries or the Asian Tigers (Hong Kong, Singapore, Taiwan and South Korea). Presumably, adoption of the Internet across all domains is a function of the technological sophistication of the underlying telephone system. However, as suggested by the following statistic, this may not be a robust determinant of rates of adoption among leading countries. The countries listed in Table 6 were ranked by the share of electronic switching capacity of total exchange lines in 1987 where this share estimate was available.[31] For the 20 countries in this sample, a Spearman correlation coefficient between the rank order of countries by share of electronic capacity and their rank order in Table 6 was calculated. The coefficient was a statistically significant -0.607. Similarly, a Spearman correlation coefficient between the rank order of 10 countries in Table 6 and the annual gross investment in telecommunications in U.S. dollars per inhabitant in 1986 was a statistically insignificant 0.19.[32]

Certainly, the state of a country's telecommunications infrastructure is not irrelevant to the use of computer networks such as Internet. For example, for the 20-country sample, the average share of electronic capacity was 35.6 whereas it was 31.5 for the entire sample of 40 countries for which estimates of average share of electronic capacity were available. Nevertheless, these results caution against an assumption that government policies promoting investment in new telecommunications capacity will necessarily vault a country into the lead in using information highway services. It is also a caution against inferring that the adoption of the Internet will proceed at anything approaching current rates for the foreseeable future. We simply don't know very much about the determinants of the relevant adoption patterns.

The Commercial Effects of Internet

While the growth of Internet usage has been spectacular, it is still a relatively limited commercial phenomenon. It is far from certain that adoption of public computer networks, such as the Internet, will be as rapid in other commercial sectors as it has apparently been in the computer electronics sector. Indeed, there are several important potential barriers to the widespread commercial use of the Internet. One is security. As a public network, the Internet is subject to greater risks of "piracy" than are private or virtual private networks. A second is the absence (to date) of an Internet "currency." That is, transactions must still be paid for using credit cards or other institutionalized forms of credit largely "off-line" for security reasons.[33] This lack of security and privacy reduces the commercial potential of the Internet.

Rapid adoption of public computer networks by commercial users will also be limited by the fact that many large commercial enterprises and establishments are already well served by private local and wide area telecommunication networks. Such networks are fairly well established in both the manufacturing and service sectors. For example, Baldwin, Diverty and Sabourin (forthcoming) examined the use of computer-based technologies in manufacturing, including the use of interconnected computers to aid in the communications and inspection processes, either by providing information through local area networks or through computers on the factory floor. Their survey also included wide area and inter-company computer networks linking plants to subcontractors, suppliers and customers. They found that the use of local and wide area networks accounted for a substantial share of the output of the manufacturing establishments. Specifically, while only 9.3 percent of establishments were using local area networks and only 10.4 percent were using wide area networks, the percentages increased to 36.7 and 35.4, respectively, when responses were weighted by shipments.

McFetridge (1992) provided evidence confirming the more intensive use of new communication technologies in the service sector, as well as the more rapid adoption of these technologies by larger organizations. Using survey data collected by Statistics Canada, he reported that some 40 percent of service sector establishments were using local area networks and 29 percent were using wide area networks. By size classes based on number of employees, establishments with over 500 employees were almost three times more likely to be using new communication technologies than establishments with between 20 and 100 employees.

Clearly, the relatively high minimum cost of private networks discourages their use by smaller firms. The lower indivisible cost associated with sharing public networks underlies the optimistic assessments about the productivity benefits of the information highway, i.e., barriers to the adoption of new communication technologies will be reduced by the emergence of public computer networks. What should be kept in mind is that the benefits of new communication technologies may not be proportionate to firm size. For example, Baldwin, Diverty and Sabourin (forthcoming) identified the elimination of many middle management positions as an important source of cost savings associated with new technologies. This is presumably less relevant for smaller organizations with minimal levels of hierarchy. The restructuring of organizations to allow greater flexibility of work and reporting arrangements – another identified benefit – is, presumably, more relevant for larger organizations.

Several other considerations suggest that new communication services delivered through existing public networks may have significantly smaller productivity impacts than implicitly contemplated in the optimistic information highway scenarios. One relates to the investments required to supply those services. The existing narrowband connection to the public telephone network that most residences and small businesses currently possess is capable of transmitting relatively crude video images. But, it is not anticipated that technology will allow full-motion video to be carried over the existing paired copper wire. Consequently, the delivery of true multimedia services to the bulk of telephone subscribers requires either the installation of fibre-optic cable into most homes and businesses or the conversion of the existing cable infrastructure into fully interactive systems.

Estimates of the costs of putting broadband fibre into Canadian homes are highly speculative: every available estimate suggests that the costs will be large. For example, Stentor estimates that it will have to spend up to C$8.5 billion to build a broadband-to-the-home network to duplicate Canada's existing 16 million telephone access lines.[34] Extrapolation from U.S. proposals suggests a cost that is as much as six times higher than the Stentor estimate. (CCTA, 1994, p. 26). Substantially higher costs imply higher charges to subscribers for access to, and use of, information highway services which will reduce potential quantity demanded and increase investment risks for the telephone companies. To be sure, if the telephone network can effectively substitute for cable TV services, the overall cost to subscribers for information highway services may be no greater than the combined current cost of telephone and cable TV services. On the other hand, pessimistic scenarios suggest that recovery of the full costs of constructing a broadband network imply expenditures by most subscribers (e.g., as much as $100 a month) that are much higher than the current combined local telephone and cable charges. Whether sufficient demand will emerge to support this level of investment is an open question.

In a similar manner, the existing coaxial cable networks operated by the cable companies cannot be readily reconfigured to provide local switched voice telephone services (CCTA, 1994). In the United Kingdom, where local cable franchisees have recently entered the local telephony market, they have done so with fibre and copper pair that is completely distinct from their cable distribution plant, although placed in the same trenches and/or cable sheath. Consequently, cable companies may be in no position to offer ubiquitous local broadband distribution services in the near future. It is also unclear how much of their existing capital stock can be converted for use in providing information highway services.

A second caveat is that the economic benefits associated with increased international trade presumably require the more widespread adoption of new networks, such as the Internet, in countries outside of North America. This rate of adoption may be relatively slow because of the limited amount of advanced telecommunications infrastructure in many regions of the world, the relatively low incomes which will limit ownership of microcomputers and the low levels of literacy and numeracy which may limit demand for non-entertainment applications of the new technology.[35]

PROMOTING INNOVATION

THE NOTION THAT THE INFORMATION HIGHWAY will promote faster rates of innovation and diffusion of technology is both intriguing and highly speculative. However, it is possible to be sceptical, at the outset, of the existence of major benefits in this regard. The major benefit of an interactive public network to the R&D process is presumably that it facilitates communication among a wider group of interested parties. In this regard, there is no evidence that the current size distribution of R&D facilities is "non-optimal" in any meaningful sense. Similarly, available evidence suggests that there are a relatively large number of channels through which technical information can be exchanged.

The most robust source of technical information for producers is typically the information provided by suppliers. While the availability of public networks, such as the Internet, may make it easier and cheaper for suppliers to communicate with users, available evidence does not indicate that lack of knowledge about the availability of an innovation is a major barrier to adoption, at least for commercial innovations.

It is also relevant to note that scientists and engineers, as well as academic researchers more generally, have had access to computer networks, such as Bitnet, for some time. The ubiquity of the information highway may add little, on the margin, if "communities of interest" are relatively small in the research community and if groups can identify their communities of interest relatively easily. Certainly, the community bulletin boards that populate the Internet add an element of serendipity to the research communication process; i.e., unexpected sources may be holders of critical information. In the fairly organized world of modern science, this serendipity would not seem to be a major contributor to faster rates of innovation.

There is no doubt that networks, such as the Internet, will promote lower cost dissemination of scientific and technical knowledge which should, on the margin, promote the adoption of innovations. These benefits may be realized in both commercial and non-commercial activities. For example, health and medical information available on computer networks may make individuals more receptive to innovative health and medical practices and procedures.[36] Moreover, faster and possibly more widespread feedback from customers to producers should promote beneficial changes to product and service features for both private and public sector activities. The issue is whether these benefits will be substantial enough, on the margin, to contribute to a significant increase in aggregate productivity growth rates to justify the associated expenditures on the information highway and software.

If investments in advanced telecommunications establish a virtuous cycle of faster innovation and economic growth which, in turn, promotes additional investment in advanced telecommunications, one would predict that the returns to investments in telecommunications infrastructure should continually diverge between richer and poorer countries. That is, countries starting out at higher levels of technological competence should realize higher returns to infrastructure investments in telecommunications.

The following evaluation of the impact of investments in telecommunications infrastructure on productivity growth was undertaken. Specifically, using data in Antonelli (1993b), the following regression equation was estimated:

$$Gp = a + bI + cY + dICA + fICL + e \tag{1}$$

where Gp is the average growth of labour productivity over the period 1979 to 1986; I is the average share of total investment in output over the period 1979 to 1986; Y is real per capita income in 1986 U.S. dollars; ICA is average share of total investment in output weighted by the average share of investment in telecommunications for 16 countries with real per capita incomes in 1986 U.S. dollars exceeding $6000 and zero otherwise; and ICL is equivalent to ICA for eight countries with real per capita incomes in 1986 U.S. dollars of less than $6000.

The specification of Equation (1) is constrained by the available data. Nevertheless, it potentially allows us to identify the relationship of primary interest.

If telecommunications infrastructure promotes innovation and technological change, a mix of capital investment more heavily weighted toward communications should have a greater productivity effect in high-income countries than in low-income countries, since the latter are likely to be relatively small performers of R&D and related innovation efforts compared to high-income countries. The I variable is relatively straightforward and should be positively related to GP. The Y variable should be negatively related to GP reflecting the income convergence phenomenon between high- and low-income countries.

The main finding of interest was robust to alternative specifications in which other independent variables were included in Equation (1) and where the Y value was specified in natural logarithmic values. Hence, only the primary specification is reported. A t-value is shown in parenthesis below each coefficient. The R-squared coefficient is adjusted for degrees of freedom.

$$GP = -.039 + .101I - .0001Y + .057ICA + .027ICL \qquad (2)$$

$$(2.29) \; (-1.90) \quad (1.59) \quad (2.68)$$

Adjusted R-squared = .722 F= 12.32.

The coefficients for the I and Y variables take the expected signs and are statistically significant at the 0.05 and 0.10 levels. The ICL variable is statistically significant at the 0.05 level, while the ICA variable is statistically insignificant. The result suggests that a higher share of telecommunications in a country's capital infrastructure is positively related to a lower-income country's growth rate but not to a higher-income country's growth rate. This latter result is not inconsistent with other findings that telecommunications infrastructure investment has a stronger impact on economic growth in low-income countries than in high-income countries (Cronin, et al., 1993b).

Clearly one does not want to make too much of such simplistic econometrics. Nevertheless, Equation (2) may be taken as yet another observation cautioning against a conclusion that the information highway will provide a major boost to Canada's economic growth rate. Indeed, in reviewing a broad set of factors conditioning the marginal impacts of the information highway, one must be highly sceptical about the hyperbole surrounding the anticipated economic benefits.

POLICY ISSUES

IT IS IMPOSSIBLE IN THIS PAPER TO PROVIDE A THOROUGH REVIEW of the main policy issues raised in the information highway context. At best, they can be identified, and the more substantive ones briefly addressed.[37]

Perhaps the overriding issue is whether there is a more active role for government to play in developing and promoting the information highway. A case for urgent government involvement is implicit in claims that there are large differences between private and social returns to investments in the information highway and related arguments that "winners and losers in the Information Age are being decided today, before they realize the information revolution has even begun. Determination of all winners and losers will occur within the next few years."[38]

Governments in Canada currently provide some funding for the Canadian Internet backbone CA*net. Through the CANARIE program, the federal government has made a relatively modest $26 million contribution to upgrade CA*net and develop new user-friendly products, applications and services. The provincial governments make more substantial financial contributions to CA*net by funding access to the provincial networks for public sector organizations such as universities and hospitals.

A specific policy issue is whether governments should increase their level of funding of CA*net on either the supply or demand sides of the market, or both. Arguments have been made that the existence of substantial externalities will lead to significant inefficiencies if the development of the Canadian Internet is left largely to market forces. Externalities of various types have been identified. One is the familiar claim that there are network externalities for users. That is, the value of joining a network is a positive function of the size of the network. Hence, the efficient price for access is likely to be less than the incremental cost of providing access. A second externality is that the productivity benefits conferred on users of the network, or non-users for that matter, will not be fully appropriated by suppliers of the network and network services. Hence, network infrastructure and network services might be under-provided by private sector suppliers. A third externality is that later suppliers will learn from the successes and mistakes of earlier suppliers. That is, there are strong "fast second" advantages in being an Internet supplier as opposed to the more conventionally assumed "first mover" advantages. As a consequence, uneconomic delays might be introduced into the provisioning of Internet infrastructure and the supplying of services by private sector participants.

A full evaluation of the role of government in promoting the development of the information highway would need to weigh the potential for government failure against market failure. One major concern about government intervention in the communications sector is that cross-subsidies will be continued long after any economic rationale for subsidization exists. This has been the experience with basic local telephone service where substantial cross-subsidies from toll usage to local access have been perpetuated (and even increased), notwithstanding that there is virtually universal access to the basic telephone network.[39]

Another major concern about government intervention is that subsidies on both the supply and demand sides of the market will likely be influenced by political rather than economic considerations. It is clear that governments are coming to view the information highway as a job creation possibility, and one must be sceptical about the ability and willingness of governments to evaluate activities to be subsidized on the basis of productivity externalities. Even efficiency-driven government bureaucrats and policy makers will find it difficult to distinguish between marginal and infra-marginal resource allocation decisions. Moreover, there is an incentive for subsidy seekers to portray themselves as being "on the margin" of participation unless government grants them financial favours, either directly or indirectly. The current threats being made by Stentor to forebear from making large investments in fibre-to-the-home infrastructures unless Stentor members are allowed to hold broadcasting licences are illustrative of the "gaming" behaviour that can be expected in a regime where ownership of valuable property rights depends critically on the outcome of political and regulatory processes.

The preceding section of the paper raised a caution against assuming that there will be large "third-party" productivity benefits associated with usage of information highway infrastructure, at least for the foreseeable future. This caution suggests that large direct or indirect government subsidies to constructing the information highway may have social costs whose present value exceeds the present value of related social benefits. Moreover, there is no evidence to support concerns that delays in investing in information highway infrastructure will permanently disadvantage Canadian firms. Indeed, the evidence suggests the opposite. Namely, that although early investments in information technology may give a company or a country some brief advantage, it is rarely sustainable, and there are comparatively few examples of successful use of information technology to gain a sustained competitive advantage (Cane, 1992).

There is also no compelling case for assuming that network externalities on either the supply or demand sides of the market for information highway services will lead to substantial market failure. For example, there are numerous instances of system integrators and network service providers directly or indirectly subsidizing access to computer networks in order to "grow" the network. In other cases, on-line services are provided without charge if the service provider can earn profits indirectly from a larger-sized network. An example is Industry Net, a special computer network for manufacturers. Any manufacturer can log onto the free network which offers advertisements, message boards, new product announcements and electronic mailboxes geared to an industrial audience. The network is used, among other things, to search across geographic markets for specific products. National and regional advertisers bear the cost of running the service by advertising their products and services (Mehta, 1994).

Rather than supplanting competitive market forces, the promotion of competition in local network distribution services might be the single most effective initiative the Canadian government and the regulator could undertake to promote the efficient growth of the information highway. Again, it is well beyond the scope of this paper to justify this claim in any detail. However, competition in local network distribution services can be expected to provide, among other things, a proliferation of services and pricing schemes more closely aligned to the tastes and preferences of different groups of subscribers. This is similar to what has happened in the case of long-distance competition. Furthermore, the abandonment of the cross-subsidy from toll to local access should encourage entry into the local distribution segment of the industry. It should also allow prices of leased lines to decline in Canada. Since leased lines form the backbone of wide area computer networks, the cost of this critical input is significant.[40]

TABLE 7

LEASED LINE CHARGES – 64 KBPS AND 1.52 MBPS AS OF JANUARY 1992, NORMALIZED TO AUSTRALIA

Country	64 Kbps	1.52 Mbps
Australia	100	100
Austria	481	269
Belgium	417	170
Canada	282	184
Denmark	188	66
Finland	137	Na
France	444	170
Germany	710	796
Greece	310	138
Hong Kong	264	39
Iceland	155	168
Ireland	150	102
Italy	358	350
Japan	258	228
Luxembourg	100	112
Netherlands	369	198
New Zealand	242	135
Norway	173	112
Portugal	201	140
Singapore	136	132
Spain	1,151	Na
Sweden	135	Na
Switzerland	296	160
United Kingdom	129	74

Source: Bureau of Industry Economics (1992, Figures 4.6, 4.7).

Table 7 reports leased line tariff charges calibrated with reference to Australia's charges as the base for two main types of leased lines: 64 Kbps (mainly for data) and 1.52 Mbps for ISDN (i.e., broadband interactive services). The table shows that Canada's charges are above average for developed countries, primarily reflecting the toll to local cross-subsidy described above. Specifically, for 64 Kbps leased lines, Canada's charges are 15th of the 24 sample countries. For 1.52 Mbps leased lines, Canada's charges are 16th of the 21 sample countries. Canada's charges for leased lines are also higher than those in the United States (not reported).

Competition in the local network distribution sector raises a host of issues related to competitive safeguards and Canadian content. In the area of competitive safeguards, a particularly important issue is how to ensure that incumbent dominant firms, particularly the telephone companies, do not engage in anti-competitive practices including subsidizing competitive information highway services with profits earned through supplying monopoly local services, and imposing network standards that disadvantage rival suppliers. Requirements to supply interconnection at non-discriminatory prices and to open up network architecture and standards should mitigate the risks of abuse of dominance, as should the use of price caps in the regulation of local service tariffs. The possibility does exist, however, that vigorous competition in the provision of information highway services may require incumbent telephone and cable companies to provide those services through separate subsidiaries. There may also be a useful role for government to play, especially in the international context, in fostering and facilitating the development of technical information standards.

Canadian content on the information highway is a clear concern of government policy makers. Indeed, Public Notice CRTC 1994-130 was a response to an order-in-council asking the CRTC to evaluate, among other things, how the information highway can be used to promote Canadian cultural content. Most of the respondents to the public notice, including Stentor, advocated the maintenance and even the extension of protectionist policies, such as Canadian content quotas, on "conventional" distribution media, e.g., cable, as well as on newer media, e.g., computer networks. Abstracting from the technical difficulties associated with implementing protectionist policies on the information highway, such initiatives can reduce the economic benefits of information highway services to Canadian consumers, by restricting their choice of services. In doing so, the rate of adoption of those services will slow down.

An additional policy issue is whether differential access to the information highway based on ability to pay will exacerbate differences across groups in Canada in terms of income levels and unemployment rates. A concern about allowing the emergence of technologically "advantaged" and "disadvantaged" groups underpins calls for subsidizing access to and use of the information highway. It also underlies proposals to provide government-sponsored training programs in the use of new communication technologies.

There is a great deal of debate about whether, and to what extent, differences in the usage of modern computer-based technologies contribute to differences in economic performance. Without assessing the merits of the positions in this debate, it seems appropriate to caution against subsidizing infra-marginal access and usage. That is, subsidies, if granted, should be targeted to "meritorious" subscribers who would not otherwise use educational and other "productivity-related" information highway services. Perhaps the most effective way to do this is through expanded access to new communications media, such as the Internet, in schools, public libraries and so forth. Lower income groups are more likely to find their access to the information highway expanded in this way than are higher income groups, since the latter are more likely to subscribe privately to information highway service providers.

SUMMARY AND CONCLUSIONS

PREDICTING THE ECONOMIC EFFECTS of the information highway is akin to predicting the effects of an earthquake as the ground begins to shake. Whether the information highway will be a minor tremor or an eight on the Richter scale is anyone's guess. The burden of proof would appear to rest with those who see major changes resulting in the economic landscape. Much of the offered proof is either anecdotal or draws on the very rapid recent growth of memberships on the Internet. Neither source of evidence is persuasive that future economic impacts of technological change in communications will be significantly different from historical experience. It should be emphasized that, just as the economic impacts of basic technology were substantial, the economic impacts of the information highway will also be substantial.

To be sure, substantial investments have been made in information highway-related technologies, including on-line services and network software. For example, it has been estimated that at least US$30 million of venture capital was invested in Internet-related projects in the second-half of 1994 alone (Churbuck, 1995). Publicly traded on-line services, such as America Online, trade at price-earnings multiples that are well above market averages, and companies, such as AT&T, are acquiring on-line services at large premiums to book values (Churbuck, 1995). One should not assume that all, or even most, of the investments being made will pay off. Nevertheless, financial optimism about on-line interactive networking cautions against being unduly cynical about the commercial prospects for new communication technologies. Put bluntly, the relatively subdued assessment presented in this analysis may prove to be incorrect, although the risk of this misjudgment is likely to be much lower in the short run than in the long run.

A key feature of the information highway is its potential ubiquity in providing interactive information services. The rate at which ubiquity will be realized is very much an open question. The costs of providing access to interactive broadband communication facilities may significantly restrict the rate of adoption of information highway services by many households and small businesses. While computer networks, such as Internet, do not provide full broadband services, they are a major source of traffic on the information highway. Yet the Internet's impressive recent rates of growth should not obscure the fact that membership has been highly selective. Specifically, individual subscribers tend to be drawn from relatively high socio-economic family brackets. Employees in educational institutions and government departments are major subscribers to on-line services. Commercial users tend to be concentrated in the computer electronics industry. In view of this fairly selective nature of on-line computer network users, it is probably quite misleading to extrapolate recent rates of growth too much further into the future.[41]

The potential economic effects of the information highway are also conditioned by the fact that private networks can provide many of the services expected to be offered on public networks such as the Internet. Hence, large companies are not necessarily restricted by available communications technology in implementing new production and management techniques that rely on high-speed broadband communication networks. Nor is it obvious that public networks, with greater security problems than private networks, will become major channels for commercial transactions, for the communication of proprietary research and development results having commercial value. In short, many of the anticipated productivity benefits of public networks, such as the Internet, assume that these networks will be clearly superior alternatives to existing communication media for a wide range of commercial activities. This may or may not prove to be the case.

The implication of this relatively subdued assessment of the economic effects of the information highway is that governments should be cautious in their expectations about what new communications technologies can and will do for economic growth and growth of real incomes. As well, the perspective that substantial government intervention is required to "manage" a techno-economic paradigm shift may be misguided. The "conventional wisdom" of relying on market forces with sufficient competitive safeguards in place and directing subsidies (where appropriate) is applicable to the information highway. Traditional government activities in the areas of education and training should also promote more effective and efficient use of this innovation.

ENDNOTES

1　Much of the discussion in this section is from Globerman (forthcoming). An excellent overview of the technical and economic characteristics of the Internet is found in MacKie-Mason and Varian (1994).

2　For example, Rogers Network Services is using Rogers Cable Company's infrastructure to provide data networking services. Such services are also provided by the telephone companies.

3　Voice communications still account for around 85 percent of total telecommunications traffic. See Bureau of Industry Economics (1992, p. 7).

4　For an analysis of the advantages of cable companies relative to telephone companies in providing switched broadband services, see Johnson (1993). Another relatively non-technical evaluation of alternative local distribution technologies is provided by Yates, Lemay and Wall (1994).

5　The Internet is actually a network linking some 10 000 networks in approximately 50 countries.

6　See "Prodigy Is In That Awkward Stage," *Business Week*, February 13, 1995, p. 90.

7　By way of comparison, Decima Research found that 72 percent of Canadians surveyed were very or somewhat interested in the idea of having access to movies on demand, with over 50 percent interested in the idea of having access to some form of electronic at-home banking service. See Rogers Communications Inc. (1995, p. 13).

8　In the business policy literature associated with Porter (1985), competitive strategy is concerned with how a firm should compete in any specified market. Corporate strategy is concerned with choosing the specific markets in which to compete.

9　This description of agile manufacturing is taken from *Business Week: 21st Century Capitalism* (1994).

10　For a brief discussion of the growth of on-line legal services, see French (1994).

11 There is an argument that very small firms may not be able to take advantage of new networks, such as the Internet, because they lack technical sophistication. Indeed, small suppliers have complained publicly about requirements imposed on them by large retailers, such as Sears Roebuck, to use electronic data interchange systems. The emergence of small consulting companies specializing in commercial uses of the Internet is a response to this situation.

12 For a discussion of virtual banking, see *Business Week: 21st Century Capitalism* (1994).

13 It is beyond the scope of this paper to address the exporting behaviour of small- and medium-sized firms. The overwhelming majority of those firms do no export.

14 The quote is attributed to Bill Washburn, former director of Commercial Internet Exchange. See "The Internet: How it will change the way you do business." *Business Week*. November 14, 1994, p. 81.

15 It is estimated that the value of goods purchased on the Internet currently amounts to roughly US$10 million a year, although it is estimated to be growing by as much as 10 percent per month. See Solomon (1995). Some observers have remarked on the disappointingly slow growth in commerce over the Internet. See, for example, Churbuck (1995). An important impediment to on-line marketing is the perception that public networks are not "secure" enough for credit card transactions, a concern that is being addressed by network service providers. At least one group (Commerce Net) claims that it will have devised a secure method for bank card transactions over the Internet in 1995.

16 For a description of several commercial computer networks linking buyers and sellers of components and other inputs, see Globerman (forthcoming).

17 The number of Internet users who browse "electronic storefronts," i.e., World Wide Web sites, is probably less than the total number on the Internet, since many individuals use only electronic mail services.

18 See "High-Tech Jobs All Over the Map." *Business Week: 21st Century Capitalism*. 1994, p. 115.

19 Ibid.

20 For an overview of studies of production location decisions by MNEs, see Globerman (1994).

21 Partial productivity indexes for specific inputs might decrease to the extent that lower communication costs encourage increased usage of those inputs. There is some evidence that the use of communication services may be complementary to the use of physical capital. See Cronin, et al. (1993a).

22 See, for example, Norton (1992) and the studies he cites.

23 Representative of this genre of evidence is Cronin (1994). There is some statistical evidence of the productivity-enhancing effects of "older" vintages of communications technology. See, for example, Baldwin, Diverty and Sabourin (forthcoming).

24 One particularly enthusiastic set of expectations is found in Benjamin and Wigard (1995).

25 See "How Many Caught in the Net?" *Seattle Times*, February 12, 1995.

26 It should be noted explicitly that the number of hosts is not equivalent to the number of users. Hosts are computers that act as "local post offices," and there are likely to be multiple users of each office. However, the geographic distribution of hosts is likely to be representative of the geographic distribution of the users. It is worth acknowledging that data describing the size of the Internet, either by number of computers, number of hosts or number of users, are "guesstimates" and should be taken as suggestive rather than definitive.

27 Data on Internet hosts were obtained on the Internet. They were supplied by Mark Lottor of Network Wizards. Identification of the nature of the host computer, e.g., commercial, educational, government and so forth, is available almost exclusively for the United States. Commercial users are the fastest growing segment of the Internet.

28 Many of the non-commercial host computers may have been part of a more specialized computer network, e.g., Bitnet, that was interconnected with (and amalgamated into) the Internet. In effect, the explosive recent growth of the Internet reflects both "acquisitions" of existing users of other networks, and entirely new users of public computer networks. The latter tend to be drawn primarily from commercial categories of users.

29 A commercial domain is essentially a post office address on the Internet used by a for-profit organization, either to sell interconnect services or to sell other products.

30 These data on commercial Internet domains were obtained from Internet Info.

31 The share of electronic switching capacity of total exchange lines was provided in Antonelli (1993a) for 17 of the countries listed in Table 6.

32 The annual gross investment in telecommunications was available in Antonelli (1993a) for only a subset of the countries listed in Table 6.

33 The Wells Fargo Bank recently announced that it has developed a secure system for credit card purchases over the Internet. See "Safe Passage in Cyberspace." *Business Week*. March 20, 1995, p. 33.

34 Stentor has indicated that any plans to build a fibre-to-the-home infrastructure are contingent on the telephone companies receiving broadcasting licences. This may or may not happen in the near future. See Stentor (1994).

35 Antonelli (1993a) presented a model of adoption of advanced telecommunications. He concluded that countries "locked in" by lower growth of output and investments and a large installed base of young vintages of inferior technology are less likely to switch to new technology.

36 There is evidence that chronically ill patients are sharing information on the Internet about new drug therapies. A concern raised is that such information is encouraging patients to change their existing medication with the unfortunate by-product that clinical trials they may have been participating in become invalid. Concern has also been expressed about the poor "quality" of medical information communicated by lay people on computer networks. See William Bulkeley (1995).

37 For a fuller policy discussion of the issues, see Globerman (forthcoming).

38 The latter is a suggestion of path dependence with a vengeance. The quote attributed to the Saskatchewan Information Technology and Telecommunications Advisory Committee is reported in Government of Saskatchewan (1995, p. 5).

39 See Stanbury, Janisch and Globerman (1995) for a recent discussion of the toll to local access cross-subsidy.

40 Information access providers will need to pay more for the local dial-up lines they use to provide access to their customers. But, capacity constraints on the trunk facilities are becoming the major bottleneck to the expansion of the Internet. See MacKie-Mason and Varian (1994).

41 Less than one third of all North Americans own a personal computer. The percentage is even lower outside of North America.

ACKNOWLEDGEMENTS

THE AUTHOR THANKS Brian Globerman of Connectivity for research assistance and intrepid guidance on the Internet. He also thanks the discussant, Roger Miller, for helpful comments.

BIBLIOGRAPHY

Antonelli, Christiano. "Information Technology and Derived Demand For Telecommunications Services in the Manufacturing Industry." *Information Economics and Policy.* Vol. 4, (1989/90): 45-55.

———. "Investment and Adoption in Advanced Telecommunications." *Journal of Economic Behaviour and Organization.* Vol. 20, (1993a): 227-245.

———. "Investment, Productivity Growth and Key Technologies: Advanced Telecommunications." *The Manchester School.* Vol. LXI, No. 4, (1993b): 386-397.

Baldwin, John, Brent Diverty and David Sabourin. "Technology Use and Industrial Transformation: Empirical Perspectives." In *Bell Canada Papers on Economic and Public Policy: Technology, Information and Public Policy.* Edited by Thomas Courchene. Kingston: John Deutsch Institute for the Study of Economic Policy, forthcoming.

Benjamin, Robert and Rolf Wigard. "Electronic Markets and Virtual Value Chains on the Information Superhighway." *Sloan Management Review.* (Winter 1995): 62-72.

Blank, Stephen, Stephen Krajewski and Henry Yu. "Responding to a New Political and Economic Architecture in North America: Corporate Structure and Strategy." *The Northwest Journal of Business and Economics.* Special Edition, (1994): 17-30.

Bulkeley, William M. "Untested Treatments, Cures Find Stronghold On-Line Services." *The Wall Street Journal.* February 27, 1995.

Bureau of Industry Economics. *International Performance Indicators: Telecommunications.* Research Report 48, Canberra: Australian Government Publishing Service, 1992.

Business Week: 21st Century Capitalism. (1994).

Cane, Alan. "Information Technology and Competitive Advantage: Lessons From the Developed Countries." *World Development.* Vol. 20, No. 2, (1992):1721-1736.

CCTA. "Submission to the Canadian Radio-television and Telecommunications Commission Information Highway Public Hearing." Mimeo. Toronto, 1994.

Churbuck, David C. "Where's the Money?" *Forbes.* January 30, 1995.

Congress of the United States, Office of Technology Assessment, *Electronic Enterprises: Looking to the Future.* Washington, DC: US Government Printing Office, 1994.

Cronin, Francis. *Doing Business on the Internet.* New York: Van Nostrand and Reinhold, 1994.

Cronin, Francis, et al. "Factor Prices, Factor Substitution and the Relative Demand for Telecommunications Across US Industries." *Information Economics and Policy.* (January 1993a).

Cronin, Francis, Edwin Parker, Elisabeth Colleran and Mark Gold. "Telecommunications Infrastructure Investment and Economic Development." *Telecommunications Policy.* (August 1993b): 415-430.

Cronin, Francis, et al. "Telecommunications and Cost Savings in Educational Services." *Information Economics and Policy.* (March 1994).

Denny, Michael, Melvyn Fuss, Charles Everson and Leonard Waverman. "Estimating the Effects of the Diffusion of Technological Innovations in Telecommunications: The Production Structure of Bell Canada." *The Canadian Journal of Economics*. Vol. XIV, No. 1, (1981): 24-43.

Denton, Timothy. "Transactions Not Transmissions: The Electronic Marketplace and the Computer Revolution." Mimeo, T.M. Denton Consultants, March 1994.

French, Carey. "Using On Line Legal Services." *The Globe and Mail*. (April 21, 1994): B7.

Fuss, Melvyn. "Productivity Growth in Canadian Telecommunications." *The Canadian Journal of Economics*. Vol. XXVII, No. 2, (1994): 371-392.

Globerman, Steven. "The Private and Social Interests in Outward Direct Investment." In *Canadian-Based Multinationals*. Edited by Steven Globerman. Calgary: University of Calgary Press, 1994.

————. "The Economics of the Information Superhighway." In *Bell Canada Papers on Economics and Public Policy: Technology, Information and Public Policy*. Edited by Thomas Courchene. Kingston: John Deutsch Institute for the Study of Economic Policy, forthcoming.

Government of Saskatchewan. "Submission to the CRTC in Response to Public Notice 1994-130." Mimeo, 1995.

Gunn, Thomas G. *21st Century Manufacturing: Creating Winning Business Performance*. New York: HarperCollins, 1992.

Harris, Richard. *Trade, Industrial Policy and International Competition*. Toronto: University of Toronto Press, 1985.

Hawkins, Donald T. "Growth Trends in the Electronic Information Services Market, Part I." *ONLINE*. Vol.17, No. 5, (1993): 98-100.

Huber, Peter W., Michael Kellogg and John Thorne. *The Geodesic Network II: 1993 Report on Competition in the Telephone Industry*. Washington, DC: The Geodesic Company, 1992.

Industry Canada. *The Canadian Information Highway*. Ottawa: Minister of Supply and Services, 1994.

"The Internet: How it will change the way you do business." *Business Week*. (November 14, 1994): 81.

Johnson, Leland. *Telephone Company Entry into Cable Television: Competition, Regulation and Public Policy*. Santa Monica: RAND Corporation, 1993.

Katsaros, John. "Electronic Commerce." *Internet World*. (July/August 1994): 41-43.

MacKie-Mason, Jeffrey and Hal Varian. "Economic FAQs About the Internet." *Journal of Economic Perspectives*. Vol. 8, No. 3, (1994): 75-96.

McFetridge, D.G. *Advanced Technologies in Canada: An Analysis of Recent Evidence on Their Use*. Ottawa: Minister of Supply and Services, 1992.

Mehta, Stephanie. "Industry Net Puts Businesses in Fast Lane." *The Wall Street Week*. (October 11, 1994): B2.

Mitchell, Bridger and Tenging Donyo. *Utilization of the US Telephone Network*. Santa Monica: RAND Corporation, 1994.

Norton, Seth. "Transaction Costs, Telecommunications and the Microeconomics of Macroeconomic Growth." *Economic Development and Cultural Change*. Vol. 41, No. 1, (1992): 175-196.

Office of Technology Assessment, Congress of the United States. *Electronic Enterprises: Looking to the Future*. Washington, DC: U.S. Government Printing Office, 1994.

Organization For Economic Co-operation and Development. *Information Networks and New Technologies*. Paris: OECD, 1992.

Orr, Dale and Ron Hirslihorn. *The Economic Potential of the Information Highway.* For Stentor Telecom Policy Inc., 1994.

Porter, Michael. *Competitive Strategy.* New York: The Free Press, 1985.

"Prodigy Is In That Awkward Stage." *Business Week.*(February 13, 1995): 90.

Rogers Communications Inc. "Submission in Response to Public Notice CRTC 1994-130." Mimeo, 1995.

Rowan, Geoffrey. "Sex, lies and commercial on-line services." *The Globe and Mail.* (February 11, 1995): B1.

Solomon, Stephen. "Staking a Claim on the Internet." *Inc Technology*, Vol. 16, No. 13, (1995): 87-91.

Stanbury, W.T., Hudson Janisch and Steven Globerman. "Riding the Wave: Developments in Telecommunications in Canada." Mimeo, University of British Columbia, 1995.

Stentor Telecom Policy. *The Information Highway.* Ottawa: Stentor Telecom Policy Inc., 1993.

Yates, Robert, Johanne Lemay and Gerry Wall. *Local Telecommunications Competition in Canada.* Verdun: Lemay-Yates Associates Inc, 1994.

Comment

Roger Miller
Hydro-Québec/NSERC/SSHRC
Université du Québec à Montréal

INFORMATION TECHNOLOGIES FEED AN INNOVATION PROCESS that appears to be a major force in the restructuring of work, firms, networks and the economy. Yet, in debates on the effects of information technology, two polarities persist with regards to attitudes. The first pole is messianic: information technology has a high potential and a positive effect on change. The second pole is pessimistic: investments in information technology have not produced the expected rates of return.

The messianic pole can be illustrated by examples taken from the information highway, Minitel and the Computer Acquisition Logistic System (CALS). The hype is proclaimed both by technologists who experience a constant flux of innovations and by non-experts who recognize the potential economic impacts. Here are illustrations.

- Industries related to the information highway are in turmoil, radically transformed by successive waves of technological developments. A new paradigm, asynchronous transfer mode (ATM) is making the concept of dedicated networks obsolete and pushing the field toward the seamless interconnection of networks. Inter-operability makes it possible for services, and the applications built on them, to work together. National borders are losing their meaning. Traffic uses the cheapest channel irrespective of national borders. Satellite transmission challenges cable networks. Dishes allow the public to capture TV signals from the satellites of neighbouring countries. New software permits voice communication in a near-telephone mode over the Internet.

- Minitel is a good example of what happens when strategic persistence and adequate technology go hand in hand. With over 6.5 million subscribers and a high level of use, the French have started the information highway with transactions between users and banks, railways, airlines and merchandisers.

- The CALS strategy is intended to accelerate the transition from paper intensive, non-integrated product development design, manufacturing and support processes to a highly automated, integrated mode of operation. Standards are developed for data storage and exchange, and for automated systems to store, manage and distribute this information to varied users across an enterprise. Concurrent engineering is supporting CALS. This is a systematic approach to develop products by considering all life cycle elements. In so doing, products, manufacturing processes and support are simultaneously defined. CALS is an enabler for concurrent engineering by providing integrated development product teams with correct, complete, accessible and timely digital product data.

Authors in the pessimistic pole of the debate ask simple but difficult questions. Where are the returns? What is the point of more options when time is a scarce factor? Let us illustrate this pole with three items.

- The information highway brings back memories of spectacular failures in Canada. Telidon and Alex are failed investments which show that, even if the technology is right, the home market may not be there. What is the point of investing millions if all you create are markets such as "messageries roses" or sex chatlines?

- The essence of CALS is technical standards for organizational change. Real implementation issues, such as the building of processes and external networks, have not been fully addressed. Major investments in information technology will need time to have substantial impacts just as electric motors took almost 40 years to change factories from the 1880s to the 1920s.

- The consensus among economists is that the impact of information technology on productivity has been somewhat limited. Additions to the capital stock by investments in information technology in the last decade have not reversed the slowdown in productivity growth. Productivity gains are not there even as firms downsize, restructure and automate.

The Thesis of Subdued Progress for the Information Technology

STEVEN GLOBERMAN'S THESIS IS decidedly on the pessimistic side of the debate. The information highway as a system of interconnected electronic networks for digitized exchanges of technical, commercial and multimedia data is not about to experience exponential growth according to him. The potential effects are not materializing because diffusion is slow and limited to specialized segments. The burden of proof would still appear to rest with those who see major changes resulting in the economic landscape. Much of the evidence is either anecdotal or draws on recent rates of membership growth on the Internet. In fact, there is little persuasive evidence that future economic impacts of technological change in communications will be significantly different from historical experience.

Private networks, the concentration of users who are in the computer electronics industry and the costs of access to interactive broadband communications will restrict diffusion of applications on public networks. The most important element of Globerman's thesis is that governments should be cautious in their expectations about what communication technologies can and will really do for economic growth. Government intervention to manage a techno-economic paradigm shift may be misjudged.

Challenging the Institutional Framework

GLOBERMAN IS RIGHT ABOUT THE INFORMATION HIGHWAY in the present context. However, the markets for products, services and applications need to be and are partly in the process of being created by entrepreneurial firms profiting from technical and regulatory changes. Technical change is feeding new possibilities and a new wave of deregulation in the information highway. Four key technologies are prodding the change process:

- micro-electronics to provide low-cost processing power;
- software engineering to provide real-time control and artificial intelligence;
- photonics to allow high-volume data flows; and
- wireless access to match the present system of wired telephone networks.

Technical change is very fertile and is leading to the fusion and convergence of once autonomous fields such as telephone, cable TV and wireless. Products and production systems are merging in the communications, computer and video-entertainment industries. Furthermore, technical change induces regulatory changes and makes possible the growth of new businesses. In spite of the resistance of regulators, technical change combined with competition is pushing toward a market-driven structure. It is now possible to deliver information to users in their home and in the most useful form: voice, data, video, images and graphics.

Many governments are making forceful investments to spur activities on the information highway. The Internet is an American creation that covers the country and is the central core of international connections. Many private value-added resellers are linked to the Internet. They offer packages, including accessible user interfaces and data banks of specialized information. Entertainment industries (picture, publishing, etc.) are positioning themselves to take advantage of interactive delivery channels offered by the web. Deregulation in the telecommunications industry has stimulated competition, leading to lower tariffs.

In his State of the Union speech of January 1994, President Clinton called for a national information superhighway that would connect every classroom, library, clinic and hospital by the year 2000. For this purpose, a national program embraces all activities related to the development of national competencies for National Infrastructure Layers in the 10 national agencies. Through co-ordinated planning, research and development, these agencies are developing an integrated infrastructure.

Ferocious battles are already taking place to protect national markets from U.S. initiatives. Canada and Europe are using tactics and strategies to allow their industries to participate in worldwide markets dominated by large American firms. Governments are under pressure to prepare new regulatory and tariff frameworks for global competition. Players with fixed assets seek open markets, while smaller players, such as cable networks, want more time to deploy forces.

The Canadian government has issued a broad but vague vision for the information highway. The Advisory Council on the Information Highway is supposed to base its strategy and recommendations on this vision. In the meantime, the federal government has committed itself to funding the development of a national backbone and to supporting the development of a private sector initiative in the development of a test network.

PUBLIC ACTION IN THE INFORMATION SUPERHIGHWAY

BECAUSE OF THE NEED FOR JOINT INDUSTRY–GOVERNMENT INVESTMENT, public intervention in the information highway cannot be limited to the traditional regulatory framework. There are two modes of action: a sound policy should be a mixture of these two options.

DEREGULATE AND LET ENTREPRENEURS BUILD THE MARKET

THE FEDERAL GOVERNMENT DOES NOT HAVE THE RESOURCES to match American and European investments. Instead of building an information highway infrastructure, the Canadian government would be better advised to stimulate Canadian firms to develop pipelines and a variety of applications. By waiting to open the field, the regulator is weakening firms which cannot now profit using low-cost channels through the United States. Weakened firms cannot react competitively but tend to seek protection.

The challenge to the regulator, insofar as the information highway is concerned, is how fast to deregulate the separation between telephone companies, cable firms and potential new entrants. With the breaking of the artificial separation, telephone firms are likely to win over cable firms. However, cable firms can survive by developing applications, new products and innovative services. Specialized firms which offer application packages using servers are likely to do well.

CREATING A PUBLIC–PRIVATE PARTNERSHIP

IT IS NOW POSSIBLE TO VIEW THE INFORMATION HIGHWAY as fibre-optic pipelines and radio communications that can carry high volumes of transactions. Instead of regulating carriers, the federal government should work in co-operation with the relevant players. Building strong partnerships with provincial and federal departments such as revenue, health and finance. Private sector firms may help co-ordinate moves and investments and create uses and markets. This approach is expensive and requires persistence. It is likely, however, that government inertia, lack of strategic will and the inability to co-ordinate with the private sector will lead to timid public actions.

Public actions need to proceed from an understanding of the techno-economic dynamics and not from ideological perspectives. Whatever choice is made, it must be remembered that the underlying market dynamics are characterized by

FIGURE 1

POTENTIAL INDICATORS OF INFORMATION-BASED KNOWLEDGE IN ORGANIZATIONS

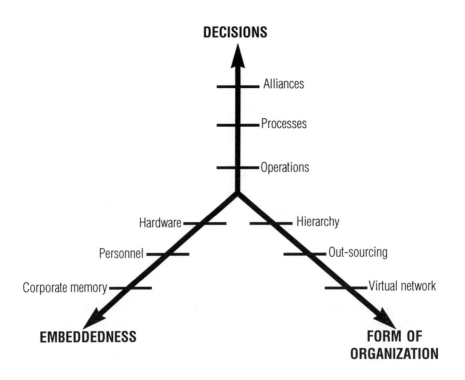

non-linear effects. Notions, such as critical mass of effort, positive feedback loops between the infrastructure and servers, network externalities or multiplier effects, must structure public action.

INDICATORS OF THE REAL IMPACT OF INFORMATION TECHNOLOGY

LOOKING BEYOND THE INFORMATION HIGHWAY, it is obvious that the changes brought by information technology are real. The pessimistic perspective is only justified when productivity figures are used. Information technology has qualitative and quantitative impacts that are badly captured by productivity figures. Workers and middle managers who have lost their jobs know that there are impacts. The flattening of organizations and the pressure to out-source supply of many products using electronic data interchange are real impacts.

Figure 1 draws a map of the potential indicators as firms incorporate more information-based knowledge into their production system. The decision axis indicates that applications of information technology can progress from automation to organizational processes to alliances. The form of organization axis goes from the traditional hierarchy to out-sourcing and virtual networks. The embeddedness of information technology progresses from hardware to personnel and corporate memory.

CONCLUSION

GOVERNMENTAL SUPPORT, TECHNOLOGY SELECTION AND REGULATION can potentially lock in on inefficient choices and weaken competition. Experimentation by many firms will create products, services and applications to operate on the information highway. New players will emerge and technologically obsolete players will disappear. In some regions, cable companies wire their territories with optical fibres to challenge telephone companies and offer new high-speed access to networks. In this turbulent environment, general trends can be anticipated, but discontinuities will occur.

Rapporteur's Comments

John F. Helliwell
Department of Economics
University of British Columbia

Conference Report

T HE CONFERENCE WAS OPENED BY HARRY SWAIN, Deputy Minister of Industry Canada, who set out two principal questions for conference attendees to consider.

- Is there theory to guide understanding of the role of knowledge in economic growth?
- Can we set out the features of public policy that are appropriate to deal with knowledge-based growth?

He then called on Peter Nicholson, Senior Advisor, Department of Finance, to report on the Canadian Institute for Advanced Research-International Institute for Applied Systems Analysis (CIAR-IIASA) conference held earlier in the week. Nicholson described the meeting between the "evolutionary" school of IIASA and the "new growth" group of the CIAR, and noted an apparent convergence of views. There is also heterogeneity within each group. He sees a two-by-two matrix: evolutionary versus new growth and theorizing in the "appreciative" style versus theorizing in a more formal style. The appreciative theorists describe what is going on, and look for regularities, while the formal theorists try to strip away the details and capture the essence. In both the new growth and evolutionary schools, technology is of central importance. The evolutionary model emphasizes the bounds of rationality, and is more biological in its orientation. It focuses on heterogeneity and gives a big role to randomness interacting with selectiveness. The new growth theory tends to emphasize intentionality, and is less historically oriented. The evolutionary school emphasizes complexity and simulation, while the new growth school tends toward analytical solutions. Nicholson saw complementarities, but not strong evidence of convergence. He suspects that the computer will help to achieve eventual convergence between the analytical and simulation approaches. He wondered both about the complexity and the lack of co-ordination in the evolutionary simulation models.

Turning to the policy implications from the earlier conference, Nicholson noted themes common to the two schools: foster diversity, accept failure and promote competition. When left alone, markets are not necessarily optimal, yet they work very well. This is potentially more contentious. Market failures are not necessarily correctable. (This sounds like Churchill on democracy: rather unsatisfactory until it is compared to the alternatives.) What is really crucial is institutional design. Intellectual property rights to basic science were seen as extremely dangerous, and there was some possibility that university research was becoming too commercialized. He saw a need for a more detailed understanding of the innovation process. Richard Nelson noted (at the CIAR conference) that the links between national labs and firms could destroy the former. Richard Lipsey argued that there could be helpful industry guidance.

With regards to the link between research and development (R&D) and productivity growth, the question was whether it is based on appropriability of the results of the R&D, or on the new flow of ideas from elsewhere into the R&D firms. The CIAR conference view favoured the latter. This tends to support a policy stance favouring open rather than proprietorial science.

SESSION 1: ON SOME PROBLEMS IN MEASURING KNOWLEDGE-BASED GROWTH

IN PRESENTING HIS PAPER, PETER HOWITT noted his concern regarding the biases caused by inadequate accounting for the role of knowledge in growth. Economic growth has always been knowledge-based, starting in this country with the dramatic increases in agricultural productivity that took Canadians off the farm. A lot of the progress in growth theory has been in transforming theories designed originally to deal with commodities into theories to deal with the production and transfer of knowledge. When knowledge is produced, it is difficult to track thereafter, since it is embodied in minds and memories, habits and practices, as well as in the codified forms of books and drawings. Just as the embodiment of knowledge is difficult to see, so is the process of its transfer difficult to measure or control. In contrast to the exchange of goods, knowledge exchange creates new knowledge since parties transmit their knowledge but still have it at the end of the day.

When a major structural shift takes place, the required investment in knowledge is great, and resources are sucked away from other productive activities. Since the new knowledge is not treated as an output, there will be an apparent decline in productivity in the course of the structural transformation. Howitt also noted that the difficulties of using hedonic measures to solve the quality improvement problem are greater in times of major structural adjustment.

The discussant, Thomas K. Rymes, queried the assumption that knowledge acquisition is not adequately recorded. Rymes argued that skill acquisition, specific to the firm, will show up as higher wages within the firm, and acquisition of more general knowledge will turn up later in higher real wages. The fact that some R&D is purchased and some is done in house is no different than the decision to rent or buy elsewhere in the economy.

Turning to the measurement problems raised by Howitt, Rymes dealt first with the knowledge-investment problem. Rymes noted that the use of hedonic price indexes for computers raises the productivity of the industry producing computers, and lowers it in industries using computers. When measured in terms of consumption goods, productivity is unchanged by the adjustment. And should the productivity attributed to the production of computers not be passed back to the manufacture of chips? The only possible understatement of long-term productivity growth is if consumer price growth is overstated by a failure to make proper quality adjustments. Rymes doubted that the net effects of these understatements add up to a great deal.

On the R&D measurement problem, Rymes commented that the measured gross domestic product (GDP) growth that would be created during a structural transformation needs to be offset by additional obsolescence created by the structural transformation. He noted that the growth-reducing effects of inflation may be offset by the effect of a tight monetary policy in drawing more resources into the design and use of transactions technology.

In reply, Howitt reasserted the importance of appropriability, or its lack, in creating a measurement problem. He agreed that adjusting the prices of capital goods simply shifts productivity to other industries, and that it is important to measure the accuracy of final prices, including those of the service industries using the lower-priced computers. He agreed that the R&D measurement problem has two sides during the adjustment to new technologies: the need to record the capital from new learning and the obsolescence created in the stock of existing knowledge.

Luc Soete also emphasized the importance of endogenous obsolescence. Howitt agreed, but noted that he was dealing chiefly with GDP rather than net domestic product (NDP), which gave him an excuse for leaving obsolescence to be dealt with in another paper.

SESSION 2: A QUANTITATIVE ASSESSMENT OF HIGH-KNOWLEDGE INDUSTRIES VERSUS LOW-KNOWLEDGE INDUSTRIES

IN PRESENTATION OF THE LEE–HAS PAPER, HANDAN HAS noted the high growth rates of gross output and employment in the high-knowledge sectors, followed by medium- and low-knowledge sectors. She also noted the faster productivity growth in the low-knowledge industries.

The discussant, Donald McFetridge, asked the rhetorical question: why are we interested in classifying industries in terms of their knowledge intensity? Is there a strategic desire to target and support these industries? Are they crucial? In what way? He surmised that these industries may be the source of positive externalities, or the split may be useful to help in forecasting the likely future demands for different types of education and training.

McFetridge then turned to the definitions used for knowledge-intensive industries. He noted the difference between the knowledge required for the design, construction and use of capital goods. He also noted, echoing Howitt, that some industries, such as many business services, produce little but knowledge, but have no recorded R&D. With respect to the performance measures, McFetridge suggested that employment growth measures may be useful for forecasting, but the productivity measures raised the problem of whether we should expect the spillovers, if they exist, to arise in the same sector or in other sectors.

In response, Frank Lee said that if it were possible to segregate industries on the basis of their knowledge intensity, and if there were externalities meriting targeted support, then the industry classifications might provide guidance for policy. This is just what McFetridge was worried about, I suspect.

From the floor, it was noted that hunters and gatherers were true knowledge-based workers living by their wits and skills. By contrast, it was suggested that the Lee–Has paper, and others, seem to associate knowledge intensity with technology. Roger Miller noted the important distinction between tacit and codified knowledge, with tacit knowledge encompassing the skills of hunters and gatherers or, as someone else suggested, the ability to ride a horse. T.K. Rymes noted the Lee–Has classification of agriculture as a low-knowledge industry, which was puzzling because of the long history of high knowledge-based productivity growth in agriculture. He hypothesized that if the input–output tables were used to transfer the knowledge intensity of seed production to agriculture, the results would be very different. In reply, Lee noted that the distinction was based on knowledge production rather than on knowledge use.

Surendra Gera guessed that alternative classification schemes would give similar rankings. Lee agreed, because the alternative ranking indexes are highly correlated with one another.

Session 3: Human Capital Development and Innovation: A Sectoral Analysis

In presenting the Baldwin–Johnson paper, John Baldwin noted that CIAR empirical research has focused intensively on the heterogeneity of firm characteristics and growth. The focus of the current paper is on the linkage between training and innovation. Joanne Johnson presented the results showing that all forms of innovation are related to training. Firms that pay greater attention to quality also do more training. Larger firms train more, while companies with a high proportion of managers or those companies based in Quebec are less likely to offer training. Firms that have a weak emphasis on innovation are less than half as likely to engage in training, especially in manufacturing. Firms that emphasize innovation and training also have the highest profit and growth rates.

The discussant, Lewis Alexander, emphasized how important the use of establishment-level data can be to help settle the debate between representative-agent and evolutionary modellers. In reference to the survey, Alexander raised the problem of selection bias: large firms were excluded, and only growing firms were included. What are the likely consequences of such a bias? Alexander mentioned a paper that attempted to offset the selection bias. This materially affected the estimates of the underlying production structure. He suspected the same issue could arise with the current survey. He pointed out that the linkage between innovation and training ties in with the more general view that there has been skill-biased technical change over the period under review.

How should the results be interpreted? The authors say they have found complementarity. Alexander would prefer to describe the variables as associated, without making the inference that they are causally connected. A relatively small number of firms grow fast and are successful. If you want to test for complementarity, you might look for the factors that determine success, and ask if it is true that firms doing *both* training and innovation are more successful than would be inferred by the separate effects of training and innovation.

D. Malkin from the Organization for Economic Co-operation and Development (OECD) asked how it is possible to link innovation and training with growth if the sample is limited to growing firms?

In reply, Baldwin agreed that sample selection is a problem. To some extent, it results from the use of a survey designed for other purposes. What they wanted to do was to look at the growing firms as a group. However, to answer the OECD point, there is still much variation of growth performance, so it is possible to link growth differences with other variables in the study. The paper was intended to look for complementarities, rather than to see how the particular combinations of chosen policies determine firm success. If the interaction effects are of great importance, then it makes it very difficult to draw inferences about whether policy should encourage one activity from among those that have been combined. Joanne Johnson noted that preliminary results with larger samples of data tended to support the findings reported in the paper.

SESSION 4: EVIDENCE AND DEBATE ON ECONOMIC INTEGRATION AND ECONOMIC GROWTH

IN OPENING THE AFTERNOON SESSION, RICHARD HARRIS presented his three-way coverage of measurement, causality and policy, in a long-run dynamic context. He noted that growth and distribution issues are intertwined, with equal attention being paid to both. In analyzing the history of the trade and growth linkage, he considered four stages: early estimates of the static gains from trade, the export-led growth hypothesis, the convergence debate and recent studies of the effects of trade liberalization. The possibilities arising from the subsequent explosion of theoretical papers on the links between trade and growth are so varied that any presumptions about the connection between trade policy and growth may not be feasible. Harris characterized the current state of play as one in which growth theory has leaped ahead of empirical implementation. He then divided the empirical research into four strands: studies of export-led growth, cross-country growth regressions with openness variables added, studies of the European growth experience and attempts to link productivity growth in OECD countries to measures of openness.

Harris then turned to dynamic general equilibrium modelling of tariff barriers, allowing for capital accumulation and, in some cases, international capital mobility. Two further classes of dynamic modelling of integration included imperfect competition models of entry and exit, and a model with externalities accruing to the accumulation of capital stock. Finally, he presented his own research emphasizing the importance of immobile human capital.

Harris concluded that it is simply too early to make any definitive conclusions about the effects of trade on growth. This is especially true in the case of knowledge-based growth.

The discussant, James Brander, professed to be embarrassed by having to agree with all of the Harris paper. Brander emphasized that the links between knowledge-based growth and trade must flow through changes in applicable technology and human capital, with the possible addition of technology embodied in physical capital. Brander focused his comments on labour force participation and changes in natural resource use per capita. He reported from his own and other research showing that demographic effects, in particular changes in dependency rates and labour force participation, explain a substantial proportion of international growth-rate differences. He did not mention one link between this and knowledge: most studies of fertility show that higher education levels help to reduce fertility rates and, hence, increase per capita growth rates.

Turning to natural resource use, Brander noted the effects of declining per capita resource stocks as a major limitation on increases in per capita income growth in many countries. Finally, he noted his recent theoretical work with Scott Taylor showing that technological progress in harvesting can exaggerate the common property problem, hastening the collapse of national or international resource stocks. Here is a case where technical progress in the hands of individual firms may be socially harmful if the institutional background is not strong enough to put the technologies to good use.

With respect to the role of education in growth, he noted the risk of two-way causation, since the demand for education rises with income levels.

If technology is important, then technology transfer should be important. Brander's first point on this is that unconditional convergence has not been taking place at a global level, but has taken place among the OECD countries. Including education and openness tends to produce conditional convergence, but Brander argued that the tendency is not as strong or as fast as technology transfer would imply.

Finally, Brander agreed with Harris that modesty was needed in the interpretation of the current evidence on the links between trade and growth, and even about growth. He noted that 30 years ago there was more optimism about growth in Africa than in Southeast Asia, while subsequent history has dramatically turned the forecast on its head.

In discussion, Lewis Alexander found the policy discussion odd. Does it really matter whether the positive effects of openness are transition or long-run effects, as long as they both take a long time?

Serge Coulombe referred to the results showing that convergence patterns among U.S. states and among Canadian provinces are fairly similar to the rates of convergence among countries. He noted that output per hour has converged more rapidly than income per capita.

Luc Soete queried the lack of a link between trade and growth and suggested that it might be more helpful to look at the structure of trade. Intra-European trade has increased much more in knowledge-intensive sectors than in other sectors. He thought this might be a negative factor for technology catch-up in the poorer countries of the European Union.

In reply, Richard Harris seconded James Brander's emphasis on natural resource endowments. On the distinction between transition and steady-state effects, the difference remains crucial for theory, and difficult for empirical and policy work. His view is that the new generation of models must take dynamic considerations into account. In response to the question about trade integration and growth, he noted the importance of establishing causal direction; hence his enthusiasm for the Ben-David study of the trade and growth aftermath of European integration.

SESSION 5: INTERPROVINCIAL BARRIERS TO TRADE AND ENDOGENOUS GROWTH CONSIDERATIONS

IN PRESENTATION, JOHN WHALLEY emphasized that the study of interprovincial barriers is part and parcel of the consideration of the larger question of the links between trade and growth. Under some circumstances, even the signs of the effects of interprovincial barriers are uncertain in endogenous growth models.

The discussant, Robin Boadway, wondered why one should expect interprovincial barriers to make much difference in Canada, given that both trade and knowledge flows are so fluid within the Canadian federation. Boadway agreed with the Whalley conclusion that it is a tempest in a teacup. But what if we extended the analysis to consider the whole policy framework? Can the policy differences make a difference? Boadway took the view that provincial policy differences may, in part, reflect barriers to trade, but regional differences in policy may respond to match local needs to local preferences and, hence, may be efficient. He noted the emphasis, in the build up to the Charlottetown Accord, on strengthening the economic union. He was surprised at the lack of support for this at the relevant constitutional conference, with negotiation being the preferred alternative.

Boadway also noted that the conversion from income to consumption taxes (which Whalley gave as an example where endogenous growth models made a big difference to policy prescriptions) mainly reflects a shift in consumption from current to future generations, with a resulting increase in the capital stock and, hence, in income. He was sceptical of the argument that interprovincial trade barriers could increase welfare. Boadway was unsure why non-convergence of provincial incomes should be treated as evidence about the effect of trade barriers.

What other federal policies affect endogenous growth? Decentralized tax policies may cause interregional distortions. Differing expenditure policies, environmental standards and the structure of transfers within provinces are likely to alter the allocation of resources, perhaps with a large impact on growth. The federal government enters the picture through subsidies to business, transportation, regional tax credits, R&D subsidies and so on. Some of these transfers, e.g., a sound equalization payments system, may improve efficiency, but others may damage growth and encourage inefficient transportation costs or subsidy shopping. Overall, Boadway judged that even the static costs of these regionally oriented policies could likely dwarf those of interregional trade barriers.

Are endogenous growth considerations likely to change these arguments or alter one's view of the evidence? Perhaps the mobility of knowledge workers has more saliency in endogenous growth frameworks that emphasize regional agglomeration effects in knowledge accumulation.

Denis Gauthier asked whether it was still true, as in Whalley's 1983 study, that barriers are still attractive to regions, given their redistributive effects? Are the likely redistributive incentives larger when endogenous growth considerations are taken into account?

Richard Harris wondered if the wide range of answers from endogenous theories should result in them being ignored or taken more seriously? Harris preferred to treat the possibility of big effects as providing a spur to more serious research.

Ed Safarian asked if there were clear linkages between some of the interprovincially challenged industries, e.g., trucking, and other industries, e.g., manufacturing, even if there were few barriers to manufactures themselves. He noted the Ottawa Valley line used to police the National Oil Policy of the early 1960s as an example of federal barriers to interprovincial trade. Finally, what about direct investment and interprovincial limits to the purchase of provincial corporations?

In reply, Whalley agreed with Gauthier that the distribution effects of barriers are indeed important, potentially more so in an endogenous growth framework. In response to Harris, he agreed that more research needs to be done, and that the policy conclusions from the models should not be taken seriously until the empirical basis for their structure and parameters is established, and convincingly so. He also agreed with Safarian that related services should be part of the story.

SESSION 6: INTELLECTUAL PROPERTY AND ENDOGENOUS GROWTH

IN PRESENTING THE ACHESON–MCFETRIDGE PAPER, DONALD MCFETRIDGE emphasized the contrast between open and proprietary science. Both give rise to research races, because of the rewards for first discovery, and both may lead to excessive activity and excessive secrecy about intermediate results. He argued that the distinction between open and proprietary science has now replaced the distinction between pure and applied science.

On the issue of strong versus weak novelty requirements, McFetridge noted the link with earlier conferences, where there was an expressed preference for a weak novelty requirement. McFetridge made the points on both sides of the issue, described some of the policy proposals to increase the access of follow-on inventors and concluded that the existing system was providing a pretty good balance between the opposing arguments, but that many specific cases would need specific treatment within the general system. It was not clear exactly what sort of empirical evidence would help to settle the debate between the more- and less-open systems.

The discussant, Jock Langford, found trouble reconciling the anecdotal evidence and policy developments in other countries with the analysis of the paper. He noted that the paper, and most models, focus on patents, while copyright tends to get ignored. Langford also noted that globalization and the information highway are big changes that might and should change intellectual property regimes. Canada has very different interests than has the United States, since Canada (along with most other countries) traditionally favours weaker intellectual property rights than would be preferred in and by the United States.

If one thinks of Canadian firms as incremental innovators, Langford argued, then narrow patents would seem to be preferable to the broader ones favoured by the United States. He noted the importance of transaction costs involved in enforcing intellectual property rights. Langford sees intellectual property in the context of a model by Vernon Ruttan, where institutions, technology, cultural endowments and resource endowments interact in the production and application of knowledge.

Geoff Oliver of Industry Canada had three questions.

- Intellectual property always weighs distribution and innovative activity. How is this different under endogenous growth?
- Intellectual property deals with rights and surpluses, and attempts by breadth and length to strike a balance. What about the related antitrust issues that arise by increasing intellectual property rights?
- Is there a fundamental difference between open and proprietary science in terms of the orientation toward fundamental research?

In reply, Keith Acheson noted that the cultural aspects of copyright tend to get lost in the shuffle. In linking intellectual property and technology, the cultural aspects were left aside. It is important, nonetheless. Competition policy does need to take into account the benefits of patent protection. Acheson noted that, with respect to the compliance costs, arrangements are often made to set up pools of users to keep administrative costs down. One problem with the endogenous growth literature is that intellectual property turns up as a single parameter which has only a weak relation to anything that is presently recognized as intellectual property. He also commented that the role of distributive considerations is a deep and unresolved issue.

McFetridge noted that competition concerns are valid, but that it is necessary to consider the trade-off between competition and innovation. How to strike that trade-off will remain uncertain.

SESSION 7: ECONOMIC AND SOCIAL IMPLICATIONS OF A KNOWLEDGE-BASED SOCIETY

IN INTRODUCING LUC SOETE, the dinner speaker, Alan Nymark, Assistant Deputy Minister, Industry Canada, noted that the policy climate, while still concerned about the deficit and jobs, was open to creative thinking about how knowledge could best be developed and harnessed to foster both growth and distribution goals.

Luc Soete saw a new, more accepting climate for the discussion of the role of technology in growth, perhaps due to the widespread acceptance of the pervasive effects of changes in communication technologies, and because of the possibility that the greater codification of knowledge might make widespread diffusion more rapid. His main focus was on the social aspects of technological change, quoting an Internet letter from David Noble alleging that the info autobahn "propaganda never mentions the road kill." He raised four issues.

- Who gains and who loses? The biggest losers appear to be the unskilled. He noted that skill-biased technical change is one of the leading suspects, at least in the United States, in the collapse in the demand for unskilled workers. It shows up as a wider dispersion of incomes in the United States and as rising unemployment among the unskilled in Europe.

- Since the application and effects of the new technologies are pervasive, and differ greatly among sectors, it would seem appropriate to concentrate policy attention on the uses rather than on the generation of new knowledge.

- Markets and property rights are not enough. Vigilance is required to ensure that needed regulations are provided and, equally important, that regulations blocking technology adoption are removed.

- What are the implications of new knowledge for firms and organizations? It is still unclear whether the virtual office has reduced economies of scale, or whether the same communication powers can be used to increase the effective control span of large organizations.

SESSION 8: A STUCTURALIST VIEW OF INNOVATION POLICY

IN PRESENTATION OF THE LIPSEY–CARLAW PAPER, RICHARD LIPSEY emphasized that technologies (or technologies+, to include tacit knowledge) operate within a facilitating set of institutions. When the technology changes, then so does the underlying institutional structure, and vice versa, so the full gains from the new technologies are not obtained until the two features of production are brought into line. Of their empirical generalizations, he emphasized the gradual infusion of technical change, the pervasive nature of Knightian uncertainty, the costs of information diffusion and the value of flexibility.

Ken Carlaw gave three of the 30 cases to illustrate their mode of attack. The three examples related to the semiconductor industry. SEMATECH was an industry-managed program to undertake precommercial research, but shifted after two years toward early commercialization and support of particular firms. This illustrated how the industry took an excessively short-term outlook and missed the potential gains from long-term research. There was a U.S.-only aspect of SEMATECH that limited the range of membership and the scope for finding appropriate solutions. Finally, the support for failing members drained resources away from the main objectives.

The U.S. military procurement policy relating to semiconductors had several key links to innovation. Firms were given lead times to develop capacity, and were given the ability to license their products for commercial sale. Finally, the firms and their customers (the military) worked closely on all design and production issues, thus reducing uncertainty at the early stages of development.

The third example is that of the Japanese Ministry of International Trade and Industry (MITI) and also relates to semiconductors. This was a catch-up policy, involving licensing arrangements with products and technologies already proven overseas. MITI chose technologies consistent with the facilitating structure and was able to influence the facilitating structure as well. Lipsey and Carlaw made parallels here with the catch-up policies adopted by Korea and Taiwan, and contrasts with the "big push" approach adopted in some of the European cases.

Carlaw noted several aspects of current MITI networking strategy.

- Co-ordination among the firms and MITI involves a shared choice of new directions.
- MITI can gather precompetitive ideas and distribute them.
- The network is used to gather information about where MITI itself should be headed. The MITI public research labs are used to produce non-patentable research fully available to member firms. Subsequent financing to firms is directly linked to commercialization. In the move from catch-up to leadership role in semiconductors, there was a need for major financing instead of seed money. The Very Large Scale Integrated Circuits (VLSI) Project failed to produce many of its technological goals, but was a large commercial success.

Overall, the MITI strategy lessens uncertainty for firms, by sharing precompetitive research and assuring that the facilitating structures will be adequate when needed.

To summarize, Lipsey spoke of goals and means. Lipsey and Carlaw are sceptical of big technological breakthroughs, which tend to be more uncertain and less flexible, as well as offering the prospect for open-ended subsidies. Catching up is best done in gradual steps, without an eye fixed on a need to leap ahead. (E.F. Schumacher would like all this.) The evidence does not favour high tech over low tech. The French made this mistake on the grand scale; it is an easy mistake to make on the small scale too.

In discussion, Gilles Paquet emphasized the apparent success of networks. Paquet supported the use of case studies on the grounds that they have often worked, that he is an inductivist and that Richard Lipsey usually chooses well.

Martin Gordon of the Department of Finance asked for advice about the Defence Industry Productivity Program. Lipsey passed, as Canadian cases have not yet been analyzed in any detail.

Richard Lewis asked about other forms of technology policy, e.g., attempts to develop common standards. Carlaw mentioned software standards in a U.S. case. Lipsey said the case studies were negative on the choice of national champions.

Steven Globerman asked about government labs versus universities. Lipsey was sure there are lessons about the best ways to encourage research, but felt it was too early to find them. Carlaw noted that the industry consortium in SEMATECH did not do effective precommercial research, while the Japanese public labs did.

Jock Langford asked about the links between intellectual property and the facilitating structure. Lipsey noted that creative innovation in the facilitating structure may have bigger payoffs than attempts to encourage specific innovations.

David Griller wondered if establishment of research goals might help. Are they subject-specific? Lipsey agreed that preferred strategies were likely to be subject-specific. In cases where MITI and the firms agreed, a listing of the points of agreement on future goals was a useful catalogue of shared views.

Luc Soete emphasized the difficulty of measuring rates of return, given that even failures provide useful lessons.

Roger Miller echoed that a narrow definition of success and failure might underplay the spinoffs in terms of developing the facilitating infrastructure. If technology is co-evolutionary with the structures, evaluation of the bits is difficult. Process is also important. Lipsey agreed, but stood by the emphasis on the development of a commercial product, plus some measure of the extent to which development costs were recovered. This can provide some measure of what the gains in facilitating structure and other benefits would have to have been to rationalize the support.

David Rose asked if there was any evidence to suggest that venture capital funds supported by taxpayers are a useful policy. Lipsey commented that they have not yet addressed issues of broad generic policies, including the notion of support for venture capital. He finished with a plea for more support for research along the same lines.

Session 9: Local Systems of Innovation: In Search of an Enabling Strategy

IN PRESENTING THE PAPER BY ACS, DE LA MOTHE AND PAQUET, ZOLTAN ACS emphasized the contrast between the pervasive view of national policies within a global context and their view of innovation as a predominantly local phenomenon. Acs noted case study results that, as globalization was proceeding, small firms were leading the way. Globalization has led to an emphasis on comparative advantage, leading to subnational specialized areas. Rising and declining regions place strains on the nation state. (I am sceptical of this, since the evidence shows convergence of per capita incomes in the sub-regions of those industrial countries where the data permit comparisons.) The authors argued that the balkanization of the national economy ought to put the emphasis on units of analysis that are smaller than the nation state. Acs, de la Mothe and Paquet also emphasized the importance of networks, especially at the local level. Acs suggested, using U.S. city and state data on innovations and high technology, and population growth, that there appeared to be a correlation between innovation, high technology and growth. No quantitative evidence was presented, beyond the list of cities and regions. Acs emphasized the variety of experiences among regions.

In discussion, John Burbidge interpreted the authors' policy preference to be for metropolitan-level industrial councils. Burbidge reviewed the literature on competition among regions, and noted that while there are some cases where the outcomes are good, there are many others where the competition is counter-productive. He queried whether globalization leads to decentralization. What about the European Union and the North American Free Trade Agreement (NAFTA)? Globalization may increase the benefits of wider markets and, hence, wider federations (but is it necessary to link markets and politics in this way). Burbidge thought there might be a role for national policies, in restricting the extent of counter-productive subsidy wars, and assuring the systems of education, transportation and communications that are necessary for enabling the regional economies to develop.

Roger Miller said that national funding and policies play an important role in developing even the local economies, and offered the example of the dependence of companies on Route 128 around Boston on defence contracts.

Luc Soete agreed that there is a need for more evidence on the costs of regional competition and gave examples of failed science parks and captured subsidies. He also advocated consideration of supranational linkages and networks, with mega-science being an obvious example.

In reply, Acs asked for equal attention for local and national systems and policies, not for complete dominance of the local systems.

SESSION 10: THE IMPACT OF TELECOMMUNICATIONS INFRASTRUCTURE ON ECONOMIC DEVELOPMENT

LEONARD WAVERMAN PRESENTED THE RÖLLER–WAVERMAN STUDY searching for possible spillovers from the telecommunications industry to the rest of the economy. The mechanism for this was a cross-country regression study of telephone penetration and GDP per capita in the OECD countries. They specified equations for the demand for, and supply of, telecommunications investment with the aim of purging their estimates of spillovers from the risks of contamination from the obvious reverse causation running from income to the demand for telecommunications.

He reported that there is no apparent effect of telephone penetration on the level of GDP in the least squares estimation, but the effects become significant in a three-stage, least squares estimation. He wondered about this functional form which seems to suggest that the more telephones you have, the greater the payoffs, apparently without limit. He proposed future research to look for limits to these additional effects. Röller–Waverman concluded that they have identified a causal positive connection between telephone investment and growth, although the revised version of the paper included in this volume is more cautious on this score, and devotes relatively more attention to surveying other studies of the same relationship.

The discussant, David Aschauer, noted the parallelism between Röller–Waverman's research and Aschauer's own research over the last several years. He noted the mixed press he has received for his own estimates of positive externalities from infrastructure growth. He tended to recommend caution. If he was critical of the paper, it should be seen in this light. It is important to do the work carefully and to be sure of the results before drawing conclusions. Aschauer applauded the author's attempt to account for endogeneity. Aschauer noted the finding of a strong non-linearity in the apparent effect of telephone penetration with the turning point being 22 percent. Since the average penetration rate in the developing countries considered is only 6 percent, the implication is that more telephones will be bad for their growth until a 22 percent penetration rate is achieved. How plausible are the results? Aschauer decomposed the estimated growth effects of telephone penetration for the United States and Canada and showed that, for the United States, telephones were estimated by Röller–Waverman to be responsible for more than one half of productivity growth over the sample period. For Canada, 80 percent of productivity growth is attributed to telephone investment, while for Sweden the result is 120 percent. Aschauer got in trouble for a public infrastructure elasticity estimate of 0.3, but Röller–Waverman have a telephone elasticity estimate of 1.43 for Sweden.

Aschauer noted that it is a big jump from the level effects estimated by Röller–Waverman to growth effects measured directly. In this context, it should be possible to distinguish transitory and permanent effects of telephones on productivity growth.

Finally, Aschauer noted the difficulties of interpreting the coefficient on telephones in the estimated production function. First, there is the question of establishing whether there are the same production functions across countries, and whether the right degrees of telephone investment have been chosen in each country. If these factors are in play, you could get the estimated Röller–Waverman effect, even if there were no spillovers of the sort being sought in their paper. For future research, emphasis on growth rather than levels is of the greatest importance. Perhaps geographic spillovers might also be important.

David Griller wondered if the results were overly affected by the data for Turkey. He also wondered if calls per capita would be a better estimate of the network effects than telephone penetration, since the number of calls per capita increases faster than penetration.

Lewis Alexander returned to the issue of how to measure telephones as they would have an effect on growth. Perhaps telephone use by business would be more appropriate if productivity is in question. Are telephones considered a public or private investment?

John Whalley wondered about the nature of the presumed externalities. Unappropriated benefits are not the same as externalities. Are penetration rates and waiting lists in commensurable units?

In reply, Waverman agreed with Aschauer that the results give estimates of the productivity effects of telephones that are too high, although he stuck to the idea that there are enormous benefits to the user far beyond the price paid. In developing their work in the context of growth, they were still wondering how to combine growth equations with investment equations. He agreed that Turkey should be taken out of the sample to see if the results are affected.

SESSION 11: THE CANADIAN COMMUNICATION EQUIPMENT INDUSTRY AS A SOURCE OF R&D SPILLOVERS AND PRODUCTIVITY GROWTH

IN PRESENTATION, JEFFREY BERNSTEIN explained the theoretical framework used to estimate the separate effects of the direct and external effects of R&D. He noted the high levels of R&D in the telecommunications industry. In analyzing costs in the manufacturing sector, he included measures of R&D capital in the Canadian telecommunications sector, and in U.S. manufacturing. In both cases, he expected to find possible spillovers. He found significant spillovers from U.S. manufacturing R&D, reflecting the OECD-level results of Coe and Helpman (1993). The effects for telecommunications R&D, while having the right sign, are estimated to be small but statistically significant.

Bernstein then turned to consider total factor productivity (TFP) growth in the communications equipment industry, and found that it outperformed the manufacturing industry as a whole by a substantial margin, matching the earlier results in the United States and Japan. He noted the anomalous result that 76 percent of productivity growth in Canadian manufacturing appeared to have come from R&D in U.S. manufacturing. I suspect that this result is being generated by cyclical variations in productivity.

From his calculations of spillover, he computed social rates of return on R&D of a very high level. Since he found similar spillovers in other industries, Bernstein does not think there is a case for specific industry-level subsidization, although there may be a case for special treatment of the activity.

The discussant, Michael Denny, described the paper as an example of a technique for studying possible spillovers, applicable to an industry. Both papers, this and the Röller–Waverman paper, illustrate the difficulties of getting reasonable estimates of spillovers. There are also difficulties in obtaining estimates of the value of the R&D that is creating the spillovers. He echoed Bernstein's plea for better measurement of key knowledge stocks. Denny was suspicious of the magnitude of the effects Bernstein estimated. He was willing to settle for improved partial results, in the absence of a fuller framework. Perhaps it needs a "macro person," he suggested, to be willing (if perhaps not able) to go further.

Michael Wolfson asked whether the problem was one of measurement of the meaning of R&D capital. A neighbour is working on a new chip that may be worth a great deal, or perhaps nothing. How should the relevant R&D be valued, and subsequently written off?

Steven Globerman noted that much of Bell-Northern R&D is done in the United States. Where is it counted?

Peter Hanel from the Université de Sherbrooke asked whether the cost function form, by putting more pressure on prices, might be a source of difficulty for the estimates. He worried that the spillovers from U.S. R&D may be capturing the effects of other collinear improvements in technology. He recommended more effort to specify the particular channels of spillover.

Thomas K. Rymes noted the estimated big differences between the private and social rates of return to R&D. To what extent do these measures depend on the extent of aggregation? If there is this large a gap, why should we not observe much greater integration of industry to internalize these large externalities?

Lewis Alexander noted that the U.S. Bureau of Economic Analysis (BEA) was now starting to publish estimates of the stock of R&D capital. Turning to national accounting issues, he noted the problems of valuing software, and depreciating R&D and other knowledge assets.

In reply, Jeffrey Bernstein noted that R&D was a good starting focus for a concern about knowledge-based growth, since at least the inputs to R&D are measured. On the choice of cost versus production functions, Bernstein was undecided. On the choice of spillover variable, he agreed that the range of choice was great, and that it needs to be guided as much as possible by other information on the source of the spillovers. To Rymes, he acknowledged the importance of aggregation in governing the difference between the private and social rates of return. On the policy side, Bernstein preferred to take the procompetitive choice, where one is available, so the finding of foreign spillover should counsel open access to ideas.

SESSION 12: THE INFORMATION HIGHWAY AND THE ECONOMY

IN PRESENTATION, STEVEN GLOBERMAN took his task as to debunk, at least partially, the exploding literature on the effects of the information highway. He stated his definition of the information highway as a set of interconnected electronic networks, owned and operated by different providers of a variety of services. He noted that almost all of what is provided is already available, to some extent, through existing public and private networks. What has been dramatically increasing has been the number of on-line services, especially since 1990. The major changes likely to flow from the increased use of the information highway include: a reduction of minimum efficient firm size, an increase of economies of scope, closer integration of markets and making productive activities easier to disentangle geographically. But how much more integrated are North American markets likely to become? Are they not already fully integrated? What about the productivity effects, as represented by the declining cost of telecommunications? Globerman suggested they are not likely to be large, given the relatively small size of telecommunication inputs in manufacturing. The information is also supposed to allow business to do things in new ways. If foreign Internet penetration is now very small, large changes in the way things are done are likely to be slow in arriving. Even in North America, the number of Internet hosts is still small relative to the number of computer users. Perhaps the biggest productivity effects will be felt in basic research, where global reach is already present. The diffusion of Internet use still needs to be modelled. His policy plea was for competition in the local distribution network. There is also a need to keep the international doors open.

The discussant, Roger Miller, placed Globerman on the pessimistic pole. On the optimistic side, the game is to get some control on the establishment of standards. On the sceptical side, the basic question is: how large a choice of options is useful before the costs of choosing rise to swamp the potential gains? One of the big changes taking place now, Miller said, is the rapid exchange of technical data between firms. Requests for proposals can be sent out to dozens of firms. This has created an earthquake in the engineering industry. Schlumberger forced the establishment of a virtual lab, by putting their labs on a fully connected basis. Yet automobile firms have not yet moved in this direction. How can you explain the high level of investment in telecommunications if the high returns are not there?

Leonard Waverman noted that Western Union turned down the patent on the telephone. What if Globerman is wrong? He is right to emphasize the open system, but why not point the finger at the Canadian Radio-television Commission (CRTC)?

Lewis Alexander agreed with the paper broadly, but noted that spectra are being sold for billions of dollars for something that is a close substitute for the information highway.

David Griller picked up the CRTC point, and warned that cross-border services will be used if the CRTC does not respond in a timely way. The shift from pessimistic to messianic modes will follow when hook-up becomes easier.

Dale Orr suggested optimism: when economies grow by 3 percent per year, a small increase will make quite a difference. Similarly, a small cost advantage, often in communications, will give non-communication firms a big edge over their competitors. Look at the way cellular phones and facsimiles have changed the way business is done. Interactive banking and international calling have grown at an average rate of 20 percent annually, over the last few years.

James Brander noted that betting on the Internet is like betting on a horse race; what does the stock market think about the issue? He asked us to remember that he was raised in the atomic age, when splitting the atom was to solve all energy problems. That did not work out, so now we call it the information age. He thus recommended continued caution.

In reply, Steven Globerman agreed with Leonard Waverman's point that the institutional framework must be right, and that the CRTC was becoming a vested interest group blocking new entrants. In this context, institutional reform may be best served by closing down the CRTC.

Roger Miller noted, in supplement, that the CRTC should be thought of as a network manager, not a controller.

Richard Lipsey agreed with the caution suggested by the atomic age example, but noted that many of these new technologies were not just a source of power, but also provided a greater variety of ways of doing things.

SESSION 13: SUMMARY AND OVERVIEW

JOHN HELLIWELL TRIED TO ASK SOME BROAD QUESTIONS, to provide a framework for the discussion.

Are there overall themes to the papers and discussions? Yes, but how do you capture them? The conference can be divided into two large sections, distinct in their subject and methodologies. The first eight papers dealt with the broad issues of knowledge-based growth, while the last three dealt with telecommunications as an industry case study.

FOUR BIG QUESTIONS AND SOME SMALLER ONES

FROM THE PAPERS AND DISCUSSIONS, at least four broad themes or questions can be posed.

1. What kind of world are we living in? Are we living in the throes of changes as fast and as fundamental as any of the last millennium, or are we in a continuation of the perennial process of time-using adaptation to thousands of overlapping and developing changes?

   Is the world becoming more local or more global? or both? In this context, what is the appropriate domain for the analysis of behaviour and policy making?

   Although there were diverging opinions, there was probably general support for the Lipsey view that changes are and have always been incremental. There may be spurts from time to time, but the spread of technologies remains a piecemeal process marked by repeated experiments, some successful and some not, rather than a steady progression. The issues of localization and globalization, and their implications for policy, are discussed below.

2. What types of enterprise are most fitted for the changing environment? Flexible ones, we were told on all sides. Whether they are large or small may be less important than how well they manage their internal networking to simulate the best that can be achieved by organizations smaller or larger than themselves.

3. What types of policy are most likely to be useful or needed? Flexible, facilitating, uncertainty-reducing.

   Policy emphasis over the last decade has been to withdraw from expensive roles as direct actors, and to leave firms and households with more cash and a solid institutional framework in which to operate. But the newer emphasis suggested by the papers in this volume and the subsequent discussions is that while the provision of facilitating institutions should remain the chief focus of policy, the amount of imagination, innovation and finesse required to do this is much greater than previously thought. With uncertain groping as the order of the day, as emphasized by Richard Lipsey, surely the required institutional support must be changed as well. Acheson–McFetridge emphasized the importance of a system of intellectual property rights that adapts to fit the situation at hand, and Lipsey–Carlaw extolled the advantages of institutions and objectives developed jointly by the innovators and the framework providers, while noting the dangers of letting the process become too cosy. Within this constraint, the need for co-ordination can be added to the key list of policy objectives.

Two more types of policy seem to flow from the previous discussion about the nature of the world and its changes.

- More consideration of the appropriate level for policy is needed, with more attention both to international institution building for the international issues and decentralization for the local ones.

- More attention to uniform standards, of the sort required, will make networking easier both across town and across the globe.

4. What types of research are likely to be most useful? Everyone agreed that more empirical research was needed, but of what sort or sorts? There was conflicting evidence. There were positive comments about the usefulness of case studies of the sort reported by Lipsey and Carlaw but, at the same time, there was ample evidence of heterogeneity of experience and behaviour, increasing the risks of concluding anything on the basis of individual case studies without their number growing impractically large. The right resolution might be a three-pronged attack, with case studies being used to generate and check hypotheses; micro-based panel and cross-sectional studies used to test particular hypotheses about the relations between knowledge and performance at the firm level; and aggregate data, both time series and cross-country, used to measure the aggregate importance of the influences identified. When all three types of evidence show a similar pattern, an idea starts to look pretty good, and when most of the opposing hypotheses have been rendered implausible, then it may be time to think of policy transfer.

TELECOMMUNICATIONS AS A CASE STUDY

RÖLLER AND WAVERMAN LOOKED FOR POSSIBLE EXTERNALITIES from telecommunications infrastructure. They noted that these spillovers may be difficult to isolate, since there is a risk of confusing two effects: that better telecommunications may encourage faster growth and that higher growth, however it is caused, will tend to increase the demand for telecommunications. They started by pointing out that the combination of these (possible) two effects gives rise to a strong positive relation, among countries, between real GDP per capita and the extent of the telecommunications network, measured in mainlines per 100 inhabitants. This correlation appears to be much stronger among the OECD countries than among developing countries.

To try to disentangle the two-way relations, Röller–Waverman specified a model in which the level of real GDP per capita depends on capital, the educated labour force, telephone penetration and a time trend. For the effect in the reverse direction, they explained telephone penetration by telephone investment, which in turn is determined by a number of variables including the level of income per capita. They found no effects of telecommunications penetration on the level of income when they estimated that equation on its own, but found what appears to be an effect that starts out negative and later becomes positive at higher penetration rates when they estimated their model as a system of equations. This is puzzling, since both effects (those running from telecommunications to growth and from the level of income to the demand for telephones) are presumed to be positive. Hence, any attempt to disentangle the two effects should reduce the size of the estimated positive externalities running from telecommunications to growth. Perhaps it might be easier to disentangle the pieces of the puzzle if the authors were to focus on the rates of growth of income, rather than on the levels, when determining the externality effect, while leaving the level effect running from income to the demand for telecommunications.

To provide some idea of how this might turn out, Figure 1 shows the relation between telecommunications penetration in 1971 (using the OECD data in the Röller–Waverman Table 3) and the average proportionate growth rates of factor productivity from 1971 through 1989 for 19 OECD countries. This would seem to avoid difficulties of reverse causation, since any growth experience subsequent to 1971 cannot feed back to influence the 1971 telecommunication stocks, while the 1971 telecommunication stocks will clearly be on hand to help determine subsequent rates of productivity growth. The figure shows a negative rather than a positive relation between telephone density and subsequent growth rates of productivity

FIGURE 1

TELEPHONES AND GROWTH – 19 OECD COUNTRIES, 1971 TO 1989

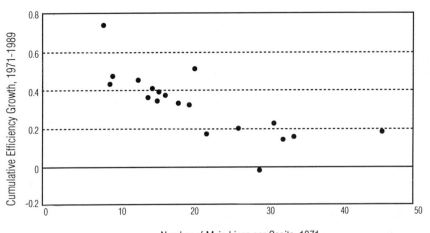

Number of Main Lines per Capita, 1971

among the 19 largest OECD economies. Regressions show this relation to be significant, and to be reduced in magnitude but still significantly negative if convergence effects are allowed for. The relation is essentially the same if growth in the 1970s is used instead of growth from 1971 to 1989, as is confirmed by the new material in tables 6 and 7 of the revised Röller–Waverman paper. More data and analysis are clearly needed. For now, I am inclined to treat the evidence as not showing any significant positive spillovers from telecommunications capital, at least as measured by telephones per capita, to aggregate growth in the economy.

Bernstein studied possible R&D spillover effects from the Canadian communication equipment industry to the rest of Canadian manufacturing, while allowing for R&D spillovers from U.S. to Canadian manufacturing. He found small positive spillovers from Canadian communications industry R&D and much larger spillovers from U.S. manufacturing R&D. Since communications industry R&D is relatively small in relation to the output of the Canadian manufacturing industry, the consequences for the estimated social rate of return in communications industry R&D are large. Bernstein estimated the private rate of return to R&D in the Canadian communications industry to be 17 percent, and the social rate of return to be 55 percent. Bernstein argued that his calculations illustrate that there is underinvestment in R&D in the communications industry, but cautions against policies that target any specific industry. He does not point out, as others have done [e.g., Bruce (1993); McFetridge and Warda (1983)], that the Canadian fiscal regime for R&D is already among the most generous among industrial countries, so the starting point is already one of extensive relative subsidy for R&D expenditure. (This is in addition to the point implicit in Howitt's paper, that the widespread mixing of R&D with other current expenditure means that many R&D expenditures are treated as current rather than capital expenditures for tax purposes, thus gaining more favourable treatment than other capital expenditures.)

If the results shown in Figure 1 had not been available, the Bernstein and the Röller–Waverman papers could have been regarded as mutually reinforcing, since they use different methodologies and data, and come to similar qualitative conclusions. However, since this does not appear to show up in aggregate productivity growth data, after allowing for possible reverse causation, more analysis should precede any conclusions.

DISCUSSION IN THE FINAL SESSION

THERE WAS SOME AGREEMENT THAT THE FOUR QUESTIONS outlined above captured some of the big issues. Peter Howitt thought it was worth flagging the emphasis on the heterogeneity of behaviour among firms and sectors, the emphasis on measurement issues and the emphasis on dealing with the detail, especially in the consideration of policies and their effects. There were several interventions aimed at clarifying the notion of knowledge-based growth. Acs wanted labour and capital to get their share of the credit for growth, and suggested that what was new now was not so much the importance of knowledge in growth but the fast growth of industries producing knowledge rather than goods. James Brander emphasized the looming (per capita) growth-reducing effects of population growth and resource depletion, Luc Soete wanted to see more emphasis on the longer-term role of knowledge in growth, and Richard Lipsey suggested identifying knowledge-based growth with the growth of technical progress, as it is normally measured in a pro-duction-function context. Bernstein agreed with the three-pronged research strategy, but wanted to make sure that Helliwell was not saying that measurement attempts in R&D should be held back just because the job was difficult. Helliwell reassured Bernstein, agreed with the rest and put Soete's suggestion briefly into practice by claiming to see the current growth in the knowledge-based service industries as another step in the long progress away from the farm, and later on, from the factory. Productivity improvements in those sectors made it possible to provide what was needed with less labour and, sometimes, with less of both labour and capital.

Dale Orr took advantage of the scope of the overview session to pose a big question: did Helliwell think that the policy framework needed root-and-branch reform or piecemeal improvement? Helliwell said that since Lipsey had argued con-vincingly that innovation is best when it proceeds in small but flexible steps, and that institutions needed to be developed collaboratively at a matching pace, that piecemeal adaptation and experimentation were likely to be the best way of making policy. Only if the existing framework and institutions were irremediably bad, which he did not think to be the case, would tearing down and starting again be the preferred course for policy reform. Flexible and collaborative adaptation were likely to serve innovation better.

There were also contributions to the telecommunications discussion. Leonard Waverman thought that important variables might be missing from Figure 1, and was only partly convinced when told that adding initial income did not change the results, and that there were relatively few other variables that were uni-formly found to be important in explaining productivity growth differences among the OECD countries. (Röller and Waverman provide more information on this score in their revised paper, finding confirmation for the results shown in Figure 1, and suggesting the need for further research reconciling these negative results with their own positive ones.) Steven Globerman noted the possibility of leapfrogging by the telephonic laggards, making 1971 to 1989 perhaps too long a period to use. He had to catch a plane, so was not able to hear that the same results are obtained if 1970's productivity growth is used instead.

OVERALL IMPLICATIONS FOR POLICY AND FUTURE RESEARCH

ONE CONCLUSION SUGGESTED BY THE PAPERS, when viewed as a group, is that research defining and measuring the linkages between knowledge and eco-nomic growth is in its infancy. An important advantage of the Industry Canada and the OECD efforts is their invitation to scholars and data providers to face up to the empirical problems, and to add missing dimensions to the definitions of the resources that firms use to produce goods and services. It might also be noted that many of the changes under study at this conference, such as the information high-way, may make the future collection of establishment-based data more difficult, since it will no longer be as easy to assign workers and capital to specific places of work. If the worker and computer are connected to each other, and to their human and mechanical colleagues, by satellite transmission, where should the output be recorded as taking place?

On the policy front, most of the papers are appropriately cautious about jumping from the theory or preliminary measurements to any conclusions about the structure of taxation and government spending. There is perhaps an underlying preference for a neutral system as between industries, either as a matter of principle or because there is not sufficient evidence to judge the proper size or even direction of departure from neutrality. In particular, none of the papers have attempted an assessment of whether Canada has an appropriate balance between public support for open science as opposed to company-based research supported by grants or special tax provisions. That is not a deficiency of these papers, since they were all focused on specific and narrower questions for which the answers will eventually improve the information base for dealing with the broader issues.

Do the papers permit any judgment about the relative importance of knowledge-based growth? In one sense, all economic growth is knowledge-based since, for centuries, the largest increases in output have come from increases in know-how rather than via inputs of matter and energy. Has growth been faster in knowledge-intensive industries? The Lee and Has results show that output per worker has actually grown more slowly in the more knowledge-based industries, although productivity levels still remain higher than in the low-knowledge (but not the medium-knowledge) industries. Do knowledge-based industries provide positive spillovers to other industries? The Röller and Waverman paper, as well as the Bernstein results, would seem to suggest that the communications industry may provide positive spillovers elsewhere in the economy, but Figure 1 would suggest that the aggregate impor-tance of these spillovers is suspect. A cautious interpretation of the evidence so far is that the case on either side is not proven.

One further specific issue invites summary, since it spans two or more papers, and is implicit in several others. What is the appropriate domain for considering the linkages between knowledge and growth, and for the design of policies that affect those linkages? At one level, the answer is easy: spillovers, like spills of other sorts, are best dealt with where they happen. If there are important knowledge spillovers across national boundaries, as the Harris analysis suggests, then they need to be encouraged by reciprocal openness and facilitating standards. For the information highway, international traffic standards are even more important than they are for motor vehicles, shipping and airlines, where they have been long established. If spillovers are mainly national, as much of the literature on growth and industrial policy has tended to presume, in the absence of much supporting evidence, then national policies may have a greater role to play. If key bits of public capital are lacking, then there will be high rates of return on their provision, and a sharp eye rather than a national policy is required. If there are important internal barriers that stop important exchanges from taking place, then they need to be removed, although Whalley's paper cautions that current barriers are not as pervasive or as expensive as others have suggested. If spillovers and networking are local, as Acs, de la Mothe and Paquet argue, then national strategies are likely to be, at best, expensive window dressing.

What is the evidence? The case studies of Lipsey and Carlaw, while mainly relating to national policies, are of such a rich variety as to show that there is no single answer to this question. Some ideas move faster and further than others, and uncertain research may be better for being done by separate groups that follow their own agendas, as long as the successes and failures are reported in a timely way, to help others to redirect their groping searches to find better ways of doing things. Coe and Helpman (1993) found international R&D spillovers that were very large relative to domestic ones, and Bernstein would probably echo that finding. However, we must not forget McCallum's (1995) startling new finding that inter-provincial flows of goods are 20 times as large as those between provinces and states, once allowance has been made for size and distance. For Acs, de la Mothe and Paquet, the heights of national boundaries would not be treated as a surprise, but how would they react to the apparent strength of the flows across the country? Perhaps the social capital and other factors which they think are important sources of local spillovers may also be shared more broadly across the country, giving rise to social and economic interdependence far greater than previously imagined. As for the relative strength of distance and national borders as determinants of trade link-ages, McCallum's results suggest that the border is more than half as wide as Canada. But are there even greater local linkages within a country? So far, there are no comparable data for the trade among local economies, but the data analyzing the relative growth of more- and less-specialized regions within the United States suggests that at least there is no predominance of local industry-based spillovers. But the level of ignorance on this matter must be regarded as large.

How about the choice among model types and assumptions, the issue that inspired Peter Nicholson's initial presentation? As John Baldwin forcefully pointed out, and others agreed, there is lots of evidence of heterogeneity of behaviour, enough to require extreme caution in the use of the assumption of the representative firm. On the other hand, there was some feeling that there were already enough untested and untestable models about, and several blanched at the difficulty of an analytical solution of models with heterogenous agents operating within an uncertain environment, each with their own sets of costly information.

In the light of the ambiguity about the current state of knowledge on the role of knowledge in economic growth, the implications for research are stronger than those for current policy. Howitt made the plea for clearer thinking and better data, supported by more direct tests of the competing views of the role of knowledge in growth. John Whalley treated the blur of answers from the endogenous growth papers as merely increasing the band of uncertainty about the answers one would continue to have to develop from other sources, with dynamic general equilibrium models being his favourite bet. Richard Harris asked whether the wide range of answers from the endogenous growth models meant that they should be ignored entirely, and then answered his own question with a preference for more research.

Each of the papers illustrates one or more issues where existing information is not strong enough to support new policy initiatives. Given both the theoretical and empirical ambiguity of the support for particular forms of industrial strategy, perhaps the best new policy would be one which required each important new subsequent policy to meet high standards of empirical support for the presumption that its costs exceed its benefits by an appropriate margin, with due allowance for uncertainty.

BIBLIOGRAPHY

Bruce, N. "The Cost of Capital and Competitive Advantage." In *Productivity, Growth and Canada's International Competitiveness*. Edited by T.J. Courchene and D.D. Purvis. Bell Canada Papers on Economic and Public Policy, Volume 1. Kingston: John Deutsch Institute, 1993, pp. 77-118.

Coe, D.T. and E. Helpman. "International R&D Spillovers." National Bureau of Economic Research Working Paper No. 4444, Cambridge, 1993.

McCallum, John. "National Borders Matter: Canada-U.S. Regional Trade Patterns." *American Economic Review*. (June 1995).

McFetridge, D. and J. Warda. *Canadian R&D Tax Incentives: Their Adequacy and Impact*. Toronto: Canadian Tax Foundation, 1983.

About the Contributors

A.L. Keith Acheson is a Professor of Economics at Carleton University. His general research interests are the economics of organization, transaction costs and property rights. His most recent project of applied research relates to different aspects of the film and television industry (with C.J. Maule).

Zoltan Acs is the Harry Y. Wright Professor at the Department of Economics and Finance at the University of Baltimore, and Visiting Professor and Associate Director of the College of Business and Management at the University of Maryland. He is also co-editor of an international journal entitled Small Business Economics. His fields of special interest are industrial organization and comparative economic systems.

Lewis Alexander is the Chief Economist of the U.S. Department of Commerce. He has held several positions with the Board of Governors of the Federal Reserve and was Federal Reserve desk officer for Russia and other states of the former Soviet Union, dealing with such topics as economic reform, currency arrangements, regional problems and options for U.S. policy. He has written on a variety of topics such as debt-for-equity swaps in developing countries, the free-rider problem in bank debt restructurings, estimating a pure-discount term structure, economic reform in post-war West Germany, the impact of German unification on the European monetary system and currency separation in the former Soviet Union.

David Alan Aschauer is the Elmer W. Campbell Professor of Economics at Bates College in Lewiston, Maine. He has been on the graduate faculties of economics and business at the University of Michigan, Northwestern University and the University of Chicago. During 1986, he was a Visiting Scholar at the Institute of Fiscal and Monetary Policy Studies at the Japanese Ministry of Finance. Before joining the faculty at Bates College, he held the position of Senior Economist at the Federal Reserve Bank of Chicago. Professor Aschauer is the author of a variety of articles on macro-economic and fiscal policy issues, and on transportation and infrastructure issues.

John R. Baldwin is Director of the Micro-Economics Analysis Division at Statistics Canada. His recent work has focused on innovation strategies, on research and development of small- and medium-sized enterprises and on human resource strategies of Canadian businesses.

Jeffrey I. Bernstein is a Professor of Economics at Carleton University and is currently a research associate at the National Bureau of Economic Research in Cambridge. His current research focuses on industrial and public economics, and on micro-economics. He has authored three books and published several articles dealing with productivity and growth, the information economy and competitiveness.

Robin Boadway is the Sir Edward Peacock Professor of Economic Theory at Queen's University. He is currently Associate Director of the John Deutsch Institute for the Study of Economic Policy. His research interests have been in the areas of public sector and welfare economics, with special emphasis on tax policy, fiscal federalism and cost-benefit analysis. His works include several books as well as articles in academic journals.

James A. Brander is the Asia-Pacific Professor of International Business and Public Policy, Faculty of Commerce, University of British Columbia. Dr. Brander specializes in the economic analysis of public policy, especially international trade policy. He is the author of a widely used textbook on Canadian public policy and has acted as a consultant for several government bodies at the federal and provincial levels, and in the private sector, mostly on matters relating either to public sector budgeting or to international trade policy. His current research interests include public sector project evaluation and environmental policy as it affects international trade.

John Burbidge is a Professor of Economics at McMaster University. Recent publications deal with redistribution within and across regions and with population mobility and capital tax competition.

Ken Carlaw is enrolled in the Ph.D. program at Simon Fraser University and works at the Canadian Institute for Advanced Research in the Growth and Policy Program where his research focuses on theoretical and applied fields of innovation, economic growth and policy. Previous research experience at various federal and provincial ministries has ranged from developing a computerized business profitability and tax burden forecasting model to an evaluation of labour relations.

John de la Mothe is an Associate Professor, Economics of Innovation, Science and Technology Policy at the Faculty of Management, University of Ottawa and an affiliate of the Program of Research in International Management and Economy (PRIME), also at the University of Ottawa. He is a regular consultant to international organizations such as the OECD and UNESCO and has been a Research Fellow at the John F. Kennedy School of Government (Harvard University) and a Visiting Scholar at the Massachusetts Institute of Technology.

Michael Denny is a Professor of Economics at the University of Toronto. He has been a consultant to both the Canadian and American governments and to private industry, and has numerous publications and reports to his credit.

Steven Globerman is a Professor of Economics at Simon Fraser University. He is also the Ross Distinguished Professor of Canada–United States Business and Economic Relations at Western Washington University. His main area of expertise is industrial organization with an emphasis on regulated industries. He has consulted widely for private and public sector organizations and has published extensively on various economic and public policy topics.

Richard G. Harris is a Professor of Economics at Simon Fraser University and an Associate of the Program on Economic Growth and Policy of the Canadian Institute for Advanced Research (CIAR). Professor Harris' area of specialization is international economics, especially the economics of integration. He is currently involved in research on North American free trade, North American currency union and the globalization of labour markets.

Handan Has is an Economic Policy Analyst with the Micro-Economic Policy Analysis Branch at Industry Canada. Research interests are in the areas of productivity and economic growth.

John F. Helliwell is a Professor of Economics at the University of British Columbia. His main interests in economics are quantitative macro-economics, national and international comparative empirical studies of economic growth, international finance, taxation and monetary policy, and natural resources, energy and environmental issues. Recently, he was the W.L. Mackenzie King Visiting Professor of Canadian Studies at Harvard University.

Peter Howitt is a Professor of Economics and the Bank of Montreal Professor of Money and Finance at the University of Western Ontario. He is also associated with the Canadian Institute for Advanced Research. His research work is in the area of macro-economics and monetary policy and growth theory.

Joanne Johnson is an Economist with the Micro-Economic Analysis Group at Statistics Canada. She has been involved in analyzing the interrelations between a variety of strategies, activities and objective performance measures and has also developed a data base on aggregate inputs (KLEMS) and outputs by industry which permits analysis of productivity issues within the context of an industry-level production function. She has collaborated with John Baldwin on a number of recent publications dealing with human capital development and innovation.

Jock Langford is a Senior Policy Analyst working on intellectual property policy at Industry Canada. Mr. Langford has contributed to recent legislative policy development initiatives such as C-91 and the GATT and NAFTA treaty negotiations. He works on a range of issues directly related to intellectual property rights such as innovation, trade, competition, regulation and investment. He is currently overseeing economic research on the patenting of biotechnology, including higher life forms.

Frank C. Lee works with the Micro-Economic Analysis Directorate at Industry Canada where he has been doing research on knowledge-based growth. Before joining Industry Canada, he was with the Department of Finance in the Fiscal Policy and Analysis Branch. His research interests are in the areas of economic growth and productivity, structural change, and income distribution and poverty.

Richard G. Lipsey is a Professor of Economics at Simon Fraser University and the Founding Director of the Program of Economic Growth and Policy of the Canadian Institute for Advanced Research. He is one of Canada's foremost economists and has worked over three decades reformulating neoclassical theory. His current research covers areas of economic growth, theory and public policy, Canadian trade policy, and spatial economics and oligopoly theory. Dr. Lipsey has contributed to pioneering theories, including "the general theory of second best," opening up new directions of research on economic policy. Aside from winning a world reputation in research, he is well known to university students for his introductory textbook in economics available in 14 languages.

Donald G. McFetridge is a Professor in the Department of Economics at Carleton University. He has also taught at the University of Western Ontario, McGill University and Quing Hua University in Beijing. He was a Visiting Research Fellow at Harvard University. Dr. McFetridge has published numerous articles and books on various aspects of industrial economics and economic policy. He has also served as an advisor to a number of corporations, public organizations, international organizations, foreign governments, provincial and federal government departments and royal commissions.

Roger Miller holds the Hydro-Québec/NSERC/SSHRC Chair in Technology Management at the Université du Québec à Montréal. He is a Fellow at Harvard University's Center for International Affairs and a Research Fellow at MIT's International Motor Vehicles Program. He has taught at INSEAD Fontainebleau, France, the Sloan School of Management (MIT) and the University of Bogota, Columbia. He is a specialist in the integration of technology with corporate strategy.

Gilles Paquet is a Professor of Economics at the University of Ottawa, Senior Research Fellow at the Canadian Centre for Management Development and is affiliated with the Program of Research in International Management and Economy (PRIME) at the University of Ottawa. He has published articles on such topics as Canada's economic history, regional and industrial development in Canada, entrepreneurship and public management.

Michael Pedersen is an analyst with Statistics Canada. He is currently working on the National Longitudinal Survey of Children.

Lars-Hendrik Röller is the Director of Research in Competitiveness and Industrial Change at the Wissenschaftszentrum Berlin. He also holds the Chair for Industrial

Economics at Humboldt University in Berlin and is a fellow at the Center of Economic Policy Research in London. His research interests are in the areas of market structures, competitiveness and competition policy.

Thomas K. Rymes is a Professor of Economics at Carleton University. His recent research has been in the area of money and banking. Forthcoming publications and articles deal with the costs of zero inflation and with monetary theory of value and modern banking.

Luc Soete is Director of the Maastricht Economic Research Institute on Innovation and Technology, and Professor of International Economics in the Faculty of Economics at the University of Limburg. He has worked in the Science Policy Research Unit at the University of Sussex, and the Department of Economics at Stanford University. His research interests include both the theoretical and empirical study of the impact of technological changes on employment and international trade and investment, as well as the related policy measurement issues. He is co-ordinating the G-7 thematic review of technology, productivity and employment for the OECD.

Leonard Waverman is a Professor in the Department of Economics, University of Toronto, and Director of the University's Centre for International Studies. He specializes in international trade, industrial organization and antitrust, energy and telecommunication economics. He has authored numerous works and has consulted widely in both Canada, the United States and Europe. Recently he was a Visiting Professor at INSEAD, Fontainebleau, France. He is a Research Associate at École Nationale de la Statistique et de l'Administration Économique, Centre de Recherche en Économie et Statistique in Paris. Recent works include an examination of costs and productivity in the U.S., Canadian, Japanese and German automobile industries (with M. Fuss), analyses of the impact of United States–Canada–Mexico free trade, an analysis of costs and regulation in European satellite service provision and an examination of the system of international telecommunications pricing.

John Whalley is a Professor of Economics at the University of Warwick, on leave from his position as Director of the Centre for the Study of International Economic Relations, Department of Economics at the University of Western Ontario. His career has spanned several different areas of economics. He was instrumental in developing the procedures that are now widely used in applied general equilibrium analysis in calibration and counterfactual equilibrium procedures. His coverage of policy interests has grown to issues in development and environmental issues. He was the co-ordinator for international trade research with the Macdonald Commission, and was involved in the early work leading to the introduction of the value-added tax in Canada. More recently, he has been a member of a dispute settlement panel under the Canada–United States Free Trade Agreement.

Corporate Decision-making in Canada

Industry Canada undertakes micro-economic studies on a wide range of subjects to provide a solid analytical foundation for the Department's policies and programs. Many of these studies are made available through the Industry Canada Publications Program, which consists of a Research Volume Series; a Working and Occasional Paper Series; Policy Discussion Papers; and a quarterly newsletter.

The research volumes draw together work by several authors on diverse aspects of a given micro-economic theme. Industry Canada appoints distinguished academics to act as general editors; they, in turn, select experts in their fields to prepare draft papers on identified issues. The papers are presented and subjected to peer review at a conference attended by representatives from the business, legal and academic communities as well as government organizations. The proceedings of the conferences are subsequently published.

The working and occasional papers have a more concentrated focus and provide a vehicle for new research. The discussion papers provide the department with important background information on micro-economic policy issues of strategic importance. All documents are reviewed by outside experts.

All of these important research and policy efforts are disseminated directly to key organizations throughout Canada. Summaries of major research findings and their policy implications are disseminated more broadly through the Department's quarterly newsletter, MICRO.

The Industry Canada Research Volume Series

- Foreign Investment, Technology and Economic Growth

- Corporate Globalization Through Mergers and Acquisitions

- Multinationals in North America

- Canadian-Based Multinationals

- Corporate Decision-Making in Canada

- The Implications of Knowledge-Based Growth for Micro-Economic Policies